William

PREHISTORIC
ARCHEOLOGY

PREHISTORIC ARCHEOLOGY

A brief introduction

FRANK HOLE

Rice University

ROBERT F. HEIZER

University of California, Berkeley

HOLT, RINEHART AND WINSTON

*New York   Chicago   San Francisco   Atlanta   Dallas
Montreal   Toronto   London   Sydney*

Portions of this book appeared in a different
form in *An Introduction to Prehistoric Archeology*
by the same authors, © 1965, 1969, 1973
by Holt, Rinehart and Winston, Inc.

Cover photograph courtesy of Thomas R. Hester.

Library of Congress Cataloging in Publication Data

Hole, Frank.
   Prehistoric archeology.
   Bibliography: p. 416.
   Includes index.
   1.   Anthropology, Prehistoric.   2.   Archaeology.
I.   Heizer, Robert Fleming, 1915–   joint author.
II.   Title.
GN740.H64   930'.1   76-53001

ISBN 0-03-089920-6

PREFACE

The subdiscipline of archeology has grown so rapidly that no person can keep abreast of all its details. With thousands of archeologists digging sites the world around and reporting on their results in as many languages as have written forms, it is impossible for even the most omnivorous reader to master the details of culture history of more than a small area or two. If we realize that concomitantly there has been an enormous increase in the development and use of scientific techniques to aid in archeological investigation and analysis, we can see how the problem is compounded, for the use of many of these techniques requires advanced and highly specialized training in fields such as chemistry or physics. A professional archeologist is expected to know some areas of archeology very well, and enough about the specialized techniques to be able to assess their appropriateness and use their results intelligently. In every sense, then, the field of archeology has become complex and highly diversified.

Over the years there has been a number of books that have to deal broadly with what happened in the archeological past. Some of these have been, and continue to be, useful textbooks for students who wish to gain an overview of human history. Needless to say, however, such books need periodic updating as new finds appear or new methods of interpretation are developed. In some extreme cases, very good books of this kind have required updating almost as soon as they have been printed. There is another problem, however, that is equally serious for the student. Any book that tells what happened in the archeological past has a kind of synthetic quality about it that results from the skimming over of the countless details that prehistory affords, and of the ambiguities and gaps that must be ignored. To read a general work on prehistory is a little like drinking a quart of milk out of a container that had been bought at the store. You can readily appreciate the product but you have a hard time imagining the creature that produced it.

In this book we try to inform the reader of what comes before the final synthesis, of the creature that produced the archeology. We take the student from the concepts that provide the theoretical basis of archeology, to the methods of analyzing archeological finds, and then to ways of interpreting them and writing about the results. In short, this book tells how and why archeology is done. In a sense we provide a behind-the-scenes look at what archeologists do before they go public with their press releases, journal articles, and books.

In the Preface to the third edition of *An Introduction to Prehistoric Archeology* we acknowledged the fact that it was possibly not suitable for all introductory courses, largely because we had set out to make the book the most comprehensive available introduction to the field. We believed that this comprehensiveness served a useful purpose, and we are happy to have found this belief validated. Nevertheless, it has seemed to both our publishers and ourselves that the story of doing archeology could be retold somewhat more simply and more briefly, without either falsifying the story or making it simplistic, and that by doing so we could adapt it to the student who is being introduced to archeology for the first time. It is a reworking and updating of the longer book, but the extensive rewriting and rearrangement, as well as the elimination of all but the fundamentals of the subdiscipline, entitle this textbook to a life of its own, for its own audience. Meanwhile, of course, its longer and older brother remains in print.

Our present book is self-contained and self-explanatory, but for those who wish to pursue topics in detail there is available an extensive and annotated set of suggestions for further reading that follow the scheme of the chapter subheads. These references are completely cited in the long bibliography that follows. A glance at this bibliography should convince the reader of the enormous amount that has been written on just the fundamental aspects of archeology. We have made no attempt to provide any systematic coverage of archeological site reports, regional reviews, and culture histories.

Our choice of citations to list in the bibliography reflects what we have read, and our own extensive experiences in the field. Most of the works would be considered basic by an archeologist, but some professors may find other useful examples from areas with which they are personally more familiar. To accommodate these interests we have tried to stress the principles that underlie archeology rather than the details that will suit all needs. Considerable leeway therefore exists in teaching an introductory course using this book.

In this bicentennial year of the United States of America, we are impressed with 200 years of change. Indeed, change has been so profound that members of the Society for Historical Archaeology are dedicated to merely elucidating our own archeology heritage. We may pause a moment to reflect that George Washington would have been perplexed if confronted with a pop-top soft drink can, let alone with a TV show of the Mars landing vehicle trying to scoop up a bit of soil from that distant planet. But our problems of looking into the past are as great as those George Washington might face if he were suddenly brought to life today. We archeologists stand on our own planet, looking back into the mystery of ancient times, with our own scoops of earth, seeking the evidence of life. There is the excitement of probing the unknown, the pleasure of devising new techniques, and the thrill of discovery in archeology. What we try to do in this volume is provide a brief introductory guide to unlocking some of the secrets of the past. We hope that some of our readers will share in the thrills of discovery as they continue the heritage of archeology by probing into the past.

Prehistoric Archeology: A Brief Introduction is based on more than a century of work, in a small amount of which we have participated, but our debt to the thousands of workers who have also labored in the trenches and laboratories is apparent in our bibliography. Nevertheless, in spite of masses of references that we may cite, books do not just happen. Encouragement and necessary prodding were provided by Dave Boynton and Andy Askin of Holt, and their persuasive arguments overcame our own disinclination to be rushed when we both felt overcommitted to other projects. It was Brian Heald of Holt whose sense of literary style steered us in the right direction and whose determination and skill in assembling a book from the parts we periodically submitted, eventually resulted in this text.

At Rice University Frank Hole wishes specially to thank Doug Whalen who assembled the final copy from our notes, queried many problematical phrases, and suggested terms for the glossary. His work was thoroughly professional and invaluable. Shirley Wetzel also provided helpful comments on parts of the text and aided us in making ideas intelligible to introductory students. Finally, when Doug Whalen left Houston his place was taken by Randy Kelley, who completed the assembly of the bibliography and the other last-minute tasks that are so vital but so tedious.

At Berkeley Robert Heizer thanks Suzanne Sundholm for her assistance.

Houston, Texas   F. H.
Berkeley, California   R. F. H.
December 1976

CONTENTS

INTRODUCING
MODERN
ARCHEOLOGY

Part

1

PREHISTORIC ARCHEOLOGY

What is Archeology?

"Archeology" evokes images of romance, foreign lands, exciting discoveries, the mysteries of the past, the skills of the ancients, the meticulous detective work, the publicity. These and more spring to mind when archeology is mentioned. There is a clamor to "go on digs,"[1] to hold ancient objects in one's hands, to imagine the "way it was," to romanticize about archeology and archeologists. "If only I could start over again, I would be an archeologist." "What a fascinating life you must lead!" "What kind of food do you eat?" "Where do you live?" "Are there snakes, bugs, heat or cold?" Do you really use dental tools and paint brushes?" "Who pays for it?"

It would seem that almost everyone knows something about archeology but few know much. **Sir Leonard Woolley**, the British archeologist whose discoveries in Mesopotamia excited the imaginations of the public and archeologists alike, said:

[1] Boldface indicates that the word is defined in the Glossary, at the end of the text.

3

FIG. 1.1 *Students learning techniques of excavation. In the initial stage of excavation rectangular pits are excavated to sample various parts of the site. The soft, sandy loam is passed through a fine mesh screen to enable recovery of all small objects. (Photo by Harry W. Rhodes III.)*

FIG. 1.2 *In remote regions archeologists may have to set up their own camps and bring in all supplies themselves. Lack of fresh food, water, heat, electricity, and so on are relatively routine problems for those whose work carries them to the frontiers of archeological exploration. This camp in Iran is battened down against a dust storm.*

There *is* a romance in digging, but for all that it is a trade wherein long periods of steady work are only occasionally broken by a sensational discovery, and even then the real success of the season depends, as a rule, not on the rare "find" that loomed so large for the moment, but on the information drawn with time and patience out of a mass of petty detail which the days' routine little by little brought to light and set in due perspective (Woolley 1932: 1–2).

The stories in the mass media usually stress the exotic setting of a field camp, the hardships of chopping through a jungle or facing the desert sands, and the story concludes with a major and valuable discovery, visible the moment it emerges from the earth. Nothing could be further from the truth. The romance lies not in these spectacular events. It lies, as John Platt (1962) says, in the excitement of science: the thrill of following out a chain of reasoning for oneself. The excitement of doing archeology is thus basically the same as the excitement and fun of discovery in any science.

In its broadest sense archeology is the study of the human past, particularly as it is revealed through material remains. It is also a set of methods and procedures for investigating the past that reflect both the data that are available and the academic training and theoretical orientation of archeologists. In American universities, archeology is a **subdiscipline** of **anthropology**, a field that seeks to study man in his various aspects: physical, cultural, social, linguistic, and historical. Anthropologists are concerned with man's **culture** and with the **cultures** of men; consequently, archeologists have been preoccupied with the changes in culture and the varieties of cultures. But archeology differs from most anthropology in that it deals with dead peoples—peoples who are often nameless— and with cultures in which individuals are seldom perceived. It differs in that archeologists study people's works—their artifacts and places of activity—rather than the people themselves. Thus, though archeology can never hope to be all that anthropology is, it can make important contributions to both anthropology and history by adding a time dimension that cannot be studied with living peoples. Archeology is part of, and ancillary to, anthropology; but its subject matter is different, its methods have little in common with general anthropology, and its interpretations tend toward the sweeping rather than the particular, concerned with processes rather than with static "slices of life."

The variety of archeology is suggested by the fact that archeologists are found in departments of art, history, classics, linguistics, and anthropology. Moreover, archeologists are employed by universities, museums, historical agencies, and the United States Park Service, and they frequently work on contract to the Corps of Engineers and highway departments. On occasion, archeologists are even employed as expert witnesses in legal proceedings. Archeology thus covers a broad range of topics and interests, and may be considered pure research on the one hand and applied technology on the other. We cannot hope to describe systematically the full range of archeology's special interests; what we shall do is concentrate on the things that all branches of archeology have in common and especially on the one that is variously called prehistoric archeology, **paleoanthropology,** or merely **prehistory.**

Until recently it was widely held that archeology is not a distinct discipline, and many still feel this way today. The argument runs along these lines: archeology has its own data and a few techniques and concepts, but most of these are borrowed from geology, history, or anthropology. As Grahame Clark (1954:7) put it, "It is often, and I think rightly, held that archeology should not be counted as a separate field of study so much as a method of reconstructing the past from the surviving traces of former societies." Evidently Clark thinks of prehistory as an extension of history. A century and a half ago J. Hodgson (1822: xvi) had the same idea when he wrote,

> The vulgar antiquary, while he walks among the ruins of a city, is struck with wonder, and fixes his observation most upon their extent, their state of preservation. . . . He is an admirer of coins on account of their rarity, their age, the beauty of their rust, or from some accidental variety which marks them. . . . He values his collection of manuscripts . . . merely because they are old. . . . But the judicious antiquary considers the various objects of his contemplation with a learned eye; and imposes a value upon them in proportion to the quantity of light they throw upon the several departments of the history of the people to which they belong.

Walter Taylor (1948:43) once stated that archeology is no more than a method and a set of specialized techniques for recovering cultural information. "The archeologist . . . is nothing but a technician." In rebuttal to this, it is worth quoting Sir Mortimer Wheeler:

> I have no hesitation in denouncing that extreme view as nonsense. A lepidopterist is a great deal more than a butterfly-catcher, and an archeologist who is not more than a pot-sherd-catcher is unworthy of his *logos*. He is primarily a fact-finder, but his facts are the material records of human achievement; he is also, by that token, a humanist and his secondary task is that of revivifying or humanizing his materials with a controlled imagination that inevitably partakes of the qualities of art and even of philosophy (Wheeler 1956:228–229).

Our own view was stated well by Glynn Isaac:

> Archeological studies are at their most significant when they attempt to elucidate the development of relations both amongst men, and between man and the material world. . . . Prehistoric archaeology is thus in its total aims not a natural science, a social science or a branch of the humanities; rather it is a distinctive pursuit in which all of these meet (Isaac 1971b:123).

One of the objectives of this book is to show that prehistoric archeology, at least, is a distinct discipline operating with a unique set of facts that can be made to tell us about the development of humanity in the past through a set of interpretive techniques and integrative concepts specially combined and tailored for this task. In stating this, we are not attempting to build a wall around archeology but merely emphasizing its special characteristics.

Prehistory

Prehistory refers to the part of man's past that was not recorded in writing—it is "before history." The prehistorian, the archeologist who studies prehistory, does so by analyzing **artifacts** that are usually uncovered through excavation.

The word "prehistoric" is so familiar and widely used that we might assume it has been in use for a very long time, but actually people have been unaware of a past that is not recorded by writing until relatively recently. The first modern use of the word dates from just a little more than 100 years ago, in 1851, when Daniel Wilson used it in the title of his *The Archaeology and Prehistoric Annals of Scotland.* Somewhat earlier, in 1833, Tournal proposed that the "Age of Man" could be divided into a "Prehistoric Period which extended from the time of man's appearance on the surface of the earth to the beginning of the most ancient traditions" and a "Historic Period which hardly dates beyond seven thousand years ago." T. Wilson (1899) wrote, in explanation, "Man may be assumed to be prehistoric wherever his chroniclings of himself are undesigned and his history is wholly recoverable by induction."

As a point of reference, history as a chronicle of events began about 3000 B.C., following the invention of writing somewhere in what is now modern southern Iraq. The language was Sumerian, and it was written in **cuneiform** on tablets of clay. The oldest tablets, those from Warka (Uruk) and from Jemdet Nasr, however, are **pictographic** (Fig. 1.3) and were hardly what we would call an effective medium of general communication. In fact, for several hundred years after its beginning, writing was used largely for keeping economic and administrative records. Full writing began around 2500 B.C. with the establishment of standardized signs and meanings. By 2000 B.C. most of Southwest Asia was politically dominated by literate peoples. By contrast, England was prehistoric until the beginning of the Christian era, and because of the lack of readable **pre-Columbian** texts we must say that the prehistory of the **Native American**

FIG. 1.3 *Two sides of a clay tablet with pictographic signs found at Warka in southern Mesopotamia. This tablet is about 5500 years old and represents one of man's first attempts to preserve records. These tablets are lists of people, animals, and things. Soon this kind of "writing" was replaced by the more stylized and versatile cuneiform script that could convey ideas and literary expression as well as economic transactions. Other styles of ancient writing are seen on the Rosetta stone (Fig. 2.3). (Redrawn from Falkenstein,* Archaische Texte aus Uruk, *1936, Plate 10 No. 202).*

ended only with the coming of Europeans in the sixteenth century A.D. We might call some of these peoples protohistoric—peoples who were living after history began but who themselves did not have writing.

For practical purposes the line dividing prehistory and **protohistory** is hard to define. Even in Southwest Asia, where writing began, only the major political centers were really within the sphere of literacy until fairly recently. Archeology is a major source of history in such places, even though the past several thousand years have been part of the historic era. If we stop to think about it, although written documents are the most important source of history, archeology can broaden our knowledge, even of the past in the United States. As James Deetz (1967:4) put it with regard to the colonists who landed at Plymouth,

> . . . no known historical documentation tells us exactly what animals were used for food by the Plymouth colonists, what types of dishes were used in the homes, when the first bricks were produced locally, or what types of nails, window frames or door hardware were used in constructing the houses. Archeological investigation of seventeenth-century house sites in Plymouth has given the answers to all these questions, fleshing out much of the bare bones of historical accounts.

Today information is recorded in diaries, books, magazines, newspapers, and official records, but still a vast amount goes unrecorded and will vanish from man's record unless it is recovered by a future archeologist. A hundred years ago, when paper was more costly and printing processes less mechanized, much more went unrecorded, and information that can supplement our written history still lies in the ground, awaiting an archeologist's interest. Thus archeology can contribute to knowledge of the whole of man's past; it need not stop where history begins.

History and Archeology

Because archeology deals with man's culture seen in the perspective of time, it is natural to assume that archeologists are basically historians. For many, particularly European archeologists, this is true. The editor of *Antiquity*, Glyn Daniel (1967a:170) states the matter forthrightly:

> We are all historians, we are all studying the past of man, whether we concentrate on Walpole, Beowulf, Stonehenge or Lascaux. Manuscripts, microliths, megaliths—it is all one. The past is the goal of the historian whether he is text aided or not . . . there are historians, in the strict sense of the word, who are frightened when they see archeologists advancing toward them with dirt on their boots and a brief case full of air photographs and Carbon 14 dates. Dugdale, Aubrey, Lhwyd and Stukeley did not think they were other than historians, and, for that matter, historians

who could be members of the Royal Society. We have taken the distinction between a history that is mainly derived from material sources and one that is derived from the aid of texts, too far.

We do not quarrel with this view as a general statement of goals, but it is useful to point out that most United States archeologists are trained in anthropology rather than in history and consequently make interpretations of the past that are different from those historians are likely to make.

A much sharper distinction can be made between history and prehistory on the one hand, and humanism or antiquarianism on the other. Historians attempt to understand life in the past; humanists and antiquaries are concerned principally with objects, and especially with their esthetic value. An example of the differences comes readily to mind. A tourist who admires the Obelisk of Luxor in the Place de la Concorde in Paris or the Elgin marbles in London is not ordinarily experiencing a historical appreciation, nor were the persons responsible for placing these treasures far from their original context acting as archeologists or historians. Similarly, collections of arrowheads in local museums contribute nothing to history unless the objects are placed in a human context. When objects—arrowheads or obelisks—are frankly placed to be admired in their own right, as objects, they have lost their historical value. As Dorothy Garrod has written (1946:27), "Man's tools are the instruments of his response to the world in which he lives, but they are much more—they are the weapons of his conquest of that world and the clue to its interpretation." **V. Gordon Childe** (1956:44–45) sees artifacts as the uniquely human means of satisfying the basic needs of securing food, shelter, and protection from enemies. In many museums, tools become works of art, and religious paraphernalia become treasures, all without value except for their intrinsic worth or beauty. Mere collection and admiration of objects are not historical activities, for though they may deal with archeological remains, they stop short of cultural or historical interpretation.

Why Study Archeology?

At a time when even the basic structure and rationale of education is questioned, it is fair to ask, "Why study archeology?" It has long been held that learning for its own sake is worthwhile, and there are many today who feel this is so. In this sense the study of archeology is no different from any of the scholarly disciplines, but there is something about it that makes it of more than esoteric interest. Grahame Clark (1970:4) expresses it well in one of his characteristically perceptive essays.

> The study of prehistory stands in no more need of justification than exploration of the physical nature and mathematical properties of the universe, the investigation of all the multifarious forms of life, or for that matter the practice of the arts or the cultivation of speculative philoso-

phy. Each in its own way enlarges the range of human experience and enriches the quality of human life.

Today when there is so much concern with the quality of life, these words are worth heeding, but there is more to it, as G. Clark (1970:40–41) again says,

> Expressed in a sentence, the significance of world prehistory is the contribution it is able to make to widening the perspectives of history in accord with the needs of today. . . . Some concern with the past is basic to humanity itself in the sense that human groups are so constituted by virtue of inheriting specific traditions. The traditional lore shared by the members of particular societies serves not only to heighten their sense of solidarity, but also to differentiate them from others in much the same way as do differences in plumage or song among birds.

Today we see a world that is divided culturally and politically but inextricably linked through a growing technological and economic structure that is global in scope. The needs of the newer nations to establish a cultural heritage along with their sense of participation in the oneness of humanity often can be accomplished solely through archeology, for in many parts of the world an indigenous history is only now beginning. In these situations, as G. Clark (1970:50–51) says,

> what we need, then, is anything but cultural nudity. On the contrary, we have to cultivate a reverence for the usages, history, and traditions of all peoples including our own—and not merely of all living peoples, but of all peoples who have ever lived. . . . Our survival depends on, among other things, our ability to view one another in a historical context appropriate to a world that shrinks in size and grows in potential danger with every passing year. History . . . is something which to a large degree determines how we behave. Let us view all histories and all prehistory in a world perspective; in honoring the achievements of our own and of all other peoples, we are after all acknowledging our own humanity.

As the historians of archeology (for example, Glyn Daniel 1971b) have rightly pointed out, we have been far too concerned with Europe and the influences of early civilizations in the Middle East. No less a figure than Gordon Childe was scarcely able to conceive of the indigenous cultures and civilizations of America, let alone those that flourished in other parts of the world. We badly need an education in world prehistory to place our own world in perspective. Thus the value of studying archeology is hardly open to question, although one may correctly question the priorities that are given to different kinds of archeological projects.

Grahame Clark raised the issue of the role of tradition in the formation of modern cultures. To what extent does the past determine the present? Can we understand ourselves and others more acutely if we know the courses of events that led to today's world? That we can is certainly one of the principal tenets of both history and archeology, yet one finds that short-range views— essentially ahistorical—dominate most political decisions. In this sense both archeologists and historians have failed to convey their messages.

Today there is a debate concerning the degree to which archeology can be scientific. Many argue that it should be, and a scientific approach would seem essential if we are to understand the processes in the past that led to the present orientation of cultures. The issues really are: What can we say with certainty? Are there principles of human behavior? Can we predict how people will behave given certain conditions? These and other questions are being raised by some archeologists who are concerned more with the general aspects of cultural development than with the particular details of any people's past. In any case, one can readily see that the interests of historically oriented scientists would be greatly aided by accurate statements of the processes that explain the historical development of a people or of peoples.

Today, many question national priorities, the direction of basic research, the uses to which the results of research are put, and the value of supporting specialist workers in a host of esoteric fields. In view of what we have said above, it should be clear that archeology does not fit neatly into a stereotype; it is done in many ways and may serve a multitude of purposes. Nevertheless, Fritz and Plog (1970:412) make a point that is valid for at least some archeological research when they say, "We suspect that unless archaeologists find ways to make their research increasingly relevant to the modern world, the modern world will find itself increasingly capable of getting along without archaeologists."

In our view the merit of archeology is that it can serve many purposes. It can produce for the **aficionado** objects of great beauty and grace; it can reveal the history of a people and of humankind; it can contribute toward an understanding of the present; and it may one day be used to test scientifically stated hypotheses about human behavior in general.

Goals of Archeology

There are many things that archeologists try to do, and they depend on the uses to which archeology may be put and the ways in which archeology can be done. Archeology has its own history which reveals that its goals have changed as our understanding of the past has developed, as chance finds of great significance have been made, and as techniques in ancillary fields have been developed for application in prehistory.

P. Watson's (1972a) brief list is a resumé of the uses to which archeology is currently put.

1. To furnish collectors' items and museum objects.
2. To furnish documentation for the study of art history or the history of architecture.

3. To attain knowledge of sequences of events and chronologies in the absence of written documents.
4. To help furnish data for much fuller historical studies (historiographic, structural, or constructive history) with **particularist/ideographic** goals.
5. To furnish independent data that can be used to help test **hypotheses** . . . about cultural process; this has to do with generalizing/ **nomothetic** goals and the general laws so confirmed provide us with understanding of history.

For the most part the first two goals cited by Watson pertain to classical and historic periods, and being largely self-evident, will not concern us here. It is toward the latter three goals that most prehistoric archeology is directed and about which there has been a considerable debate in recent years. Nearly everyone agrees that archeology can provide us with a kind of historical documentation of what happened in the past. Some may find this the central and most important goal of prehistory, but there are others who feel that such activity is theoretically weak. Moreover, they maintain that one can go much further—toward the explanation of prehistoric events rather than merely their chronicling.

Here are some views of archeologists. Glynn Isaac (1971b:129) writes, "Archaeology ought to be what archaeology already is. The problem is how can we improve our ways of doing it." Glyn Daniel (1971b:149) says, "Our aim now, surely, is to describe, as best we can with the material at our disposal at the time when we write, the life and times of prehistoric people." Watson, LeBlanc, and Redman (1971:171) state, "One important goal is the explanation of particular events and processes in the past"; and "The understanding of past cultures, and the explanation of the differences and similarities found among them, is generally agreed to be the goal of anthropologically oriented archeology." Lewis Binford (1962:217) emphasizes explanation as one purpose of archeology: "Most will agree that the integrated field [of anthropology and archeology] is striving to explicate and explain the total range of physical and cultural similarities and differences characteristic of the entire spatial-temporal span of man's existence." Fritz and Plog (1970:405) are of the opinion that "All archaeologists employ laws in their research. Those of us who are interested in **processual analysis** have made the formulation and testing of laws our goal."

There should be no doubt that most archeologists are concerned, as Daniel said, with describing the life and times of prehistoric peoples. This is now and always has been a central concern of prehistory, and it is certainly the foundation upon which it will continue to build in the future, whether it reconstructs culture histories or tests hypotheses of lawlike generality. It should also be clear that the goals of archeology are in many ways similar to those of anthropology, except that archeologists deal with long spans of time and frequently encounter situations that are unique and unavailable for study in the laboratory of modern cultures.

What Archeologists Do

Archeologists do everything from digging ancient cities and tombs, to deciphering extinct languages, to carefully cataloging piles of broken pottery, to experimenting with ways things were done in the past, to studying modern peoples, to devising tests of general laws of culture, to diving on shipwrecks, to speculating about visitors from outer space. There is a broad spectrum of interests in the archeological past and in the motives that stimulate people to investigate it. In spite of this range of possibilities, however, there are some underlying activities that characterize most of archeology. Archeologists are concerned with **sites** (places where people once lived or carried out special activities), with the regions surrounding the sites, and with periods that have been identified in the past (the **Paleolithic**, Spanish colonial, or Roman). These are studies which are usually carried out in the **field** rather than in the laboratory or library. Consequently, archeologists talk about "**fieldwork,**" and consider themselves "fieldworkers."

Sites

In the popular view each archeologist has a site or a notable discovery. Howard Carter's finding of **King Tut's** tomb in Egypt, or Heinrich Schliemann's of Homer's **Troy** in southern Turkey are vivid examples that reinforce this kind of thinking. More typical, however, is the archeologist who labors for years exposing an anonymous ancient temple, a camp of hunters and gatherers, or the remains of simple villagers. For these archeologists the discovery of a site is only a small first step. Most of the work comes after the digging, in the analysis and interpretation of the things removed from the ground.

Still, the excavation and interpretation of sites is at the core of archeology and is regarded by many as a goal in itself, for it is in the analysis of a site that one brings to bear all the aspects of archeological theory and technique. The excavation of a site provides the raw material of prehistory, but it also serves as the principal means for the training of students. The reasons for excavating a particular site will, in consequence, range from the role it is presumed to play in a key historical or theoretical problem to its value in teaching techniques of digging and methods of analysis.

Most sites lie buried under earth that has accumulated through the centuries, but there are others that lie under water. In recent years a whole branch of archeology called nautical or underwater archeology has grown up, chiefly to investigate shipwrecks but occasionally to study port cities and other settlements that have sunk below the waters of the oceans. Nautical archeology's sites are usually ships, frequently known from history and often bearing valuable cargo. It is reported, for example, that the **Nuestra Señora de Atocha,** one of 28 Spanish ships which sailed from Havana in 1622, sank off Florida along with eight of the other ships two days later. The cargo of the *Atocha* was 901 silver ingots, 250,000 silver coins, 161 pieces of gold bullion, 582 copper planks, and 350 chests of indigo. By today's standards this is a fortune that has attracted the attention of divers for many years. The wreck was finally discovered in 1973, and the treasure was salvaged, but the disposition of the material still waits final word in the courts: both the United States government and the **salvor** claim the cargo.

The lure of wrecks like the *Atocha* has attracted divers the world around. Most of these divers are simply archeologically untrained adventurers, although they are doing some of the things archeologists do. They are akin to the much-despised "pot hunters" on land, who are in turn like the countless thoughtless people who rip souvenirs from parks and public places. The harm that people like these do to our cultural heritage is incalculable.

Nautical archeology, however, is also a serious and scholarly discipline with close ties to maritime history and studies of technology. The work is quite different in many respects from that done on land, however, so that its methods, which are well described in many books, will not be dealt with here. (Topical bibliographies are given for each chapter at the end of the book.)

Regional Studies

In contrast with the excavation of one site, which may occupy the attentions of archeologists over several generations (for example, the great mounds at **Cahokia** near St. Louis, or some of the major cities in Southwest Asia) and become a focal point of vigorous and intensive research, are the more general regional surveys coupled with limited excavation. Although the layman usually thinks of the site and the dig and identifies an archeologist with it, professionals recognize the need for the more general areal overviews that are gained through systematic reconaissance as well. Indeed, the basis for intelligent work on any particular site depends a great deal on knowledge of its place among other sites and in its relationship to geographic features.

The overview may require extended fieldwork with very little return in objects for museums or even in immediate publication, and partly for these reasons the tendency has been to avoid it. However, in recent years there has been a growing appreciation of the importance of knowing patterns of settlement and of understanding them in relation to the social and physical environment of the prehistoric peoples (see Chapter 12).

Although we find the broad regional approaches increasingly popular, they are not new. What is new is the systematic manner in which they are now being carried out. Universities as part of their teaching programs, museums to augment collections of local culture, and to a lesser extent, amateur archeological societies sometimes set as their goals the discovery of the archeological resources of their state or region. During the Depression years extensive work of this kind was carried out by the federal government, although the goal then was as much to provide jobs for the unemployed as to reveal prehistory. The effect, nonetheless, was to provide a corpus of systematically collected data about a region. Much of this work remains unpublished even today, although it has provided the basis of a number of regional surveys and is available for study.

In principle, regional studies set out to discover and record all the sites in an area. Follow-up work may include excavation of important sites in the attempt to build a coherent sequential picture of prehistorical occupation. Often there is little urgency to such survey, and it is not necessarily keyed to future excavation, although it should be obvious that if sites are to be protected as a matter of policy they must first be found.

The selection of an area to survey may be carefully considered in advance with relation to a problem that interests a particular researcher, but often regional studies are simply carried out near where archeologists live or where there is a suitable supply of students or other manpower. The point is that regional studies, while they are of great importance in archeology, may be carried out with definite, problem-oriented goals, or they may simply be thought of as taking advantage of a local opportunity.

Culture History

It is often the more glamorous digs uncovering spectacular tombs or the skeletons of early forms of men that capture the attention and imaginations of the public, but relatively little archeology is actually devoted to these ends. For the most part archeologists have shown a strong interest in tracing the histories of cultures, and when these histories approach the present, names of peoples can be attached to the archeological remains. Out of this we find a growing interest in ethnic history, or the culture history of a particular people. Indeed, it is correct to say that recently archeology in some countries has been encouraged precisely to serve as an adjunct to history. In this sense it is national pride and ethnic identity that is served. Grahame Clark (1957:256–261) has discussed the interest in archeology displayed by the newly liberated countries of Europe following the First World War, and a similar interest is rapidly emerging in many of the world's developing nations. In consequence of this sense of nationalism, officials in some countries discourage "foreigners" from digging, feeling that the study of local prehistory is a prerogative of the peoples who live in the country.

Tracing the history of particular cultures has some decided advantages in that one starts from the present and works back in time, using such historic records as are available, with the keen appreciation of the local culture that only a native **ethnographer** or historian can have. Work of this kind is common in the United States whether we deal with Native Americans or early Western settlers. Incidentally, one of the side effects of the concern over ecology, especially the depletion of our natural resources, has been the stimulus to do both prehistoric and historic archeology lest all tangible traces of our own ancestors be swept into spoil heaps or paved over with asphalt.

A reaction to ethnic archeology has emerged in some areas, however. For example, in the United States some Native Americans are expressing their concern over what they feel to be the violation of the graves and living spots of their ancestors. Although some have attempted to prevent digging, most archeologists consider it important to conduct scientific examination of Native American prehistory. Whatever the ethical merits of either side, the legality of the issues is being examined anew. Usually legal restrictions on disturbance of the dead cover only the remains of known persons or of bodies lying in marked graves, but in some areas this protection has been extended to older aboriginal sites and native cemeteries.

Although some archeological studies may be stalled in the immediate future through moral suasion and legal means, it is safe to say that in the future more archeological attention will be paid to relatively recent remains and to remains that are relevant to a current sense of heritage than has been true in the past. It is to be hoped that an accommodation between Native Americans and archeologists can be realized. The study of American prehistory ought to be encouraged by Native Americans since it is their own past that is the objective.

Key Problems in Human History

Although most archeology has been focused on single sites or relatively small areas, there have been some notable large-scale efforts to gain an understanding of the crucial turning points in human history, which transcend modern cultural and geographic boundaries. These projects have a central theme and are carried out by investigators who, although they may or may not be working closely together in the integration of their separate projects, are nevertheless working on a well-defined problem of considerable generality. Two examples come readily to mind: the recent work by multinational teams of workers into the origins of man, which has ranged from Africa to India with the most intensive work now being done in East Africa, and the investigation of the origins of agriculture, which has been carried out in considerable detail in Asia and the Americas.

One notable aspect of these projects is that from the start they have included multidisciplinary teams of scientists and have achieved in the process a level of cooperation and mutual stimulation among the specialists that is unusual in archeology. Research teams have begun to replace the traditional one-man operation that has characterized and still characterizes much of archeology. Second, these projects have sought explanations for the crucial changes in human history. These explanations have tended to be phrased in terms of ecology: in the systematic interplay between people as biological and cultural beings and the physical and social environment in which they find themselves and to which they must adapt.

A similarly interesting problem, which has worldwide examples and consequently wide appeal, is the emergence of urbanism and the factors that gave rise to it. This is a subject that has attracted historians and philosophers as well as archeologists, but it is only now being investigated systematically in the field, which is surprising in view of the great amount that has been written to suggest the possible factors accounting for the phenomenon. Now that work on these problems is being carried out in earnest, it is apparent that the range of factors which may account for the developments is exceptionally broad; however, there appear to be some that are more crucial than others. To determine this it was necessary to have constant interaction among the specialists, each working on his own facet of the problem but aware of the overall goals. The merit of this cooperative effort is seen in the wealth of new ideas that are expressed in print each year and in the way fundamental conceptions have changed. One sees a convergence of opinion on the methods of procedure, and it is conceded that the goal of understanding these major changes in humankind is within reach, once sufficient well-conceived and implemented projects have been carried out.

Perhaps one of the most remarkable aspects of these studies is that there has never been one person in charge of all the work, though it is easy to point to leaders who gave the initial stimulus and achieved some of the first important successes. It has been the challenge of intellectually interesting projects and the well-defined methods of approach that have attracted specialists out of various backgrounds into the common cause, resulting in exceptionally rapid attainment of important objectives. It is also in these projects that one can most readily find examples of the interplay between ideas, fieldwork, and experiment, together with innovation in analysis. In short, in these projects it has been the attractiveness of the problem rather than the lure of a particular site or regional history that has drawn specialists together, and it is in such team-oriented studies, which are not restricted geographically, that the best of traditional archeology and modern innovation will be melded in the years to come.

Testing Hypotheses

Archeologists usually go into the field with the expectation of finding something. They may be looking for sites, or investigating the relationships between types of soils and the occurrence of agricultural villages, or checking the chronological association of certain groups of artifacts. The point is, they are looking for something in particular and can usually tell when they have found it. In recent years, however, there has grown up a kind of archeology that deserved the term "new" during the 1960s but that has more recently entered into the mainstream in various forms. The central idea behind "new" archeology was that one should establish and test hypotheses and that to do so requires the explicit statement of the relationship between theory and archeological data; that is, the setting up of an appropriate research design so that the results, like those from any good experiment, give definitive answers.

Few of the newer studies have been carried through to published completion to illustrate the process that has been so much discussed. There are, however, some older examples that may be cited. One such hypothesis concerns the way one can determine the age of a site by means of the artifacts it contains. George Brainerd (1951:304) states the theory that "each type [of artifact] originates at a given time at a given place, is made in gradually increasing numbers as times goes on, then decreases in popularity until it becomes forgotten, never to recur in an identical form." From this theory and from considerable data archeologists have deduced that there is a directional change (for example, from simple to complex) in the artifacts from any particular archeological sequence.

F. Hole and M. Shaw, with reference to chronological **seriation,** state (1967:4):

> It follows that each period is characterized both by its unique assemblage of artifacts and by the relative frequency with which each type of artifact occurs. . . . Hence, presence or absence and relative abundance of artifacts are two tools with which one can work in seriation . . . , [and] sites showing the greatest degree of agreement either in the occurrence of artifacts or in their frequencies will lie closest in time.

Many archeologists accepted the theory as fact and proceeded to carry out elaborate seriations of their data, thus presumably arranging them chronologically. What had not been done, however, was to test the theory against material of known age and with artifacts of different kinds. Critics of seriation were correct in saying that any data will seriate and there may be many reasons for changes in artifacts not related to the passage of time.

To test the hypothesis that seriation is a useful and accurate tool, Hole and Shaw used data from a well-stratified, long archeological sequence in which the chronological order of the material was known. They then seriated these data using various methods that had been proposed and found that in the test case some artifacts (most notably pottery) seriated very well while others (like flint tools) did not. Moreover, they found that some methods of seriation work better than others. Future studies can now build on these results and perhaps test some of their implications.

Another example of the testing of hypotheses is the study done by Robert McC. Adams (1962) of the relation between irrigation and the emergence of urban civilization in Southwest Asia. The hypothesis was that societies with complex administrative hierarchies arose in response to the need to organize and administer irrigation projects. Adams however, found the opposite: that complex societies arose long before the irrigation systems had developed to the point that they required elaborate administration. Although this point is disputed by some authors— for example, Sanders and Price (1968), dealing with other areas—it appears to hold for Southwest Asia, and only similar testing in **Middle America** will tell whether the situation was the same there.

The studies mentioned above dealt with real archeological data and actual archeological problems. There are some archeologists, however, whose interests are much more theoretical, who seldom do fieldwork, and who deal very little with sites or artifacts. These people are concerned with fundamental issues of human behavior and the relation between this behavior and the things we may find archeologically. For example, Michael Schiffer (1976a) has been attempting to establish some basic rules or laws of human behavior so that general statements which are true irrespective of time or place can be made. The implication of this is that such laws may be discovered in any cultural context and need not necessarily be derived solely from archeology, ethnology, or sociology. When one has sufficient understanding of the relationship between two or more variables and can therefore make a general statement expressing this relationship, he is armed with a "law." This law, which may be quite explicit, should pertain to all situations where the same conditions are present, whether it is today or at some time in the past.

Schiffer (1976b) illustrates these ideas with the following example, which is derived from George Zipf and has been tested in part by Schiffer (1972, 1973). Zipf (1949:73) writes:

> . . . The most frequent[ly used] tool . . . which tends to be the lightest, smallest, oldest, most versatile and most thoroughly integrated tool in the system, will also be the most valuable tool in the sense that its permanent loss would cause the greatest cost of redesigning and of retooling. Hence it is most economical to conserve that most frequent[ly used] tool . . . we see that the value of conserving any given tool is directly related to its relative frequency of usage.

Because the relationship between tool use, frequency of use, and cost is stated as a general principle, it can be studied in any cultural context. It should be as applicable to today as to the past and Schiffer has devised various schemes for testing such "laws" by studying modern people.

The kind of investigations that Schiffer's studies exemplify represent one of the frontiers of archeology. They represent an explicit attempt to make archeology a science, and in so doing remove some of the exotic aura from the field by suggesting that the past is neither unfathomable nor especially exotic. As Schiffer (1976b) puts it, "the laws of nature are constant." By extension he would reason that since man is a part of nature, the laws governing his behavior are likewise constant. It is only the particular episodes in the past, which illustrate the workings of the laws, that are unique. Most archeologists, however, are concerned with these unique episodes, and out of them they build the story of man's past.

Experiments

The testing of hypotheses is experimental in a sense, and much of it involves observations of modern peoples. The connotation of experimental archeology, however, is much wider. Most such studies fall into the category of what Robert Ascher (1961a) characterizes as "imitative experiments . . . in which matter is shaped and used, in a manner simulative of the past." Rather than using archeological materials directly, experimenters try to duplicate artifacts or archeologically known effects. Of these there are a great many examples. Another kind of experimentation is examination of the ways of modern peoples for the information this gives on how the tangible artifacts prehistorians may find relate to cultural behavior. A third general type of experimentation is simulation, in which one builds a theoretical model that is like a prehistoric situation in certain crucial respects and then allows the model (for example, of the effects of population growth) to run through time so that the effects of different conditions built into the model can be observed.

Imitative experiments are the easiest to understand, and lend themselves to participation by almost anyone. They are especially useful as classroom exercises. The best-known such work concerns the methods by which prehistoric peoples made their stone artifacts (Graham and others 1972). Except for the making of gun flints and some use of stone tools by peoples in remote parts of the world today, the arts of chipping stone had nearly died out until some investigators began systematic studies. In this country the work of Don Crabtree at the Idaho State Museum has been particularly significant because he has been able to duplicate, after several decades of experimentation, the process by which Native Americans made **fluted points**. One may wonder how this information was lost because Native Americans were chipping flints when the first European colonists arrived, but by that time the art of **fluting** had disappeared among even the Native Americans, as the use of bows and arrows had long since replaced spears and darts. Nevertheless, Crabtree found the decisive clue to the process from a historical record—from a Spanish priest who witnessed Aztec Indians making long knife blades from obsidian. Adapting the technique described— pressing a blade from the obsidian core with a T-shaped "crutch" placed against the chest to deliver pressure to a precise point on the edge of the obsidian core—Crabtree was at last able to remove the fine channel flakes from the bases of **Folsom points**. Since that discovery other modifications of the method have been developed. Figure 1.4 shows one such being carried out by Bruce Bradley, a student who worked with Crabtree.

Studies to determine causes of particular effects are also exemplified by studies of edge wear on chipped stone tools. It is commonly held that when tools made of chipped stone are used their edges get dull or scratched. If this is true, it would be archeologically interesting to know what kinds of use produce what kinds of recognizable wear. Then we could determine the wear and infer the behavior that caused it. We would be relieved of wondering whether a bladelike object had been used as a knife, a saw, or a spatula. In principle such studies should be relatively easy and informative. The Russian archeologist S. A. Semenov pioneered such studies but his results have been hard to duplicate. Other workers have introduced more formal controls into the experiments and have been able to reach more dependable conclusions. Although these studies are far from being universally valid, the groundwork for systematic interpretation has been laid (Tringham 1974).

A much longer-term experiment is the construction (Ashbee and Cornwall 1961) in 1960 and the subsequent observation of the experimental **earthwork** on Overton Down, Wiltshire, England. The intent was "to study the changes which take place with time in a **bank** and **ditch**, and in selected materials buried within the bank" (Dimbleby 1965). After only four years, significant archeological implications had been derived, although the experiment is expected to run up to 128 years with partial excavation at regular intervals (Jewell and Dimbleby 1966).

FIG. 1.4 (top) *Bruce Bradley demonstrating a method of making obsidian blades, using a clamp to hold the obsidian core and an antler flaker to press off the blades. When the blades spring from the core they fall onto a rabbit skin. A pile of blades lies in front of the skin.*

(bottom) Bradley demonstrating a method of pressure flaking, using an antler flaker on the edge of an obsidian biface.

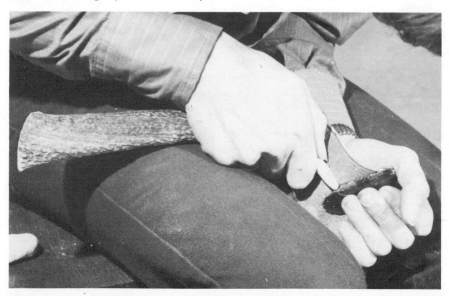

Further removed from tangible reality than the cases cited above are simulation experiments. This technique has been widely used in many fields of science and is coming into more general use for problems in social science where large populations and long times are involved. Of primary importance is the fact that such simulations are abstract models based on mathematics and are designed to operate with relatively few variables, largely because of the extraordinary mathematical difficulty of incorporating all possibly relevant variables and because of the difficulty in assigning a quantitative value to variables. Nevertheless, one may examine such single factors as population increase and its effects on demographic pattern. Such an example is given by Ammerman and Cavalli-Sforza (1972a), where they postulate that the spread of agricultural peoples, because of increasing population (**demic expansion**), may be likened to a "wave of advance," that will progress radially at a constant rate. The authors contrast the wave of advance with colonization, which could also be considered a result of population growth. In order to test which of the two hypotheses is correct in the instance of the spread of farming peoples into Europe, they needed to be able to plot the times at which farming peoples arrived at successively more distant points from the presumed origin. Thus they were able to plot points on the wave front to the center of diffusion and thereby estimate the radius of the wave front at various times. When they plotted these distances against time, if their wave of advance model were correct, the radius of the wave front should have varied linearly with time. This was found to be the case within the limitations of the data presently available.

The importance of the experiment lies not only in an explanation of the process by which Europe was colonized, but also in the deductions that may be made from using this model about other matters, such as a population densities at different places and times or the genetic composition of population involved in the spread. In short, while it has not been adequately tested as yet, and does not completely exclude other factors, the model has suggested a strong hypothesis to account for the process of population expansion and has provided some corollary hypotheses to test with archeological data.

We have seen how experimentation in archeology may take many forms and provide an opportunity for students having a wide variety of talents and interests to contribute to the field in ways that are not usually thought to be traditional. Indeed, it seems likely that much of the future of archeology will be closely linked with advances made through experimentation.

Ethnoarcheology

The study of modern peoples for the light their practices may shed on prehistory has become a current focus of research. In one way or another, **analogy**, in which we compare something from the past with an object in use today, has long been used as an aid in interpreting the past, but **ethnoarcheology** goes well beyond the usual limits of analogy. Analogy has been used chiefly to identify the uses of artifacts, such as arrowheads, hide scrapers, and stones for grinding grain. Analogy is possible because people have observed and recorded the use of such implements, and we can infer that similar objects were used in the same way in the past.

Ethnoarcheology, which is the study of peoples specifically for the information they may give on archeological matters, carries such interests forward and also adds a dimension of potential interpretation. These studies are usually carried out by archeologists themselves, whereas formerly it was usually ethnographers who studied the customs of other peoples. Archeologists eventually realized, however, that ethnographers often did not return with the kind of information that archeologists need: they were more interested in marriage practices than in the kind of houses people lived in; or in their religious rituals than in the tangible traces that religious activities might leave. In fact, most questions that an archeologist would ask, would not occur to an observer of the fully functioning society. What archeologists need are clues in the living community as to how material objects and the places they are used relate to specific activities. Then these findings can be compared with remains that may be thousands of years old, to answer such questions as how many people lived here, what was their social organization, their basis of subsistence, and so on?

An issue of *World Archaeology* (1971) was devoted to the topic, archeology and ethnography. From that issue the article by Nicholas David is particularly apposite in the present context. David begins with the statement,

> That a degree of fit exists between households and their domestic buildings is an ethnographic fact and an assumption necessary for the reconstruction of past social organization. . . . In this paper I attempt to demonstrate the fit that exists between compounds at the village of Be on the Mayo (River) Kebbi (N. Cameroon) and their settled Fulani inhabitants, and go on to discuss the problem facing the archeologist who wishes to crack their building code (David 1971:111).

David's study was basically ethnographic in that he resided in the community and was able to determine the kinship of the people, their residence patterns, and activities, along with the tangible artifacts and remains that related to these practices. To augment his analysis he drew a map of the settlement, and from this, another that shows only remains that would be potentially recoverable archeologically. He then invites the reader to try to interpret the significance of these remains much as an archeologist would try to interpret the plan of features at a site he has dug. The exercise, in other words, is not sterile but rather an important example of the kind of reasoning that every fieldworker goes through.

Much of David's paper is an explanation of the actual ethnographically known circumstances of the village. He then makes the point that it would be impossible for archeologists to make accurate intepretations of some of the features, though not of others. To cite a simple example of the failure of commonsense expectation to be borne out, "wealth was never expressed in hut size." Rather he found hut size a function of "expected frequency of white ant infestation" (David 1971:126–127). "When a roof might be eaten in six months or less, the smaller the hut, and thence the roof, the easier it is to replace."

More complicated kinds of interpretations may lead to even greater imprecision, as David (1971:128) points out:

> Even in the test case, doubly unreal since the rules were known and everything preservable and not easily portable was left without disturbance, imprecisions, and ambiguities inherent in the data made accurate deductions of household groupings impossible or at least not unequivocally demonstrable. How much more so when a site is not protected by clean sand, but has been eroded, built over, pitted and plundered by later occupants, and tunnelled by rodents?

A study like David's provides a sobering appraisal, through "testing" a modern situation, of how much one can hope to infer from archeological remains. One should not, however, despair that any interpretation can be made. Rather his study provides us with a set of solid data to use in judging how far we may allow interpretations to go, and it extends our range of useful information concerning reasons houses may be of a certain size and duration, to cite only one example given by David.

A similar investigation, the Garbage Project, has been underway for several years in Tucson under the supervision of William Rathje. By analyzing the garbage discarded by samples of families from different social and economic backgrounds, investigators have been able to test certain assumptions about dietary habits, and to learn about a wide range of behavior that is usually not recorded but whose residue appears in the trash. The investigators hope to be able to relate their findings in modern garbage to what archeologists normally deal with in their ancient trash heaps and abandoned cities (Rathje 1976)

There has been a tendency to regard studies in ethnoarcheology as "cautionary tales." That is, the investigators have come back from the field with all sorts of reasons why they cannot make valid interpretations of prehistoric behavior based only upon the tangible remains found in archeological sites. One reason has been that there are many possible causes for a single effect, and another is that archeologists have tended to focus too specifically. The former problem may be illustrated by pointing out that a stone tool which is finally worn out and discarded may have been used in its lifetime as a knife, a scraper, an awl, or a backscratcher. By observing patterns of wear, even microscopically, one could never deduce all of these uses. The other problem relates to the fact that modern peoples may not be doing things just as they were done in the past. Thus, the use of iron pots is not quite the same as the use of pottery vessels. There is, in this instance, no direct analogy possible between modern pots and those we find in prehistoric sites.

In spite of such limits, ethnoarcheology has great potential for informing on general patterns of behavior and their relation to artifacts, and for giving us a view of how people with quite different technology and social organization do things. The latter simply gives us a wider range of options in imagining how things were in the past. The former is the kind of thing Schiffer is attempting with his testing of cultural laws through the study of modern behavior.

Ethnoarcheology can also help with specific archeological studies when the ways of life of modern peoples are sufficiently similar to those of the past and when there simply aren't any adequate studies of certain interesting ways of life. A case in point is the study of pastoral nomadic peoples in Luristan, Iran, which was carried out by F. Hole in support of an archeological project that concerned the origins and development of domestication. Traditionally, it had been assumed that pastoral nomads leave few traces that can be found archeologically and that their way of life is a relatively modern specialization which depends greatly on the use of horses, donkeys, or camels for packing baggage. Since nomads have no written history of their own, there was no way to tell how old the way of life was. Therefore it was necessary to study nomadic people to find out about their way of life and what it might leave for archeologists (Figs 1.5a, b). Then it was necessary to use this information to search for sites to find out how old they are. This work resulted in the finding of a nomad camp which is about 8000 years old.

We can see from these examples that ethnoarcheology has much potential. It is as varied as circumstances and the imaginations of archeologists allow. Certainly its present popularity is a reflection of the continuing close relationship between archeology and other branches of anthropology and between the practical and theoretical aspects of our science.

A Mission for Archeology: Cultural Resource Management

The most recent development in archeology in the United States is to direct it toward national and local goals of conserving the environment. The impetus for this has come largely from those agencies of the federal government that are involved in managing our natural and cultural resources. In this sense, the agencies are mission-oriented and insofar as they are involved in archeology, it too has become mission-oriented in contrast with its traditional academic orientation. Within the framework of mission-oriented archeology is (1) the evaluation of resources and of the impact that construction and other activities might have, (2) the development of plans to mitigate losses that might occur, and (3) the management of archeological sites for conservation, for public education and enjoyment, and perhaps future excavation. In the broad sense, this development is a response to the threat of destruction of sites (which are nonrenewable resources), and it is a reflection of general concern over protecting our environmental and cultural heritages.

There has been, of course, a long history of public concern with archeological resources, as the Antiquities Act of 1906 and subsequent legislation indicate. Nevertheless, there has never been a comprehensive inventory of archeological sites on federal land, nor, until recently, much concern over the loss of sites during construction of highways, dams, and the like. What applies to federal lands is even more true of sites on state and private lands, which have

FIG. 1.5a Sometimes archeologists find it most efficient to study contemporary people whose way of life resembles that of ancient peoples. Here nomads in western Iran are the subject of an ethnoarcheological study.

scarcely been protected, let alone managed. State antiquities laws have become common only in the last decade, and most states still have inadequate staffs to manage their resources. Thus, we suddenly find that while there are now laws requiring archeology, there are too few persons to do the jobs and still less a broad understanding or consensus of what the problems and responsibilities are.

The 1906 Antiquities Act was followed by a number of other acts, the most notable having to do with the preservation of historic sites. Prehistoric sites were not much considered in these acts, although various federal agencies undertook archeological work when major resources seemed to be threatened. This was the case during the great periods of dam building, the most recent of which resulted in the River Basin Surveys of the Plains states. The act with the most far-reaching consequences, however, was passed in 1974. This is known as the Moss-Bennett Act (Public Law 93-291) and officially as the Archeological and Historical Preservation Act of 1974, which was enacted by Congress to provide a covering rationale and the means of funding archeological work in the public interest. Although the guidelines for the way this act will be applied are still being worked out and the Act itself will come up for reevaluation in 1979, it has already had a tremendous impact on archeology.

Since both the federal and state governments have enacted legislation

FIG. 1.5b Archeologists try to discover how the kinds of activities the people engage in relate to things we may find in ancient sites. Details of dwellings, fireplaces, cooking utensils, location of campsites and so on are all objects of archeological inquiry.

concerning the need to protect archeological resources, a large proportion of archeologists have shifted their attention from academic projects to **contract work.** That is, the archeologists are now hired by an agency or company to carry out investigations that are required by law. This work is ordinarily very specific as to area to be covered, the type of work that must be done, the deadlines that must be observed, and the nature of resulting reports. Thus, the philosophy, pace, and accountability of the work are quite different from what is traditional in academic archeology.

The philosophy of **cultural resource management** (CRM) is to make the wisest use of our resources. To begin, this requires an inventory of what there is that might be affected by construction or other use of the land. When this has been determined, an **environmental impact statement** (EIS) is required, a part of which deals with archeological sites. This describes the possible effect of proposed activities on the resources, and it makes recommendations about ways to mitigate the impact of these activities on the sites. The emphasis during the days of **salvage archeology** was to dig. Now the emphasis is on alternatives to digging. Are the sites worth saving, and if so, how can they be saved without digging them? The philosophy of management is directed **not** toward digging so much as it is toward maintaining sites.

The new philosophy now requires archeologists to take more into account than just their personal interests or even the broader academic interests of archeology. They are now called upon to place archeology in a wider context. Environmental assessments are evaluations of the worth of many things. Are trees or sites or clean streams worth more than bridges or dams? Is one archeological site more important to dig or preserve than another? One of the challenges in modern cultural resource management is learning to make such decisions intelligently. The future of archeology and of our cultural heritage depend upon wise choices and responsible management.

As one might expect, there have been numerous responses to the new needs in archeology. Foremost among these have been programs at universities to teach students how to enter into cultural resource management. These programs depart from the standard archeological curricula chiefly in providing a thorough working knowledge of legislation affecting archeology, ways and means of developing working relations with agencies, bidding on jobs, drawing up research proposals, and writing reports. There is in these programs an emphasis on management as it involves both cultural resources and a businesslike approach to contracted projects. In these programs there is the explicit assumption that efficient administration is as important as competent archeology. Indeed, without the latter one can hardly hope for the former.

We also find that many archeologists have set up teams to do contract work. Usually such teams are affiliated administratively with a university or museum but individuals also do contract work, sometimes as their exclusive occupation. The complexities of the work—which include liaison among government agencies, private companies, archeologists, concerned citizens, and legislators, as well as handling payrolls, logistics, taxes, analysis of material, and writing of reports—ordinarily are more than one person can handle. The tendency therefore seems to be to develop teams of people who have an array of skills and various levels of academic achievement, which can be brought to bear on particular projects.

Because there is such a large and rapidly growing amount of relevant legislation and procedures, it is impossible to give a succinct resumé of the total situation or even to provide information that will remain up-to-date. The book *Public Archeology*, by Dr. Charles R. McGimsey of the University of Arkansas, is the most comprehensive effort to provide a nationwide review of state programs, but this work is now out-of-date. Information on new developments in cultural resources management is now being distributed by a newsletter from the American Society of Conservation Archaeologists, a group of archeologists and others who are involved in contract work. The most complete and up-to-date summary of the background on CRM is in *Guidelines for the Profession: The Airlie House Reports*, a publication sponsored by the National Park Service and the Society for American Archaeology. The history of legislation preceding the Moss-Bennett Act is included in this work, along with guidelines and ideas concerning other related matters in archeology.

Certainly cultural resource management promises to become the most important innovation in archeology of this decade and perhaps of this generation. Nevertheless, as these words are written one can only guess precisely what the future may hold and it is too soon to report just how profound the effect will be on all of archeology, whether in the United States or in England where there are parallel concerns, or in other parts of the world where archeology is coming to be seen as an important aspect of public policy.

It is much easier to look back into our own history and it is not inappropriate to do so when we are caught up in a whirl of change that seems so very new.

As early as 1627, Charles I of England officially declared that "the study of antiquities . . . is very serviceable to the general good of the State and Commonwealth." And positive action was being taken to preserve sites a hundred years ago in Britain, when a Roman amphitheater was sucessfully saved from destruction because it stood in a railroad right-of-way. In 1899, when the **Aswan Dam** was built by British engineers, the proposed water level was reduced by 55 feet in order not to submerge the island of Philae with its magnificent stone temple (Ward 1900:256). This is one of the earliest examples of consideration being paid to archeological sites threatened by great engineering projects. The spate of dam building in the United States in the past 35 years has inevitably led to the submergence of thousands of prehistoric archeological sites. Despite the concern of federal authorities over this loss and their efforts to recover materials, much more has been lost than learned, and regional archeological histories will forever be deficient to the extent that information was not obtained while there was still time. It is principally because of this belated recognition that the concept and practice of cultural resource management has developed.

Chapter 2

A SHORT HISTORY OF ARCHEOLOGY

In the first chapter we dealt with what archeologists are doing today. The present chapter, in briefly reviewing the history of archeology, attempts to set the modern activities in the field into their own context and perspective.

As an academic discipline, archeology has a history of only a little more than 100 years, but a few persons were practicing a form of archeology by the end of the fourteenth century. Early archeologists, spurred by an interest in ancient Greece and Rome, directed their work mainly toward recovering coins and objects of art. The emphasis was on collecting and cataloguing, usually for personal rather than for public pleasure. But as long ago as 500 years there were "royal cabinets" consisting of ancient items. Many of these later formed the nucleus of national museums, which began to be founded after 1800.

It was this interest in the past that gave birth to the concept of the romance of archeology. In fact, some of the finest tales of adventure and exploration stem from the romantic lure of discovering and collecting. The words of early travelers who happily faced privation, disease, and sometimes death as they sought their treasures across the globe quicken the pulse even today. This is true even though, as Wheeler (1956:241) remarked, ". . . romance is merely adventure remembered in tranquillity, devoid of the ills and anxieties, fleas, fevers, thirst, and toothache, which are liable to be the more insistent experience."

Without doubt, the most persistent motive throughout the history of archeology has been to collect antiquities. Sometimes excavation was needed; at other times, not. Sometimes collection was an end in itself; at other times it was a step toward a broader end. Whatever curious turns archeology has taken, collection has traditionally been at its center. But the emphasis has shifted. Today private collecting is done mostly by amateurs and persons of means, and is actively shunned by professionals.

Although recovering objects is a central activitiy of archeology, when these artifacts—whether they are cuneiform tablets, Greek statues, flint tools, or bits of pottery—are collected, archeologists must describe, classify, record, and interpret the information recovered. The differences among the various kinds of archeology that are practiced today are largely in the geographic areas and particular times studied, and in the way the data are interpreted. The following sections will describe some of these kinds of archeology as they have developed historically.

Dilettantes, Bargain Hunters, and Deep-Sea Divers

The history of "treasure hunting" is highlighted by cultivated gentlemen of the arts, brash performers for fame and prestige, highwaymen with official backing, cowboys, and submarine adventurers. At their best, these men stirred the imaginations of a complacent and self-centered Western world; at their worst, they wrought irreparable damage to the record of man's past.

The history of treasure hunting must be viewed against the slow development of archeology, the emergence of a conscience about how it should be done, and the appearance of an educated public and appreciative governments who acted to protect their ancient remains from destruction. We shall want to judge the men involved, but we must remember that our criticisms of their work depend on knowledge not available a hundred or more years ago. Were we to judge work done in 1800 or 1900 by the standards of today, we should generally find it damnable, both in its execution and in its conception.

The earliest record we have of archeology was actually discovered by archeologists of a much later day. The first archeologist who appears in history is **Nabonidus**, last of the kings of Babylon (555–538 B.C.) and father of Belshazzar. Nabonidus became intensely interested in the past of Babylonian culture and conducted excavations of ancient buildings, saved what he found, and established a museum in which his discoveries were displayed.

Tombs, with their lure of buried riches, have long attracted both looters and archeologists. In fact, excavation for the jewelry and precious metals contained in princely tombs began long before the advent of anything approaching archeology in Egypt. As W. Emery (1961:129) neatly observes, the Egyptians believed "you could take it with you," and as a result they buried a wealth of materials with their dead. Belzoni (whose work is described later) and others of his ilk were doing nothing new when they entered these tombs, for they often found they were several thousand years too late to salvage the prizes they sought. The ancient Egyptians themselves were always conscious of the temptations that royal tombs offered to looters, and they took elaborate precautions to protect them. The precautions were often fruitless, however, and as early as 1120 B.C. there was an official investigation and list of tomb robberies made in Egypt. But the practice or robbing was worldwide. The historian Strabo mentions that when Julius Caesar established a Roman colony for veterans of his campaigns on the site of ancient **Corinth**, former cemeteries were discovered and looted for bronze vessels, which were sold to Roman collectors who prized items of Greek manufacture. The Spanish **conquistadors** in Mexico, Panama, and Peru soon learned that they could "mine" ancient cemeteries for gold objects, and they proceeded to do so as soon as the native peoples were conquered. Fernandez de Oviedo, a Spanish chronicler, wrote a detailed report on the opening of a tomb in Darien in 1522, and if we are willing to call this archeology, his is one of the earliest archeological reports from the New World.

In the fifteenth century, 2000 years after Nabonidus, the large-scale collecting of art treasurers began in Italy and flourished, especially in Rome, under the example of popes such as Sixtus IV (1471–1484) and his immediate successors. To supplement the techniques of merely removing standing monuments, Alexander VI, who was pope between 1492 and 1503, began excavating to add to his collection. During the fifteenth century it became fashionable for influential men of affairs as well as of the church to furnish their homes with the abundant ancient statuary. These men of the Italian Renaissance were known as **dilettanti** (Italian for *delighting*), to describe their delight in the fine arts.

The collector's spirit did not remain confined to Italy. With the spread of the Renaissance, collectors from all over Europe began to accumulate objects that would later become the nuclei of many of the world's famous museums. It was during this time that the city of **Herculaneum**, buried under a thick deposit of volcanic material thrown out of **Vesuvius** in A.D. 79—at which time **Pompeii** was also buried—was "mined" for Roman sculptures, which were sold to rich collectors.

When **Thomas Howard, the Earl of Arundel**, visited Italy in the early seventeenth century, he began his extensive collection of art from Greece, Italy, and Southwest Asia. His example of travel and collection was not lost on other young Englishmen of means who, for the next 200 years, were to follow Howard to the Mediterranean. The extent of Arundel's zeal can be seen today in the Ashmolean Museum in Oxford, England, which retains the nucleus of his once much larger collection of marbles. Howard's collection, not as greatly appreciated by his descendants, was partly destroyed and then dispersed.

By the beginning of the nineteenth century, the scene of large-scale collecting had begun to shift to the sites of the forgotten civilizations of the Near East. There on the desert valleys of the Nile, Tigris, and Euphrates, the great feats of treasure hunting were performed. Until the end of the eighteenth century, the Western world knew little of the riches that awaited discovery in Southwest Asia. A few mud bricks with undecipherable inscriptions on them, a handful of cylinder seals, and tales of certain imposing cities in ruins were all that had reached Europe after the **Crusades.** The establishment of a British consulate in Baghdad 1802 marked the opening of Southwest Asia for the Western world and its treasure hunters.

The occupant of the British Residency in Baghdad for most of its first 25 years was **Claudius Rich**, a precocious student of languages and an astute politician. Rich's wide interests were shown in his careful surveying of prominent archeological sites and especially in his collecting. After his untimely death in 1821, some 7000 pounds of antiquities—including ancient coins, Syriac manuscripts, and about 1000 pounds of clay tablets, cylinders, and bricks with cuneiform inscriptions gathered by him—were deposited in the British Museum in London.

A contemporary of Claudius Rich, **Henry Creswick Rawlinson**, was a British (Indian) Army officer, horseman, adventurer, and student of ancient languages. With remarkable energy and devotion, Rawlinson visited virtually every ancient monument of consequence in what is now modern Iran. His interest was mainly to collect samples of the ancient writing that had not yet been deciphered. As evidence of his travels one frequently finds Rawlinson's name carved into cliffs that were once reserved for the inscriptions of kings. But Rawlinson's fame lies not in his arduous journeys nor in his artistry with a chisel, but in his recording and translating of the long-lost inscriptions that describe Persia's former opulence. By 1837, working in his spare time, he had accomplished the translations that were to gain him the title, "Father of Cuneiform."

The earliest archeology had been done as a hobby by men whose primary business lay along quite different lines, but by the middle of the nineteenth century archeology received an impetus that it had not hitherto enjoyed. Both the French and British, sensing the great treasure that awaited the enterprising, supported men whose sole job was to recover antiquities.

One of the first of these men was **Austen Henry Layard**, who, under British auspices, undertook to dig the site of **Nimrud**, Mesopotamia, one of the ancient Assyrian capitals. (Actually he had mistakenly identified the site as **Nineveh**.) As Layard approached the task, his expectations mounted and he recorded a dream he had as follows: "Visions of palaces underground, of gigantic monsters, of sculptured figures, and endless inscriptions, floated before me. After forming plan after plan for removing the earth, and extricating these treasures, I fancied myself wandering in a maze of chambers from which I could find no outlet" (Lloyd 1955:126). When two palaces were discovered during the first day of excavation, the news spread rapidly, and soon the French entered the scene. With the lure of gold for the taking, agents of the two countries frantically dashed around, staking claims on sites about whose contents they knew nothing.

In spite of the promise of treasure for the British Museum, Layard, in contrast to his French counterpart, Paul Emile Botta, was never able to finance properly a really serious excavation. He was reduced to an expedient more the rule than the exception in those days. It can be stated simply: "to obtain the largest possible number of well-preserved objects of art at the least possible outlay of time and money" (Lloyd 1955:133). Though he sorely regretted it, as he dug through Nimrud, Layard saw many of the treasures disintegrate before his eyes. Frescoes, sculpture, and metal work frequently crumbled to bits when exposed to air and handling. Layard, in common with his competitors, had no knowledge of how to preserve the priceless objects and no time in which to experiment on techniques of conservation.

Although much information was lost in these excavations, they were remarkable accomplishments when we consider that they were carried out with very little money (Layard paid his workers 6 cents a day), in sites of impressive size (Kuyunjik covers 1850 acres; the Khorsabad palace, 25 acres; Nippur, 445 acres), among warring Arab tribes (witness the destruction of Peters' camp and equipment at Nippur in 1889), and at a time when medical knowledge was minimal (C. Bellino, C. Rich, and G. Smith died in the middle of their fieldwork from cholera or dysentery) (Lloyd 1955; Pallis 1956). Books by Layard—as much about adventure as about archeology—became bestsellers in their day.

In the ensuing years French and British archeologists even vied with each other at the same site. In 1853 a British subject, **Hormuzd Rassam**, who was Layard's successor, anxiously watched as French diggers approached a particularly likely looking spot on Kuyunjik, one of the palace mounds at Nineveh. When his envy over the prospects of a rich find grew unbearable, Rassam took his workmen and had them excavate at night, stopping at dawn before the French came on the scene. By this simple subterfuge Rassam's men discovered a picture gallery and library in the palace of Ashur-bani-pal, an Assyrian king who lived between 669 and 633 B.C. Lacking time and funds, the men hacked their way through the palace, preserving little that was not obviously intact and thereby losing much. Rassam (1897:395–396) wrote,

> Early the next day I . . . examined the localities where collections of un-baked clay tablets had been discovered, and was glad to find that important relics had crowned our labors. I found, to my great vexation, that a large number of the records had crumbled to pieces as soon as they were removed, as they were found in damp soil impregnated with nitre. Had I had an Assyrian copyist with me, we might have preserved, at all events, the history of the documents, though part of the originals would have been lost.

Rassam later learned that mud tablets could be baked and thus preserved, and wrote, "Our excavations at Aboo-Habba were carried out without much interruption for eighteen months altogether, during which time we must have discovered between sixty and seventy thousand inscribed tablets, a large number of which fell to pieces before we could have them baked."

The great public interest in these ancient records written in cuneiform on clay tablets made them particularly desirable to collect, and the Arab workers were quick to realize this. The natural result was large scale plundering of Mesopotamian sites by local people searching for tablets, which they sold to dealers in Baghdad who in turn sold them to archeologists and museum collectors. G. Smith bought 2000 tablets from Sippar in 1876; Budge in 1890 purchased 9500 tablets which had been illegally dug from Dêr, and after Sarzec's departure from Telloh in 1900 the local natives opened up the ancient tablet chambers (that is, libraries and record rooms) and were able to remove 35,000 tablets in sufficiently good condition for dealers to purchase. The search for the tablets continued, and in 1931 it had gotten so out of hand that Royal Air Force planes were used to drive away the Arab plunderers (Pallis 1956:284).

The style of digging that was done more than a century ago in Mesopotamia is expressed in Loftus's (1858:52–53) account of his efforts to collect glazed coffins from the site of Warkah (Uruk) in southern Mesopotamia:

> The object of my second visit to Warkah was to collect a series of such antiquities as it afforded, and more especially to obtain one of the glazed coffins which might be sent to the British Museum. As the colour of those near the surface is affected by exposure, I tried to procure a good specimen from below; but, the deeper I dug, the more saturated with moisture and brittle they became, so that, the moment an attempt was made to move one, it fell to pieces. Finding it impossible to succeed at any depth, I came to the conclusion that the only chance for me was to try at the surface. As the Arabs were much more adept at digging with their spears and hands than with the spades which I had brought with me, I permitted them to follow their own mode of searching. Their cupidity is attracted by the treasures contained within the coffins, to procure which many hundreds are broken and searched every year. Their method of proceeding is simple enough: they pierce the loose soil with their spears, until they chance to strike against some solid substance: by the vibration produced, the Arab knows at once whether he has hit upon a coffin or the vault containing one. The spear is then thrown aside, and, after the fashion of a mole, the wild fellow digs a hole with his hands. If an obstacle presents itself, the spear is again had recourse to, and in this manner perseverance secures the object of search. When the coffin is rifled, a hole is broken through the bottom to ascertain if there be one below. In riding or walking over mounds considerable care is requisite on account of the innumerable holes made by the Arabs, who of course never take the trouble to fill them up again.
>
> During every day of my stay several coffins were uncovered, and numerous expedients adopted to remove one unbroken: but notwithstanding every precaution, they broke with their own weight. Pieces of carpet and Arab abbas were tied tightly around them, the earth inside was either partially or wholly removed, and poles were placed below to give support; all however to no purpose.

As if these feats of looting and mass destruction were not enough, a crowning blow to the developing discipline of Assyriology occurred in 1855 with the destruction by Arab vandals of some 300 cases of antiquities collected by Place from the Palace of Sardanapalus. Disappointed in the cargo, the Arabs capsized the rafts carrying it as they were about to enter the Persian Gulf below Baghdad, and there they await recovery by some enterprising archeologist who can locate and raise them from the mud (Fig. 2.1).

In writing of the history of excavation in Iraq, Lloyd (1963:35) recalled his impressions of the great site of **Khafajah** in southeastern Iraq. "When we first visited it, [it] looked like a battlefield. The main mound . . . was completely honey-combed with holes large enough to be shell craters, surrounded by mountains of discarded earth." Lloyd also records that since 1930 in the Lurish province of western Iran between 400 and 500 burial grounds, each containing about 200 graves "have been excavated commercially [for bronze objects] without any assistance from archeologists" (Fig. 2.2).

The looting of ancient graves for the precious metals and jewels they con-

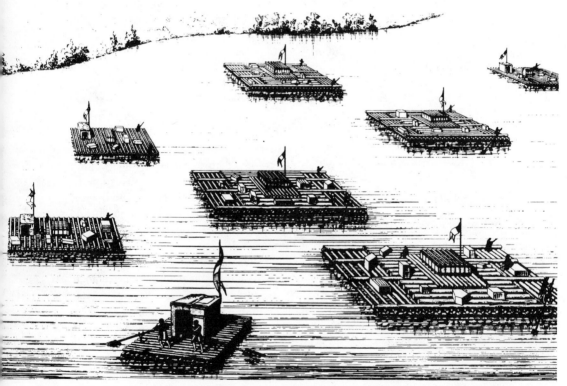

FIG. 2.1 *Transport by V. Place on the Tigris River in 1855 of Assyrian sculptures. The* kelek *rafts are made of inflated animal skins decked with logs. The entire shipment of about 300 cases, except for a colossal bull sculpture and a winged figure now in the Louvre, was lost when the rafts were sunk by Arab brigands. Illustration from V. Place,* Ninève et Assyrie. Paris, 1869.

FIG. 2.2 In the foreground is an archeological site in western Iran that was systematically looted of the bronzes in more than 1000 graves. The site is pockmarked with vertical shafts that lead to the tombs, leaving the site worthless for archeological exploration.

tain has been practiced for thousands of years. As scientific interest in antiquities developed, however, much material which had been of no interest to tomb robbers began to acquire pecuniary value. Egyptian mummies (the word derives from "mumiya," the Arabic word for a raw pitch) were much in demand in the fifteenth and sixteenth centuries in Europe where they were ground into powder and taken as medicine. Mark Twain in *Innocents Abroad* reports that on the Egyptian railway "the fuel they use for the locomotive is composed of mummies three thousand years old, purchased by the ton or the graveyard for that purpose, and . . . sometimes one hears the profane engineer call out pettishly, 'D—n these plebians, they don't burn worth a cent—pass out a king.' " We remind the reader that this is humor, not fact.

In Egypt, collecting of antiques was begun during the fifteenth century by Italian humanists who were interested in the religious texts that the Romans had reported being on the **obelisks**. A by-product of these activities was the pillaging of sites and tombs. This interest in the ancient Egyptian language received its biggest boost with the discovery of the **Rosetta Stone** in 1799 (Fig. 2.3). It was discovered by one of Napoleon's field officers, André Joseph Boussard, who was directing excavations for fortifications at Fort Rachid (later Fort Julien) about 7 kilometers from Rosetta (near Alexandria) in the Nile delta. The Greek inscription was soon translated by archeological experts attached to the French forces, and it was thus learned that the stone referred to a general synod of Egyptian priests at Memphis in honor of Ptolemy V. The importance of the stone was realized, and it was entrusted to General Jacques François de Menou, who kept the stone for safekeeping in his house. When the British army in 1801 forced the surrender

FIG. 2.3 The Rosetta stone is a slab of basalt found at Rosetta, at the western mouth of the Nile. A decree of Ptolemy V (196 B.C.) was written on the stone in Egyptian **hieroglyphs,** *a cursive form of Egyptian called Demotic, and in Greek. Study of these parallel texts enabled Champollion to decipher the Egyptian hieroglyphs at the top.*

of General Menou, included in the articles of capitulation was the provision that all Egyptian antiquities collected by the French should be delivered over. General Menou, in an attempt to save the Rosetta Stone, claimed it as his personal property, but the English commander, Lord Hutchinson, through his envoy, Turner, ignored this nicety and seized the stone, which was taken off to England in 1802, and deposited, with the Elgin Marbles, in the British Museum in London.

Rubbings of the trilingual inscription of the Rosetta Stone, made by the French before it passed from their hands, provided scholars with what they needed. While the British worked hard at finding the key to the Rosetta inscriptions, so also did the French, and the answer was finally provided by Jean François Champollion in 1822 (Fig. 2.4).

No history of archeological treasure hunting should fail to mention one of the most extraordinary persons ever to be called an archeologist. **Giovanni Battista Belzoni** was perhaps the most outrageous and audacious looter of them all. Working in the early 1800s, partly under the auspices of the British Consul in Cairo, Belzoni capped his richly varied life as circus strong man and hydraulic engineer by dedicating himself to robbing tombs. Belzoni, whom Mayes (1961: 296) somewhat inappropriately described as "the man who laid the foundations of an English Egyptology," was a physical giant of a man whose deeds assumed gigantic proportions.

Belzoni's career in Egypt began in Thebes. His first efforts are described as follows "Every step I took I crushed a mummy in some part or other. When my weight bore on the body of an Egyptian it crushed like a bandbox. I sank altogether among the broken mummies with a crash of bones, rags and wooden cases . . . I could not avoid being covered with bones, legs, arms and heads rolling from above" (Daniel 1950:155–156). Moving from tombs to outdoor projects, Belzoni excavated Abu Simbel, he opened the Second Pyramid, he recovered the 8-ton head of Rameses II from Thebes, and he probably would have succeeded in the prodigious engineering feat of sending the Philae obelisk out of the country had he not been intercepted by a better-armed band of

FIG. 2.4 Jean-François Champollion (1790–1832) deciphered the Rosetta stone in 1822 and unlocked the mystery of the ancient Egyptian hieroglyphic writing.

brigands who claimed it for themselves. But Belzoni was not altogether a crude wrecker and collector, if we may judge him by his time-consuming efforts to make wax castings of the interior of two elaborate Egyptian tombs with the aim of bringing them back to Europe and making exact reproductions for showing to the public. Belzoni was not the seed from which British Egyptology sprang but the autumn brilliance of a leaf that was soon to wither and fall. Howard Carter, famous for his excavation of the tomb of Tutankhamen in 1923, had this to say about Belzoni's day: "Those were the great days of excavating. Anything to which a fancy was taken, from a scarab to an obelisk, was just appropriated, and if there was difference with a brother excavator, one laid for him with a gun" (Carter and Mace 1923–1933:Vol. I, p. 68).

Austen Layard certainly believed in this principle. In 1842, his equipment was plundered by Arabs. After appealing to the authorities, a procedure which had no effect, he took matters into his own hands. Bonomi (1853:34) describes how he handled the matter:

> In three or four days he learned who were the robbers, and he deter-
> mined to make them feel that they were not to carry their incursions
> into his quarters with impunity. Taking with him two trusty Arabs, expert
> at their weapons, he came upon the guilty sheikh in the midst of his fol-
> lowers, and politely asked for the missing articles, some of which were
> hanging up in his sight. When the sheikh and his party had stoutly denied
> the possession of the goods in question, one of Layard's two attendants
> handcuffed the old man in a moment, and, jumping on his horse, dragged
> him out of the encampment at a most uncomfortable pace. The sudden-
> ness of the performance paralyzed the by-standers, who were well sup-
> plied with arms. The sheikh was carried to Nimroud where he thought
> it wiser to make a full confession than to journey to Mosul and confront
> the Pasha. Next morning the missing property, with the addition of a kid
> and a lamb, as a peace offering, made their appearance: the sheikh was
> therefore liberated, and Layard had no subsequent reason to complain of
> him or his tribe.

Experiences of this sort were the rule rather than the exception in the early days of archeology in the Middle East, and we can only admire the fortitude and capability of these early excavators. But that is not to say that uncomfortable, and often dangerous, confrontations do not occur on archeological digs today. Both of the authors of this book have had such experiences in Mexico and Iran.

By the end of the nineteenth century, archeologists had come to recog-
nize the part that texts would play in unraveling the history of the area, and they began to dig primarily to recover the ancient writings. Some of the inscriptions were on stone and clay, but others (especially from Egypt) were **papyrus** rolls containing Egyptian texts as well as Greek and Roman literary writings. With this change in emphasis, archeology took a historical bent and became more leisurely and scholarly than it had been in the days when the museums were empty and the excavators were chiefly collectors.

While the history of ancient civilizations occupied scholars in the Near East, in Europe a fascination with the extreme age of cave-dwelling man, whose remains dated from the latter part of the **Pleistocene**, or Ice Age, developed just over a century ago. By the end of the nineteenth century many sites, the scenes of occupation lasting thousands of years, had been systematically "quarried." Gangs of workmen were hired to obtain the few carvings of bone and ivory, figurines of clay and stone, and superbly made tools of lint and bone that had been produced so many thousands of years before. The lure was not so much the intrinsic value of the artifacts as it was the great age that they implied. During those times, men such as Otto Hauser, a Swiss dealer in antiquities, became wealthy collecting and selling material to the museums that would bid the highest. In 1908 he sold a skeleton from Le Moustier in France for 100,000 gold marks to the Museum of Ethnology in Berlin. All over the continent and England as well, gentlemen spent their holidays excavating in the local sites. But these looting operations gradually died out as the historical importance of the antiquities was recognized.

There was a time when public interest in ancient cities was so great that whole sites might be purchased. In 1840 J. L. Stephens, acting privately, though an official of the U.S. government, made a serious effort to purchase the **Classic Maya** site of Palenque (Heizer 1969:219–226), and J. E. S. Thompson (1963:222) quotes a letter from Lord Palmerston to Frederick Chatfield, British representative to the five Central American republics, asking him to make an attempt to secure some of the famous carved **stelae** of Copan, saying,

It appears that these ruins are held in little or no estimation by the natives of the country, and it seems possible, therefore, that the chief difficulty to be encountered in removing specimens of the sculpture would consist in providing means of transporting them to some place of embarcation. You will be careful, therefore, that in making inquiries in pursuance of this instruction, you do not lead the people of the country to attach any imaginary value to things which they consider at present as having no value at all.

Fortunately neither Stephens nor Chatfield succeeded in removing the antiquities of Palenque or Copan, two sites now generally agreed to be the most beautiful of all **Mayan** cities.

A happy and early exception to the prevailing rule was the famous and successful research team of Henry Christy, an English banker, and Edward Lartet, a French magistrate who abandoned the law for paleontology. Between 1863 and 1865, when Christy died from an illness contracted in digging a cave in Belgium, the two men excavated in the famous French Paleolithic sites of La Madeleine (from which the **Magdalenian** culture was named), Le Moustier (type site of the **Mousterian** culture), Les Eyzies, Laugerie Haute, and others (Fig. 2.5). Their cooperative work was intelligently done, and among their important accomplishments were the first recognition of Paleolithic engraved art, recognition and definition

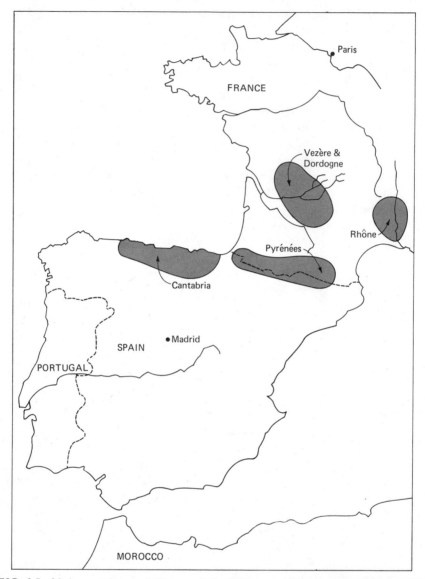

FIG. 2.5 *Major regions of Upper Paleolithic art in western Europe. The Vezère-Dordogne region is sometimes called "The Capital of Prehistory" because of its wealth of Upper Paleolithic sites, which include La Madeleine and the cave of Lascaux; Altamira is in Cantabria; and Niaux in the Pyrenees.*

of the **Upper Paleolithic** as distinct from the **Lower Paleolithic**, and the first classification of Paleolithic cultures based on associated fauna.

In the United States there was a similar pattern of events. After the Mexican War, and when the West had been wrested from the Indians and opened to cattle grazing, cowboys became pioneers in archeological discovery. At the successful conclusion of the Mexican War, engineers of the United States Army were dispatched to the newly acquired territories of the southwestern United States, and their reports contained descriptions of prehistoric sites that were soon to encourage American archeologists to investigate them. In the late 1800s members of the Wetherill family, early settlers in Colorado, discovered at **Mesa Verde** some of the most impressive and best-preserved prehistoric remains in the Western Hemisphere (Fig. 2.6). In 1888 Richard Wetherill and Charley Mason, looking for a stray herd, came upon one of the largest cliff dwellings ever built —"Cliff Palace." After their discovery the Wetherill brothers explored the Mesa Verde canyons in detail, and archeologists soon followed suit. A Swedish archeologist, Baron Gustav Nordenskiold (1895), wrote the first comprehensive account of the ruins in 1893, and, in retrospect, this seems to have been an open invitation for looters to try their luck also.

Central America and Peru, centers of the New World civilizations, have been the scene of even greater looting. There is scarcely an art shop or decora-

FIG. 2.6   A cliff dwelling at Mesa Verde. Masonry houses were built on ledges in the vertical sides of the mesas. Although defense may have been an important consideration in the placing of these settlements, most of the population lived on top of the mesas or in other easily accessible places.

tor's atelier in the United States that does not feature some pieces of pre-Columbian art, usually finely modeled pottery, stone sculptures, or jade carvings. These antiquities are still smuggled out of the countries of their origin; conveniently, the rural natives dig them up in their free time, thus sparing a modern collector the burden of becoming a latter-day Belzoni.

Nevertheless, both exportation and importation of pre-Columbian archeological objects are prohibited by treaties recently put into effect between the United States and Mexico and the countries of **Central America.** These laws and the prosecution of offenders by the United States government are being vigorously contested by associations of art dealers, although most museums have agreed to cooperate with the spirit of the law.

The insistence of many dealers and of collectors that the importation of antiquities to the United States is not only moral but necessary today is expressed by Andre Emmerich, a dealer in pre-Columbian art, who was quoted by Ann Holmes in a feature article in *Zest*, the Sunday supplement to the *Houston Chronicle* (May 14, 1972, p. 37):

> I believe totally in the preservation of the art of the past. But I do not support the narrow nationalism, the possessiveness involved in the position of some of these countries. Is Homer only for the Greeks? . . . Is Shakespeare only for the English? Rembrandt only for Dutch eyes? . . . Should descendants of the Turks who ran the Greeks into the sea be the sole possessors of the Greek treasures found there? . . . The United States has bought its art and has not acquired it by conquest. We have paid our moral debt, furthermore, by sponsoring and paying for many important archaeological explorations and by contributing about 75 percent of the literature on pre-Columbian art.

In response to the statement of Harvard University, which controls the Dumbarton Oaks Museum in Washington, to the effect that it will work to eliminate black market purchases, Emmerich said, "Certain museums in the east can be pious about things like that. They are already overflowing with fine examples. But what about the empty museums of Texas and California?"

Our response to such nonsense, which is merely that of a commercial dealer in antiquities trying to justify his activities, is that laws prohibiting unauthorized export of antiquities should be observed by everyone as a matter of principle. The commerical trade in antiquities has and continues to encourage the destruction of evidence and has even resulted in murder. If Texas and California museums remain empty of stolen contraband objects from other countries, we will be, as Texas and California citizens, happy. If the antiquities dealers go out of business or get thrown in jail, we will not be saddened. Today it is possible to arrange for the loan of objects, and reproductions that are recognizable as such only to experts can be made relatively easily. Thus there seems little reason to continue looting, smuggling, and other illegal activities merely to obtain objects for display.

One more aspect of treasure hunting should be considered. As practiced underwater to recover objects long since sunk, it has been called with some derision "archeological salvage." Particularly in the Mediterranean, where traders have been moving goods by ship for thousands of years, there are numerous wrecks lying in relatively shallow waters that are easily accessible to divers. Soon after the invention of the aqualung in the 1940s, a growing group of sportsmen-adventurers discovered that treasure awaited their search. It was exceedingly simple. For example, as Borhegyi (1961:10) wrote:

> As soon as word got out that an archeological discovery (a sunken ship) had been made at Antheor, amateur divers rushed from all parts of the French Riviera and with thoughtless enthusiasm carried off hundreds of souvenirs of their visit. One day in 1949 an American yacht anchored over the wrecks, and the owner arranged a special show for his guests. He put the davits of his ship at the disposal of the divers swimming there so that they could bring up heavy articles from the sea bottom.

In citing this example, we do not wish to imply that all underwater archeology is disreputable, any more than we imply that all archeology on land is treasure hunting. Nevertheless, of all of the kinds of archeology practiced today, the one which seems to appeal most to the adventurer and treasure hunter is diving on sunken ships. Small wonder. In recent years millions of dollars worth of coins, cannons, hardware, silver bars, jewelry, and more have been wrested from wrecks around the world. Truly there is a potential for treasure hunting in shipwrecks, as certain popular magazines are quick to announce.

With modern equipment, such activities are relatively easy, but it is interesting to note that many of the Spanish vessels which are searched for today off Florida and elsewhere were salvaged in their time by crews sent out specifically to recover the vast amounts of wealth. Long ago the potential of underwater archeology, as distinct from mere recovery of valuables, was also recognized. Sir Charles Lyell (1872, 2, Chap. 46) cites a considerable number of known instances of submarine archeological materials, and his list of the numbers of British vessels wrecked between 1793 and 1829 povides a hint of the possibilities for archeology that exist on the ocean bottom. Lyell concludes by saying, "It is probable that a greater number of monuments of the skill and industry of man will, in the course of ages, be collected together in the bed of the ocean than will exist at any other time on the surface of the continents."

For persons living in the fifteenth or even during much of the nineteenth century, looting, as we call it today, was a wholly respectable practice, but when it was shown that serious archeological study could pay dividends in knowledge ultimately far greater than the price an object alone might bring, educated persons engaged in looting have found themselves working against the main stream of public conscience. When measured against the life history of archeology, looting is the activity of thoughtless children; adults are expected to be better informed and to set a creditable example. Evidence of man's past is destructible and, once destroyed, can never be restored.

Texts, Temples, and Tombs

The title of this section recalls the previous one, for most of the treasure hunters were dealing with temples, texts, and tombs. But the important thing is the purpose toward which the work is directed. Here we shall deal with studies of the ancient civilizations of the Middle East and Mediterranean. Such work is usually done by persons trained in the humanities.

Classical archeology received its greatest impetus from Heinrich Schliemann, whose single-minded diligence proved that places named in the Homeric epics actually existed and were not just poetic fiction. His reading as a child of the sacking of Troy during the Homeric period so impressed him that after he made his fortune as a merchant, he began to study ancient history and set as his archeological task the finding of Homer's Troy. In spite of ridicule from scholars and difficulties in obtaining permissions to dig, he was eventually able in his several seasons of personally financed excavations, between 1869 and 1889, to find a convincing Troy (Hissarlik) on the southwestern shore of Turkey, and other great sites. He was also responsible for bringing to light the first traces of **Mycenaean civilization**. His finding of treasure in Mycenaean shaft tombs was described by Glyn Daniel (1950:138) at the time as being "one of the most important discoveries of past human civilization that has ever been made." He also found remains of an even earlier, previously unknown, prehistoric Greek life and so opened a whole new world for classical scholarship. But Schliemann's influence was most effectual in that he opened the eyes of the world to the possibilities of excavation directed toward solving problems rather than solely toward the recovery of objects of art.

As a matter of fact, Schliemann's techniques are hardly to be dignified with the term "archeology." His impatience with getting to the bottom of sites left him with little taste for working out precise stratigraphic associations. In his later years his associate, Dörpfeld, and more recently, Mellaart, brought a certain order to his digs, but his early work amounted to little more than the recovery of objects. By contrast, Schliemann's predecessor, Giuseppe Fiorelli, who excavated Pompeii in 1860, attempted to restore a picture of the whole Roman city. Fiorelli said that the discovery of art objects was of only secondary importance; yet it was Schliemann, not Fiorelli, whose work was followed by the world and whose example was emulated by later workers. Although Schliemann's excavation methods left much to be desired, his conception of what archeology could be was much more perceptive than that of his contemporaries in the eastern Mediterranean.

The recent history of **classical archeology** has been one of continuing discovery and interpretation. The Egyptian **hieroglyphs** had been deciphered by Schliemann's time, and Greek writing could be read, but other ancient scripts have not been deciphered to this day. A pre-Greek civilization, **Minoan**, was responsible for two forms of writing, the more recent of which, Linear B, was shown only in 1952 to be a form of ancient Greek. The earlier form, Linear A, is still to be deciphered adequately. Early cuneiform inscriptions from Mesopotamia, writing on Hittite documents from Anatolia, and the written **Mohenjo-daro** script of the Indus Valley civilization still cannot be read.

Writing is not the only concern of Classical scholars. Art fascinates many students, and some study coins; others prefer architecture; and, of course, there is the old mainstay of most archeology, pottery, which serves as a means of determining chronology as well as cultural connections between different societies. In spite of the diversity of topics and approaches, when ancient civilizations are studied, the emphasis usually rests on the esthetic qualities of civilization —art in its various forms, monumental architecture, and literature.

Schliemann's work set the tone of what is still being done. The significant changes since his time have been in the development of more precise techniques for acquiring information. As knowledge has accumulated, it has been possible to plan excavation more intelligently. As better techniques for excavating, recovering, and preserving antiquities have been developed, archeologists have been able to learn more. Classical archeologists have defined their aims and devoted their time to recapturing history in ever more sophisticated ways. It is not stretching a point to say that in the last generation more scientific skill and technical aid have been expended in Classical archeology than in any other branch.

Prehistory and Protohistory

It is customary to separate prehistoric from historic times. People who did not write things down or keep records that we can read, have no history as such. They did not tell us about themselves as the literate Romans or Greeks or Chinese did. Thus we say that these people are *prehistoric*. Sometimes, however, people like Native Americans who had no writing were described by other people who did, such as the colonists of North America. We say that the Native Americans who were described are *protohistoric*. These terms—prehistoric and protohistoric—are convenient labels, and they suggest something about the kinds of information that we may find about ancient peoples. But they are like many other labels that we use in archeology in that they tell only part of the story. They are not precise in detail. Sometimes people with writing did not tell us very much, and sometimes those without left a wealth of information of other kinds. The way these ideas of dividing up the past developed can be seen by taking a brief look at the history of archeology.

Christian Jurgensen Thomsen (Fig. 2.7), curator of the National Museum in Copenhagen in 1836, devised a method for sorting and displaying the antiquities in his charge. His method was to display separately the objects of stone, bronze, and iron. This was the birth of the **Three-Age System**, in which all mater-

FIG. 2.7 C. J. Thomsen (1788–1865) devised a system of arranging archeological materials for display in the National Museum of Denmark. This classification was based on the materials out of which the objects were made: stone, bronze, and iron. This later came to be known as the Three-Age System when it was found that the use of these materials followed one another historically.

ials were attributed to the **Stone Age**, **Bronze Age** or **Iron Age**. It soon became apparent through the excavations carried out by Thomsen's associates, among them J. J. A. Worsaae, that in Denmark there was an actual stratigraphic succession of flint, bronze, and iron. With this clue it was natural for archeologists to conclude that mankind had gone through these three stages almost everywhere.

The principle of **superposition** or **stratification** (sometimes called **Steno's Law**) was first devised by Nicolaus Steno (1638–1686), a Danish medical doctor attached to the court of Ferdinand II, Grand Duke of Tuscany. The principle was described in *Prodromus*, published by Steno in 1669. When this idea was employed (it has been used consistently only in the last 70–80 years), archeology could be used to extend local history by recording evidence of past cultures in their proper chronological order. Building on this foundation, enterprising archeologists in Europe turned their attention to uncovering their national past and in the process gathered information that showed the spread of civilization across the Western world.

When archeology deals with people who had no written documents or no writing which can be deciphered, it must create history out of other evidence. This kind of archeology discovers lost or forgotten civilizations such as the Minoan of Crete, the Hittite of Asia Minor, and the Harappan of India–it literally creates these. The Scythians of South Russia, who had no writing, were, however, pretty well described by the Greek historian Herodotus, and when we combine Greek documents and archeology, we can learn a great deal about the Scythians. Archeologists in western Europe, unlike their colleagues who were working with Greek and Roman materials, could not even name the peoples whose past they were excavating. True enough, the British had historical knowledge of the Celts and the Angles and Saxons, but before them, nothing. And in most of Europe there was no knowledge at all of who the early inhabitants had been. Modern national names would not describe the peoples who, thousands of years earlier, had not been grouped into the same political allegiances. With nothing to fall back on, archeologists named prehistoric people after some of their most characteristic artifacts. Thus we have the curious spectacle of the "Beaker-folk," whose movements have been traced to the Rhineland, Holland, and finally, by about 1800 B.C., to the British Isles. Another group, perhaps having its origin in the steppes of central Asia, was named the "Battle-axe Culture." Somewhere in Europe the Beaker-folk and the Battle-axe people met, and both seem to have entered Britain at about the same time. It is anybody's guess what these people called themselves or what their language was. Although they lived at a time when civilization thrived in the Mediterranean, they are usually regarded as prehistoric, because they were not described by writers.

In the Western world the dominant civilizations were in the Mediterranean and Southwest Asia, and these centers had a strong influence on outlying areas for much of their history. Accordingly, it has been natural for scholars concerned with peripheral areas to study their material in terms of the influential civilizations. How otherwise could they compare one area with another, or interpret fragmentary data that were only complete in the centers of **diffusion**? As early as 1836 Thomsen saw clearly that the later prehistory of northern Europe would have to be understood as derivative from the Mediterranean area of civilization, although this view reached its extreme form in Childe's *The Dawn of European Civilization* (1957). Dawkins earlier (1880:447) also saw the possibility of dating the later prehistoric cultures of Europe by referring them to the dated remains of the Mediterranean area when he wrote,

> . . . it is a question equally interesting to the historian and to the archaeologist, to ascertain the extent to which the light of their culture [that is, of Egypt, Assyria, Etruria, Greece, and Phoenecia] penetrated the darkness of central, western, and northern Europe, and to see whether it be possible . . . to bring the Historic period in the Mediterranean region into relation with the Pre-historic period north of the Alps.

This relation was not understood until G. Montelius in the last decade of the nineteenth century effectively tied the two chronologies together. Montelius carefully studied artifacts from both Europe and the Mediterranean and worked out a chronology based on the types of tools. His division of the Bronze Age into chronological segments numbered I–V enabled archeologists working from the British Isles to the Aegean to date their material relative to one another. Recent assessments of radiocarbon dating by C. Renfrew, however, show these ingenious correlations to have been at least partially incorrect (see Chapter 8).

Archeology in Palestine, which has derived inspiration from references in the Bible and other contemporary sources, has been a great aid to history through discovering in the ground evidence to support many brief or cryptic comments on sites, peoples, customs, and historical events. In the Migration period (or Dark Ages), after the decline of Rome in the third century A.D., northwestern Europe lost direct contact with the literate Mediterranean world, and for a period of about half a millennium lapsed back into what was essentially a "nonhistorical" phase, which we know mainly from traded goods found in archeological sites rather than from documentary evidence. The study of protohistory has therefore been closely allied to the **humanistic traditions** that produced the classical scholars.

Piggott (1959a:Chap. 5) has provided us with an excellent discussion of the degrees to which societies can be called historic. Peoples lacking writing (or whose writing cannot be deciphered) but who lived in the penumbra of literate civilizations may be known to us by name, and something of their history may have been recorded by their neighbors. The Scythians of South Russia, described by Herodotus and Strabo, the occupants of the Land of Punt (Somaliland), with whom the Egyptians traded and whose customs they recorded, and the Celts of Europe, known from writings of Caesar, Tacitus, and others, belong to the category of nonliterate barbarians living beyond the borders of the civilized world where writing and reading were practiced. But the fact that they are named and described, and the knowledge that certain events of ancient history involved them, bring them into focus as "real" and identifiable people rather than as people belonging to that shadowy, nameless kind of group (so familiar to the prehistorian) whose very existence is a fact discovered by archeologists. This kind of knowledge about preliterate societies is not limited to the peoples living on the fringes of the Greek, Egyptian, and Roman worlds, but indeed is equally true of all the primitive cultures of the Old and New Worlds that are known to us from the writings and museum collections compiled by travelers, explorers, and ethnologists. For example, in the New World the great native empires of the **Aztecs** and **Incas**, which were brought to a sudden and bloody end by the Spanish conquest in the early sixteenth century, managed to incorporate some of their history in Spanish accounts. These "histories" take the form of traditional genealogies of important families and main events in the lives of certain individuals, including the ruling dynasties. Thus, for the Peruvian rulers there are lists of emperors that are very useful in identifying and dating archeological sites of the late Inca period.

Similarly, the Homeric epic was a memorized tale that happened to get recorded in writing while it was still remembered in detail, and it has been argued that the *Iliad* describes an actual historical situation referring to the end of the Bronze Age. Piggott (1959a:104) uses the term "conditional literacy" to characterize the surviving written records of societies such as that of the Mycenaeans in Linear B script—tablets that are almost exclusively bookkeeping accounts recording the amount of production or inventories of goods. These official business records, made by clerks who were a specialist minority in the society, can tell us a great deal about the economic and political structure of the Mycenaeans, but they do not contain literary or historical accounts. The famous Peruvian knotted-string mnemonic records called **"quipus"** were probably similar in function. The surviving books (**codices**) of the Maya and Aztec peoples, though known to represent only the barest fraction of such records existing at the time of the Spanish conquest, are of the greatest importance in our understanding of the later history and calendars of these societies. Thus, a variety of situations is involved when we refer to a society as historical.

Adam and Beyond

Unlike other kinds of archeology, prehistory is closely allied with anthropology, which developed at about the same time, and with geology, which supplied evidence of the great age of man. From the beginning, then, prehistorians have attempted to develop a scientific study of mankind by using the concepts of the social sciences and the methods, concepts, and techniques of the natural sciences. A concern with history enters because we trace the careers of extinct cultures, but this concern takes two forms: evolutionary studies that deal with the development of culture generally and studies of the culture history of archeologically identifiable groups of people.

The geological ideas of the great age of the earth and the concepts of biological evolution have a fairly long history, but they really became important for archeological studies only after the time of Darwin.

Quite by chance, the year 1859 marked both the publication of Charles Darwin's great book *On the Origin of Species*, which presented the theory of evolution by natural selection, and the birth of Paleolithic archeology. In that year several British geologists (John Evans, Joseph Prestwich, Flower, and H. Falconer) visited Amiens, France, where they verified the claims made by Jacques Boucher Crêvecoeur de Perthes (Fig. 2.8) that rude flaked stone implements (Fig. 2.9) occurred at great depths from the present surface in the Pleistocene (then called "**antediluvian**") gravels of the Somme River. Such ancient and crude tools fitted well with the idea implied (but not stated) by Darwin of the progress of man from lower forms. No primitive fossil human bones were known in 1859 except for the first of the **Neanderthal** skulls, discovered in 1856, about which a controversy was raging over whether it was the skull of a primitive form of man or that of a pathological idiot.

FIG. 2.8 Jacques Boucher Crê-vecoeur de Perthes (1788–1868), the father of Paleolithic archeology, who attributed flint implements found in the gravels of the Somme River to the work of ancient man.

FIG. 2.9 (left) *The first published illustration of a hand ax (scale 1:2) (Hearne's [1715] edition of Leland's* Collectanea *l:lxiv). This implement is described in the Sloane Catalogue: "No. 246. A British weapon found, with elephant's tooth, opposite to black Mary's, near Grayes Inn Lane" (as quoted in J. Evans 1897:581).*
(right) *The same hand ax reproduced as a woodcut in J. Evans,* Ancient Stone Implements *1897: Fig. 451 (scale 1:2).*

The early prehistorians recognized that the remains they were digging up had their closest counterparts among living primitives rather than among civilized peoples, so that it was natural for them to turn to anthropologists, and especially ethnologists, who were gathering information on primitive peoples, rather than to historians and humanists, for their inspiration and interpretation. The development of man's technology from simple to complex over the long span of his existence was readily attributed by writers like G. de Mortillet (1867) to cultural evolution. Since then, many prehistorians have been more concerned with discovering and interpreting the universal trends of cultural evolution than with working out the details of short-range local sequences of cultures. The earliest attempts at describing cultural evolution were based largely on analogy with living primitives, who were thought to exhibit various "stages" of cultural evolution. Though this notion has been persistent, detailed work on particular sequences has demonstrated that human history has been remarkably varied and cannot be described by any single system of stages of development.

Generally speaking, the further back archeologists push into the past, the harder it is to recover evidence about the people of the times. Even though geology provided archeology with the concept of **stratigraphy**, and with certain fundamental ideas about the age of the earth, it offered no direct methods for recovering archeological material, or for interpreting the physical conditions of times past. These ideas and techniques were provided by an array of other sciences, some of which were also facing the problem of reconstructing the ancient world. Kidder (quoted by Wauchope 1965:157) put it this way:

> . . . [Archeologists] will find that other sciences are grappling with the problems of plants and animals, of weather and rocks, of living men and existing social orders; collecting, classifying, winnowing detail, and gradually formulating the basic laws which render this perplexing universe understandable. Beside and with them the archeologist must work if his results are to be more than the putterings of the antiquary.

Archeologists have, therefore, grown accustomed to cooperating in research projects with chemists, physicists, botanists, zoologists, geographers, geologists, geomorphologists, and astronomers when the special knowledge of these scientists can be made to reveal information about prehistory. The same is true of the cooperation with physical anthropologists who are interested in the physical characteristics of extinct populations, with human evolution, and with other biological characteristics of man. The impact of culture on the early development of man is not always very apparent, and archeological interpretations of fossil man as frequently draw on theories of biology as they do on anthropology.

In America, archeology drew on different interests when it was beginning. Legends of lost cities and of mysterious **mound builders** were reinforced by spectacular finds in **Meso-America** as well as in North America. But archeologists had neither history nor legend to give a clue as to the extent of time man had been in the Americas or of the changes he underwent after his arrival. The prevailing opinion has been that man is a relatively recent comer to America and that he arrived in fully modern form. Thus until very recently the idea of fossil man in America has been given little consideration. The earliest proto-men in Africa are now dated back some 5 million years and modern men in Europe to about 35,000 years. By contrast, there are no remains in America that can be argued as dating to earlier than about 40,000 years ago, and these are disputed by many scholars. Thus, there has been essentially no interest in the biological evolution of Native Americans, although it is now clear that major cultural transformations took place. In fact, the cultural changes are parallel to and fully as dramatic as any seen in the Old World.

The archeology of Native Americans is almost prehistoric in spite of a few native books and accounts by Western observers. The basic effort of archeologists, therefore, has been one of working out regional sequences; that is, attempting to put prehistoric events into their proper chronological order region by region. This has been essential in laying the ground work for more recent studies, which attempt to see local developments in terms of the evolution of cultures throughout the continent.

Prehistory can be contrasted with treasure hunting, art history, philology, history, and even protohistory in its goals and methods. This contrast holds in spite of the fact that the ends of these studies—to understand man's past—are superficially the same. We have therefore entitled this book *Prehistoric Archeology: A Brief Introduction* rather than *An Introduction to Archeology*. The aims, methods, and results described in the remainder of the book for the most part pertain to prehistoric archeology.

Landmarks in Archeology

We often think of spectacular discoveries that set off a rush of activity in some branch of archeology: Schliemann's finding of Troy, Stephens' and Catherwood's descriptions and pictures of Mayan cities enveloped in tropical jungles, Carter's announcement of the opening of King Tut's tomb in Egypt, and the Leakeys' finding of **Australopithecines** in **Olduvai Gorge**. In their own way each of these discoveries set in motion vigorous archeological activity and stimulated popular thought. They, and a handful of similar finds, are "landmarks" in archeology. But this is not quite what we have in mind here. Our interest is in the ideas and techniques that have influenced the development of prehistory as an intellectual discipline.

In the history of archeology, there have been many landmarks in technical innovation and in theoretical orientation, but progress in the two areas has run neither smoothly nor coordinately, and it seems that one is often out of phase with the other. This probably results from the fact that the leaders in these two areas are ordinarily different people. The "idea people" tend to be impatient with the tedious task of meticulous excavation and recording of data, and the "technical people" regard the theorists as armchair visionaries. In fact, most archeologists probably have some interests in each area, but the balance is rarely equal, as the following quotations from an obituary of A. V. Kidder will illustrate.

About his early career and his Ph.D. dissertation, Wauchope (1965:152) says, "Although Kidder is best known during this early period (ca. 1915) for his stratigraphic and typological techniques and space-time reconstructions, here we see what may be even more remarkable for the time: hypotheses regarding the sociocultural significance of ancient pottery." Wauchope (1965:157–158) also cites Kidder's own words:

> Study of the Maya from the earliest times to the present involves consideration of age-long and world-wide problems: the relation of man to his habitat, the spread and interaction of nascent cultures, the origin of higher civilization, the decay and fall of social orders, the clash of native and European races, the adjustments between conquerors and conquered, the impact of Twentieth Century ideas upon backward peoples.

And another quotation:

> In the past many facts appeared to be mutually contradictory. Modern

learning, however, shows that all truths are interrelated. Chemistry and physics are striking downward to common fundamentals; zoology and botany are rapidly merging and the resultant newer biology is joining hands with the physical sciences. Similar tendencies are becoming manifest in the human field, where geography, ethnography, sociology, and psychology are constantly drawing closely together.

Later Kidder spoke of the time when we shall "be in a position to approach the problems of cultural evolution, the solving of which is, I take it, our ultimate goal" (Wauchope 1965:159).

In view of Kidder's perception of the goals of archeology, which are strikingly modern, we may be surprised to learn that "he did not attempt to answer these questions or to marshal his data bearing on them . . . . He was certainly aware of anthropology's concern with specific culture processes and specific cultural dynamics, but he was obviously not interested in them sufficiently to investigate them empirically and in depth himself" (Wauchope 1965: 163). Rather, Kidder pioneered in and provided archeology with excellent examples of field technique and methods of analyzing artifacts.

We may be tempted to look at Kidder's perception of goals as an illustration of the idea that even great men cannot do everything, but at least we can consider the possibility that Kidder may simply have been too far ahead of his time. John Platt (1962:17) put it this way: "It is just as sure a recipe for failure to have the right idea fifty years too soon as five years too late." Max Planck (1949:33–34) made a similar point: "A new scientific truth does not triumph by convincing its opponents, but rather because its opponents die, and a new generation grows up that is familiar with it."

In Kidder's time the greatest strides were being made in technique, and especially in gathering new data. Archeology paralleled anthropology generally in this sense and in this concern. Improvements in these areas were easy to conceive and to execute, whereas few could see the ways to approach an understanding of culture processes. Although such problems have certainly been very difficult to deal with, we take the position now that the time is right to work as diligently in theory as in technique. To put our contention into some historical perspective, we shall review some of the landmarks in technique and interpretation.

Techniques

A casual visitor to archeological excavations at half-century intervals in 1860, 1910, and 1960 might not detect many changes in technique, but if he observed the operations carefully he would recognize several fundamental differences. The improvements in the last hundred years have come from the ways archeologists dig and in the knids of information they think will be able to extract. There is mutual interaction between these two parts of the operation. Better techniques enable us to recover more information, and as we do so we develop new techniques to give us still more and different kinds of information.

Historically, the most important technique was that of stratigraphic excavation. In essence this means removing soil and the artifacts in it by layers. The oldest layers are at the bottom because they were deposited first. Nevertheless, though the principles of stratigraphy were learned early, they were inconsistently applied, and one still finds them ignored in isolated instances. Apparently Thomas Jefferson in 1784 was one of the first, if not the first, to apply the principles of stratigraphy in excavation, but as Wheeler (1956:59) notes, "Unfortunately, this seed of a new scientific skill fell upon infertile soil." The same author, in describing the excavation of the Roman town of Silchester in the 1890s, says, "It was dug like potatoes" (Wheeler 1956:150), and he quotes Petrie's comment about certain excavated sites in the Near East that are "ghastly charnel houses of murdered evidence" (Wheeler 1956:112). It was not until 1914 that American archeologists led by N. C. Nelson routinely began to excavate in such a way that the stratigraphic relations of buried materials could be demonstrated.

As we discuss later, the importance of stratigraphy is that it enables archeologists to keep things from different periods separate. Our understanding of stratigraphy has come a long way in recent decades, partially as a consequence of the use of new techniques for discerning it, and partly in the recognition that sites can be dug by their **natural levels** rather than arbitrary ones. The increased sophistication in the use of stratigraphy can best be exemplified by work now being done in Paleolithic sites where, in the absence of convenient strata or structures, levels as thin as a few centimeters, representing brief encampments by hunters, are now being peeled off. This is sometimes termed **micro-stratigraphy**, and it illustrates the close interaction between the development of techniques and theory. It had been customary to dig Paleolithic sites by the gross recognizable layers that were separated by marked changes in color or composition, but when archeologists began asking new kinds of questions about the size of groups occupying the sites and about the differences in kinds of artifacts in several parts of the same site, it became necessary to devise methods of isolating artifacts from smaller and smaller spatial and chronological units of the site. The goal now sought, and being reached in some instances, is to isolate each separate occupation. Armed with data from such digs, archeologists can now enter an entirely new realm of interpretation. It is safe to predict for the future that there will be more refinements along these lines. In Part III of this book we take up these issues more fully.

The second area of technical development concerns the invention and routine use of processes for preserving artifacts and for analyzing them. The greatest innovations have come since 1950 with the advent of radiocarbon dating and the interest that scientists in physics and chemistry have displayed in applying their skills to archeological problems. These topics are treated later in the book; thus they will not be described here. It is useful to note however, that the fascination with technical applications of several types of unusually complex apparatus has probably tended to diminish interest in more theoretical things. Archeologists have suddenly become overwhelmed by the wealth of data now available or potentially available, and it is not surprising that they have turned to the use of computers to help manipulate them.

Somewhat less obtrusive, but still of fundamental importance, are techniques of **survey** and **sampling.** Again, these are examples of feedback between the need for new kinds of knowledge and the development of techniques to obtain it. Modern archeologists recognize the value of extensive and detailed surveys (Fig. 2.10), especially of settlement patterns and their relation to geography, trade routes, sociopolitical structure, and the like, but they did not become customary until recent decades. An early example is Braidwood's survey of the Amuq, Syria, in the 1930s but the full power of the techniques was appreciated only in such studies as Adams' *Land Beyond Baghdad* (1965), which undertook to relate settlement patterns to hydrological, social, and historical factors. Here again, however, the future holds more promise as surveys become more detailed and exact with respect to the kinds of information desired. It should be added that

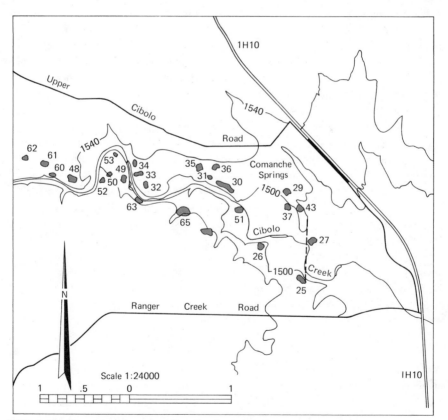

FIG. 2.10 Map showing the distribution of Indian sites in Texas with respect to the terraces of Cibolo Creek. The interval between contour lines is 40 feet. (Kelly and Hester 1976, Fig. 1.)

Adams' survey depended heavily on the use of aerial photography, a technique that received its greatest development during World War II, but which has received a new boost with satellite photos and new methods of interpreting them.

Sampling can also be regarded as an important technique in both excavation and analysis. This topic will be taken up in various contexts in later chapters, but we can point out here that the use of sampling techniques in archeology stems from ideas about patterning in culture. Sampling techniques are used in two ways: to help select sites for excavation, and to obtain reliable groups of artifacts for analysis. They are important because they enable an archeologist to make intelligent decisions about what, where, and how much to dig as well as about the quality of his data.

The amount of information that one can get out of a site is quite amazing. As an example, there are two kinds of techniques which, by recovering a great deal of new information, have opened up whole new areas of analysis and interpretation. First is **flotation**, a method in which water or another fluid is used to separate things like bone, pieces of charred plants, shell, and other small bits from the dirt in which they were hidden. The use of this technique has added a whole dimension to interpretation that even the most sophisticated workers of the 1950s could not have imagined. Aside from just a huge quantity of small and relatively unimportant things that turn up in properly washed soil, entirely new kinds of things of which archeologists were largely unaware, such as seeds, fishbones, beads, and bits of metal are also found. The major problem now is how to analyze the vast amount of small bits. It is a situation ready-made for sampling.

Another new area of recovery concerns analysis of pollen from archeological sites. Pollen, which is given off by plants when they flower, is microscopic but nearly indestructable. It may therefore lie in the ground for thousands of years and be recoverable in archeological sites. Although pollen has been studied throughout the century, primarily for the information it gives of regional vegetation and past climates, only recently have techniques of capturing pollen from most archeological sites been devised. Using these techniques, it is possible to get much more information about plants that were available to people and eaten in the prehistoric past.

These techniques are examples of the general trend toward recovering increasing amounts of information from sites. Today we can often learn a great deal more from small test pits in a site than was once learned from its total excavation. Field work has thus become more economical of time but the amount of time devoted to laboratory analysis has expanded correspondingly.

A final innovation is the use of multidisciplinary teams in archeological research projects. Although it has long been acknowledged that archeologists must draw on the advice and information of specialists in other fields, it is relatively new to include these people in a field party. The newness of this concept can be realized by reading Wheeler's (1956:153) statement: "The staff of an archeological excavation on any considerable scale includes a director, a supervisor for each area under excavation, a trained foreman, a small-find recorder, a pottery assistant, a photographer, a surveyor, a chemist, a draftsman, and, according to need, an epigraphist or numismatist." Naturally, Wheeler would change the composition of the group somewhat for a dig in the Paleolithic, but it is noteworthy that he did not include a botanist, a zoologist, or a geomorphologist. These people, and others, are now being included almost routinely in modern large-scale operations. Although, as he notes, Braidwood was not the first to use them, it is largely to him that we can attribute the rise of the multidisciplinary approach; and the reasons should be clear. He was concerned with the origins of agriculture, a topic that no archeologist could hope to solve on his own. As research projects have become more "problem-oriented" they have come to include more and more of the specialists without whose help the problems cannot be solved. We must also mention that it is necessary to have these people work in the field with the archeologists so that each can evaluate the problem on the spot. It is hard to overestimate the degree to which congenial colleagues seeking a solution to a common problem can stimulate one another to more penetrating insights and consequently to better results.

Interpretation

All archeology is based on the idea that there are ancient remains of human activity to be found. This may sound simple-minded, but, considered in the context of the history of archeological theory, it is basic. Until people knew there was a human past long enough to be interesting, there could be no archeology. Thanks to history, educated people were aware of some antiquity long before archeology started, but they commonly believed that the earth was only about 6000 years old. They had little knowledge of people vastly different from themselves in the modern world, let alone in the ancient, and consequently no interest in digging to expose the past. Had this situation continued to prevail, archeology would have developed as a branch of history with a special interest in the civilizations of the Mediterranean and Near East. Schliemann and others of his time were digging to find things they knew once existed. The real breakthrough came when scientists found that the earth is millions rather than thousands of years old, and when they discovered that life in the remote past was far different from life today.

Geologists and paleontologists were responsible for these ideas, which became important for archeology when the stratigraphic association between crude stone tools, geologic age, and extinct animals was demonstrated. Hard on the heels of this discovery came the ideas of biological and cultural evolution. When these ideas had taken hold, they showed scientists the potential of archeology and gave them a goal to seek: the missing link. A rash of activity followed, particularly in Europe, which resulted in the first syntheses of Pleistocene prehistory in the late 1880s.

Although techniques of digging saw little improvement during the first 50 years of archeological activity, the important concept of **sequence** (or chronological order), which was itself borrowed from geology and history, had become clear and was effectively used in the early general accounts. The seminal idea was that the sites contained continuous records of change that could be arranged chronologically to give an idea of the development of cultures. These records were pieced together from evidence that was recovered stratigraphically, although the stratigraphy was crude by modern standards. The discovery of sequences led naturally to an awareness of differences between areas, and this awareness in turn to the idea of distinct archeological cultures that prehistorians likened to modern "tribes."

By virtue of hindsight we can see two important concepts implicit in these findings. Both concern culture systems. First, there is the idea of cumulative and directional change in the technologies of the ancient peoples, and, second, the idea that because each culture has its distinct set of traits the boundaries of separate culture systems can be inferred. The use of these concepts can be seen clearly in such archeological classics as Breuil's *Les subdivisions du paléolithique supérieur et leur signification* in 1912 and A. de Mortillet's *La classification paléthnologique* in 1903. Both of these works had a profound influence on archeological thinking, in that they made it clear that a history of mankind generally, as well as of particular cultures, can be deduced from archeological findings.

When the results of the preceding decades' work were compiled into a systematic chronological-developmental form, the way was paved for making inferences about intangible aspects of prehistoric life. The artifacts of the Paleolithic had been made by hunters, and it was assumed that these people led lives like those of modern hunters. But the aspect of prehistoric life that attracted most speculation was art. The early prehistorians avidly excavated—and sometimes looted—sites to recover engraved bones and stones, and caves were systematically searched for paintings. When the splendid paintings on the ceiling of the cave at **Altamira**, Spain, were discovered in 1879, they stimulated a chain of speculation about the intellectual capacities and interests of prehistoric man, a subject that still intrigues a number of authors, as we can see from the quantity of books that not only illustrate the art but attempt to interpret its mental, religious, magical, technical, and intellectual implications (Fig. 2.11).

Although these ventures into the inner life of early man are ingenious and interesting, they can scarcely evoke the ring of credibility that studies of diet and even of social organization can. Grahame Clark's pioneering work, *Prehistoric Europe: The Economic Basis*, published in 1952, showed the way for investigations of subsistence, settlement, and technology that continue today. But Clark did more: he effectively integrated concepts of ecology into archeology by showing how economy is "an adjustment to specific physical and biological conditions of certain needs, capacities, aspirations and values." He says,

> There are thus two sides to the equation—on the one hand the character of the habitat, itself to a greater or less degree influenced or even conditioned by culture, and on the other the kind of life regarded as appropriate by the community and the resources, in the form of knowledge, technical equipment and social organization, available for its realization.

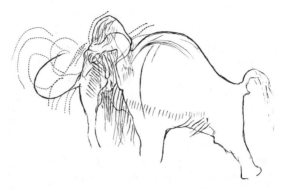

FIG. 2.11   *Engraving on a cave wall of a charging mammoth. The viewer gets an impression of an animal in action. Such art is widespread across the earth. Examples like this from western Europe date back about 13,000–18,000 years.*

> The relation between man and external nature is thus a dynamic one and the development of culture viewed in its economic aspect is indeed one of man's growing knowledge of and control over forces external to himself (G. Clark 1952:7).

The importance of these concepts is that they treat man as a variable in a natural world—one element in an **ecosystem**—and that man's culture, as seen in artifacts, is adaptive. The idea of culture as an adaptive system thus emerges, and with it a sense that the artifacts can be viewed as tools used by man to cope with his world. A change in emphasis could then be made from the delineation of technical sequences, which had often been viewed as examples illustrating evolution, to an interpretation of the processes by which this evolution had taken place. Archeologists continue to use these concepts, and they have been reiterated in a number of books that explicitly use the term "ecology" or "economy" in the title.

The next step, which is being developed today, is to attempt to reconstruct the social systems operative in the past. To do so, ecological theory and a thorough knowledge of the way modern social systems work are required. Archeologists can thus make use of their reconstructions of the physical environmental conditions, their knowledge of prehistoric settlement patterns, and the hunting or gathering practices of the people, to make a number of reasonable inferences about the kind of social organizations. The inferences stem from the idea that under specified conditions people have a limited range of cultural possibilities (or responses); then it is often possible to make more specific inferences and say what these responses are.

These concepts partly stem from, and partly lead into, an interest in general systems that requires archeologists to look at ever-wider geographic areas to try to reconstruct the interplay of people in the several separate groups comprising an effective network of interaction. The view thus shifts from the local group in isolation to the local group in a context of both natural and social environments.

In the decade of the sixties, an explicitly scientific approach to prehistory, "new archeology," emerged as a potent force. Some (for example, R. Adams 1968:1187) call it a revolution in thought. The ideas behind the new archeology are as old as science itself, yet they came as a fresh breeze to a discipline whose leaders some had accused of being afraid to open their windows lest an idea waft in (Wauchope 1962). Science in fact, though not in ideal, has been slow to take hold in archeology, very likely because most prehistorians have not been trained as experimental or theoretical scientists, although many are well acquainted with the natural or inductive sciences. There is, however, a world of difference between zoological systematics and theoretical genetics, just as there is between accurately predicting the moon's eclipse and discovering the laws that govern the orbits of planets.

For years archeologists have talked of scientific archeology, usually contrasting it with the bungling attempts of amateurs. What most scholars had in mind was the technical control they exercised over an excavation. "We dug the site with strict scientific controls" was an oft-heard phrase; or, "We made a rigorous scientific analysis of our pottery," when what they did was dig by 4-inch levels and classify **sherds**. To be sure, strict control, accurate keeping of records, and classification are all parts of good experimental or of natural science, but in themselves these technical operations are not science. Additionally, in archeology there is a long tradition of numerical manipulation, whether it be the calculation of descriptive statistics, the interpretation of frequency curves as artifacts change in time, or the use of inferential statistics and sampling that aid intuitive judgment. These are part of science but their use does not make archeology a science. Neither does the use of electronic calculators or computers, which rapidly and accurately perform the routine calculations that so plague the empiricist, make of archeology a science any more than it guarantees the accuracy of the inferences drawn from the calculations.

Science is not a set of operations but a reasoned, logical inquiry into a problem whose solution is within reach. Science is usually characterized by a series of sequential steps that lead to an answer, but these steps may be evaded and avoided on occasion as insight wins over logic, and impatience over routine. Still, the test of a conclusion is its reproducibility and its capacity to take account of relevant factors that would negate the hypothesis or conclusion deduced from an experimental result.

New archeology, discounting its first feeble cries (for example, uttered by W. W. Taylor in 1948 and Willey and Phillips in 1958), really became important when Louis Binford was able to persuade a number of graduate students and young colleagues to begin to state archeological problems in scientific terms. Among these people there was a great emphasis on the logic of scientific inquiry and on the ability of science to solve most problems. The theoretical position taken by these archeologists has been described by **logical positivist** philosophers such as Hempel (1952, 1965, 1966), Hempel and Oppenheim (1948), and T. Kuhn (1962). Out of this welding of ideas from philosophy with archeology came the belief—some called it the dogma—that archeology can and should be science, done in one manner only. The arguments that arose centered on the question of the nature of explanation and on the operations needed to achieve it.

The "new archeologists" rapidly achieved a position of prominence, largely by speaking bluntly of the potential of scientific archeology and of the evils that had been masquerading as scientific work. An immediate reaction was one of defense by the older archeologists who were criticized and of renewed vigor in the attack by those who were winning the verbal debate.

The furor has now settled down, although the discussion remains alive through occasional articles in archeological journals. Ideals and procedures of new archeologists have achieved wide acceptance, although in more moderate form than their initiators had hoped for. Still the most readable and thoughtful single volume expressing a *view* of new archeology is *Explanation in Archeology: An Explicitly Scientific Approach* by Watson, LeBlanc, and Redman. As they put it (1971:x), "If the term 'new archeology' is to be used, it should be equated with explicitly scientific archeology." The contrast with other forms of archeology "lies in the strong emphasis of the theoretically oriented archeologists on explicit definition of a problem, of data needed to solve it, and of techniques necessary to collect the data" (1971:120). In the same vein they say (1971:32), "Whatever one thinks of the sometimes pretentious expression of this insistence on self-conscious use of scientific method, one lasting beneficial result will be that archeologists henceforth will be forced to make their assumptions explicit." They agree (1971:159), however, that all archeologists need not be scientists. "There is no more reason for all archeologists to be scientists than for all historians to be sociologists, psychologists, or anthropologists."

Much of the writing of new archeology has been concerned with the distinction between the **inductive** (nonrigorous, intuitive insight) and **deductive** (formally logical) approaches, but in truth scientists work with both. Some prefer to begin with data and to infer their meaning; this is induction. Others prefer to work theoretically, devising hypotheses or laws and then testing them with data. No one, however, can operate entirely without data in hand, for he would have not the least idea what kinds of laws or hypotheses he might test. By the same token, an inductive approach that begins with data, whether it be accidentally or deliberately derived, can make its hypotheses credible only through adequate testing. By whatever means the hypotheses are ultimately derived, the procedure for testing them follows strict scientific method; the sequence for testing presented below follows Platt (1964:347):

1. devising alternative hypotheses;
2. devising a crucial experiment (or several of them), with alternative

possible outcomes, each of which will, as nearly as possible, exclude one or more of the hypotheses;

3. carrying out the experiment so as to get a clear result;
4. recycling the procedure, making the hypotheses or sequential hypotheses to refine the possibilities that remain; and so on.

> Steps 1 and 2 require intellectual inventions, which must be cleverly chosen so that hypothesis, experiment, outcome, and exclusion will be related in a rigorous syllogism. . . . It is clear why this makes for rapid and powerful progress. For exploring the unknown, there is no faster method; this is the minimum sequence of steps. Any conclusion that is not an exclusion is insecure and must be rechecked.

Although this procedure is standard, many scientists (archeologists included) do not follow it because they become method-oriented or they fall in love with their pet theory. As Chamberlin (1965:755) put it,

> The mind lingers with pleasure upon the facts that fall happily into the embrace of the theory, and feels a natural coldness toward those that seem refractory. . . . There springs up, also, an unconscious pressing of the theory to make it fit the facts, and a pressing of the facts to make them fit the theory.

An all-important point is made by Platt (1964:350):

> There is no such thing as proof in science—because some later alternative explanation may be as good or better—so that science advances only by disproofs. There is no point in making hypotheses that are not falsifiable, because such hypotheses do not say anything: it must be possible for an empirical scientific system to be refuted by experience.

If we may characterize a compromise and scientifically sound approach for new archeology, it would be to postulate relationships among variables that can be tested using data derived from prehistory. A satisfactory explanation for the crucial data will then consist of the hypothesis that cannot be excluded after it has been tested along with alternative hypotheses. An explanation thus represents the best we can do at the present state of our knowledge.

Trends of the Future

Glyn Isaac, in an article, "Whither Archaeology?," wrote, "It is safe to predict that branching and the establishment of liaisons with an ever-widening range of disciplines will continue to be one of the most conspicuous trends." Within archeology there will be greater specialization as students receive better training in technical aspects of analysis and in the ancillary supporting fields. In combination these two factors will make archeology at once more complicated and better able to contribute more accurate reconstructions and interpretations of the past.

Both of these trends will stem directly from the awakened appreciation of the possibilities of doing archeology scientifically, but it is unlikely that an explicitly scientific approach will ever override the more strictly historic and humanistic aspects and rationale of archeology. The ability to discover the processes by which culture developed and to establish laws of human behavior depends in large part on the capability of archeologists to make accurate assays of both the relative and the absolute time elapsed and to determine the nature of an archeological episode during a discrete segment of its history. The linking of these episodes through time by means of causal processes depends in large part of the primary data and will often come late in the archeological study of an area rather than at the beginning.

It is important to remember that one of the chief attractions of archeology, both for archeologists and for the public that supports it, is in the reconstruction of local histories and the display of the things people used. One may predict, therefore, the increasing popularization of archeology by archeologists themselves rather than by writers of fiction, and the growth of displays and other educational media to convey the message of human heritage. For most people the fascination of archeology is in the seeking and compiling of clues and in the deductions drawn from them. Archeological reconstruction is like the summation given by detectives of the solution to an intriguing mystery.

We must remember that whatever archeology may become in the future, it can only be nourished by evidence that can be found in the ground. In many areas the very existence of such data is imperiled through thoughtless looting of sites, through erosion and degradation, and through various kinds of construction. It is ironical that the population increases that have spurred some of the recent rapid increases in prehistoric research have also created a need for more housing, more roads, and more industry, thus destroying the very subject matter of the field. Alarming statistics can be produced to show that sites are disappearing by the tens of thousands annually through these combined factors of attrition. Of these, perhaps only a fraction of a percent are excavated or even seen by professional archeologists. It seems clear, therefore, that a major effort of archeology in the future must be directed toward the management of its resources. As a reflection of this new thrust, two organizations of archeologists and others concerned with the management of archeological resources have been established: the American Society of Conservation Archeologists and the Society of Professional Archeologists. As needs develop in this rapidly changing area of archeological interest, these organizations will attempt to develop appropriate responses.

THEORY
AND DATA

Chapter 3

BASIC CONCEPTS IN PREHISTORY

It is sometimes said that anthropology and archeology are fields in which theory is poorly developed. This is a fair criticism if we take it to mean that the fundamental concepts have not been adequately defined, consistently used, and systematically taught. It is not going too far to say that as archeologists we have failed to get our concepts across to many students. That this is true is apparent when students who have sat in class for a semester and mastered all manner of trivial data cannot conjure up any reasonable statement of how these data can be used, much less how one converts data in the form of artifacts fresh from the ground into statements about people who lived in the past. The problem seems to be that few archeologists say much about how they arrive at their conclusions. This point has been stressed repeatedly in the writings of new archeology: we must make our assumptions and procedures explicit. If archeology is to develop as a rational science that follows orderly procedures it is absolutely essential to make the underlying assumptions clear. For students and professionals alike, this means continually asking: What do we know? How do we know? And what difference does it make?

Throughout this book we try to explain why archeologists do the things they do. Many of the concepts we use are derived from other fields and adapted for use in prehistory. We have borrowed from geology, anthropology, and biology, to name only a few, and it is to these fields that one must turn for supplementary reading on points that we discuss only briefly here. Students who have substantial backgrounds in these fields may consider our treatment of the concepts oversimplified, but we are interested in the way the concepts are used rather than in their substantive content. Thus, we do not belabor our discussion of biological processes; instead we try to show to what degree they are analogous to cultural processes. Similarly, we look at the biological and cultural aspects of humankind for the purpose of showing that archeological interpretation depends on which of the concepts we choose. As research in biological and cultural anthropology continues, some of the concepts will change and archeologists will change their ideas accordingly. It is important, therefore, to show in this chapter what concepts are currently accepted and how they are put to use.

Antiquity and Change

As we discussed in Chapter 2, the idea that humans have an antiquity that goes well beyond recorded history was slow to develop. This is a profound concept and essential to all prehistoric archeology, but the concept itself is not obvious. Although most people have a sense of the past through family histories and perhaps through seeing ruins of structures built by forgotten peoples, they usually feel that the past was very much like the present and that it was not very long. Consequently the past holds little interest for most persons. It is fair to say that most people are more concerned with the present and the future than they are with the past.

Change is an equally profound concept: the idea that man has not always been as he is today. From history one knows of changes in the political fortunes of people and of changes in technology, but the idea that man himself was once fundamentally different was not apparent until some chance finds were correctly interpreted. Without prior knowledge that the earth is very old and that it, too, has undergone major changes, it would not have been possible to interpret the finds of ancient tools and human fossils correctly. As we mentioned earlier, there was considerable debate about these discoveries; most scholars believed that the tools belonged to early historic times, or were natural phenomena, and that the fossil bones were those of abnormal modern people. Archeology did not invent the ideas of antiquity and change, but when they had become sufficiently well established in geology to overcome the prevailing beliefs, it capitalized on them.

Geologists observed that landforms change, and rightly postulated that the processes responsible had been going on since the earth was formed. Similarly, paleontologists were able to discern differences among the fossils in strata of different ages. As the fossil record became clearer, they could see that species replaced species and that forms of life greatly different from those of today had once roamed the earth. It was but a small step to apply these concepts of biological change to man himself. It remained to discover the mechanisms that govern such changes, but after Darwin most scientists accepted the possibility of the evolutionary development of all forms of life. After this time man's past took on an entirely new interest for scholars.

Today there are still some who do not accept the theory of human evolution. For these persons studies of fossil man are meaningless, and for them a major portion of prehistory does not exist. Thus they would deny archeological interpretations that depend on ideas of great antiquity and fundamental changes in form or quality. It is important to point this out because it illustrates very well how dependent we are in any kind of analysis on initial premises. Before we can study anything we must make an operating hypothesis that it exists and that it has certain properties. The existence and properties of anything are observed or deduced, and until our conceptions of them are confounded by the evidence, we continue to accept them.

Stratigraphy and Sequence

Closely related to ideas of antiquity and change is the concept that there is a continual deposition on earth as things are discarded and as soils erode from higher land and are laid down at lower elevations. Where people discard things they also tend to accumulate in layers, as in a garbage dump. These layers, whether they result from geologic or human activity, actually are the record of the sequence of events (Fig. 3.1). Thus, if one digs through these layers, he encounters successively older material as he goes deeper. In archeology this is important because we can put things in their proper chronological sequence if we can isolate strata that lie above one another. This concept leads to one of the principal methods of **relative dating**, the establishing that one thing is older than another (Part IV). It was largely through the use of stratigraphy, the interpretation of the strata, that geologists were able to deduce the antiquity of the earth. By analogy with modern events, they could see that it took a long time for layers to build up and for changes to occur.

Uniformitarianism

Without the concept of uniformitarianism—that the present is a guide to the past because the processes of geology (for example, uplift, erosion, deposition) are constant—geologists would not have been able to infer that it had taken millions of years for the layers now seen on earth to have accumulated and

FIG. 3.1 *The Rösch sandpit near Heidelberg produced the famous Mauer jaw, which is also known as Heidelberg Man, in 1907. The jaw, of a* Homo erectus *form of fossil man, was found 80 feet below the surface and has been dated to the Mindel glaciation (roughly 350,000 years ago) on the basis of fauna found at the site. There were no stone tools or other cultural remains found at the site with the jaw.*

changed. The same principle is applied by prehistorians, who regularly use analogy with modern peoples as a guide to interpreting prehistoric ways of life (Chap. 10). With regard to human behavior in the past, however, it is now acknowledged that it may have no exact counterparts among even "primitive" modern peoples. This is especially true with fossil forms of man. Behavior aside, if we look at the processes of biological change, scientists agree that the same processes affect all forms of life and have been constant since life began. Thus the principle of uniformitarianism applies directly to studies of human biological evolution.

Cumulative Change

A basic idea in anthropology is that human culture is learned and transmitted from one generation to the next. This means that changes in culture can be, and often are, cumulative. Thus we find that cultures have tended to become more complex as human history has advanced. Some scientists also believe that life systems in general change in similar fashion, from relatively undifferentiated toward more diversified (Chap. 15).

These concepts are useful to prehistorians chiefly as an aid in relative dating, especially when change can be expressed in artifacts. Thus sites with simpler **assemblages** of material are *likely* to be older. That this is not necessarily true is explained later (Chap. 9). The concepts also stimulate consideration of the question why change tends to be toward increasing complexity through diversification and specialization. It is in the principles of ecology and general system theory that we find the explanatory working hypotheses in use today.

The concepts mentioned above make the discipline of prehistoric studies possible and set forth certain rules of procedure. Below we raise concepts that define the subject matter of prehistory and serve to differentiate it from related fields such as history These concepts also set the stage for the interpretation of man's behavior in antiquity in terms used by ethnologists and ecologists. Much of the work being done today in archeology in the United States depends on concepts derived from ethnology and biology. This text is not the place to give a thorough review of these studies, but we will briefly mention those that are important in the present context. Concepts that relate specifically to interpretation will be discussed in Chapter 10.

A number of basic concepts concern the nature of man. We often say that he is both a biological and a cultural being, and to this we should add that man in the singular, if not necessarily collectively (and there is some debate on this point), has his psychological, intellectual, spiritual, and mystical characteristics as well. Together these comprise the facets of mankind that we can presently perceive and hope to analyze. In prehistory most analysis focuses on the material expressions (artifacts) of man's culture.

Biological Aspects of Man

Like other animals, man must deal with the problems of eating, protection, and reproduction. Because he reproduces through mating between the sexes, offspring share characteristics of both parents. For this reason biological change between generations is inevitable, although within any population over the short run it may not be noticeable. In the long run the random combination of genes in a population will introduce changes that are noticeable. Thus, even if we were to assume biological continuity, no population today would resemble one of 5000 years ago in the total configuration of genetically controlled characteristics. Even if closed breeding populations had been maintained over such a long time, no population today could be identical with any 5000 years ago. It is not implied that such changes are for the better or worse, only that they must exist.

The chief factors that cause changes in the biology of populations are **genetic drift, mutation, natural selection**, and **gene flow**. Genetic drift is a change by chance or accident in the gene frequencies in a population. Mutation is the unpredictable spontaneous alteration of genetic material that would eventually bring about some changes in the genetic structure of populations even if drift were not a factor. Although most such mutations are thought to be deleterious and consequently have a low probability of remaining in the **gene pool**, others may be inconsequential or even beneficial and thus be heritable. Many feel that mutations create the potential for adaptation to circumstances of stress in populations by providing the genetic material that preadapts a segment of the population for survival under conditions of change. Natural selection works by culling out that segment of the population that cannot reproduce rapidly enough to keep it viable. The result is that certain genes may be eliminated from a population. Organisms are said to be well adapted when they can maintain their breeding population at a high enough level to support stability or growth. It is through natural selection that mutations may be removed from a population or increased at the expense of other, less adaptive, genes. The final factor, gene flow, is the introduction of new genetic variants from other populations.

These various factors ensure that there will be changes over time in the genetic makeup of human populations. Some maintain that culture removes much of the pressure of natural selection and consequently allows greater genetic diversity to exist, but one may also make the point that the biological organism must adapt to culture itself. In the history of mankind, culture, with its accumulating requirements, has probably acted upon the genetic makeup of populations through favoring the survival of persons with greater intelligence and manipulative skills, to name only two obvious traits that have some biological basis. It is likewise true that people may select sexual partners according to physical characteristics, and if this practice were systematically followed, it would serve to cull out certain "undesirable" genes, as they are defined in that particular culture.

Throughout this discussion of biological factors we have stressed populations, for it is only in dealing with them that we can see genetic factors at work. The science of genetics is based on populations and on the probability that one thing will lead to another. It does not in any way deal with the certainty that anything will happen to an individual.

Adaptation

As far as prehistory is concerned, the most important biological concept currently in use is that of **adaptation**. Many authors, especially those interested in the processes of culture, see changes in the archeological record as evidence of adaptation. What is frequently not stated is that the evidence consists of cultural events inferred from artifacts; these are only loosely analogous to biological processes. Moreover, in emphasizing adaptation, archeologists often neglect to consider that changes may be spurious. That is, they may only seem to have occurred because our knowledge of the past is too limited. To a great extent the question is whether we have a large enough sample to make accurate judgments. If change actually does exist, however, it may be maladaptive or neutral. To state that change is necessarily adaptive is to prejudge the case, a matter that we discuss more fully in Chapter 15.

The fact that there has been biological change, as evidenced in the fossil record, is important in interpretation, for it raises the possibility that early forms of men did not have the same biological capabilities as men of today, whose behavior is usually used for purposes of analogy. To deal with this problem some anthropologists have studied other primates, such as chimpanzees, gorillas, and especially baboons, which are the easiest to observe and which occupy an **ecological niche** similar to that of the early forms of men. The assumption is that the earliest forms of men were more similar than modern man in mentality and in behavior to those nonhuman primates which have only the most rudimentary "culture."

Recent research in this branch of anthropology has taken an even more biological turn through the investigation of the degree of genetic relationship between species. The attempt has been to determine through serological studies, the sequence and chronology of events that led from ancestral forms to modern man and apes. When consensus has been reached over how the findings should be interpreted, these studies will no doubt have considerable bearing on the kinds of archeological analogies that will be made in the future and on the kinds of interpretations that will be considered useful about the behavior of fossil men.

In brief resumé, for the most part prehistorians take man's biological heritage into account only peripherally. This is an area of theory that badly needs further consideration so that the assumptions that are usually made implicitly become explicit and amenable to serious discussion and testing.

Psychological and Intellectual Aspects of Man

Archeologists have usually ignored psychological and intellectual factors in their interpretations of human history. For that matter, the subject is not very popular in other anthropological studies, partly because the factors are extremely difficult to assess and because they pertain more to persons than to populations. In contrast, humanistic historians often invoke creativity and decadence in explanation of phenomena under their investigation. Others have attempted to attribute success or failure of a culture to biological factors that affect intelligence and creativity. None of these approaches has found much support among anthropologists or even among geneticists. Likewise, statements about peoples' accepting or declining challenges, or about their acting in accord with some vision of self-determination, have been severely criticized by historians and anthropologists alike. Nonetheless, the persistence of such ideas suggests there is something to them, if not in fact, in that people believe them to be true. We might compare this with findings of psychologists that children whose teachers are told they are smart are likely to do very well in school. The interpretation is that the teachers "saw" and attempted to nurture the talent they believed was there, when, in fact, they had been deliberately misled about the test scores of the students for purposes of the psychological experiment. In these and perhaps in most cases students performed up to their teachers' expectations.

Seldom are historical explanations phrased in such rational terms, however, and it is this that makes them so difficult to handle systematically. The same is true if we deliberately try to discover rationality in human behavior. Much of new archeology is dedicated to finding the rational basis of human behavior, either through laws that govern such behavior or through a mechanical description of the ways in which various behaviors affect one another. When one postulates relationships between definable and measurable variables, he can test their correctness with appropriate experiments. But the concept that underlies such hypotheses is that the relationships are in some way determined and rational. Thus the postulated relationships must conform to logic. The alternative is seldom mentioned.

A recent development, sociobiology, confronts some of these issues head-on. The field first came to wide attention after the publication of a textbook, *Sociobiology*, by Edward O. Wilson, a curator in entomology at the Harvard Museum of Comparative Zoology. Although the book is almost entirely devoted to a discussion of social behavior among such forms of life as slime molds and ants, rather than among mankind, one of its central conclusions, that behavior is genetically determined, has been seized on by critics. The criticisms are based largely on the idea that to admit a genetic basis of human behavior is to condone and accept the idea that there are important differences among the races, an idea which to many is untenable. Thus a scientific proposition has been attacked on basically political grounds. The point in the present context, however, is that ideas like those alleged to be contained in *Sociobiology* are commonly held, but they have not been subjected to scientific testing.

Ultimately, science can hardly afford to dismiss out-of-hand factors that are thought by most people to be important, even though they do not lend themselves to easy analysis. However, in the present state of archeological science, we must work with the kind of data we have and can hope to control. There will be plenty of work for future generations as we accumulate well-founded concepts and results.

Culture

To begin, we must make a distinction between *culture* as an abstract concept and *cultures* as particular groups of people who are named. For example, we speak of culture in general, of American culture, or Hopi culture, or, in archeology, the La Tene or Adena cultures. Because the same word is used for two rather different concepts, we must define each separately. This initial discussion will deal with *culture in the general sense* as a distinctly human phenomenon.

It is often said that humans have culture whereas animals do not, but the distinction has become less clear with intensive studies of nonhuman primates and other forms of life that behave in noninstinctive ways. To clarify the nature of culture as an abstraction we may contrast it with strictly biologically controlled behavior. Kluckhohn and Kelly (1945:97) define culture as "historically created designs for living, explicit and implicit, rational, irrational, and non-rational, which exist at any given time as potential guides for the behavior of man." Humans have many of these socially transmitted patterns of learned behavior, while animals' behavior is more genetically controlled and instinctive. Animals cannot pass learning from one generation to another except by example, and they are relatively inflexible in learning itself. On the other hand, some human behavior is thought to be biologically determined, so one might express the distinction between the species in the proportion of behavior that is controlled through either learning or instinct. Nevertheless, there is a vast difference rather than a simple gradation between humans and animals.

At the base of this difference is the fact that culture is transmitted by symbolic communication (abstract thought through speech). This fact has two important implications: culture is uniquely human because other animals are not equipped for language as we know it, and cultures (in the specific sense) may change abruptly in ways that appear to defy our generalization that it is learned from preceding generations. It is symbolic communication that allows the rapid transmission of knowledge and experience from one group of people to another, so that, for example, the Manus Islanders studied by Margaret Mead can leap in one generation from the Stone Age to the twentieth century.

The contrast with biologically transmitted behavior lies in the fact that biological information depends on the reproduction of matter, while culture depends on the transmission of learned behavior and is not constrained by the same physical laws. Thus, the mechanisms of biological change and evolution do not pertain except metaphorically to cultural change and evolution, as Huxley points out.

Very little archeological discussion concerns culture in the general sense. Indeed some anthropologists (such as Mellor) have questioned whether there is any validity to the concept at all (Mellor 1972). Still, most of us accept the existence of culture even though it may be an abstraction constructed out of experience and intuition. L. A. White and others have written extensively of this intangible concept and made it a central focus of anthropological studies. In archeology we are much more concerned with the material remains of particular cultures and the ways they change or the reasons they are different. In order to discuss these matters, however, we must consider the properties that culture (in the general sense) is thought to have.

Pattern. Culture is usually thought to be patterned, or ordered in a systematic way such that the component parts fit together harmoniously. Looked at this way, culture consists of various subsystems: technological, social, religious, ideological, and economic. The underlying assumption is that these subsystems interact in ways that are mutually supporting or at least not harmful. We may infer from this that people must behave consistently so that they do not upset the working of the system. When people behave consistently, we may say that their behavior is patterned. People in different cultures behave in somewhat different ways; their patterns of culture are different.

Archeologically we see evidence that these concepts are valid in the way artifacts are distributed in sites. The artifacts themselves show patterning, a fact that has been tested through the use of various analytical techniques. To demonstrate that patterning exists is only the first step, for archeologists would like to use this fact to infer what behavior causes it. This is not easy, and it must ultimately depend either on direct ethnographic analogy or on general hypotheses about the relationship between artifacts and behavior that are themselves derived from a study of the modern world.

Change. Another property of culture is that it keeps changing. The ways it changes are loosely analogous to the ways biological organisms change, but there are important differences. We have already mentioned that culture is transmitted through **extracorporeal** means, which allow for rapid and dramatic changes. We should also remember that the anthropologists' conception of culture was inferred from observation of peoples' behavior and the discussion of a particular culture usually focuses on an ideal set of patterns. In the beliefs of any people there are proper ways to behave and proper ways to manufacture things. To some degree, people who are brought up (enculturated) in that culture adhere to these ideals, but there is typically a considerable range of variation in their actual behavior. For this reason we find what we may call *random change*, a process that is analogous to genetic drift. The learning of appropriate or ideal behavior patterns cannot be perfect, so there will inevitably be some differences between generations that may not be noticeable in the short run but that may accumulate over time as long as populations remain somewhat isolated.

Diffusion is one of the primary mechanisms of cultural change. Because culture is transmitted largely through symbolic communication, it is possible for aspects of it to be exported over long distances, as in the case of the Manus Islanders. Although it would be rare for entire cultures to be so transmitted, certain patterns of behavior and customs may be introduced into another culture and adopted. Conversion of peoples to foreign religions is a case in point; here a set of behaviors of foreign origin replaces or mixes with native traditions. There is no direct biological counterpart to this kind of change, although hybridization through gene flow is somewhat analogous.

Invention is also a primary mechanism of change. The usual implication is that people consciously and purposefully invent things they need. That invention need not be deliberate, however, was discussed at length by A. L. Kroeber in an article that attributes many inventions to man's delight in play. Manipulative and intellectual "play" is fun and sometimes results in inventions of importance. However, whether inventions are deliberate or not, insofar as the things invented become a part of a culture and affect the overall cultural patterns, we may say that the culture has changed.

Accidental discovery is closely related to invention and can be considered an agent of change if the value of the discovery is recognized and the resultant invention put to use. Accidental discovery is analogous to mutation and is probably only infrequently of value or recognized to be of value and hence retained as part of the culture.

The importance of the processes enumerated above is that they produce variability (expressed as behavioral alternatives), which, like genetic diversity, may be critical to survival of the species under rapidly changing circumstances.

However, unlike biological change, the material out of which changes can be effected need not lie in the culture itself, but can be borrowed from another culture. Thus, the ability to transmit and borrow useful behavior from outside one's own culture is extremely important for humans, and has resulted in the exceptionally rapid development of the inventory of culture. We may say that the pace and magnitude of cultural evolution today far outstrips the pace of biological change in the human species.

   Adaptation. Aside from its ability to transmit information through symbolic means, culture is seen primarily as an agent of human adaptation in much the same way as the ability to run fast may confer a selective advantage on certain animals. In this sense, culture is a biological phenomenon (G. G. Simpson 1964). Ordinarily, however, culture is seen as standing between biological man and the physical and organic environment that surrounds him. Today it is unthinkable for man to exist without culture, for he is no longer equipped to survive solely through his biological equipment. His basic needs of subsistence, shelter, and reproduction are largely satisfied through learned behavior and effected through the spoken communication with his fellow men that leads to cooperation.

   Consider how ill-equipped the newborn infant is; even if he were of adult size and strength, he could not cope with the world about him. He lacks the basic tools for survival. Compared with the predators who would find him succulent quarry, he lacks the speed, size, and strength that would help him defend himself, and he would find it hard to keep warm and obtain suitable safe shelter. Man survives because of his culture: tools, equipment, social behavior, skills, and knowledge, and these are learned or acquired after birth. To say that culture is adaptive does not imply that people always behave adaptively, but only that without culture they would not survive. The adaptive aspects of culture are a matter that will be explored in greater detail in Chapters 10 and 15.

The Relation between Biological and Cultural Processes

It is incorrect to argue that biological change is no longer important in man simply because culture can take care of most biological problems. What should be said is that there is feedback between biological and cultural change, each affecting the other. Washburn, Lancaster, and others (for example, Bordes) have made a strong case that increments of culture had a profound effect on man's early development, and this position is not seriously challenged today. What has been debated is whether biological change is important today or whether, in fact, man is changing biologically. A fair assessment of the situation points to the probability that culture has altered the adaptive value of certain genes. For example, it is no longer essential to have good eyesight, or the ability to run fast, or to hear or smell well. People with gross deficiencies in these abilities can survive, breed, and consequently add to the relative numbers of persons with these

problems. On the other hand, in industrial societies there is increasing dependence on the ability to use the mind, to communicate effectively, and to manipulate things with dexterity. One might think that selection would favor persons
with these skills, but success in a society need not be only in the biological sense
of reproduction. In fact, the biological analogy fails, for, as Simpson says, "Natural selection solely and always favors relative efficiency in reproduction. Artificial [cultural] selection may, and usually does, favor other and conflicting goals
(and here they *are* goals)" (G. G. Simpson 1964:151). That is to say, people are
at least as concerned with matters such as quality of life as they are with quantity of offspring, and the former goal competes with the latter.

As examples of the interplay between biology and culture, W. Bray
(1972:88) enumerates a number of cultural factors that may affect biological
change in man: (1) population size, (2) assortive mating, (3) the degree of inter-
population mobility, (4) control and regulation of childbirth, (5) disease, and (6)
alteration of mutation rate (for example, through use of drugs). "Genetic changes
have brought about increased ability for adaptation by cultural means, and this
cultural adaptation has changed environmental conditions in such a way that
new selective pressures have arisen, giving rise to further genetic changes in
the population."

Archeological Cultures

The preceding discussion concerned culture in general; of much greater relevance to archeologists is the concept of the archeological culture. It follows
from the principle of uniformitarianism that if modern man is a cultural animal
and people today have cultures, there were also cultures in prehistoric times. In
archeology we deal not with patterns of behavior (including customs, language,
and speculative thought) but with artifacts, and from them we must infer the existence of cultures. V. Gordon Childe (1947:51) defined the relationship in the
following way:

> An archaeological culture is an assemblage of artifacts that recurs repeat-
> edly associated together in dwellings of the same kind and with burials
> of the same rite. The arbitrary pecularities of all cultural traits are assumed
> to be concrete expressions of the common social traditions that bind to-
> gether a culture. Artifacts hang together in assemblages, not only because
> they were used in the same age, but also because they were used by the
> same people, made or executed in accordance with techniques, rites or
> styles prescribed by a social tradition, handed on by precept and exam-
> ple and modifiable in the same way.

Thus, for archeologists cultures exist in the form of tools, pottery, burials, styles,
ornaments, and art, because these things are repeatedly found together. Artifacts
are part of a people's material culture, but an ax is not culture, nor is a burial
or a house. It is only when certain kinds of axes, burials, and houses are found

together in several sites that archeologists refer to the repeated associations of artifacts as evidence of a culture. All these statements imply a kind of grouping an ethnologist would call a "tribe," or a "people," or a "society." We expect that people who occupy a common territory and share a common material culture will also share such things as language, ideas about right and wrong, preferences in art, religion, and other intangible traits. These elements of non-material culture are not recovered by prehistoric archeologists, but every effort is made to make inferences about the social or nonmaterial aspects of the re-mains they examine. In this sense archeology is "paleoethnology."

In most archeological writing, cultures are inferred from things that are found in excavations. The most important of these are artifacts, tools and other things made or used by man. Artifacts are then ordinarily classified into types that serve to identify their variety and to simplify their description. An arche-ologist can then characterize an excavation by the types of artifacts it produced. Should the artifacts be different from those found in other excavations, he may decide to let them stand for a culture and give it a name. This method is not precisely the same as that used by ethnologists to identify cultures, because it does not take into account such intangible and important considerations as language, religion, or political relations; nor does it imply any knowledge of the way the culture was organized. The closest analogue to this procedure is the drawing up of **trait lists** in ethnology in order to determine which people are related most closely. The judgment in this instance would be based on the number of items that two or more groups of people shared without any particu-lar weighting of the importance of the artifacts held in common. The definition of an archeological culture in this way is traditional and serves important func-tions for comparing excavations, but it does not necessarily lend itself to some of the questions that archeologists now think relevant.

It is possible to deal, as Childe did, with culture largely as a **taxonomic** device for ordering archeological evidence in time and space, but modern approaches emphasize the behavioral aspects of prehistoric cultures. What were the people doing? What were they like? Why did they change?

There is consensus among archeologists that artifacts are "fossilized" evi-dence of human behavior. If this assumption is true, it follows that we *may* (but not necessarily will) be able to infer the behavior from the artifacts. As Binford has pointed out, there are three kinds of behavior on which artifacts may inform: technological, sociological, and ideological. If all artifacts relate to one or more of these kinds of behavior, we may be able to infer the behavior if we can cor-rectly identify to which uses the artifacts were put. A prehistorian interested in behavior will therefore keep in mind the possible relevance of his data to these categories and structure his analysis accordingly. However, although one can easily conceptualize these three important areas of behavior, and in specific instances relate artifacts to them, it is quite another problem to verify the rela-tionship between most artifacts and the behavioral context within which they were used. Logically we cannot do this solely with archeological material, for we would only be correlating inferred evidence with assumed behavioral patterns.

We could hardly fail to find ourselves correct. One way to overcome this problem is to study modern peoples to see how their behavior relates to the tangible traces that can be found archeologically. The study by David (1971) referred to earlier is one example, and *Approaches to the Social Dimensions of Mortuary Practices* (1971), edited by James Brown, goes into considerable detail on the possibilities of making inferences about the intangible aspects of culture from burial data. However, even in regard to burial practices, which have been described and analyzed since the early days of anthropology, there has not emerged a systematic set of concepts and procedures for their archeological analysis in behavioral terms.

In shifting the emphasis from cultures to cultural practices, we avoid one dilemma but raise some problems. We avoid labeling archeological remains with names of cultures that imply distinct social groups when we have not the slightest idea whether such groups are manifest in the criteria we use to identify them. To confess the lack of tangible support for such labeling casts into doubt all the historical reconstructions that speak of migrations, wars, and other kinds of interaction among prehistoric peoples. This does not suggest that such activities did not occur, but only that the identity of the groups—their sociocultural characteristics as well as their distribution in time and space—is in question.

If instead we speak of cultural practices, we raise another problem; namely, to determine the relationship between archeological data and the behavior. What we gain, however, is precision of focus and the possibility of discovering the relationship through a study of living people. We cannot do this with prehistoric cultures because many of the criteria on which cultures today are defined are intangible or unlikely to leave archeological remains (language, religion, dress, political organization, and so forth). The archeological culture thus remains a typically archeological construct in which validity can be tested only with reference to the concepts that underlie it. In short, archeological cultures are not analogous to the cultures an ethnographer describes and should not be treated as if they were.

The concepts discussed in this chapter are basic to an understanding of archeology as distinct from history and the humanities. Archeologists, like anthropologists, take the view that man is only one part of the organic world, and he exists in a context that is both social and physical. The thing that sets man apart is his culture, but that too can be seen as a biologically based phenomenon in the sense that people have the biological capacity to symbolize through speech and thus transmit abstract thoughts. Still, in important ways man is an animal, and his biological and cultural qualities affect one another through mutual interaction.

In order to understand the special nature of archeology, one must recognize that the data themselves to a large extent determine the kinds of things archeologists can investigate. It is commonplace to assert that archeological remains represent only a portion of the things used by people in a culture, and that even if we were to include all things, we would still omit a great deal of the essence of a culture. Under these circumstances archeology cannot be all that anthropology is nor can it routinely employ concepts of anthropology. Prehistorians must adapt these concepts to their particular data; for example, an archeological culture is analogous to, but not the same as, an ethnographic culture.

Because of the problems inherent in dealing with archeological material, some prehistorians have preferred to deal with archeological data exclusively in their own terms. One could, for example, develop a science of artifacts without any reference to the peoples who made and used them. This would, however, be a rather sterile and unsatisfying study, unrelated conceptually to anything of social consequence. One could arrange the artifacts in time and space and study their characteristics, but the question would inevitably be raised, "So what?" Much archeological research has been conducted essentially on the level of a self-contained study of artifacts, but prehistorians inevitably use these studies as the basis for making inferences about the behavior of peoples. It is at this point that the need for accurately stated assumptions becomes critical, and it is here that a great deal of archeological research should be directed.

THE EVIDENCE OF PREHISTORY

The story of archeology centers on sites, places that were used by people in the past, and on their excavators. But the story of prehistory concerns the people who lived at the sites and the things they did. What we know about these ancient peoples depends on the sites we have found and dug and on an interpretation of the artifacts and other things found in the sites. The site report, a technical paper describing the excavation and its results, is the first step in presenting information about the past that will eventually be compiled into a story of ancient peoples. Therefore, when we consider what archeologists do and what they have to work with, it is natural to begin with sites. They are precisely placed on the landscape, and their locations can be plotted on maps; they have definite sizes and shapes; they have certain periods of occupation; and they represent the leavings from particular kinds of use by peoples of antiquity.

Archeological Sites

In reading prehistory we find references to ceremonial sites, hill forts, graves, trading centers, and camps, and in looking at the modern world we recognize similar diversity. Some settlements may be primarily manufacturing centers, others market towns, still others suburbs or rural hamlets. We also have centers of transportation and of fishing or agriculture. Still, apart from their special functions these sites are usually inhabited as well, and they serve multiple needs of their residents. How would you characterize New York City? Is it a center of industry, of commerce, of shipping, of transportation, or of population? It is, of course, all of these and more, depending on what aspects you want to emphasize. Why is it then that we confidently ascribe specialized functions to prehistoric sites?

We do so for two reasons. First we have a conception of how people live and behave. Through ethnography we know that some contemporary peoples with simple ways of life actually have complex settlement systems. In the course of a year one group of people may use a number of sites that principally serve specialized functions. Hunters frequently observe game from lookouts; religious activities are often carried out in places of solitude and obscurity; winter villages may be placed with protection from wind and the availability of fuel in mind, and summer encampments may be in quite other parts of the territory. People who travel continually may have favorite overnight campsites as well as sites for their permanent villages. Manufacturing typically may be carried out near sources of raw material. One could expand this list indefinitely, but the point is that before most people were permanently settled and before rapid and efficient transportation and communication were possible, people took themselves to the things they needed. Today we bring the products to the people. Thus, we reason, in antiquity there were many more specialized sites than today. Ethnography also tells us what kinds of sites we may expect to find among people who have ways similar to our primitive contemporaries.

Second, we may examine the contents of the sites themselves. That Pa Sangar rock shelter in western Iran served as a butchering station or that Yafteh Cave (see Figs. 4.1 and 4.2) was a base camp can be inferred from the kinds and quantity of material left by their inhabitants (Hole and Flannery 1968). It would be even more obvious to find a fort with arrows imbedded in the walls and the bodies of slain defenders in testimony of the last battle. But even without the arrows or bodies, the absence of domestic refuse and geographic context (perhaps on a defensible ridge away from evidence of settlements) would imply a very specific use of the site. Although we find more examples that are ambiguous than obvious, we do have reason to ascribe singular functions to many sites in prehistory. This chapter summarizes the kinds of sites that have been described.

FIG. 4.1 *A typical rock shelter that was used some 15,000–25,000 years ago by hunters in West Iran. The shelter, Pa Sangar, offers minimal protection from the elements, but it affords a panoramic view of the valley below where the food supply lived.*

Kinds of Sites

A site is any place, large or small, where there are to be found traces of ancient occupation or activity. The usual clue to a site is the presence of artifacts. There are millions of sites on the earth, some of which are as large as a city, others as small as the spot where an arrowhead lies. The number and variety of prehistoric sites are limited only by the activities of prehistoric men who lived and left their

FIG. 4.2 Yafteh Cave in West Iran was used as a base camp by hunters some 35,000 years ago. The cave is large enough to accommodate about 20 persons, and it overlooks the length of the Khorramabad Valley.

equipment scattered over the full breadth of the earth, and by the conditions of preservation.

We could hardly comprehend prehistory if we regarded each site as unique; therefore archeologists customarily group sites into convenient categories. A reader of a general work on archeology will see reference to Paleolithic sites, early Bronze Age sites, or Desert Culture sites. These sites have been classified by the kinds of artifacts that are found in them: stone tools, bronze tools, and a variety of milling stones and hunting equipment, respectively. Another way to classify sites is to emphasize their locations. Thus we see reference to open sites (villages), cave sites, lakeside sites, and valley-bottom sites. A third way is to name the activity represented by the remains, such as kill site, camp site, quarry site, and living site. We can also refer to the duration of use by such designations as permanent, seasonal, or intermittent. Finally, we can refer to the archeological context of the sites: stratified, nonstratified, or surface find. These designations could be expanded, but none of them can account for all the possible kinds of sites. To convey some idea of the variety of archeological sites, we shall describe a number of different kinds of sites that are grouped by the activities they represent.

Some sites are clearly more important than others, but the importance of any particular site may not be evident to the layman. The importance of a site lies in how much information it can provide in answer to some questions or problems. Thus, a tomb may be valueless if we are concerned with questions of trade or the problem of the origin of a people. On the other hand, tombs often preserve the finest objects in an unbroken condition. Which sites are the most important, therefore, depends on your perspective and on the amount of archeology that has been done in an area. We would not know very much about Maya civilization if only the hamlets of poor peasant farmers had been dug. As it is, we know relatively little about the "poor peasant farmers" precisely because attention has been given to temples, palaces, and other buildings in monumental style. In this case, a good study of rural Maya life would be more important now than clearing the jungle from another temple and probing its innards for a tomb. One would hope in most work to strike a balance so that a sample of all the kinds of sites in use at a particular period could be obtained to give a balanced picture of a prehistoric people's way of life.

Habitation Sites

The most commonly sought and excavated sites are the places where people lived, for the simple reason that these sites were a focus of prehistoric activities. In a sense, all archeological sites imply habitation, though it may have been relatively short, but for convenience here, a habitation site is a spot around which a group of people centered their daily activities. Habitation sites that were occupied the year round frequently have the remains of houses, but people may also have lived in caves or rock shelters, or even open areas in which no trace of a permanent shelter remains. Seasonally occupied sites generally have fewer traces of architecture. Prehistoric men made various kinds of shelters such as temporary brush windbreaks, lean-tos, tipis, semisubterranean houses made of logs and earth that could be lived in year after year, and mud-brick or rough masonry houses. Some pictures of modern settlements and prehistoric sites that illustrate this variety are found in Figures 2.5, 4.7 and 4.15. In areas where shelters were not needed, habitation sites may show nothing more than the remains of fire and a scatter of refuse and artifacts. Special sites that are usually close to settlements are agricultural fields and terraces, irrigation canals, roads, bridges, aqueducts, and cemeteries. Occasionally habitation sites served the dual purpose of dwelling and defense. Such examples include the cliff dwellings in Mesa Verde (Fig. 2.5), and the remains of actual fortresses in the Mexican and Peruvian highlands.

Middens

Along seacoasts and rivers, a very common kind of site is the **midden**, an accumulation of shells, bones, and cultural refuse (Fig. 4.3). Middens are usually found where people ate shellfish, snails, or quantities of fish and sea mammals. All these food sources leave a great amount of debris that was customarily piled up where the food was cleaned and eaten. People sometimes lived on the middens but more often their shelters were close by, away from the stinking heap of garbage. When deaths occurred, the middens were sometimes used as burial sites, perhaps because a relatively secure grave could be made by covering the body with shells. For the most part middens should be considered evidence

FIG. 4.3 Excavation of the Cerro Colorado refuse midden at Taltal, northern Chile, where a test trench revealed the slope of natural strata. When the stratification had been determined, a large block of the midden was isolated and stripped layer by layer, as shown in this photo. (Photo courtesy of Junius Bird.)

of temporary occupation rather than permanent habitation sites. They were probably used seasonally as people made their annual round, hunting and gathering the various species throughout their territory.

Quarry Sites

Sites where minerals were mined (often for trade) are common throughout the world, although they are seldom excavated. Examples include the Alibates Ranch (now a state park) in Texas, where prehistoric men quarried for a widely used multicolored flint; flint mines, dug into the chalk deposits at such places as Grimes Graves, are well-known sites in England. Mining for metal ores has also left sites. In grim testimony of the dangers of mining, archeologists have uncovered the bones, and sometimes the bodies, of miners who were crushed by falling rock.

Kill Sites

It is common in the United States and elsewhere to find kill sites, places where one or more animals were killed by hunters, who had no permanent dwellings. At kill sites archeologists find the bones of the animals, spear and arrow heads used for killing them, and the tools for butchering. In some cases where the bones have been well preserved the pattern of butchering the animals can be reconstructed in considerable detail.

Trading Centers

Trading centers have been reported from a few places, though they are hard to recognize with certainty. Trading on a scale large enough to necessitate trade centers must have been unusual for prehistoric peoples, but sites centrally situated between the Maya and Aztec areas have been identified as ports of trade, though of course they were habitation sites as well. Often the geographic location of a site is the best clue as to its function as a trade center. A site in Turkey which is on land that could not be farmed was favorably placed for the salt and obsidian trade, and the widespread trade in the latter commodity and in copper raises the possibility of finding definite evidence of mining and manufacturing sites if they are deliberately sought.

Ceremonial Sites

Ceremonial sites include the imposing **megalithic** construction at Stonehenge, and the much older caves in France and Spain where remarkable paintings, carvings, and reliefs are found. All the major civilizations have erected temples or other monumental architecture. Some of the most impressive examples are in Meso-America where the enormous ceremonial precincts, such as Teotihuacan near Mexico City, evoke admiration the world around (Fig. 4.4). Ceremonial centers need not be attached to habitation areas, but if they are monumental in

FIG. 4.4 View of the Pyramid of the Moon, Teotihuacan, Mexico, a site built and abandoned during the Classic period. This enormous city and ceremonial center covers approximately 8 square miles.

size they cannot have been far from a supply of labor. Ordinarily, however, there are no dwellings other than those of political or religious officials and their retainers within the area of a ceremonial site.

Burial Sites

Burial sites have attracted looters since early historic times, and many archeologists concentrate their efforts on cemeteries because they often contain useful information about social practices. Burial sites range from isolated burials in shallow holes to elaborate masonry constructions and earth mounds.

Burials may also be found in the garbage dumps of large villages; they may be under the floors of houses; or they may occur singly, away from habitation sites. At times certain cemeteries, or sections of a cemetery, may have been reserved for persons of one sex or age or social rank. Usually, however, cemeteries contain a sample of the whole population that died in the period of the cemetery's use. Examples of special cemeteries are those for children in Pennsylvania (Farabee 1919); separate cemeteries for men in the Desert Fayum (Caton-Thompson and Gardner 1934); the Roman cemetery at Ziegelfeld in upper Austria, where special areas were reserved for children, for victims of epidemics, and for persons belonging to "an elevated social group, very like the clergy" (Kloiber 1957); and the Carter Ranch site in eastern Arizona, where the burials were grouped by descent line and status (Longacre 1964).

Surface Scatters

Surface scatters are sites that have a geological or geographical context (Chap. 5) but no archeological associations; that is, the sites are simply denoted by the presence of artifacts lying on the ground. Although there is a limit to what one can infer from such evidence, in the United States knowledge of the distribution of early big-game hunters is based largely on a plotting of isolated projectile points and other artifacts found by farmers while plowing in their fields or by persons who accidentally came upon them while walking. Although most such sites cannot be classified by activity, flints are sometimes found on the surface in situations that suggest activities. For example, in West Iran, in hilly country on the edges of large valleys, one frequently finds flints on the tops of hills, as though hunters had waited and watched for their quarry there.

Petroglyphs and Pictographs

Petroglyphs and pictographs are pecked or painted pictures of animals, men, mythical beings, or geometric and curvilinear designs whose meaning has not been interpreted with any reliability. They are usually found on exposed, flat rock surfaces, either in the open air or on the protected walls of caves and shelters. Pecked or painted designs are spread over most of the world, and vary from the painted caves of Lascaux and Altamira in France and Spain to rude designs pecked on boulders in the western United States. In general these painted or pecked designs seem to have been associated with magico-religious activities rather than being pure expressions of artistic-esthetic impulse. However, we are all familiar with the propensity of tourists to carve, scratch, or paint their names on monuments, public walls, and the like. The practice was apparently just as common in antiquity, and the inscriptions of Spanish and American explorers on the cliffs of Morro Rock, New Mexico, actually constitute a valuable historical record. In the same way an intimate insight into the life of the common people at Pompeii is afforded by a careful study of the graffiti on the walls of that city. A graffito copied from a wall in Pompeii and inscribed there about 2000 years ago (Fig. 4.5) reads: "Successus the weaver loves the innkeeper's maid servant, Iris by name. She, however, does not return his love. But he begs her to take pity on him. Written by his rival. So long" (Tanzer, 1939:87).

Large "**intaglio**" figures of animals, humans, or geometric forms constitute a special kind of pictographic site, as do the giant desert figures along

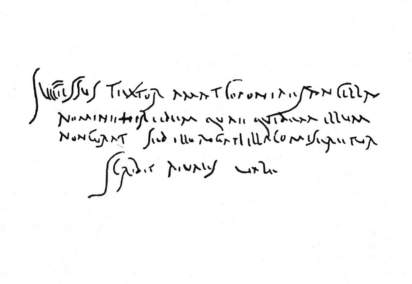

FIG. 4.5   A grafitto from a wall in Pompeii. (See text for translation.)

the lower Colorado River, the "medicine wheels" and effigy figures in the Great Plains, the immense figures on the coastal desert of Peru, and the giant, turf-cut figure in Wessex.

How Is a Site Made?

Two questions frequently asked of archeologists are, "How is a site made?" and "How do you know where to look for sites?" In principle, the answers to both questions are easy, but sometimes a little explanation and illustration are required to put the point across.

Sites are the result of human activity, and as a consequence, one might think they would be easily recognizable, but so few persons have seen an archeological site that they would be unlikely to recognize one unless it were a pyramid or some other obvious ancient structure. Most sites look at first glance like natural hills or they may even be entirely covered over by dirt, grass, and trees. These sites can not be "seen" but their presence can be recognized by a trained archeologist. How did this happen? Why does human refuse in a cave often attain a depth of 50 feet, or a village leave a mound that rises 100 feet above its surrounding plain, or a settlement become buried under several feet of sterile dirt? Each of these is a separate situation and requires its own explanation.

Take the case of caves and rock shelters where continued occupation over thousands of years has left a layered deposit of debris some tens of feet in depth. What caused this deposition? At first it may be hard to understand how persons, living a normal life, could eventually pile up so much dirt. The answer, though, is really very simple. We should recognize, to begin with, that ancient cave dwellers were ordinarily less particular about cleanliness than we are. Second, through natural geological processes such as falling rock, blowing dust, and running water, dirt is continually added to the floor of a cave. The accumulation of debris in caves thus can be explained as the joint result of man and natural processes. A family moving into a cave might bring in some branches or grass to cover the damp, hard floor where they wanted to sit and sleep. They might even bring in some rocks to sit on. They would bring in wood and branches to build fires. The hunters would kill animals and bring their bodies into the cave. When they had finished their meals they would throw the bones to one side. On muddy days they would track in dirt. They would never sweep out the cave. As natural erosion of the cave or rock shelter took place, bits of rock and dirt would flake off the ceiling. Sometimes a major rockfall would bury the whole floor. Dust carried by wind might add appreciable quantities of fine soil over long periods of time, and water-carried sediments might also add to the filling process. If occupation together with natural events continued for thousands of years, the cave might finally be filled to its top.

The great mounds (**tells**) that have accumulated in some parts of the world, especially in the Near East, represent a similar story, except that natural processes have sometimes done more to take away than to add material (Fig. 4.6). There are mounds in Turkestan that were occupied between the tenth and seventh centuries B.C., where the depth of deposit is as much as 34 meters (about 114 feet). At Ur in Mesopotamia, Woolley dug more than 90 feet to reach the base of the great mound, and Sultantepe in Anatolia rises to a height of more than 150 feet. How do such huge accumulations form?

These mounds occur in parts of the world where the chief building material is mud. The people make bricks or layers of sun-dried mud and they lay poles across them to form a roof on which they pile brush or matting, and cover the whole with a thick layer of mud that is practically impervious to what little rain falls in these regions (Fig. 4.7). Despite the low rainfall and consequent slow rate of erosion, the houses ultimately deteriorate and eventually become unsafe for continued use. Then thrifty villagers scavenge the scarce poles used in the roof and reuse them in a new structure. After this, the bare walls standing there against the wind and rain rapidly disintegrate and eventually leave a featureless mound where the old house stood (Fig. 4.8). After minor leveling, new houses are often built on the same location, frequently with a floor several feet higher than the original house. One may wonder why people—as they customarily do in the Near East—chose to build on top of old houses rather than pick a spot on level land. The reasons seem to be that, with agricultural fields beginning at the edges of the settlements, there was no room to expand, and often defensive walls were built around the towns, preventing lateral expansion except at the cost of

FIG. 4.6   The mound of Farukhabad rises some 22 meters above the Deh Luran plain. The sharp profile on the right has been caused by the adjacent river undercutting the mound. Farukhabad was occupied intermittently for about 4000 years beginning about 4000 B.C.

extensive renovation of the **circumvallation**. A diagram that illustrates how mounds grow is found in Lloyd (1963:Fig. 1).

The mound is such a conspicuous feature of the landscape in Southwest Asia and so conspicuously absent by comparison in the rest of the world that one must ask why. Childe (1962:56) wrote that there "are no tells in the woodland zone of Eurasia, north of the Po valley and the Hungarian plain." There are at least two reasons for this. First, the building material in Europe was usually wood; and, second, the sites in Eurasia generally have not been occupied for so long as those in Southwest Asia. In Europe, outside of caves, an occupation of 1000 years duration is almost unknown. Where wood is used in building, it disintegrates and does not leave a mound. Where stone is used, it is frequently reused for new buildings; therefore there may not be the constant addition of new material. Under these conditions only small mounds accumulate. In modern cities, when old buildings are razed, they are rarely leveled to their original surface. In the course of repaving, street levels are raised. And so, even in the United States, mounds are growing. J. C. Wylie (1959:9) calculates that in our own civilization "every thousand people . . . discard nearly a ton of rubbish every day of their lives." Some of the refuse remains in the living area and thus adds to the rising surface of our cities.

FIG. 4.7 Detail of a recently abandoned Near Eastern mud-walled house, showing the position of roof beams.

This discussion has so far excluded the conscious building of mounds by the deliberate heaping up of dirt or stone. The practice of building mounds on which to place houses, public buildings, and temples was common in the eastern United States as well as in Meso-America (Figs. 4.9, 4.10, 4.11). Native Americans in the Upper Mississippi Valley region of the United States often made mounds for purposes of burial, some of them being effigies of animals, birds, and serpents.

These examples show how mounds come into being. The other problem is how sites become buried. In the category of buried sites are most of the so-called Early Man sites in the Americas, as well as such examples as Olduvai Gorge, where the early African **hominids** (early forms of man) have been found. These are covered by geological strata, and the circumstances of burial are often very similar the world around. As typical examples, consider sites like Naco and Lehner in the American Southwest. There, some 9000 years ago, hunters killed mammoths alongside a stream. They left part of a carcass at the edge of the

FIG. 4.8 Mud brick and stone walls gradually eroding and forming a mound of rubble of the type that constitutes many archeological sites.

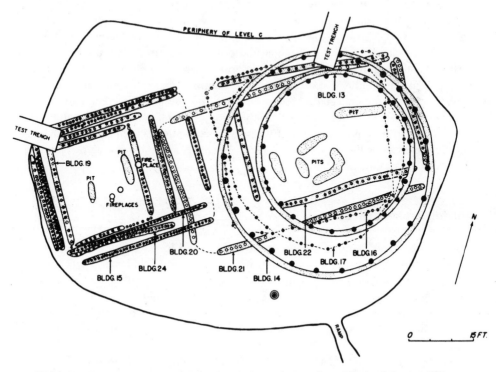

FIG. 4.9 Plan view of summit of mound in the Southeast United States (Hiwassee Island), showing the remains of superimposed buildings. The entire village, of which this mound is a part, was surrounded by a defensive stockade. (T. M. N. Lewis and M. Kneberg, 1946, Hiwassee Island. By permission of the University of Tennessee Press.)

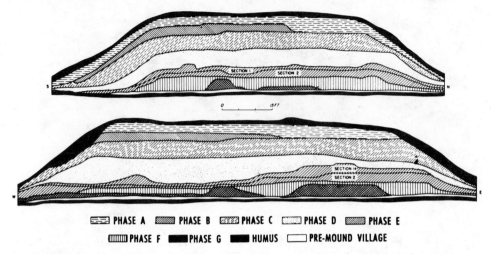

PHASE A   PHASE B   PHASE C   PHASE D   PHASE E
PHASE F   PHASE G   HUMUS   PRE-MOUND VILLAGE

*FIG. 4.10 Section through the mound at Hiwassee Island, showing the succes-
sive stages of construction. (T. M. N. Lewis and M. Kneberg, 1946,* Hiwassee
Island. *By permission of the University of Tennessee Press.)*

water, where it was buried as the river flooded and deposited a load of sand
or silt over the bones. In time, the river deposits buried the site under many
feet of dirt. Thousands of years later, when the river began to degrade its channel, the site was exposed again, this time in the vertical bank of the new stream.

This example implies that the absolute depth of a site below the modern
surface has no bearing on its age. The question, "How deep did you have to dig
to find a site that old?" is meaningless. The depth of deposit over a site is related to geomorphological processes, whereas the depth of accumulation of
human refuse within a site reflects a combination of cleanliness, type of material
used in structures, the desirability of the site for continued settlement, and such
natural processes as the disintegration of cave ceilings and the washing or blowing in of sand or dirt.

Recognizing Archeological Sites

A wide array of techniques, ranging from walking and looking at the ground to
aerial photography to magnetic prospecting, can be used to find sites. Fortuitous
discovery of sites will always be important, though perhaps not so dramatic as
that of Adaura cave near Palermo, Sicily, which was opened by the demolition
of artillery ammunition during World War II, and that of the hitherto unknown
sites on the northeast coast of Nuka Hiva in the Marquesas Islands, which were
exposed by the action of a tidal wave.

Most archeologists, however, decline to wait for luck to strike, and they
deliberately go out and look for sites. There are two approaches we can use.
We can start with an area we like or happen for other reasons to be in, and ask,

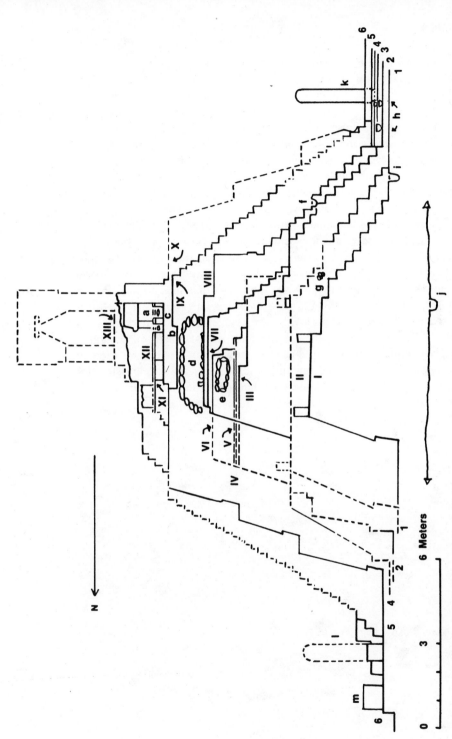

FIG. 4.11 *North-south section of pyramids within Pyramid A-I Complex at the site of Uaxactun, Guatemala. a, Sanctuary; b-c, Cists; d-f, Crypts; g, a burial; h, cache of five pottery vessels beneath Stela A-7; i, Cist; j, empy hollow cut in limestone bedrock; k, Stela A-7; l, Stela 7; m, Altar 1–XIII, pyramidal platforms; 1-6, floors at bases of pyramids. (From Carnegie Institution of Washington Publication No. 456—Smith, Plate 10.)*

"What kinds of sites are here?"; or we can begin with a kind of site in mind and ask, "Where can we find one?".

To begin to find sites in certain areas, a person must first familiarize himself with the landscape and its potential for supporting different kinds of human activities. It is helpful also to have some general ideas about the kinds of sites that are likely to be found. For example, a person would normally look in somewhat different places for sites of hunters and for sites of farmers (Fig. 4.14). He would also know that hunters usually lived in relatively small camps, in impermanent dwellings, that they moved regularly in pursuit of game, and that such sites as they did occupy would have been in places where water, game, and perhaps fuel could be obtained. Farmers, in contrast, ordinarily lived in permanent settlements and chose their sites with an eye toward **arable** land.

Armed with this kind of knowledge, a person can then survey the land-scape for suitable places. Then comes the difficulty. How do you recognize a site when you see one? A person who takes the time to familiarize himself with an area will soon learn what is natural there: how the hills look, how the grass grows, where the trees are, and the location of sources of water. If he pays at-tention, he will begin to notice when things look out of place. An unnatural contour to a hill, an unusual kind of vegetation growing in a particular spot, or soil differing in color from that of the surrounding areas are all clues to sites (Fig. 4.12). In short, the observer must train himself to look for the unusual.

FIG. 4.12   *An ancient irrigation canal is recognized by the growth of grass in the filled-in channel. A test pit has been dug across the canal to reveal its size and shape.*

Direct inspection of suspicious or "unnatural" features of the landscape should then tell whether or not a site is present. If the unusual contour is strewn with flint or pottery, or is a heap of shell, it indicates an archeological site. If the grass grows more luxuriantly in the outlines of a rectangle, it may mark the borders of an ancient ditch or house, and occasionally the walls of houses may be exposed on the surface (Fig. 6.3, p. 154).

Some archeologists get in the habit of watching wherever building construction involves the moving of a lot of dirt. But we need not always wait for construction crews to expose sites. Rivers may do the same thing. Perhaps the -most spectacular such site is Olduvai Gorge in Tanzania, where many hundred thousand years of hominid occupation along the edge of a lake can be seen in the sides of the eroded gorge. As one goes from the top to the bottom of the gorge, each successive layer is older than the preceeding one. Similar finds, though less impressive, are often made in the United States by persons who scan the cut banks of streams looking for flints, bones, and layers of charcoal that may be weathering out.

Caves should also be examined. Men usually lived toward the front of caves, sometimes leveling a terrace in front to give themselves room to work in the daylight. If the archeological deposit has been covered by rockfall or soil after the abandonment of occupation, artifacts will at times be found just below the cave, where they are eroding out of the steep or rocky slope. Caves of hunters are often situated on hillsides or cliffs where the men could survey the surrounding countryside (Fig. 4.13), but caves occupied by gatherers of plant food are located where the food is and may offer no attractive vistas for overlooking the landscape (see Fig. 4.14). Cave dwellers were not much interested in deep and dark underground caverns such as Mammoth Cave in Kentucky, except for special ceremonial purposes.

Instead of random searching, many archeologists decide what they want to find and then go out to find it. A discovery comparable to Schliemann's finding Troy was made by a Dutch doctor, Eugene Dubois, who went to Java in 1890 to find a fossil man, and did—"*Pithecanthropus erectus*" (now included in *Homo erectus*). Ordinarily, deliberate discovery of particular kinds of sites depends on careful evaluation of available information. It is a case of narrowing down the possibilities to select the most probable.

An example taken from modern archeological research is the seeking of sites that will shed light on the origins of agriculture. In these investigations archeologists have worked closely with botanists and zoologists to determine where the most likely spots in the world to find out about the history of agriculture would be. Obviously, maize had to be domesticated somewhere near where it grew in the wild, and the same is true for wheat or for goats or cattle. The process is one of eliminating the areas where domestication could not have occurred and then trying to narrow the field still further by identifying the most favorable locations within the possible areas remaining. Then it is time for field work, beginning with surface survey to see if relevant sites can be discovered. If they can, excavation ordinarily follows; if they cannot, it is necessary to reexamine the premises on which the areas were selected.

FIG. 4.13 (top) *Kunji Cave in West Iran was a base camp that housed hunters more than 40,000 years ago.* (bottom) *From the cave entrance hunters could scan the valley floor on which wild oxen, onagers, and elk grazed. These animals, plus the goats that scaled the cliffs above the cave, comprised the bulk of the diet for the hunters.*

FIG. 4.14   *Edible seeds of thorny plants that ripen in late summer and fall in the dense forest in the Oaxaca valley, Mexico, were harvested by food collectors. Fruit of the organ cactus, prickly pear, and the pods of several leguminous shrubs and trees provided a varied and abundant source of food. Sites of the prehistoric people are caves, rock shelters, and open camps. Compare the terrain and vegetation with Figures 4.2 and 4.13, where hunting rather than gathering plants was the principal occupation.*

Here is where archeologists must depend on the talents of specialists in other fields. When our knowledge of the present does not lead us directly to knowledge of the past, it is usually because the natural environment has changed. The world's present climatic pattern is only a few thousand years old, and what is now pleasant country may have been under ice during the period we are interested in investigating. Or land that is now grassless rock and sand dunes may have been well watered not too long ago. Archeologists must therefore know not only in what kind of environment sites would be found, but also what kind of environment existed when the sites would have been occupied. For information about prehistoric environments archeologists depend on geologists, paleobotanists, and paleozoologists, who study plants and animals and the countryside in which they lived.

Archeological Evidence

For the most part archeological evidence is tangible. It can be excavated, handled, weighed, measured, photographed, and described. Such evidence consists of artifacts and of the sites in which they occur, the strata or levels in the site, and distributional maps of their spatial occurrence. Data may also consist of counts, measurements, and descriptions of the primary evidence. Evidence is found in the earth itself, in pollen contained in it, in the bones of animals, and in various forms of economic and industrial waste found in sites. Data also consist of the relationships between and among things. What is archeological evidence to one excavator, or at one time, may not be considered as such by another. Thus, carbonized wood was not usually saved as data for dating until the radiocarbon process was invented. Similarly, until techniques of flotation were developed, archeologists overlooked the seeds that might occur in the soil. What constitute data thus depends on what the archeologist thinks data are, as well as on their actual occurrence. We can usefully make three categories: (1) raw data as they appear before analysis; (2) analytic data that concern the physical, numerical, and relational aspects; and (3) conclusions that give the meaning of the raw data as they have been interpreted by a prehistorian after analysis.

What are considered data, regardless of the techniques available for obtaining them, depend also on the goals an archeologist has set for his project. When we reviewed the history of archeology, we mentioned excavations that were carried out with the single goal of recovering objects for display in a museum. In the case of most nineteenth-century excavations these objects were simply quarried from the sites and few records were kept of their context (Chap. 6). In the museums objects from many sites and many cultural periods were often displayed together so that a viewer was able to gain no appreciation of the range of material that was found in any site or at a single period. The objects were considered valuable as works of art and examples of craftsmanship rather than as sources of information on a wider range of interests. When objects are removed from sites and treated in this manner, a great deal of what archeologists with other ends in view would regard as data is ignored. When collectors purchase artifacts from sites that have been looted of their monuments and art objects, they thus heedlessly continue these old practices and contribute to the destruction of primary archeological evidence. Once removed from their context, such objects may no longer be of much archeological value, however much they may be prized as objects for display.

We stress the matter of the nature of archeological evidence because it emphasizes the difference among the approaches used by the various disciplines that study the past. We especially deplore the wasteful looting that now seems rampant throughout the world. It is a little ironic that as we develop better ways to recover and interpret archeological evidence, it is disappearing at a frightful rate.

What Is Preserved?

Accurate reconstruction of prehistory depends on the preservation of archeological evidence. How much is preserved depends on the conditions it has been exposed to and the ability of an archeologist to recover it. Data that lie in the ground but cannot be recovered by an archeologist are, for practical purposes, unpreserved. In a given environment we can predict what kinds of things may remain after a certain time; yet frequently, by accident, only a small part of the potentially preserved material will remain; also frequently, from the viewpoint of archeology, the wrong things will be preserved. Man lives in a world composed of plants, animals, minerals, and other people (societies or cultures), and we are looking for data that will help us understand their interrelations. Naturally, of these, minerals are the most likely to be preserved under any conditions, but even metal may rust and fired clay may disintegrate. With the exception of stone and gold, very few inorganic artifacts last under adverse conditions, so that archeologists are literally at the mercy of the elements. Only sophisticated understanding of natural destructive processes and ingenuity in designing technical aids for the recovery of evidence give prehistorians a chance of success in their more complicated endeavors. To illustrate what we mean, consider our world today. Large buildings, being framed with steel, will soon disintegrate if left untended; our automobiles will be reduced to window glass and spark plug insulators; our tools will rust, our books and papers will rot, our landscapes will be littered with imperishable plastic containers, and "throwaway" bottles rather than beer cans. Without historical records, an archeologist in 50,000 or 100,000 years would have to use a great deal of imagination to recapture a reasonably accurate picture of what life is like today. Wylie (1959:106–107) in his excellent book on the disposal of modern wastes, tells of some of the ways trash, most of which is perishable, might be informative:

> Times change and the character of refuse changes with changing habits in home and industry; the stream of refuse flowing from any community provides material from which a comprehensive record of the life and interests of the people could be written. Local and national newspapers still clean and legible would furnish relevant facts, while these along with periodicals and magazines would reveal reading habits and interests. The

quantity of tins would indicate a decline in home cooking and the economic strain that is forcing an increasing number of housewives to go out to work. The quantity of coal and ash and cinders would surely indicate the inefficiency of the open fire and the certainty of a polluted atmosphere. Bottles and, still more revealing, their metal caps, would establish drinking tastes while scraps of food, decaying vegetable wastes would reveal what the people ate. Discarded clothing, household furnishing, and odd surprising things would supply all the evidence required to complete the story.

Rarely would most of these things be preserved, but under some conditions our cities would survive virtually intact. It would happen only if the climate suddenly changed to permanent below-freezing conditions, or if rains stopped suddenly and deserts took over, or if clouds of fine dust from massive volcanic eruptions filtered into every crack and buried the city. Although these circumstances are only theoretically possible, they do illustrate the point that the best environments for preservation of organic remains are the very wet, the very dry, and the very cold. If oxygen can be excluded, very wet environments may even preserve metal. The worst environments are those that are alternately wet and dry, hot and cold. Preservation thus depends on a complicated and little understood chemistry that determines how the environment will affect particular artifacts. From the standpoint of preservation, the tropics have the worst environments. Their heavy rains, acid soils, warm climate, vegetation, insects, and erosion combine to destroy almost everything built or droppd by man. Because of this, even spectacular monumental architecture and art has been destroyed in Southeast Asia. Even with any conceivable techniques, the archeologist will never learn very much of prehistory from that area.

Destruction does not take long. Archeologists clear jungle from Mayan temples only to watch them disappear back into the forest after a few years. W. H. Holmes records that the site of Chichen Itza in Yucatan was cleared in the last century, but in 50 years the jungle growth had completely covered it again (cf. Fig. 4.15). As vegetation takes hold, its prying roots slowly tear the structures apart. Heavy rains have long since washed most of the plaster façades from the buildings, and paintings are rarely preserved. But there is always the exception. Surprisingly, some Maya paintings have been preserved just because of the humidity. At Bonampak, water has deposited a thin film of lime that excludes air and dirt from the paintings. The same thing happened in southern France with some of the 10,000–20,000-year-old cave paintings at Lascaux. But nature is fickle on this score, for if too much lime is deposited, paintings are obscured or obliterated.

The best preservation under wet conditions is in northern Europe, Scandinavia, and the Arctic, where bogs have sealed artifacts in wet and airless tombs or low temperatures have prevented decay. Whole bodies have been found in bogs. The Tollund man, buried with the noose that strangled him still around his neck, is a famous example. His preservation was so perfect that the species

FIG. 4.15 The ruins of a palace at Palenque, a Maya site, have been partially cleared of the jungle vegetation that rapidly engulfs a site and gradually destroys it. (Rickards 1910:10.)

of plants he ate for his last meal could be identified in the contents of his stomach. Schlabow and others describe in detail two bodies found in a bog at Windeby in Schleswig-Holstein, Germany: one, a female who still wore a blindfold (Fig. 4.16); the second, a male who met death by strangulation with a hazel-root rope. The circumstances suggest that the persons were put to death for transgression of laws, probably those dealing with adultery, and were buried in graves dug into the swamp. They date from the early post-Christian Iron Age in the second or third century A.D. In Switzerland and neighboring countries the remains of villages once situated on lakeside marshes but now found beneath the water surface have remained waterlogged and well preserved for several thousand years. The evidence recovered from the mucky slime of one such well-preserved site may give more information than that from hundreds of poorly preserved sites.

A remarkable example of how man unwittingly helped nature comes from Russia, where tombs of Scythian warrior horsemen yield the complete burial furnishings. Two thousand years ago Scythian inhabitants of the Altai buried their leaders in log tombs more than 12 feet deep. After the tombs were lined with logs and covered with rocks, moisture rapidly filled the shafts and froze during the first winter to such a degree that they never completely thawed during the summer. The deep freeze thus created has preserved even the most fragile silk,

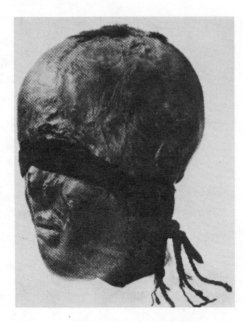

FIG. 4.16 Head of Windeby Bog-body No. 1 with blindfold. (K. Schlabow et al., "Zwei Moorleichen Funde aus dem Domlandsmoor," Praehistorische Zeitschrift, *Vol. 36.)*

felt, wood, leather, metal, and, of course, the bodies of men and animals that were interred with them. The preservation of human bodies was so perfect that the designs of complicated tattooing could be readily copied (Fig. 4.17).

Another instance of unusual preservation of wooden materials which had been waterlogged since burial is that of the thousand-year-old Oseberg Viking ship in Norway. The entire ship, 65 feet long, used as the coffin of a Viking queen, was buried beneath a mound of earth. Excavated in 1904, it yielded wooden sledges, four-wheeled carriages, a bed, a chair, buckets, and two female skeletons, one of which is believed to have been a bondwoman who was selected to accompany her royal mistress into the afterworld (Fig. 4.18). The ship burial is dated at A.D. 800.

Almost perfect preservation also occurs in exceptionally dry environments. Even without mummification, Egyptian bodies would have been well-preserved by the dry atmosphere of much of Egypt, as we can see from the naturally preserved bodies that have been found in the American Southwest in caves, and in graves along the coast of Peru. In all these places even the most fragile textiles, basketry, and wood and leather objects may be preserved. Possibly the most spectacular example of preservation was the consequence of the eruption of Mt. Vesuvius in A.D. 79, which buried Pompeii and Herculaneum in a flood of mud and ash. Although bodies were not preserved, their casts were. Inorganic objects remained in a perfect state, and the carbonized remains of complete loaves of bread, so perfectly preserved that they still bear the name of the baker stamped on them, have been recovered. Sometimes, as was true of the scrolls found in 1753 at Herculaneum and those found by Bedouin in dry caves near the Dead Sea, suitable techniques for unrolling them, preventing them from

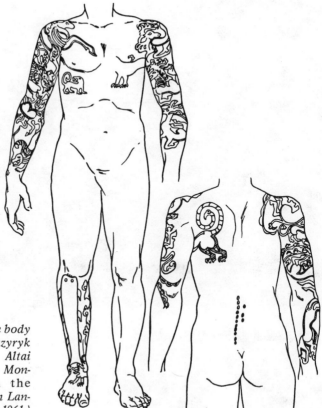

FIG. 4.17 Tattooing on the body of a man from the Pazyryk burial ground, in the Altai Mountains of Russia (A. Mongait, Archaeology in the U.S.S.R., *Moscow: Foreign Languages Publishing House, 1961.)*

decomposing, and even of reading them with the aid of ultraviolet light had to be devised before they could truly be said to be preserved.

Most archeologists work with poorly preserved sites, even in very dry areas, such as Southwest Asia and the American Southwest, where very little is preserved unless it has been isolated from the small amount of moisture that does occur. To witness the torrential rains and flash floods that seasonally soak such areas makes one appreciate how accidental is preservation. In areas of extreme cold, if there is any thawing at all, rot will occur, and if wet areas should dry, new oxygen will enter and with it destruction. A fact that is sometimes not appreciated is that in many arid areas, such as the Near East, rains fall during the cooler winter months, when the effect of the small amount of precipitation is relatively much greater than it would be during the hot summer months. Except in the most unusual circumstances, sites anywhere that are exposed to the weather are subject to alternate wetting and drying, and organic materials disintegrate or are destroyed by bacteria in a fairly short time. For this reason, caves in dry areas often provide the best chance of finding perishable remains.

If one counts the number of objects recovered from a dry cave in the western United States, one cannot fail to be impressed with the large amount

FIG. 4.18 (top) *The Oseberg Viking ship when first uncovered.* (center and bottom) *A wagon and sledge from the Oseberg ship.*

of perishable items made of horn, leather, or vegetal materials that would rapidly disappear in an open site (Fig. 4.19). Table 4.1 presents the count of items recovered from six sites where dry conditions have preserved organic materials that would normally have disappeared. The two sites from Chile are from the very dry north coast where conditions of preservation are similar to those prevailing along the narrow Peruvian coast. The two sites in New Mexico are from protected caves in a dry region where conditions of preservation are optimal, and the same situation holds for the two Nevada cave sites. The average annual rainfall in these areas ranges from less than 1 inch to not more than 8 inches. Table 4.2 summarizes the counts in Table 4.1 and presents the proportional amounts in percentage of total number of items of perishable and imperishable pieces. It is easy to see how deficient our knowledge of material culture items would be for an open site in Nevada, for example, where not more than 10 percent of the items that find their way into the trash layers are of durable materials.

In the dry deposits of Lovelock Cave, Nevada, cordage was perfectly preserved, and details of the size and mesh of nets could be determined. One hundred and forty-two pieces of braid gave evidence that the prehistoric occupants of the cave knew how to braid 3, 5, 6, 7, 16, and 18 strands; and 404 knots proved to belong to 8 types (mesh or sheet-bend, overhand, reef, granny, slip, clove hitch, "necktie" or timber-hitch, and wrap knots). Details of the methods of stringing shell beads were also preserved (Fig. 4.2D). This listing of some of the details observable about cordage illustrates clearly the degree of complexity in one single aspect of prehistoric technology that is ordinarily totally absent in open sites.

The fact that so much is lost in most sites affects the way we can interpret prehistoric cultures. For example, if a technique or type of artifact does not make its appearance after a considerable amount of archeological investigation has been carried out in an area, it may be permissible to suggest that the prehistoric peoples did not know or possess that technique or tool. But if the technique or implement is of the kind that would not leave any palpable trace, even under relatively favorable conditions, the archeologist would have to admit that there was no way of telling whether it may or may not have occurred in the area he is interested in. A case in point is that slings made of cordage were widely known ethnographically in the New World, but they had not appeared archeologically up to 1960 in North America, even in collections secured from dry cave deposits. Arguing from this negative evidence, one author proposed that the sling was introduced to the Indians of North America in historic times. Although this explanation seemed unlikely, there was no way (except possibly through linguistic analysis, which was never done) to verify or disprove the recent spread of this weapon. Now, however, at least three prehistoric North American slings (all from dry caves in western Nevada) are known, and the theory of historic introduction is shown by archeological facts to be incorrect.

A discussion of the preservation of artifacts should not omit sites themselves. They are constantly undergoing change as a result of the actions of people who live on them, the burrowing of animals, weather, erosion, the deposition

*FIG. 19*a.   *Three flint knives in wooden handles from Humboldt Cave, Nevada. Length of specimen on the left is 22.4 cm.*

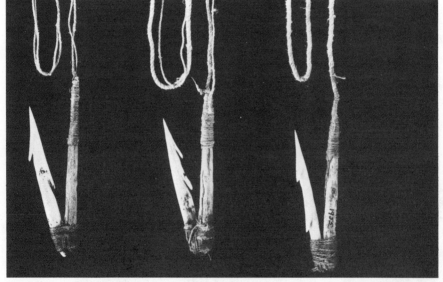

*FIG. 4.19*b   *Three prehistoric fishlines from a single cache in Humboldt Cave, Nevada. The string is Indian hemp (Apocynum); the hooks have bone barbs and wood shanks. Note the similarity of the three composite structures as well as the variation in details. Length of wood shank of center example is 9.0 cm.*

TABLE 4.1

	Playa Miller, Chile	Punta Pichalo, Chile	Cordova Cave, New Mexico	Tularosa Cave, New Mexico	Humboldt Cave, Nevada	Lovelock Cave, Nevada
Imperishable						
Stone	494	6389	1577	1546	87	95
Metal	17	1				
Pottery	28,871	1414	751	5470		
Shell	1	222	2	4	2	7
Bone	29	228	23	55	272	530
Antler			8	1		
Perishable						
Wood	55	945	394	762	113	310
Rush, cane, twine basketry	323	1552	628	3473	2982	7535
Skin, wool, feather	750	442	40	594	49	320
Vegetal food	299	48	2000	28,000		
Hoof, horn				3	15	20

Occurrence in six dry open or cave sites of perishable and imperishable objects. Two Chilean open sites from Bird (1943:191–216, 253–278); two New Mexico cave sites from Martin and others (1952); two Nevada cave sites from Loud and Harrington (1929), Heizer and Krieger (1956). Unworked stones of various kinds reported as found are included; unmodified food animal bone is counted; human burials (2 at Playa Miller, 42 at Punta Pichalo, 2 at Tularosa Cave, 32 at Lovelock Cave) are counted each as one bone. (We are indebted to Mr. Ronald Weber for preparing this and the following table.)

TABLE 4.2

	Imperishable		Perishable	
Sites	No. Items	Percent	No. Items	Percent
Playa Miller	25,412	95	1427	5
Punta Pichalo	8253	73	2987	27
Cordova Cave	2361	43	3062	57
Tularosa Cave	7296	19	33,832	81
Humboldt Cave	361	10	3159	90
Lovelock Cave	632	7	8285	93

Summary of Table 4.1, showing total numbers of imperishable and perishable items from six sites. In many open sites perishable items are totally absent. The two largest figures (at Playa Miller and Tularosa Cave) are ascribable, respectively, to the great abundance of potsherds and maize cobs.

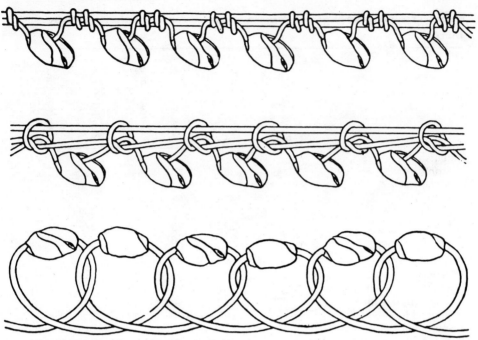

FIG. 4.20 Beads recovered from Lovelock Cave, Nevada, showing details of their stringing. The dry environment of the cave preserved organic material—in this case the actual vegetal cord on which the beads are strung—that would ordinarily be absent from archeological sites. (Loud and Harrington, "Lovelock Cave," University of California Publications in American Archaeology and Ethnology, Vol. 25, No. 1, 1929.)

of sands or soil, and so on. These processes steadily destroy or rearrange the contents of sites and they even affect the shape and size of the sites themselves. When archeologists begin to dig, the sites are usually quite different from what they were when people lived in them. Ideally for archeologists, the occupants of a site would decide on the spur of the moment to abandon their homes and leave everything in its place, taking nothing with them. Even under these ideal circumstances, which rarely happen, we would still have to contend with natural disintegration of materials and with the various geologic processes.

Among other things, sites may be buried gradually as soil builds up over a site, or they may be buried quickly under drifting sand, or under mud after a catastrophic flood, or by lava and ash after a volcanic eruption. Such buried sites may be very hard to find and are, even if found, often very hard to dig because of the depth of material over them. Some sites alongside rivers are washed away by high water; others along lakes or seas may be eroded by wave action; and in some areas rising sea levels or subsidence of land may cover the sites with water. Sites are also affected by earthquakes that destroy buildings and that sometimes loose rockfalls and mudslides that can bury or even move entire settlements. When we consider all the things that can happen to sites, we begin to appreciate how difficult archeology can be.

What Is Willfully Destroyed?

As we have seen, man himself destroys many sites and artifacts. His destructive powers have probably never been greater than now, however, with the building of networks of highways, the spread of urbanism, and the construction of dams, not to mention the continued practice of looting archeological sites. During the Paleolithic, when the few people on earth made a living by hunting and collecting, they may not have had much impact on the earth's surface. But when man became a farmer and acquired a tool kit that allowed him to quarry stone, dig ditches and pits, and domesticate animals—which in some areas turned wooded country into deserts by overgrazing—man began to make profound changes in the earth's face. It seems that the more sophisticated he becomes in technology, the more damage he does. In recent history, sites have been regarded as quarries of objects and material and as obstacles to be removed. Today, even in the United States, where laws have begun to respond to popular contrary sentiment, both of these attitudes are still prevalent. It is not surprising, therefore, that in most countries conservation of sites is generally given a low priority.

As Claudius Rich (1819:40) wrote, "A ruined city . . . is a quarry above ground." The unfortunate truth of this pithy statement can be documented by hundreds of instances of the pillaging of ancient buildings for construction materials. In southern Utah, J. W. Powell (1961:107–108), in referring to a three-story pueblo ruin at the mouth of the Kanab River where it enters the Colorado River, wrote, "The structure was one of the best found in this land of ruins. The Mormon people settling here have used the stones of the old pueblo in building their homes and now no vestiges of the ancient structure remain."

Some sites where stone was employed have been leveled and others so greatly damaged that they are like the Abbey of St. Martin in Tours, of which Henry James in *A Little Tour of France* says, "What we see today may be called the ruin of a ruin." The Greek Temple of the Giants at Agrigentum, Sicily, was partially destroyed in the eighteenth century to provide material for a breakwater, and in about 1800, great sculptures of Nineveh were broken up to furnish materials to repair a bridge. The great pre-Inca site of Tiahuanaco in the Bolivian **altiplano** near Lake Titicaca contained immense quantities of beautifully sculptured stone blocks. The nearby village by the same name consists of houses with sculptured doorways taken from the ancient site (Fig. 4.21), and the large church, built in the seventeenth century by Pedro de Castillo, is constructed entirely of stones carried from the nearby ruins. When the railroad was built between La Paz and Guaqui, Bolivia, on the shore of Lake Titicaca, the site of Tiahuanaco provided a convenient source of stone for building bridges, and Posnansky (1945:166) records the fact that "an immense statue around which there was entwined a snake from the chest to the feet, was divided and set in cement in bridges." Many of the stones at Tiahuanaco proved to be too heavy to transport (some weigh 100 tons), and, it being beyond the imagination of the local people after the Spanish conquest to understand how such large stones had been brought from distant sources, the belief grew that these colossal stones were made of concrete and must contain gold. Accordingly, many of the great blocks

FIG. 4.21   Prehistoric sculptured basalt doorways from the site of Tiahuanaco removed for reuse in the nearby modern village.

were split open with steel chisels in order to find the gold. A few failures did not seem to be sufficient evidence that the story was untrue, because everywhere on the site one can see scores of these sundered blocks. The lure of gold was so great, the Tiahuanaco site so impressive, and the imagination of ignorant people so active, that a Spanish miner in the seventeenth century went to the great effort of digging a hole more than 20 feet deep, 120 feet wide, and 250 feet long in the top of the Akapana, a great, flat-topped mound of earth. Local recollection of this activity having been lost, the pit (which contains water) is now believed by the townspeople to be the ancient reservoir that served the prehistoric occupants of the city.

Such behavior was not confined only to recent times, as Winlock (1942:11) tells. He found clear evidence of the nearly total destruction in ancient times of an immense mortuary temple at Deir-el-Bahri, Egypt, and it is recorded in Egyptian texts that the magnificent mortuary temple of Amenhotep III of the Eighteenth Dynasty was destroyed in the reign of his successor. Archeologists have excavated the temple area and found only some column bases and fragments of shattered statues.

Wars have also caused immense destruction to ancient sites. One of the best-known instances is the Parthenon in Athens, which, while being used in 1687 by the Turks as a powder magazine, received a direct hit by a Venetian shell, which blew out the interior.

When religious iconoclasm inspires the destruction of the sacred monuments of other religions, it leads to destruction of archeological evidence. Moorehead describes the defacement of Egyptian monuments by Coptic priests, and Duignan records that by 1531, roughly 10 years after the conquest of Mexico by Hernando Cortes, the Franciscan priests had torn down 500 Aztec temples and broken up 20,000 stone idols. Inca religious sites in Peru suffered a similar fate, and a book by Father Joseph de Arriaga, in 1621, records the destruction of large numbers of various types of native temples and shrines: 477 Chapkas, 603 main Huacas, 3410 Konopas, 617 Halkis, 45 Mamazuras, 180 Huankas, and so on. By contrast, religious sanctity of a spot may serve to protect a site. Rawlinson (1850:419) wrote that an ancient site opposite Mosul, Iraq, had not been excavated because "the spot, indeed, is so much revered by the Mohammedans, as the supposed sepulcher of the prophet Jonas, that it is very doubtful if Europeans will be ever permitted to examine it." On the other hand, Layard at Nimrud noted that his Arab workmen were continually trying to batter out the eyes of sculptured animals and persons because they were the idols of unbelievers. Stephens (1842:187) tells a tale of the President of Guatemala, who about 1810 received a present of a small gold image from the archeological site of Santa Cruz de Quiche. Intrigued with the possibility of getting gold, he ordered "a commission" to explore the site for hidden treasure, and in the process the palace was destroyed. The Indians, roused "by the destruction of their ancient capital, rose and threatened to kill the workmen unless they left the country."

In spite of resolutions of professional societies of archeologists, laws, and treaties between countries, there is still an enormous traffic in antiquities which have been looted from sites. Such collecting goes back to Classical times, but today, among wealthy persons who can afford it, very high prices are paid for prehistoric stone sculptures, metalwork, and ceramic vessels. The availability of a market encourages surreptitious and illegal digging, often by needy local people who usually realize very little for their labors. The looting of sites is a regular business in many countries of the world where ancient civilizations flourished. Although the objects found may be brought to light intact, in the course of changing hands through dealers and collectors, their context may be forgotten. Then identification of their source and age can be determined only by referring to similar pieces in archeological reports or museum collections. Most countries have very strict laws governing the excavation, and prohibiting the unauthorized export, of archeological materials, but these regulations usually are observed only by reputable archeologists. On the other hand, antiquities dealers encourage unauthorized digging and manage quite successfully, through the simple expedient of bribes, to remove vast quantities of material to their galleries in New York, San Francisco, Los Angeles, London, Paris, Rome, and other capitals of the art-conscious world.

Professional anthropologists in the United States, through resolutions approved by the membership of such organizations as the American Anthropological Association and the Society for American Archaeology, have taken a position against the illegal traffic in antiquities. UNESCO has formally approved a resolution on the Means of Prohibiting and Preventing the Illicit Import, Export, and Transfer of Ownership of Cultural Property, and the United States has treaties with many countries of Latin America. These are all steps in the right direction, and one would hope that the abolition of the marketing of contraband antiquities would lead to the cessation of plundering of sites.

What Is Recovered?

Much remains preserved in the ground that is not recovered from ordinary excavations. Belzoni, or even Schliemann and Layard, recovered only a small part of the available information. When Sir Leonard Woolley went to Mesopotamia in 1922 to excavate at the great site of Ur, he discovered the royal cemetery within a few weeks, but kept it secret until four years later. It took Woolley all that time to train his men and himself so that he was confident of doing a good job. His excavation still stands as a model of technical skill. In one instance he was able to restore a completely disintegrated harp by filling with plaster the open cavity in the ground where it had lain (Fig. 4.22). But for all his skill, he still discarded much that might have been saved by a later generation of archeologists.

People often ask, "Is there still anything to dig in Egypt?" The answer for Egypt and almost anywhere else is a resounding "Yes." The fact is, that for all the palaces and tombs that have been excavated around the world, there has been little or no effort in most of the ancient centers of civilization to find out how people lived. We know much more about their burial habits and ideas of an afterlife, or about their places of religious ritual, than we know about government officials, artisans, and farmers and laborers. Excavation has been confined in some places solely to the spectacular monuments. We can scarcely say that we know much about the civilizations on that basis!

When an archeologist has the option of digging a rich tomb or a peasant's house, he will usually choose the former. And, of course, it is rich objects from tombs that people like to see in museums. A bias toward the spectacular is thus understandable, if somewhat regrettable. A hint of what is missing sometimes comes quite by accident. A number of Egyptian tombs have now been excavated in which there are models of houses and other buildings: carpenter shops, butcher shops, bakeries, and the like, all stocked with the tools of the trade and figures of the artisans going about their tasks. These models, together with some of the elaborately decorated scenes on the walls of noble tombs, give us an unusually complete picture of some of the more mundane aspects of life (Fig. 4.23). But the more usual situation is that we do not even know what the people ate, let alone anything about such intangibles as the effects of civilization on the lives of the common people. The available information about the early civilizations comes mostly from texts and sometimes from pictures, but only rarely from the excavation of houses. This preoccupation with one kind of information—art, architecture, epigraphy—implies a corresponding blindnesss about other kinds of data.

FIG. 4.22 The queen's harp from Ur as it was reconstructed by L. Woolley. Height is 1.07 m.

We should not like to give the implication that prehistoric archeologists also are not sometimes blind, but theirs is a blindness that comes not so much from a lack of interest in all kinds of information as from a lack of knowledge that such information exists or can be extracted.

To illustrate this point—that there is no preservation unless adequate techniques for removing buried material are available—we can take the excavation of Ali Kosh in Iran. There, after making a test pit into the mound, Hole and Flannery reported (1962:125) "plant remains were scarce at Ali Kosh." The few seeds that did come to light were found accidentally in the cleaning of a radiocarbon sample, but the clue that they might be found in ashy deposits raised the possibility that more such remains could be found if the ash were treated by water separation. Fortunately, considerable pioneering work in this technique was being carried out in the early 1960s, and in a subsequent season of work at Ali Kosh hundreds of ashy samples were poured in water to separate the carbonized organic material from the silty matrix. As a result, tens of thousands of

FIG. 4.23 Wrestling scenes and warfare depicted on a painting at Beni Hasan, Egypt, and dating from about 2500 B.C. The wrestling scenes depict two Egyptians, one painted in a clear red, the other of a red-brown hue, probably so colored in order to distinguish the entwined arms and legs of the two men. Although these rows of individual scenes are not precisely like a motion-picture film strip, nevertheless in a number of cases it is clear that a continuous series is represented. (P. E. Newberry, Beni Hasan. Archaeological Survey of Egypt, Egyptian Exploration Fund, London, 1893, Part II, Pl. XV.)

seeds were found in deposits where they had not been noticed before and where they could rarely be seen even by careful separation of the dry material. A simple recovery technique thus resulted in the effective preservation of invaluable clues to the history of agriculture.

The foregoing examples have dealt mostly with the recovery of artifacts, but there are other kinds of data in sites. It is just as important to record the spatial distribution of artifacts with respect to the stratigraphy of the site and with respect to one another as it is to pick them out of the ground and count them. These data are often ignored, but they are essential if we are to reconstruct the uses of artifacts and of different areas within the site, or the ages of different structures. Moreover, as was true of the seeds, there are "nonartifactual" remains that will yield information. Men trained to pick up bronzes and potsherds will blithely hack through bones, charcoal, and fragmentary traces of perishable material (Fig. 4.24). Hired laborers or students under the supervision of an unimaginative archeologist will more often than not miss just the kind of information that we need for modern analysis.

Just as an archeologist must take care to recover what is preserved he must preserve what is recovered. Countless objects have been destroyed within a few hours of their excavation because they dried out or fell apart. Metal will often turn to dust; in fact, it may appear only as a rusty stain in the ground. Basketry, textiles, and wood may dry out and disintegrate. Almost all excavated objects are damp when first taken out of the ground, and a few minutes in the hot sun may destroy them. Objects taken from bogs are subject to shrinking and cracking that can be countered by proper use of preservatives. Bones that threaten to fall apart can be reinforced with plaster, papier-mâché, glue, or plastic compounds. There is no lack of techniques for preservation, but the excavator must know enough to use them and have them available when he needs them.

What Is Reported?

If there is a big difference between what is preserved and what is recovered, there is a bigger difference between what is recovered and what is reported. Archeologists are notoriously slow in reporting the results of their excavations. Many reports are never written, and many that are written are never published. It is safe to say that there is much more excavated material unpublished than published, and for practical purposes this information is lost. Because the sites were destroyed in the process of excavation, if there is never a publication, the information is lost forever.

It is not uncommon for an excavator to publish only part of his material. He may do the pottery or temples, or may report on only the very finest objects from among a large group. In this regard it is common to see a group of artifacts labeled "typical" or "characteristic" of the site in question, but it would often be more accurate to say that they were the finest, the most elaborate, or

FIG. 4.24   *A workman at Chagha Sefid, Iran, carefully exposing the inorganic traces of a floor mat that remain more than 8000 years after the fibers had decomposed.*

the most exotic. Mud bricks are typical; gold pins are not. Another archeologist might dig for years and never find one of the so-called "typical" objects. Such reporting can be a misleading weighting of the evidence.

More will be said about excavation technique and report writing in other chapters; this short discussion should point up that what we understand about prehistory is based on many variables. Part of the archeological context is the human filter through which information about preserved antiquities must pass before it is eventually described in print.

ARCHEOLOGICAL CONTEXT

One reason why archeologists get irritated when people come in with arrowheads, skulls, and pieces of pottery is that most of the people either do not know where the objects came from or will not tell. Then they want to know of the archeologists, "How old is it? Who made it? Is it genuine? And how much is it worth?" Answers to any of these questions depend a great deal on precisely where the object came from. Was it in a site? What kind of site? Where is the site? Which level of the site? What else is there in the same level? Uncomfortable silence usually follows questions such as these.

Even professional collectors sometimes fail to have the answers to these fundamental questions. One of the most infamous examples of this problem was the purchase in 1972 of the Euphronios vase, a **calyx krater**, which is thought to have come from somewhere in northern Italy. The Metropolitan Museum of Art in New York paid one million dollars for this old pot, whose **provenance** (place of origin) has never been officially determined. This is such an extreme case that a book, *The Grand Acquisitors*, by John L. Hess, deals with it at length, and two television programs on BBC, *The Plunderers* and *The Hot Pot*, described the scandals and international intrigue surrounding the acquisition of the vase. In this instance, the Museum spent this extraordinary sum for a pot that has been described as the finest in existence, but for which there is not one iota of solid evidence of its provenance.

What happens all too often with collectors and dealers to museums is that they seize upon objects with singleminded fascination and forget, if they were ever aware of, their contexts. On the other hand, archeologists depend on careful interpretation of the sites and layers of earth in them, as well as the kinds of objects in the layers, to help them establish things such as age, culture, and activities implied or represented. To an archeologist, an object has many messages and implications other than simple novelty or artistic elegance.

Context is the environment within which things (artifacts, sites, and even cultures) are found or within which they operate. Consequently, part of the definition of archeological things is a specification of their contexts. It is only when we can specify the three major contextual variables—time, space, and human activities—that we can make inferences bearing on historical problems. For other kinds of problems we may need to know only one or two of the contextual variables. For example, if we wish to describe a sequence of technical innovation we need only know time and space. To make inferences about the uses of artifacts we find that space and behavioral context become relevant, whereas time may be largely irrelevant.

All sites have geographical contexts (that is, contexts in space), and if the sites or the artifacts in them can be dated, they have contexts in time. The archeological culture represented in the sites is defined in terms of the kinds of artifacts found, their date, and the location of the sites.

A single arrowhead found on the surface ordinarily cannot be dated, nor can it be associated directly with other artifacts, even though it is of a named type (for example, Folsom). It therefore has, properly speaking, no archeological context. By contrast, all objects found and recorded as occurring in one level of a cave can be related to one another and to other finds in the levels above and below. Such an association of artifacts may also be referable to similar associations at other caves. It is easier to interpret the significance of an assemblage when there are other similar assemblages from several sites. It should be clear, therefore, that the context in which any artifact is found determines the extent to which one can make interpretations about it.

Stratigraphy and Stratification

During excavation we attempt to place the evidence (artifacts, houses, trash heaps) in their time and space contexts. We do this chiefly through stratigraphic excavation. That is, we attempt to dig according to the layers that were laid down during human use of the site. If we can separate these layers correctly, we can easily record the occurrence of artifacts in them. This gives us a sense of time because the layers are normally successively older as we dig deeper. This is the principle of stratification: if there are layers, those laid down first will be on the bottom. This idea is so simple that most authors give only passing reference to it; yet interpretation of stratification is one of the most difficult jobs for the excavator (Fig. 5.1). As Sir Mortimer Wheeler, a British archeologist who established standards of excavation for a generation of diggers, put it, "The first rule about stratification is that there is no invariable rule" (Wheeler 1956:62).

The words "stratigraphy" and "stratification" are often used interchangeably, but they have somewhat different meanings. We consider stratigraphy to

FIG. 5.1 *One of the earliest instances of the recognition of stratigraphy in American archeology. The painting, done in 1850, shows a Mississippian mound being excavated under the supervision of Dr. Montroville Dickeson. (Courtesy of the City Art Museum, St. Louis.)*

be the actual sequence of events in a site, whereas stratification refers to the levels (natural or arbitrary) that are excavated. Stratigraphic layers in a site may consist of many things. In a cave or rock shelter, debris from daily living may accumulate as it is packed down under foot. If the cave should be abandoned for some time, chips and flakes falling from the roof and walls as a result of natural weathering will cover the debris left by people with a sterile layer, or wind or water may wash in a layer of soil that contains no artifacts. The result is a series of superimposed natural and cultural layers that can be seen as the cave is excavated. Occupational debris, likely to be rich in organic matter and to contain charcoal, is usually dark in color, whereas the sterile accumulation deposited by nonhuman agency is generally lighter colored (Fig. 5.2).

FIG. 5.2 *Excavation of Kunji Cave, Iran, showing the clear-cut layering of the deposits. The dark bands were caused by the decomposition of organic material, whereas the lighter strata are composed largely of disintegrated stone from the roof of the cave. The age of these layers extends back more than 40,000 years.*

One must remember that sites may not have been lived on continuously, and that the camping or housing areas shifted from one part of the site to another. Under such conditions the stratigraphic record will have gaps or temporal discontinuities, and the archeologist may or may not be aware of these lacunae from a simple visual inspection of stratigraphic **profiles** (Fig. 5.3). His chief hint of a discontinuity may come from his analysis of the artifacts that are known, or

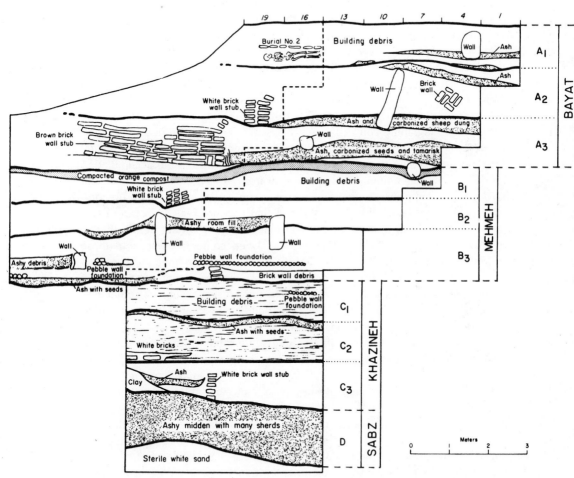

FIG. 5.3   *Profile of one side of the step trench in Tepe Sabz, western Iran. The trench began at the highest point on the site (dashed line) and was stepped back toward the outside of the mound to permit easier access to the trench but still maintain a continuous stratigraphic sequence. After the trench had been stepped back five times, the remaining depth was reached via a shaft 5 by 3 meters in extent and some 5 meters deep. The profile shows the way successive stratigraphic levels were grouped into cultural phases, each with subunits called zones. Each phase is characterized by a unique assemblage of artifacts.* (F. Hole, K. V. Flannery, and J. A. Neely, Prehistory and Human Ecology of the Deh Luran Plain. *Museum of Anthropology, University of Michigan, Memoirs, 1969.)*

assumed on other grounds, to follow a different pattern of change. Failures to recognize hiatuses in a sequence are of course usually more common in the early stages of investigation of an area, and when they are discovered, they illustrate the important point that archeologists should work systematically toward establishing a chronological sequence before they tackle other tasks.

In sites where there have been permanent buildings, the layers usually consist of house floors, and because they are successively rebuilt on top of old floors, there is usually a discernible gap between them. The floors thus serve to isolate and demarcate material below them. Frequently in such sites people dumped their trash among the buildings. As a result, one may find an ashy layer lying under dirt from disintegrated buildings that, in turn, is under a floor or wall foundation (Fig. 5.4). These are all examples of layers that, taken together, comprise the archeological stratigraphy of a site and allow us to give our evidence a relative age.

The words "layer," "level," and "**horizon**" are used by various authors to denote the stratigraphic context in which artifacts are found. *There is no uniform size or time duration to a level*; it may be only an inch thick or several yards thick, depending on the circumstances; it may represent the accumulation of a day or of a millennium. Levels are set off from one another by the fact that they look different from adjacent levels (that is, are darker or lighter or are composed of different materials), or by the fact that they are sealed off from other levels (by a rockfall or a floor), by the fact that they are a certain depth (that is, arbitrary levels), or by the fact that their analyzed contents differ from those found in adjacent levels. The word "level" and its synonyms thus mean several things. One must be careful to understand how they are being used in each instance. As "level" is used here, it refers to the excavation unit, whether it is natural (geological), cultural (for example, buildings), or arbitrary (excavation techniques), and to the associations of artifacts in the level.

Some sites do not have visible natural stratification, but consist of homogeneous deposits that are essentially the same from top to bottom. These sites are often referred to as "unstratified," the term here meaning that they do not show natural stratification. Such sites are usually dug by arbitrary levels (10 cm, 6 in, and so on). If analysis of artifacts that have been collected from these levels shows that there is a difference between types of objects found at different depths, the archeologist may then speak of cultural phases or levels. At the bottom of the site there may be an early cultural phase that is different from a late cultural phase found in the upper deposits. One may even go so far as to speak of the site as being culturally stratified, although this use of the term is not common.

When an archeologist deals with an unstratified deposit in which he can distinguish no differences in texture or color, what must he do? Does he treat the entire deposit as a single unit of deposition and simply record his finds as occurring within this homogeneous matrix? The method widely used by an archeologist in excavating such sites is to establish arbitrary levels and to treat each level, which may be as thin or as thick as he deems desirable, as though it were a natural stratigraphic level. It is a method of establishing some kind of

FIG. 5.4 *Stratification in Tepe Ali Kosh, Iran. Dark layers are composed of organic material, and the lighter layers of clay from the disintegration of houses. The dark, ashy deposit can be seen butting up against the partly collapsed brick wall of a house in the lower right. On the left side the ash layers rode over the eroded stub of a wall and eventually became horizontal as erosion of exposed features and filling in of depressed areas on the site proceeded. After the house had been abandoned for some time it was completely covered by layers of trash as the village continued to be occupied.*

stratigraphic control, even though it be an arbitrary one, in the absence of visible layers. One of the authors (Hole) has seen rock shelters in Iran with as much as 15 feet of archeological deposit, representing thousands of years of occupation, which have no apparent natural stratigraphy (Fig. 5.5). Any cultural succession in

FIG. 5.5 *Deposits at Gar Arjeneh, Iran, showing the lack of visible stratifica-*
tion that is common to rock shelters of this sort. The bulk of the deposit is
composed of disintegrated rock that has fallen from the overhang. Tools and
bones are interspersed throughout. The deposit is partly contemporary with
that in Kunji Cave (Fig. 5.2).

such sites is demonstrable only by analysis of the artifacts, which have been
collected by arbitrary levels, or by plotting layers of artifacts which are separated
by layers of dirt in which there are no artifacts.

Wheeler (1956:70) refers to the method of arbitrary or metrical stratigraphy as an "old outworn system," and he is absolutely correct in saying this if
the system is employed in archeological deposits that are composed of distinguishable natural levels or layers. He is not so correct, and in fact, may be wholly
wrong, in referring to the system as outworn if he is referring to unstratified
deposits. Collections made and recorded by arbitrary levels, when analyzed,
often show differences in artifacts from level to level. These differences, which
result from differences in cultural practices, are as "real" as anything that can
be determined by following natural layers.

In most instances where natural stratigraphy exists it is wrong to dig a large area by arbitrary units, because no horizon in any site is absolutely level throughout its extent. Contemporary houses may often be built on different absolute levels; thus excavation by arbitrary depth units will cut through strata of different ages and mix them (Fig. 5.6). The inappropriate use of a system of absolute levels has been effectively depicted by Wheeler (1956:Fig. 11). In Wheeler's drawing, pits have been dug into lower levels. Later filling of the pits introduced more recent material to the same level as older artifacts.

Usually, archeologists begin to dig in small areas (called **test pits** or **test trenches**) until they have determined the nature of a site and of the layers in it. Then they may proceed to remove the layers over a wide area so that they can learn about the horizontal variation. Although a small pit may reveal the layers, and consequently the passage of time, only a broad horizontal excavation will tell what the composition of an entire layer is. A small test pit might dig through a house or a trash pit, or a courtyard, or a temple, but it would not uncover all of these in one level. Only a wider lateral exposure can hope to reveal all that was going on at any particular time. This is just as important an aspect of context as the successive stratigraphic levels.

Digging is a complex process that requires innovation at nearly every site to accomplish the objectives. A problem faced by most excavators is that sites

FIG. 5.6 A horizontal exposure in the step trench at Chagha Sefid, Iran, reveals the foundations of houses and work areas. The trench is 5 meters wide.

are too big to dig entirely. How, then, does one establish vertical and horizontal context efficiently? All professional excavation reports describe these matters in great detail, but it is worth mentioning some examples here.

In digging the very large sites (tells) in the Near East, effective use has been made of the **step trench**, a technique that allows archeologists to plumb the total depth of the mound with a relatively small excavation. When a mound is 100 feet high, there obviously are problems in digging a vertical pit! The step trench starts toward the center of the mound with a pit of convenient dimensions. This pit is dug down to either an arbitrary or a natural building level and then shifted slightly toward the edge of the site, where the new area is taken down another level. This ultimately results in a long trench whose interior face is a series of steps that gradually move outward until sterile subsoil is encountered (Figs. 5.3, 5.7).

A good deal of archeology is small-scale work, however, and if an archeologist is limited with regard to funds, size of work crew, or time, he may be able to excavate only a series of test pits or a trench. Lloyd (1963:64) describes the method of one archeologist who covered sites with test pits. Although these

FIG. 5.7 *A step trench, 45 meters long and 5 meters wide, was used to expose successive levels at Chagha Sefid over a vertical depth of some 18 meters.*

pits were dug with great care, and all finds were meticulously recorded, Lloyd concludes that "this process could have been prolonged indefinitely without any prospect whatever of coming to understand the anatomy of the mound." The choice of the two alternatives (area exposure or test pitting) is clearly stated by Kathleen Kenyon, a leading British archeologist, who says (1957:41–43),

> There was a phase in Palestinian archaeology in which expeditions set out with the aim of excavating a site completely, and of removing each occupation level over the whole site from the uppermost to the lowest. This was a reaction against earlier methods in which pits or trenches were sunk which never gave an adequate idea of any of the phases discovered. The aim of this total clearance was to gain a complete picture of each successive period. There is something to be said for this idea. But it has two serious disadvantages. Scientifically, it has the disadvantage that nothing is left for posterity. I have already stressed the fact that archeological methods are always improving, and should continue to do so. Therefore, material should be left for future excavators to test the results of their predecessors on all sites of major importance, though the complete excavation of smaller sites is desirable in theory. The second serious disadvantage is that though a number of long-term plans have been made to carry out the complete excavation of a large site, no single one has ever been carried through. Changes of circumstances, in the resources available to the expedition, or due to political events, have always suspended operations, with the result that much time has been spent on preliminaries and in dealing with less important superficial areas and the really interesting levels have hardly been reached.
>
> We have now come back to the idea of more limited excavation. But the limited excavation must be to a set plan. We must decide what problems we hope to solve and how that solution can best be attained. I have already referred to the problems which were uppermost in our mind in deciding upon Jericho as a site for excavation. They concern in fact the beginning and end of ancient Jericho, the question whether the end of the Bronze Age occupation could be ascribed to the period of Joshua, and the examination of the extremely early occupation revealed by Professor Garstang. In between lay many long centuries in which Jericho was a very important town, on which our excavations would undoubtedly throw light, but our initial operations were planned to throw light on these two main problems.

As Kenyon points out, important sites often must be restudied as techniques improve, and this study can be done most effectively if an undisturbed block of the original stratified deposits remains. Museum collections from archeological sites may easily be restudied whenever the occasion requires, but from reexcavation, new insights can be secured that inspection of already collected material can never supply—*because it has been divorced from its context.*

Another way to preserve the stratification, so that one can refer back to it after the excavations have been concluded, has been developed by soil scientists. The method is to secure a vertical sample of the stratification by attaching a heavy cloth or board to the sides of the excavation, fixing the soil to this backing with an adhesive, and then removing the backing with a thin layer of soil attached. The vertical panel can then be removed to the museum and used to check texture, color, and other features of the original profile at leisure.

Deriving Stratigraphy from Stratification

A practical problem for all field archeologists is to decide what the observed stratification indicates. Does it accurately reflect the sequence of cultures? Are two or more cultural horizons mixed, or are the strata reversed?

A striking example of reversed stratigraphy was found in the American Southwest, where, at the large site of Chetro Ketl in Chaco Canyon, New Mexico, the prehistoric people excavated their garbage dump in order to build a large semisubterranean ceremonial chamber (**kiva**). The excavated garbage dump, thus overturned, formed a new dump that had the most recent material on the bottom and the oldest on the top. N. M. Judd cites a similar instance of partly reversed ceramic stratigraphy at Pueblo Bonito, New Mexico. Judd, who knew in general what to expect in the way of changes in ceramics from the work of earlier investigators, accidentally selected the prehistoric dump as a spot at which to make a stratigraphic pit. Recognizing that pottery types were not appearing in their correct sequence, he sought for, and found, the cause of the reversal in the kiva pit that had been excavated nearby. It is fortunate that N. C. Nelson, who carried out the first systematic stratigraphic examinations in refuse heaps in the American Southwest, did not happen to select an overturned refuse dump to demonstrate the method!

Although reversed stratigraphy is rare in archeological deposits, archeologists can expect it to occur in a variety of circumstances. Winlock (1942:75ff.) describes an apparent instance of Eleventh Dynasty Egyptian materials overlying deposits of the younger Eighteenth Dynasty. The "reversal" of order resulted from a misinterpretation by the archeologist of the order in which two buildings were constructed. A more unusual example of reverse stratigraphy was found at the site of Muldbjerg in Denmark (Troels-Smith 1960). The site had been built on **peat** at the edge of a lake. When the water level in the lake rose, the peat rose with it, breaking away from the bottom of the lake. In this instance, artifacts from the site were found on top of and below the peat, although the peat itself, which was sandwiched in the middle, was older than the site.

Another situation that is often found on relatively shallow but extensive sites is that the areas actually lived on shift from time to time. This results in a "horizontal stratigraphy," which can sometimes be recognized and disentangled by observing pits or other features which were dug through floors of previous houses, or by noting where different kinds of artifacts occur. Examples of horizontal stratigraphy would be likely to occur in places where there is shifting agriculture, campgrounds that are used irregularly, and in sites where certain edifices such as temples remain in place and in use although the buildings around them are changed or abandoned.

There are many examples of horizontal stratigraphy, especially at some of the very large **Neolithic** sites in Europe where farmers tended fields near their houses for 10–15 years and then moved nearby to fresh fields. This kind of settlement is usually associated with slash-and-burn agriculture where the fertility of the fields is maintained through allowing them to lie fallow for a number of years, after which the trees that have grown up in them must be cut down and burned. These farming systems are usually found today in wet areas where soil fertility is low and there is rapid regrowth of vegetation.

The more usual problem in a site is that the contents of layers have become mixed. For example, in one carefully excavated level there will be found pieces of pottery from several adjacent levels. This kind of thing happens when the former inhabitants dig pits for burials or storage, when animals burrow into sites, when trees growing on sites die and become uprooted, and so on. What all of these activities do is to cut holes through otherwise intact layers and to move the artifacts from their original stratigraphic context to a new one. Except in rare instances of complete reversal, this usually means that artifacts from several layers will be mixed so that there is no apparent order in their occurrence. As one example of this, sherds were carried down from the surface to a depth of more than 20 feet by mice burrowing in the site of Ali Kosh in Iran.

Because of difficulties in analyzing stratigraphy, archeologists must use the greatest caution in drawing conclusions. Almost all interpretations of time, space, and culture contexts depend on stratigraphy. The refinements of laboratory techniques for analysis are wasted if archeologists cannot specify the stratigraphic position of their artifacts. Pyddoke (1961:17) writes,

> The vertical side of any excavator's trench displays a section through superimposed strata, and almost every archaeologist today will record the thickness and extent of these layers and carefully note the exact position of his "finds," but an excavation report is not complete unless the writer sets out to explain the manner in which the layers were deposited. To understand his site properly the stratigrapher must always ask himself how his finds reached the position in which he discovered them; his little sequence of strata can no longer be regarded just as a heaven-sent means of separating cultural levels, nor can deposits be regarded as meaningless and "barren" simply because no recognizable artifacts or organic remains are discovered in them. They are equally important parts of the continuing record.

A further point should be stressed. Once the stratification has been determined, it is still necessary to verify the association of the objects in each horizon. We generally assume, usually correctly, that objects found associated together at one level in a particular layer in an archeological site were made and used at the same time. By "the same time" is meant, of course, a period such as 10 or 15 years or even a person's lifetime. If this were not true, association of objects would mean little to the archeologist.

The rule that associated objects are contemporaneous may be upset, however, by the preservation of heirlooms or curiosities that finally come to rest in association with much younger objects. In certain societies valued goods are handed down from generation to generation. The Yurok tribe in northwestern California passed valuable obsidian blades from father to son, and it is conceivable that examples of these blades seen by ethnologists around 1900 may have been a century old. On the other hand, Foster conducted an "age census" of pots used in the households of the Mexican Indian town of Tzintzuntzan and found only one vessel whose age was as great as 40 to 50 years. Foster's observations bear out the assumption made by archeologists that pottery vessels have a relatively short life.

Two instances of the deliberate copying of ancient artifacts serve to illustrate another possible source of confusion for archeologists. In the Late Period in the seventh century B.C., in Egypt there was deliberate imitation of Old and Middle Kingdom relief carving and of literature dating from 1000 to 2000 years earlier. On the basis of style and content alone it would be very difficult to determine the age of these reliefs. Such a determination would have to come from the *total context* in which the reliefs occur. A similar example of copying was reported by J. Ford. He found that modern Eskimos of Point Barrow had copied the pattern of a prehistoric boot that had been shown to them by an archeologist. Again, without knowledge of the total context, one could not ascribe a certain date to the boots.

Objects from antiquity are also used by later peoples, sometimes in ways that can be misleading. For example, an archeologist might assume that the ancient quarries were still being worked in the fourteenth century A.D. when he found a Cairo mosque built of the same limestone that covered the great pyramid—an assumption that would be wrong because it is known that Sultan Hasan, in A.D. 1356, stripped off large amounts of the outer limestone casting of the pyramid of Cheops to build the mosque. R. B. Dixon (1905:136–137) noted that the Maidu Indians of northern California used stone-bowl mortars to grind acorns in, but that these mortars were always archeological pieces which they had found on ancient sites. A final example is that provided by Gadow (1908:17), who observed Mexican Indians making clay figurines in prehistoric molds and selling them to tourists.

It is generally assumed that the objects found in graves represent pieces that were made and used during the lifetime of the person buried. Ordinarily this assumption is true, but a special situation is presented by family tombs or collective **sepulchers** that may have been used as a depository for corpses over several generations. In this instance, the offerings placed with the bodies may pertain to a long period, and it will be difficult to isolate the styles of artifacts typical of any particular part of the period, because they will be mixed indiscriminately.

We may appear to be belaboring the point of stratigraphy, but it is extremely important to recognize that normal deposition of layers is subject to a wide variety of disturbances. Archeological deposits must be carefully studied; assumptions that relative age of material can be determined from relative depth may be misleading. *Depth in itself tells nothing about age.* With all of these caveats in mind, it should be easy to see why archeologists get exasperated when collectors come in with objects that they have just "found."

Time

When an archeologist asks, "How old is it?", his question is more than a matter of idle curiosity, because for many kinds of interpretation he must know where an object fits in time. He may need to know the calendar date of an object or only whether it came after A and before C, but in any case he needs some chronological context. Any kind of study of culture change or of evolution, for example, depends on knowing which find is the earlier. The question of age is vitally important also in evaluating the cultural significance of two things. For example, the similarity of two objects of the same age at distant sites may imply trade, whereas the similarity of two objects of widely different ages may suggest a long cultural tradition.

One of the most interesting examples of the effects of knowing relative ages of distant sites has recently been described at length by Renfrew (1973). He discusses the implications of the new calibrations of radiocarbon dates with calendar dates (see Chapter 8) on the interpretation of Stonehenge, a world-famous site in southern England. This impressive monument consists of a circular area enclosed by a ditch and bank, in the center of which is a circle of huge upright stones. Within this circle is a horseshoe-shaped group of five uprights and lintels, also of huge stones. The amount of labor required to move some of these stones more than 100 miles without machinery is impressive and has caused people to wonder what the site was used for and who built it.

Until recently it was thought to be contemporary with the Mycenaean civilization in Greece, about 1800 B.C., and that it had been built under the influence of these civilized people. The date of Stongehenge was based on both radiocarbon and on some artifacts found in nearby graves. That it could have been built by the Neolithic farmers and herders of England was considered unthinkable. It was still more unthinkable when Gerald Hawkins, an astronomer, deduced that Stongehenge was actually an instrument which could be used to sight important solar and lunar events as well as to predict eclipses. Still more exciting was the finding that what we see today at Stongehenge is the latest of a long series of constructions, of which the earliest clearly precedes Mycenaean civilization. The date of the early construction has been pushed back still further by reinterpretation of the radiocarbon dating itself. Now it is unequivocal that Stonehenge, far from having been influenced by a more advanced civilization in the Mediterranean, actually shows evidence of more advanced intellectual activity in England.

At the outset it should be noted that two kinds of time—relative and absolute—are important in archeology. In fact, this is only a convenient distinction, for all dating is *relative*. Absolute dates are those that are keyed to our modern calendar. Our calendar is based on recurring astronomical events, but it is arranged relative to the date of Christ. The ancient Maya, for example, had a different system that was just as absolute as ours.

A relative date tells us simply that one thing is older than another; in archeology, material is dated in relation to other archeological material. For example, Stongehenge is old in relation to Mycenaean Greece. Absolute dates automatically give relative ages; thus, by reading the birth dates of George Washington and Abraham Lincoln, we can tell immediately that, relative to Washington, Lincoln was more recent.

There are differing degrees of accuracy in all dating, whether we call it absolute or relative. With some modern techniques we are able to give dates that are expressed in terms of the Christian calendar, but such dates are absolute only within a mathematically expressed margin of error. Sometimes, because of the possible error, the dates would be less useful to archeologists than sound relative dates would be. For example, when two closely similar sites are found, it is useful to know which is earlier. If the absolute date (carbon-14 years before present) of each site (for example, 5200 ± 200 and 5100 ± 200) has a margin of error of 200 years more or less, the archeologist can never be really sure which is earlier, because the true date in these illustrations will fall between 5000 and 5400 years in one instance and 4900 and 5300 years in the other, the overlap being between 5000 and 5300 years. By contrast, if the archeologist can find some way to date one site relative to the other, rather than relative to the Christian calendar, he can tell which is the older.

Besides the methods for dating one must also consider what is to be dated. The best method is to date the article—a site or an artifact in the site—itself. Another method is to date the immediate context in which the artifact or site lies, for example the beach deposit which contains a site, or the hearth in which an artifact is found. If so, we then infer that the artifact is the same age as its context. The third, and least accurate, method is to date similar occurrences. Thus, if the beach in which a site is found cannot be dated, a similar site elsewhere may be dated; or sometimes the geological stratum in which a site is found can be dated some miles from the site; or, in some instances where geological formations have been traced around the world, it may be possible to get a date from another continent that will give an estimate for the age of a site. In short, although absolute and relatives ages can be given for many archeological occurrences, the dependability of these age determinations may vary considerably.

An interesting example of geological cross-dating comes from Java, where **tektites** (also called billitonites)—small, chemically distinct drops of glass of cosmic origin—fell during the Middle Pleistocene. Conveniently for archeologists, they have been found in the upper Trinil beds in Java, where *Homo erectus* fossil human remains were found, and also in the Philippines in association with the teeth of stegodons and elephants (von Koenigswald 1956:104–105). The age of the tektites of Java has subsequently been determined because some of them underlie the basalts, which by the potassium-argon method can be shown to be 500,000 years old. *Homo erectus* and the stegodons and elephants, therefore, are older than 500,000 years.

Cultural Association and Space

In Chapter 3 we discussed the concept of culture as it is used in archeology. In most instances we speak of archeological cultures or of the way artifacts relate to behavior; we will call this "**cultural association**" to emphasize that we are inferring from our data an abstraction that is something like what anthropologists call culture or cultural behavior. As prehistorians we associate our data with these concepts. This important distinction should be kept in mind in the following discussion.

Cultures exist only in a context of time and space. As stated before, the one thing that keeps a Parisian or a tourist from enjoying a historical appreciation of the obelisk of Luxor, which today stands in the Place de la Concorde, is that it has been removed from the context that would have given it correct historical meaning and placed instead in the middle of the heavy Paris traffic. In Luxor the obelisk was among the ruins of which it was a part. Enlightened probing of these ruins has revealed the cultural context into which the obelisk fitted. In addition, at Luxor there are the sun and the sand and the Nile; these comprise the geographical context. Inserted into the contexts of culture and geography, the obelisk has far different meaning and evokes far different appreciation than it does in Paris surrounded by fountains, palaces, automobiles, and tourists. As Childe (1956:5) put it, with a different example (the Elgin Marbles) in mind, "Indeed we tear down the frieze from a temple in a sunny clime and set it at eye-level in a room in murky London to appreciate its beauty."

An archeological culture (the reconstruction we make from archeological finds) represents a social system that existed in a definable area and whose members shared certain artifacts, ways of life, and ideas. The contextual variables of time and space are thus intimately linked when we deal on the level of cultures, but if we want only to describe the distribution of an artifact, we can ignore culture. If, however, we wish to interpret the distribution of the artifacts or to examine their nature, we must infer the way they were used. It is only when we treat space as uninterpreted geographic data that we can ignore culture. This use of the spatial context is so obvious that it requires no further discussion; accordingly, we shall focus on cultural association as a dimension of archeological context.

A normal procedure in archeology is to lay bare a level in a site and plot the occurrence of artifacts with respect to one another and to the other features in the stratum. We do this for two purposes: to discover the kinds and numbers of artifacts in a particular assemblage, and to enable us to infer their uses. These goals follow from our ideas that culture is patterned and that arti-facts are tangible evidence of prehistoric behavior (Chap. 3).

Moreover, we assume that most artifacts were used for a rational purpose —or at least one that we may be able to infer from the context within the sites. Characteristic sets of artifacts will have been manufactured and used at the scenes of the activities to which they pertain. A careful examination and analysis of context and associations will therefore tell us something about the activities carried out by the prehistoric peoples.

Moving from the general to specific cultures, we can find other uses to which the concepts of archeological culture and space are applicable. When assemblages from contemporary sites are compared, some are more alike than others. Accepting the ideas that cultures are patterned and transmitted symboli-cally, it follows that sites having more similar assemblages of artifacts are likely to have been more closely related so long as they are found within a restricted geographic space. These similar assemblages are then conventionally taken to be representatives of archeological cultures, a term that is akin to the popular use of "tribe" when it is used to describe modern peoples. There is considerable question regarding what constitutes similarity among assemblages, but we shall ignore this problem for the time being. It is worth noting, however, that there may be exceptions to the rule that related cultures are found within restricted geographic areas. Recent mass migrations and exportation of ways of life negate the generalization. However, it is to be doubted that in prehistoric times one could find a parallel to transplanted modern English culture in such widely spaced places as Hong Kong, Nairobi, Sydney, and Victoria, B.C.

In the absence of history, an archeologist must give an arbitrary name to the cultures. He may name them after the region in which they are found (for example, Desert Culture), after the site in which the assemblage was first identi-fied (Badarian after the Egyptian site of Badari), or after a characteristic artifact industry in the assemblage (Beaker Culture after the kind of pottery). As a per-son goes back in time he finds he can distinguish fewer and fewer separate cul-tures. The reason for this is that at each period man has a limited fund of knowl-edge and technical skills, and he must draw on these when he invents new things. The farther back in time we go, the smaller the inventory of possibilities man had. The earliest forms of men naturally had the smallest inventory of ideas from which to draw; so they were exceedingly restricted in what they could do. As the inventory grew larger with passing time there was more possibility for innovation; and as men spread across the earth they faced different problems, which required unique solutions. Groups of people in separated locales there-fore developed somewhat different habits and skills. Cumulatively, the inventory of ideas increased slowly, but significant differences can be seen as early as the Middle Pleistocene between peoples living in Africa, Europe, and Asia. These differences are in contrast to the earlier situation, when the artifacts are very similar wherever they are found. In the earliest times, we can identify only one archeological culture, whereas later we find striking differentiation. (See Chapter 3 for a fuller discussion of culture change.)

Countering tendencies toward divergence, and acting to increase the stockpile of ideas of each separate group, was diffusion of ideas, which took place through imitation, symbolic communication, or migration. But the pooling of ideas made it possible for more divergence, a fact that becomes especially noticeable in recent times as people developed highly specialized ways of dealing with local situations. We find as we approach the present that differentiation proceeds more rapidly and that archeological cultures become more restricted geographically. The tendency has only recently been counteracted with the invention of rapid communication and transport, with the result that many cultures are losing their uniqueness and being subsumed under more dominant, expansive cultures.

Many of the cultural differences that we observe now in Europe between people living in various countries might not be obvious archeologically. Evidence of such things as dress, language, and art—in the absence of graphic arts—would not ordinarily be preserved. Even though people over most of Europe used similar tools during the early stages of the last glaciation and are therefore hard to differentiate archeologically, we have no reason to assume that they spoke the same language, told the same legends around their campfires, believed in the same gods, or painted their faces in the same way. *As archeologists we can distinguish cultures only when we can distinguish differences.* Many peoples in the past left us very little with which to distinguish differences. Specific ways for identifying cultures from artifacts, and the ways to interpret archeological data in cultural terms, are given in Part V of this book.

The boundary lines we draw between cultures are arbitrary. People living along the Rhine share elements of French and German culture; in many ways they are not typical of other groups of French or Germans living further west or east. For every culture there is a center in which it finds its clearest expression. Groups on the geographic edges may grade indistinguishably from one culture to another; there are few clear-cut lines. All archeologists could read with profit Kroeber's and Driver's discussions of the problem of defining culture areas, how to draw boundaries between culture areas, and how to define the climax group within a culture area.

In summary, context, with its aspects of time, space, and culture, is central in archeological studies. The use of stratigraphy to establish associations and relative ages of artifacts allows interpretations to be made about culture. An archeological culture consists of repeated associations of artifacts as they occur in time and space, and archeologists use the concepts of culture generally to help them understand the processes that led to the development of archeologically identified cultures.

ACQUIRING THE FACTS OF PREHISTORY

Part III

The prehistoric past exists in the form of archeological remains, but each item and each fact must be discovered and recorded before it can be said to exist meaningfully.

Mankind had emerged by 2.5 million years when the first recognizable stone tools were made by hominids. Since that time man has changed biologically, behaviorally, socially, and, in the largest sense, culturally, and by this extraordinarily complicated process of change through time he has expanded in numbers and colonized all the inhabitable portions of the earth. Wherever man has been he has left some evidence of his presence. It is the archeologist's first job to locate the places where this record of the human past occurs. The search for these locations is called "site survey." Many sites are found by accident rather than by deliberate search; others are discovered by applying certain general principles that archeologists have learned by trial-and-error method. Careful inspection for surface remains by persons walking over the ground is the most widely used method of site survey. We would guess that any fairly active archeologist has, between the age of 20 and 50, walked about 4000 miles looking for sites.

Once sites are found, their age and contents must be determined—not at first with great precision, but to the extent that their general chronological position and what kind of materials are contained in them can be estimated. Artifacts found on the surface will provide some clues of the site's contents. Its size, depth, or location may give a hint whether it is recent or ancient. There are devices that can, as it were, look beneath the surface and inform the operator about buried walls, house floors, stone sculptures, and the like. The **magnetometer** is one of these pieces of apparatus that provide information on some of the kinds of things that lie buried beneath a site's surface. Everything learned about sites on a survey is recorded in notebooks, and at the conclusion of the survey the archeologist is in a position to select for excavation any sites that seem to offer the greatest amount of information of the sort he is interesed in.

Excavation that follows survey is a complicated, usually expensive, and time-consuming procedure. There are well-developed methods for digging small open sites, closed occupation cave sites, large open sites, sites with abundant architectural remains, shell mounds, and so on. Each kind of site requires a particular approach, but all sites are dug in the same way to the extent that the investigator must dig from the top down to the bottom and thus be digging backward in time. Systematic exploration is always necessary, and it involves due attention to recording the occurrence of everything found, so that when the excavation is concluded the site as such (or that portion of it which was dug) has been translated into the photographs, notebooks, maps, and specimen catalogue that the excavator makes.

Once an excavation is finished and the archeologist is back at his home base with his records and collections, he will write a report on his findings and provide his opinion on how they contribute to the understanding of the regional development of prehistoric culture. Archeological reports are difficult and time-consuming to prepare, and a year's fieldwork may require three years of careful study and writing before the archeologist can tell himself that the project has been completed. In this process of studying his finds the archeologist proceeds systematically, and usually treats different classes of objects separately. Pottery, stone tools, architectural remains, bone implements, animal bones used for food, and similar objects are presented in a separate section of the report. Trade, probable site-population numbers, social organization of the prehistoric inhabitants, hunting and collecting, or farming patterns are also discussed from the standpoint of what inferences can be drawn from the excavation data. Animal bones must be identified by a competent zoologist; vegetable remains, such as burned seeds or charcoal or pollen, must be studied by botanists; stones used for tools or in building construction will be studied by a **petrographer** in the hope of discovering the geological sources of the various kinds used; chemists, physicists, and **pedologists** may also be consulted to give their opinion on some aspect of material or soils.

The archeologist's main activities can be summarized as those of finding sites, excavating them, making records of all finds, analyzing in a systematic way (usually through application of typology) the materials recovered, and writing a report to interpret the human occupation at the site or sites he has investigated.

Chapter 6

SURVEY AND EXCAVATION

Archeology combines discovery, excavation, interpretation, and, in part, destruction of its only sources of evidence, sites and their contents. Two major problems in archeology, then, are to find sites and to use them judiciously. The former is largely a matter of applying time and up-to-date techniques. The latter requires careful interpretation, good judgment; and exacting excavation and analysis. In both cases, a permanent record that others can build upon should be a primary goal and outcome of the work.

It is worth repeating that even the most careful excavations at least partially destroy sites. As a general rule, therefore, excavations should add to knowledge about man's past. Better still, they should add something new. In some cases this means looking at new areas and in others looking at old sites with new techniques or new ideas. It may also mean that an archeologist will deliberately search for the mundane rather than the spectacular. Laymen sometimes wonder why an archeologist will avoid digging temples or tombs in favor of searching jungles or deserts for ancient hamlets. Most people probably think that the latter is less important work, but the point we wish to make is that importance can be judged only in terms of what questions are important to answer and not in the intrinsic worth of objects that may be recovered. The crowns and jewels of royal tombs offer only the merest glimpse of man's history, a glimpse that may be no broader or more important than that afforded by the contents of a hunter's camp. However, it would be remiss to ignore the possibility that a tomb may provide the best glimpse of *many* aspects of an extinct society.

Archeologists have traditionally followed one of several procedures: they dig sites that happen to have been found, they deliberately search for certain kinds of sites, and they deliberately look in particular places to see if any sites are there. The latter approach is typical of much of cultural resource management. Simply stated, it means inventorying the archeological resources.

In prehistoric archeology, it is relatively rare now for a person to dig a site just because it happens to have been found. Indeed, such a policy would be considered disreputable. Unless the site has an interesting context that raises or would help solve certain problems, it would be both a waste of time and destructive to dig it. More constructive and usual is for the prehistorian to look for certain kinds of sites both to inventory them and to have available a series from which he may choose one or more for excavation.

Since most archeologists are basically concerned with history, they usually think in terms of historical problems. "Where did these people come from?" "When did they borrow or invent pottery?" "How did agriculture begin?" "What factors were involved in the origins of the early civilizations?" "What people lived in this area?" "Were these people influenced in their development by people from Egypt?" "Why did this civilization decline?" "How were these people affected by climatic changes?" The list can go on indefinitely. When questions such as these are asked, however, they immediately suggest limited ways of finding the answers. Successful archeologists move quickly from the question to finding evidence, to interpreting it in terms of clearly stated hypotheses, and then to additional questions that have been suggested by the first results. Needless to say, the larger questions such as were posed above must be broken down into manageable smaller ones whose answers will contribute to the solution of the larger problems. The point is that the work is both systematic and cumulative.

Finding Sites

Archeology is a source of historical and anthropological data, and for the most part the evidence is found in sites and in the patterns of their distribution over the land. Therefore, when an archeologist has a problem in mind, he usually must go out and find sites that will help him solve it. Or, to turn the matter around, the archeologist may just be searching a hitherto unexplored area to see if there are any sites and, if so, what kinds. In either case, his problem is to find sites. To accomplish this he usually carries out a survey or reconnaissance which is designed so that he can cover the ground efficiently and find the things he is looking for (Fig. 6.1). The problems of doing this are far from trivial; the kind of survey he will make depends on the kinds of information he wants to

ARCHEOLOGICAL SITE SURVEY RECORD

1. Site .... 2. Map .... 3. County ....

4. Twp. .... Range .... ¼ of .... ¼ of Sec. ....

5. Location ....

....

.... 6. On contour elevation ....

7. Previous designations for site ....

8. Owner .... 9. Address ....

10. Previous owners, dates ....

11. Present tenant ....

12. Attitude toward excavation ....

13. Description of site ....

....

14. Area .... 15. Depth .... 16. Height ....

17. Vegetation .... 18. Nearest water ....

19. Soil of site .... 20. Surrounding soil type ....

21. Previous excavation ....

22. Cultivation .... 23. Erosion ....

24. Buildings, roads, etc. ....

25. Possibility of destruction ....

26. House pits ....

27. Other features ....

28. Burials ....

29. Artifacts ....

....

....

30. Remarks ....

31. Published references ....

32. UCMA Accession No. .... 33. Sketch map ....

34. Date .... 35. Recorded by .... 36. Photos ....

FIG. 6.1   An example of an archeological site survey record form.

obtain, the kind of terrain and vegetation, the availability of maps, aerial photos, personnel, equipment, and time and money. For a variety of reasons, it is impossible to conduct surveys that will locate everything, so an archeologist tries to strike a balance and do the best possible job in terms of his goals and resources.

There are several general principles to keep in mind when looking for sites. The most important thing is to learn to recognize the unusual, something that is not "natural." For example, a mound where one should not be, a place where vegetation grows differently than it does in surrounding areas, straight alignments or sharp contours, potsherds or chipped stone lying on the surface, layers of ash in the bank of a stream. These are the kinds of things a person who is familiar with an area will recognize immediately. When he examines them closely, the presence of artifacts tells him that the unusual feature is a site.

Another important principle is that people in the past had many of the same needs that we have today. They preferred to be close to water, have access to fuel and food, have shelter from inclement weather, and level land to sleep on. If we know that people were doing certain things, it gives us clues where to look for their remains. Farmers live near their fields, hunters close to where there is game, miners near the mines, traders along routes of commerce, and so on. Many times we find that ideal picnic spots were also campsites of prehistoric people.

Many times an experienced archeologist can look at a **topographic map** and get a pretty good idea where sites are likely to be found. The clues are the natural features such as rivers and springs, hills, vegetation, and so on. Sometimes, the surveyors who made the maps labeled ancient sites as "ruins," but more often the presence of sites must be inferred from the topography and distribution of natural resources. Aerial photos are a useful supplement to topographic maps because they show the actual vegetation, location of agricultural fields and sometimes ruins of buildings, abandoned roads and canals, and other recognizable features (Fig. 6.2). A skilled photointerpreter can make a very accurate assessment of the things that an aerial photo shows if he is familiar with the area.

Most site survey is done on foot and most sites are found by just walking over them. In fact, only with this sort of intensive survey can one hope to find most of the sites, because modern vegetation or recent accumulations of soil have hidden them from all but the closest scrutiny. It is very revealing to see how many sites are often found when the archeologists decide to walk all of the land. Naturally most such sites are small and were of short duration, but they are no less important than larger sites in terms of the total picture of ancient habitation.

Although the principles of finding sites are easy to comprehend, actually carying out a survey is often very difficult. Take a typical situation, the survey of a river basin that will be inundated when a flood control dam is installed. The archeologist is requested to determine how many sites will be affected by the flooding and to propose ways to mitigate the damage before the reservoir is

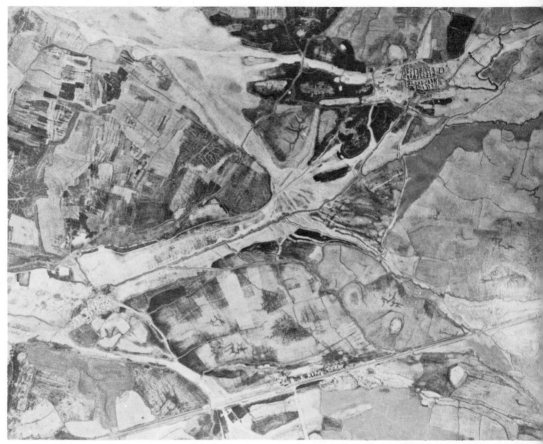

FIG. 6.2   Aerial photos are often used as an initial aid in discovering sites and they also help to show the locations of sites in relation to streams, roads, trails, agricultural fields, and vegetation. Sometimes large sites can be mapped accurately from such photos because ruined buildings may be easier to see from the air than from the ground. This photo shows both modern and ancient sites as well as roads, streams, and agricultural fields.

filled. The mitigation in this case would probably be to excavate some of the sites, a sample that would be an accurate reflection of all the sites.

In cases of this sort, the reservoirs are frequently put in areas of farmland and woods where the land is hilly and perhaps cut through by broad rivers and deep valleys. The time available for such a project is usually quite limited, perhaps a year, during part of which the ground will be covered by snow or by grass cover that obscures the surface. Typically one also finds that some or all of the land is under private ownership and access to it must be negotiated with each owner. Finally, much of the land may be very hard to reach because there are no roads, or permission to do the survey cannot be obtained. If the reservoir is tens of miles long and encompasses thousands of acres, the task is formidable.

What an archeologist actually does in a case like this depends on how well the area is known already. If there has been a lot of prior work, he may know pretty well what to expect. On the other hand, he may be stabbing in the dark. Keeping in mind that he wants a sample of sites which will give him a maximum of information about the total picture, he must devise a strategy, a research design, which is appropriate to the conditions that he faces.

In principle the problems are similar to what any person doing survey research finds. We are all familiar with companies that take polls to find out who will probably win elections, how many people watch a particular TV program, or which ad for toothpaste sells better. Most people are surprised to find out that the outcome of a national election can be determined by asking only a few thousand voters whom they favor. The secret, of course, is in the choice of the people who are questioned. The pollsters have discovered that there are patterns in voting behavior and they design their survey to find out these patterns.

In archeology we recognize patterns in human behavior too, some of which are expressed in the location, size, and type of sites occupied by any given people. We also admit that there are many things we do not know, and consequently we have to be on the lookout for the unexpected. In designing surveys, then, archeologists try to make maximum use of what they know and still allow for the chance of learning something new. This means, for example, that if all known sites lie along rivers, the survey should make a thorough search of the riverbanks. At the same time, however, land away from the rivers should be examined on the chance that there was something more going on than previous work had recognized.

In a typical reservoir pool area there is much more land away from the present rivers than along them, and this may include some of the hardest terrain to cover because of vegetation, hills, fences, and so on. Usually it is impossible to walk over all of it. By contrast it may be relatively easy to run a survey along a river by using a boat.

There are a number of techniques currently in use to deal with the many problems of survey under all imaginable conditions. Although this is not the place to deal with such techniques in any detail, it is useful to mention some of them in a very general way. Walking the banks of rivers or using a boat is an obvious strategy that attempts to find all the sites in a very narrow strip of land. Since sites are most likely to be found along water, such a procedure assures the finding of a large percentage of the total sites. The remainder of the area, however, poses quite different problems.

For example, it is often varied as to topography and altitude (floodplain, hills, valleys, marsh, plateaus, and so on), vegetation (grassland, forest, mixed, and so on), and resources (food plants and animals, fuel, minerals, and so on). What these distributions of features mean is that some areas were better than others for the living purposes of prehistoric peoples. What many archeologists do is divide the area according to the way these things are distributed and take a sample (conduct a survey) from each of the divisions. This means that perhaps not every ridge top will be closely examined, but some of them will be. The same holds true for such features as floodplains, narrow valleys, and sources of flint.

If surveys such as these are carried out, a tentative picture of the way sites are distributed should soon become clear. As the pattern emerges, the research design can be improved to take advantage of new opportunities or fill in obvious gaps in information. Eventually, if everything works well, the archeologist should be able to predict with considerable accuracy where sites will be. If he can do this, he may have a large enough sample. He would then have accomplished essentially the same thing as the pollster who predicts who will win the election.

This all sounds quite simple. Go out, look at the ground, tally up the sites, make some shrewd inferences, and describe the site location pattern and what it means. Unfortunately it is never this simple. In practice, it is very hard to cover the ground that you want to see. Moreover, once you have found the sites by their characteristic contour, growth of vegetation, or bits of flint or pottery, it is hard to tell how old or how big they are, how many times they were occupied, or whether they were campsites, villages, or work stations. Such information is crucial to the archeologist whose task is to inventory the resources and make recommendations about which sites to protect or dig. Unless he can make these determinations, he cannot fulfill one of his major obligations.

Judging the Contents of Sites

Age and Cultural Association

There are a number of clues to the age of a site. They can include such diverse things as the location of the site in relation to potential resources; location in relation to changing features such as rivers, lakes, and seas that have altered over time; size; overall shape; visible remains such as remains of buildings; nature of the site soil; and artifacts (Figs. 6.3, 6.4). The latter are usually the most direct clues and must always be considered before a final determination is made; potentially they give the most accurate dates. From the list above it can be seen that many clues about age can be simply recorded on a map or written down in field notes. These clues are visually obvious, although their specific implications in any instance may be in question. The same is not true, however, for artifacts. They must be found, and therein lie many problems.

During survey, artifacts are usually collected and then studied to determine their age and cultural association. These determinations are usually based on previous excavations that have shown the chronological relationships of different kinds of artifacts and have, however roughly, outlined the geographic areas in which particular cultures are found. Even the lack of previous work is no insurmountable problem, for one can often establish at least a tentative chronology with small excavations. The problem for site surveyors is whether the artifacts found on the surface are truly representative of the ones that lie buried. Archeologists usually assume that some artifacts from each period of occupation will

FIG. 6.3 *Surface indications of a house in the Deh Luran valley, Iran. The upper part of the walls, made of clay, has completely eroded away, leaving only the stone foundations. See Figure 6.4 for a plan drawing of the house.*

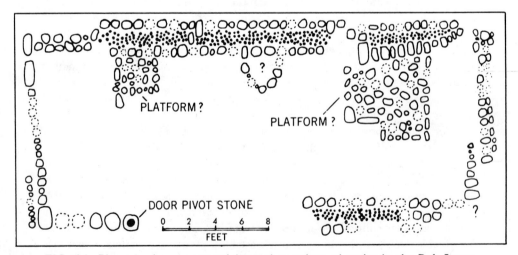

FIG. 6.4 *Plan of a house mapped from the surface of a site in the Deh Luran valley, Iran. The man in Figure 6.3 is examining what would be the upper left-hand corner of this plan.*

find their way to the surface through disturbance by later people, burrowing of animals, uprooting of trees, erosion, and similar factors, but we know that this assumption is often inaccurate. Indeed, it runs counter to one of our firmest principles, that the older things should be on the bottom. What we must remember is that in general, both principles hold, but that in particular instances, neither may. The following examples will illustrate this point.

The kinds of artifacts found on the surface of sites vary with the age of the site, soil chemistry, climatic conditions, vegetation, and previous survey. Caves that have been abandoned for hundreds or thousands of years may have few or no artifacts lying on their surfaces. The upper part of the fill may be sterile rock, dirt, and, as is so often the situation in many parts of the world, dung dropped by animals that are kept penned in the shelter. In order to find surface indications of human occupation there, it is often necessary to crawl on hands and knees for some time before finding the first signs of human habitation. As one walks up to caves and rock shelters, it is usually best to begin the search for occupation evidence on the **talus**, a good bit below the cave opening. Flints and sherds that are deeply buried are more likely to be exposed on eroded talus slopes below the cave's opening than on the present exposed floors of the caves. The surface finds may be few and unencouraging, but their paucity is not necessarily an indication that the cave's yield will also be meager. If the caves were cleaned out by ancient occupants, *all* the artifacts from deposits that were formerly part of the cave fill may have become part of the talus. Sometimes previous occupants swept out the dirt. It is necessary to excavate to find out.

The surface signs on open sites may also be misleading. Mounds or middens may be covered with pottery and flint, or their mass may be barren. In Southwest Asia it is usually hard to find artifacts on mounds that are covered with close-cropped turf. Centuries of trampling by sheep and goats have usually beaten the surface into a hard layer and broken all sherds into small pieces. But it is not always easier to find sherds in newly plowed mounds. In fact, we have surveyed mounds of which one-half was recently plowed and the other fallow, and found no consistency to tell us which half contained the greater amount of material. We have also seen mounds that by shape, size, and position must have resulted from human habitation, but on which no artifacts could be found.

Conditions for collecting also depend on whether a site has been looted or eroded. If graves have been looted, pottery is frequently thrown out onto the surface. Sites situated along streams may be cut by the water; fresh sections, thus exposed, usually yield good examples of pottery.

The degree to which precise information about the age and cultural association of sites can be learned from surface finds is closely related to the techniques used in making the collections. Probably the most widely used technique is to gather materials selectively. If the archeologist has any knowledge of the area, he will be able to recognize certain types of pottery and stone tools and he will emphasize these in his collections. Thus, painted sherds may tell him more than unpainted ones because he can tell more accurately the time period when they were used (Fig. 6.5). Unpainted pottery sometimes changes

FIG. 6.5 *Pieces of pottery (sherds), picked up during surface reconnaisance of archeological sites, can often be used to date the site or the periods during which it was occupied. These sherds, from a site in western Iran, are about 6500 years old.*

very little over long periods, whereas the styles of painting may change very quickly. By studying artifacts that he knows well, an archeologist can break his collection down into smaller dated units (parts of assemblages), each of which is defined by its diagnostic types of artifacts.

This method of selectively collecting material seems to make more sense than simply picking up everything made by man that lies on the surface. Indeed, on very large sites where artifacts are abundant, it might be possible to pick up tons of sherds. This would clearly be impractical. Nevertheless, the procedure that seems to make the most sense is not necessarily the best. The reason is that deliberate selection of type artifacts can lead to undue emphasis on certain types and neglect of others, possibly leading to misinterpretation. Furthermore, when there are no easily datable type artifacts, changes through time may be best seen in the relative frequencies of different types. For example, during the early occupation of a site, artifacts of type A may have been most abundant, with type B in the minority; later type B may become dominant, with some type A remaining and some type C beginning to appear. Still later, all type A may be gone, type C dominant, and types B and D minor elements. The differences between the phases are seen in the differences in the frequencies of types. On the surface of a stratified site it would be very difficult to separate assemblages, but where sites were occupied for only a short time, it may be possible to determine the frequency of the various types for one moment in time. It is not possible to do so by deliberately selecting only the most attractive or familiar examples.

The way to avoid the massive collections implied by picking up everything is to sample the site's surface. The usual method for systematic sampling is to **grid** the site and pick up only the pottery within certain randomly selected grid squares. All pottery in these selected grids is collected. When the material has been lumped, the percentages of various types can be calculated. It is assumed that pottery of all types was distributed evenly across the site and that it occurs on the surface in the same proportion as in the ground. But even random sampling, which is designed and carried out in such a way as to eliminate the subjective element in collecting, may not produce all the types of materials that could be recovered, nor does it necessarily give an accurate estimate of their relative abundance.

No serious archeologist would contend that the surface of a site is always a microcosm of its contents. The only way to tell whether it is, is to sample the surface and then dig the site. A few archeologists have examined in particular— by comparing surface potsherd collections with collections made from test pits dug in the same sites—the assumption that the surface materials do represent a sample of the pottery contained in the deposit. From our own experience, we have found that the presence of artifacts on the surface is dependent on so many variables, both natural and cultural, that it is unwise to use surface indications as more than a rough guide to a site's contents.

A technique to supplement surface survey is to test-dig a site; in other words, to dig a small exploratory pit that plumbs the depth of the site. Such a pit is called a **sondage**, a French term meaning a sounding probe into the soil. Its purpose is to find out the stratigraphic relations of artifacts and to provide a basis for judging whether the site is worth extensive excavation. This is a particularly valuable technique where surface material is sparse, or when it includes very little material from what are thought to be the earliest periods of occupation.

Structural Features

Once a site has been found and some estimate has been made of its age, it is useful to find out if the nature of its contents can be determined. This can help with assigning a function to the site and will also help if excavation is contemplated.

Sometimes it is possible to make a topographic map of the visible features of a large site and attain a good idea of its layout and the sort of activities that were carried on there. This would be particularly true of sites whose buildings lie close to the surface and where there are bits of walls exposed or changes in vegetation that show where buried walls are. Aerial photos have been particularly useful in mapping sites of this kind because they give an overview that shows the pattern of structures more clearly than can be seen at ground level. Even when it is not possible to see the site from above, however, if features can be seen at the surface, they can be plotted on maps to compile an overall picture. An experienced archeologist may be able to detect even minute clues as to subsurface features that would be effectively invisible to the beginner.

There are some other simple, direct methods for discovering what is below the surface without digging. The simplest and most widely used of these is probing. The probe is a rod made of spring steel that can be pushed into the ground. An experienced operator can often tell what kind of object he is hitting by the feel and sound, which is transmittted through the probe to the handle. An auger may also be used to bring up small samples of subsurface material, and sometimes solid cores that preserve the stratification are taken.

Cameras have also been used to look inside unexcavated underground Etruscan tombs. The tombs are usually found by probing or from visual indications. Then a hole is drilled in its top and a miniaturized camera with flash gun is lowered down to take pictures of the interior. When the contents have been thus revealed on film, one can decide whether to dig or not.

There are also methods that are less obvious and direct. One of these is magnetometry, or "magnetic surveying." This method uses the proton magnetometer, a sensitive instrument that measures the intensity of the earth's gravitational field directly below the instrument. When readings are taken at intervals across a site, the presence of underground archeological features may be indicated by variations in the strength of the magnetic field. The readings are usually plotted as a profile of magnetic intensity across a site. When there is much variation, the plot shows pronounced peaks and valleys that can be interpreted as archeological features (Fig. 6.6). In a site that is predominantly of dirt, a large stone wall should cause a change in magnetic intensity. Similarly, a ditch dug into the earth under a site will register differently from the remainder of the site. The problem is that in many cases it is not possible to determine what the changes in magnetic intensity mean. That is, one cannot always tell ahead of time whether a wall will appear as a peak or as a valley on the record of intensities.

Magnetometry is widely used in geologic prospecting because changes in intensity (anomalies) relate to changes in the structure or composition of rocks beneath the earth's surface. The instruments are often carried in planes and can thus be used to detect mineral resources over large areas. The instruments are also used to detect metal beneath water. A recent archeological ap-

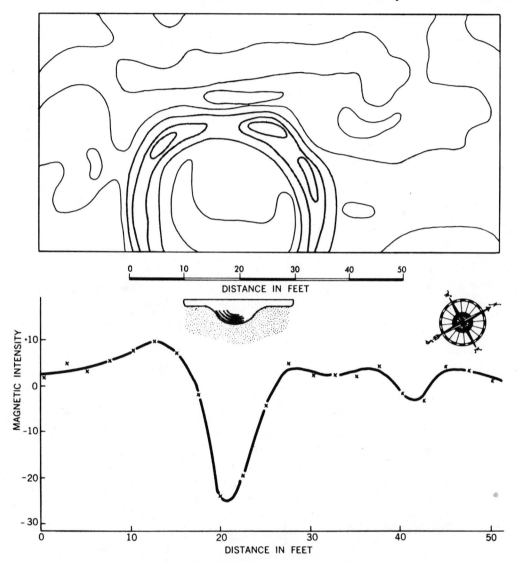

FIG. 6.6 *Magnetometer survey of a ring ditch at Stanton Harcourt, Oxon. A magnetic contour diagram is given with a sample magnetic profile and sketch-ditch section. The ditch was cut down into natural gravel and filled with mixed gravel (dotted) and then uniform loamy earth (solid black). (R. E. Linington, "The Application of Geophysics to Archaeology,"* American Scientist, *51(1963):60.)*

plication is in surveys of the outer continental shelf where there is now much exploration for oil. Prior to drilling, companies that lease these tracts from the government are required to determine whether there are any cultural resources present. The towing of a magnetometer and a **side scan sonar** (a device that gives a "picture" of the ocean bottom) has enabled archeologists to discover some shipwrecks this way because the metal in them has caused distinctive anomalies in the magnetometer records (Fig. 6.7).

Magnetometers are expensive instruments and sometimes difficult to use because of local magnetic interference and the fact that there may be no detectable anomalies in most sites. In some instances, however, they may be very useful, as at La Venta, a site in Mexico where there is a large pyramid that was suspected of having ceremonial offerings or perhaps tombs inside. A magnetic survey clearly indicated that there are stone constructions inside the pyramids, but their nature remains to be determined by actual excavation.

Finally, we may mention **resistivity surveying**, a technique that measures the electrical resistance of the earth. The method depends on the water content of the soil and thus lends itself well to sites where there are several kinds of subsurface structures. For example, stone walls have a higher electrical resistance than the surrounding soil or clay has. The equipment needed is more cumbersome, and its application generally more time-consuming, than that for magnetometry.

The technique involves placing metal electrodes in the ground at regular intervals and sending an electric current through one of them. The amount of resistance in the ground between two electrodes is measured as the ratio of voltage across the electrodes to the current flowing through them. The system requires the use of at least four electrodes, an electrical source, and a measuring device. When operated by two persons, this method is as efficient as magnetometry, though it may be more time-consuming.

There have been relatively few applications of resistivity surveying, although in theory it should be useful in many circumstances. The major problems are that rain-soaked ground and a high water table will seriously affect the readings. Natural geological phenomena may also cause trouble. For example, pockets of clay or soil in surrounding rock may be indistinguishable from archeological features. Rocky soil also causes trouble, because the interference caused by rocks may be taken for archeological features.

It should be clear from this discussion of survey and ways of determining what is in sites, that much information must remain ambiguous because it is incomplete or subject to more than one interpretation. The way to solve these problems is usually excavation.

Excavation

Judging from the way people talk, digging is the exciting part of archeology. Above all, it implies discovery, perhaps of something spectacular, and it may imply exotic settings in faraway lands or merely the beauty of the outdoors. This attitude is a holdover from the days of looting, when the collecting of fine objects was all that mattered. Although it is true that digging may be exciting for the reasons expressed above, today we regard excavation more as a last resort than as the first objective. There are several reasons for this. Most importantly,

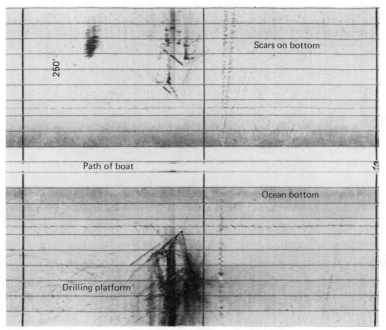

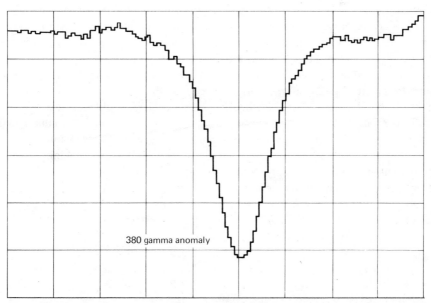

FIG. 6.7b *A magnetometer towed behind the boat at the same time as the sonar detected a large anomaly at the location of the drilling platform. A magnetometer detects differences in the intensity of the magnetic field such as are caused by large metallic objects like drilling platforms and sunken ships.*

since by excavation sites are destroyed, they should not be squandered on personal whims. As we pointed out before, there is still a lot to learn from survey as well as continued analysis and interpretation of material already dug. Finally, digging takes a great deal of time and money, commodities that are both in short supply in archeology. Today, although the techniques and rationale are different, archeologists still try to adhere to the motives that drove Claudius Rich: to obtain the greatest amount of useful information for the least cost.

Archeologists select sites for excavation that they hope, usually for good reason, will provide information to illuminate some inadequately known part of prehistory. The only justification for excavating a site is that new information can be secured from it. The clever use of advanced techniques for excavation and analysis is wasted if it is not directed toward, and designed for, the solution of a particular problem. The suitability of approaches and the scope of the dig should develop naturally out of an archeologist's intention. As R. J. C. Atkinson says in *Stonehenge* (1960), in a review of the development of archeological thought about this impressive site, "It is now no longer considered sufficient, or even justifiable, to excavate a site in a repetitive manner, merely waiting, like Mr. Micawber, for something to turn up. On the contrary, every excavation and every part of one must be planned to answer a limited number of quite definite questions."

Digs that are routinely carried out in the hope that "something will turn up" are almost invariably a waste of time. Unless there is immediate reason for digging, sites should be left alone because archeologists in the future will probably find no more justification than we do for the reptitious results. What we often find is that new questions and new approaches to interpretation require new kinds of information which, not having been appreciated in the past, were not collected. For example, when W. H. Sears attempted to draw inferences about the social and religious systems of prehistoric Native North Americans, he found that the older literature was grossly deficient in relevant information. The same could be said for almost any area: what we want to know today cannot be answered fully by the information recovered in the past. This does not mean that the older work is irrelevant or that the archeologists did it badly. What it does mean is that archeological results, like those of any science, are cumulative and progressive. We build on the past and move forward into the future.

The points made above are so important that it is worth making a strong statement expressing their implications. Digging simply to "salvage" information from a site that may be threatened seldom satisfies immediate interests and will almost certainly contribute very little to future ones. Archeologists should be as prepared to justify why they want to dig at all as well as why they want to dig a particular site.

These remarks are not intended to give the impression that there should be no excavation; indeed, without it archeology could not advance. Under what conditions, then, is it appropriate to excavate? Before an archeologist can make an intelligent decision about a site's potential, he must have studied it thoroughly from the surface and related what he can see to what is known about other sites in the area. Essentially this means that he should be an expert in the local archeology (or as expert as one can be given the state of knowledge). He should have read all the publications, talked with archeologists knowledgeable about the area, and studied collections of related artifacts. As a result of this prior study, he should have clearly in mind what archeological problems need to be solved before further progress can be made. On the basis of all these considerations, he can make a decision about whether to dig any particular site and, equally important, how to dig it.

Sometimes many sites in an area are worth digging, and the problem of selecting one becomes difficult. Some archeologists compare archeology to a military campaign because of the many factors that must be balanced before the best approach can be selected. Starting with a problem and some sites that will help solve the problem, the archeologist has to consider the difficulty of digging each site, the time available for excavation, sources of equipment, cost, and the number and quality of workmen and supervisors available. After these factors have been considered, one or more sites will then be selected as best suited for digging. The presence of a good access road or permission to dig from a landowner may tip the balance in favor of a particular site. Often the choice is not so clear-cut, but it is unusual, after evaluating all of the available facts, to have a number of equally promising sites.

When a decision is made to dig, it is especially important to pick a job that can be completed. This sounds trivial, but there are probably hundreds of sites whose excavations were never finished. Sometimes the situation was unavoidable, but more often the archeologists merely bit off more than they could chew. There is a tendency to assume that very large sites will take many years to dig and then to proceed on a leisurely course of excavation. At the huge site of Susa in Iran, French excavators have been digging nearly continuously since the 1880s, and they still have not solved some very basic questions of the history of the site. They have, of course, exposed vast areas of some historically important periods, but the period when the site was founded is known only from some very small and very deep pits. At least the archeologists are still working! It is all too common, however, for money to run out, archeologists to die, political circumstances to change, and so on, leaving the excavation in an unsatisfactory state of incompletion. When this happens, much of the proposed value of the work is never achieved.

It is well to point out also that unless the results are published there will never be much useful information from a site. Archeologists who do not publish their results are little, if any, better than looters who destroy sites without keeping records.

The elements of a military organization are evident in the actual excavation: there is the training of labor; the orderly assignment of the men and supervisors; the procurement of equipment and supplies; and the recording of data. Above all, the job should be done with precision. As Wheeler (1956:80) noted, it is axiomatic "that an untidy excavation is a bad one." In order that the excavation be carried out smoothly, efficiently, and without loss of information, there must be enough trained supervisory personnel on hand. In a dig where college students are providing the labor, trained supervision may not be a problem, because students can be readily trained to observe and record finds or to ask for assistance when they need it. In Mexico or Egypt or Peru or Africa, however, where untrained labor is available in quantity and the pay scale is low, the archeologist may be able to carry off an excavation of rather larger magnitude than in an area where labor is expensive. But with the larger crew of workers, the head archeologist will need more assistants to supervise and maintain a careful watch on the progress of the excavation. Big digs are always more difficult to carry out than small ones, and anyone who has managed an excavation with 50 or 100 pick-and-shovel workers has learned that shirking, stealing finds, labor agitation, internal dissension among the workers which must be adjudicated, and a dozen other problems tend to eat up precious time and cause frayed nerves. By the end of such a dig the archeologist is usually willing to swear that he will never return to the same area and submit to such frustrations another time. But when all is done, and the accomplishments are evident, such experiences seem worth while, and it it not six months before our archeologist is planning a follow-up dig. About the only thing that really causes archeologists to give up digging is when their creaky bones cannot take it any more.

How to Dig

As Sir Mortimer Wheeler (1956:36) said, "There is no method proper to the excavation of a British site which is not applicable—nay, must be applied—to a site in Africa or Asia." Grahame Clark (1954:7) is more specific when he says that all archeologists, whether they work with the Paleolithc or with Greek art, should have training in prehistoric archeology because it requires greater discipline to recover a maximum amount of data. Neither author recommends definite procedures, and perhaps that is just as well. In fact, there are no invariable rules for digging any particular kind of site. but there are some general principles that must be followed using the techniques available. Above all, it is important to remember that each site is unique in some respects and will require some individuality of approach.

This book is not the place for a detailed discussion of how to dig. There are several books designed to teach students and laymen techniques, and most excavation reports deal with the subject as it pertains to particular excavations. It is more important here to discuss some general principles that express the reasons why particular techniques are used.

The essential underlying idea in digging is that one is removing the dirt which covers objects so that we can see them where they lie in their correct relationships to one another. This means that we want to dig so that the horizontal and vertical positions of all objects are observed and recorded. If this is done carefully, we should be able to rebuild the site as we found it. Of course, the ideal cannot be completely achieved, nor is it considered necessary for all purposes. Nevertheless, the more closely this ideal is approached, the more exact and useful the results are likely to be.

Briefly, the reason we want to keep track of the spatial relationships of all artifacts and traces of human activity in the site is so that we can tell what goes with what. Which objects are older? Which tools were used to butcher the bison? What work was done inside the houses? And so on. These are questions whose answers depend on our knowing spatial relationships. If we were simply to move a site with a bulldozer into a powered shaker screen and pick out the objects that remained after the dirt had shifted through, we would have no contextual information even though we might have all of the objects.

With our basic principle in mind, we are then ready to deal with our site. The first question that arises is "where to dig?" This depends on what we are trying to do and on what we have observed from studying the surface. Naturally we want to dig where we think we will find what we are looking for. If we want to see a cross section of the history of the site, we might dig a pit or trench into the deepest part; if we want to expose houses of a particular period, we will dig where we find surface traces of remains of that period. If we cannot see much from the surface, we may find it necessary to sample various parts of the site until we find an area that is suitable.

Assuming that we have selected a place to dig, another obvious question is, "How big or what shape shall the excavation be?" The former part of the question is more difficult than the latter. An observer of excavations will quickly realize that pits, of whatever size and proportion, are rectangular (Fig. 6.8). This shape follows from the need to maintain records of vertical and horizontal position. To accomplish this, sites are gridded. Usually before the digging starts, a map of the site is made and several datum stakes are fixed in the ground. These stakes become the basic reference points for all horizontal measurements. Usually, for convenience, they are laid out along north–south and east–west axes. They form the basis of the grid, which is a set of squares that covers the site. Often these squares are 5 meters or some similar size on a side. If a stake is put at each corner of all of the squares, any excavation pit can be quickly related to the grid and in turn marked on the map of the site (Fig. 6.9).

For convenience, pits are often the same size as the squares laid out in the grid, although they need not be. The important thing is to make the excavation units large enough to enable workers to get inside them comfortably and large enough so that they will expose what is being sought. That is, if you want to dig houses, the pits should be large enough to include substantial parts of houses. If the pit is dug through a midden that contains no architectural remains, it might be suitable to dig squares two meters on a side to sample the contents.

The next question is usually, "How deep should we dig?" If we are going to keep accurate records of spatial relationships, we must dig slowly rather than in large bites. The vertical units that we dig by are usually called "levels." When there is stratification easily visible in the site, the levels may conform with it. When there is no visible stratification, the levels may be of arbitrary thickness. It

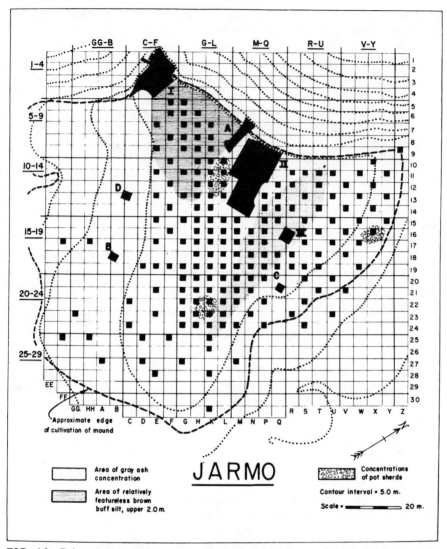

FIG. 6.8 *Prior to excavation, an archeological site is usually mapped to establish the topographic contours, and gridded to provide baselines so that the
areas excavated can be related to one another. In this example the grid was
used as a basis for sampling the entire surface of the site with small pits in
the attempt to detect and trace the upper layer of architecture without the
necessity of digging the entire site. (R. J. Braidwood and B. Howe,* Prehistoric
Investigations in Iraqi Kurdistan, *Fig. 6.)*

should be pointed out, however, that levels help the diggers maintain some
orderly procedure. The ideal is still to make a record of the occurrence of each
object where it is found within a level. In cases where the soil is hard or the
quantity of materal is too great, or the objects too small to see in their earthen
matrix, the contents of each level are usually put through a screeen so that the

FIG. 6.9 *General view* (top) *and close-up* (bottom) *of the excavations at Tia-huanaco, Bolivia, showing the technique of excavating large areas and leaving regularly spaced balks to preserve evidence of stratigraphy. (Centro de Investigaciones Arqueologicas en Tiwanaku.)*

dirt sifts through leaving the artifacts behind. What we have then is a group of artifacts whose vertical and horizontal positions are known by square and level, but no more precisely than that. Often this is sufficient and it is standard procedure on many digs.

The kind of pits you dig depend on what you want to accomplish and on the nature of the site itself. The problems are quite different in digging waterlogged sites in marshy areas, shell middens a meter or so in depth along a river, cities where the architectural remains cover hundreds of hectares, earthen effigy mounds, or temple pyramids. The more you can see from the surface, the easier it is. The deeper the site, the more difficult it is. In general, you can expose much more of the upper layers of a site than of the lower layers, and this is one reason why sites should be selected with great care.

Whatever methods are chosen, it is usually wise to leave at least some portion of a site unexcavated. This is particularly true of sites that are unique, because workers in the future who have new techniques may want to come back for another look. Such periodic revisits have been carried out in one notable example, at the site of Jericho in Palestine, and most of the great mound is still intact, awaiting the research of future generations of archeologists.

Keeping Records

Precise and careful excavations are carried out in conjunction with precise and careful keeping of records. Both depend on skilled observers: the staff of the dig.

When a site is ready for excavation, it is usually mapped and laid out with a grid. This constitutes the first step in keeping records and also serves to delineate the areas of responsibility of the staff, each of whom is ordinarily assigned to some portion of the site. Individual supervisors are then responsible for keeping track of what goes on in their own area of work. The records they keep become the primary references for all of the objects found in the site. And the objects themselves are usually tagged or marked with a notation that indicates where they were found. The idea behind keeping records is that everything of importance should be noted so that the sites could be "reconstructed" if necessary (Fig. 6.10).

The precise methods of keeping records vary from site to site and there is no point in going into detail here. Large projects frequently make use of preprinted forms and require each supervisor to keep track of very specific information in addition to noting unexpected and unusual things. Often, written notes are supplemented with photographs or sketches and in some cases, these illustrations may serve as the primary records, especially of horizontal relationships (Fig. 6.11). As the digging proceeds downward, sections are drawn of the vertical relations of the strata and record visually what the levels include (see Fig. 5.3).

Whatever the precise nature of keeping records entails, it should be emphasized here that excavations should be kept neat. Messy digs lead to messy recording. On the other hand, students who read reports where photographs of

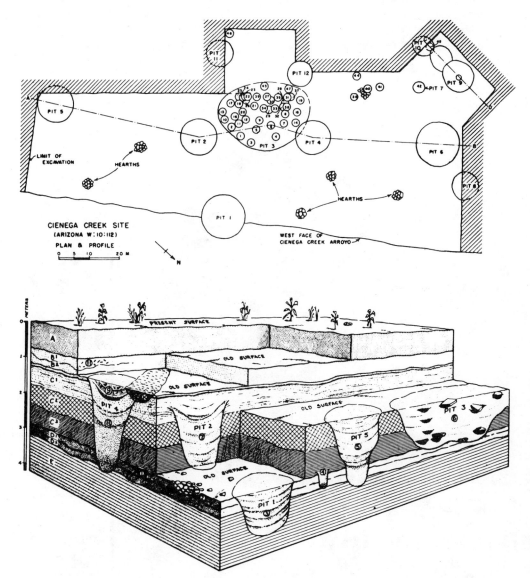

FIG. 6.10 Plan (top) and block diagram (bottom) of the Cienega Site, Arizona, showing the deposits both horizontally and vertically. The block diagram summarizes the sequence of cultural features in relation to the geological stratigraphy. Excavators must establish controls on the digging that will allow them to reconstruct the deposits in this manner. (E. W. Haury, "An Alluvial Site on the San Carlos Indian Reservation, Arizona," American Antiquity, Vol. 23.)

the work in progress show meticulously clean digs should also be aware that the situation is atypical; that is, the site has been swept clean for purposes of taking the picture. An excavation can never be kept completely clean although it should be neat at all times. This is not just fussiness. It is very hard for a super-

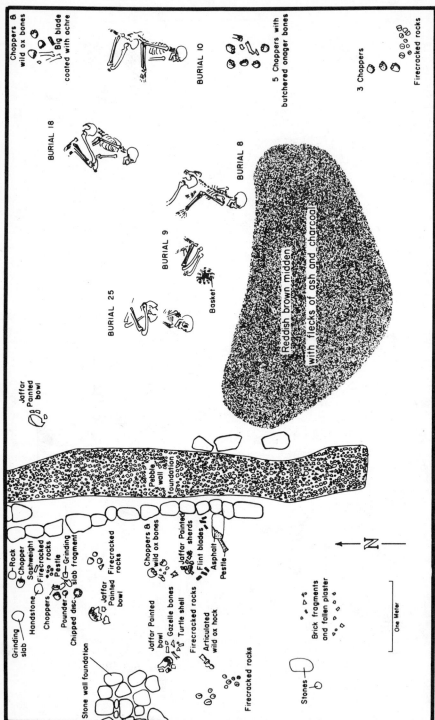

FIG. 6.11 Artifacts, skeletons, and architectural traces are all plotted where they were found in Ali Kosh, Iran. The distribution shows household debris inside the house and burials in what was probably a courtyard. Some of the burials had been partly destroyed by later people, who used the eroded mound for a cemetery. (F. Hole, K. V. Flannery, and J. A. Neely, Prehistory and Human Ecology of the Deh Luran Plain. Museum of Anthropology, University of Michigan, Memoirs, 1969.)

visor to see and record things if the area in question is messy. At the very least, it needs to be cleaned at regular intervals and these are good times to take pictures.

From what we have said, it should be clear that good excavation requires good teamwork and coordination among a skilled staff. Sir Mortimer Wheeler, who organized his digs like a military staff, had a hierarchical series of administrative and technical personnel. His staffs consisted of "a director, a deputy director, a supervisor for each area under excavation, a trained foreman, a small-find recorder, a pottery assistant, a photographer, a surveyor, a chemist, a draftsman, and, according to need, an **epigraphist** or **numismatist**" (M. Wheeler 1956: 153).

Wheeler was concerned with historical sites. For prehistoric sites he would have had to add a zoologist, a paleobotanist, a **palynologist**, a geologist, a mineralogist, a pedologist, and possibly others as well, and could have left the epigraphist and numismatist at home. There is not less need for specialists at prehistoric sites; indeed, there may be need for a greater variety, because the prehistorian must rely on the natural scientists for recovery and interpretation of basic information much more so than the historian (Fig. 6.12). On a practical basis, one person may well control two or more specialities, so that a mere listing does not indicate the number of persons involved.

It is only under especially fortunate circumstances that a prehistorian can

Scientific
  theoretician
  integrator
  evaluator

Fieldwork
  dirt archeologist
  stratigrapher
  detective
  photo interpreter
  explorer
  recorder

Ancillary Scientific
  botanist
  ethnologist
  geographer
  geologist
  palynologist
  pedologist
  zoologist

Editorial
  writer
  editor
  layout and design

Administrative
  executive director
  expeditor
  foreman
  politician
  secretary
  accountant

Analytic
  research assistant
  statistician
  computer programmer

Technical
  surveyor
  draftsman
  photographer
  restorer
  carpenter
  machine operator
  mechanic

FIG. 6.12 *Jobs required to carry out an archeological project.*

take such a team of specialists to the field with him. Most analyses are made by technicians in their home laboratories, though it is common for them to visit sites being excavated. In fact, it is important that these persons have a chance to do work at archeological sites. Only in this way will they be able to appreciate the conditions under which samples are obtained. At the site they can also make valuable suggestions about collecting samples and preserving specimens. Furthermore, as a guide to what is happening in the site, an archeologist will find useful a running analysis of the plants and animals encountered.

Excavations are chronically understaffed. For most sites the deficiencies lie, not so much in labor, but in too few supervisory personnel and in inadequate numbers of specialists who can identify such things as animal species from bones, pollens extracted from soils, and so on. In Wheeler's organization, like a military chain of command, each man is assigned responsibility for a certain segment of the operation and supervision of a certain number of workers. However, no matter how the staff is organized, care must be taken to ensure that someone is present at all times in all areas under excavation. In this way proper records can be kept. Routine excavation is often dull work, which requires little supervision, but, when the unexpected occurs, prompt and efficient supervision is necessary. Under loose supervision an incalculable number of artifacts have been broken or thrown away by careless workmen or stolen by dishonest ones.

Like every archeological operation, the selection of a staff must be planned with due regard for the unique circumstances of each dig. No factor is as important to the outcome of an excavation as the cooperative efforts performed day after day by the group of individuals who, collectively, comprise the staff.

TECHNICAL DESCRIPTION AND ANALYSIS

As Stuart Piggott said, the evidence of archeology is inevident. In fact, the question of whether something that we find is the result of human or of other factors remains important today even though we have long since gone beyond the question of whether hand-axes were thunderbolts or tools of ancient man. Now we know that the characteristically shaped stones found in European river gravels are tools, but there remains debate on cruder pieces of chipped stone in many places around the world, on some concentrations of fractured bone, and on certain alignments of stone. In cases like these, when the observed effects *could* have been created by natural processes, it becomes an archeological problem to determine whether they *were* created by human activities.

Most of us, however, deal routinely with evidence in the form of neatly chipped stone, cut and polished bone tools, carefully shaped milling stones, and bits of pottery or whole vessels. These are all clearly made by the hands of artisans. What is inevident is how they were used and how they fit into a picture of

a prehistoric society. We also deal routinely with evidence of spatial relationships between artifacts in sites and between the sites themselves. Although
these data are easy to record, their implications are not necessarily evident.
Finally, we often find quantities of objects that are man-made but whose use is
almost impossible to deduce.

One particularly vexing example of this is the lightly fired strips of clay,
often with impressions of matting on one side, which were found by the thousands at Chagha Sefid in Iran (Fig. 7.1), in an ashy midden where it looks as if
the contents of fireplaces had been dumped. One can say the following about
these enigmatic artifacts: (1) they are very numerous, occurring in densities of
about 1000 per cubic meter, (2) they were made quickly and without great care,
(3) they were often made by pressing one side against a mat, (4) they were used
in or around a fireplace, (5) they were probably only sun dried before they were
fired during their use, (6) they were used only once and must have been considered cheap and expendable, (7) they have never before been found at an
archeological site, (8) they date to about 5800–6000 B.C. Although there is more
information on their context, their use has not yet been determined. The evidence, then, is clearly inevident.

Or, to cite another example of inevident data, take the sculptured monuments at the site of Abaj Takalik on the south coast of Guatemala. An initial exploration of the site revealed sixty stone monuments of various forms (stelae
and altars). A minority are sculptured, and of these some are in Olmec style

0   5 cm

*FIG. 7.1 Enigmatic artifacts from Chagha Sefid, Iran. These are strips of
lightly fired clay that often have impressions of matting on one side and finger
impressions on the other. They occurred by the thousand in ashy trash deposits.*

(dated elsewhere around 600–1100 B.C.) and some are in early Maya style, dating from a century or two before and after the beginning of the Christian era. Most of the monuments of shaped stone are plain—that is, are not sculptured. Why are they neither sculptured nor painted nor in any way embellished, so far as can be determined? To what style or period do these plain monuments belong? Why are they plain? Why are there so many of them? If the people who occupied the site were capable of doing beautiful relief sculptures on such stone, all of them brought to the site from a distance, why were only a minority carved and the rest left undecorated? There are no answers to these questions now, and even with further fieldwork they may remain problematical.

It would be nice if the finding of "ceramic strips" and plain monuments and equally inevident evidence were not so common, but the fact is that much of what we find in a site falls in that category. We are in the position, as prehistorians, of trying to discover and recreate the history of cultures whose "language" (as it is expressed in artifacts) we cannot yet read with any great clarity. As a consequence, we often resort, at least initially, to description and comparison of objects from many sites, rather than to very profound or insightful interpretation. When we do this we present a record of what we have and of how it compares with records from other sites.

A description usually focuses on the external characteristics of objects from sites. In many instances, however, it is useful to make analyses of the composition of the clays or metals, or to study the manufacturing techniques. It may also be helpful to look at the organic remains like bones of animals and seeds or pollen of plants, and, finally, we may wish to study the sites themselves for their chemical composition, structure, and geologic history.

Most of the descriptive studies can be carried out by an archeologist, who is usually well trained to deal with artifacts. The other kinds of analyses are usually assigned to specialists who have the special training and laboratory facilities to carry out these technical studies. No matter who does the work, however, the objective is to reduce the ambiguity concerning the artifacts and to put the miscellaneous cultural and technical information into a form that can be interpreted and related to the story of past human activities.

Description

When the archeologist has finished with the digging of a site and has returned to his home base with aching back, equipment, notebooks, maps, photographs, and artifacts, he has accomplished only the first half of his research. The second half is to write a report. Actually, considerably more time is required to analyze material and write reports than to excavate a site. A conservative estimate is that it takes from two to three times as long to prepare a good report. In the report all the finds must be described and illustrated, and the site map and stratigraphic profiles must be presented and discussed. The report should also provide information on the age of the cultural materials found, and the culture disclosed should be compared with other archeological cultures in an effort to determine how similar and how different it is. The report, when published, makes the particular body of information available to everyone interested. Some archeologists would rather dig and discover than write reports of their findings, but those who fail to do the latter are avoiding a responsibility. Archeological data that are not analyzed and reported might just as well have been left in the ground.

Classification

We all classify. In our lives there are cars, trees, houses, people, clouds, and so on. When we are crossing a street and attempting to avoid being run down, we care little to make a distinction between a Buick and a Benz. What is important is that a car and not a tree is heading our way. If each brand of car (indeed, "brand" is another classification) required a unique solution to the problem of how to avoid it, chances are that most pedestrians would soon be dead because they would be unable to recognize the model and calculate the necessary evasive tactics quickly enough to do any good. Instead, what people do is lump all cars moving toward them together as a category to be avoided. Similarly, we classify spiders, mosquitoes, ants, and roaches together as "bugs" and deal with them in this gross category. When we do so, we reduce our uncertainty about specifics and we group together those things toward which we plan to behave in the same way.

Archeologists excavate and record thousands of objects and bits of information. For convenience in sorting it all out, they usually consider that there are three kinds of data: artifactual, nonartifactual (for example, bones, soils, and charcoal), and the geographical or chronological positions of the site. Within each of these broad categories, of course, an archeologist will make subdivisions. Among the artifacts will be those of bone, chipped stone, polished stone, ceramics, matting and basketry, and wood. Bones might include those of cattle, mice, bats, dogs, deer, and bears. A rough sorting quickly establishes these subcategories and sets the stage for more detailed analysis.

When they consider artifacts, most archeologists attempt to establish types, the most frequently used unit of classification and comparison. A "type" is a particular kind of artifact in which several attributes combine or cluster with sufficient frequency or in such distinctive ways that the archeologist can define it explicitly and recognize others like it. What this procedure does is to establish categories that can be distinguished from others. For example, in a site there may be red pottery and gray pottery. The attributes of color are mutually exclusive and serve in every instance to distinguish between two types of pottery. The pottery might, however, be subdivided still further by noting whether it carried painted designs or not, and according to the shapes of the pots.

Classification is a tool that can be made to work for many purposes. Theoretically, there is an almost infinite number of typologies for any body of material. Different typologies can help in understanding chronology, the relation of one part of a site to another, or the relations among sites or areas. Unfortunately, as G. Clark (1952:1) says, "The overwhelming proportion of archeological evidence has been gathered rather by accident than by design, and studied more as an exercise in classification than as a source of history." It is quite possible to get lost among the trees of typology and never see the forest of which they are a part. There has been considerable controversy over typology and whether typology as we are about to describe it is even worthwhile.

The important question, however, is, "What kind of information is desired?" Do we want to simply describe what is present in a site? Do we want to detect minute changes through time in the way artifacts are made? Do we want to record how techniques change? Do we want to be able to distinguish the work of individual artisans? Different goals require different approaches to classification. No single method of classification will serve all purposes.

The recognition and naming of types serve many purposes. First, as we have said, they are a means of introducing order or system into a varied assortment of objects. The array of archeological materials recovered thus becomes capable of being understood and handled in a meaningful way. Second, artifacts and nonartifactual materials from an archeological site are the concrete and palpable evidence of human action, because all these items had to be carried to the living area and were then modified by men in some way. Let us illustrate this by taking two excavated items. A flint projectile point may have involved the following human actions: obtaining the flint at its geological source; carrying it back to camp; securing a chipping implement (hammerstone); shaping the rough material by flaking into the finished weapon tip; mounting it on the end of the projectile shaft; searching for game; shooting the animal. The leg bone of a deer, not in itself an artifact, may have come from an animal whose taking and utilization may have involved these actions: killing of the animal by a hunter (or team of hunters) who used a deer-head decoy disguise; the killing effected with a bow and arrow; the dead animal skinned and butchered; the skin and carcass parts carried to camp; distribution of part of the meat to village mates; cooking the meat in baskets by heated stones or roasting it over the open fire; eating the cooked meat; dressing the skin and sewing it into a garment; use of some of the animal's bones to make tools (scrapers, awls, harpoons, and so on); ritual disposal of certain bones; using the food scraps to feed camp dogs—the list is almost endless.

We can see from these two constructed and much abbreviated examples that an object found in an archeological site is in reality an historical document of past human action. Who made the projectile point, why it came to be buried in the site, and who killed and ate the deer, are questions one can ask of these stones and bones but not have answered by them. But more general questions of what *people* used points and what they killed and ate for food can be answered, and typology is a useful aid in framing such questions. As typologies become more refined, the archeologist learns that at a certain time in prehistory (which he may label as Period IV) a certain group of people (which he may label the Olmec Culture or Beaker Culture or Folsom Culture) used a certain series of forms or, in other words, made and used certain things in certain ways. In a later period, the archeologist observes that new or modified forms are being made and used. He will look for the reasons for the changes he sees, and he may then discover that they are caused by altered habits resulting from changes in climate, which in turn led to altered requirements in tools, to different cultural practices such as the acceptance of farming, or simply to quite arbitrary modifications in style that arise through the mental activities of their makers. Changes in type over time are therefore a main road to studying the course of events in prehistory.

Functional Types

"What is it?" Whenever we see something that is unfamiliar, we ask that question. This is why there are labels on objects displayed in museums and why works of art often have explicit titles, even though the piece may be so abstract as to defy rational interpretation. Many people are satisfied to learn that a curious-looking object is a "celt," but others will want to know what you do with one. Until we know what you do with one, we can hardly make a very accurate interpretation of how celts fitted into the lives of a people. This is why many archeologists use words like "axe" or "adze" or "hoe" instead of "celt." The stone object that is called a "celt" looks something like axes, adzes, and hoes, depending on your point of view. The problem is, are celts really any of these and, if so, which?

Archeologists find it easy to classify a bow and arrow if they are lucky enough to find them preserved. They are able to recognize and know their use because they know that similar tools are used by living peoples. However, if they should find several variations of bows and arrows at one site, they will have a hard time trying to decide whether they should take notice of the differences. They will wonder whether variously shaped arrowheads were used for different kinds of game or resulted from accident in manufacture or from the preference of their makers. In short, once archeologists get beyond very gross classification of material or known use, they run into difficulty. Classification of stone or bone tools is even more difficult. One can call a piece of chipped flint a "knife" and still be in doubt whether it was really a knife, a javelin tip, a scraper, or something else. It is common for some archeologists to name artifacts after their presumed use, even though there is no way to check the guess. This practice has resulted in a great deal of misunderstanding by uncritical readers. Furthermore, giving an artifact a name carries the implication that it served a particular use; this kind of attributed function often leads to inaccurate comparison. For example, when a person reads the term "knife" in several reports, he is likely to assume that the same implement is being described in each instance. A check of accompanying illustrations may reveal that very different objects are being described by the same term.

The greatest pressure for giving functional names to artifacts usually comes from people who know the material the least. Archeologists tend to avoid such names *in their basic reports* unless they can establish without doubt what the objects were used for. The problem is that uncritical readers might otherwise accept a tentative identification and subsequently make inappropriate use of what they consider to be fact. In many instances it is possible to determine how objects were used, a matter we turn to later in this chapter. Until that is done, however, it is important to retain a clear distinction between basic description of artifacts and interpretations of their function.

Convenient Types

An opposite approach to naming functional types is to define types as being whatever variations of artifacts can be used to make comparisons. Sir Flinders Petrie, the famous British Egyptologist, for example, was less concerned over how the ancient Egyptians used different styles of jar handles than over the fact that he could set up a chronology based on their changes. Similarly, when American archeologists describe projectile points, they go to great lengths to discern differences that may help define geographical and chronological versions of cultures. An aborigine who was given a handful of different "types" might, unlike an archeologist, see no noteworthy differences among them. However, the aborigine's opinion is irrelevant because typing helps the archeologist. As Jennings (1957:98) remarks, "I view . . . types not as synonymous with cultural truth but as an invention of the analyst for his own convenience." A similar idea was expressed by Burkitt (1955:59) when he wrote,

> The classification of gravers [burins] is a matter of some controversy. They can be classified according to type, or they can be classified according to the method of their manufacture. Neither of these systems is perfect, and, indeed, the student must always remember that he is not making rules for prehistoric man, but deducing laws from facts. He is in the position of a grammarian, not of the inventor of a language.

Convenient types are probably the most commonly used in archeology. Whenever a report lists types without giving any basis for them, the reader is justified in assuming that the archeologist finds it convenient to group his material in such fashion; he probably has no other rationale behind his classification. Unfortunately, the use of purely arbitrary types results in different archeologists' choosing various types to describe the same assemblage. Because of this, more than for any other single reason, it is hard to compare archeological data. Most archeologists assume that they are doing a good job and that other archeologists understand what they are doing. Unfortunately, this is not always true. A person who wants to sum up the results of many excavations must himself handle the material or at least be sufficiently familiar with the excavators and their techniques to make judgments about what they report. Too often synthesizers overlook the extremely variable quality of reporting as it pertains to describing artifacts.

Cultural Types

People make things according to patterns, whether these are in the form of blueprints or simply in the mind. This is not to say that there is assembly-line type manufacture of nearly identical artifacts, but only that people who live and work together have similar ideas about what a knife, a soup bowl, or a bathtub looks like. If several of these people were asked, they probably would give very similar descriptions. Moreover, what they would describe would be a kind of average of the class of objects rather than some unusual example they knew about.

Because people have these ideas about how things should look, it follows that an archeologist may be able to deduce what the ideal is from examination of the examples he finds. His types, then, are intended to be the ideal toward which the artisans were striving in their imperfect manufacturing process. In the basic description, ideal types are not functional types. Deetz (1967) suggested one way to look at the cultural type when he related artifacts to language. In his view the makers of artifacts have a "mental template" that tells them what a tool should look like. The finished object is made up of many parts (attributes) whose occurrence in combination makes the tool a particular type of object. Deetz likened the attributes to elements of language, morphemes and phonemes, which speakers combine to produce meaningful communication. Deetz, like Burkitt (1955:59), thinks that if we analyze the "grammar" of artifacts we shall be able to learn more than if we look just at finished pieces.

Another way to discover cultural types is to use statistical analysis to discriminate clusters of attributes that occur in significant frequencies. The method depends on the fact that people do things by habit and preference. Most artifacts are the result of several separate stages of manufacture. Very likely there are alternate ways to accomplish each stage, and the way chosen may have no significant bearing on the use to which the artifact is put. Nevertheless, the particular way a piece is made can, to a large degree, show the peculiar notions the maker had about how the job ought to be done. Some methods of manufacture are characteristic of individuals or groups of people. If archeologists can distinguish these differences in method of manufacture and end result, they have an easy way of distinguishing between cultural groups *even though to all intents and purposes the finished artifacts are functionally identical.* In many instances the archeologist may pay more attention to the attributes of artifacts, for example, to shell tempering of pottery or the lost-wax casting process, than to the whole pieces, because it is the technique rather than the object that helps him solve his particular problem.

To discover types statistically, artifacts must first be described by their attributes. Attributes are recognizable features such as size, shape, color, material, and decoration. A single pot has many such attributes, and in one industry there may be several shapes and sizes of pot, two or three different kinds of tempering material, and a dozen or more kinds of decoration. Analysis attempts to discover which combinations of attributes are found in association in such frequency that they are probably not accidental. Archeologists look for "a consistent assemblage of attributes whose combined properties give a characteristic pattern. . . . Classification into types is a process of discovery of combinations of attributes favored by the makers of the artifacts, not an arbitrary procedure of the classifier" (Spaulding 1953:305).

Description and Illustration of Artifacts

Description of artifacts goes hand in hand with classification. Good descriptions should be brief, readily understood, and comparable with other descriptions to the extent that essential information is provided. All descriptions begin with words. Purely verbal descriptions, however, are easily misunderstood even by speakers of the same language. Translations to other languages are even more difficult, because descriptive terms frequently have no direct counterparts in other languages. Verbal descriptions are most precise when they define the attributes of artifacts.

Graphic Descriptions

The most common, and in some ways the best, kind of description is a drawing or photograph of the artifact. However, the ideal sought is seldom attained. To draw artifacts requires the hand of a skilled draftsman, just as photographs require the skilled use of a camera.

Drawings can show details that will not appear on photographs, but they are highly susceptible to personal interpretation. Artists usually emphasize the features that archeologists wish them to show. Photographs can also be used to show significant details, but good photos may be harder to achieve than good drawings (Fig. 7.2). In the hands of a skilled operator the camera can be made to do what the archeologist wishes, but like a drawing, a photograph can misrepresent.

FIG. 7.2   The style to be used in illustrating tools depends on their important attributes. Outline drawings are sufficient when the gross shape of a tool is important; techniques of chipping can be depicted best by a careful drawing of the details; a photograph shows texture and color differences.

If the shape of an artifact is important, it is common to represent it by an outline, which is a stylized description. Stylized drawings are ordinarily taken to be ideal types and they may not duplicate the outline of any single specimen. Such drawings are easy to make and easy to understand, but many artifacts cannot be understood by their shape alone. For these, one must use a more representational technique. The usual practice is to draw particular artifacts as faithfully as possible, emphasizing archeologically significant attributes.

Statistical Descriptions

Statistical descriptions may be simple tabulations of data or descriptions of the combinations of attributes of artifacts. All reports that present basic data should contain a numerical listing of artifacts, and most will also have a calculation of the frequencies in which various artifacts occur. The use of statistical techniques often permits more exact description than do words or illustrations alone, and may help to discriminate between associations of attributes or artifacts that are not readily observable by any other method.

Mention has been made of the use of statistics in discovering artifact types, a process that follows logically after basic description. However, statistics are also used for basic description. For example, it may be useful to describe the size of certain artifacts. Statistics may describe the range, the mean, and the standard deviations in size. These three statistics may be sufficient to describe an artifact type or may help to discriminate between variations of a type found at different sites. That is, even though the same type may have been used at different places, two different sizes of the type may have been made, and the demonstration of this fact may lead to significant cultural interpretation.

Statistics can also help tell whether the observed variations seem to be random and accidental, or nonrandom and purposeful. This information is especially useful because it will help the archeologist avoid the error of emphasizing attributes that are the result of accident rather than design.

Less complex numerical and graphic techniques have been used to describe entire industries. For example, a segment of the French Paleolithic has been described by Sonneville-Bordes by classifying all the flint tools into types and plotting their frequency in each site on a **cumulative histogram**. Visual comparison of the histogram shows how closely one site conforms to another in terms of relative frequencies of various types. Bohmers describes a method of comparing the percentages of a series of clearly defined artifact types whose mean measurements are represented graphically. These data, represented by a series of vertical histograms, are ranged next to one another for convenience of visual comparison.

Symbolic Descriptions

There has been considerable concern over whether it is possible to describe and classify artifacts entirely objectively. The main problem is not over the philosophical or technical possibilities of description, but that all workers are not consistent in their use of basic terms.

Ignoring the question of whether true objectivity can ever be achieved, several workers conclude that, to the extent to which each analyst can understand and apply a standard terminology, the resulting descriptions will be comparable. The easiest way to achieve agreement of description is to define the most minute attributes of artifacts in the simplest fashion. Measurements of length, width, shape, and weight are examples of attributes that can be easily defined. It is also possible to define design elements, and combinations of elements, by using a symbolic notation. When description has been reduced to a formal language of symbols, it is easily stored in a computer and readily compared with other similar descriptions (cf. Whiteford 1947; L. Binford 1963).

The advantage of recording each artifact mechanically is that unlimited numbers of attributes can be accommodated and that the data, readily available for retrieval from the file, can easily be extracted. If one is interested in learning the association of axes with convex bits, holes for hafting, and trapezoidal sections, he can do so quickly by requesting the computer to print out the information. By this method it is possible to change the constitution of types without a basic reanalysis of the artifacts. Each worker can select whatever attribute clusters he wishes, and no change will have been necessary in the basic description.

The advantages of mechanical recording and statistical analysis are obvious. As archeologists become more aware of their possibilities, they will be used more frequently. It takes a great deal of time to create the descriptive system on which the recording must be based and for each analyst to learn the system. For the present, these are the two most important obstacles that prevent universal adoption of such techniques.

To develop complete files of coded data, however useful, would represent a staggering amount of effort, especially in areas where collecting has gone on for a long time. Such files might require governmental sponsorship. Few would argue against the proposition that archeology has now secured such a mass of material that no individual can study all the available items of even one class of artifact, such as projectile points, pottery, or basketry. The compilation of complete files provides one of the directions in which the present authors think archeology will eventually move. The sheer magnitude of accumulating files on, say, projectile points, stone axes, or ceramics, is so staggering that it will take more time, workers, and funds than one can imagine will be available.

In spite of archeologists' traditional preoccupation with classification, a universally accepted system has never been devised. Until one is developed, archeology will continue to be plagued by descriptions that are not comparable with one another. It is clearly worth the effort to develop and learn better methods of handling basic data.

Determining the Uses of Artifacts

As we mentioned earlier, classification and description often precede an archeologist's knowledge of what the artifacts were used for. The "ceramic strips" are a case in point; they can be classified easily as being similar to one another and different from any other objects. The question remains, however, "What were they used for?" We might even ask that question of an object whose primary use we can name. Think about all the ways we use screwdrivers. There is no reason to assume that many of the artifacts made by prehistoric peoples were not also used for multiple purposes. If that is the case, we may have trouble inferring functions because we have only a limited set of clues to work with. These clues are the shape, size, and material of the object; its context in a site; evidence of wear or use on it; and analogy with the way similar objects are used today.

As an example, let us consider a **hand-stone (mano)** made of a hard, coarse rock that is used for grinding seeds. Its size, shape, and material as well as analogy readily help us infer this. Context in the site might also be useful, especially if it was associated with a **metate** (basal grinding slab) and a mealing bin where corn was ground. The same stone, however, may have been used on occasion to crack open bones to remove the marrow, to throw at a camp dog stealing food, to break firewood, to grind a lump of red ochre into paint powder, to pound a tent-peg into the earth, and so on. Most of these uses could not be recognized in the clues we can observe, so that our inclination is to relate the tool to its most obvious use, in this example, the grinding of seeds.

As we have seen before, evidence available does not give us sufficient information to determine the use of "ceramic strips" and other objects are equally ambiguous. Because they are relatively rare, such objects are usually ascribed a place in the ceremonial or symbolic culture. Judd (1959b:290) has written: "Unusual pieces are the sore thumbs of an archeological collection. There is no taxonomic pocket into which they can be dropped conveniently. Their very uniqueness makes them conspicuous and tempts the finder to specu-lation." As a result of speculation, one frequently finds these artifacts labeled "ceremonial object" in archeological reports.

Ideally we would like to be able to look at a tool and "see" its use in the signs of wear. A promising line of investigation in this regard is the micro-scopic examination of the edges or working areas of tools. Through this kind of analysis it may be possible one day to tell whether a long pointed object of chipped stone is a tip for a spear, a skinning knife, or a saw. Although this kind of study is still in its infancy, perhaps through the analysis of some of the large museum collections of ethnographic stone tools, whose method of use is definitely known, we will be able to identify positively the distinctive wear pat-terns occurring on meat-cutting flint knives, skin-dressing tools, fiber-shredding implements, and the like.

Ethnographic Analogy

When we say that an object looks like an axe or loom weight or whatever, we are employing analogy. That is, we think an artifact looks like something that we know and use ourselves or that other people have been described as using. Since prehistory is preindustrial, the closest analogies are to be found among people who today are living or were recently living under what we would call primitive conditions. People who still make tools of stone, who hunt and gather wild species for their food, or who practice farming with only simple equipment, are likely to use implements that are similar to what we find archeologically. By observing the tools such people use and their ways of life, archeologists can often identify objects found in sites and get much better ideas of how ancient peoples may have lived.

In this chapter, our principal interest is in the identification of tools and how they are manufactured or used, and in most cases this is a simple, straightforward process. In some instances it is still possible to carry out fieldwork among people who use analogous tools, but in most cases, archeologists depend on the extensive descriptive ethnographies, accounts by travelers which were written during the great era of world exploration since the fifteenth and sixteenth centuries, and museum collections of artifacts. As a matter of fact, some of these early travelers themselves saw the possibility of using their observations as a guide to the past. Père Lafitau in his *Moeurs des sauvages americains comparées aux moeurs des premiers temps* (1724) produced one of the first attempts at a systematic comparative ethnography by comparing the Native Americans' tools and customs with those of "antiquity," by which Lafitau meant mainly the peoples described in Homer's *Odyssey*.

Ethnography is one of the subjects that student archeologists are usually expected to study. The point is well made by MacAlister (1949:99) in a book on the archeology of Ireland, in which he says,

> It is not too much to say that a study of the contemporary cultural ethnology of the South Sea Islands must now be regarded as a *necessary* preliminary to any serious study of the cultural ethnology of Ireland down to at least 1500 years ago. A student of Prehistoric Ireland may go to school under the instruction of a lowly Arunta of Central Australia, without the least sense of incongruity; and he will assuredly come back from his teachers enlightened with an illumination which he could never have drawn from any other source.

It may seem rather extreme to compare aborigines in Australia with the prehistoric Irish, and in many details it certainly would be. Most archeologists would restrict interpretations by analogy to cultures that have a similar subsistence level and approximately the same ecological background. In this way, it would be appropriate to use modern Eskimos as a guide to the way their ancestors lived, and perhaps to the way Ice Age man lived during the Upper Paleolithic. But it would be much less revealing, and perhaps not at all relevant, to compare Eskimo artifacts with those made by aborigines in Australia or Bushmen in Africa, even though all of these people are still in the "Stone Age."

We are on much surer grounds in interpreting the way or ways in which a prehistoric object was used or the processes by which it was produced when there has been historical continuity of culture. The study of prehistory is considerably aided by citing persistences, in the peasant or folk cultures of the

modern period, of forms or practices that are similar to archeological occurrences. This is sometimes called the "direct-historical approach," and it provides
the opportunity, if one works back in time from historic sites occupied by identified groups, to determine historical continuity of culture complexes that have
been ethnographically identified. An archeological example is Kehoe's (1958)
attempt to settle the problem of the function of rings of boulders found in the
Great Plains area. By gathering ethnographic examples he was able to demonstrate that the stone circles are **tipi rings.**

Context

When archeologists have the good fortune of finding artifacts where they were
used, they have an excellent chance of determining their function. Unfortunately,
prehistoric peoples, like ourselves today, kept their houses clean, used their belongings until they were worn out, and then discarded the remains in trash
heaps. A lot of archeological finds consist of just this: worn out artifacts lying
where they were disposed of. The context tells us this even if the appearance of
the artifacts might not. Sometimes, however, people abandoned their belongings
where they were being used and then never returned. When we find these kind
of sites, we can often tell how objects were used by their context.

Take a simple object like a bone awl. This is a splinter of bone that has
been polished down to make a slender point at one end. The name we give it
suggests that it was used to poke holes in leather, separate fibers in weaving
baskets, and so on. Since most of these are found broken and discarded, we can
seldom do more than suggest their use. Such implements are known, however,
to be used today by women as applicators of eye makeup. If they were found in
a site along with a palette of cosmetic colors in the women's part of a house,
we would be able to do much more toward reconstructing the way of life and
the activities that took place than if the bone had been found in the trash. In
this example, context has allowed us to narrow down the possible uses of the
bone "awl."

Context frequently allows us at least to tell in what area of activity certain ambiguous objects may have been used. It is sometimes said that when
archeologists cannot tell what something is, they call it a "ceremonial piece."
If such an object is found in a temple or by an altar, such a supposition may be
supportable. At least the context would tell us that the objects were used in
places where religious activities were carried out. If they are not found in houses
and in domestic refuse, the case may be stronger. Once again, context has enabled us to narrow down some possibilities, although in this example it has not
necessarily told us how the particular object was used or what it is.

For the most part, unless we have very good ethnographic analogies, we
can only guess at the chief uses of many objects we find in sites, because the
contexts in which they are found are not themselves specific to particular tasks
or uses. Household debris that includes tools, toys, and garbage, left by all
members of a family of all ages and sexes, is not sufficiently precise. We should

also bear in mind that identifying an object is not the same as understanding its use. Many objects that we regard as mundane and worthy of no special attention are involved in seemingly esoteric rites of which we could have no guess without firsthand knowledge. For most of prehistory, these social correlates are, of course, lost to us, but when we read some of the modern ethnographic accounts we can imagine that they did exist. In illustration, we cite the paper by Sandin (1962) on the "Whetstone Feast" of the Iban of Sarawak. Among the Iban, after several bad harvests or because new families must have ceremonially blessed whetstones to sharpen iron farming tools, perhaps 30 separate rituals are performed during the ceremony. The events that together form the "feast" include making offerings to the good spirits; bloody sacrifice of pigs and chickens; making small ceremonial huts for storing farm tools; collecting and offering worn-out household tools to the spirits; washing, cleaning, and oiling of old whetstones; playing music; singing and dancing; combing the hair of live pigs; feasting and wine drinking; bathing of pigs; and divining future agricultural success from the whetstones. This ceremony may be taken as one example (how typical it is we do not profess to know) of the complexity of social action that can involve a simple tool the archeologist would normally assume to be merely utilitarian. The complicated ritual of the Iban would not be in the least inferable, either as a general fact or in any detail, from the whetstones as archeological specimens. Only if the institution of blessing whetstones by farming people was widely observed would an archeologist have reason to suggest the possibility that the Iban whetstones (if they were found as archeological examples) may have been ritually sanctified, but even this would be the sheerest guess. The only hint we would have, and this is a very slim one, would be the recorded fact that whetstones are sequestered in the loft of the house after the farming season is over. Archeologically speaking, the association of the whetstone with the housefloor might come about with the abandonment and disintegration of the house, provided, of course, that the occupants of the house did not take with them their sacred whetstone when they moved out.

Replicative Experiments

Many archeologists have attempted to duplicate methods by which artifacts were made and to carry out activities in which they were used. The best-known of these are the experimental flint chippers who have succeeded in duplicating virtually every technique known to prehistoric man. The consequence of this has been that archeologists now have a very much heightened appreciation of what skills and materials are actually necessary to produce different effects. This in turn will be of aid to typologists who need to know which attributes of stone tools are important.

The experiments that go further and use the tools are also enlightening. Some archeologists have become proficient at everything from skinning and butchering bison to making pottery, from building log cabins and lean-tos to drilling holes in shell beads. In many cases these experiments have served only to show how something could have been done, without proving that prehistoric people did it that way. When these experiments are carried a step further and consider the traces of use on the objects, they may permit positive identification of artifacts. Thus, if the skinning of buffalo results in a particular kind of edge wear on a flint knife, this wear can be compared with wear on "knives" found at prehistoric bison-butchering sites. If the wear on both sets of "knives" is the same, then the prehistoric ones were presumably used in the same way as the experimental ones. On the other hand, if the prehistoric artifacts show a different kind of wear, either the experimental process must have been different or the prehistoric objects were used for something other than skinning.

Analysis

Artifacts and the places where we find them are the tangible clues of ancient activities. The artifacts themselves represent a series of actions, decisions, and uses. At some time, the material for each artifact was chosen, it was made according to a plan, it was used, and then eventually discarded and finally found by an archeologist. The artifacts tell us many things about a people or about particular persons if we learn to read the messages they bear. To help in this task, archeologists depend on many technical analyses that can be made by metallurgists, chemists, physicists, geologists, botanists, and zoologists. Some of these specialists study artifacts to determine the origin of their raw material, the processes by which they were made, and the uses to which they were put. Other specialists examine the plant and animal remains for clues of diet, domestication, and local environment. Sites themselves may also be studied to tell how they were formed, how long they were occupied, and perhaps what they contained when visual traces have disappeared.

In studying the ways things were made and the ways people used materials, one gets very close to seeing actual artisans at work. A stone tool or a pot becomes an object that was crafted for a purpose and used. When we determine through replicative experiments or by analytic techniques what went into the making of an object, we gain an appreciation that is impossible if we look only at the external form of the artifact. How many of us can feel what it is to stand before the forge and force hot iron to yield to our hammer? How many of us can "hear" the knappers chipping out arrowheads around the campfire? How many of us can feel the exertion of moving a 30-ton boulder 100 miles without benefit of wheels and motors? How can we understand the way the locally available material enabled one people to prosper and left another frustrated? What is it like to wield a bronze sword against an attacker whose weapon is steel?

What practice, what discipline, what strength, what industry was required to make and use the objects that sustained life in the past? We scarcely know how our own forebears lived without automobiles, telephones, running water, and refrigeration, let alone what life is like without paper. Our history books and television programs are remarkably uninformative on these matters and only by *doing* can we get the feel for what was involved. In some instances we can do ethnography and participate in cultures where ancient practices are still being carried out; in most we must depend on analyses that help us determine how things were done, and on experiment that allows us to try it out.

There are dozens of sophisticated laboratory and instrumental analytic techniques available for study of archeological remains, and with a little encouragement there might be dozens more. The problem is not so much in devising ways to look at objects, but rather to find techniques that will help us solve archeological problems. It matters little how elegant an analysis is if it tells us nothing we want to know. The following pages serve only to give some impression of the range of things that one can learn through technical analysis.

Analysis of Pottery

Classification of ceramics depends on knowledge of their attributes. Such attributes as shape, texture, and design are readily identified visually by an archeologist, but there are other qualities whose presence may be equally valuable for identification. Among these are the way pots were made, firing conditions, nature of the paste or glaze used, and other surface finishing. Such data may help to distinguish among wares at one site, or to determine the place where the pottery was made. Other qualities, such as hardness, porosity, luster, strength, color, and mineral content, can also be readily determined, but often such details are of little use to archeologists.

The main tools used by a ceramist are binocular and petrographic microscopes, with which he can identify most of the culturally important attributes of sherds. A binocular microscope is necessary for identifying paste and tempering material, and often nothing more is needed. If more detailed analysis is required, the petrographic microscope will reveal the mineral composition of the tempering material used in the pottery. Spectrographic analysis and differential thermal analysis are two other techniques for identifying the chemical composition of sherds.

What these analyses do, primarily, is chart changes in the ways pottery was made and help determine where the clays were obtained or the pots made. In many instances, for example, one may suspect that a pot was traded into a site. With proper analysis, it may be possible to say that the pot was not made from local clay or that it was made from clay found at another site. Analyses of pottery may also include studies of the temperature at which it was fired, the kind of minerals used in its paint or glaze, and studies of the use of the pots through an examination of residues still clinging to the insides.

Analysis of Metal and Stone

Quantitative chemical analysis of metal or stone artifacts can yield valuable information about techniques of manufacture and composition. Such knowledge can lead to information about where the artifact was made and where the stone or metal or ore was obtained. Techniques of analysis are varied, and the investigator chooses the one that promises to provide information needed to solve the problem. Relatively simple chemical analysis may be sufficiently precise to enable the technician to determine the relative proportions of the major components of a smelted metal object. Such data may be of small value, however, if the archeologist, in the hope of showing whether a single find may have been secured by trade, wishes to compare a metal object found in one region with those found abundantly in another region. Here a more precise quantitative analysis of a series of elements present will be secured either by the neutron-activation analysis or x-ray fluorescence methods. The place of origin of copper artifacts can be determined by identifying a similar trace-element composition in copper ores.

It is equally interesting to learn how metal artifacts were made. Details of manufacture that cannot be determined by simple visual inspection may be discovered by photomicrographic examination of portions of artifacts. Such discoveries go a long way toward enlarging our knowledge of the technical skills of prehistoric peoples. As an example, we can cite the study made by Prof. Cyril Smith, Massachusetts Institute of Technology, of a copper bead dating back to about 6500 B.C., found in Tepe Ali Kosh. Because it is one of the earliest copper artifacts known, a study of its manufacture is of considerable interest. Metallographic and microscopic analyses clearly show that the artisan cold-hammered a lump of native copper into a thin sheet, that was then cut with a chisel and rolled to form the bead. In other words, the technology involved was very simple and required no knowledge of metallurgy.

The identification of places where stones were secured for making tools, ornaments, or large sculptures can tell the archeologist something about ancient procurement activities. If the source for a certain kind of flint occurs in an outcrop 10 miles away, he may conclude that the local people simply walked there when they needed more implement material, whereas if the source proves to lie at a distance of 200 miles, he will probably assume that the material was secured through a system of intertribal trade. Extensive studies of obsidian in the Near East have provided similar detailed information about the sources from which the stone was derived and the pattern of its distribution. From this kind of evidence of interregional context, archeologists have gained clues about the relations among early sites—clues that were not at all apparent from only a visual or typological study of the obsidian tools.

Analysis of Textiles

In dry refuse deposits of occupied caves or rock shelters of the American West, in dry desert areas such as Egypt or the Peruvian coast, or in acidic peat bogs, woven cloth and baskets may be preserved even though made of ordinarily perishable materials. The imprints that textiles leave on wet clay that was later baked may provide information about prehistoric cloth or basketry.

Analysis of textiles can provide a wide range of information. To begin with, it is often possible to identify the material used. Study of the fibers may lead to conclusions about whether plants or animals were domesticated. Identification of the fibers may show that they are not native to the area. Analysis of the dyes tells a great deal about the technical skill of prehistoric people, and may also give several clues about trade if the pigments are identified as originating in an area other than that in which the textiles were found. Study of the kind of weaving and type of loom used to produce a kind of cloth gives data on technical skill and, in many instances, on cultural relations. Where actual basketry that was once present has not survived, impressions or casts of basketry may be recorded on soft clay that was later fired, and by a study of these imprints a great deal about the basketry techniques may be learned. For example, in the Tehuacan Valley sites it was found that, as time passed, people learned different techniques of knotting and basketry (MacNeish, Nelken-Terner, and Johnson 1967).

Analysis of Soils

Analyses of soil help date sites, indicate how deposits were formed, and tell something of the environment at the time of formation. The persons who study soil are called pedologists, but similar work may also be done by geologists, geographers, and geomorphologists.

It is often evident how a site accumulated and was buried; if not, the information may be obtained through detailed analysis of the sediments. In most instances one can discover whether sites resulted from natural or man-made deposition; the pedologist can distinguish among water-laid, wind-laid, and man-laid deposits. This analysis is important because it helps to show whether the artifacts are *in situ* and provides information about the environment at the time of deposition.

The soil is a very important part of the ecosystem, and, as the physical base on which man lives and works, may be expected to be modified by addition or subtraction of physical and chemical constituents in accordance with the specific practices followed on the spot. Thus, a living site will ordinarily experience the addition of inorganic and organic trash incidental to the occupation process.

Human organic wastes are rich in nitrogen, phosphorus, and calcium, and where people of minimal sanitary practices have lived these elements will be concentrated in the soil. There will be a gradual loss of these constituents over time in an open-air site; therefore quantitative differences in soil chemistry may be a means of relative dating (Cook and Heizer 1965).

Every single item of organic origin that has once been present in a site in complete form but has decayed into a formless chemical residue can, theoretically, be determined by chemical analysis. The present authors believe that chemical techniques now available could be used to analyze the soils of prehistoric sites and could produce information on the kinds, and to some extent the quantities, of perishable items once present. Practically nothing has been attempted along this line, and it stands as one of the great opportunities for future development in prehistory. For example, it is known that the maize plant has an affinity for absorbing zinc, copper, and aluminum in the form of trace elements from the soils in which the plants grow. If the population of a site ate large quantities of maize, the soil of the living site should show higher than ordinary levels of these trace elements. There are numbers of large and important prehistoric sites in Meso-America where it is assumed that maize was the staple food item, but no concrete evidence (pictorial, carbonized seeds, and so on) has been recovered. If trace-element concentrations could be established, we might be able to follow the chemical trail back in time to sites where maize was first being eaten and thus know we were dealing with people who were the first corn farmers.

Pedologists, through chemical analysis of the soil, may also be able to tell whether an observed feature in the earth is natural or man-made. For example, there may be a question whether a hole once held a post or resulted from a burrowing animal, or perhaps just from the digging by the inhabitants of a site. Analysis of the humic content of the pit compared with soil nearby may tell whether a wooden post rotted there. In acid soils, bone is usually destroyed by chemical action, but Solecki (1953:382–383) was able to show in the Natrium site, West Virginia, from a very high phosphate concentration in what were believed to be grave pits—but in which no visible signs of bone were apparent —that the pits had at one time contained bones, presumably human skeletons.

There is no shortage of similar examples in archeological publications, but the point should still be made that chemical and other analysis of the soils in sites remains one of the most promising avenues for research. Unlike the traditional studies of artifacts, some of these techniques will afford us the chance to see into the past where nothing is literally visible.

Analysis of Animal and Plant Remains

Aside from artifacts, bones and remains of plants are the most abundant materials usually recovered from sites. These remains, when properly identified and interpreted, provide information on diet, the presence or absence of domestication, prehistoric environments, and special cultural activities. The identifications and analyses are usually made by zoologists and botanists whose special interests are in archeological problems that, because of cultural practices, make interpretation of these remains especially difficult.

The initial and simple step in studying bones is to identify the species present. When this is done, we have a rough idea of what people were eating and which domestic animals they may have had. If the analysis can be taken a step further to compute the relative proportions of each species, we can infer how important each was in the meat element of the diet. In turn, this information gives us an impression of the activities required to obtain the dietary meat. Since animals occupy specific environments within an area, people had to go there to hunt them. Thus we also get an idea of the territories exploited by people in gaining their subsistence.

The animal bones may also tell us something about the environment at the time the site was occupied. Many animals have very specific requirements for food and are confined to places where the temperature, rainfall, vegetation, and terrain are suitable. When zoologists have discovered through studies of modern species what their environmental requirements are, they may use this information to help infer the environments required by the prehistoric animals. This is especially important when the archeologist thinks that climate or environment may have changed and had an effect upon the human populations of an area. It is unfortunate, however, that most species of animals hunted by man are tolerant of a wide enough range of environment so that relatively small local changes, which might have been important to man, are not detectable in the presence or absence of particular species.

In addition to telling which species were eaten and in what proportions, careful study of bones may also tell a great deal about hunting, butchering, and cooking practices. As we mentioned earlier, some sites are small camps where hunters sat waiting for game, and when it was killed, these sites were sometimes used as butchering stations. There are some excellent examples of hunting and butchering sites on the edge of the Great Plains where bison or mammoths were trapped in dry stream beds and then butchered. In some of these instances, the reconstructions are so detailed that archeologists can infer the month of the slaughter, the direction the wind was blowing, and the precise sequence followed in cutting up the animals. At many sites, the subsequent methods of cooking and smashing of bones for marrow can also be detected.

Potentially, then, there is a great deal of information in bones, both in their context (as at the bison drive sites) and in the bones themselves. This potential is sometimes not realizable, however, for a variety of natural and cultural reasons.

The preservation of bones depends partly on the chemistry of the soil and on the mechanical breaking the bones are subjected to. As one might expect, bones from different parts of the body are affected differently by these factors. In general, teeth are the most resistant, but do not always convey the most important information.

Cultural factors are even harder to deal with. Among some people, it has been observed that they ritually dispose of certain bones of species that are considered important and thus prevent their incorporation in the refuse archeologists are likely to dig. Another kind of social practice that would be hard to interpret archeologically occurs in the Mt. Hagen district of New Guinea, where great feasts are held at intervals of several years. At these times numbers of pigs are killed, roasted, and eaten. There is a record of 1100 animals being killed at one such feast (Riesenfeld 1950:425; Salisbury 1962). Because pigs are eaten only on such festive occasions, the great accumulation of discarded bones that one supposes results from such a feasting orgy would refer to one single event of this sort. Only certain villages hold such feasts; therefore there would eventually be a great concentration of pig bones in these sites and not in others.

A final caution is sounded by V. Watson (1955), who calls attention to the situation (also in New Guinea) where meat resources are rare and considerable reliance is placed on small feral mammals, worms, and insects that would not leave any bones. Thus, to infer that because no animal bones were found in archeological sites the people did not eat meat, or had a protein-deficient diet, would be incorrect. The example points up once more the incompleteness of the archeological record and reminds us that there may be a number of alternative explanations for either the presence or absence of some element in the refuse deposits of an archeological site.

Plant remains serve very similar purposes in archeological analysis. Although parts of plants are less likely to be preserved than bones, techniques have been devised to improve the chances of recovering them. The most important of these is flotation, where water is used to aid separation of carbonized seeds and other plant remains from the soil of the site. Perhaps more useful in the long run, however, will be pollen studies, because pollen is likely to be preserved under a greater range of conditions than seeds themselves. At this time, the difficulty of extracting the pollen from its earth matrix and of doing the microscopic analyses prevent the technique from being more widely used.

Plants are especially useful in helping make environmental reconstructions because they are more likely to be limited to narrow sets of conditions than mobile animals are. On the other hand, people might go some distance from a site to harvest plants and thus make it seem as if they were in the local environment. Again, then, cultural factors intervene in any interpretation of what these remains mean.

Both flora and fauna can give information that a site was occupied at a certain time of year. When caches of ripe seeds are found, one infers that the site was occupied during or soon after the harvest season. If animals of a certain age are found, it may indicate seasonal slaughter or that the animals were domesticated. When migratory birds are found, one can determine the seasons when they would have been present and killed. It is easier to tell when a site was occupied than to say that it was not occupied at a particular time.

Valuable clues to diet may also be derived from analysis of human feces. These **coprolites** are preserved in desiccated form in dry sites and may contain the bones of small mammals, fish, or insects, together with seed and vegetal matter that can be identified. For analyzing coprolites preserved in dry archeological sites, the late E. O. Callen of McGill University, Canada, perfected a technique of soaking for 72 hours in a 0.5 percent aqueous solution of trisodium phosphate. The softened mass is then sedimented, and a detailed microscopic examination and separation is made of all the solid matter that remains.

Coprolites of humans and other animals preserved in dry deposits usually contain pollen grains, which may indicate the season of the year when the feces were voided as well as provide an indication of the variety of local flora.

Not only would the archeologist usually like to know what the dietary range was—that is, the list of edible materials available to and exploited by the people he is studying—but in addition he would like to know the relative amounts of each food resource. He probably can never hope to secure very precise data on these subjects, but he should at least go as far as he reasonably can toward this end when collecting and intepreting the archeological facts. There are ethnographic studies reporting the percentages of animal and vegetal food in the diet of modern hunting peoples who live in a similar environment and follow a way of life similar to prehistoric people. These studies (Table 7.1) provide the archeologist with data he can compare to those he has recovered from excavations. Dry cave sites, of course, will offer nearly ideal conditions of preservation, so that by combining food residues found in refuse deposits with information on diet from coprolites a reasonably complete picture of ancient diet can be reconstructed.

Much has been written about what is termed "cultural ecology," the interaction between man and his natural environment. Man as part of the ecosystem, the triple combination of biome (plants and animals), habitat (soil and climate), and culture, must never be lost sight of in the study and interpretation of archeological materials. All general archeological reports employ the ecological approach, whether or not the author uses the word, because it is not possible to write about culture and what people did without referring to the biome and habitat. Economic systems are a result of the direct application of culture (hunting or farming tools, types of crops grown, kinds of animals hunted, and the like) to the conditions and available plant and animal life (biome). Size of the human population in an area is a reflection of the existing natural features exploited through the use of tools and cultural practices.

TABLE 7.1 Percent of Main Dietary Resources in Five North American Tribes (Data from Driver (1957), Powers (1877), Stefannson (1937), and R. White (1963)).

	Agricultural products	Wild plant products	Fish	Animal products
Colorado River Yuma	40[1]	35[2]	15	10[3]
South California[4] Inland Luiseno	—	75[5]	05	20
South California[4] Coastal Luiseno	—	40[5]	50	10
Pyramid Lake Paiute, Nevada	—	25	50	25
Arctic Eskimo	—	—	30	70

[1] Maize, beans, pumpkins
[2] Mesquite, screwbean, river and desert plants
[3] Rabbits, wood rats, ducks
[4] Estimated from variable percentages
[5] Includes acorns, seeds, greens

Technical analyses are ancillary aids to archeology (Brothwell and Higgs 1963; Hammond 1971b). In themselves they provide data that only archeologists can interpret. Before archeologists begin to dig, they should have a clear idea of the kinds of information they may be able to recover, and if they are adequately "briefed" they will have a better chance to recognize what they see, because its appearance will suggest some human action in the past. For this reason the archeologist should have read as widely as possible the findings of other excavators, so that, when he digs, as little as possible will escape his eye. This suggestion is particularly appropriate for archeologists who analyze chemical vestiges, which may not appear to be important by themselves, but which, after they are analyzed, may provide important information.

The Problem of Hoaxes and Fakes

Most archeologists will not be bothered with the "planting" in their site of specimens that do not belong there. Occasionally, however, a malicious individual or a person who does not understand the serious nature of archeological investigation will play a practical joke and bury, for later "discovery" in apparently undisturbed ground, a specimen he found elsewhere. Most archeologists will simply not stand for this kind of horseplay, and, if discovered, the practical joker will be told to leave. The most notorious instance of faking and planting of objects—in this instance, human bones—in a deposit is that of Piltdown Man. The story of this hoax has been told by J. S. Weiner (1955), who, with admirable courtesy, restrains himself from drawing the logical conclusion and naming the perpetrator. The demonstration by analytical chemical methods that the bones were forgeries was made by K. P. Oakley and his colleagues in the British Museum. An earlier instance, in which a human lower jaw was said to have been discovered in Pleistocene gravels, involved the father of Paleolithic archeology, Boucher de Perthes. Having offered a reward for finds of bones to the quarry workers in the Moulin-Quignon pit, the temptation was too much for one worker who, in 1863, presented the jaw to Boucher de Perthes and claimed, and received, his reward. The jaw was finally shown, by application of fluorine tests, to be more recent than it was alleged to be (Oakley 1964a:111–116). What is probably the earliest instance of an attempted archeological hoax in the New World concerns the sixteenth-century planting of Roman coins in a site, "discovering" them, and citing these as evidence to bolster the theory of the Old World origin of Native Americans.

Many forgeries make their appearance in museum collections, where they may be taken as genuine until someone becomes suspicious of their authenticity and examines them from a new viewpoint. It was actually for this reason that the Piltdown hoax was exposed, because it became increasingly difficult to see how the morphological anomalies of the bones could be reconciled with what was otherwise known of human evolution. More recent examples are the discovery that the remarkable Etruscan terra-cotta warrior statues in the

Metropolitan Museum of Art in New York are recent forgeries (Von Bothmer and Noble 1961) and that a well-known cast-gold figurine representing Tizoc, an Aztec lord, was of modern manufacture (Easby and Dockstader 1964).

It appears to be relatively rare for fakes to be planted in archeological sites, but most collectors who buy objects on the market are wary that they might purchase one. It was for this reason, in fact, that the technique of dating pottery by **thermoluminescence** was invented. Now there are many other techniques with which suspect objects may be tested. Some of these, such as x-rays and **xeroradiography**, look inside the object and show details of its manufacture. Other techniques examine the composition of the materials. In either case, the attempt is made to determine whether the object could be of the age ascribed to it. If the making of the object required techniques or alloys not known in ancient times, then it must be a fake. Similarly, if thermoluminscence shows a pot to have been made in the 1920s, it could not be "Aztec."

The problem that both archeologists and collectors have is that modern artisans can duplicate all the processes used by the ancients. What they lack, however, is the time and patience, so they often resort to modern methods. When they do so, they usually give themselves away to close scrutiny. This is not to say, however, that all fakes can be identified. Most archeologists would agree that when the context of a piece is gone, there is often no way to tell if it is genuine or fake. And in many cases too, the cost of finding out is not worth the effort.

DATING
THE EVENTS
IN PREHISTORY

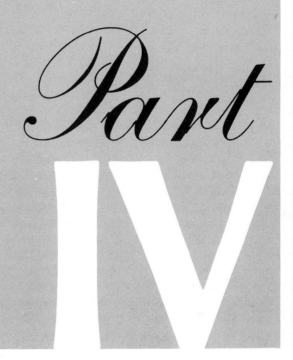

Many important problems in archeology cannot be solved at present because our techniques for deriving chronology are not well enough developed to give results of sufficient precision. This difficulty is immediately evident to anyone who has worked on a problem whose solution depends on precise dates. Such problems have to do with origins, influences, diffusions of ideas or artifacts, the direction of migrations of peoples, rates of change, and sizes of populations in settlements. In general, any question that requires a definite statement of the type, A is earlier than B, depends on dating. Then, if it can be shown that A is earlier than B, and not contemporary with or later than B, the two alternative hypotheses can be ruled false. An enormous amount of ambiguity in archeology would be removed if answers to such apparently simple questions could be obtained readily. Unfortunately, often they cannot.

The recent corrections in radiocarbon dating give a good example of the degree to which changes in dates themselves affect interpretations of cultural developments. Renfrew (1969, 1970a, 1970b) discusses some of the ways in which corrected radiocarbon dates have entirely changed conceptions of the relationship between the Neolithic and Bronze Age cultures of Europe and those of the Aegean. It had been customary to interpret the building of megalithic tombs in western Europe in terms of colonization and influence from the Mediterranean. Now it is known that these structures *precede* those that were thought to be the prototypes. For example, the final building of Stonehenge and the nearby Wessex burials in southern England had been attributed to Mycenaean influence; now they have been shown to be some 500 years older. The reversal of relative dates thus requires a complete change in the theories that were offered earlier in explanation of the building of these structures. "The moral which we should not fail to draw, however, is that the new dates should not simply change our chronologies. They render meaningless so much that has been written in recent years that there must have been serious inadequacies in our whole approach to the past, not simply in our chronology" (Renfrew 1970a:209).

Archeology is unique with respect to the other branches of the social sciences and humanities in its ability to discover, and to arrange in chronological sequence, certain episodes in human history that have long since passed without the legacy of written records. But the contributions of archeology to this sort of reconstruction depend largely on our ability to make chronological orderings, to measure relative amounts of elapsed time, and to relate these units to our modern calendar.

Few cultural interpretations in archeology and none that have unique interest with respect to anthropology generally can be made without reference to time. Moreover, none can have demonstrated validity if the chronology used is not accurate and appropriate— accurate in the sense of correct, and appropriate in the sense of applicable in the situation under study. This remark is unfortunately not trite, because there are examples in most archeological journals where its tenets were ignored. It is not pedestrian nit-picking to ask that time be controlled when it is a priori obvious that many answers (all of them if they have historical implications) depend absolutely on it. We would go further and say that there cannot be "proof" of a theory about cultural process unless time can be controlled.

Time is treated in most serious general works on archeology, but the discussion usually centers on the technical aspects of its determination; for example, how to do **tree-ring (dendrochronological)**, radiocarbon, or **cross dating**. Relatively little attention is paid to exploring the properties of time derived from each method. Because of the pronounced differences among the premises on which the various methods of dating are based, it is useful to discuss briefly the nature of archeologic time and its implications for interpreting the past.

Concepts of Chronology

Most authors (for instance, Oakley 1964b) make a basic distinction between relative and absolute chronology, but this is actually irrelevant for all uses except establishing rates of change; otherwise one always wants relative chronology, and absolute dates are decidedly secondary, if of any real interest at all. Absolute or chronometric dates state the age as the exact number of years that have elapsed since a fixed beginning date, in the fashion of a calendar. Thus, the year George Washington entered the White House as President was 1789; the year Abraham Lincoln entered the White House was 1861. Second are *relative* or *indirect* dates where the age is given, not in terms of years, but as "younger than" or "older than" some other event. For example, we can say that relative to Lincoln, Washington's presidency was earlier. Stating this relation does not tell us how much earlier, but the two events are fixed *in their proper sequential position*. Most archeological datings are of the relative type, where it is known that Culture *A* is older than Culture *C*, but how old *A* and *C* are, or how much later *C* is than *A* in terms of number of years, is unknown.

For purposes of discussion we can distinguish four bases on which all dating methods stand. Three are as follows: cyclical events such as the movements of the sun and moon, on which most calendars are based; constants such as the speed of light or the rate of vibration of quartz crystals (at the moment of no particular interest in archeology); and progressive or cumulative change as in the decay of C^{14} molecules, the cumulative increase in the hydration layer of obsidian, or changes in the form of artifacts. A fourth basis for dating is stratigraphy. Because the relation among dating methods is not always obvious, we shall try to point out what the implications of their use in archeology may be.

Absolute Time

All of us are familiar with calendars and clocks that are based on the observed periodicity of certain natural events. Calendars give elapsed time measured relative to the movements of heavenly bodies; clocks are ultimately related to the same cycle, and time consists essentially of subdivisions of it. The important point about these measurements (and more precise measurements now in use) is that they depend on the repetition of events at uniform intervals. In this sense, a day is a day without regard to the year in which it occurs.

With calendar and clock time, it is easy to date the succession or synchrony of events anywhere in the world. It permits placing of chronologically successive but geographically separate events, and ultimately establishes the basis for studies of rates of change, differential development in separate areas, and the identification of the geographic sources of widespread cultural influences. Analogous use of time in our daily lives allows contest judges to award the prize to the first entrant with the correct answers and to pick the fastest runners in three separately run heats.

Cumulative or Progressive Change

Several of the dating methods described in Chapters 8 and 9 are based on natural phenomena whose changes can be measured and made to yield a date. The most familiar of these is radiocarbon dating, which depends on the fact that the C^{14} **isotope** decays at a known rate. Knowing the rate and the amount present in a sample enables one to calculate how many radiocarbon years have elapsed since the death of the organism whose remains are being dated. Obsidian-hydration dating also depends on progressive change: that the hydration layer on glass grows progressively deeper. A measurement of the hydration layer is thus a statement about age and can be translated into either relative or absolute dating, depending on the circumstances.

The important thing to remember about dates that are based on progressive change is that they need not be, and usually are not, directly translatable into calendar years. These are dates in their own system (for example, radiocarbon years, or obsidian-hydration years), and it is a matter for further investigation to determine the correlation between such dates and the calendar.

Relative Dating

The use of stratigraphy is ultimately the most important method for establishing relative dating (Chap. 3). It depends on the fact that earlier deposits lie under later deposits. Usually stratigraphy gives the relative ages of deposits only within a single site, although special circumstances (such as the deposition of ash layers from a single eruption of a volcano) may allow one to relate the stratigraphy of two or more sites with as much precision as one can ordinarily attain within one site.

Although stratigraphic levels give chronologic relations, they tell very little about absolute amounts of elapsed time or even of relative amounts of elapsed time. A statement that one find is "older by a foot or two" (Napier 1964:88) tells nothing about elapsed time. Stratigraphic levels represent unequal lengths of calendar time, and two such units are only accidentally of the same duration. The kind of chronology that one can derive from stratigraphy is thus limited to telling which unit is earlier, and one can infer only the barest information about relative lengths of time. Thick layers *may* have taken longer to accumulate than thin layers, but this is not always true. It should be evident that stratigraphic units in themselves cannot be related to calendars.

If the archeologist is unable to relate levels in several sites to one another by stratigraphy, he must turn to other methods, of which the most important is known as *cross dating*; it involves the comparison of artifacts found in the stratigraphic levels (Chap. 9). Stated in its simplest form, the idea behind cross dating is that similar artifacts are approximately contemporary. The greater the similarity, the closer the ages. Cross dating depends on the fact that certain artifacts—coins, types of pottery, and arrowheads—have a limited occurrence during the life of any culture. When "identical" artifacts are found at separated sites, the principle of cross dating states that the two sites are roughly the same age, namely, within the span during which the artifact was used. Some artifacts have a much shorter life span than others have, and as a consequence are better **index fossils** or **horizon markers.**

Using the occurrence of artifacts, and/or their frequencies, one can compare isolated stratigraphic units and judge whether they approach contemporaneity. In the absence of a known stratigraphic sequence somewhere, however, it may not be possible to tell, from the artifacts alone, what the relative ages of the deposits are. It is thus necessary to use stratigraphy and cross dating together to determine relative ages of sites that are separated; that is, there must be some way independent of the two occurrences in question to decide on the relative ages.

It often happens that *trends of change* can be distinguished in the archeologic record. The trend from the use of stone to bronze to iron is a simple illustration. A site in which one found flint arrowheads would ordinarily be judged earlier than a site in which one found bullets. Knowing trends of this sort, one can resort to "typological" dating, at times an exceedingly useful technique for the rough ordering of materials that are temporally exclusive and distinct in time.

Segmenting Time

Archeologists are accustomed to dividing time into periods, phases, levels, and the like; for example, "all specimens are of Mousterian or Acheuleo-Mousterian age." Periods and phases ordinarily include deposits that have several levels—in other words, the larger groupings are usually based both on stratigraphic breaks and on the changes in the content of the levels. Most students of history would agree that although change is continuous there are times when its rate or impact is increased or lessened. The exploitation of a new power source, a period of warfare, and similar discontinuous events may leave traces in the archeological site that enable one to recognize distinct periods in a cultural continuum.

For historical periods, it is not necessary to use periods or ages except as a shorthand device to denote a certain kind of activity within a certain range of time. Archeologists, however, frequently use their periods as though they were equivalent to units on a calendar. A phase comes to be thought of as we think of a decade or a century, except that instead of being so numbered, it is usually named. It is well to note, however, that such terms as "phase" are not defined by all archeologists to mean the same thing. Thus, although phases segment time, they do so differently for different archeologists.

Implications of Archeological Time

In fact, there is no such thing as *an* archeologic time. From the preceding discussion, we can see that there are many kinds of time that range from years of known and constant duration, to the life span of an artifact type that is of unknown and unpredictable duration, to the stratigraphic levels of a site whose principal chronologic significance is that they demarcate earlier from later strata. In practical terms, archeologists use and must interpret dates from a wide variety of sources whose degree of precision is highly variable and whose correlation to absolute chronology is uncertain and not mutually commensurable. Much of archeological dating, in other words, represents more a statement of faith than a sober appraisal of proved evidence. It can hardly be stressed too strongly that this is a sad statement of affairs for scientists whose chief claim to fame is their ability to interpret unique and long-forgotten records of man's past. It is not going too far to say that many professional archeologists have overstepped the bounds of credibility in assigning relative and absolute dates to sites that on closer inspection have yielded only the most tenuous evidence of the claimed age. It is especially true that many interpretations that absolutely depend on accurate dating assume a precision that is far greater than warranted. It is also true that archeologists have begun to pose questions that require far more accurate dates. The chapters that follow will describe the present state of the art of dating archeological remains. But by this time the student should be sufficiently warned that, in spite of occasional impressive sophistication in techniques, most dating methods are far too imprecise to help us much with a number of the most important problems we now are grappling with. Even today, despite a full century of digging, analyzing materials, and publishing findings, archeologists are not in possession of enough facts to do more than sketch the history of man in any except the broadest terms.

Chapter 8

DATING BY PHYSICAL-CHEMICAL METHODS

Radiocarbon Dating

For archeologists, one of the most important discoveries of the twentieth century was made just after World War II. In 1949 a method for determining the absolute age of certain ancient and previously undatable organic materials was announced (Fig. 8.1). The method was devised to measure the amount of low-level radioactivity of carbon remaining in ancient and dead material of organic origin. With this measurement it was possible to tell when a plant or animal had died. Thus archeologists could learn the approximate year in which a tree was cut for a house beam, how long ago a man represented by a mummy had died, or when the fire had been burned in a fireplace. The immediate enthusiasm of archeologists went far beyond the limits of the method as it was first developed. Most archeologists had had "guess dates" for their materials, and they were aware that a system of absolute dating would probably invalidate

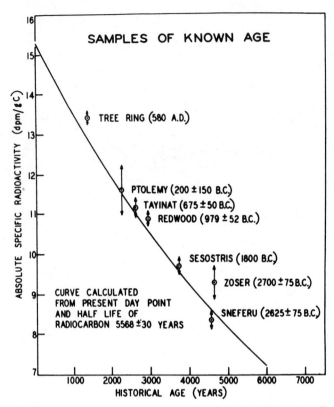

FIG. 8.1 W. F. Libby's first results in testing the reliability of radiocarbon age measurements with samples of known age from Egypt (W. F. Libby, Radiocarbon Dating, Fig. 1.)

some of their guesses. Unfortunately, some of the new dates were so far off the expected, and many so internally inconsistent, that some archeologists simply chose to ignore them. After this pendulum swing of enthusiasm, more sober judgments prevailed, and the "bugs" in the system were largely worked out. The radiocarbon method for dating has proved itself useful when the laboratory uses all possible care and the archeologist supplies material that has been collected with proper methods. In view of its importance, carbon-14 (C^{14}) dating will be described here in some detail.

In essence, radiocarbon dating is based on the following argument. Neutrons produced by cosmic radiation enter the earth's atmosphere and react with the nitrogen isotope N^{14}. The reaction produces a heavy isotope of carbon, C^{14}, which is radioactive and has a half-life of about 5730 years.[1] Libby's (1955:2) equation describing the reaction is

$$N^{14} + n = C^{14} + H^1$$

[1] The original Libby value for the half-life of C^{14} was 5568 ± 30 years. Research currently being carried on at several laboratories will result in final agreement on determination for this constant. For the present, the Fifth Radiocarbon Dating Conference,

Chemically, C^{14} seems to behave exactly as ordinary nonradioactive carbon, C^{12}, does. Thus, the C^{14} atoms readily mix with the oxygen in the earth's atmosphere, together with C^{12}, and eventually enter into all living things as part of the normal oxygen-exchange process that involves all living plants and animals. As long as matter is living and hence in exchange with the atmosphere, it continues to receive C^{14} and C^{12} atoms in a constant proportion. After death the organism is no longer in exchange with the atmosphere and no longer absorbs atoms of contemporary carbon.

After the death of an organism the C^{14} contained in its physical structure begins to disintegrate at the rate of one half every 5730 years; thus, by measuring the amount of radiocarbon remaining, one can establish the time when the plant or animal died. Half-life (t ½) is measured by counting the number of beta radiations emitted per minute (cpm) per gram of material. Modern C^{14} emits about 15 cpm/g, whereas C^{14} 5700 years old should emit about 7.5 cpm/g. In the disintegration the C^{14} returns to N^{14}, emitting a beta particle in the process. Thus:

$$C^{14} = B - + N^{14} +$$

There were several assumptions about the process that had to be verified before it could be used with confidence; for example, that the rate of cosmic radiation through long periods of time has remained constant; that the concentration of C^{14} in the reservoir of exchangeable carbon on the earth and in the atmosphere has not changed; and that C^{14} is distributed evenly throughout the atmosphere and living matter. Verification of these assumptions involved such things as possible errors in the calculation of a half-life, instances of differential levels of C^{14} among living things, the effect of atom bomb explosions on the production of new C^{14} by atmospheric enrichment ("atom bomb effect"), and the effect on the ratio of C^{14} to C^{12} of burned fossil fuels such as coal and oil, which add nonradioactive carbon to the atmospheric reservoir ("Suess effect").

For a number of years it was thought that the possible errors mentioned here were of relatively minor consequence, but more recent intensive research into radiocarbon dates, compared with calendar dates, shows that the natural concentration of C^{14} in the atmosphere has varied sufficiently to affect dates significantly, especially for periods older than 1500 B.C. The principal variables in the production of C^{14} are thought to be solar activity, climatic change, and variations in the magnetic dipole of the earth. Because scientists have not been able to predict the amount of variation theoretically, it has been necessary to find a parallel dating method of absolute accuracy to assess the correlation between C^{14} dates and the calendar.

The latest research in radiocarbon dating has centered on the attempt to correlate the dates with tree rings. At the present time it has been possible to

---

Cambridge, 1962, has accepted 5570 ± 30 years (the original value) as the half-life of radiocarbon, and made the decision to use A.D. 1950 as the standard for computing dates B.P. (Before Present). The best value now obtainable for the half-life is, however, 5730 ± 40 years. To convert published dates to new half-life, multiply them by 1.03 (*Radiocarbon 5*, 1963, "Editorial Statement").

extend a correlation back as far as 8200 years, although the data for more recent times are much more complete. The older dates depend on the few trees of great age, principally bristlecone pines, that still remain. The corrections that are presently available (Table 8.1) show that radiocarbon years and calendar years begin to diverge significantly after 1500 B.C., and from then until the limits of the correlation method are reached, the radiocarbon dates get progressively younger with respect to calendar dates. Thus, a radiocarbon date of 2200 B.C. is about 500 years too young, according to the best estimated calendar age. There is some question whether the trend shown in the radiocarbon dates can be extrapolated to still older periods; if it can we may expect to find an error of 20–30 percent, or 2000–2500 years, in the dates of older samples. It is important to stress, however, that *"it is presently impossible to determine on theoretical ground, what the relationship is between a radiocarbon date and the true age of a sample"* (Stuiver and Suess 1966:536). Thus we should adopt the habit of dating events in *radiocarbon years* rather than in calendar years, except when it is possible to use the correction factor. In all cases, however, the radiocarbon date should be included so that the reader will be aware that correction has been applied.

Charred wood is the material most often used for radiocarbon dating because it is the likeliest to be preserved and found in sites. Charcoal is chemically inert and will last forever if it is not broken, pulverized, and dispersed. Organic material that is not charred will usually rot away except in dry sites where wood, soot, grasses, dung, paper, and bark may all be present. It is also possible to date antlers, tusks, shells, calcareous **tufa** formed by algae, lake muds (gyttja), and peat, all of which are of organic origin.

For many years it has been known that burned bone often gave anomalous results when compared with dates derived from charcoal. The problem had to do with the fact that bones absorbed some radioactivity from ground water through a chemical exchange. This problem was resolved, and in the process an important technique of radiocarbon dating developed, when it was determined that collagen, a bone protein, could be extracted and dated. This process deals with bone that has not been burned, and it has the advantage of dating the bone rather than its association with charcoal. That is, it is possible to date a skeleton directly, even though it was placed into deposits of another age, as is often the case when people bury the dead in archeological sites.

The amounts of organic material required to make a reliable age determination vary with individual laboratories. For example, Geochron Laboratories[2] (Cambridge, Mass.) operates as a commercial service,[3] having a fixed charge per age determination. It recommends the following amounts of material: charcoal,

---

[2] All radiocarbon dates are numbered in a lineal series by each laboratory. The laboratory is identifiable by the prefix letter(s); thus, for example, GRO = Groningen. Since 1959, dates from all laboratories are published in *Radiocarbon* (Vol. 1, 1959; Vol. 2, 1960, etc).

[3] A complete listing of laboratories, including those that do commercial contract dating, may be found in *Radiocarbon*.

TABLE 8.1 MASCA Correction Factors. Suggested Method of Adjustment of Radiocarbon Dates to Calendar Dates Based on the Determination of Average Deviations for 250-Year Periods in the A.D. and B.C. Eras Except for the First and Last Two Periods Which Span Longer Intervals of Years. C¹⁴ Dates are Calculated with the 5730 Half-life (Michael and Ralph 1971:28, Table 1.5).

Time Period Represented by Radiocarbon Dates	Average Deviation of C^{14} Dates (+ = younger, - = older)	Calendric Period Represented by Precisely Dated Tree-Ring Samples	Number of Samples
A.D. 1525 – 1879	+ 50	A.D. 1500–1829 (329 years)	12
A.D. 1250 – 1524	0	A.D. 1250–1499	7
A.D. 975 – 1249	0	A.D. 1000–1249	8
A.D. 700 – 974	– 50	A.D. 750– 999	4
A.D. 450 – 699	– 50	A.D. 500– 749	11
A.D. 200 – 449	– 50	A.D. 250– 499	9
25 B.C.–A.D. 200	– 50	A.D. 1– 249	7
225 B.C.– 26 B.C.	0	249– 1 B.C.	7
450 – 226 B.C.	+ 50	499– 250 B.C.	7
675 – 451 B.C.	+ 50	749– 500 B.C.	7
900 – 676 B.C.	+100	999– 750 B.C.	8
1125 – 901 B.C.	+100	1249–1000 B.C.	10
1325 – 1126 B.C.	+150	1499–1250 B.C.	4
1550 – 1326 B.C.	+200	1749–1500 B.C.	9
1750 – 1551 B.C.	+200	1999–1750 B.C.	6
1900 – 1751 B.C.	+300	2249–2000 B.C.	12
2050 – 1900 B.C.	+400	2499–2250 B.C.	4
2225 – 2051 B.C.	+500	2749–2500 B.C.	6
2450 – 2226 B.C.	+550	2999–2750 B.C.	6
2650 – 2451 B.C.	+550	3249–3000 B.C.	7
2850 – 2651 B.C.	+650	3499–3250 B.C.	5
[3700 – 2951 B.C.]	+700	[4395–3645 B.C.] (750 years)	11
[4366 – 4060 B.C.]	+750	[5116–4810 B.C.] (306 years)	9
		Total	176

8–12 grams; wood, 10–30 grams; shell, 30–100 grams; peat, 10–25 grams; bone, 20–100 grams. (For more complete lists, see Polach and Golson 1966:Table 3, and Ralph 1971.)

Libby's original laboratory apparatus was primitive compared to that now in use. He used what is called the "screen-wall" technique, in which he reduced the organic material to carbon and then smeared it on the inner surface of a specially built Geiger counter. By contrast, modern methods change the carbon to a gas—carbon dioxide (CO_2), acetylene (C_2H_2), or methane (CH_4)—and count its level of radioactivity in a proportional counter (for photographs of apparatus, see Briggs and Weaver 1958). There has been a considerable gain in accuracy and reliability over the older technique, because the sample is not handled after it has been made ready for conversion to a gas. Thus the danger of radioactive contamination from the atmosphere, a disruptive factor introduced by twentieth-century atomic bomb tests, has been eliminated. With the gas-proportional counters, a much smaller sample is needed to make an age determination.

Some laboratories use Geiger-Muller counters or liquid scintillation spec-trometers. Neither of these methods has yet proved better, for routine work, than use of the gas-proportional counter.

Another important refinement is isotopic enrichment. With the original methods, the effective range of radiocarbon dating was about 30,000 years. With the more modern systems, 40,000–50,000 years is the practical limit, but for sam-ples of great significance an elaborate, expensive, and time-consuming process of isotopic enrichment can be carried out that will enable the scientist to ascertain the age of material as old as 75,000 years (Grootes et al. 1975). However, the problems of contamination are much greater with very old samples, as a prac-tical example will make clear.

The addition of 1 percent of modern carbon to a sample that is 5570 years old increases the specific radioactivity by 2 percent, so that the measured age of the sample is too small by 160 years, an error of 3 percent. For a sample that is 23,000 years old, the addition of 1 percent of modern carbon increases the specific radioactivity by 16 percent, corresponding to 1,300 years, an error of 5 percent. But for a sample that is 67,000 years old, the addition of 1 percent of modern carbon makes the radioactivity 40 times what it should be. The indi-cated age would be 37,000 years; this bears no relation to the true age and depends only on the degree of contamination (Aitken 1961:97).

Quite apart from matters of possible contamination, no sample is worth dating unless it is archeologically dependable. Archeologists must make sure that their samples are from undisturbed deposits. They should be prepared to tell the laboratory technicians how the sample was collected, the kind of deposit in which it was found, the kind of pretreatment they have given it—washing or sorting out of foreign material by hand—whether there were roots or humus-rich soil horizons near the sample, and anything else that might bear on its dependability. Here the responsibility rests squarely on the shoulders of the archeologists, who must take care to submit only samples of high quality.

It is necessary before leaving the subject of radiocarbon dating to men-tion two more topics. The first is the statistical expression of the dates and what it means. All dates are expressed in terms of a plus-or-minus factor. In the case of a date given as 3621±180 years before the present, the plus-or-minus 180 is the range of one standard deviation; it indicates that 68 percent of the time the true age of the sample will lie between 3441 and 3801 years—that is, 3621 + 180/3621 − 180—before the present. If we double the plus-or-minus factors, there will be a 95 percent probability—19 chances of 20—that the true age lies within these limits (that is, 3261–3981 years before the present). But "there are *no* limits within which the true age lies with absolute certainty" (Aitken 1961:98). We thus see that although the radiocarbon method is usually referred to as a method for securing absolute dates, it is in fact not an exact or precise time-determination method. At best, it provides dates that are more probably correct than wrong within the plus-or-minus standard deviation.

The second matter is the use of B.P. (Before Present), as opposed to B.C. (Before Christ) or A.D. (Anno Domini), when stating the age of a sample. For archeologists, the use of B.P. dates makes little sense. The machines count the years that have elapsed since the time the organism died, but archeologists need not. When dates are written B.P., persons reading them must continually update them. The compromise adopted in 1962 by the Fifth Radiocarbon Dating Conference—to use A.D. 1950 as the standard for computing dates B.P.—is not entirely satisfactory, although it is decidedly preferable to using a constantly changing date. The main problem that will arise from using A.D. 1950 is that dates published before the agreement have to be adjusted. (The index to radiocarbon dates assembled by Deevey, Flint, and Rouse [1967] makes this adjustment.) A second problem is that archeologists as well as nonprofessionals have difficulty adjusting their thinking about the past when they must use several time scales. The mistakes made when one must shift between A.D. and B.C. are annoying at best.

Radiocarbon, published by the American Journal of Science, lists dates determined by the half-hundred active radiocarbon laboratories, and an index to these for the years 1950–1965 has been published (1967). Since 1969 an annual index of radiocarbon dates has been published in *Radiocarbon*.

Other Radioactive Dating Methods

Several other methods of dating depend on radioactive decay of elements. Many of these techniques cannot be applied to archeological materials because they are only effective on extremely old materials or because they are based on material ordinarily not found in archeological sites. One method that is valuable for dating very old archeological deposits is based on the decay of potassium-40.

Potassium-Argon Dating

The potassium-argon (K-Ar) dating method was widely hailed after its development in the 1950s because it promised to yield dates in the span between C^{14} and the time of the earliest traces of man. Its value was soon proved in connection with the dating of volcanic materials associated with human bones and artifacts at Olduvai Gorge. In the last decade, there have been a number of refinements in the methods of measuring the ratio of potassium to argon in samples, as well as the development of a new potassium-argon method.

The original method measured the ratio of potassium-40 (K^{40}) to the gas argon-40 (Ar^{40}). This method depends on the fact that radioactive K^{40} decays at a known rate (t $\frac{1}{2} = 1.3$ billion years) to form Ar^{40}. By measuring the ratio of K^{40} to Ar^{40} in a mass spectrometer, one can calculate the age of the rocks. K-Ar dating also depends on these assumptions: that no argon was added or lost during the lifetime of the sample, and that measuring techniques are accurate. Of the three assumptions, the second is known to be incorrect in many instances; certain rocks leak argon at a greater rate than others do. For example, mica retains 80–100 percent of its argon, whereas feldspars retain 40–85 percent. Accurate dating of some of these minerals must await clearer definition of the factors that cause the leaking.

The new method measures the ratio between Ar^{40} and Ar^{39}, using a more complicated laboratory technique that involves placing the sample in a nuclear reactor and bombarding it with a beam of fast neutrons that convert some of the K^{39} to Ar^{39}. The ratio of Ar^{40} to Ar^{39} can then be calculated to give an age estimate. There are three advantages in using the new method, even though it is much more difficult technically and is no more accurate for good samples than the conventional K-Ar method. The advantages are: (1) many dates can be taken from one sample, thus reducing the statistical error; (2) samples that are weathered can be dated; and (3) contamination of samples may be detectable and if so may be corrected for.

The value of the K-Ar dating is that potassium-rich rocks or ash deposits laid down by natural means before or following occupation of a site may be dated. Thus far the major application of the method has been on archeological sites in East Africa, such as Olduvai Gorge in Tanganyika, where L. S. B. Leakey has found some of the oldest known fossil hominid bones. At Olduvai the beds containing the fossils are composed of volcanic **tuffs** (consolidated volcanic ash) alternating with clays. It appears from the freshness of the tools and bones that vulcanism occurred repeatedly while the site was being occupied, and that the material was covered by ash soon after it was laid down. The tuffs make excellent dating material. The K-Ar dates from the lowest levels at Olduvai average 1,750,000 years. This age is much greater than would have been expected by many workers, and it has been questioned on stratigraphic and technical grounds. More recently stone artifacts excavated from what is interpreted as a former ground surface within a volcanic tuff layer east of Lake Rudolf, Kenya, have been dated by the K-Ar content of pumice pebbles enclosed in the tuff, which provides an age of 2.61±0.26 million years (Isaac, Leakey, and Behrensmeyer 1971; Curtis 1975:206). These are the oldest dated stone tools recovered through excavation.

Most archeological sites cannot be dated by K-Ar. It would do no good to date rocks brought into a site by man because they might well be millions of years older than the site. The major application of this method to archeology would seem to be only at sites where there has been volcanic activity that has caused the deposition of potassium-rich materials either shortly before or shortly after occupation by man.

Thermoluminescence

In 1960 Kennedy and Knopff announced a potentially useful method of dating archeological materials. This method was based on the fact that objects such as pottery that have been heated more than 400–500°C in the past could be dated by measurement of their thermoluminescent (TL) glow. Although the principle of thermoluminescence was well known, it was necessary to verify the practicality of routinely dating archeological materials. The theory seemed sound enough, but attempts to apply it to dating ancient pottery were unsuccessful in so many instances that the high hopes of many archeologists, having been raised by overconfident (and at times quite uninformed) persons, were dashed. As has occurred so often in natural science studies, what was required to develop a reliable procedure had to proceed at a slow step-by-step pace, where each of the variables could be identified and compensated for, so that gradually a controlled technique would result. Such is often the way of success in science when an idea is conceived, the theoretical basis is examined, and enthusiasm over anticipated results exceeds early test-findings. Then there is a reaction when optimism ebbs, but the effort at proving the proposition continues. Finally, with one small gain after another, the method is perfected and everyone is once more happy. The opposite, of course, may occur, when continued effort at correction fails at every step and the matter is then abandoned as beyond the technological capabilities of the generation to make the theory successfully applicable.

So, in a rough way, it has been with thermoluminescence dating, but now, after more than a decade of laboratory experiment, some reliable dating results have been achieved (Winter 1971:133–146).

By way of explaining the principles of TL dating we quote from Mazess and Zimmerman's (1966:347) article:

> Thermoluminescence (TL) is the release in the form of light of stored energy from a substance when it is heated. The phenomenon occurs in many crystalline nonconducting solids, and has been suggested as the basis of a dating technique for rocks and minerals. Naturally occurring radioactive elements in these materials are a nearly constant source of ionizing radiation. It is assumed that some of the electrons excited by this radiation become trapped in metastable states, a few electron volts above the ground state. Released from their traps by heating, the electrons return to the ground state, emitting light.
>
> Pottery accumulates such trapped electrons with time, and the amount of natural TL produced by a sherd therefore depends on the

time elapsed since its last firing. The amount of natural TL also depends on the amount of ionizing radiation present, and on the nature and number of electron traps in the material (which determine the material's sensitivity to radiation-induced TL). By taking these factors into account, natural TL has been used for dating limestones, lava flows, ice, and pottery.

There are still many problems with the method, and various laboratories have taken different approaches to their solution. As one might expect under the circumstances, there is no standard set of methods for processing and analyzing ceramics, nor is there general agreement on whether the method should be used for relative or for absolute dates. Among the problems currently under investigation is the possible contamination of the sample by the addition of radioactive particles from the soil in which it was buried, or from exposure to cosmic rays. Other studies are aimed at using thermoluminescence for the dating of non-ceramic materials. There has been some success in dating obsidian from El Chayal, Guatemala, but experiments with glass show that the potential of the method depends heavily on the amount of uranium the glass contains (Ralph and Han 1971).

Aside from dating, one application of the method is in detecting modern ceramic fakes, because it is easy to determine that a pot was recently made when it fails to show an accumulation of TL.

At the present time active research on thermoluminescence is being carried out in laboratories at the following institutions: The University Museum, Philadelphia; the University of California at Los Angeles; the University of Wisconsin; the Research Laboratory for Archaeology, Oxford; Nara and Kyoto Universities in Japan; and the Danish Atomic Energy Commission, Roskilde, Denmark.

Natural Low-Level Radioactivity (Beta Activity)

Buried archeological materials vary in low-level radioactivity in the form of beta and alpha activity measured with a proportional-flow counter. Correlations between radioactivity of the soil-matrix environment and the material (bone or teeth are excellent subjects) can be determined.

The method shows great promise as a means of making distinctions in the relative age of two finds, of detecting intrusion of recent bones into older deposits, and of checking archeological materials for their fit with postulated climatic history.

Applications of the method have been made to a number of alleged or possible finds of early human remains in order to learn whether they are contemporary with the soil layer where they were (or are said to have been) recovered, or whether they are later intrusions. Such finds as the bones of Midland Man, Texas; the Piltdown bones; Arlington Springs Man, Santa Rosa Island, California; human osseous remains from the Llano Estacado, Texas; and the Lagow

Sandpit remains from Texas have been examined by radiometric assay, and sometimes the results have enabled the investigators to decide that the bones are either ancient or relatively recent.

Lead-210 with a t ½ of 22 years is present in recently refined lead, which is a source of paint pigment. A number of forged old masters have been detected by age-dating the Pb^{210} content of the paints used (Keisch 1968). This technique has no readily applicable archeological utility but is interesting from the methodological standpoint.

Fission Track Dating

A method for dating glassy materials such as obsidian that was exposed to high heat in ancient times, glass, pottery glaze, and a wide range of rock types

> . . . depends on the spontaneous fission of U^{238} atoms contained in glass taking place at a constant rate, and leaving fission tracks (that is, detectable damage trails of nuclear fragments). Once formed, the fission tracks in a glass disappear if the glass is heated above a critical temperature. It may be assumed that the density of spontaneous fission tracks of U^{238} atoms in a glass is proportional to the lapse of time after the glass was either produced or last heated above the critical temperature, and to the density of U^{238} atoms contained in the glass. The latter can be determined from the density of U^{238} atoms which are induced by bombarding the glass with a known dose of thermal neutrons. Then the lapse of time is given approximately by the simplified formula [Time $= 6.12 \times 10^{-8} \times$ dose of thermal neutrons $\times$ (density of U^{238} fission tracks $\div$ density of U^{235} atoms)] (Watanabe and Suzuki 1969).

Fission track dating remains in the experimental stage, although several applications have been made in archeology. The most important of these was the corroboration of the K-Ar date for Bed I of Olduvai Gorge, where the Leakeys found two varieties of early man. The K-Ar date of 1.75 million years, which was much older than expected at the time, was substantiated by fission track dating of volcanic pumice from the same geologic bed. The fission track age was two million years (± 0.3). Another archeological application may eventually help resolve one of the most vexing questions in American prehistory: When did man arrive in the Western Hemisphere? In that connection, ages between 270,000 ($\pm 100,000$) and 600,000 ($\pm 170,000$) years have been obtained from volcanic pumice and ash in geologic beds above and below archeological remains at the Mexican site of Valsequillo. In this instance, the association of the site with the geologic beds remains in question, but it provides an instructive example of the reasoning involved in deciding on dates. If the site was occupied after the lower bed was deposited and before the upper, then it is between 270,000 and 600,000 years old. On the other hand, if the site is intrusive into the geologic beds, it is younger than 270,000 years. It may also be that the geologic beds have been redeposited through water action so that they have come to enclose a site which is only several thousand years old. If this is the case, the age of the geologic beds may have nothing whatsoever to do with the age of the archeological site.

Since fission track trails will begin to accumulate on the surface of a freshly chipped piece of glass such as obsidian, it is possible to secure a rough dating of the time when the obsidian artifact was flaked. For younger materials there will probably be better methods for dating such artifacts, but for very ancient examples this method can be useful, as Watanabe and Suzuki (1969) demonstrate.

Amino Acid Dating

The newest of the chemical dating techniques uses the relation between elapsed time and the degradation of proteins in fossils as a basis for estimating age of shells, bones, and teeth. The fibrous protein collagen in bone contains L-amino acids which, over time, undergo **racemization** (or **epimerization**) and change into D-amino acids. The racemization reaction involves the change of L-isoleucine to the nonprotein amino acid D-alloisoleucine. Fossil bone contains both L- and D-amino acids in proportion to the age of the bone; thus age can be calculated from the L-D amino acid ratio.

Racemization is a chemical reaction and is consequently affected by temperature and the amount of water to which the bone has been exposed in the ground. These factors present very difficult problems as far as archeology is concerned: the rate of racemization of each sample must be calibrated according to the estimated temperature and humidity. To some extent, this problem has been overcome by radiocarbon dating the collagen of a bone and then determining the L-D amino acid ratio. On the assumption that the C^{14} date is correct, the rate of racemization can be calculated and used as a basis for determining other L-D dates from the site.

Much of the research into amino acid dating has been done under controlled laboratory conditions that clearly show the factors involved in racemization rates and emphasize the magnitude of problems inherent in the technique. At this time, the dates determined for archeological material cannot be considered reliable in the absence of independent checks. Nevertheless, there is great optimism that additional research will result in improved methods of estimating age by this method. In principle, L-D amino acid dating is very attractive because it can bridge the gap between radiocarbon dating at about 40,000 years and K-Ar and other methods that are most effective on the order of hundreds of thousands of years. Further, L-D dating requires only minute samples of bone, so that for practical purposes it is nondestructive.

Recently, amino acid dating has been employed on some of the most controversial material in North America, some allegedly ancient skeletons of man. Some five skeletons from California have now given racemization dates in the range of 40,000–50,000 years, based on correlations of racemization rates determined from C^{14} dating of bone collagen. The temperature and humidity estimates on these old samples are, however, still open to question. P. Hare, one of the pioneers in developing the method, says "Probably few, if any, of the published amino acid dates are reliable. Some are possibly off by an order of magnitude (Hare 1974)."

Paleomagnetic Dating

Magnetic dating can also give absolute dates, *potentially* with an accuracy of a few decades. The method depends on changes in the earth's magnetic field. Variations in the angle of declination between magnetic north and true north and in the angle of dip of a magnetic needle have been recorded for 400 years in London and for shorter periods in other cities (Fig. 8.2). These measurements have shown that the magnetic field of the earth, as expressed in terms of angles of declination and dip, has changed, although not in easily predictable ways. Other studies have shown that a record of past angles of declination and dip is trapped in baked clay and in various kinds of sediments in lake beds. In unfired clay the magnetic fields of the magnetite and hematite grains occur at random. When clay is fired, the grains are aligned with the magnetic field of the earth surrounding them. On cooling, the alignment of grains is "frozen" and can be recorded as long as the clay is preserved intact. This permanent alignment of grains is called **thermo-remanent magnetism.** Where records of past angles of declination and dip have been kept, it is possible to compare the values obtained from a piece of clay with the plotted values of historic records and arrive at the date of the archeological specimen of fired clay.

In practice the method is severely restricted by inadequate records. In addition, for any given time the angles of dip and declination vary considerably from place to place. Reference to Figure 8.2 will show how the values for the same years in Boston, London, Rome, and Paris differ. Thus, one must not only have good records of change but also have them for areas near archeological sites. One thousand miles is a maximum distance for extrapolation of data, but there are ways of getting around this limitation.

The problem for the archeologist is to obtain samples of baked clay that can be dated by radiocarbon or some other means. When a number of such samples from one area has been recorded, a curve that shows the variation in angles of dip and declination through time can be plotted. When a series of clay samples of known dates has been measured, one can measure samples that have no independent dates. By comparing these with the scale, their ages can be calculated.

Research has focused on Japan, Central Europe, South America, Mexico, Arizona, and Canada, where considerable data concerning the meanderings of the earth's magnetic poles have been obtained. Many of these data are presented in tabular or graph form by Bucha (1971). In summary, Bucha (1971:84) says,

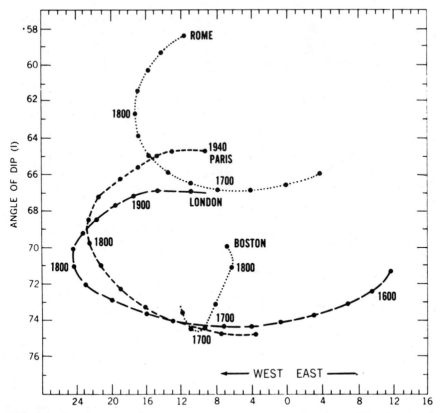

FIG. 8.2 *Secular variation—London, Paris, Rome, and Boston. The time scale is indicated by dots at 20-year intervals. The curves up to 1900 are those obtained by Bauer (1899), who used recorded observations of declination and dip to determine an empirical formula. Bauer's extrapolations into periods when only declination was measured have been omitted. Subsequent to 1900 the data have been taken from Vestine and others (1947). (M. J. Aitken,* Physics and Archaeology. *Courtesy of John Wiley & Sons, Inc., 1961.)*

> The application of the archaeomagnetic method is still restricted to those areas for which the archaeomagnetic curves have been determined, but it has been extended to Mexico and Arizona on the basis of fundamental geomagnetic characteristics . . . covering the past 3000 years. In this area, the method can improve the dating of the sherds of unknown age and substantially facilitate their classification.

Magnetic dating has thus proven useful in a number of instances and will gain in importance as the basic data on shifts in the magnetic poles are gathered for more areas and over longer periods.

There are many difficulties in magnetic dating. Some of these result from the problems of accurate declination-and-dip measurement and some from the nature of thermo-remanent magnetism. For example, the best material for dating is that which remains in the precise position where it was fired. Fireplaces and pottery kilns are ideal. On the other hand, bricks and pottery have ordinarily been removed from the place where they were fired so that it may be impossible to align them in their original positions. In addition to this problem, pottery is often a poor medium for measuring because it was frequently traded over great distances. On certain types of pots, however—glazed pots or those with considerable plastic decoration—it is possible to measure the angle of dip because it is almost certain that they were fired standing on their bases and hence on a fairly level surface. Nevertheless, their angles of declination cannot be measured because there is no way of knowing what their alignment with respect to geographical north was when they were fired.

The measurements themselves are usually made in a laboratory with special equipment. Only two determinations are made in the field: calculation of the sample's horizontal position (determined with a spirit level), and true north. Both of these readings are recorded while the sample is in undisturbed position in the ground and before it is sent to the laboratory for measurement of thermo-remanent magnetism. Measurements in the laboratory are done with several kinds of sensitive magnets. Under certain circumstances there may be some alteration of the thermo-remanent magnetism. Laboratory methods have been worked out to allow for these and to determine whether the sample is suitable for measuring.

Chemical Analysis for Fluorine and Nitrogen

The most important of the chemical techniques for bone analysis are determinations of the fluorine and nitrogen content. Quantitative differences in the amount of fluorine and nitrogen may permit archeologists to reach a decision on the relative age of buried bones, and in many instances, where there is a demonstrable association of the bones of extinct animals with those of man, to determine whether the human and animal bones are of the same or different ages. Buried bones and teeth gradually absorb fluorine from the ground water. The absorption of fluorine occurs through the alteration of hydroxyapatite, the phosphate of which bones and teeth are mainly composed, with the result that a chemically stable compound, fluorapatite, is formed. The amount of fluorine can be determined by chemical analysis or through the x-ray crystallographic method. Whereas the fluorine content increases with age, nitrogen decreases in amount with prolonged burial, owing to the disappearance of collagen in bone. The conditions of burial of bones at different depths, in different soils, and in different places make it impossible to establish a rate for fluorine uptake or nitrogen loss. Therefore no generally applicable dating method can be devised that is based on quantitative determination of these elements in buried bones.

Analyses of organic material help to determine the relative ages of bone specimens from one place. However, because of the complicated and poorly understood chemistry involved in the absorption of organic elements by bone or in the disappearance of organic matter, it is not possible to compare specimens from different places with accuracy. Bones, teeth, and antlers may take up fluorine at variable rates. It is known that temperature and humidity affect the chemical action, and environments differ greatly in their chemical makeup. In spite of the many limitations, chemical analyses may be very useful in helping to establish stratigraphy or association of one bone with another. There is as yet no method for deriving an absolute chronology from such chemical analyses.

Schoute-Vanneck (1960) describes a method of relative dating of coastal shell middens. Shells of mussel (*Mytilus*) are dissolved in acetic acid, and the ratio of conchylin (a substance similar to chiton) to calcium carbonate (lime) is determined. There is proved for South African coastal sites a progressive loss of conchylin over time. The method is now useful for relative dating, but if in the future the rates of decrease of conchylin can be determined, an absolute or chronometric dating method could be devised.

Progressive chemical changes occurring in animal skin (or leather) are claimed to follow a rate by which the age of ancient skin can be determined. Burton, Poole, and Reed (1959) describe a technique in which collagen fibers extracted from ancient skin are mounted for microscopic viewing. When the fibers are heated, they begin to shrink, and the older the specimen, the lower the shrinkage temperature. Fragments of the Dead Sea Scrolls, written on parchment, were found to produce "collagen fiber shrinkage temperature dates" that agreed with paleographic and radiocarbon-age determinations. In theory, almost any ancient preserved material will differ in its chemistry from modern material. Sometimes the process of change can be invested with a rate or tempo and thus provide a means of calculating the age of older materials. At other times all that can be said is that there are differences between what are clearly older and clearly younger materials. But even this knowledge can be useful because it provides a means of relative dating.

Patination

It has long been observed that the surface of rocks exposed to the atmosphere undergoes chemical alteration. The altered surfaces are said to be patinated. Many writers have suggested the possibility of using the amount of patina on stones as an index to their age. A evaluation of this method (Goodwin 1960) lists so many variables involved in patina formation that one must agree that absolute dates cannot be determined. Nevertheless, for certain problems, observation of the amount or color of patina on a stone may be of use. In sites where there is a long sequence, the flints in the bottom levels of a site may have more patina than those found in the upper levels. This difference is especially common in river gravels and terraces of rivers or lakes. When one has a large series of tools from several levels, it is sometimes possible to see clear-cut differences in the relative amounts of patina. With this knowledge it is then possible to assign dependable relative ages to artifacts from the same area. The famous Belzoni, referred to in Chapter 2, noted three distinct types of patination on the sculptures on the granite cliffs at Aswan in Egypt, and suggested that by dating the sculpture of one style or age, the age of the other two degrees of patination could be calculated (Belzoni 1820:Vol. 1:360–361).

The variations between areas and even on the same tools greatly limit the use of patina for age determination. When patination is used, it must always be with a firm basis in stratigraphy; it is no substitute for excavation.

Glass that has been buried in soil or submerged under water will undergo surface alteration and form microscopically thick bands or layers, which can be counted. Some studies suggest that these bands are annual, and that their total number is a register of the number of years the glass has been buried or immersed. Ages of nearly 1600 years have thus far been determined for certain archeological specimens (Brill 1961, 1963).

Hydration of Obsidian

Potentially one of the most useful methods of dating sites and artifacts is through measuring the hydration layers of obsidian. Obsidian, a natural volcanic glass with a high aluminum content, does not weather rapidly, but a freshly exposed surface of obsidian will take up water from the atmosphere to form a hydrated surface layer. The dating system depends on the fact that the hydration layer grows progressively deeper. It is therefore possible to estimate the age when the hydration began if the rate of its development can be determined.

The method is not quite as simple as once believed, however. It has now been demonstrated that there is no single rate of hydration for all obsidians nor even of all obsidian found within a given region. Rather, rates of hydration are specific to the sources of obsidian, each of which has a somewhat different chemical composition. Therefore, in order to apply the method, it is necessary to determine the source and composition of the obsidian in each instance.

The precise process involved in the development of the hydration layer is still under investigation. At the moment, the most practical procedure is to identify the source of each sample and work out calibrations of the hydration rate, using radiocarbon or other methods as an independent source of dates. In this way, it should be possible to arrive at rates that have local application.

The advantages of working with obsidian hydration are chiefly that the method is inexpensive and that it dates artifacts rather than the context in which they occur. In this way, problems such as the age of the artifacts at Valsequillo, whose geologic context was dated by fission track, could be resolved.

Chapter 9

OTHER METHODS FOR DATING

Dating by Use of Artifacts

For the most part, artifacts by themselves cannot be used to establish a date. The only exceptions to this rule are instances when coins or other objects have dates marked on them. One can then assume that the objects were made at approximately the date indicated, even though this does not automatically enable you to say that the coin accurately dates the context in which it occurs. The reason, of course, is that ancient coins may be collected or otherwise find their way into contexts of quite different age than those indicated by the dates on them. By definition, however, we do not have objects in prehistory with their dates stamped on them, so that any estimates of their age must be based on other characteristics. The most important of these are those which can be shown to change through time. We are all familiar with this principle if we have even the most casual appreciation, for example, of how automobiles change year by year. Some may only be able to say that "it looks like an old car," whereas others may quickly identify it as a 1947 Ford Super Deluxe. An archeologist familiar with the area should be able to peg his artifacts to time as the auto buff did the Ford.

In the long run, artifacts tend to change in predictable ways so that even though they do not imply very accurate dates, they may help establish a relative chronology. The old museum classification that separated objects of stone, bronze, and iron into different cases, implicitly arranged them chronologically. In man's long history, these three materials have been used successively for tools and common objects. Somewhat more specialized, but similar, classifications deal with sequences of events locally. For example, in France during the late Paleolithic, which is toward the end of the "Stone Age," there was a succession of industries named Mousterian, Aurignacian, Solutrean, Magdalenian, and Azilian. Each of these has its characteristic types of tools, so that an archeologist who is familiar with the situation can look at a group of tools and tell whether they are Mousterian or Magdalenian, and probably ascribe them still further to one of the many subdivisions within these categories. This knowledge of how artifacts change is developed through stratigraphic excavation, which has established the order in which the various types of tools appear.

Although knowledge of this kind may enable an archeologist to specify quite exactly what the age of some artifacts is, in most instances it is not possible to be very precise. For example, people began using bronze tools while they were still using stone tools. It might be possible to say that a bronze tool cannot be older than a certain date, but it may be much harder to say that a stone tool was not used after a certain date. In fact, there are people in the world who are still in the "Stone Age," a fact which only points up the general principle that you need to know both the overall trends of change and the details as they affect particular areas.

What archeologists often do is dig a series of sites where they can obtain a stratified sequence of artifacts. In this way, they establish a chronology for an area based upon changes in artifacts. They can then use this information to date sites or collections that do not occur in stratified contexts. The dating of sites found during surface survey is most often done this way.

Pottery has traditionally been the most important artifact used for purposes of dating. It is durable, being made of fired clay, and therefore will accumulate in quantity rather than decay and disappear after it is broken and discarded. It is a medium of artistic and esthetic expression, because the moist clay can be manipulated into different forms and can be decorated by surface impressions in the form of stamping, molding, incising, or painting. Like any aspect of culture, the manufacture and functions of pottery are subject to patterning. That is, any single social group will usually settle on a limited variety of shapes and decorative styles so that the pottery becomes definable and recognizable as a ceramic pattern of the society. Like all other parts of a culture, pottery changes over time; by detecting these trends of change, an archeologist can trace associated cultural changes and make short-term time distinctions after careful study of the ceramic remains.

The recognition of the importance of potsherds as a guide to chronology in archeology could not come until reasonably exact excavation methods had been developed. Albright (1957:49ff.) tells us that Furtwangler, who was primarily an art historian, was the first to see and use the significance of painted pottery for chronological purposes in classical studies, and that Petrie, in his report on the excavation of Tell-el-Hesi (Lachish) in 1890, was the first archeologist to appreciate the importance of unpainted pottery for purposes of determining chronology (Petrie 1891:14–15, 40–41). Petrie wrote, "once settle the pottery of a country, and the key is in our hands for all future explorations. A single glance at a mound of ruins, even without dismounting, will show as much to any one who knows the styles of the pottery, as weeks of work may reveal to the beginner" (cf. Kroeber 1916).

Sir Flinders Petrie, an Egyptologist whose work in Egypt began in 1881, developed the technique known as **sequence dating**. Predynastic Egypt was almost unknown, and the graves that Petrie excavated at the site of Diospolis Parva could not be dated. The pottery from the graves was varied, but certain types were habitually found together. Petrie reasoned that different assemblages of pottery were of different ages. With this in mind, he analyzed change, progressing from functional entities to mere decorations. The changes in pots were then correlated with changes in other artifacts from the graves, and he finally ended with a series of numbered pottery stages that he labeled "Sequence Dates." His series ran from S.D. 30 to S.D. 80, but Petrie had no way of telling what this range meant in terms of calendar dates or elapsed years. He began with S.D. 30 because he assumed (correctly) that he had not found the earliest Egyptian pottery. As a guess, Petrie suggested that S.D. 30 should be about 9000 B.C. We now know that S.D. 30 occurs at about 3500 B.C. (W. Emery 1961:28).

Dating by seriation, a variety of sequence dating, depends on the fact that types of artifacts change in their style and in their relative abundance. The fact has been used by many workers to obtain relative dates for the deposits they find in several sites in an area. A simple illustration of the idea behind seriation follows. It frequently happens that in a site of long duration with many stratigraphic levels, certain objects are confined to particular levels. Artifact a may occur in levels 1–3, artifact b in levels 3–8, artifact c in levels 2–4, artifact d in levels 4–9, and artifact e in levels 4–6. If a nearby site has a stratigraphic unit with artifacts a,b,c, one assumes that the unit is contemporary with level 3 in the first site, because this is the only level in which all three artifacts were found (Table 9.1). If a different combination of artifacts had been found, it might not have been possible to relate a level in one site to a single level in another site. For example, b and d were found alone in levels 7–8, but there may be no other site in which the same combination has been found. If this situation exists, the relative dating cannot be as precise.

The preceding example assumed that the presence or absence of artifacts is the criterion one uses for seriating cross-dating sites, but one can also use the frequencies in which artifacts occur in the various levels. Taking artifacts b and

TABLE 9.1 Distribution of Artifacts by Stratigraphic Levels

Stratigraphic Levels	Types of Artifacts				
	a	b	c	d	e
1	X				
2	X		X		
3	X	X	X		
4		X	X	X	X
5		X		X	X
6		X		X	X
7		X		X	
8		X		X	
9				X	

d in Table 9.2, for example, we find that they occur in different relative frequencies in the two levels. If, in a comparison of levels, one found 30 percent of b and 70 percent of d, he would assume that he was dealing with a level contemporary with level 7. When one has enough information (that is, a sufficiently large sample), it is likely that each period can be characterized by the frequencies of artifacts that occur in it (Fig. 9.1).

Earlier we compared the methods of dating artifacts to the recognition of automobile styles and their temporal significance. The analogy was, however, only a loose one because many artifacts, like pottery, change in different ways from autos. Ever since pots have been made, their sizes and shapes have been related to use and methods of manufacture. As a consequence, pottery is seldom improved, but it is often changed according to notions of style. By contrast, autos have changed in response to new uses, better roads, new materials, style, safety, affluence, and many other factors. In the case of autos, it is relatively easy to chart the chronology of changes by observing technical innovations. This is not the case with pottery, where it is often hard to tell which among a series of pots is the oldest. The best made or most artistically decorated, or most

TABLE 9.2 Relative Frequencies of Artifacts of Each Type in Each Stratigraphic Level

Stratigraphic Levels	Types of Artifacts				
	a	b	c	d	e
1	100				
2	75		25		
3	50	40	10		
4		60	5	10	25
5		70		15	15
6		40		50	10
7		30		70	
8		10		90	
9				100	

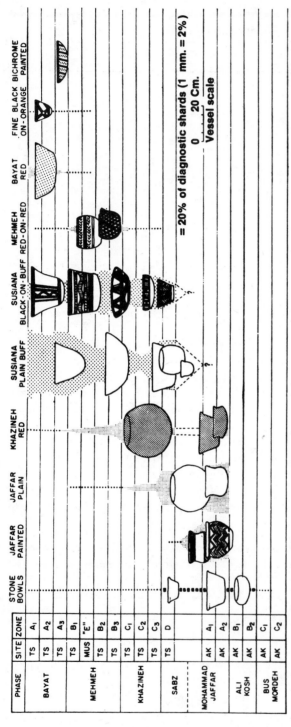

FIG. 9.1 Frequency polygons showing changes in percentage of various pottery types through time in the Deh Luran sequence, Mohammad Jaffar through Bayat Phases. The phases are characterized by the relative frequency of each type of pottery and also by the presence or absence of certain types. Drawings indicate typical vessels of each period but do not represent the full range of variations. Temporal distribution of stone bowls is shown for comparative purposes, but percentages are not calculated versus pottery. (F. Hole and K. V. Flannery, "The Prehistory of Southwestern Iran: A Preliminary Report," Proceedings of the Prehistoric Society, Vol. 33 (1968):Fig. 10.)

functionally diverse pots may belong to any age and they may occur at the same time with the worst examples. The point is, there is no "natural" sequence of pottery. Sir Flinders Petrie was fortunate in being able to anchor one end of his sequence of predynastic Egyptian pots to later pots of known date, but there was much room for error in the earlier periods. At best, therefore, sequence dating gives good relative dates, and these have to be checked by independent means.

When the sequence of changes in artifacts has been established, it can be used as a reference against which artifacts of unknown age can be compared. It is generally assumed in archeology that things which are similar are about the same age. Obviously, this assumption needs to be checked by independent methods in cases where it is necessary to come to definite conclusions.

If pots or artifacts of a particular style were manufactured in one place and traded to another, there would be a way to tie the two areas together chronologically. If objects are known to be of a certain age in the place where they were obtained or manufactured, the context in which they are found elsewhere cannot be older than the context in which they originated. This is the idea that underlies the technique of cross dating. It was through tracing traded goods of known age that archeologists worked out the chronology of European prehistory, and especially the spread of cultures across Europe from the Mediterranean area.

Cross dating works best when two groups exchanged easily identifiable and distinctive objects. What is more often the case, however, is that one group exchanged durable goods such as pots or axes for perishable materials such as wine, grain, or fabrics. Moreover, in some instances the traded durable goods might remain in use for centuries after the exchange took place, and might even have been traded subsequently to groups still farther removed. Thus both the chronology and inferences about the nature of the exchange between the groups might be in error.

A curious example of the movement of artifacts from one place to another that has no implications for either prehistoric trade or contact between widely separated groups is the transshipping of flint from Europe as ballast in ocean-going vessels that was dumped in the harbors of the American east coast. A person finding artifacts among these might erroneously assume contact between Europe and America during the Paleolithic. Such examples of what have been termed "travelers" or "wayfarers" are, of course, of no value for showing ancient diffusion or cross dating, but serve only as traps for the unwary archeologist and the uncritical speculator.

Dating by Using Plant Remains

Man is an intimate part of the natural environment by virtue of the fact that he uses plants and animals, both wild and domestic, for food as well as for industrial materials. The residue from this activity, discarded as trash, can often be recovered by an archeologist and used to date the archeological deposit. Further, the natural deposits on which the archeological site rests may yield faunal and/or floral evidence that, if datable, can tell an archeologist the maximum age of the site. When a site has been abandoned and the spot reverts to its original condition as part of the natural environment, the faunal and/or floral remains that accumulate may, if datable, provide the archeologists with the information on when the site was abandoned.

Studies of ancient botanical and zoological materials are termed **paleobotany** and **paleontology**, and from their results we learn about distributions of plants and animals of the past. When this information is correlated with that secured by geologists, geographers, climatologists, and ecologists, the natural environment and chronology of the past comes into focus.

There are at least four circumstances that enable archeologists to use plant and animal remains to date sites.

1. If extinct species are present, an archeologist can say definitely that the site is not recent, and he may be a great deal more precise if he knows from other information when the species lived.
2. If plants and animals that are no longer able to live in an area because of climate occur in archeological sites, an archeologist can infer that the climate was different when the site was occupied. If he can determine what the climatic preferences of the species were, he may be able to determine during which period in geologic history the climate would have been suitable to the animals and from this infer the site's age.
3. If some species, especially domesticates, have undergone osteological or morphological changes incident to domestication, it will be possible to say at least that the site was not occupied prior to a certain date. Sometimes enough may be known about the physical changes to enable an archeologist to narrow the time down to a few hundred years. These methods give relative ages that may be capable of refinement, but they are far from precise, and a person must be very careful in using data derived from one location to make inferences about other areas. For example, at present it is not possible to say that all **mastodons** became extinct at the same time; there may be a period of several thousand years during which they gradually disappeared, first from one locality, then another, and so on. The same sort of caution must also be applied to climatic changes, especially when they were caused by the advance and retreat of glaciers. Finally, our data on domestication are still too few to permit us to say with confidence that after, say 5000 B.C., all goats looked alike.
4. The most accurate method is tree-ring dating, which gives absolute dates directly correlated with our calendar. These dates are of such precision they are currently being used to check radiocarbon dating.

Palynology

Pollen analysis (palynology) was first developed in 1916 by the Swedish botanist Lennar von Post, who was interested in forest trees. Twenty years later the technique was extended to all plants that produce and release pollen. It has subsequently been developed into a highly refined method for identifying **Quaternary** and post-Pleistocene climatic changes and their chronology.

Accurate analysis depends on whether plants distribute their pollen widely and whether the grains are sufficiently well preserved to be identified. Pollen analysis is tedious and painstaking work, based on the microscopic identification of pollen from modern plants. When these modern grains have been identified, it is possible to take a standard number of grains from samples in a geological or archeological deposit, and count the number from each species of plant. By plotting the relative frequencies of various species through time, the analyst can make a pollen diagram describing the changing vegetation for the area involved (Fig. 9.2).

Deevey (1944:138–140) lists four conditions that must be fulfilled in order to apply the technique of pollen analysis to problems of chronology in prehistory. These are: (1) there must have been, within the period encompassed by human occupation of the area, vegetational changes resulting from areawide

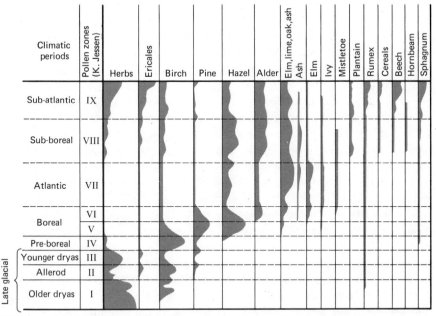

FIG. 9.2 *Diagram showing development of vegetation in Jutland since the re-treating ice sheet uncovered the land. The diagram depicts the relative frequencies of pollen from each of the plant species listed. (G. Clark,* Archaeology and Society. *Cambridge: Harvard University Press. London: Methuen and Company, Ltd., 1947.)*

causes; (2) pollen grains must be properly preserved in the deposits; (3) the investigation must first establish a "standard pollen sequence" through study of natural deposits such as lakes and swamps; (4) the investigator must possess a knowledge of the regional plant ecology in order to interpret properly the pollen sequence in terms of vegetational and climatic changes in the past.

If pollen analysis is relatively simple in theory, it is often disappointing in practice, because under many conditions pollen is not preserved. The best conditions are in highly acidic bogs with a **pH** below 5.0, where pollen has remained damp from the time it was deposited. It is simple to cut sections from peat bogs and plot the pollen diagrams. In Scandinavia, after several hundred such diagrams had been constructed, certain characteristic "zones" in the late glacial and postglacial sequence stood out. These zones are easily identifiable between sites and can be used to indicate climate and chronology. Radiocarbon dating of the peat, combined with pollen analysis, gives the best chronology in the world for the period.

Prehistoric sites found on the edges of bogs or objects found in bogs can thus be dated. However, even though a site is not in a bog, if pollen has been preserved in soil in the cracks of implements collected long ago and stored in museum trays it can often be identified, and the soil layer originally enclosing the artifact can be identified and thus dated (G. Clark 1957:47, 1963). Pollens in soils underlying or overlying archeological areas may be correlated with the already known regional pollen sequence, and the age of the site thus "bracketed."

Deevey's dictum that standard sequences must be established has been partly superseded by careful examination of pollen from archeological sites whose period of use is not long in the usual palynological sense. Studies carried out in the Southwest and in Meso-America show that relatively minor changes in plants around a site can be seen palynologically, with the consequence that accurate relative dating within a small area sometimes can be accomplished.

Pollen analysis can be very useful for both relative and absolute dating. Where only broad outlines of the climatic-floral history of a region have been worked out, it is often possible to identify pollen from a warm interglacial or cold glacial period without specifying the date. Where the chronology has been worked out in greater detail, one can place pollen profiles in terms of hundreds of years to give a rough absolute chronology.

The dating of sites through the use of pollen usually requires a long sequence of strata in which changes can be detected. These strata themselves must be dated so that the age of the pollen in them can be dated. This causes particular problems for palynologists who work with pollen from dry areas, because, unlike bogs, inorganic sediments cannot be dated by radiocarbon. There are also problems in dealing with pollen from archeological sites. In sites, much of the pollen may have been from species brought to the site by man and thus it will not necessarily reflect the natural vegetation. Second, sites are often disturbed through digging, so that pollen may sometimes get moved from one context to another. All these difficulties can be overcome eventually in most areas, but the prospects for immediate useful results are not always good.

Dating by Using Animal Remains

The study of bones in archeological sites may also give a rough basis for chronology, if it is realized that change in climate can cause migration or extinction as well as bring different animals and different plants into a region. What is more, certain species of animals have become extinct since man appeared. Taking these two factors into account, we may use paleontology to establish relative dates. Thus, we can assume a temperate climate if such species as *Elephas antiquus* (a forest elephant) are present, whereas *E. primigenius* (a steppe elephant) indicates a steppe or tundra environment of almost glacial conditions. For some periods during the Pleistocene even such gross estimates of dating as these can prove valuable. For the later stages of the Pleistocene it is often possible to get much finer distinctions. In France, for example, an alternation of the forest and steppe varieties of reindeer suggests the alternation of warm and cold stages during the final glaciation (Movius 1916:564; Bordes 1966).

In North America there was a sequence of extinction of mammals whose remains are found associated with those of early man. The mammoth, horse, camel, and several species of bison all became extinct after the arrival of man in the New World. Although the exact dates for the final extinction of these forms are not yet known, the sites where mammoths are associated with tools of man are an average of 11,250 years old. It has recently been proposed (Mosimann and Martin 1975) that mammoths may have become extinct within a few hundred years of man's arrival owing to his deliberately selective hunting of these animals. The problem with most animals that became extinct is that they did not all die at one time. Thus, except for the possibly special case of mammoths, it is hard to prove that an animal in a site was not one of those which lingered on in isolated refuges for hundreds or even thousands of years after the species had been decimated. Dating by means of faunal association is thus inexact and may at times be decidedly misleading.

Smaller species of animals may give better evidence. Rodents and birds are often more sensitive indicators of climate than are larger mammals. Some molluscs and forms of snails are exceptionally sensitive to changes in climate (Lais 1939). Their presence or absence in archeological sites may therefore record the changes of climate in an area. When these changes can be related to **varves**, pollens, or soils, it may be possible to date them and the human remains found in association.

The chronological and climatic significance of bones found in archeological sites must be interpreted with caution, because the bones were usually brought there by hunters and are not a random sample of the species around the site. If hunters chose one species as their favorite quarry during one period, and then shifted to another species, the findings may appear to indicate climatic change. Such a possible example is provided by caves in the Levant, where early workers reported an alternation in the abundance of *Dama mesopotamica* and *Gazella* (indicating moist and dry habitats, respectively [Garrod and Bate 1937]).

Later work by Hooijer on the fauna from Ksar Akil concluded with the statement, "I believe it is only correct to say that what we see reflected in the refuse parts is accessibility of game, and food choice of the men who occupied the rock shelter, rather than climatic changes, the evidence for which is geological" (Hooijer 1961:61).

This warning should be remembered, because many animals can live in a wide range of climate and environment. It is also noteworthy that if the environment is highly varied many different species may live within easy walking distance of a hunter's base camp. The archeological consequence is that the animal bones in archeological sites may be a partial and selective sample of the total number of zoological species known to, and even used by, man. To use inferences derived from such data as the basis for determining the ages of deposits may therefore be highly inappropriate.

In places where men could choose among many species of game—anything from jackrabbits to mammoths—they may have hunted mainly or even exclusively one species. Thus, a hunter living at the base of a mountain might habitually secure his food from the slopes of the mountain rather than from a valley or plain. If the hunter had a choice of food from a forest or plain, the ancient selection of the former would lead the archeologist to believe he is dealing with people living in a forest environment. In reality, both forest and tundra might have been within easy hunting range; yet they imply very different climates.

One must also remember that inferences about the climatic tolerance of a species assume that the tolerance has not changed over the millennia. This is not necessarily a safe assumption. Also, many species have a much greater range of tolerance than of preference. That is, some animals prefer one kind of environment, but under certain conditions may be able to live in a different environment with little visible effect. The preferences and tolerances of various living species, and all the more so for extinct species, are not in fact very well known, and judgments about environment at the time archeological sites were occupied must be made with great caution.

If climate can be deduced from paleontology, it should be obvious that the climatic phase to which it refers may be fitted into a dated sequence derived from other kinds of data.

Dendrochronology

Tree-ring dating, or dendrochronology, is potentially the most accurate of all methods for dating archeological materials. It depends on the fact that under suitable environmental conditions, trees add one growth ring each year, and that, because of fluctuations in rainfall and temperature, the rings are of different widths. When a tree is cut or sampled with a borer, the rings can be counted and their pattern of narrow and wide rings recorded. This pattern then serves as the identifying "signature" for a particular block of time. Like fingerprints, no two such "signatures" are identical.

The method was developed and has received its greatest attention in the American Southwest, where climatic conditions were suitable for the growth of characteristic tree rings and where the prehistoric people made extensive use of wood in their houses. Recently, however, it has been found that trees in many other parts of the world are equally suitable, and detailed tree-ring histories are being developed in various parts of Europe, in Turkey, South America, and Mexico. Part of the stimulus for these studies is due to the recent use of tree-ring dating as a method of helping calibrate C^{14} dates.

The method of tree-ring dating now in use was conceived about 1913 by Dr. A. E. Douglass, who was trying to determine whether tree rings held a record of past climate that could be related to sunspot cycles. Knowledge that some trees grew a ring each year and that by counting the rings one could determine the age of the tree had been known since the time of Leonardo da Vinci. Dating by dendrochronology depends on the fact that trees growing in temperate zones have clearly defined annual rings of growth. After a winter period of dormancy, new growth cells are formed in the spring and continue to be added, though at reduced size, during the summer. If a person examines a cross section of a tree trunk he can see these annual increments preserved as a series of concentric rings. To tell how old the tree is, you count the number of rings.

To get a chronology suitable for dating archeological materials it is necessary to match series of rings from trees of various ages. The dendrochronologic sequence for the American Southwest, which extends back to 322 B.C., was developed by means of cross dating some 20,000 dates from 1000 sites. Because the size of tree rings depends on the weather from year to year, one can match similar series of rings from one tree to another. The relative sizes of rings for a given time will be similar and recognizable in properly selected samples. The system of cross dating is illustrated in Figure 9.3.

In principle the method is simple, but there are some practical problems. These are listed by Bannister and Smiley (1055:179) as follows:

> The establishment in any given area, of a satisfactory tree-ring chronology, permitting the dating of prehistoric materials, is possible only when the following four conditions are met:
>
> 1. There must be trees that produce defined annual rings as a result of a definite growing season.
>
> 2. Tree growth must be principally dependent upon one controlling factor.
>
> 3. There must have been an indigenous prehistoric population that made extensive use of wood.
>
> 4. The wood must be well enough preserved so that it still retains its cellular structure.

Traditionally, conifers were used for dating, especially Ponderosa pine (*Pinus*

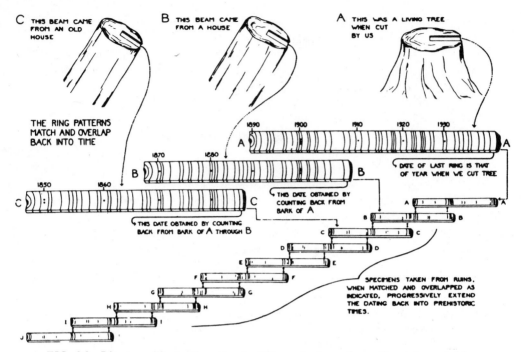

FIG. 9.3 Diagram illustrating the building of chronology through matching tree rings from successively older samples. (W. Stallings, Jr., 1939, "Dating Prehistoric Ruins by Tree Rings." Santa Fe, N.M.: Laboratory of Anthropology, School of American Research, General Series, Bulletin 8.)

ponderosa), which grows widely in the Southwest. However, other trees, such as oaks in Europe, have proved equally valuable. Many other trees might be used, but unfortunately they were not as commonly used by man and are consequently of less value in dating sites.

The use of tree rings for calibrating C¹⁴ dates is not subject to this limitation, however. For this purpose, the bristlecone pine (*Pinus aristata*), which grows in some of the western states of the United States, has been used. In particular, the White Mountain region of eastern California has been important because there are living trees there as much as 4600 years old, and dead trees have been found that extend the series of rings back 8200 years. There seems to be good prospect of eventually pushing the series back about 10,000 years. Fortunately, there are trees of equivalent age in subfossil conditions in parts of Europe that can be used to check on the American results.

In testing whether atmospheric C¹⁴ had remained constant, wood from tree rings of known age was dated by radiocarbon. This independent dating method revealed that the radiocarbon dates did not always agree with the tree rings. This finding led to a very protracted and extensive sampling of hundreds of tree rings. The results, which have had a profound impact on archeological interpretation, have fully justified the effort, because it is now possible to give a much more accurate calendar equivalent to radiocarbon ages. It is especially important to mention that all the laboratories engaged in this research have reported essentially identical results. As a consequence, it has been possible to publish tables that indicate how C^{14} dates should be corrected to conform with calendar dates back some 6000 years.

It should also be mentioned that tree rings may help with other kinds of archeological problems. Since they preserve a record of climate, it is sometimes possible to reconstruct a picture of even minor changes in rainfall within a region. This has been done in the Southwest, where climatic changes have often been suspected of causing changes in the activities and settlements of the prehistoric Native Americans.

Other uses include the dating of sections of buildings such as cathedrals, by analyzing tree rings of beams used in their construction, and even the authentication of paintings by dating the rings of wood used in their frames.

Tree-ring dating thus has many kinds of uses. It also suffers from inherent problems that prevent its universal use. The most important of these is the availability of suitable wood. Even when wood is found, however, it may not date the structure in which it is found. Assuming the log is intact and not trimmed or squared, the outermost ring tells when the tree was cut. This does not, however, necessarily tell when the log was used. In areas where wood was scarce or had to be felled with primitive tools, it was reused repeatedly. There are instances in the Southwest where Native Americans are using roof beams today that were cut several hundred years ago.

Dating methods using plant and animal remains include both the most precise and the least exact methods for determining chronology currently at our disposal. It seems safe to say, however, that as more evidence accumulates in palynology and paleontology, in some areas it may become possible to obtain dates on biological species which are nearly as accurate for relative dating as is the cross dating of artifacts today.

Dating by Geologic Effects

Because man lives on the earth's surface it is not at all surprising that his bones, tools, and other evidences of his former presence are commonly found on the surface. The houses, buildings, roads, canals, scatters of trash, and everything else that we strew over the landscape today will become, in varying degrees of preservation, the archeological materials of the future. The earth's surface is continually subject to change by erosion and deposition, as well as by a multiplicity of other processes that we call geological. The same processes account for the fact that things which once lay on the surface have been moved or buried, or that things once buried have again been exposed to view. In all instances where archeological materials occur in a context that can be called geological, the archeologist may be able to determine the chronological placement of the find by one or another of the methods of **geochronology**. Some of these methods ultimately rest on the principles of stratigraphy, but others have to do with the location of a site in relation to geologic features. The various methods that can be used to establish a geochronology are numerous and we make no pretense at mentioning more than some of them.

Varve Analysis

Varve analysis, the oldest technique for geochronology, was described in 1878 by the Swedish Baron Gerard De Geer, who did most of the pioneering work, although somewhat earlier Heer (1863:453-455) had recognized that varves are annually deposited layers of silt. Varve analysis depends on the fact that certain clayey deposits are laminated. These laminations, or varves, as they are called in Swedish, are annual layers of sediment deposited in lake basins by the runoff from melting glacial ice. By a process similar to that used in tree-ring analysis; it is possible to measure the relative thickness of the varves and obtain a series to which one can compare and correlate new sections as they are discovered (De Geer 1912; Heizer 1953:9–12).

Varves are composed of a double layer with coarse sediments at the bottom and fine sediments at the top; the finer sediments settle during the winter while the lake is frozen over, and the coarser material is deposited in the summer when it is warmer and melting is increased. Varves may range in thickness from a few millimeters to almost 40 centimeters, though these maximum and minimum values are seldom reached.

Varve analysis can be used indirectly for archeological dating. Sites are not often found in glacial lakes, but sediments in glacial lakes may be correlated with other geological features, such as beaches left by varying water levels. When the lake levels, and hence their beaches, can be dated by reference to varves, it is possible to date archeological material found in the beaches. The method lacks precision, however, because it is possible for archeological materials to have been incorporated into beach deposits long after the beaches were formed.

The application of varve dating is restricted by several factors. First, because varves accumulate only near ice, there are no varves in most of the world. Second, in many places ice that was present during the Pleistocene has receded, and no longer supplies basins with sediments. Outside Scandinavia, therefore, it is difficult to find a continuous sequence of varves reaching the present. Nowhere do varves linked with the present extend very far into the past. The longest sequence known goes back only 17,000 years. The reason is that places where there are now lakes were covered by ice during the height of the Pleistocene glaciation and therefore were not receiving sediments. A final reservation is that varves are not invariably annual; depending on the pattern of melting, layers may be deposited more or less frequently than annually (Flint 1957:293–297).

Beaches, Terraces, and Dunes

During the Pleistocene (the glacial epoch or Ice Age), which ended about 11,000 years ago, there were major advances and retreats of ice across the continental land masses. The effect of this was to alternately take water from the oceans and leave it frozen on earth, or to let the water flow back into the oceans when the ice melted. This resulted in alternate raising and lowering of the sea, called **eustacy**. Changes in sea level of at least 300 feet occurred many times during the Pleistocene. When the sea levels changed, new beaches and sea cliffs were created. Some of them were left "hanging" above a lowered sea level, whereas others were buried by rising sea levels. In principle, then, there is a record of changing sea levels preserved in coastal features such as beaches, sand dunes, and sea cliffs. Eustacy was often accompanied by a movement of the land masses, called **isostacy**. Under the weight of the ice (which was often several thousand feet thick), land masses were depressed, and, when the ice retreated, the land sprang up again. In some places this isostatic action raised the land so high above sea level that traces of old, once much lower, shore lines are visible; without isostasy they would now be submerged. Outside glaciated areas, **tectonic** action—movement of land masses whether or not they were covered by ice—has exposed Pleistocene shore lines. Some beaches that would have been submerged are now readily seen, but the opposite is also true—some land areas are now submerged that might not have been were it not for tectonic action.

Geologists have been able to date many of these seaside geologic features, and when archeological sites are found in association with them, they can be dated indirectly. Although such dates are not precise, they do enable us, for example, to say that a site is not older than a particular beach formation. Often there are also ways to tell that a site must be older than a certain age because of other geologic changes. Among these are the encroachment of water over sites, a phenomenon which has happened in many places since the end of the Pleistocene. It is not uncommon as a consequence to find remains of Native American sites under water on the continental shelf of the United States. This is an area, however, that is understandably little explored as yet.

Along the eastern Mediterranean coast is has been possible to relate certain kinds of sand dunes, or **weathering horizons** within them, to Pleistocene chronology. Sometimes archeological sites can be related not only to beaches but to dunes as well. Even better, in the Baltic, shore lines can sometimes be correlated with varve sequence, and in this way absolute dating can be given to the beaches. In some instances the sinking or rising of shore lines provides a means of dating archeological sites when there is some idea of the rates at which the changes in elevation are taking place. These situations have been studied in Tierra del Fuego, Chile, Arctic North America, and New England.

Terraces, former flood plains formed along streams as a result of the changing regime of the river, can be used in the same way that shore lines are used. During periods of aggradation a river will deposit silt and gravel and build up its bed, where at other times the river will degrade or cut into its bed.

During periods of relative stability a stream may cut a valley sidewise by flooding or meandering. Alternatively, it may build a flood plain by depositing silt and gravel in the river valley. Either process results in a relatively level valley floor over which the stream spreads during floods. Later degradation leaves remnants of the flood plain suspended well above the river. The lowering of the bed of a river ordinarily takes a long time and in the natural course of events the flood plain should wear down at about the same rate as the stream bed. However, sometimes bits of the old flood plain are preserved at the margins of the valleys where meanderings of the river have failed to remove them. After a time a series of flood plains at different elevations can be distinguished (Flint 1957:Fig. 12-4).

Under certain conditions the heights of these remnants can be used as a means of correlating one terrace with another. This method is the same as that used on shore lines, but it is much more difficult to make correlations with rivers; in practice it is even difficult to identify parts of the same terrace on different stretches of the same river (D. Johnston 1944). If the aggradation or degradation of a river can be directly related to an ocean or lake, it may be possible to date one by the other. Just as archeological materials may be found in association with shore lines, so they are often associated with terraces.

Rivers that flow over a wide flat flood plain may change their courses, or meander. At times the meander changes may be unidirectional, with the result that over a long period of time the river will leave behind it a series of abandoned channels which can be detected and plotted either by topographic surveying or aerial photographic mapping (**photogrammetry**). The most extensive application of a meander chronology to which a rate or tempo has been determined is in the lower Mississippi Valley, where the main stream's former locations have been plotted at 100-year intervals for the last 2000 years (Fisk 1944). The plotting has been done through extrapolation of data on river changes between 1765 and 1940. Sites located on a particular meander channel can be dated as being no older than that of the channel when occupied by the river. However, sites on abandoned channels may be much younger than the time when the channel held the main stream of the river. Some abandoned channels, if blocked at two separated points by silting, may collect water and form a lake that will provide an attractive location for settlement. If this did occur, the archeologist might readily recognize it by noting that the water-associated fauna (fish, waterfowl, molluscs) used for food and recovered by him from the site was of the lake rather than river type.

Correlation of Pleistocene Features

Some of the best evidence of the Pleistocene climatic succession is preserved in Europe and along the Mediterranean coasts. A considerable amount of prehistoric archeology has been done in the same area; European and Russian scholars have therefore been the leaders in correlating Pleistocene events with prehistoric man. By contrast, in North America there was relatively little habitation that can be related to the glacial stages of the Pleistocene. Substantial traces of man do not appear in this hemisphere until the end of the last (Wisconsin) glacial phase. Many claims of older material denoting man's presence have been advanced, but none has been generally accepted. There may be, even probably is, more ancient evidence of man in the Western Hemisphere, but it awaits either finding or the kind of demonstration called proof.

Moraines (lines or piles of rock and dirt scraped and pushed by the bull-dozer effect of glaciers) and outwash features from the melting ice are well-known geologic features. Ordinarily, however, because of their nearness to glacial ice, which was not a very favorable place for man to live and find his food, they are not directly associated with human habitation. Areas suitable for man lay beyond the immediate margins of the ice. In much of the northern hemisphere this was **loessland**, in some places several hundred feet thick. Loess "is a sediment commonly nonstratified and commonly unconsolidated, composed dominantly of silt-size particles, ordinarily with accessory clay and sand, and deposited primarily by the wind" (Flint 1957:181). The loess that covers large portions of southwestern Russia, East Europe, and middle-western United States is thought to have been derived from moraines and other glacial debris.

The development of soil horizons in loess is exceptionally important in helping to establish the late Pleistocene chronology of Europe. In theory, loess is deposited during glacial periods, whereas soil horizons are developed in the loess during the warmer phases when plants grow better. When these soils are buried, as they were during the cold (ice advance) and warm (ice retreat) alternations of the Pleistocene climate, a layered sequence is built up. Because some soil horizons are deeper than others, a characteristic sequence of thinner and thicker soils can thus be compared, from one locality to another. Sometimes loesses include fauna that helps to identify them. For example, the snail, *Helicigona banatica* (among others), is found in a soil in central Europe.

Loess regions were grasslands, especially suitable for grazing animals such as bison and mammoths. Hunters of these animals left their camp sites in the loess, and these sites can sometimes be associated with particular loess horizons. A striking example of this association is in southern Moravia, where Dolni Vestonici and Pavlov, both sites of mammoth hunters, are associated with the "Paudorf" soil formation (Zeuner 1955b). The soil, now a marker in the Pleistocene chronology of the area, is estimated to have lasted approximately 4000 years, from about 27,000 to 23,000 B.C. The estimate is based on radiocarbon dates made on charcoal from the sites, as well as humus from the soil (Movius 1963:132).

By slowly compiling knowledge of local time sequences, geologists have begun to establish reliable chronologies for the latter part of the Pleistocene, but for most of the Pleistocene—now thought to be about two million years long—the dating is much less precise. There are two reasons for this: either datable remains have not been found, or they do not occur in many areas. Such gross traditional distinctions as the four Alpine glacials—Günz, Mindel, Riss, and

Würm—are of little help to archeologists, because they are individually of long duration, and they cannot be easily correlated with geologic features elsewhere. Moreover, each of these Alpine glacials is now subdivided, and it is now known that there are more than four, each of which had its own relatively minor fluctuations of climate. In short, except for the very end of the Pleistocene, when radiocarbon dates and varve sequences are useful in making correlations, chronology based on geologic features is imprecise. This fact is overlooked in many publications on the subject.

Rate of Chemical Changes in Site Soils

Soils undergo changes over time in chemical and physical characteristics as a result of climatic changes, which in turn will be reflected in vegetational change. The soil will modify in accordance with these shifts. Because the chemistry and morphology of soils that have been altered in the past are not readily reversed, soils may contain a record of several past climatic changes as in the Paudorf soil mentioned above. Rates of soil development are variable and not at present well understood, but the fact that change does occur over time makes soil a potentially useful source of chronology.

Archeologists have been slow to seek the advice and technical assistance of soil experts (pedologists), and the future will probably see increased interest in this subject.

Rate of Accumulation

Archeologists often estimate the duration of a site by its depth of deposit, but any such estimate is likely to be little more than a guess. It is really not possible in most cases to say that a deposit in a cave has accumulated at the rate of 15 inches per 1000 years, or that a shell midden accumulated at the rate of 2 feet per 100 years. When such guesses have been checked with radiocarbon or other dating methods, they have usually been proved wrong. On the other hand, if the depth of deposit and the length of time it took to accumulate are both known, one can say that, on the average, N centimeters of deposit were added per century. Even with such statistics, however, it is not possible to extrapolate these data from one site to another, because there are too many variables to control. Geological deposition is as complex as deposition in an archeological site, and its short-term characteristics are not easily measured.

There is no justification for assuming that the rate of the growth of the soil of any particular site was constant throughout its occupation. Increase or decrease in population, the use of several debris dumps, the lateral expansion of a site, and similar factors will all skew deductions. An interesting example is that supplied by Fowler (1959:19–20) with reference to Modoc Rock Shelter in Illinois. Total depth of the archeological deposit was 27 feet, and from the several layers 11 charcoal samples were collected and dated by radiocarbon. Fowler, accepting the correctness of most of the radiocarbon dates, has examined the vertical position of each dated sample with reference to the amount of refuse between it and the next higher dated level in an effort to calculate rate of accumulation. He found that the rate of deposition was constant at about 1 foot per 500 years for the period 8000–5000 B.C.; increased to about 1 foot per 300 years between 5000 and 3600 B.C.; increased to 1.7 feet per 100 years between 3600 and 3000 B.C.; and decreased to 1 foot per 400 years between 3300 and 2700 B.C. These variable rates discourage any attempt in this particular site to apply a single rate of increment, but, having discovered the fluctuations, the archeologist is presented with an intriguing problem of why this variation occurred. Fowler found it necessary to reexamine his total information to learn whether variable rates of accumulation were caused by such factors as climatic conditions, differences over time of number of occupants, variations in living patterns, and so on.

There are times, however, when an archeologist is forced to rely on rate of accumulation because no other means of dating is available to him. Wheeler (1956:45) says about rate-of-accumulation dating: "Such calculations have, if any, a purely academic or abstract interest. They make no allowance for the intermittencies and vagaries which, alike in human and in geological history, defy the confines of mathematical formulae." This is a rather positive statement, whose effect is to deny any possible validity or utility in increment dating. Actually, Wheeler himself has, in at least one instance, made use of the method in attempting to determine the duration of time involved in the six successive building phases of the platform of the Harappa citadel that he excavated in 1946 (Wheeler 1947:81).

Location of Sites

In the desert portions of western North America water was scarce; for this reason sites usually occur in the vicinity of springs or creeks. The presence of chipped flint tools on the shore-line terraces of dry lake basins in the southern California desert has led to the supposition that the stone tools date from the time when the lake held water, and that if one can date the time the water was there, the cultural materials can be dated. This idea seems reasonable, but there are at least two other possibilities that should be considered before the assumption that the age of the lake waters is the same as the age of the implements can be accepted. First is the fact that some of these lake basins occasionally fill even today as a result of very heavy rains. In 1938, for example, the basin of normally dry Lake Mohave received enough water in a period of 13 days to form a lake 16 miles long, 2.5 miles wide, and 10 feet deep. In prehistoric times, say as recently as 150 years ago, such a lake would certainly have attracted Indians of the vicinity to its shores, where they would have camped and left traces of their contemporary occupation, however brief, until the lake dried by evaporation. Thus implements found on the surface around the lake margins might be 15,000 years old and date from the Pleistocene when the country was better watered and the lake permanent, or they might be 150 years old. Mere surface associations of this sort between implements and a geological feature may or may not be related in a single way and may refer to only a single event, or to a series of events.

Ethnographic evidence provides another reason why lack of proximity of sites to water may also be misleading. This is illustrated by J. H. Steward (1937: 105), who writes,

> In the southern end of Eureka Valley, near the northern end of Death Valley, California, there is a site bordering a **playa** and extending several miles. Thousands of flint flakes with relatively few artifacts mark it as predominantly a workshop, though the source of the flint is several miles distant in the mountains. The nearest water is a spring 3 to 5 miles away. There is no apparent reason why anyone should choose a place lacking water, having virtually no vegetation, and in fact, devoid of any-thing of apparent use to man or beast, for a workshop or other purpose. Nevertheless, the presence here of large spherical stone mortars of the type used by Death Valley Shoshoni and at last one arrow point of the Shoshonean type is presumptive evidence that the Shoshoni visited the site, though it does not, of course, prove that they used it as a workshop. Although Mr. and Mrs. Campbell (1935, p. 26) have never found a camp site more than 3 miles from a water hole in southern California, the writer has repeatedly received accounts from Shoshoni and Paiute in-formants of camps maintained by entire families and groups of families for days at a time 10 and even 20 miles from water when seeds, salts, flints, edible insects, or other important supplies made it worth while to do so. Water is used sparingly and when the (basketry) ollas in which it is transported are empty one or two persons make the long trip to replenish them. Remoteness from the present water, then, is not, per se, the slight-est proof that a site dates from the pluvial period.

It is sometimes possible to give a maximum age for a site by noting where it lies in relation to a datable geological feature. The date of the penetration of the Upper Great Lakes area in North America by early hunters using fluted dart points has been estimated in this fashion. Geologists have calculated the dates when the Wisconsin glacial ice receded and when the various glacial lakes waxed and waned; it is therefore possible to say that man could not have lived in certain places before a certain time. By similar reasoning it has been possible to date Mousterian occupation of caves on the Italian peninsula. During the Pleistocene, when the level of the Mediterranean Sea rose, some caves that lie close to the water could not have been occupied. Knowledge of sea levels and their approximate dates thus gives archeologists a date before which the caves could not have been lived in.

Although there is a variety of methods for dating archeological materials by means of geology, none of the methods is simple. It is always better to have several independent methods for dating particular events. Used alone, any method that depends on far-reaching correlations of geologic stratigraphy is likely to be undependable because of weak links in the chain of observations. Archeologists should use geochronologic dating but be aware of its many possible sources of error.

The various methods of dating sites should be regarded as complementary When possible, sites should be dated by several methods that are independent of one another. Many times this practice helps resolve difficult questions, such as the one posed by the K-Ar dates of Bed I at Olduvai Gorge. Although the date seemed too old at first, it was substantiated by fission-track dating, and the great antiquity of man has been accepted. On the whole, it is probably better to trust dates derived from archeological–cultural remains because they tend to be better controlled and it is easier to tell when they are consistent with other evidence. Nevertheless, in order to obtain absolute dates or even an order of magnitude for most very old cultural material, it is necessary to rely on physical-chemical methods. The reason for this is that the oldest cultures were the simplest and we can see very little change during long periods. Tools made a hundred thousand years apart may be virtually identical and give no clues in themselves of even their relative ages. In later times, when cultures changed more rapidly, it is often possible to obtain more accurate dates by examining details of artifacts than it is by using radiocarbon. The important points to remember are that each technique of dating has its own uses and limitations, and the more we can cross check among these methods, the better off we are in establishing the true age for a site.

RECONSTRUCTION AND PROCESSUAL INTERPRETATION

The central concerns of prehistory have always been to document a chronological sequence of man's changes and to describe the variations in ways of life in different places. These reconstructions lead to historical narrative. Another approach is to examine the workings of past cultures to determine how and why they operated as they did, and to attempt to find general laws that explain the courses taken by mankind. Some authors see these two approaches as part of a normal sequence of investigation. Willey and Phillips (1958:3–7) refer to three "levels of analysis," with only two of which we are concerned here—"description" and "explanation"; "observation" (the lowest level) was discussed in preceding chapters. These authors say,

So little work has been done in American archaeology on the

245

> explanatory level that it is difficult to find a name for it. . . .
> Perhaps it is fair to say that there has been a lack of progress
> in processual interpretation in American archaeology to date
> precisely because unit formulations have been put together
> with so little reference to their social aspect (1958:5–6).

As Willey and Phillips emphasized, archeologists often fail to appreciate that archeological remains which represent the activities of people must be interpreted with this fact in mind. In both historical reconstruction and processual interpretation we make interpretations, but the intents of the studies are different.

It is useful to keep in mind the difference between historical reconstruction on the one hand, and analysis and interpretation of changes on the other. When we excavate a site and describe its contents, we deal for the most part with synchronous events. Archeologically we observe a slice of life in the history of a people in much the same way that an ethnographer might study a people over the course of a year or so. We see the houses, burials, work areas, and the artifacts associated with them, and in so doing we gain a glimpse of a way of life. Translated into three dimensions, such a picture is analogous to a museum diorama that is really a scale model of a community with the people engaged in their daily activities.

In contrast with this descriptive approach, and after some of these slices of life have been described, we may concern ourselves with changes and the processes that enabled them. Our attention turns from the study of things to the study of the way artifacts and sites relate to the behavior of prehistoric people to one another and to the surrounding world. We are interested not in charting the development of ceramic technology, but rather in the reasons for changes in the culture of the people who made the pots. How do we explain the shift from hunting to agriculture? Or from villages to cities? Or why some cultures seem not to change over long periods? These are questions of process which must be answered in the light of theory pertaining specifically to stability and change; they cannot be answered by reference only to the immediate archeological situation. As Flannery (1972) said, "The way data are collected to answer inductive questions of culture history may make it impossible to do processual studies later." In other words, one can do a splendid and convincing three-dimensional reconstruction of a village and yet know nothing of the way it was organized, how the people related to others around them or to their environment, or how they came to be as they were found. Were they in the throes of change? Did they have a long-lasting adaptation? Were they declining from a previous "higher" level? Were they about to become extinct as a viable culture? The question "why a people were as they were" nags at the archeologist interested in process and cannot be answered solely in terms of the immediate situation. Thus studies of process draw on different bodies of theory and express quite different goals from those concerned primarily with reconstruction. It is important to bear in mind that although the two approaches are not mutually exclusive, they are not necessarily complementary either; and one cannot shift readily from one to another unless he has an adequate understanding of how they differ and how they may be mutually supporting.

The studies that reconstruct prehistoric ways of life are more readily understandable than are studies of process for two reasons. First, the former studies deal with tangible things and lend themselves to visual representation; second, they appeal to the common sense. A person can literally imagine himself living in a prehistoric village. Processual studies, on the other hand, dealing with organizational interrelationships and changes over long periods of time, lend themselves more to abstract graphic rather than to representational depiction. It would be very hard for a person to imagine himself acting out a thousand generations of a culture's history. For these reasons we shall present the concepts that deal with reconstruction first.

Chapter 10

CONCEPTS RELATING TO RECONSTRUCTION

Earlier (Chap. 3) we discussed the concepts that make a study of prehistory possible and how they relate to the data and goals of archeology. Now that we have reviewed the ways archeologists obtain and analyze data we must turn to their interpretation. We shall try to make clear the premises on which historical reconstructions are based; in later chapters we will show how they are used in specific instances. The basic interpretive concepts are few, but each has a variety of implications that illustrate how the concepts are interrelated and how they may be used in archeological interpretation.

Although some of the concepts relating specifically to reconstructing prehistory have been mentioned previously, they have not been discussed explicitly in the context of interpretive reconstruction. The concepts are basically concerned with how it was in the past and how we know. They are: data, uniformitarianism, analogy, system, culture, adaptation, ecology, evolution, and model. From most of these concepts there follows a particular view of culture and of data and a set of possible interpretations.

Archeological Data

In many respects, doing archeology is like groping around in a dark and unfamiliar room trying to grab something familiar in order to get oriented. Orientation in a dark room requires fixing on something you can identify that in turn will allow you to predict finding something else, such as a wall or door. Testing of these subsequent predictions will eventually lead to an accurate picture of the room, because the world is predictable—it consists of patterns or relations of objects. Some of the patterns are essentially timeless, having come into being with life itself; others have been added in the long course of human history. But patterns of organization are common to all things and to all life. If we understand this we can use minor clues and incomplete evidence to help us reconstruct prehistoric life.

Archeological data consist of mud, clay, stone, bone, and fibrous objects, and so they will remain unless they are given a cultural interpretation. Then they become bricks, pottery, projectile points, remains of meals, and basketry, used and discarded by living peoples in the normal routine of gaining a livelihood. The basic and tangible data we use are derived from the survey and excavation of archeological sites. The data might be treated simply as objects, but if we did so we should not be able to use them in reconstructing prehistoric cultural **systems** (as described later in this chapter), because the essence of a system is its organization. What we must look for in archeological data, therefore, are the attributes that pertain to organization. They are distribution, relative size, number, spatial arrangement, and hierarchy. These aspects are important with whatever archeological data we are studying, be they sites, houses, artifacts, or burials.

A typology of projectile points, an analysis of settlement patterns, or a reconstruction of the structure of a prehistoric social system—all begin with an analysis of the spatial and quantitative relations of the component parts. In a previous chapter we treated space as one dimension of context, a dimension that should be recorded by measurement and hence become a datum or fact. When we wish to use these data for cultural reconstructions, however, we are concerned with a further dimension—pattern or relation—because these are the attributes that inform on the organization of prehistoric culture systems.

Data are necessary, as we have already mentioned, but they exist only when we think they do and can be obtained only when we have the techniques to find them. The former is the more formidable problem, as was neatly expressed by Mulvaney (1971:239, quoting A. Kenyon 1927:282) in his review of the history of archeological studies in Australia. Work was not done there until recently because it was thought:

> Aboriginal material culture was static through time and space, so that excavations were pointless, and in any case sites were shallow and unstratified. "Culture" was a misnomer, because of the essential local causative factors in every instance . . . our black brother . . . was a poor, primitive creature, who allowed the material available to govern him.

If preconceived notions about an entire people and their history could stifle archeological study for half a century, consider how dependent we must also be on conceptions of what is interesting to investigate and what our data will tell. For example, "It is ironical that archaeology should be so highly prized by votaries of the materialist interpretation of history, when so few of the outstanding monuments or even of the finest artifacts revealed by excavation can, in fact, be explained in material terms" (G. Clark 1970:143).

We should bear in mind Clark's caveat, but a contrary view is often expressed. For example, in his reconstruction of prehistoric social organization in the American Southwest, J. Hill (1970:48) says,

> It would appear . . . that virtually all aspects of prehistoric behavior are amenable to discovery—given appropriate methods and techniques. While I have attempted to argue this and have presented a methodological approach that should be useful in this regard, I am by no means prepared to argue that there are no limits at all! On the other hand, it would be presumptuous to attempt to state with any degree of precision what the limitations actually are; we simply do not know. It is clear, however, that some of the commonly *believed* limitations are not as limiting as they have been thought to be.

Hill (1970:50–52) goes on to state what he thinks the limitations may be. First, most aspects of behavior are intangible. However,

> most of the things the archaeologist is interested in *do* leave . . . remains —the problem is in knowing what kinds of evidence a particular item of behavior might be *expected* to leave in the archaeological remains . . . , and what kinds of methods and techniques can be used to discover this evidence. [Second,] most elements of behavior have more than one or two material correlates, and relatively few of them may be needed to demonstrate the prehistoric existence of behavior. If we begin thinking less about the significance of individual artifacts and more about the *sets* (or clusters) of data that might be associated with a particular element of behavior, we can begin to make (and test) inferences that are presently not believed possible.

Hill concludes his discussion of the limitations of data with a statement that is not controversial and with which we would emphatically agree: that we are limited at present not so much by our data as by our theory and by our techniques for gathering and analyzing data.

Uniformitarianism

Earlier we discussed the concept of uniformitarianism, especially with regard to geologic processes and ethnographic analogy. The underlying idea is that the present is a clue to the past because all things on earth behave or interact with their environments in ways that are determined by certain principles. The important point is that there are processes that affect all matter. If we can determine what these processes are, we can use this knowldge as a key toward unlocking the unknown. As Sanders and Price (1968:221–222) put it, "The broad justification for archaeological inference is in effect, the principle of uniformitarianism; but taken alone its explanatory and predictive-retrodictive powers are limited." However, for specific examples they make the point that "similar causes produce similar effects, independently of historical or lineal relationships of cultures." Trigger (1970:33) says much the same thing: "Products of processes that went on in the past can be interpreted in terms of processes that can be observed at work at the present time." For archeology, of course, the products of the processes are archeological sites and the things that are contained in them, which can be interpreted as residue left by people engaged in their activities, with subsequent modification through the degradation of these remains since they were deposited.

Two concepts are implicit in the foregoing. First, the processes of change are controlled by certain factors. Thus, we may speak of cultural evolution, which has been likened to biological evolution and is effected through somewhat analogous processes. Second, people behave in basically similar ways when confronted with certain situations. Thus patterning in site residues can be related to our understanding of the principles of behavior. Here it is that ethnographic analogy is important.

It should be clear that if uniformitarianism is not correct—if the processes or principles that we can observe today did not pertain in the past—then our interpretations of the past will be skewed or even completely invalid. Because cultural change depends in part on the nature of biological man, we cannot assume that all of the principles of behavior that we may discover in today's world pertain to the past. At the same time, the processes of biological change and of changes in the earth itself could follow a strictly uniform line. Because we know that man has not always been either biologically or culturally identical to what he is today, it follows that there are limits to the application of uniformitarianism in making inferences about material remains and interpretations about the ways of prehistoric peoples. Still, without the concept we would have no guidelines at all toward interpreting cultural changes. We would be left with a study of sequential changes and variety in physical remains, a science of ancient things in their own physical terms alone.

Ethnographic Analogy

One of the facts that makes us believe in and use the concept of uniformitarianism is that we can find striking parallels between people today and those known through archeological remains. Even today there are still a few people who live in a "stone age," and in historic times such people have been widespread across the earth. In terms of equipment and ways of life, these people appear to be very similar to the hunters of ancient times. In some instances the parallels are so close that one can assume direct continuity from the past into the present. In most cases, however, resemblances are more general and the study of modern peoples gives only guidelines for interpreting the past.

Analogy is one of the most commonly used methods of interpretation. When we see something unfamiliar we ask ourselves what it looks like and try to find a category to put it into. If we have before us a thorny plant and conclude that it must be a cactus, we have applied our knowledge that cacti have thorns and reasoned that thorny plants are therefore cacti. The reasoning may be incorrect, but it is an example of the use of analogy.

In archeology we use analogy in three basic ways: to determine the uses of objects, to give us an idea of how people in the past may have lived, and to help us discover how particular behavior relates to remains found in sites. An example of the latter, which is the most difficult to understand, is to study modern Pueblo Indian potters to see whether designs and styles of pots reflect their customs of marriage and postnuptial residence. Another example would be to study the ceremonial activities of a group with the intention of discovering how we could infer these activities from the archeological evidence that would remain.

The use of a modern primitive group as an example of the way a prehistoric people may have lived has had a long and useful history beginning as early as 1865, when Lord Avebury wrote *Prehistoric Times, as Illustrated by Ancient Remains and the Manners and Customs of Modern Savages.* The technique was popularized and captivated an international audience in Sollas's work, published first in 1911, *Ancient Hunters and Their Modern Representatives.* One of the most recent examples is a well-illustrated book by Grahame Clark, *The Stone Age Hunters,* whose contents are chiefly a description of prehistoric cultures but whose illustrations contain analogous examples drawn from modern Australian peoples living apparently similar ways of life. This approach has the advantage of presenting living examples of ways of life that otherwise are scarcely credible to many people raised in urban-industrial surroundings. Vivid photographs, motion pictures, tape recordings, and examples of artifacts used in hunting or preparing food tell much more to the average student of prehistory than do pages of drawings of projectile points, floor plans of post molds, and tables of bones listed in Latin by genus and species. The expression, "the dry-as-dust facts of archeology," is only too oppressively real to a novice who is working his way for the first time through the tedious presentation of data in a typical site report. For him a boldly drawn analogy with a living people may be his only convincing clue that the whole business is not just an unfathomable and jealously guarded secret kept by a coterie of strange men in pith helmets.

In spite of the obvious value of ethnographic analogy for popularizing prehistory, it must be used with considerable caution, because prehistory deals with the past, and things were different then, the more so as one goes farther back in time. This statement applies both to the environment (even if climate has not changed) and to the ways people lived. Modern-day cultures are the products of their unique histories and inevitably must be different in some respects from all other societies. We should remember also that every human invention and kind of organization had its historical "first." When to this realization we add the fact that communication was far from instantaneous, we realize that prehistoric peoples had far fewer potential alternatives of experience to draw on and were thus more limited in their possible actions than are people today.

If we wish to use analogy to help with particular archeological problems, it is well to keep in mind some rules concerning its use. Dozier (1970:203–205) lists six such rules.

> *First*, it is important to have the temporal factor in mind. The shorter the time gap between a prehistoric site and the living site, the more likely that the inference will be a reliable one.
>
> *Second*, . . . the sociocultural level of the prehistoric and ethnologic groups must be matched—at least roughly. For example, analogies between band-level societies and tribal ones may be made only with caution . . .
>
> *Third*, . . . it is important to compare societies having the same type of subsistence economy: hunting-gathering with hunting-gathering ones, agricultural with agricultural ones, . . .
>
> *Fourth*, inferences about societies widely separated in space can be made only with extreme caution . . . The initial work on inferences with analogy to ethnologic groups should be restricted to contiguous areas where the history, prehistory, and distribution of sociocultural and linguistic groups are fairly well known.
>
> *Fifth*, in making inferences, language affiliation should be given low priority (that is, languages may differ while culture does not).
>
> *Sixth*, . . . some measure of how conservative the ethnologic culture has been over time should be established . . . (that is, those that have changed the least are the most dependable analogs).

Culture Systems

"One of the most important ideas in modern science is the idea of a *system;* and it is almost impossible to define" (Hardin 1968:455). One speaks easily of systems and finds them everywhere he looks, but to be useful a concept must be accurately defined. A. Hall and Fagen (1956:18) put it this way: "A system is a set of objects together with relationships between the objects and between their attributes." A system can be subdivided into subsystems. Systems can be physical, biological, and cultural; their common denominator is organization—the way in which the objects interact or relate to one another.

The central concept in scientific and historical studies of cultures or culture, past and present, is system. The term has various shades of meaning which we will discuss below. In anthropology, culture is often said to be patterned; it is systematic in a predictable way. We may also see cultures as examples of life systems that have the same properties and are affected by the same processes as all life systems (Chap. 15). The two uses of the term system are conceptually different and are based on quite different traditions of thought.

The general anthropological view, which is concerned little with long-term changes, sees culture as composed of interrelated parts that are mutually interdependent. Thus, anthropologists may see relationships among settlement pattern, subsistence techniques, social organization, and religious beliefs. All these and other aspects (subsystems) of a culture "hang together" in a consistent way, lending stability to the way of life and ensuring a measure of predictability in the behavior of individuals in the culture. "If a society is to survive, the gears of its culture must mesh, even though they may growl and grind" (Hoebel 1972:26). A good bit of social anthropology is aimed at describing and interpreting the interactions among the parts of a culture in terms of their mutual effects.

The anthropological view of the systemic nature of culture derives from the fact of variation among cultures and the attempt to understand it. How can we account for the way a people reckon kinship? How does it happen that two peoples speaking closely related languages have quite different cultures, or that peoples who are linguistically unrelated share many basic elements of culture? What is it that makes cultures distinct and how may the distinctions be characterized? These are some of the questions anthropologists have asked and attempted to explain through viewing culture as "the integrated system of learned behavior patterns which are characteristic of the members of a society and which are not the result of biological inheritance" (Hoebel 1972:6). Basic to the concept of culture is that:

1. Every culture represents a limited selection of behavior patterns from the total of human potentialities, individual and collective.
2. The selection tends to be made in accordance with certain postulates (dominant assumptions and values) basic to culture.
3. It follows that every culture exemplifies a more or less complete and coherent pattern, structure, or system of actions and relationships (Hoebel 1972: 26–27).

Culture is thus frequently discussed only in terms of its own properties and without explicit reference to a theory of systems. It is assumed that systematic relationships exist in cultures and that the nature of these relationships is to be found in the particular situations and explained in terms of the overall goals of survival and satisfaction. There typically follows a description of a culture in terms of its central tendencies, norms, or idealized patterns of how things ought to be done. The assumption is that most people behave as they should (at the very least, consistently) or else the culture in question will lack both coherence and, in the long run, endurance.

This is not to imply that there is no variation within a culture, only that norms do exist and that these can be discovered archeologically in the patterned remains found in sites. What is important is that there may be considerable variability within a site. In archeological fieldwork, one must sample a site to attempt to discover what the intrasite variability is and what it relates to. The implication is that variation itself is patterned and that the different patterned behaviors represented in archeological remains are related to one another in a systematic fashion that has as its underlying rationale the maintenance of the system.

Aberle (1970:216) makes the essential points in the following way:

> (1) culture is systemic; (2) it is an energy-harnessing system that articu-
> lates a human population with its environment; (3) by virtue of the na-
> ture of the productive activities and the social organization of produc-
> tion, there will be nonrandom variation within settlements as a result of
> (a) different practices in different family or larger kinship groupings, (b)
> differential locus of various activities, (c) status differentiation, if any,
> and (d) other reasons; (4) in an archaeological site, these differences ap-
> pear in nonrandom variability of artifacts, styles, leavings, and so forth.
> So, (5) it is insufficient for purposes of archaeological analysis to type a
> site and let it go at that.

The systemic view of "culture" is described by R. Thompson and Longacre (1966:270).

> We view culture as systemic and thus composed of various highly inter-
> related subsystems such as the social system, the technological system
> and the religious system. . . . All of the material remains in an archae-
> ological site are highly patterned or structured directly as a result of the
> ways in which the extinct society was organized and the patterned ways
> in which the people behaved. Thus our first task is to define the archae-
> ological structure at the site and then from that infer the organization of
> the society and aspects of behavior.

The process of making the inferences may become quite complex, but the goal, of course, is to attempt to explain how a cultural system works.

In examining cultural subsystems we focus our attention for the first time on people, not as individuals, but as members of once-living communities. However, we are not able to comprehend people in all of their facets. We may be able to say little about politics or theology, but we can perceive some of the ways to reconstruct how they were organized. All things are made up of organized parts; it is one of our jobs as social scientists to try to discover the principles of organization that make viable societies of collections of people. As archeologists we must try to reconstruct the organization of the people whose remains we can handle, count, measure, and draw.

It is probably fortunate that organization has emerged as one focal point of behavioral studies, because archeologists are able to find information in prehistory that relates to organization. The sites, the artifacts in them, and especially the way in which sites and artifacts occur, give clues to the organization of the society that left them. This conviction follows from our belief that cultures are patterned and adaptive. A particular culture represents a system whose parts, largely because of the requirement of adaptation, are organized in a cooperative, mutually beneficial way. Therefore we should be able to discern the patterns of interaction and describe the structure and organization of the system. We state this as a general hypothesis; it clearly needs to be tested with regard to cultures, but it seems to hold true for other communities of biological organisms. The hypothesis has important consequences for anthropology, but its value for archeology may not be obvious at first. Simply stated, it means that objects we find archeologically are remnants of behavior that was carried out in the context of the social system of the time. Therefore, from the artifacts, we can infer human activities. The hypothesis means, moreover, that we can seek interpretations of the material we find, in the expectation that it played an understandable role in an adaptive system. It is here that hypotheses about the operation of systems generally are important, for if we know some of the elements in a culture system we can make reasonable hypotheses, based on our knowledge of how similar systems operate, about other cultures. It needs to be stressed emphatically here, however, that we are talking about hypotheses and not about facts. It is our job to use the hypotheses for the insight they may give us about what to look for and, above all, to use them as accurately phrased questions that are capable of being definitely answered.

We have just written as though the single culture system is the basic unit of our analysis. It is not. Systems operate within systems, and virtually every human group known lived in contact with other human groups and within a context of a circumscribed physical arena. An adequate description of a social system and an understanding of its operation thus require a perspective that transcends the village or tribe and encompasses what we might call the symbiotic, nuclear, or key area that defines the effective universe of interaction for people in the system. At this point we find the concepts of human ecology relevant.

Adaptation

The centrality of the concept of adaptation can hardly be overstressed in either reconstruction or processual interpretation. Sanders and Price (1968:221) put the matter succinctly: "What is adaptive survives." Poorly adapted cultures, like poorly adapted biological organisms, are weeded out through natural selection. "The thesis I would seek to propound is quite simply that man and his way of life as this has developed down to the present day are both ultimately the product of natural selection" (G. Clark 1970:61). Freeman (1971:1197) makes the point even more strongly: "In our attempt to understand man's physical and behavioral evolution, we are at long last learning to distinguish Evolution from the concept of Progress and to equate it, as rightfully must be done, with Adaptation."

Alland (1970:40–41) discusses two aspects of adaptation. First are the long-range changes that maintain the viability of a system in relation to its environment. Second are the short-term adjustments that may or may not be carried through in the long term. An analysis of the way of life of a prehistoric people as found in a site describes an adjustment or adaptation to the circumstances of the time. An interpretation of the long-term changes as seen in evidence from many sites is an example of the first sense in which we may analyze adaptation.

Anthropologists, even those who have explicitly disavowed interest in culture history, tend to view social organization as a means of adaptation. A quotation from Radcliffe-Brown (1952:8–9) illustrates this very well.

> [Adaptation] is a key concept of the theory of evolution. It is or can be applied both to the study of the forms of organic life and to the forms of social life amongst human beings. A living organism exists and continues to exist only if it is both internally and externally adapted. The internal adaptation depends on the adjustment of the various organs and their activities, so that the various physiological processes constitute a continuing functioning system by which the life of the organism is maintained. The external adaptation is that of the organism to the environment within which it lives. The distinction of external and internal adaptation is merely a way of distinguishing two aspects of the *adaptational system* which is the same for organisms of a single species . . .
>
> When we examine a form of social life amongst human beings as an adaptational system it is useful to distinguish three aspects of the total system. There is the way in which the social life is adjusted to the physical environment (ecological) . . . There are the institutional arrangements by which an orderly social life is maintained (social) . . . there is the social process by which an individual acquires habits and mental characteristics that fit him for a place in the social life and enable him to participate in its activities (cultural) . . . What must be emphasized is that these modes of adaptation are only different aspects from which the total adaptational system can be looked at for convenience of analysis and comparison.

There is a tendency in anthropology to consider almost any kind of behavior adaptive simply because we believe that culture, through its institutions, serves as a means for man to adapt to his environment. Indeed, some anthropologists have gone to considerable lengths to justify in adaptive terms what the man on the street would regard as bizarre, stupid, or perhaps offensive behavior. Such studies are usually carried out by cultural ecologists and will be discussed in more detail later. For the present the important consideration is how to judge whether behavior is adaptive. In biology, adaptation is related strictly to reproduction. The more organisms that can be raised to maturity and supported, the better adapted that species is. By analogy, in cultural terms we might say that the more people a culture can support, the better adapted it is.

Although the link between biological and cultural adaptation can thus be measured quantitatively, one should beware of two pitfalls. First, adaptation depends partly on competition. If there is no competition for an ecologic niche, a culture may continue and be considered adapted; however, if competition develops, the former culture may find itself at considerable disadvantage and in the new circumstances cease to exist. This was the case for the native way of life of Native Americans after settlement of the continent by Europeans. Second, what gives a momentary advantage may not be viable in the long run. For example, an adaptive change (that is, one that allows for population growth, such as the adoption of firearms by a hunting people) may in the long run result in such a depletion of game that the system cannot withstand the shock when it occurs. Similarly, one could mention intensive farming or grazing practices that have seriously depleted the land, or the drawing of excessive amounts of ground water for irrigation from arid regions. One could also point to the effects of crowding that results from large increases in population; these are problems that have both psychological and physiological implications even if supplies of food and shelter are adequate. In all these cases, short-term advantage may lead to long-term disaster.

Ecology

Properly speaking, ecology is the scientific study of the interrelations of organisms with each other and within a specified physical environment. More generally speaking, however, the term "ecology" denotes a concept developed in biology to define the relations of an animal to its organic and inorganic environments. The concept implies a concern with how an organism relates to its inanimate environment and also with the interrelationships among organisms who live together in mutual interdependence. The mutual interdependence implies organized relationships and consequently a system, or ecosystem as it is usually called. Parenthetically it should be stressed that the well-advertised concern among conservationists for "ecology" is not the same thing. There is always an environment, whether polluted or not, and there are always organisms adapting to their environments. Ecology cannot be killed, although specific niches may be fouled. "Ecologic niche" is also a useful concept; it is the particular animate and inanimate sphere within which an organism carries out its life. Classic studies in ecology have often focused upon specific niches—ponds, stumps, forests, or grasslands. A culture's niche is likewise circumscribed, although usually not so narrowly.

The relationships within a niche may be described in terms of who eats whom or who benefits from the others. We can describe the food chain in these terms; it begins with the lower organisms, which convert solar energy through photosynthesis into vegetation, which is then eaten by the animals that constitute the next links in the chain, and are themselves consumed by "higher" forms of life. These are predatory relationships; one animal benefits and the other does not. We may also find commensal relationships in which one species benefits another. These relationships are neutral in effect. Finally there are relationships in which both species gain from their mutual behavior. We might, for example, see animal husbandry as an example of mutualism; in this instance man protects the animals and allows their numbers to increase so that he can harvest them for his advantage.

Cultural ecology is a subfield within anthropology that seeks to understand the workings of culture systems in ecologic terms. It is clear that man has relations with his animate and inanimate environments, but in addition his culture serves to relate him to others of his own species, including people outside his immediate group. The ecologic niche within which people operate is thus broader and more complex than among other animate species.

> The cultural ecologist sees the culture of a given people as a subsytem in interaction with other subsystems. He argues that the key to understanding the developmental processes of the cultural subsystem lies in this interactive relationship. The total network of relationships between subsystems has been called the "ecological system" or "ecosystem." It includes three subsystems—culture, biota, and physical environment (Sanders and Prince 1968:171).

The focus of attention in cultural ecology is in the interaction among these three subsystems. Sanders (1965) presents eight postulates (somewhat abridged here):

a. Each biological and physical environment offers particular problems to human utilization.
b. Diverse environments offer different problems; therefore, the response by man (that is, the development of a cultural subsystem) will be different.
c. There is an almost unlimited number of possibilities but a limited number of probabilities in the way in which a people may adapt to a given environment. . . .
d. Response to environmental challenges may be technological, social, or ideational. . . .
e. In a broad sense men living in similar environments solve the problem of adaptation in similar ways: in differing environments, in different ways. . . .
f. There is some overlapping of responses and solutions even in cases of strikingly dissimilar environments. . . .
g. Cultures are dynamic, as are all of the components of an ecological system, and the degree of integration of a cultural subsystem to the total ecological system will vary. . . .
h. The culture of a given people, therefore, can be considered essentially as a complex of techniques adaptive to the problems of survival in a particular geographic region. . . .

Cultural ecology is derived from general ecologic studies in biology. Somewhat more restricted in view is an approach pioneered in archeology by Grahame Clark and effectively presented in his classic work, *Prehistoric Europe: The Economic Basis.*

> One of the principal attractions of prehistory is the opportunity it offers for studying the interplay of social aspiration and environing nature over long periods of time. The economy of any community may be considered as an adjustment to specific physical and biological conditions of certain needs, capacities, aspirations, and values. . . . There are thus two sides of the equation . . . the character of the habitat . . . and the kind of life regarded as appropriate by the community (G. Clark 1952:7).

Clark's use of the concepts of ecology can be considered restricted only in the sense that he chose for reasons of the availability of evidence to emphasize the economic aspects (subsistence, trade, technology, and so on) of prehistoric life. Also, he regarded economy as of fundamental importance. "The economy of any community . . . is . . . the product of an adjustment between culture and environing nature" (G. Clark 1952:7). Clark has emphasized the economic subsystem of culture, an approach that has been especially fruitful although not as comprehensive or as informative as studies that examine the ecosystem in its broader aspects. Examples of both approaches are given in succeeding chapters.

Models

Models are conceptual structures that (a) organize and guide our thinking (heuristic), (b) describe the relationships between variables (explanatory or legal), or (c) describe a situation in graphic form (illustrative). Most models used in prehistoric interpretation are primarily heuristic and consist of labels like "the Bronze Age," or "the Archaic." This is like saying the Elizabethan Age or the Golden Age of Rome. Such labels are informative in that they connote a vast range of information to a person trained to understand them, but they are of no value to the neophyte. Another kind of heuristic model is exemplified by the concept "pattern." We take as a truism that all cultures are patterned and from that it follows that pattern in the distribution of artifacts is meaningful. Thus we have structured our thinking, established some guidelines for fieldwork, and partially determined the results of our analysis by employing the concept "pattern." We have not explained anything; we have only structured our thinking.

Prehistorians often employ ethnographic analogy as illustrative and heuristic models to aid in the interpretation of their data. Present-day Pueblo Indians may serve that purpose for archeologists working in the Southwest; modern hunters and gatherers may even help in understanding prehistoric men who lived thousands of years ago. Thus analogy is a form of model in that it structures our thinking.

Models, then, are nothing mysterious. We all use them in everyday life. Indeed, it is this ability to conceptualize categories of things and their relationships that enables us to carry out our daily lives effectively. We see this readily in the normative aspects of culture itself, both from the point of view of a participant who knows what ought to be and from the point of view of the outsider who abstracts from observation of collective behavior a model of a culture. These models are called ethnographies.

The remaining chapters are devoted to employing the concepts we have discussed here, sometimes with fuller discussion of their implications.

Chapter 11

SUBSISTENCE AND ECONOMIC SYSTEMS

In attempting to understand people in prehistory, one might ask, as Childe (1956) did, who the people were, when they lived, what their culture was, and how their culture changed. The questions might be approached frontally in the order given (as they were by Rouse 1965), but our present purposes, which ultimately tend toward the same information, lead us to put the questions in another form. Who, what, when, and how are questions of very different magnitude, requiring different orders of interpretation, and it seems most reasonable to begin with the simpler and work toward the more complex. Moreover, Childe's approach was more nearly in the tradition of historiography, working as he was with European prehistory, which could be linked with historically known peoples. Our approach is more nearly akin to anthropology, where culture, rather than cultures in the specific sense, is important. Accordingly, we are more interested in what was happening and in how ways of life changed than we are in precisely who the people were.

The simplest topics to deal with, and those for which interpretations are the most straightforward, are technology, subsistence, and economy. In fact, one can reasonably treat them as aspects of the same thing under the general term "economy."

What Is Economy?

Prehistoric man did not have a money economy such as we are familiar with today. His economy consisted, not of buying, selling, and consuming, but of acquiring, distributing, and consuming. The different words show that basically similar actions and transactions are implied but that the basis of the economy was "do-it-yourself," "reciprocity," and "barter." Prehistoric economy consisted of the way in which man hunted, fished, and collected food; the way he farmed, harvested, and prepared food; the way he used or distributed these products; the shelters in which he lived and the tools he used; the trade he carried on for raw materials; and the manner in which he traveled. In short, prehistoric man's economy was multifaceted, reaching into the technological, environmental, and social spheres of his life.

To begin with the simple, we can consider the landscape, which offered opportunities and set limitations on what man might do. The landscape can be studied easily in the present, but two questions arise when we consider its relation to prehistoric man. First, how does today's landscape compare with that in the past, and second, what skills did man have to exploit the resources that were potentially available? Bearing these two questions in mind, we can consider the role of the landscape in general.

Man lives in a world of plants, animals, minerals, the soil, weather, and people. Taken together, they comprise the elements of an ecosystem whose operations or organization archeologists try to reconstruct in their descriptions of prehistoric ways of subsistence and economy (Figs. 11.1, 11.2, 11.3). Plants are basic to man's life, and they in turn depend on climate and soil. Vegetation is dispersed in accordance with climatic zones, and the animals that feed on the plants are thus restricted in their distribution. In turn, man was constrained in his hunting and gathering by the well-defined distribution of species around the world. For most of his prehistory man was not able to move plants and animals from their natural environments to places better suited to his purposes. Such manipulations were possible only after the domestication of plants and animals.

Even with an environment full of plants and animals, man had to be able to use them. He needed the technology for killing his food, for butchering or otherwise preparing it, and for storing and distributing it. Mastery of food procurement came quickly; even today we have not adequately solved the last two problems. Although most of the history of prehistoric man is the story of his increasing efficiency in acquiring food, man still remains at the mercy of his environment to the degree that he can grow only certain crops in any particular

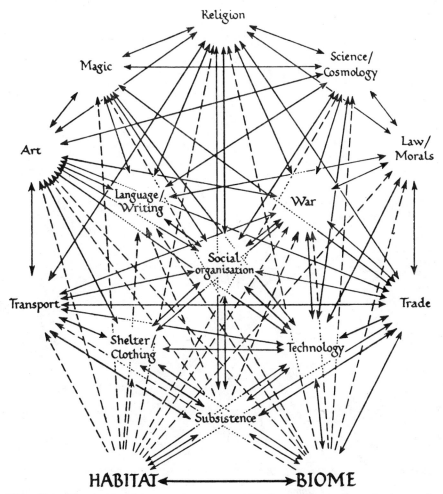

FIG. 11.1 The habitat-biome-culture network that characterizes the interrelations of man with his environment. (G. Clark 1953b, Fig. 6.)

area. Where modern man has produced plant hybrids, irrigation, and fertilizer, prehistoric man was largely nonscientific and was forced to get along with what luck and trial-and-error experimentation could produce.

No single environment, delimited by the distance a man might walk in his yearly round of hunting or farming, could supply all the material he might wish to use or might require. In many places this limitation meant that he did without or was forced to settle for a substitute. He may have wished for obsidian to make sharp blades but have had to settle for flint.

Prehistoric people could adjust to a wide range of opportunities, but they were not always able to maintain life in all places the year round until they had developed sufficient capacity for acquiring items that might be scarce, and the means of storing or otherwise protecting them. One of the principal means

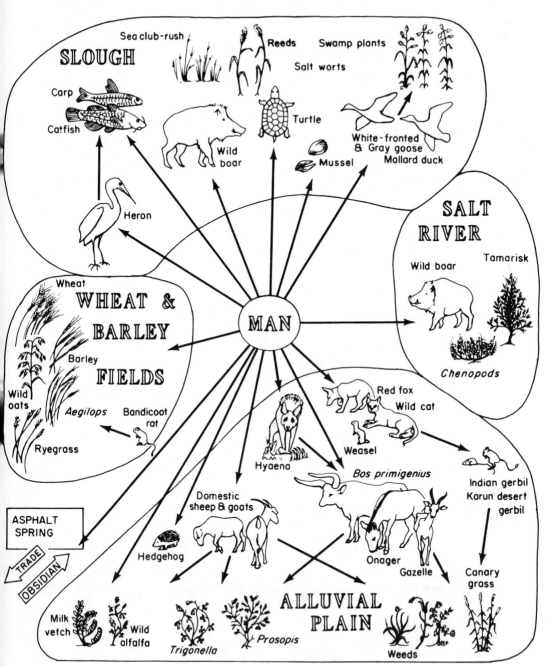

FIG. 11.2 *Simplified diagram of man's exploitation of wild and domestic re-sources in northern Khuzistan during the seventh and eighth millennia B.C. Also shown are major imports, exports, and a part of the food chain of some of the animal species involved, by "microenvironment."*

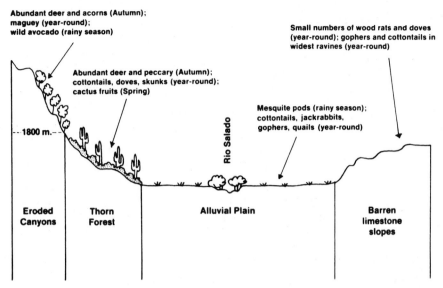

Abundant deer and acorns (Autumn);
maguey (year-round);
wild avocado (rainy season)

Small numbers of wood rats and doves
(year-round); gophers and cottontails in
widest ravines (year-round)

Abundant deer and peccary (Autumn);
cottontails, doves, skunks (year-round);
cactus fruits (Spring)

Mesquite pods (rainy season);
cottontails, jackrabbits,
gophers, quails (year-round)

Rio Salado

-- 1800 m. --

Eroded	Thorn	Alluvial Plain	Barren
Canyons	Forest		limestone
			slopes

FIG. 11.3   The diversity of ecological zones that may be found in a limited area is illustrated by this idealized east–west trans-section of the central part of the Tehuacan Valley, Puebla, Mexico. (See Fig. 4.14, which shows a Mexican thorn forest.) The seasons in which food is available in each zone are indicated. East is to the left. The length of the area represented is about 20 kilometers. (M. D. Coe and K. V. Flannery, "Microenvironments and Mesoamerican Prehistory." Science, Vol. 143 (1964):Fig. 1, pp. 650–654. Copyright 1964 by the American Association for the Advancement of Science.)

developed was domestication of plants and animals, whose effect was to bring necessary foodstuffs into an area and keep them there until they were consumed. Under preagricultural conditions, people may have been able to stay in one locale only a short time until they had to move on in pursuit of food. What this illustrates is the dual roles of natural resources in a landscape and the ability of man, through technology, to exploit and manipulate the resources for his special purposes.

During much of prehistory it appears that the major concerns of people were acquiring food and protecting themselves by building shelters. These activities required weapons and tools of stone and they left easily recognizable traces in the ground. Consequently, we probably find more information that we can confidently relate to technology and subsistence (economy) than to any other aspect of life in ancient times.

Diet

If preservation is good, we can tell quite a lot about diet, especially of the animals eaten. Because of their poor preservation it is much more difficult to tell what plants were consumed, although techniques like flotation and new methods of extracting pollen have helped greatly in recovering evidence of dietary plants. The identification of species is a routine process of matching bones, seeds, cells, or pollen with examples from the modern flora and fauna. What is much more uncertain, however, is what these remains mean with respect to diet. There are several relevant considerations: what percentage of the total diet was made up of any single source of food, what was the seasonal variation in abundance and in variety, what was the nutritive potential, what was the capacity of the food to be stored and of the people to store it, if we consider their technology and degree of mobility.

These kinds of information help us understand subsystems and the processes of culture generally. The relative proportions of meat to plant food, or of wild to domesticated resources, can tell us about the stability of a group, the area it must control or exploit, and its potential for growth. These answers will lead to speculation about the necessity or desirability of trade or interaction between groups of people who exploited somewhat different sets of resources. The data will also permit us to infer the number of people who could be supported, and this estimate in turn gives us some idea of the kind of social organization that might have regulated the population in the acquisition, distribution, and consumption of food. It is only when we consider all these aspects of activity that we can imagine a system operating to satisfy the basic necessities of life for a particular group of people.

Man's diet has ranged from almost complete dependence on animal food, as with certain Eskimo groups, to societies such as Brahmin Indians, who place practically complete dependence on vegetable foods; its scope ranges from the extremes of hunting—or better, scrounging—to full domestication and controlled food production.

Until man became adept at special techniques for catching animals, he was geographically restricted. The earliest man had no bows and arrows, or even spears; he had to rely on the crippled or small animals he might catch by hand, carrion from the kills of carnivores, or animals trapped in bogs. He could not afford to be too choosy about what he ate. Specialization—in the face of varied possibilities—presupposes considerable know-how and the ability to produce on demand what is needed. The earliest man, therefore, must have been largely omnivorous, depending greatly on plants for food and supplementing his diet with meat when he was lucky. A mouse was probably important in his diet to a degree that would have been laughable to the skilled hunters of big game in later times.

Studies of bones can tell many things about man's way of life as well as specifically about his diet. The species of animals represented tell about both the resources available in an area and man's use of them. The bones can also tell the ages of animals and their relative sizes so that we can infer the time of year when people hunted and what contribution to the diet each species made. We can also get some impression of man's skill as a hunter by observing which species were taken, the numbers of animals represented, and their ages. A study of the bones may also reveal in great detail just how butchering was carried out and subsequently how the food was prepared for eating. Finally, bones tell us when there were changes in the animals of the type we associate with domestication.

Identification of species and of their archeological implications is a task that is ordinarily carried out by trained zoologists who are thoroughly acquainted with comparative anatomy. When dealing with bones from archeological sites, most zoologists depend on collections of skeletons of known modern species and try to match the prehistoric bones to them. Obviously this is not possible for extinct species, although for the most part those found in sites are likely to be similar to their modern counterparts. There are, however, many very subtle differences between species, whether viable or extinct, whose recognition may have profound effect upon an archeological interpretation. It should be emphasized, then, that faunal identifications and interpretations must be handled by properly trained persons.

It is relatively easier to learn about man's meat diet than about his vegetable diet. Plants are seldom preserved—and then rarely ever beyond 10,000 years. On the other hand, the charred remains of plants may last indefinitely. Charred seeds, for example, retain their morphological characteristics and can thus be identified by a specialist; unless they are subjected to mechanical destruction—breaking or crushing—they should last forever. The problem appears to be one of finding the seeds rather than of having the plants themselves preserved. The widely used technique of flotation, in which carbonized bits of vegetable remains and seeds are separated from the earth through the use of water or another chemical, has enabled the recovery of an extraordinary amount of information where it had previously been thought not to exist. Unfortunately, flotation does not work in all situations. Apparently it works best where the plant remains have been protected by a cushion of fine-grained dust or alluvium. Coarse-textured matrices crush and abrade the seeds.

Evidence of seeds and of parts of plants may also be found in impressions in the clay of pottery or bricks of buildings. They may be found in coprolites (Fig. 11.4) and in the stomachs of mummies and bodies buried in acidic bogs. There may also be evidence in depictions on pottery, walls, and caves. Even teeth, through patterns of wear, may carry dietary information. Archeologists have inferred the cutting of grains from the presence of sickles in sites, and hoes and digging sticks can be similarly used to indicate horticultural activities. Finally, most archeologists attempt to discover what foods the environment offered prehistoric men and then they may make some guesses about actual diets, based when possible on ethnographic evidence.

A great deal of ingenuity has been expended in the attempt to extract useful dietary information from archeological sites, and both techniques and interpretation continually undergo review and revision. We have emphasized that it is possible to learn much about diet, but the situation varies so much from site to site that the particulars are of little concern here. What is more

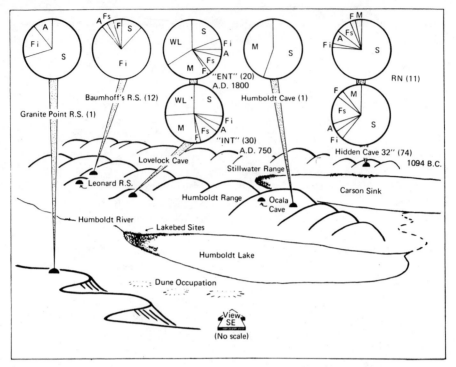

FIG. 11.4 *Prehistoric diet as determined from identification of food items in coprolites from dry cave and shelter sites in the Humboldt-Carson lakes region of western Nevada. The pie diagrams indicate percentages of types of food: S, seeds; Fi, fiber; Fs, fish; F, fauna; M, miscellaneous; WL, weight loss of coprolite material carried off in solution during rehydration process. Dates are radiocarbon ages. Numbers in parentheses indicate number of coprolites analyzed. (For details see Napton 1969.)*

important is that even with good preservation, bones and seeds must still be related to prehistoric ways of life. This implies determining relative emphases and daily, seasonal, and annual food-gathering practices.

Unless we can uncover caches that indicate how much food could have been harvested or collected, we have no good way of estimating surplus production or acquisition. The absence of bones, or the presence of only a few, may indicate that vegetable products were more important than meat. In the few instances where quantitative studies have been made on the bones from several sites, it has been possible to distinguish clear-cut differences in the diets of groups of people who, it might otherwise have been assumed, lived on identical foods.

J. T. Davis (1959) has critically reviewed a number of generalizations made by Southwestern archeologists about the relative importance of animal versus vegetable food in the diet of the occupants of specific prehistoric sites, and has shown that these for the most part rest on very tenuous grounds. The archeologist must not only use judgment in reaching inferences on the basis of what is present, but also keep in mind that a great deal more evidence has disappeared without any trace. It is this requirement—that the prehistorian balance what is known against an indeterminate amount of information that is not known—that makes the job of interpretation so difficult. As A. L. Kroeber once wrote, the training of anthropology consists of "learning to discriminate between better and worse judgments and better or worse evidence."

It is probably safer to make inferences from ethnography about subsistence and economy than about any other aspect of prehistoric life, but even these safer inferences are subject to error, as can be shown from an example that combines the use of ethnographic analogy and the direct historical method. The example concerns the data from Lovelock Cave in western Nevada. Ethnographic studies made around the 1930s of the Northern Paiute Indians indicated that the subsistence pattern involved small groups of people who ranged widely, seasonally collecting pine nuts, kutsavi fly larvae, and cuyui sucker fish, which could then be stored and consumed over the lean winter months. Surprisingly, prehistoric coprolites from the cave showed nearly total dependence on plants and fish present in Humboldt Lake, about 2 miles from the cave; no pine nuts, larvae, or river fish are present in the remains from the cave. A search of historical records showed that the local Indians were dislodged from their prehistoric sites and forced to change their way of life only after 1833. Hence an apparently stable pattern of life, which had been recorded ethnographically and on which many analogous reconstructions were based, is in fact an artifact of the white man's recent encroachment on Indian territory (R. Cowan 1967).

That the subsistence pattern had been inferred incorrectly leads one to question whether other reconstructions of the social organization of the prewhite period are valid. Following Steward's studies in the Great Basin among Shoshonean speakers, most anthropologists conceptualize small family groups scattered over the countryside, moving from grass harvests to grasshopper hunts, to acorn or piñon harvesting as the ripening plants and the seasons dictate. Altogether it is a hand-to-mouth existence. But now it seems that some of the groups, like those at Lovelock Cave, had a much more stable existence. What then does this do to our usual view of the social organization? The wandering bands had a simple family organization having patrilineal descent, with no formal leaders. Can we say the same of a larger settled group? This matter clearly needs further investigation; it is mentioned here chiefly by way of example.

Evidence of diet is won from the soil only with the most diligent effort and exercise of ingenuity by the archeologist. Often techniques must be invented or perfected in the hope that something may be found. A case in point is the flotation process, a technique that was suggested by a botanist (Hugh Cutler) to an archeologist (Stuart Struever) to help him find remains that he thought should be in refuse pits but were invisible to the naked eye. In fact, although Struever (1968a) reported that almost all the small seeds and bones had passed unnoticed through the usual dry screen, after flotation at one site, tens of thousands of nut shells, seeds, and fish bones were recovered; the result was a picture of the local subsistence economy that was completely different from what had been imagined. Although these results may seem to have been attained by the use of a simple technique, the process now in use was developed only after several years of work involving many hundreds of man-hours of hard labor.

We might tell much the same story about the botanists who have strained their eyes during thousands of hours at the microscopes to learn the criteria that signal the difference between wild and domestic cereals, or the characteristics of the pollen grains that serve so well to give a picture of the local environment. The important thing is that, before any cultural interpretations can be made, somebody must get the data out of the ground and identify them.

Technology

Studies of diet lead directly into studies of technology, because the two aspects of economy are often intimately intertwined. When technology is known in detail, it is possible to infer that certain kinds of hunting or farming were practiced. For example, when an archeologist finds sickles at a settlement he usually infers agriculture, although sometimes sickles may have been used to cut plants other than cultivated grain. Bows and arrows indicate hunting of animals; a study of the kinds of points used may indicate what kind of game was being hunted. Bolas (stones tied to long cords for entangling the feet of game) are an old invention; they were probably nearly as effective as spears or arrows. However, it is not always possible to tell what was hunted merely by looking at the tools: absence of a tool may mean nothing. In connection with the use of bolas is the interesting suggestion that their habitual use might leave some skeletal evidence in early man. Wells (1964:134–135) describes modifications of the humerus that result when slings are used, and it may be that similar motor habits, such as hurling bolas, would leave tangible evidence in the modification of bones.

As we know from a few rare finds, people who lacked spears tipped with stone could have used perishable bone or wood points. One of the Mousterian skeletons at Mt. Carmel, Skhul (IX), showed evidence of having received a hip wound from a four-sided wooden spear (McCown and Keith 1939:2:74–75, 373), and from this we can verify what has seemed highly probable; namely, that the Mousterians used simple wooden spears. What is more, some people may have preferred to snare animals or to catch them in deadfalls or other traps rather than to shoot or spear them. If people had no bows and arrows or **atlatls,** they were limited to trapping or hunting at close range. Such a situation might altogether preclude the killing of certain types of beasts. Negative evidence for various types of weapons is useful primarily where sites show good preservation and a variety of wooden and bone tools; then it may safely be inferred that a number of other tools, such as stone spears, were not used.

Without the means for storing food, people had to spend considerable time in its acquisition. This condition probably existed during most of human history, but it was relatively more of a problem for collectors of plants than for big-game hunters. Furthermore, people who had to carry burdens on their backs were limited in the amount they could carry and in the distance they could cover. Sometimes the carrying of burdens prevented extreme dependence on one source of food that might have been favored. For example, for many Native American groups the bison was only seasonally important before the use of the horse on the Great Plains. After that time, Plains Indian economy was revolutionized, and the people became almost totally dependent on the bison for the necessities of life. This is merely one illustration of the interplay between technology and subsistence; and the correlates in social organization are also striking. Lack of certain tools also prevented people from exploiting rich farm land. Before the moldboard plow was invented, people who could not break the sod were prevented from farming the prairie grasslands—and much of the world's best farm land needed first to be cleared of forest with axes and fire.

Such instances serve to illustrate a point: it is difficult to make inferences about diet from technological evidence alone. We know only some of the ways of obtaining food; many others must have been developed and forgotten. Furthermore, we are at the mercy of preservation, and we can rarely be sure that we have the total picture. The biggest and ever-present problem in archeology is how to fill the gaps in the record that have been caused by the disappearance of organic materials.

There are many aspects to technology, not all of which relate to the food quest. First and foremost, a study of technology reveals the steady increase of man's skills. Thomsen devised the Three-Age System—Stone, Bronze, and Iron —and it was applied to describe the cultural evolution of man. As Childe (1944b) has pointed out, each of the three ages indicated a significant technological advance that allowed man to do many more things than had been possible before. Today most of the stages of prehistory have been defined on the basis of technology. Put into a series, the stages indicate an ever-better mastery, through tools, of the environment. As man learned to do new things with the resources about him, his economy was enriched. In some instances it meant that he was able to live better, that is, with less worry about food shortages. In other instances he was able to move into new areas, and in still others he was able to surround himself with luxuries. These advances in technology and the fruits derived from them eventually contributed to craft specialization, population increases, large political groupings, and social hierarchies. The culmination was the increasing complexity of society and the increasing technical mastery of the world that has led to civilization as we know it.

The study of technology can lead to inferences about man's cultural progress, but it is also informative about his relations with other people. For more recent prehistoric times it is often possible to trace the spread of technological knowledge into an area and to note the effect it had on the people there. For example, a study of sites in Europe indicates that farming was not accepted by all at first and that a hunting and fishing way of life died slowly (Fig. 11.5) (G. Clark 1952). Even though a population might try to perfect a particular

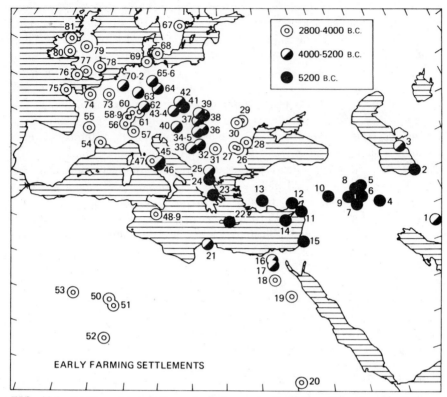

FIG. 11.5 Radiocarbon dating of early agricultural settlements in Europe, which illustrate the slow northwestward spread of farming. (From G. Clark 1965. For a recent assessment of the true ages of the dates given here see Renfrew 1970b.)

subsistence economy, it might not always be able to count on its productivity. Total commitment to a specialized economy by prehistoric men was often hazardous, and as a consequence, seasonally different economies must have been fairly common; yet they are difficult to identify from archeological materials.

Study of technology may also reveal where and how objects were made. Metal tools, containers, and ornaments as well as some pottery were manufactured by specialists whose skills were beyond those of the common folk. When especially distinctive wares were made, it is possible to trace their trade throughout an area. When this trade has been charted, we can ask what was traded in exchange. Such inquiry may reveal that grains, skins, or raw materials were being exchanged for finished products. Exotic items always imply trade, and because trade—as opposed to tribute—usually follows a two-way road, it gives us the best opportunity for finding direct evidence of the extent to which any particular group of people was isolated. Precise knowledge of the geographic limits of trade enables us to plot the areas of effective intercommunication or interaction for each group of prehistoric people; this knowledge in turn lets us make reasonable guesses about the sources of influence and the nature of the contacts between areas.

Caches of an artisan's tools or paraphernalia of a specialist may throw light on the association of many items that otherwise occur only singly (Fig. 11.6). A few examples may be cited. W. Emery (1961:137–139) mentions a number of burials that were deposited on the perimeter of the tomb of a queen of the First Dynasty of Egypt. The bodies in these graves were those of special craftsmen, such as sculptors, artists, sailors, and butchers, each one accompanied by the characteristic tools of his trade. Dawkins (1880:384–388) provides a list and description of the items in a bronzesmith's hoard found at Larnaud, France. The hoard contained 1485 pieces, of which 163 are items used directly for smelting or working bronze, 266 are tools and implements, 211 are weapons, and the remaining 845 are personal ornaments. This hoard, if analyzed by modern spectrochemical methods and compared with the rich body of museum materials, would yield an important story of where the individual items originated and provide hints as to the ways in which it was accumulated.

Mention may also be made of the marvelous models of daily life, activities, and familiar objects that are found in Egyptian royal tombs and from which much specific and detailed interpretation can be extracted (Winlock 1942:25ff.;

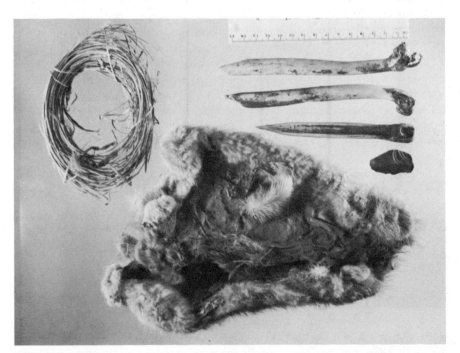

FIG. 11.6 Basketmaker's kit from Lovelock Cave, Nevada. Foxskin pouch contained the coil of weft material, one complete bone awl, two split bones to be made later into awls, and a sharp-edged flint flake that presumably served as a knife.

1955). The varied activities, such as sowing, reaping, fowling, hunting, and warfare, shown on Egyptian tomb paintings provide us with pictorial evidence of what and how things were done in dynastic times, and we can reconstruct from them many aspects of the technology of these ancient people. On the other hand, W. S. Smith (1958:13) cautions against assuming that the Egyptian paintings and engraved reliefs are always literally exact when he writes,

> Because the Egyptian's pictorial record was unique among his contemporaries, it is now infinitely precious, but his remarkable powers of observation have paradoxically laid him open to criticism for his carelessness. Obviously he was not impelled by a scientific interest in the modern sense and was capable of all sorts of inconsistencies. Hence, there is a danger in drawing too exacting conclusions from his work.

Trade

In our own experience we usually think of trade as consisting of buying and selling in the market place or between nations, but more useful connotations for most of prehistory would be exchange, barter, and swapping. Although such dealings are without money they may be far from simple and in fact may require the most delicately balanced sets of conventions or rules. What is more, such exchange may literally be noneconomic, in the sense that no gain is expected nor any economic necessity fulfilled. As we can document from ethnographic sources, many modern means of redistributing goods cannot be understood by reference to our own Western industrial concepts of economy. Yet a careful analysis of trade in a prehistoric context can inform us, perhaps, more quickly than any other means, of the scope and nature of the effective sphere of interaction in which the people who lived at any one site were participating.

It is easy enough to recognize "foreign" objects in a site, but much harder to demonstrate that they were traded and to pinpoint their origin. The examples that follow will point up some of the problems.

The simplest sort of trade must have involved the casual meeting of two groups of people or their representatives, who bartered or exchanged goods. This sort of exchange would be expected among nomadic peoples. Before the use of metal or pottery such trade must have been limited, but we know of instances in which certain kinds of flint, calcite crystals, stalactites, sea shells, and obsidian were traded. None of these were necessities to the people who obtained them, although the imported flint and obsidian made better tools. It is worth noting that we do not find evidence of regular trade before the end of the Pleistocene, but sporadic finds indicate that at least a desultory trade in nonsubsistence items was going on. Saint-Perier (1913:49) lists molluscan species that are present in Upper Paleolithic sites in Lespugne, France, and finds that three species come from the Mediterranean and two from the Atlantic. Here, where there is no other hint of trade relations with these two coastal areas, both of which are about 200 kilometers distant from the site, one cannot make a definite decision on whether the mollusc hells occur at Lespugne through trade or because the occupants happened in the course of time to visit both coasts and collect the shells. A similar find in Pa Sangar, Iran, only piques the curiosity about the mechanism of transmission; the find by itself does not provide the details to fill in the picture (Hole 1970).

Objects for decoration and ritual were probably the most favored trade items, because prehistoric man was ordinarily self-sufficient so far as his basic food and tool needs were concerned. Luxury items were avidly sought and widely traded. Gold, copper, amber, and shells were traded at great distances, and their record provides archeologists with insight into the extent of man's known world. Such trade also tells us something of his acquisitive instincts and esthetic sensibilities. Trade in weapons and luxury goods has left a clear picture of the emergence of class differences and the relation of an "international economy" to the tribal status seekers.

Some very concrete evidence of the extent of such trade networks has been obtained from analyses of objects from many areas of the world. In the Near East, the trade of obsidian from sources in Anatolia to early village sites some hundreds of miles distant has been clearly documented, and opens up a realm of inquiry concerning the role of such trade in the spread of agriculture (Renfrew, Dixon, and Cann 1966; J. Dixon, Cann, and Renfrew 1968) (Fig. 11.7). Similar extensive networks of trade are seen in North America, where the Ohio Hopewell Indians traded for obsidian, mica, and other exotic materials from the Atlantic Ocean to the Rocky Mountains, a distance of perhaps 2000 miles or more. In Meso-America, trade routes were well established at the time of the Spanish conquest (Fig. 11.8), but objects in Olmec sites, where some of the earliest pyramids are found, also document a remarkably wide area of interaction for the time. In one of these large Olmec sites (La Venta), obsidian, which can be shown to have come from at least five separate sources, three of which are identified as occurring in Guatemala and in the state of Hidalgo north of Mexico City, enlarges our information on the geographical extent of Olmec commerce. A picture of trade contacts extending at least as far distant as 200 miles south, 350 miles east, and 300 miles north thus emerges from these simple facts. Therefore the Olmecs, who lived on the Gulf Coast plain between 1000 and 600 B.C., are seen to have lived in a larger world of contact and communication than might have been supposed, and any interpretation of their culture must take this fact into account.

The documentation of trade depends on the identification of sources of objects found in sites. Although this information often allows us to chart routes of transmission with some accuracy, it does not necessarily point to the nature of the exchange. We do not wish to imply that trade is always a kind of economic transaction, although that would certainly be suggested if we used our own market-oriented society as a model. Fortunately, we have abundant ethnographic evidence of other kinds of transaction that are probably more appro-

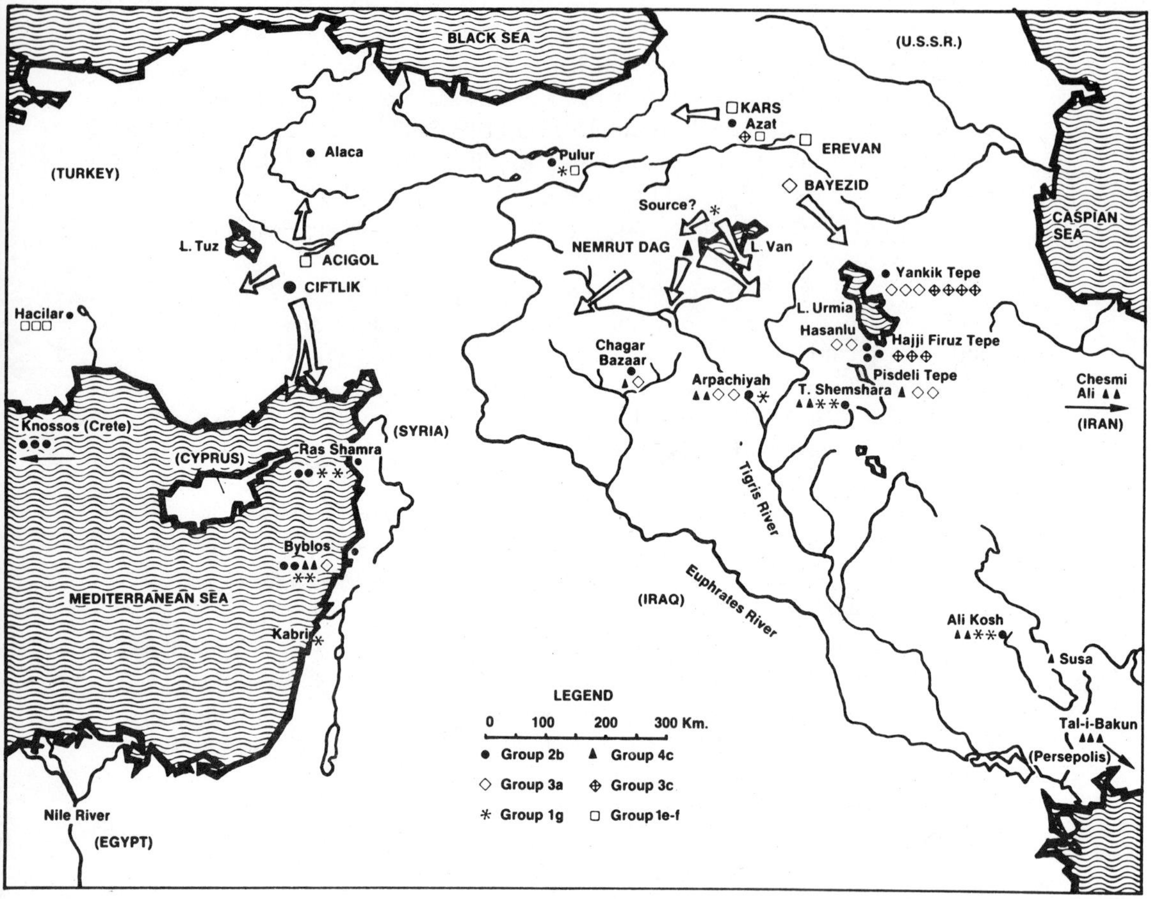

FIG. 11.7 *The obsidian trade in the Near East from the fifth to the second millennia B.C. (sources in capitals). Obsidian was one of the first raw materials to be systematically distributed by prehistoric men. The sources from which obsidian came can be determined precisely by several techniques: x-ray fluorescence, optical spectrography, and neutron activation. (C. Renfrew, J. E. Dixon, and J. R. Cann, "Obsidian and Cultural Contact in the Near East,"* Proceedings of the Prehistoric Society, *32 [1966]:Fig. 6.)*

priate models with which to view prehistory. Merely to cite some examples, we can mention that in some societies it is customary for people to pay tribute to their leaders and thereby bring in exotic items from far afield. Sometimes, too, we find that leading families exchange gifts among themselves in a way that is not at all representative of the society at large. A classic example of exchange is the "Kula-ring" described by Malinowski (1932), in which trading partners exchange coral for shells. These objects are exchanged in a regular cycle so that shells move in one direction around a circle of islands and coral in the other.

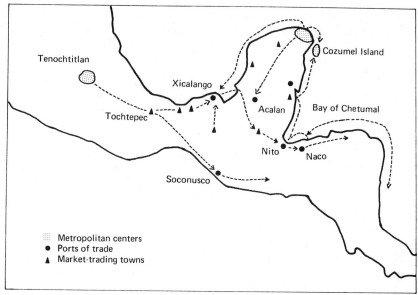

FIG. 11.8 Some main trade routes and trade centers in Meso-America at the opening of the Spanish Conquest.

The objects are kept only temporarily and then are passed on in an endless ring. Although this exchange takes place during trading sessions, in itself it cannot be considered "economic," and it would be extremely difficult to detect its underlying rationale through archeological methods.

The point to be made is that exchange implies social interaction. Without additional evidence, we cannot easily specify the nature of this interaction if we have only the objects that were exchanged or obtained by other means from afar.

Unless a site is the indisputable place where trade goods were made, it is often difficult to determine that certain items were traded. For example, pottery could be made by almost anyone, and for the most part trade pieces were probably only the finest wares, which were made by specialists. However, this statement need not necessarily be true. In Meso-America today there are villages where the people make pottery for a whole region, carry it to market periodically, and distribute it widely. In Crete (Xanthoudides 1927:118) and in Peru (Bruning 1898; Donnan 1971) there are itinerant potters who travel about the country and settle down for a time where good clay occurs and a profitable market exists for their wares.

In some cases traveling potters will bring with them a supply of dry, prepared clay. Such pottery, in archeological context, would not be distinguishable from pottery imported from outside. When their sojourn is no longer profitable, they move on. In antiquity such practices may have occurred and might account for some of the distributions of prehistoric pot forms or styles. Itinerant Bronze

Age smiths (perhaps like the Sleib or Solubiyeh, traveling tinkers of the Syrian desert) in Europe have long been recognized as one of the agencies of diffusion of metal-working techniques, as well as of types of ornaments.

Standards of Exchange

Minted metal coins were not used for exchange in prehistory. For the most part, the world was on a barter or exchange system, but there are a few instances in which a form of currency was in use (see Loeb 1936; Bessaignet 1956). The Aztecs and Mayas used the cacao bean (Chapman 1957). Some Indian groups in California measured wealth in tubular sea shells (*Dentalium indianorum*), the longer being the more valuable. We know that today tribal peoples in many countries reckon wealth in the numbers of livestock they own. When they make large purchases, a certain number of animals is judged to be an equivalent value. For example, in such systems so many chickens may equal a pig, and so many pigs may equal a cow. There is an element of barter economy in this exchange, but at the same time quite arbitrary values are given to things, and these values need have little relation to the intrinsic worth of an object. Thus, a pig with particularly well developed tusks may bring more than one with small tusks.

Without some system of arbitrary value-units, trade would not flourish, because it would be limited by the amount of real worth a person could pack on his back. The use of coins relieved man of having to tote a load of bloody hides home in trade for a copper ax—unless, of course, he happened to want hides. The use of coins enabled much more diversified exchange. A man with hides could sell to a man who wanted hides but who did not have axes to trade. The seller of hides could in turn buy an ax from a man who did not want hides.

On a surprisingly simple cultural level we note specialization of labor, where certain individuals or families work to produce finished products such as arrowpoints, fishnets, and bows and arrows, which they trade to their village mates for other finished items or for food. Ordinarily such craft specialization is found in settled village populations, who support themselves by agriculture, but the Indians of central California, whose economy was based on salmon, deer, and acorns and who are therefore nonagricultural, did practice craft specialization. An archeologist should not assume, therefore, that craft specialists come into existence with farming villagers.

Shelter

To the degree that people could shelter themselves they could live in areas that were too hot or too cold for constant exposure. Earliest men, like certain peoples living today, were content to lie under a shady bush or tree during the day and to huddle in a burrow during the chill of the night. We do not know when men first learned to build shelters or to clothe themselves with skins. However, once they had done either, they could vastly increase their geographic range. The use of fire not only supplemented their shelter but also enabled them to cook food. Some of the most ancient shelters built by man are the curved stone piles found in Olduvai Gorge at the site of the camping spot of "Zinjanthropus" (*Australopithecus*), whose age is determined by the potassium-argon method as about 1,750,000 years (Curtis 1961; Gentner and Lippolt 1969). The oldest unequivocal remains of huts occur at Terra Amata, a site in Nice, France, that was salvaged for archeology during the construction of an apartment building. These huts were apparently temporary shelters of poles and skins that were erected seasonally on the beach at a favorable location during the Mindel glaciation some 300,000 years ago (de Lumley 1966). The oldest known use of fire by man is at the site of Choukoutien, where the bones and tools of Peking Man (*Homo erectus*), dating from the Mindel glaciation, about 350,000 years ago, were excavated. Attested use of fire by man in Africa came somewhat later (Oakley 1955a; Heizer 1963) in Middle Acheulean times just before the Riss glaciation, about 200,000 years ago.

In one sense man's houses show his capabilities as a food getter. The camps of hunters are ordinarily small and temporary. Usually impermanent shelters seem to have been favored. There is some evidence, however, that the reindeer hunters who settled so successfully in the rock shelters of France during the Pleistocene may have constructed a sort of shelter under the rock overhang to give additional protection. At best this would have been a framework of wood overlaid with skins, but it may have lasted from one season to the next. The animal bones in the rock shelter deposits suggest that some of the groups stayed in one place the year round—for all we know, groups may have stayed in one shelter for generations. It is certain that these men could not have carried a shelter very far with them if they migrated, because they had no pack animals. Hunters on the loesslands of Central Europe used the bones of mammoths as framework for their houses and probably roofed them over with skins. Even wood was scarce there, and the people burned oil-rich mammoth bones for fuel. If these men had not known how to build houses and to make fires, they could not have lived in these regions.

One of the best adaptations to varied climates is the earth-covered house. In prehistoric times some of these houses consisted of pits dug into the ground and roofed over with wood and branches covered with mud or skins. The low-lying houses were sheltered from the wind and were well insulated from heat and cold by the thick layers of dirt on all sides. Of all the houses built in temperate-to-cold climates, these underground houses have enjoyed the longest popularity. In fact, some of the dwellings of the Paleolithic mammoth hunters of Russia were essentially pit houses, and our own pioneers in the West built similar houses of sod.

Many kinds of houses are made of mud. Slabs of mud dried in the sun can be piled on one another as bricks, or indeed, bricks can be made in wooden forms and baked. Mud can also be layered on a wall, a little bit being added vertically each day, and allowed to dry in the sun. Another system is to build forms for the walls and to tamp mud between them, allowing it to harden in the sun. Still another way is to build a framework of sticks in the form of loose matting and to plaster this with mud to build up a substantial wall. Such houses are ordinarily roofed with beams laid across the walls. The beams are then covered with sticks or brush and packed over with mud or earth. The result is an economical house that serves admirably in a hot, dry climate. Rain will eventually ruin such houses, but with reasonable care a mud house will last 15 to 50 years.

The use of stone for building seems to have been a rather late invention, but some of the earliest Mesopotamian and Anatolian mud houses were reinforced, especially at their bases, with stone (see Fig. 5.6). However, successful stone construction demanded either careful shaping of the blocks so that they could be laid dry, or a knowledge of mortar. Stone houses were often plastered on the inside, but where mud was scarce skins could be hung to keep out drafts.

The kinds of houses depended largely on what building materials were present, but even with limited resources there were alternatives (Fig. 11.9). One of the most unusual villages ever constructed has been excavated at Beersheba in Israel (Perrot 1955a, 1955b). The houses, built entirely underground, resemble an ant colony with passages leading to the rooms. The excavators reported that it was pleasant working underground during the baking heat of the day because there was good ventilation and the heat did not penetrate the earth. In these houses no wood was needed though some passages were lined with stone slabs.

As G. Clark (1957:197) has pointed out, there is often a close correspondence between the size of settlement and the kind of economy practiced by prehistoric man. Almost invariably the settlements of farmers are larger than the settlements of hunters, because there is a limit to the size of the group that a purely hunting and gathering economy can support. (For some relevant statistics,

FIG. 11.9 The outline of a prehistoric house at Nørre Fjand, an early Iron Age site in West Jutland, is revealed by the line of post holes and the shallow wall trench.

see Table 11.1.) The limit depends largely on the number who can live through the worst season or through a succession of bad years. This number, in turn, depends on the amount of game and vegetable food, and the efficiency with which the people can secure it.

The size of a settlement is also partly a matter of preference. Some people preferred to live in large groups, whereas others preferred smaller units. We see these differing attitudes in the homesteading farmers of the United States, as opposed to the pueblo-dwelling Native American farmers of the Southwest. On the one hand, each family lives on its plot of land; on the other, all families live in a central village, and the farmer walks to his fields. One system stresses independence of action; the other stresses community living.

The size of a settlement may also depend on other preferences. Some areas were probably always more active socially, whereas others were more isolated or frontier areas. Sites at a distance from established trade routes may have seemed less attractive to some peoples, even though the level of subsistence may have been equally favorable.

Despite all the sociological reasons for the different sizes of settlements, however, other things being equal, there were great inequalities between the lives of hunters and farmers. The latter had an assured food supply unless they had settled on poor land. They could readily grow a surplus, and it could be stored against want in the future or traded for goods and services. Population would therefore increase. The history of food-producing people is one of population expansion and the colonization of "underdeveloped" areas.

Transport and Travel

Trade, colonization, and migration imply transportation. For most of his history man had to depend on his feet for travel and on his back for transport. Lack of transportation severely restricted, although it obviously did not prevent, his movements. What it did was to preclude the frequent movement of large amounts of material. Prehistoric man, like most hunters and gatherers around the world, went himself to the supplies or resources rather than bringing them, or having them brought, to him. Man's mobility was greatly enhanced when he invented boats to enable him to cross rivers. The importance of such craft may be forgotten until a person faces the problem of negotiating a body of water that he cannot wade across. The location of towns in our own countries at convenient fords reflects this importance, even to people who have a sophisticated technology. Consider the plight of a westward-moving pioneer in his covered wagon who had to cross one of the major rivers that drain the West. With equipment too heavy to carry and water too deep to ford at most places he was literally incapable of crossing what we all too often think of simply as scenic attractions or sites of recreation. Boats were probably the first improvement in man's means of travel. Simple rafts and dugout canoes were among the first conveyances, and they were followed by vessels with oars and sails. Actual remains of boats are

TABLE 11.1 Relation Between Economy and Size of Site (Area in Square Meters)

Site	Economy		
	Hunting-Gathering (Mesolithic)	Early Farming (Neolithic)	Developed Farming and Technology (Bronze Age)
Nøore Sandegaard II, Denmark	100		
Nøore Sandegaard III, Bornholm, Denmark	290		
Oakhanger, Hants, England	160		
Star Carr, England	240		
Teviec, Morbihan, France	240		
Windmill Hill, England		93,080	
Fort Harrouard, France		68,760	
Aichbühl, Germany		6,300	
Moosseedorf, Switzerland		1,000	
Robenhausen, Switzerland		12,100	
Wasserburg Buchau, Germany			15,000
Gournia, Crete			24,280
Gla, Greece			97,120
Los Millares, Spain			50,590
Troy II, Turkey			8,000
Averages	206	36,248	38,998

The figures listed above should be taken as general indications only. Precise calculations of sizes of settlements are difficult. Comparisons between sites is hazardous because of particular topographic or environmental conditions, and the kind of houses or shelters present. Reports frequently fail to state sizes of settlements, and where sites were occupied over long periods it is hard to state precisely what the size of settlement was for each period. After effective agriculture, there begins a great disparity in the size of sites even within one cultural tradition. Some sites, for economic or social reasons, become more important than others and are not strictly comparable with them.

This chart was taken from a much larger list compiled by Ronald Weber, a student at the University of California. It includes the largest and smallest sites of each economy in Weber's list, together with three of intermediate size.

rare and not very old, but there is good evidence that watercraft of some sort were in use 50,000 years ago. The evidence is in the fact that people had reached New Guinea and Australia by this time, and had to cross many miles of open water to get there. Animal transport, so far as we know, came late, although it is conceivable that the dog was used for packing or traction by the end of the Pleistocene. The animals used for transport include the reindeer, elephant, dog, horse, donkey, ass, ox, water buffalo, sheep, goat, and llama.

The extent to which culture change may be effected by adoption of an efficient means of transport is illustrated by the use of the horse (from Spanish stock) in the Plains-Plateau area of North America. A careful study of the Blackfoot tribe by Ewers (1955) discusses in detail the cultural changes engendered by the horse.

The use of wheeled vehicles caught on very slowly because they require the services of a draft animal, and because most areas require extensive preparation (such as roads) before carts can be moved easily. It was also important to have something worth transporting. Forests, mountains, swamps, and sandy areas are virtually impassable for primitive carts. The hard-packed deserts of Mesopotamia and Egypt and the grassy steppes of Eurasia were most suitable for traverse, and the animals and the incentive to move goods were present there early. It is likely that the first wheeled vehicles in Mesopotamia were reserved for the use of persons with high status and social prerogatives, and not for routine transport of goods. Even today, as the modern traveler to the area is surprised to learn, the rural villager makes little use of the wheel.

Of course, one might consider all the various devices that have been used to enable or enhance mobility in various parts of the world. Chief among those we have so far omitted are devices that can be used in snowy regions: sleds, skis, and snowshoes for overland travel, and kayaks for water traffic. Incidentally, it should be noted that travel over ice is relatively easy, certainly easier in today's arctic than travel over the spongy expanses of the semithawed tundra that characterizes much of the area in the summer. Travel is easy, provided the ice is firm and not interrupted by crevices or ice wedges. These barriers are as effective in stopping a sled as a river is in preventing the passage of a covered wagon.

The foregoing has considered relatively small-scale movements that were probably typical for most prehistoric men. It is worth noting in addition the deliberate as well as accidental migrations of people who sailed the Pacific in search of islands to settle. In accomplishing these feats with relatively simple boats and navigational equipment they populated the last remaining uninhabited desirable areas of the world, which, until some 3000 years ago, were effectively out of reach of man.

By interpreting evidence on climate, geography, plants, animals, and artifacts, the archeologist can learn a great deal about prehistoric man's economy—his struggle to live and improve his lot. However, man's past was not merely a matter of technology and environment; he was a social being. By the painstaking and imaginative examination of archeological evidence, we can learn something about the less tangible aspects of his life.

Chapter 12

PATTERNS OF SETTLEMENT

Spatial arrangements of man and his works are constantly before us and they make intuitive sense to us all. It is obvious why some things are where they are. The fact that things in space are readily observable lends them to graphic representation in the form of the distributional map, which can be studied indoors and out and virtually endlessly plotted, copied, colored, and analyzed. Spatial studies reduce some of man's most fundamental traits to graphic two-dimensional expressions. This combination of simplicity and significance makes geography—the "map science"—and its related discipline, settlement archeology, appealing areas of study.

History of Settlement Studies

In his appraisal of *Settlement Archaeology* Willey (1968b:224–225) said,

It seems safe to say that an interest in, and an awareness of, the settlement dimension will continue and increase. In the past decade, archaeological articles on, and monographs taking account of, site, regional, or areal settlement patterns have appeared with regularity . . . A variety of attitudes or approaches has been addressed to settlement pattern study . . . The prehistoric settlement form or pattern is one important part of this whole past . . . It is now, I think here to stay in archaeology. . . .

The term "settlement pattern" has become a part of the vocabulary of archeology and ethnology, and there is general agreement among anthropologists that settlement pattern studies are worth doing. In archeology the settlement approach has encouraged a shift in focus from a study of individual artifacts and sites to culture areas and relationships among sites and areas. But although everyone agrees that settlement pattern studies will be part of the more sophisticated investigations of the future, there is no consensus on the concepts necessary for such studies, how they are to be used, what constitutes a settlement or community, what is meant by settlement pattern, or even what we can hope to find out by studying settlement patterns.

Like many terms used in archeology, "settlement pattern" has too many connotations to be useful in scientific discourse. A cursory review of the literature will show that settlement pattern is variously considered (a) a trait indicative of a culture; (b) a valid research objective—for example, "we will survey for settlement pattern"; and (c) a theoretical viewpoint that implies a particular kind of interrelationship among the elements in the distribution of settlements. A brief look at archeological history will illustrate how the term has been used.

Following Trigger (1968c:54), we can distinguish two approaches to settlement pattern: the first, often called an ecological approach, deals with the distribution of sites and seeks relationships between sites, subsistence, technology, and environment; the second is more concerned with the distribution of features within a single site and the inferences that can be made from these data about social, political, and religious organization.

Ecological studies are numerous in archeology, having a history that goes back to Julian Steward's suggestion to Gordon Willey that he investigate settlement pattern because of its close relation to subsistence and environment (Willey 1953:xviii). Since Willey's Viru Valley study was published, there has appeared an impressive list of similar reports that describe the interrelations between environment and settlement pattern. In most of these, "settlement pattern" is considered a trait of the culture or cultures in question, and is as much a characteristic of the culture as its pottery. Struever (1968c:286) sums up the views expressed by most of the authors:

> Culture is viewed as a system of functionally interdependent parts in which change in one aspect is related in specifiable ways to changes in others. Explanation for change in a cultural system requires understanding of these linkages. Cultural variations in space are seen in terms of the differing adaptive requirements of specific environments; accord-

ingly, varying ecological potentialities are linked to different exploitative economies and the latter, in turn, to different integrative requirements and therefore to different forms of social structure, etc.

The theoretical position adopted in ecological studies is that culture is adaptive; consequently its physical manifestations can be seen as examples of adaptation. Although this view clearly oversimplifies the actual situation, it is generally taken as an approximation in ecological studies, without any checks on its accuracy. The assumption of adaptation is a "working conclusion."

The second orientation in archeological studies views the distribution of features within sites as clues to elements of nonmaterial culture.

It is clear that "there is an obvious relationship between social structure and spatial structure of settlements, villages, and camps" and that social systems may be studied through "objective and crystalized external projections of them" (Fitting 1969:360, quoting Lévi-Strauss 1963:284).

Once again spatial distributions and relationships of architectural features are treated as traits, this time not just of a single culture but as traits revealing behavior that may be common to many cultures. A number of novel and imaginative studies of this kind have emerged. The most convincing are those dealing with Southwestern Pueblos, where abundant ethnohistoric data inform on cultural practices of great antiquity, and where few substantial changes can be detected in architecture.

R. Naroll's work (1962) and similar studies by S. Cook and Heizer (1968) on the correlation between floor space and population in certain California groups are also convincing, based as they are principally on ethnohistorical data. More speculative are observations on the psychology of site orientation. As Eric Reed (1956:13) put it,

It surely must reflect something basic in personality structure, outlook, national character—or something comparable to the Spanish inward-facing patio-type house on the edge of the street and our front-facing dwellings with the lawn on the outside.

Granted there may be aspects of personality in this, but most archeologists will continue to use the information on orientation as a trait and leave the speculation, as Reed suggests, to psychologists, architects, or social commentators.

In the ways in which archeologists have practiced the study of spatial aspects of their data we see two contrasting approaches: the broad ecological overview that stresses man–land relationships, and the view that relates the nature of structures in sites to social and/or psychological factors. Although settlement studies have not stimulated a radical departure from previous practices, they have encouraged examination of regions rather than of single sites, and of systematic relations, whether within or among sites. Expressed this way settlement pattern studies support ecological approaches.

Concepts of Settlement Analysis

Analysis of settlement was pioneered and developed by geographers, who have defined a set of concepts to provide them with a theoretical basis for conducting spatial or locational studies whose goal is to explain how things are arranged and associated in space. Three concepts underlie these studies: **direction**, **distance**, and **connectivity**. *Direction* is orientation. *Distance* can be calculated in time or in units of measure such as miles. Location thus becomes directed distance: the direction and distance from a point of origin. *Connectivity* is the relationship between locations, whether it be in terms of movements of people and goods, or communication. Although geographers often explain patterns of settlement in terms of economic activities, they do so with accurate knowledge of actual connections between settlements. It is much less easy, and perhaps entirely misleading, to infer the nature of connectivity from the spatial distribution of settlements.

Geographers who are interested in locational analysis have developed a series of abstract models based on the three concepts mentioned above and on premises concerning the reasons why people take spatial relations into account. These premises have to do mostly with cost and ease of transportation and communication, on the assumption that people behave rationally. Archeologists, on the other hand, are much less concerned with abstract models than they are with putting to use the relationships that have been modeled by geographers. There has therefore been great interest in archeology in "locational analysis." It does not take much study of the literature to discover that archeologists have failed to define concepts analogous to those used by geographers. In other words, they have not developed independently a field of spatial analysis; this suggests that attributes of space per se, especially distance and direction, have never been important in archeological problems. However, connectivity or analogous concepts of relationship have been emphasized. Of these perhaps the most important is *adaptation*.

The fundamental difference in the way archeologists and geographers approach the problem is that while archeologists have been preoccupied with man–land relationships which are believed to operate as part of an adaptive system, geographers have been more concerned with man–man relationships which operate in an economic or information network. The difference, it seems, stems from the following facts. First, archeologists have been primarily concerned with primitive non-Western cultures, whereas geographers have traditionally studied modern Western, economic-oriented societies. Second, while archeology is concerned with real data, manifested principally in sites arrayed over a landscape, locational analysis has dealt with statistical data input into abstract models. Finally, in archeology the fundamental premise of adaptation has overshadowed alternative kinds of relationships that geography routinely uses as instances of connectivity. In a real sense, then, spatial analysis in geography has been able to ignore terrain, the basis of the man–land relationships that have loomed so large in archeology. The basic difference lies in the approach.

Archeologists have traditionally sought to explain the particular instance, whereas geographers have attempted to understand a general class of events through the use of abstract models. In archeology neither the data nor the concepts have been precise enough for constructing analogous models.

If we were to try to define our concepts more clearly, we could readily copy *direction* from spatial analysis. *Distance*, as noted earlier, is more of a problem, and an adequate definition for archeological purposes must consider the kind of relationship as well as the mileage. In order to have an effective way to use both distance and direction, we need to be able to specify the point or area on the map from which we will measure. This involves dealing more meaningfully with some basic matters that are familiar to all of us.

Activity locus, site, settlement, community, and territory are all used to designate the spatial coordinates of certain kinds of human behavior, but they do not all mean the same thing; or perhaps we should say they embody several distinct concepts. Consider the following common archeological problem. A village consisting of an area of closely spaced houses surrounded by miles of terrain without houses is easy to identify as a site and its position on the map is its center. But what is the location of a city 3 by 5 miles in extent? If you want to measure the distance to another city, what point do you use? Or how do you determine the limits of sites marked by seasonal occupations that over the years may accumulate a thin scatter of material over a mile or more? Should we treat as a single site the entire territory occupied by a group of hunters and gatherers over a year? Such a site would consist of many activity loci and campgrounds. These are just some of the issues for which we need operational definitions if we wish to relate spatial analysis to the archeological world.

To return to *connectivity* again, when we speak of settlement patterns we prejudge the matter of relationship. We assume patterns, but there are at least three senses in which pattern is used in archeology: (a) a *distribution*, as the simple plotting of locale; (b) a *statement of relationships*, as traits of culture functionally interrelated. In archeology we deal exclusively with physical remains and the relationships among them. For us patterns consist of seeing the same set of variables in different circumstances and we often conclude that the elements in the set are functionally interrelated; (c) a *model*, an abstraction that can include statements both of distribution and of relationship.

In settlement pattern studies the first two uses of pattern are common but the second requires more discussion. As we have noted before, archeologists tend to assume that adaptation or adaptive behavior underlies the man–man or man–land relationships. This is a major assumption that is no less reasonable than the assumptions ordinarily made by geographers. What is more to the point is that all these assumptions can be stated more profitably as hypotheses to be tested, and explicit effort should be made to find alternative hypotheses. In fact, whether we are interested in settlement patterns or not, it would be useful for archeologists to focus their attention on the general question of connectivity. As archeologists we are often interested in the linkages between peoples in different sites or regions. Trade, diffusion, symbiotic relationships, interaction spheres, warfare, migration, and the like are the subjects of much archeological discussion. These are statements about connectivity, but we understand relatively little about the factors that would go into such relationships. Part of the reason may be that ethnologists have given little attention to such matters; our principal sources in this regard are historical, not anthropological. And part of the reason may be that the questions have not been investigated through the means of testing hypotheses. Archeologists have not assiduously tried to *disprove* hypotheses, nor have we devoted sufficient effort to establishing what kinds of evidence we will find acceptable. These are matters of the utmost urgency in archeology.

In summary, settlement archeology grew out of an ecological concern with man–land relationships, and in consequence adaptation has been used to explain observed phenomena. By contrast, locational or spatial analysis has emphasized the spatial arrangement of phenomena and the extensive use of abstract models of settlement systems.

Archeological Studies of Settlement

Following the concept of adaptation, most archeologists feel that the location, spacing, size, and kinds of sites are determined by the natural environment, by social factors, and by biological factors. Of these we can deal most effectively with environmental and social factors.

Patterns of settlement can be described statistically; in doing so, size and spacing of sites are emphasized, together with the number of people who live in the sites. This concern with vital statistics is usually called **demography**. Patterns of settlement can also be interpreted in terms of their relevance to human behavior. In this area concepts of ecology are important.

Trigger (1965:2) writes,

> The settlement pattern . . . directs attention toward developing a methodology for the systematic study of the social and economic organization of ancient society. The settlement pattern is the order which the members of a society observe in their utilization of space. It is the plan according to which houses, shelters, fields, markets, temples, forts and cemeteries are distributed across the landscape. When the actors leave the stage, the social, political and economic activities disappear with them, but the settlement pattern, like the set and properties of a play, remains behind. In this basic sense the settlement pattern is an expression of the societal aspects of ancient cultures. The study of changes in settlement patterns thus becomes a study of the development of social and political organization, while the study of change in phase-archaeology is largely a study of the invention and diffusion of various items of material culture.

For archeologists, both description and interpretation of settlement patterns are important, but it should be stressed that interpretation is our ultimate goal. Interpretation must be based on careful recording and description, and the latter can be done effectively only if the archeologist has some idea of how he may want to use his data. This chapter will thus deal with how settlement data are used in archeological interpretation.

Demography

Demographic data are usually quantities that express the number of persons comprising a certain population, together with the relations among categories (for example, occupation and status) of persons. These can be used to calculate both relative and absolute sizes, as well as rates of changes. Basic to obtaining demographic data in archeology are careful surveys of sites, with an adequate control over dating, and either extensive or sampled excavation of sites to gain an accurate picture of their size and internal structure. Surveys of sites or of areas will reveal the pattern of the space occupied by people and hence represent a description of one area of prehistoric human behavior.

Probably few kinds of archeological interpretation have more systematically built-in sources of potential error than have estimates of population, yet such figures are commonly given and used for making further inferences. It is safe to say that, because our concerns in archeology turn more and more toward reconstructing social systems, we shall have to devise methods of obtaining better demographic data.

Many estimates of population begin with an estimate of the size of sites, because there is some relation between number of people and the area they occupy. The precise relation can be determined through ethnographic analogy, which sometimes may be relatively simple. Such analogies are possible when there is ample ethnohistorical evidence to indicate that the archeological people are direct ancestors of historically known groups. This condition is met, for example, in parts of the Southwest. Here the archeologist can make accurate estimates of the total population if he knows how many houses there are. The problem becomes more difficult when there is no historically known descendant group or, in either instance, when the number of houses occupied at one time is not known.

Several methods have been proposed to calculate the number of people who occupied a site. One method of obtaining a general estimate was proposed by Naroll (1962), who examined a sample of ethnographic sources and determined that the ratio of enclosed floor space per person is a relatively constant 10:1. That is, if there are 100 square meters of floor space there will be 10 people occupying it. Subsequent very careful examination of California data for a large number of sites fully confirms Naroll's conclusions (Cook and Heizer 1965, 1968). These figures probably apply principally to permanent settlements that have substantial houses, and they are likely to be inaccurate if applied to brush huts, **tipis**, and other forms of impermanent camp shelters. Moreover, the ratios are averages and the range of variation within the samples is large.

Another approach is to try to relate the total surface area of the site to the number of occupants (Cook and Treganza 1950:231–233). A small sample of sites in California showed that there was a relation of the type:

$$\log \text{population} = \text{constant} \times \log \text{area}.$$

Although the reasons for this relation are not clear, it does seem to hold. Further work (Cook and Heizer 1965, 1968) indicates that the precise relation between surface area of a site and the population is itself related to the ecologic area in which the site is found, and to social factors. Somewhat different relations were obtained for sites in hill, coast, and desert environments, and also for sites in which houses were for single families and those in which multifamily dwellings were common. In other words, if archeologists can calculate the relation between area and population they can use this formula for other similar sites in a homogeneous environment. Summarizing their findings on the California sites, the authors say, "As far as village area or space is concerned, there are three very distinct groups, whereas when floor space or house area is considered, all the regions form an unbroken exponential continuum."

Another important method of roughly estimating the population of a site is to calculate the number of people who could have existed there. This sum can be determined by figuring the amount of food consumed (as represented in the refuse) and determining how many people it would have fed, or by figuring how many people an area could have supported. The former method is illustrated by R. Ascher's (1959) analysis of a California shell midden in which he calculated the amount of protein represented by the shells. Assuming that each person consumed 5 gm. per day, Ascher divided the day-units of protein by the length of occupation of the site, and concluded that over a 25-year period, the population varied between 21 and 53 persons. One should remember in such interpretations that the remains found in the site may represent only a portion of the total food consumed and may, in fact, represent only a small part of the total diet.

Although these methods are potentially useful, before they are even attempted there are several purely practical problems that must be solved. The first of these is how much to dig. Since one seldom digs a whole site, it is rarely possible to specify the total number of houses, fireplaces, or pits, or even the total area of the site. This situation is especially true for large sites and sites in which there are many levels.

Consider the problems in digging a site like Grasshopper Ruin in Arizona, a "masonry pueblo consisting of more than 500 habitation and storage rooms" (R. Thompson and Longacre 1966:259), some of which were two stories high. The site also includes large open courtyards, cemeteries, and numbers of kivas. It would make no sense either scientifically or economically to excavate the whole site; instead, a method for sampling it had to be devised. Sampling a site such as this is no small problem; it requires several years' work, which must be followed by excavation of the sample. The first step is to prepare a map of the site that shows every structure, a task made possible by the fact that the masonry walls lie on or near the surface and can be traced with a minimum of digging. With the number, kinds, and sizes of rooms recorded, it is then possible to design a technique for sampling them. The judgment of what constitutes a reliable sample is aided by excavations already completed and by the analysis of mutual variation among the data.

The other practical problem is in judging how many houses or what portions of a site were occupied at one time. The solution to this problem is not obvious for most sites. There may be rare instances where techniques such as obsidian-hydration or tree-ring dating will allow one to assign relative dates to separate rooms on one occupation level, but other dating techniques are too coarse to help.

Accurate demographic data are hard to obtain, yet they are vital if we are to understand trends of stability or change, and they are very useful in helping assess the nature of a particular society. Accordingly, demographic data are one aspect of archeology that needs a good deal more emphasis in the future so that better techniques and more accurate estimates can be developed.

Factors Affecting Population Size and Its Distribution

The size of populations depends on both social and environmental factors. The environmental limitations are obvious, because, with a given population of plants and animals, there is a theoretical maximum human population that can be supported. If all the food could be used, one would have only to total up the calories, minerals, and vitamins available and calculate how many persons could live on this quantity. However, our knowledge of social factors prevents our even taking the first step in this direction. Man cannot, and may never be able to, use the total food in any environment. For one thing, if he did so, there would be nothing left for the next year; we see this today in places where certain livestock are literally eating themselves out of a future. People could do the same thing.

These considerations reflect certain theoretical parameters affecting population size, but one cannot get very far with such abstract discussions. It is more meaningful to deal directly with actual examples. We know that man's use of the land will depend on the resources and on his ability to use them. We are dealing with the interrelations between man and his environment, or, in general terms, an ecosystem. The question that needs to be asked about an area is, "Can man live there?" There are a few regions beyond the ability of man to tolerate, but this is a statement made in the abstract. Much more to the point is whether man can extract from this environment the necessities to sustain life. Is there sufficient food or the potential for agriculture? If wild, how is the food distributed across the landscape, and how is it available seasonally? Are the food sources sufficiently close to drinking water? A good exercise is to take the map of an area, see what resources are available, and then put man there and try to figure how he would exploit the land, granting him several different levels of techno-logical sophistication.

Technology is consequently another important part of the ecosystem. What does man have with which to exploit the resources? Does he have the tools to flense a whale or skin a hippo? Can he cut, thresh, and grind the wheat? Has he suitable utensils to cook or boil food? Can he rid the acorns or manioc of their acids and thus create for himself a dietary staple? Can man tap the water, provide adequate shelter, and find fuel? It was technology that converted the plains hunting ground into the breadbasket of America. Today, with the same environment, but a different technology, the area can support a population many times the size of the total number of Native Americans in North America at the time of first contact by Europeans.

What we have just said has to do with whether it would be at all pos-sible for man to live in an area, but more usually it is pertinent to ask what limits the environment places on settlement. As many writers have pointed out, hunters make extensive use of the land, ranging far wider on the average than do people who collect plant food or who plant crops. The density of hunting groups depends on the density of animals and the number required to feed the people. That is to say, a human population may fluctuate considerably, because the population of game fluctuates over a period of years. Moreover, if the game is migratory, sometimes it does not migrate near where the people are waiting. Mobility is thus important for hunters and tends to keep the ratio of people to area fairly low. Usually with hunters the social organization is such that it permits both rapid and easy splitting of groups when the occasion de-mands, and coalescence if desirable. The exigencies of the hunt and the nature of the terrain thus exercise strong controls over the size and distribution of a population. The same is true whether the people are farmers, hunters, or fishers, but it becomes less true as people gain control over the environment by means of technology.

We can also consider the importance of social factors. First, the group must be large enough to carry out all the necessary tasks of subsistence, shelter, and procreation. The size of the group will depend on environmental factors and perhaps also on such intangible factors as the desire for companionship, a consideration that could vary from group to group. The socially acceptable upper limits of settlement size and density probably also vary from group to group. Early villagers in western Iran seem to have split after their communities reached 100 to 200 persons. Subsequently the worldwide trend in the Near East and in many areas has been toward larger and more compact cities. It is relevant to note that external factors such as the encroachment of outsiders may also have an effect on settlement or group size. As Elman Service (1962) has shown, a tribal level of social integration is largely a result of external pressure; there seems little reason to doubt, for example, that the density of settlement in the stockaded Indian villages of the Eastern Woodlands was protection against the threat of attack.

Trade, or commercial activities generally, can affect settlement either by permitting people to live removed from certain vital resources or by creating different types of settlements. Diversification of mutually interdependent types of settlements is one of the characteristics of complex societies. Complex societies have religious or political capitals, market centers, rural villages, fishing or farming communities, military garrisons, industrial or mining centers, and the like. It is important to note that it is the organization of a social system that permits such specialization and welds the diverse parts into a viable whole. The pattern of settlement thus can be seen to be both a result of, and a contribution to, social complexity.

A final set of factors limiting settlement sizes relates to custom, belief, and religion. Returning to subsistence, we can easily bring to mind a variety of food taboos around the world. We have no idea how old these practices are, but we do know that man today willingly restricts his diet and that there are very few persons who eat the full range of nourishing food found in their environment. For the most part the reluctance to make use of everything available stems from beliefs in what is good to eat. For example, pigs, snails, snakes, and insects are not eaten by most persons in Southwest Asia. Such exclusion of good food is not always the result of an abundance of other foods. Many peoples have certain animals that are clan totems, and in most instances members of the clans are forbidden to eat these creatures.

Preference rather than taboos also rules out certain food except in unusual circumstances. For example, in Southwest Asia sheep and goats are said to be "warm" animals and good to eat, but cattle are "cold" and not so good to eat. We have records of people who abstain from certain foods that are thought to leave persons with a characteristic odor offensive to themselves and detrimental to hunting. Social reasons for particular choices of food could be listed at great length, but these few illustrations should serve to show that any inferences we might make about hypothetical maximum populations, based only on a simple tally of the available food, are very likely to be wrong.

Warfare, the enslavement of war captives, and ritual human sacrifice were probably not factors of major importance in the regulation of most prehistoric populations, but they were in some areas, especially Meso-America. At the time of contact by Spanish conquistadores and for an unknown time before, ritual sacrifice was carried out in highland Mexico on a scale that was certainly consequential for the population. A variety of ethnohistorical sources suggest that there were enough ritually induced deaths to affect population trends. S. Cook (1966:291) estimates that "the mean annual sacrifice rate of 15,000 would have augmented the death rate by roughly fifteen percent, a quantity which, over one or two generations, could have been of material significance in aiding to control the population density." Although recent estimates of the population of Meso-America are considerably higher than the figures Cook used in his calculations, his point still has some validity. We need not think of such numbers of deaths, however, to recognize that even modest-scale warfare could be important. As we describe later on, under trends of change, the calculated growth rate of population during the Neolithic in the Near East would have been offset by one additional death by sacrifice or a war every 10 years, in a population of 100.

Kroeber (1963:148–149) proposed that warfare among Native Americans of the eastern United States was the most potent factor operating to keep the population from expanding, and that warfare further prevented the emergence of the state. His discussion, based on ethnographic evidence, constitutes an interpretation that archeologists could test. Kroeber says,

> [The eastern tribes] waged war not for any ulterior or permanent fruits, but for victory; and its conduct and shaping were motivated, when not by revenge, principally by individual desire for personal status within one's society. It was warfare that was insane, unending, continuously attritional, from our point of view; and yet it was so integrated into the whole fabric of Eastern culture, so dominantly emphasized within it, that escape from it was well-nigh impossible. Continuance in the system became self-preservatory. The group that tried to shift its values from war to peace was almost certainly doomed to early extinction. This warfare, with its attendant unsettlement, confusion, destruction, and famines, was probably the most potent reason why population remained low in the East. It kept agriculture in the role of a contributor to subsistence instead of the basis of subsistence. On the other hand, such farming as was practiced yielded enough of added leisure, concentration, and stability to make pretty continuous warfare possible. A population of pure hunter-gatherers would probably, except on the immediate coast, have been too scattered in minute bands, too unsettled in a country of rather evenly distributed food possibilities, too occupied with mere subsistence, to have engaged in war very persistently. . . . Agriculture made their wars possible; but their warfare kept the population down to a point where more agriculture was not needed.

Trends of Change

Some useful statistics are relative population sizes at various periods and the implied rates of change. Today we are impressed by the rate of population growth and by the dire predictions that accompany it, and we vaguely apprehend that the rate is unusual. But is it? Some perspective on modern conditions was given by Carneiro and Hilse (1966), when they considered the rate of population increase during the so-called Neolithic revolution, when, with the advent of food production, population grew far beyond previous levels. What is surprising in their figures is that the population growth was not rapid; "it was, in fact, only on the order of one-tenth of one percent per year" (Carneiro and Hilse 1966:179). This rate of increase would be unnoticeable to a person whose life expectancy was on the order of 30 years, because in his lifetime only 3 persons would have been added to a village of 100.

Such figures are, of course, subject to many errors, including the fact that they are based on the assumption that one rate of change characterized a 4000-year period, but they do have important implications when we consider the effect that an increasing population may have had on social institutions. Today we are faced with many problems brought about by a seemingly endless supply of people who strain existing facilities and for whom we cannot plan adequately. Our social institutions are literally being torn apart by excessive demands. Such would not have been the situation during the Neolithic, when the populations were relatively fixed residentially and the social organization was based on kinship and personal face-to-face relations. The strains would have come when the populations grew beyond the limits of personal recognition and familial control, and when access to wealth or productivity became unequally distributed. In part a contributing factor and in part a by-product would have been the growth of technological and administrative specialists who eventually comprised an entirely new kind of segment of society. But before this, the first 3000 years of population expansion in Mesopotamia would have seen the budding off of small communities as they reached an optimum size—provided that there was sufficient virgin land available for new settlement under the existing system of extensive, rather than intensive, use of the land. From an archeological view, the change from many small settlements to a pattern where some if not most became significantly larger would be the clue that a change in social organization was in the offing or already present.

Perhaps no contribution of archeology is more important than its ability to reconstruct the course of change over long periods, but these examples point out clearly that one must look very carefully at the details of the situation before leaping into the realm of speculation and interpretation that might easily be colored by our own experiences during a time of truly exceptional population growth.

Composition of Sites

Most sites consist of a number of discrete areas that represent different kinds of activities. Houses, pits, and work areas characterize even simple sites, whereas more complex sites have palaces, temples, aqueducts, wells, houses, and the like. One major archeological problem is to isolate and describe adequately each of the areas of a site and to try to see the whole site as a set of structures and spaces that were used by people. With a small site, the problem of obtaining a total site plan is not too great, but we have already seen what the comparable problems are for a site as large as Grasshopper. For a very large site, one might question whether extensive sampling is really worth the effort, or even possible. A decision would have to depend on the site itself and on what kinds of information a person wants to obtain. There are clearly arguments for and against extensive excavation.

One example is given by the magnificent and uniquely large mound of

Çatal Hüyük in Anatolia, which covers some 32 acres (450 meters long and 275 wide) and is at least 19 meters deep (about 60 feet), making it "the largest Neolithic site hitherto known in the Near East" (Mellaart 1967:30). Çatal Hüyük covers an area about 10 times as large as Grasshopper and has a series of buried levels spanning 600–700 years. How is one to sample Çatal to obtain an intelligent idea of the community pattern? Mellaart did what most archeologists would have done: he picked an area where the walls of burnt buildings were exposed at the surface and began digging down. When this resulted in some of the most spectacular finds in all Near Eastern prehistory, he simply continued to dig in the same area.

> In the area excavated which covers about one acre—a mere thirtieth of the entire surface of the mound—a great number of houses and shrines with their storerooms have been found, but no workshops or public buildings. It must be assumed that these were located in a different part of the mound and the quarter on the west slope was evidently the residential, if not the priestly quarter of the city. One need hardly point out that Çatal Hüyük was not a village (Mellaart 1967:71).

The evidence at Çatal is so well preserved that the excavator can begin his interpretations on much surer footing than is possible at most sites, but no less ingenious sets of postulates and their testing are required to get at the vast amount of information that Çatal must hold. Appropriate models must be conceived to help us understand the many unique features of this site: Why is it so precociously large? Why is access to the settlement via the roofs rather than through doors? What is the relation between houses and shrines? What kind of social groups occupied the houses? What was the internal differentiation of the community? What was the role of Çatal with respect to other contemporary communities? These are only a sample of the questions whose answers will require a careful consideration of the total community pattern, the areal settlement pattern, and the local sources of resources. In short, Çatal must be viewed as the home of a community that lived in the context of a definable and understandable environmental and social system.

No less perplexing examples come from the Americas. Intrasite variation has long interested Maya archeologists, although it is only recently that they have worked out accurate site plans for the major centers, and, more recently, good surveys of regions. The ancient Maya have long confused archeologists because these people seem not to have lived in cities, and remains of domestic structures are relatively rare at the major ceremonial centers. What is more, within the ceremonial centers there are buildings that have been called temples and others called palaces. An exceedingly important question that still has not been answered satisfactorily was asked by Willey (1956b:107): "What were the size and composition of the Maya living community, and what was the relationship between the living community and the ceremonial center?"

Haviland's (1965, 1967, 1969, 1970) work at Tikal and Ricketson's (1937) investigations at Uaxactun, about 10 miles away, have shown that there are large numbers of house mounds surrounding the main temple-plaza zones, which are taken to be the religious activity centers of the sites. Another pertinent question concerns the role of different sizes of centers to one another (Bullard 1960). Questions of this kind seem capable of solution by intensive investigation of the community (or better, here perhaps "dispersed community") patterns with special attention to the spacing, size, and mutual variation among all classes of structures and artifacts. An answer to the question of the function of the "palaces" is perhaps less clear, but one has the overriding impression that they have been studied more as examples of architecture than they have as loci of activities. If this is true, one would expect an intensive study of the distribution of artifacts throughout one of the ceremonial centers to reveal patterns of difference among palaces, temples, and domestic structures. Unfortunately, these structures at most of the major sites have been thoroughly cleaned of artifacts and restored as architectural displays. New information must come from as yet unexcavated lesser sites where the prospect of finding artifacts *in situ* remains.

It seems reasonable to suppose that a great many similar archeological problems would vanish if only they were investigated seriously rather than remarked on in passing. First, the problem must be recognized as one capable of, or worth, solving. Solutions will rarely be found, however, if the archeologists are content to study the objects removed from sites rather than try to determine the social context in which they occur.

Interpreting Patterns of Settlement

The distribution of sites is an important datum for archeological interpretation because it gives the facts, which in turn suggest questions. It tells where the sites are and demands an answer to why they are where they are. Patterns of settlement give us information that is very closely related to environment, technology, and social organization—in short, to the ecologic relations that obtain in any social system.

To illustrate these ecological relations we can take a complex situation, the nature of the Hopewellian occupations that centered in Illinois and Ohio. Various authors have referred to Hopewell as "a culture type, a culture phase, a temporal horizon, and a form of burial complex or cult" (Struever 1964:87). It is represented by mounds, earthworks, villages, burial sites, and trading centers and identified principally through a shared group of artifacts made of exotic materials that were imported from sources in the Rockies, Great Lakes, and Gulf Coast.

Around 100 B.C. Hopewell appeared abruptly in restricted locales in the Eastern Woodlands. Casting this appearance into ecological terms, Struever (1964:90) suggested that it might attest "to the expansion of a dominant mode of adaptation at the expense of less efficient ones." If this were true, what was the new mode of adaptation? Parenthetically, one should note that when problems are phrased properly they lead to questions that can be answered by finding specific kinds of information—in this example, on subsistence. Supposing that the Hopewell peoples may have initiated agriculture in the area, Struever assessed the distribution of sites with respect to agricultural potential. He found

> that localities manifesting Hopewellian forms can be correlated with a series of ecological zones ranging in increasing specificity from the entire region lying south of the 140-day frost line, to the flood plains of the major rivers, to (in the case of habitation sites) the immediate environs of shallow backwaters and stream banks in and immediately proximal to the alluvium. It can be postulated that this distribution reflects a correlation between these cultural events and the importance of a simple, mud-flat horticulture, an hypothesis that sees a low-level, technologically simple cultivation as an important feature conditioning the degree to which Woodland expressions in different locales underwent a shift to a higher level of complexity exemplified in the Hopewell mortuary expression (Struever 1964:99).

We normally think of agriculture in the New World as involving maize, beans, and squash, but such was clearly not true at many, if any, Hopewell sites. Quite the contrary (and incidentally this is where Struever's experimentation with flotation really paid off), the people in Illinois seem to have been cultivating the locally available wild *Iva* marsh elder, *Chenopodium* lamb's-quarter (or goosefoot), and *Amaranth,* all plants that do well in the mud-flats bordering streams and sloughs.

The facts fitted the conditions in Illinois very well and immediately suggested that they be tested in other areas. Even at the time of Struever's writing (1964) it could be determined that other nearby contemporary people, who were outside the specific ecological niche of Hopewell, did not participate in the logistics network that distributed exotic raw materials, nor did they have the distinctive burial complex. It seems clear, therefore, that the Hopewell peoples had a more efficient subsistence base, which allowed their population to expand at the expense of other peoples, and that their social organization consequently became more elaborate, as is evidenced in the variety of their artifacts and mortuary practices.

Such conclusions represent only a beginning in understanding Hopewell and contemporary cultures. In particular, such questions as the nature of the social organization responsible for promoting the logistics network, and the nature of the interaction that resulted in raw materials and designs being distributed, remain to be answered. It is obvious, however, that such questions must be approached with a view to the total system as it can be seen in the patterned occurrence of its durable remains.

Another example of the value of studying patterns of settlement is both simple and useful for its practical implications in field work. In Iran, where do you look for caves that may have been occupied by Paleolithic hunters? Caves occur in some limestone ridges; it is necessary only to find the ridges to find the sites. A plotting of settlement pattern on a two-dimensional map would, however, be very misleading, for two reasons. First, caves are relatively rare, and people must have lived elsewhere; thus the map really shows the distribution of caves and not the distribution of human settlement. Second, all caves are not the same, as one learns from excavation. Some caves are large, others small; some sites are rock shelters, and others surface scatters in the open. At least three types of settlements occur: base camps, butchering stations, and transitory camps. Had a functional difference between these sites not been seen we should have to consider them separate settlements rather than several loci of activities of one group. Hence an estimate of the total population would have to consider that several sites might be the result of one band of hunters. Once the interpretation had been made, however, it was possible to calculate roughly how much space was used by each group and thereby to figure a total population for the area.

Another example comes from Oaxaca, Mexico, where sites of the Early Formative period are located in the center of the valley near the Atoyac River (Fig. 12.1). The obvious interpretation is that people during the early stages of agriculture preferred to work the good soils of the flood plain and to live close to surface water. However, the interpretation failed to explain why other areas of the valley that enjoyed the same advantages did not also have Early Formative villages. The apparent explanation emerged following studies in which it was shown that all the early sites are situated on land where the water table is within 3 meters of the surface. The location of the sites was determined by the depth of ground water rather than by quality of soil or availability of surface water (Flannery and others 1967).

Sometimes a careful examination of settlement data will lead to questions or suggest possible lines of investigation. Archeologists often find sites where they do not expect to find them, and this contingency demands an explanation. Such anomalies are regularly overlooked, however, when the total pattern of settlement is not considered. Examples would be trading outposts or mining centers that are far away from the major concentrations of settlement and may in fact be in country so poor that it permits only a precarious existence without the support of subsidies, tribute, or taxes. Such examples are admittedly rare, but few archeologists would be willing to state that all the sites they know of are just where they would have predicted them to be. In short, the archeologist should train himself to look for reasons why things are as they are.

Robert Adams (1962) provides a good example of such speculation. He found in his survey of Khuzistan, southwest Iran, that all early villages were located inside the 300-millimeter rainfall **isohyet**. This suggested to him that the villagers were still dependent on rainfall farming. During a later period, however, villages were in areas of lower rainfall. Adams thus concluded that some farmers were then practicing irrigation. In subsequent years it was possible to prove the correctness of his conjecture by excavating key sites in the area.

These examples point up the need for thorough (either complete or

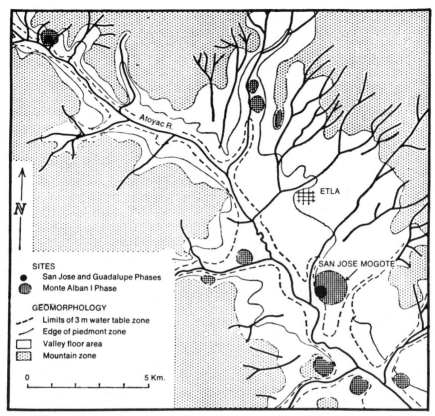

FIG. 12.1 *"Pilot" survey area in the northwestern part of the Oaxaca Valley, Mexico, showing the distribution of Early Formative archeological sites with regard to physiographic areas and water resources. Early Formative sites are found exclusively on the high alluvium, where the water table is within 3 meters of the surface. Later sites spread up the tributaries of the Rio Atoyac into the piedmont zone. (K. V. Flannery, "Farming Systems and Political Growth in Ancient Oaxaca,"* Science *Vol. 158 (1967):Fig. 5, pp. 445–454. Copyright 1967 by the American Association for the Advancement of Science.)*

sampled) studies of large areas and the testing of a selected range of sites that promise to be useful in the understanding of crucial shifts in way of life. Often when we work in a new and unknown area we have no sure guidelines around which to construct our pattern. Demographic data can often provide us with the first clues to grasp as we grope in the darkened room of prehistory.

Territoriality

Enough examples have now been cited in this chapter to show what may be done with systematic observation coupled with pertinent hypotheses. In every instance the work leading to the examples was done by archeologists, and inspired either by archeological problems or by ethnographically known situations that were thought to be recognizable archeologically. It remains to consider the role of other fields of study in suggesting suitable approaches and in providing models for testing.

Two of these readily come to mind. The first was mentioned by Vogt (1956:173) as a possible area of inquiry, but it has not been followed up explicitly in archeology. This is the question of "territoriality," which has been studied extensively by ecologists and other students of animal behavior. Territory can mean many different things, and there are consequently various facets to consider. For any particular human group, where does it live? What territory does it exploit, depend on for survival, defend against outsiders, or use for special (for example, ceremonial) purposes? We can see that there is a variety of kinds of territories implied in the mere fact of group or community existence. We might also consider the sequential use of territory, which implies that only certain persons or groups have access to portions of the same territory at different seasons. Finally, we can get down to the individual level and consider how much space a person needs or uses. Edward Hall's book, *The Hidden Dimension* (1966), takes up the psychocultural factors that determine man's interpersonal space requirements. These are not the same in every culture, and because they seem to be deep-seated and enduring, could conceivably be used by archeologists to help in determining historical continuities in populations. The hypothesis would be that people of different cultures would have different spatial arrangements for their daily activities.

The question of how to define territory archeologically is certainly an important one for archeologists, who usually resort to pottery styles or cultural traits, such as the building of burial mounds, as criteria for lumping or segregating people in different sites. The rationale for this tendency, as Klopfer (1962: 140) pointed out, is that "the fixity of the territorial boundary implies that there is a training of the young by their parents, a training that involves teaching the offspring the extent of the family territory." In aboriginal Australia and California, for example, children were taken on tours of the territorial border of the tribelet, and landmarks such as prominent rocks were pointed out. How common this practice was among hunting-gathering societies we do not know, but it seems probable that most such groups in the prehistoric past did something of the sort. For human beings, such teaching might be aimed at recognizing group-specific styles or artifacts. L. Binford's (1962:219–220) "ideo-technic" artifacts are of this kind. They are

> items which signify and symbolize the ideological rationalizations for the social system and further provide the symbolic milieu in which individuals are enculturated, a necessity if they are to take their place as functional participants in the social system. Such items as figures of deities, clan symbols, symbols of natural agencies, etc., fall into this general category.

In addition to the ways already mentioned, territory is denoted by such things as rivers, mountains, field boundaries, walls of cities, collective burial tombs, walls of dwellings, rooms, courtyards, and fences. A logical question to ask on finding any of these "barriers" or symbolic structures is what they mean in the social system. What kind of behavior or necessities caused the people to delimit themselves as they did? Mellaart saw the blank façade of Çatal Hüyük as a defensive mechanism, but one must then ask whom these rich and powerful people had to fear. Courtyards have been suggested by some persons as a way of keeping animals penned and by others as a way to keep the family activities from the prying eyes of inquisitive neighbors. Some have viewed keeping dogs in the house as a means of preventing strangers or unwelcome persons from entering the premises, and the traveler in many parts of the world who has been confronted by one of the snarling beasts would be inclined to agree.

An interesting example of the use of archeological data to infer territoriality is found in Bradley's (1971) article on the relationship between competition in trade and the distribution of artifacts. (Some of the implications of his reasoning are discussed further in Chapter 15.) Bradley has applied the concept of *opportunity* to the study of trade networks. In essence the concept suggests that traders will avoid one another so that they will not be in direct competition. He states that

> the amount of interaction over a given distance will be directly proportional to the opportunities existing at that distance, and inversely proportional to the number of intervening opportunities. In its application to trade, this should have the effect that the field of any particular traded item may be restricted by the presence of a competing business in the area. On the other hand, in a region where there are no "intervening opportunities" of this type, we should see the uninhibited extension of this field. In practical terms its effect should be this: that a trader avoids an area where he must share his business with a competitor and instead extends his operations into an area where he can secure a monopoly. The distributions of the traded items will almost appear to repel one another. (Bradley 1971:347–348)

In a short review of archeological situations where trading was a factor, Bradley found his principle to operate. Consequently one may see in this behavior some aspects of territoriality.

It is fair to say that concepts of territory are important for all people, but it is by no means clear what they will be or how they will be expressed. If the delineation of territory has been neglected by archeologists, it is to some degree because territory is a more difficult topic to deal with than, for example, the subsistence basis of the Hopewell people.

Attributes and Implications of Settlement Systems

Settlements, as the physical loci of human activity, strongly reflect various aspects of the social systems that used them. We find, for example, that the complexity of social organization can often be inferred from settlement patterns. In illustration of this point, we know from ethnographic studies that one aspect of increasing social complexity is specialization. In a human society this may mean that some persons take over certain activities, that some families are in charge of certain resources or rituals, that one community may manufacture spears, and another baskets for trade, that the leaders may have "capitals," that market centers may appear, and so on. Specialization and division of labor among people or subsets of communities are two of the most characteristic features of human social organization. Such specializations occur as aspects of adaptation; it is a reasonable solution to the problem of supply, demand, and distribution.

Speaking generally, there are two things that relate to overall settlement pattern: the activities needed to exploit the resources, and the social organization itself. Even on a very low level of social complexity there may be a differentiated settlement pattern. We noted in the Iranian Paleolithic, for example, a minimum of three types of settlements: base camps, butchering stations, and transitory camps. Such a situation would be typical for most hunting and gathering peoples. To take another example, Struever (1965) identified five types of Middle Woodland settlements in the lower Illinois Valley. He found base settlements, summer agricultural camps, regional exchange centers, Hopewellian burial sites (mound groups), and burial sites with associated mortuary camps. Here again we find a settlement system divided into specialized components, but here are clearly implied more differentiation of status and a greater range of activities than we have for the Iranian Paleolithic. In both examples the settlements reflect adjustments to patterns of activities carried out in a particular environmental arena. The exact location of the agricultural camp would be related to farming; the base settlement to other considerations, and so on. But wherever the Hopewell settled they had common requirements, and one could expect to find a common set of parts comprising the settlement pattern.

The Yurok tribe of northwestern California provides us with an interesting ethnographic example of land and resource ownership. Here villages are permanent, house sites are owned individually, and each house is named. Private ownership included such economic resources as sections of ocean beach where surf fishes could be dip-netted, sea mammals hunted, and where occasionally a dead whale might be thrown ashore; groves of oak trees that yielded one of the food staples, acorns; pools where salmon could be speared or netted; and favored spots on deer trails where these animals could be snared or noosed. Yurok diet was based on acorns, salmon, and deer, and Yurok territory held these resources in abundance. Villages did not collectively own or control the economic resources in the vicinity of the settlement—rather, choicest hunting, fishing, and collecting locations were individually and exclusively owned. A highly structured system of property rights and inheritance rules encouraged the development of the Yurok system outlined here. Elsewhere among Californian Native Americans, similar individual or family rights to land products were known, but the Yurok emphasized this more than any other tribe. As an illustration of one man's private resource holdings, see Figure 12.2.

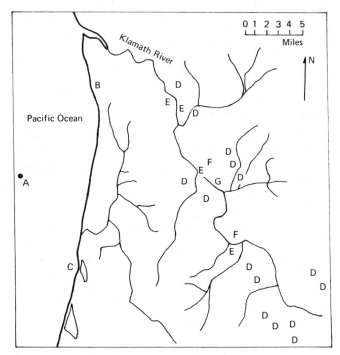

FIG. 12.2 Property and exclusive use rights of one Yurok Indian. A, offshore rock for sea lion hunting; B, C, stretches of ocean beach; D, fifteen groves of acorn-producing oak trees; E, four salmon-fishing pools; F, two deer-snaring localities. G is the man's house in Qo'otep village. (After Waterman 1920, Map 3.)

We do not suggest that situations of this sort are very common among hunter-fisher-gatherers, and we do not know whether they existed in Paleolithic times. But if private ownership or exclusive gathering-hunting rights were vested in individuals (or families) in Pleistocene times, it would invalidate interpretations that resources were available to all who might want to make use of them. This in turn would affect an interpretation of the carrying capacity of the land.

In reconstructing a settlement pattern an archeologist focuses on the interrelations of the various parts. If, for example, there is a trading center or site of some other specialized activity, it is imperative to try to see it in a context of other communities that support it and in turn take from it. As a general rule, when social organization becomes more complex and wealth (surplus) becomes greater, the area of interaction or influence of any people grows. In other words, there is no way to make a reasonable interpretation of prehistoric life by concentrating one's analysis on a *site*. Environmentally, a site is only a locus on a landscape; socially, the community living there is only one among many that are linked by marriage, trade, or language, and consequently influencing one another. We must make every effort to find the nature of such influences if we are to make any sense of our archeological cultures.

Social organization also directly influences settlement, though its influence may be relatively weaker than economic or subsistence factors. The most notable examples in American archeology would be the Maya pyramids and, to a lesser extent, the Woodland and Mississippian mounds in North America, all of which seem to have something to do with veneration of persons of high status. This association is especially clear in the Maya area, where pyramids are thought by some to be memorials for chiefs and their lineages (some would say rulers and dynasties). The particular kind of structure—private monumental and "nonutilitarian"—can be seen as a normal outcome of at least the following circumstances. The society has the capacity for producing agricultural surplus, but the area is relatively homogeneous and especially lacks the differential distribution of raw materials that characterize some other regions and lend themselves to trade. Therefore wealth is basically food, which can be used to "buy" labor. Labor is the universal and abundant commodity because farming takes relatively little time. A person who aspires to status must work with what the system has: unskilled labor. He uses labor to build himself monuments. Pyramids are a natural form because they are impressive and, more importantly, require little skill other than piling up dirt and rubble; only the façades require expertise. The leader of such a system can put his pyramid center wherever he likes, because it bears no important relation to the settlement pattern of the peasants who built it, other than being close to both labor and material.

Quite the opposite is true of commercial centers, whose location is very strongly influenced by matters of transportation and politics. (But see the example of territoriality in trade cited earlier.) This aspect of settlement pattern has been studied in great detail by geographers, who have produced a few interesting models of optimization in which the circumstances that lead to optimum location of settlement can be stated in very precise terms. That these circumstances are really important is underscored by the fact that capital cities are rarely moved if they are commercial as well.

The reasons for abandonment of village sites are usually difficult, if not impossible, to determine from archeological evidence alone. A survey of ethnographic information on why villages were abandoned in California (Heizer 1962c) indicates that disease, floods, fear of enemy attacks, bad dreams, dread of ghosts of former inhabitants, accumulation of filth, plagues of fleas, escape from malevolent witchcraft practiced by neighbors, shortage of food in the vicinity, and mere instability of residence patterns are among the causes. This transient occupation in terms of initial settlement, abandonment, and reoccupation, which involved hundreds of villages, would also have some effect on tribal territory as a whole. It would be useful to archeologists to have other regional surveys of this sort from other continents in order to gain some perspective of the range of human occupational stability.

The optimization theory of the location of sites is probably valid for all people. The location of a site is based on a number of factors that must be weighed. We can infer some of these factors but can probably never guess all of them. Some ethnologists and archeologists have succeeded in treating settlement pattern as an example of game theory, where the placing of sites is regarded as the best payoff under given circumstances. To state that there are "natural" patterns of settlement is only to emphasize what we have already said, that there is a predictable pattern in human behavior.

Some Suggestions for Applying Locational Analysis

We have already indicated that geographers work with a distinct set of concepts and a body of theory that is largely derived from the modern world. They tend to emphasize aspects of communication rather than ecological relationships and to work with abstract models rather than with particular cases. Nevertheless there are some concepts in geography that relate specifically to ecology: networks, nodes, and hierarchies. In essence these express the ecological relations among the subsets of settlement systems. As we have already said, all communities have relations with others through a network of communication links, and we should look for ways to determine this archeologically. One can assume that there will be a route or routes between two interacting communities, and conversely, there may be no route between noninteracting communities. There are instances where we know the route of trails, but for the most part such evidence is long gone. Archeologically there are three ways to approach the problem of routes: to note where sites are, to examine traded goods to see what communities were actually in interaction, and to postulate the most reasonable routes. The first two are easy, and the last may be too if a river, a line of springs, a steep cliff, or other natural features predisposed people to movement in certain directions. Geographers point out that roads or trails seldom take what appears to be the fastest route, but they also note—using the theory of optimization—that any route represents a series of compromises and often is a suitable solution to a problem of locating routes that serve several settlements or different purposes. This is especially important if we consider the spread or expansion of population. Where will the people go? Expanding populations must frequently have remained on routes of communication, trade, or irrigation rather than simply heading for the nearest vacant space. Or, vice versa, if we could plot the spread of prehistoric settlements, we might learn something about preexisting networks of communication. Always, of course, we must bear in mind the dictum "all other things being equal."

An interesting archeological problem that would require very intensive survey of a large area, and unusually accurate relative dating of sites, would be to plot the history of settlement, starting with the parent communities and working out a "kinship" or descent chart showing the pattern of development. To be considered would be the kind of units that comprised the first settlement, how and where they expanded, whether greater or lesser differentiation followed, whether new units were duplicates of the original settlements, whether some settlements assumed focal points, and whether the sites were in a hierarchy of importance.

Site location also involves the question of nodes, another geographic term meaning "the junctions or vertices" on a network of settlement (Haggett 1965:87). A node is a focal point and, depending on the nature of the analysis, may range from an isolated farmstead to a city.

Geographers struggle with problems of building models to predict where foci will be, but we are interested here more in the fact that there are such things as focal points of settlement. A moment's reflection will indicate that all people have a "center," which is the locus of influence in their lives. A center may be a base camp for hunters; this is the place where the whole group exists in interaction, and it comprises the minimum social unit for the culture. A center may also be a city or even a mobile phenomenon like a chief whose physical residence may change regularly. A center has two aspects; it is a focal point drawing people in, and it is a force that influences people who may not be physically present. It follows, therefore, that centers are different from other kinds of sites; recognizing this fact, we should be able to determine which is which. Such a determination then becomes a statement about the organization of a prehistoric society.

A final consideration is hierarchy. How are the various settlements ranked relative to one another? Three ways to determine rank or importance seem obvious. First, one can regard nodal settlements as more important, because nodal settlements have subsettlements in their sphere. One might also rank nodal settlements by the same criterion. Second, one can regard relative size of settlements as the criterion of ranking. Finally, internal differentiation of a site may indicate its importance. Hierarchy is important, however, only if it means something. One supposes that its principal meaning is difference in function. This distinction would be especially true of large settlements that, at least in modern times, "have a far greater range of service functions than smaller centers" (Haggett 1965:116).

If a settlement system has a number of sites of different sizes, one may find that there is a regular ratio between the sizes such that, for example, the largest sites are twice as large as the next size. The sizes would imply considerable differences in function, just as a landscape of settlements of uniform size would suggest lack of differentiation in function.

A pattern of settlement is a workable solution to human problems at one moment in history. In time settlement patterns adjust to changes in the working of the social system or to changes in the physical environment. When we examine settlement patterns archeologically, we are therefore coming as close as possible to working with evidence that bears on the processes of culture and of human development.

Chapter 13

SOCIAL, RELIGIOUS, AND INTELLECTUAL SYSTEMS

In the preceding chapters on subsistence and settlement we dealt tangentially with matters of social organization and religion. In this chapter we deal explicitly with how social, religious, and intellectual systems may be deduced from archeological data. It is often difficult to distinguish between remains that indicate social and religious activities, because they were frequently aspects of the same thing. Nevertheless, we can make a few inferences about the various religious and ideological matters that can be distinguished from their organizational aspects.

Part of this chapter consists of practical examples of how we deduce information about intangible systems from archeological data, and part is theoretical, in which the reasons for certain organizational forms are discussed. We consider peoples and cultures, socioeconomic units, social differentiation, correlates of social organization, religion, ideology, and intellectual developments.

Prehistoric Peoples and Cultures

When an archeologist finds artifacts he may remark that they belong to the "Basket Maker" culture or to the "Azilian" culture or to one of the many hundred such "cultures" that have been distinguished (see Chap. 3). An archeological culture is usually defined as consisting of a certain assemblage of artifacts, so that if the archeologist finds the same types of pottery, arrow points, and houses in several sites he will say that they all belong to the same culture. Archeological cultures are thus different from the cultures anthropologists study. Anthropological cultures usually consist of people who share a language and various customs and have some feeling of unity, either political or ideological, that separates them from other people. In other words, the people can define the limits of their own group. It often happens that neighboring groups who speak different dialects of a language or who follow different leaders are antagonistic toward one another. In the minds of the people the neighbors do not share the same culture. They are not the same people. Archeologically, we may not be able to discover such nuances of differences, because the preserved remains of neighboring peoples might be identical. In spite of this limitation, there are times when it is desirable to recognize a general category like "Plains Culture," which denotes a way of life of many distinct peoples who for other purposes should be identified as members of Apache, Cheyenne, or Crow tribes.

The question of the precise identification of prehistoric peoples is only a central concern for most archeologists when their sites have a historical link to modern times. Then archeologists try to define their cultures as ethnologists or historians would. There are relatively few places where such an attempt would have any prospect of success and still fewer where it has been tried. The techniques used by these archeologists are ethnohistory and linguistics. The former method was outlined by Steward (1942) and the latter by Traeger (1955) and Sapir (1916). One linguistic technique is to look at the distribution of speakers of a language. If the people are scattered and intermixed with speakers of other languages, it can be assumed that some migration has taken place. A good example is the Navaho, who speak an Athabascan language and who, with the Apache, represent linguistic foreigners in the Southwest. A linguistic map shows that most Athabascan speakers are in interior Canada, and this is assumed to be the place from which the Navaho originally came. Of practical importance for archeology is the fact that, by using another linguistic technique, **glottochronology**, the Navaho entry into the Southwest can be dated to about A.D. 1500; sites from an earlier period therefore cannot be Navaho.

Techniques of glottochronology and **lexicostatistics** allow linguists to tell within limits when groups of people split from other groups. Researchers can do so by measuring the degree of divergence between two dialects or languages. By applying a formula that expresses change in terms of years elapsed since two peoples split, it is possible to get an estimate of the date of migrations or separation of peoples. We should note, however, that not all authors agree on the validity of the method. Even when provable relations in the languages of geographically separated populations may be taken as evidence of migration, it is often difficult to find archeological evidence to support it.

Linguistics can also help by finding words in peoples' vocabularies that do not fit their present environment. In the legends of many peoples there are references to places or things that no living person in the group has seen. As an example, which is presently considered an hypothesis rather than a proved case, Thieme (1958) located the homeland of the original Indo-European language community as lying between the Vistula and Elbe Rivers in Europe; and by applying archeological dates to certain words (for example, metals and domesticated animals known to the original speakers) suggested this homeland was occupied toward the end of the fourth millennium B.C. In the absence of other kinds of evidence, such ideas can never be proved, and it seems unlikely that there was only one locale at one moment in prehistory that gave rise to modern European languages and cultures.

It is not possible to discover the names or language groups of most prehistoric cultures; instead, they are usually named after the geographic region, the major site, or characteristic artifacts. For most of prehistory distinct assemblages of artifacts are the criteria used to identify cultures. There remains, however, one more method that has limited application. A person can consider racial characteristics if he has enough skeletons to determine what a population looked like. This area of archeology has received relatively little attention in recent years, but several general reviews by Neumann (1952), in which Native Americans are divided into racial groups, illustrate what was at one time considered an important method for identifying genetically related people. Howells' (1966) recent analysis of the races of Japanese skeletons substantiated the archeological data that differentiated sites of different cultures. Although attempts along this line are scattered and of variable quality, there are many reports in which the skeletal characteristics of populations are discussed and used as a basis for helping reconstruct movements of people, and contact between groups. One difficulty with this approach is that there are relatively few skeletons at most sites; the range of variation of any single population is therefore hard to ascertain.

The purpose of trying to identify separate peoples at all is to reconstruct some details of history in the sense of asking, "What happened?" This question is usually asked when dramatic change is evident in a sequence of events—when a new kind of pottery, house style, or settlement pattern appears suddenly in the record. It is often assumed that "outsiders" brought the new traits and that we can tell who they were if we can find the traits manifested earlier elsewhere. Reconstructions of migrations thus form a major concern of many archeologists.

Instances of migrations in the American Southwest and South America are detailed in articles in the volume edited by R. Thompson (1958b), where Rouse (1958:64) proposes five requirements for the demonstration of a prehistoric migration. These are (1) identify the migrating people as an intrusive unit in the region it has penetrated; (2) trace this unit back to its homeland; (3) determine that all occurrences of the unit are contemporaneous; (4) establish the existence of favorable conditions for migration; (5) demonstrate that some other hypothesis, such as independent invention or diffusion of traits, does not better fit the facts of the situation.

It should be clear that we can scarcely hope to deal with many of the complex questions of culture history unless we can distinguish among the cultures that compose it.

The Socioeconomic Unit

Basic to any society is its home base, and basic to the home is the family or, put another way, the **minimal socioeconomic unit**. It is preferable to consider the socioeconomic unit rather than family per se because of the great variety of social arrangements that constitute the family around the world and because the family does not always carry out the social and economic functions we have in mind. We cannot generalize from our own typical pattern, in which the family consists of mother, father, and children who together form a residential, economic, reproductive, and socializing unit. We call this the **nuclear family**. Of course, the pattern in the United States is typical only in the statistical sense, because there are many variations, including a common one in which grandparents and married brothers or sisters and their families live "at home." Still, we find that most builders expect nuclear families to occupy their houses. Accordingly they put one kitchen and two, three, or four bedrooms in most houses —just what a nuclear family needs. Even in apartment buildings the individual apartments are divided much like houses for the use of single nuclear families. An archeologist who repeatedly found floor plans of the kind we have in the United States would infer that a basic socioeconomic unit of society resided in the homes.

One archeological task is to identify the spatial context of the minimal socioeconomic unit. For most prehistoric peoples, it consisted of single-room houses; multiroom houses whose rooms can be distinguished functionally; apartmentlike structures made up of separate units; or a group of from two to four rooms around a patio. As we have already mentioned, in many modern societies there is also a constant ratio of floor space to number of people. With these two kinds of clues it is relatively easy to make inferences about the minimal group of people who habitually dwell together. The difficulty is that the people who habitually dwell together may not be either a biological family or a socioeconomic unit. As anthropologists have discovered, there are many possible variations of kinship, residence, economic function, and socialization. As in our own society, they may be combined in the nuclear family, or they may be parceled out to other kinds of social arrangements, and it is not easy to judge such things archeologically except when there is good ethnographic evidence for choosing one form of socioeconomic unit over another. A few examples of how archeologists have deduced living arrangements will help illustrate these points.

We usually assume that the cook for each nuclear family has her own fire, an assumption that is borne out by ethnographic data. It was for this reason that Grigor'ev (1967) inferred that the "long house" at Kostenki, a community of mammoth hunters who lived along the Don River in European Russia 12,000–15,000 years ago, was occupied by a number of nuclear families. In this instance there were 10 hearths along the central axis of a shelter or house. Earlier, Efimenko (1958) had inferred that the house was occupied by a **clan**, a social unit of related people. He had assumed that the large dwellings were typical and that a clan-based society existed during the late Pleistocence in Russia. Subsequent work, however, has shown that long houses with multiple hearths were not typical; rather, small, circular, single family huts were. In those instances where there were two or three hearths in the same shelter, the average area of floor that went with each hearth was 5 meters in diameter. It would appear from these kinds of evidence that groups of nuclear families lived under common roofs as separate and equal partners.

Grigor'ev suggested that conservation of building materials, a factor that may have been important on the Russian steppe, could explain the multifamily dwellings. One can also consider the possibility that the social organization was not exclusively based on the nuclear family. In many societies, it is customary for aged parents, and unmarried or widowed aunts or uncles, to live with a viable nuclear family. These families are called "**extended**" if the custom is the rule and separate generations habitually live together. In such homes separate fireplaces may be maintained by each of the females. Another possibility is that some of the Paleolithic hunters had more than one wife, a practice that we sometimes find even among people who have a simple subsistence economy. Today it is common for extra wives to have their own separate huts, in which they raise children and carry out other domestic tasks as though they were a nuclear family, but the same duties could be accomplished under one roof. The reason for not suggesting this possibility for the Kostenki hunters is that plural marriages are usually thought to be a recent innovation. However, if plural marriages are based on economic considerations, there is no reason why the mammoth hunters could not have had extra wives.

The mammoth hunters of Kostenki were a simpler society than the Southwestern pueblos studied by J. Hill (1966) and Longacre (1964). There, the size of the community, the durability of the buildings, and the agricultural base of the subsistence system all suggested that the societies were more complex. Ethnographic evidence shows that the Western Pueblo Indians have clans and **matrilineages**, social devices for keeping property in the family and for integrating groups of people who may not be closely related biologically. Both Hill and Longacre supposed that lineages and clans might have been present in the prehistoric pueblos, and by means of careful analysis of the mutual variation among types of rooms, features and artifacts within the rooms, and style of pottery designs, they tried to determine whether it was true. Both authors made the assumption that "if there were a system of localized matrilineal descent groups in the village, then ceramic manufacture and decoration would be learned and passed down within the lineage frame, it being assumed that the potters were females as they are today among the Western Pueblos" (Longacre 1964:1454).

At Broken K Pueblo, factor analysis (a mathematical technique of multi-variate analysis) of the kinds of data enumerated above suggested to J. Hill that the pueblo was divided into five localized residence units. The basis for this statement is that the rooms in the other units showed greater similarity to one another than to rooms in the other units. Hill then used ethnographic analogy with modern Pueblo Indians to conclude that the data suggested five "uxorilocal residence units." This means that "husband and wife live in the vicinity of wife's maternal relatives" (J. Hill 1966:fn.7). Hill permits himself this inference principally because artifacts related to female activities are distributed nonrandomly in the pueblos. "Of all residence systems known, only uxorilocal and duolocal systems should be reflected by highly nonrandom distributions of female-associated items or stylistic elements; and in the latter case, one would expect male-associated items to distribute in a nonrandom manner also" (J. Hill 1966:21).

Hill was unwilling to declare that descent was matrilineal, although he did conclude, because of the strongly traditional nature of the style of artifacts within each residence unit, that inheritance was within the unit. That is to say, descendants of the original settlers continued to occupy the houses of their birth.

Longacre's (1964) analysis of the Carter Ranch site was similar in technique to Hill's, but it introduced several different kinds of interpretations that are worth noting. At Carter Ranch there were two main groups of rooms, each associated with a kiva (ceremonial room). Analysis of pottery showed that each kiva was associated with a block of rooms, and that certain stylistic distinct vessels were associated with kivas and with burials. Analysis of the burials, which were in three separate areas of the site, showed significant differences in orientation of the bodies and of the ceramics associated with them. Two of the burial areas pertained to two of the residence units, but the third was mixed, containing bodies from each. The skeletons in the latter area also had twice as many vessels per burial as the burials in the other areas, a discovery suggesting that persons of high status in each main segment of the site were buried in a common plot, whereas the remainder of the people were buried in their "family" plots.

Longacre also found that weaving implements occurred with male burials and in the kivas. This finding shows similarity with modern Pueblo practice, where weaving is largely a male activity that is carried out in the kivas. Continuity in this aspect of culture thus seems to have obtained for some 700 years.

During the occupation of both Broken K and Carter Ranch the environment deteriorated. This factor was used to explain an apparent shift toward intracommunity integration, as seen in the development of larger communities but fewer separate settlements after A.D. 1250, and in the shift from lineage kivas to community kivas, whose members would have been drawn from all segments of the society. The increase in size of kivas began about A.D. 1000, with an accompanying decrease in the number of kivas, compared with residence rooms. The increase in aggregation of separate settlements and intra-village integration is seen as an adaptive mechanism to cope with decreasing yields of agricultural products, a trend that continued until the time of contact with the Spanish in 1540. At that time there were only three major groups of Pueblos, and ethnographic evidence shows each of them to have a high degree of intragroup integration, which is maintained through various ceremonial societies.

Social Differentiation

Specialization

One of the most basic aspects of society is that people are assigned different tasks. The number of distinct tasks is a measure of size and complexity, but even in very simple societies there is specialization. It is only in a theoretical social sense that "all people are equal." Some are men, some women, some older, some stronger, some more adept, and so forth. Jobs tend to devolve on people who can do them best.

It seems likely that in prehistoric times some tasks were more often done by women and others more by men. On the basis of ethnographic analogy, hunting was usually but not exclusively a man's job. This division of labor, of course, has a biological basis in that women find it hard to chase animals when they are pregnant or caring for young children. The result is that tasks that must be done in and around the home—collecting firewood, caring for children, basket making, cooking meals, and so on—are usually female activities. Necessary activities that require hard work and travel, such as animal hunting and aggressive warfare, are customarily male activities. The fact is that in many societies both cooking and hunting take so much time that one person can hardly be expected to do both. Archeologists usually assume that there was some division of labor based on sex, but because it is practically impossible to determine whether a man or woman made a particular artifact in antiquity, detailed interpretation of archeological materials in this regard has not been done often.

Specialization, beyond that which is merely sex-determined or allocated, involves skills known to only a few persons in any community or area. Such things as metalworking, weaving, mining, specialized pottery making, and jewelry manufacture were carried out by persons, either men or women, who traded their handicraft for food. That craft specialization can occur on a very simple cultural level is illustrated by an old Australian man who served as the weapons repairer for his group and was supported in return for his services (McCarthy and McArthur 1960:148).

Another kind of specialization involves whole communities. For example, there is a traditional division between farmers, herders, and fishers in many parts of the world, and in the more complex societies the intracommunity specialization can be extreme. Culturally distinct groups might sometimes perform the complementary specialized occupations, but segments of an ethnically homogeneous community can also be employed. Consider our own civilization, in which most persons have a single occupation that is so specialized that they cannot provide themselves directly with the necessities of life, but must have the help of many others. With us, the specialization does not follow any particular ethnic or class lines, but in some civilizations it does. However, in prehistory most persons were much less specialized: herders may have done some farming themselves or had close relatives who did; and persons of whatever specialty were probably capable of gaining their own subsistence livelihood if necessary.

Trading relations that are vital for survival occur among people whose way of life is surprisingly simple, and they provide another example of specialization. When two groups such as farmers and herders depend on one another for products they do not produce, the relation is said to be symbiotic. An extreme example, where the breakdown of such trade resulted in the migration of a people, is related by Spencer (1959:28–29, 201, 203), who describes the disappearance of the inland Eskimo of the Point Barrow region. These Eskimos depended mainly on caribou for food, but could survive in the interior region only if they could secure whale or seal oil for fuel from the coastal Eskimos. In prehistoric times a two-way trade of caribou hides in return for oil was mutually advantageous, but when clothing could be secured by the coastal peoples from whaling ships or traders, they no longer needed the caribou skins. As a consequence, they abandoned trading with their neighbors, leaving the latter in a position where they could not continue to survive. The interior people have thus been forced to migrate to the coast.

Even though specialization was not as extreme in prehistoric times as today, it is something we should look for, but we must admit that recognizing specialization archeologically can be difficult. The difficulty lies in the fact that detection of specialization requires extensive knowledge of intrasite and intersite variation. There are few examples of either. As evidence of specialization one would expect to find areas within a site where artisans worked, where business or ritual was done, where political or religious leaders lived, and where the common folk resided. For every area one would hope to find a different set of artifacts or features that could be ascribed to the specialized activity. In principle this is no different from trying to identify activity areas within sites, although we assume that occupational specialization implies something more in a social sense than the fact that animals were butchered in one place and pottery fired in another.

The kind of variation that indicates full-time specialization will occur only if the population is sufficiently large and wealthy and if the technology is sufficiently well developed to permit the exploitation of different opportunities. Specialization is a consequence of both social and technological factors.

Specialization is an aspect of status that is closely linked to the roles people play—the jobs they do. Status is the respect or recognition a person earns from playing a certain role, whether the role be that of hunter, chief, or old man. With every role is a status, and in many societies it is reinforced by tangible "status symbols." As we have already seen, whether or not the status is specifically rewarded, there are likely to be artifacts related to particular roles. Therefore, a way to find out about the roles people played and the status they enjoyed is to see what characteristic artifacts go with the jobs.

Rank is another aspect of social differentiation that implies more social distance between members. In a ranked society "positions of valued status are somehow limited so that not all those of sufficient talent to occupy such statuses actually achieve them" (Fried 1967:109). In these societies we usually find that persons of certain rank have access to prestige items not available to all. Because many of the prestige items are tangible, we stand a good chance of being able to recognize status and rank archeologically.

We are all aware that some of the things we have relate to our work, to our pleasures, to our beliefs, and to our status. Hammers and typewriters, boats and balls, icons, and dress-up clothes or automobiles are examples. It follows, then, that if we can identify artifacts whose type or pattern of occurrence suggests that they were used for one of the classes of activities listed above, we can make a few inferences about the way of life of the people who used them. L. Binford (1962) has indicated this possibility, but in a slightly different way. He says that people have the following classes of artifacts: *technomic*, meaning that they are utilitarian; *sociotechnic*, meaning that they relate to status or rank; and *ideotechnic*, meaning that they are principally symbols or insignia indicating group membership. The important thing stressed by Binford is that artifacts must be considered in the light of our knowledge of their having functioned in one or more of the several subsystems in a particular society. In other words, it is important to view the artifacts as tangible remains of roles enacted in a cultural and environmental context. Their presence is related to something that more often than not can be determined through careful consideration of the alternative explanations.

Binford's interpretation of an apparent enigma (1962) provides a good example of the way in which one can analyze artifacts with respect to the various subsystems of a culture. The enigma was that copper implements were found in Old Copper culture sites of the upper Great Lakes but disappeared in the later Early Woodland period. On the assumption that copper tools were better than stone tools, their disappearance made little sense. Binford proceeded to examine the environmental situation, the setting in which the copper occurred (graves), and relevant models of social behavior as derived from anthropological studies of modern people. The location of the Old Copper culture sites and the remains in them suggested that the people were pursuing land-based hunting and gathering, whereas in the Early Woodland period a marked shift to exploiting water resources is seen in the settlement pattern, food remains, and subsequent population increase.

By analogy with modern peoples who live in small groups and pursue a hunting-gathering way of life it seemed very likely that the social organization was simple and egalitarian. Looking at it in another way, because the copper was found in graves and in the form of utilitarian objects Binford (1962:222) inferred that the Old Copper culture represented an instance of an egalitarian society in which "status symbols are symbolic of the technological activities for which outstanding performance is rewarded by increased status." In other words, a copper knife represented the symbol of achievement of a man whose aspiration did not exceed being recognized for his technological (for example, hunting) proficiency: it was sociotechnic. Had the copper knives been found commonly outside graves, one would have argued that they were primarily utilitarian: that is, technomic. Binford (1962:223) concluded, however, that "the Old Copper copper tools had their primary functional context as symbols of achieved status in cultural systems with an egalitarian system of age grading." Their later disappearance then can be explained by reasoning that there was a shift in the form of society in Early Woodland, a reasonable conjecture in view of the new subsistence pattern and larger population. Thus there is no enigma in their disappearance, and one must look for a different way of expressing status in the new society, a way that may or may not be found among the durable objects recovered by archeologists.

Analyses such as these may prove to be incorrect when there is more information, but it is important for archeologists to learn to try to test their material in the light of the cultural systems that may be operating. It should be clear that there are two facets to such analysis. One is that, knowing certain circumstances, an archeologist can form an hypothesis about what kind of things to expect; or he can infer general principles of social organization from the pattern of occurrence of artifacts.

That burials, together with the material placed in them alongside the dead, provide information on status and social relationships is not new in archeological thinking. Still, there has been relatively little attention paid to the sometimes vast numbers of burials that have been excavated from large sites. Such burials number in the hundreds and sometimes thousands from sites in Southwest Asia, Europe, and America; yet there are few publications documenting and analyzing the associations of material found with each burial. Publications tend rather to describe in some detail the "royal" burials or to give illustrations of the finer objects found in all of the burials. In short, archeologists have tended to treat burials descriptively rather than analytically.

In the study of mortuary practices prehistorians are faced once again with a paucity of explicitly stated concepts but no shortage of ad hoc opinions. L. Binford (1971) has reviewed traditional assumptions about burials and found them wanting; he has also pointed out that burial is both a technical and a symbolic act. It is primarily the symbolic nature of burial customs that interests us here. According to Binford's reasoning, symbols are an arbitrary assigning of meaning to form; therefore the form of the symbol need not denote its meaning, nor need the symbol determine its tangible form. Thus, the same form of symbolic representation may be used in different cultures to denote different social symbols. For example, two peoples may employ the same set of symbols, as in cremation, but one may use it for chiefs and the other for criminals. Without additional information one cannot infer status from the fact of cremation.

There are two kinds of information ordinarily conveyed by symbols in society and in burials. First, the social persona,

> a composite of the social identities maintained in life and recognized appropriate for consideration at death. Second, is the composition and size of the social unit recognizing status responsibilities to the deceased. We would expect direct correlations between the relative rank of the social position held by the deceased and the number of persons having duty-status relationships vis-à-vis the deceased (L. Binford 1971:17).

With these concepts in mind Binford turned to ethnographic evidence for material with which to test some propositions, two of which are given below.

> 1. There should be a high degree of isomorphism between (a) the complexity of the status structure in a socio-cultural system and (b) the complexity of mortuary ceremonialism as regards differential treatment of persons occupying different status positions.
> 2. Among societies of minimal complexity, the major dimensions which serve for status differentiation are based on the personal qualities of the individuals involved: age, sex and differential capacities for performance of cultural tasks. On the other hand, among more complex socio-cultural systems, status positions may be defined in terms of more abstract characteristics related to the culturally designated and symbolized means employed for partitioning the socially organized human aggregate.

Although the data Binford used and the tests he employed were admittedly crude, his hypotheses appear positively reinforced if not demonstrated. The propositions may seem simple and commonsense to many readers, but Binford had a clear purpose in stating them. His point was to show that burial data may not be used to support hypotheses of diffusion of ideas or customs surrounding mortuary practices. Rather burial data "must be understood in terms of the organization properties of the cultural systems themselves" (L. Binford 1971:25).

Probably the clearest evidence of status comes from graves that are unusually well stocked with luxury goods, weapons, food, or religious objects. The Royal Cemetery of Ur, the shaft graves at Mycenae, and King Tutankhamen's tomb are famous examples of rulers' burials that have their less elaborate counterparts in many societies where the implications of status are no less clear.

Many of the persons who repose in rich tombs were political leaders who commanded a large following, but religious leaders often have an equally high status and may be as richly buried. Especially in the earlier civilizations and other complex societies, there is good reason to believe that political and religious authority were often vested in the same person, although this custom might not be obvious archeologically. The finding of temples and elaborate ceremonial structures is evidence, however, that the society supported a number of religious specialists and that they or another authority was responsible for organizing the construction of the temples. An example might be the pyramids and buried offerings found at La Venta (Fig. 13.1), which, though difficult to relate to an individual, may have served to commemorate religious beliefs. Whatever the

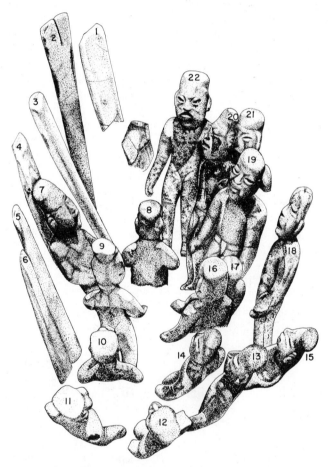

FIG. 13.1 *Offering No. 4 from the Olmec site of La Venta, Tabasco, Mexico. These figures, which were buried carefully, seem to be engaged in some kind of ritual. The figures were carved of jade.*

object of the offerings, it is clear that persons of considerable status were responsible for planning and overseeing the construction of the site. The inference that the society was complex enough to support ceremonial specialists and craftsmen is clear, even though the details of the nature of the system itself remain unknown.

In prehistoric sites we would be more likely to find burials of **shamans** or **medicine men**, who are well known from ethnographic sources to occur in most societies where full-time specialization is not the rule. These are persons who have special powers based on a connection with the supernatural world, but they are not exempt from earning their own subsistence. Thus there is no great difference in status between them and other members of the society. If an archeologist dug the sites where such people lived he would expect to find some religious or magic paraphernalia (for example, medicine bundles) but not expect to find rich tombs or temples. He would more likely find such remains if the society had full-time priests whose knowledge of the supernatural had been gained through long-term study, and who were free of the obligations of supporting themselves. Incidentally, this situation would occur only among peoples whose agriculture was capable of producing considerable surplus.

The analysis of burial data holds a great deal of promise in the areas we have just enumerated, and they can inform on other aspects as well. For a long time, burials have been used to determine racial affinities, although such studies have waned with the realization that there is a great degree of variation within most culturally homogeneous breeding populations. Thus, the analysis of a few skulls cannot tell much about kinship. However, striking enough differences may be introduced into local populations to be recognizable in instances of invasion, migration, and colonization, or in the use of slaves. A relatively easy task of identification is in the Americas, where local Native American populations were invaded by Europeans; burials side by side in a cemetery usually leave little doubt of the affinities of the deceased. We might also consider whether such archeologically documented cases of migration and invasion as occurred throughout Europe since the advent of farming might not show up in the skeletons.

Recently, in a dramatic case, the identification of siblings was verified through examination of remains some 3000 years old—the mummies of King Tutankhamen and Smenkhkare, both youths of about 20 years of age. Both had been assigned by Egyptologists to the 18th Dynasty, but considerable debate had ensued over the interrelationships of pharaohs during this period. An analysis of cranial morphology, stature, and blood grouping "suggest close kinship; in fact a relationship sufficiently close as to suggest that the two pharaohs are brothers" (Harrison and Abdalla 1972:13).

These findings are of more than technical interest, as was explained by Fairman (1972:15). The importance of this identification "lies principally in the contribution it may make to the solution of one of the most intractable and hotly disputed problems in the history of Egypt—the family and chronological relationship of the later kings of the 18th Dynasty. . . ."

Correlates of Social Organization

Social organization is a description of the way people act toward one another, and it can be seen, in turn, as the way a group of people has chosen to behave collectively in adapting to its physical and social environment. Social organization is thus closely related to factors external to the culture. Following anthropological theory, if we can specify some of the external factors, we can infer something of the social organization. When we couple these inferences with archeological data that bear directly on social organization we may be able to make accurate reconstructions of it. Settlement data and the distribution of artifacts within sites are two of the main kinds of data. With regard to the former, Vogt (1956:174) neatly summed up the range of interests we consider in this chapter:

1. The nature of the individual domestic house type or types;
2. The spatial arrangement of these domestic house types with respect to one another within the village or community unit;
3. The relationship of domestic house types to other special architectural features, such as temples, palaces, ball courts, kivas, and so on;
4. The over-all village or community plan; and
5. The spatial relationships of the villages or communities to one another over as large an area as is feasible.

Any environment offers certain opportunities and sets limitations on human behavior, but the way people exploit it depends on their technology and on their social organization. There is abundant evidence from ethnography that among most primitive people social organization is strongly shaped by the environment and by the technological skills of the people. It follows that if we can assess the environment and the technology we can make inferences about social organization, although in more advanced or complex cultures the relations may be less precise. The usual assumption is that there is a limited number of basic types of human organization that can be used to enable the society to adapt to its situation. The stress here is on organization—sets of interlocking roles—rather than on details of kinship, marriage practices, and the like.

Steward's work (1936, 1937, 1938) is basic to this discussion. He found (1937:101–102) that more complex social organization generally goes along with more favorable economic potential. As paraphrased by Eggan (1952:38),

> A low culture and/or unfavorable environment prevents dense population aggregates. It produces groups which, barring special contrary factors, are unilateral, localized, **exogamous**, and land-owning. Descent is male or female largely according to the economic importance of man or woman in that culture.

It seems to be the rule that people whose subsistence occurs in unpredictable quantity and location from year to year must keep to relatively small groups that will often break down to their lowest denominator, the nuclear family. It follows, therefore, if we find a settlement pattern of dispersed small camps, which were seasonally occupied at intermittent intervals, that the social organization was probably no more complex than the nuclear family, which might be joined seasonally by other families, each preserving its autonomy and flexibility of movement.

Among sedentary agriculturalists there can be found a close correlation between capacity for producing a surplus, distribution of resources throughout the general area, form of social structure, and degree of stratification. As Sahlins put it (1958:247),

> The interaction of a particular technological system with a given environment is the basic adaptation of a culture. It is held that the basic adaptation effected by any culture will be reflected in the social structure, because of the organization requirements of manipulating the technology and distributing life-sustaining goods.

The potential value of this for archeology is given in the following quotation from Sahlins (1958:203):

> If these deductions be correct, empirical evidence (other factors being constant) should show ramified systems in islands in which there is a variety of scattered resource zones differentially exploited by families or small groups of families. Or, inversely, where a single patrilocal extended family could not efficiently exploit the total range of available resources on a high level. However, where resource areas are clustered in time and space so that a single familial group could cope adequately with the total range of available exploitative techniques, descent-line systems would be most frequently found. As a further corollary, we should expect to find ramified systems most often in association with a scattered, hamlet type of settlement pattern, while descent-line systems might frequently be found with a nucleated, village type of settlement arrangement.

Sahlins' survey of ethnographic data from Polynesia showed these relations to hold true, and one might use the facts archeologically to reconstruct possible types of social organization from an evaluation of the resources and a study of settlement pattern.

Michael Coe's (1961) analysis of the Maya takes this kind of inference somewhat further. Following Durkheim (1949), Coe distinguished two types of society, mechanical or unilateral, and organic. The former societies are relatively undifferentiated in that the subunits are all similar. The solidarity is one of likeness, in which religion provides the sanctions for orderly behavior. Organic societies are those in which the parts of society are different and bound together by their common dependence, which is usually expressed by exchange. "Exchange is the social glue itself, and is ultimately based on the division of labor; in its highest and more effective form it consists of large-scale trade" (M. Coe 1961:66). Although these are recognized as polar types that may have no pure representatives, it is also clear that certain environmental circumstances dispose a society to tend toward one or the other pole.

Organic societies tend to develop in areas that are environmentally differentiated, have a highly productive agricultural system, and adequate transportation. In these areas urban centers develop early as focal points of trade and have a high proportion of merchants and administrators, who exercise political influence in selecting or controlling the leader. The bulk of society consists of peasant farmers.

Unilateral or mechanical societies are found in undifferentiated areas where transportation is difficult; they tend to produce the same crops throughout at the same seasons. Lacking the need for trade, such people are nonurban. Political control devolves unilaterally from the leader, who does not have competition from a group of economically important merchants and administrators.

Following this analysis, Coe found that the Maya correspond to a unilateral society (Fig. 13.2), whereas the people of highland Mexico were organized into

FIG. 13.2 The famous Maya murals at Bonampak, Chiapas, Mexico, show persons of high status, servants attending them, prisoners of war, and members of the military, all dressed in elaborate costumes.

organic units. The same kind of comparison can be extended fruitfully to the differences between Mesopotamian and Egyptian societies, which also seem to conform to the two polar types for similar environmental reasons. The old enigma of why some civilizations lacked cities thus seems to have a rational explanation. In an analysis like this it is important to remember that the ideal types pertain to early civilizations; they are early stages of adaptation that became modified, especially under the growing influence of organic civilizations, until some of the "normal" behavior typified by unilateral organization was forced to change to meet the competition.

In the organic civilizations, wealth and prerogatives are spread more widely among the population. Archeological indications of this would be that "royal" tombs or houses would not be substantially richer or larger than those of rich citizens, and that there would be a continuous gradation from the wealthiest to the poorest citizen. In the unilateral civilizations, the leader would be dramatically richer than even members of his court, and there would be a great difference between the kinds of goods found in his and in his followers' tombs. One characteristic of such societies is that any trade tends to be for luxury goods that emphasize the leader's difference from the populace, and because trade was a royal prerogative, no merchant class developed.

These basic differences between unilateral and organic civilizations may help explain why some civilizations disappear and others continue in one form or another throughout history. In explanation, M. Coe (1961:83–84) paraphrased Durkheim:

> The relative form of mechanical solidarity is quite weak and powers based on it are subject to rapid overthrow. A social order founded on the sanctions necessary to enforce tribute and corvée labor is extraordinarily brittle to social change, whether internal or external. . . . The unwritten charters of urban, organic civilizations, being based on inter-regional dependence and therefore on interests which are mutual and universal within each society, are by their nature more resilient and adaptable to outside pressure.

Religion and Ideology

Most archeological inferences about the nature of religion or ideology are highly speculative because they concern areas of behavior for which few rules of interpretation have been developed. Or they may concern the interpretation of artifacts that could be explained by reference to kinds of behavior entirely different from the intellectual. It is an archeological joke that strange things which otherwise cannot be explained are called "ceremonial"; it is probably true that many things that ought to be explained in more mundane ways are called religious.

Perhaps the kinds of artifacts that are most commonly referred to religious belief are figurines and other forms of art, on which there is an enormous literature and volumes of published illustrations. In spite of the amount of thought that has been given to Paleolithic art (of Europe during the Upper Paleolithic, some 10,000–30,000 years ago, and to a lesser extent in other parts of the world), there have been few interpretations that seem conclusive to the majority of reviewers. One reason for this situation is that a great deal of art is notoriously hard to date, with the result that a consideration of trends in style or technique is premature. Perhaps a more basic reason is that most art has been studied as art—in terms of its style, design, and composition—and relatively little attention has been given to considering its context in a society. This statement excepts the oft-repeated idea that most cave art is hunting magic. The fact is that until recently no one had systematically analyzed the physical distribution of art in caves. Leroi-Gourhan's (1967, 1968) attempts in this direction suggest new ways to date and interpret the pictures, and if we can judge from the success archeologists have had in analyzing the spatial occurrence of other kinds of human remains, the prospect of obtaining additional insights into Paleolithic art seems good.

Figurines of humans and animals are likewise enigmatic. Most authors refer to the human females as "Venuses," with the obvious implication that they represent female fertility. Somewhat akin to this is the idea that they are "mother goddesses," which would imply that the female was venerated in a religious sense, perhaps as the mother of all living things. If the figures are fertility symbols, one would expect them to look like the contemporary ideal of feminine sexuality. An exception to this assumption would be made for the figurines that may show pregnancy. If the figurines were mother goddesses, however, they might more reasonably be expected to portray older mature women, as many in fact do.

Because figurines have been made in many areas of the world over tens of thousands of years, in vastly different cultural contexts, it is unwise to generalize very much; this discussion is confined to the European Paleolithic. The figurines show a remarkable variety, contrary to what one generally assumes and occasionally reads, "obese naked figurines of women sculptured in the round" (McBurney 1961:110). The fact is, although some are obese, others are slender, and some are in the round, whereas others are simply engraved in rock. They are carved and modeled in a variety of media ranging from limestone to ivory to coal to clay. It seems unlikely that a single interpretation will account for the differences in this group, although it must be admitted that they share the fact of having been made, during a relatively short time, by people who are tenuously related (in the sense of sharing certain tools and subsistence). This is a problem, once again, that needs a thorough restudy in the light of the style of the figurines themselves, and the context in which they occur. It may be that there is more pattern in their occurrence than usually meets the eye.

Peter Ucko (1962) gives a useful review of later figures found in Neolithic Crete and other nearby contemporary cultures. As he pointed out, it is inappropriate to mix periods and cultures when making interpretations. "Any assumption regarding the desirability of numerous children, for example, in an agricultural (neolithic) society may well be quite mistaken for a hunting (paleolithic) society" (Ucko 1962:30). His description of the ways in which figurines are used in modern cultures is especially useful for the range of possible interpretations it suggests. Among these, and the interpretations he suggests as possible explanations of the Cretan figurines, are that they were used as dolls, made by and for children; as teaching devices to instruct initiates; and as vehicles for sympathetic magic (Ucko 1962:47). None of these theories considers that the figurines are mother goddesses, an interpretation that Ucko rejects on several counts. According to his interpretation, contextual evidence, coupled with an analysis of the artifacts themselves, rules out the mother-goddess hypothesis.

Intellectual Developments

The last decade has seen a number of studies that infer the capabilities of prehistoric man in geometry, mathematics, calendrics, and symbolic notation. The best known of these is the study of Stonehenge by an astronomer, Gerald Hawkins, who published a definitive work, *Stonehenge Decoded* (1965a). Stonehenge (see Fig. 13.3) is a megalithic monument in southern England built in stages during the third millenium B.C. Basically, the monument consists of an outer bank and ditch in the form of a circle with a diameter of 380 feet. Inside this circle the most notable features are: a ring of "Aubrey Holes" just inside the bank; still closer to the center are large standing stones comprising, as one moves toward the center, the "Sarsen Circle"; a "Bluestone Circle," most of whose stones are now missing; the "Trilithon Horseshoe" consisting of enormous upright stones capped with lintels; and finally the "Bluestone Horseshoe." Many legends have surrounded Stonehenge, and it has been used by Druids in recent times to celebrate the annual summer solstice. At this time the sun rises on a line between the center of the circle and the "Heelstone," which lies just outside the encircling bank.

FIG. 13.3 Stonehenge in southern England has been called a "Neolithic computer" by Gerald Hawkins, an astronomer who has determined the uses to which the megalithic monument may have been put in making astronomical sightings.

Prevailing archeological theories were that Stonehenge was built by late Neolithic and Early Bronze Age people for reasons that were essentially unfathomable, although the possibility of using the structure to aid in sighting the sun at its solstices was generally accepted.

Hawkins, who had been intrigued with Stonehenge since his youth, investigated its astronomical significance with the aid of a computer that enabled him to make rapid calculation of the correspondence between possible lines of sight through various of the features of Stonehenge and past astronomical events. His results were spectacular in that he found it possible to sight all the important solar and lunar cycles and to keep track of them systematically though the years by placing markers in the Aubrey Holes. Further, he deduced that one could predict when significant lunar events such as eclipses would take place.

Hawkins's deductions were met at first with stiff resistance from archeologists, who felt the sophistication implied far exceeded the capabilities of the people who had built the monument. The consensus now is that Stonehenge and many other less known monuments were used to observe the movements of the sun and moon, to keep track of time, and to help in predicting the occurrence of eclipses. Hawkins (1965a:1) said, "If I can see any alignment, general relationship or use for the various parts of Stonehenge, then these facts were also known to the builders." As a result of subsequent work by Hoyle (1966) and especially by Thom (1967, 1971), there now seems little doubt that Hawkins's conclusions are essentially correct.

The implications are that people 5000 years ago, who incidentally built many other similar structures of wood and stone, made systematic and prolonged observations and records of the heavens. As Thom (1971:5) has said, "As the investigation advanced it became evident that I was not dealing with monuments orientated for some ritualistic purpose but rather with the remnants of a scientific study of the Moon's motion." The uses to which they may have put this knowledge still escape us. Far from being "howling barbarians" as was once thought, these pastoral and farming peoples were evidently making significant intellectual contributions at about the same time as the great pyramids were being built in Egypt.

Great Britain has many nearly circular alignments of standing stones in addition to Stonehenge, and their study has occupied the attention of Alexander Thom for many years. He has been concerned especially with the method used to align the stones with what seemed an unusual degree of accuracy, apart from the impressive task of transporting and erecting the monoliths themselves. In essence Thom (1964, 1966, 1971) has deduced that the builders had a unit of measurement of 2.72 feet, which he calls the "megalithic yard." Thom found that the circular alignments were set in such a way that the circumferences were integrals of the megalithic yard. This is no mean accomplishment today even with the use of calculators, and it certainly required considerable trial and error on the part of the builders, who were restricted to the use of stakes, ropes, and perhaps "yardsticks." What this seems to imply is a fascination with proportions, a rather abstract intellectual exercise.

Additionally, Thom (1966), T. Cowan (1970), and Hutchinson (1972) have determined various methods for scribing the rings of standing stones. To construct these, still maintaining the relationship between circumference and the megalithic yard, required the use of the pythagorean triangle or an equilateral triangle, depending on how the figure was scribed on the ground. In some instances it seems that designs were first scribed on rocks and used as the plans for the megalithic constructions. What is interesting about these is that they were drawn to a scale of one fortieth the size of the monuments. The unit used in the plans was 0.816 inch.

It is certain that some of the stone rings were used for lunar observations (Thom 1966:128), but equally impressive is the builder's apparent concern for perfection, so that the measurements were laid out in integral units of "megalithic yards." Thom (1966:126) said, "One can only surmise that, having no pen and paper, he was building in stone a record of his achievements in geometry and perhaps also in arithmetic."

A final set of examples of prehistoric man's early attempts at symbolic notation and at keeping records goes back into the Upper Paleolithic at a time when peoples were hunting and living in caves and temporary shelters. Alexander Marshack (1964, 1972) has pioneered in the study of engraved bone and stone, some of which he thinks were used to record lunar cycles. His initial study was based on microscopic examination of two bone objects—one from the Magdalenian (some 13,000–16,000 years ago) and one from the Aurignacian (perhaps 10,000 years older)—and of a painting on a rock wall in Spain (between 4000 and 13,000 years old). In each instance a series of marks could be interpreted as denoting the passage of one or more lunar cycles, with the various phases of the moon recorded symbolically.

More recent work by Marshack (1969, 1970a, 1970b, 1970d, 1972) has dealt both with the methods of analysis he has developed and with the interpretations of the significance of the markings on prehistoric objects. One such example is the Baton of Montgaudier (Marshack 1970a, 1970c), an engraved antler of Magdalenian age estimated to date to more than 12,000 years ago. On this baton were engraved a salmon, two schematized ibex heads that had been "crossed out," a series of plants in various stages of growth, two seals, and an enigmatic sluglike creature. What is impressive is the extraordinary attention to detail that enables one to follow the growing season from start to finish in the characteristics shown on some of the species. As Marshack (1970a) says,

> What we have, then, is a composition in which diverse species from separate realms (oceans, river, ground and mountain) are differentiated according to their season of appearance, sex, and stage of maturation. All the images are of the spring and summer. We can conjecture that the precision of rendition had a complementary vocabulary for naming and

identification, and that it probably also included a lore with which the hunter explained the seasonal reappearance of the species involved and probably the general rebirth of spring and summer.

Marshack (1969) has also shown that other objects were repeatedly engraved, in effect accumulating a record of their use over time. Marshack's interpretations, which have been widely acclaimed for their originality, have also been criticized (Rosenfeld 1971; Marshack and Rosenfeld 1972; Marshack 1972).

It is certain that Paleolithic man had skills in drafting that matched his ability to observe anatomical characteristics of the species in his environment. What is uncertain is his motives for making the engravings and paintings. Whether they were hunting magic, art for art's sake, or an attempt to keep permanent records is still open to discussion.

Chapter 14

HISTORICAL RECONSTRUCTIONS IN ARCHEOLOGY

In this chapter we deal with what happened in history. Before an archeologist can interpret changes in man's past he must find out what the sequence of events was. As we have already indicated, most archeology is essentially descriptive of what was found in sites and how the sites relate to one another chronologically. With a large enough geographic and chronological perspective such a description amounts to a history of events. But a mere relation of events in their temporal order says nothing about causes; about the best that can be done is to identify moments when major transformations occurred, and some of their characteristics. Working with such data we can pose hypotheses and seek relevant data that will prove or disprove them. In any event, most archeological writing has followed the former procedure, and it has remained at an essentially descriptive and inferential level. The various ways in which this work has been done are related here.

From our modern viewpoint prehistory describes foreign lands and faceless people. It may deal with the culture of a people, with a region, or with what was happening in the whole world through time. Neither archeologists nor historians have the ability to see the past as it was to those who lived it. We can see it only in ways that are familiar to us, either through our own experience or through our knowledge of other cultures. We judge the artifacts by what we know today. We can describe prehistoric environments and the tools used to cope with them, but we can only guess what man thought of himself or of the world. We can deal with the past only on our terms, and our terms are not those of prehistoric man.

Prehistoric men had no real sense of history or of their place in the larger world of man, for these imply a conception of the progression of time and events, as well as a familiarity with geography and culture. Most men in prehistory expected tomorrow to be like today and another generation to be like the last. A prehistorian views the past as a series of changes, and his job becomes one of finding out both what happened and how and why it happened. To learn these things it is necessary to find out what the chief events of the past were. With this knowledge a prehistorian can see what prehistoric men could not, namely from where they came and where they were going. Having this kind of perspective enables an archeologist to begin making hypotheses concerning how and why certain changes in the past occurred. Such hypotheses depend on a knowledge of the physical environment—its opportunities as well as its changes; of the cultural environment—its pool of technical skill and the possibilities for intercultural exchange; of the interaction between these factors that in the end tells us how cultures change. Knowing how cultures changed is different from knowing why they changed. Ultimate causes of particular events are perhaps unknowable; yet with our scientific predisposition we are led to ask why, and we try to answer with some statement of cause and effect. It need not invalidate our answer to recognize that prehistoric men would probably not have been able to answer the question. The interpretation of human history is a job for a historian, not for the man who lives, experiences, and inquires about only a small part of it.

Prehistorians are concerned with the daily life of prehistoric men, and also with the existence of the many kinds of prehistoric life and how these related to the gradual development of cultures or civilization. Prehistorians are interested in the annual rainfall and probable number of frost-free days 20,000 years ago in a valley in France, not for the sake of this knowledge alone, but for the way changing patterns of weather affected men and their relations with the plants and animals. Prehistorians are interested, not in the quarry from which prehistoric men obtained their flint, but in the development of social and technical skills that enabled them to live in and exploit any environment. Prehistorians are interested, not in the size of a man buried in an African cave, but in man as a biological organism gradually acquiring the features that we recognize as human. Prehistorians examine the relations between culture and biology, and how, in the past three million years, man has become king of the beasts. In short, prehistorians are interested in the history of man, not of particular men.

Historians who deal with literate societies are sometimes impressed with the role played by great men, and their histories therefore emphasize people. Other historians are more interested in the broad outlines of cultural development and see history as a series of technological or social trends. Still others wonder about the influence of environment on man and write their histories to demonstrate a causal relation between the two. Prehistorians have different choices. They cannot see particular persons because their human subjects are impersonal, but they can see evidence of societies or cultures in the archeological record, and they can tell something about the environment.

Both history and prehistory are based on primary documentation. An archeologist's history will stand or fall on the quality of his basic documents—reports on the excavation of sites. If site reports are adequate, it is possible to arrange the data contained in them in a variety of ways, depending on the aims of any particular interpreter. We should stress, however, that data gathered solely for descriptive purposes may not lend themselves to every kind of interpretation.

Site Reports

Grahame Clark (1957:107) says that "the archeologist with little or no experience of excavation is ill qualified to interpret the results of other people's digging." In spite of Clark's stricture, there are several criteria that identify good and bad reports. Professional archeologists and even students must try to evaluate the reports they read, both to learn how archeology is done and to see if the writer's conclusions really follow from the evidence presented. There is no substitute for reading basic reports, and students interested in archeology should begin early to immerse themselves in the reports on the area of their interest.

A site report should tell what was found in an excavation. It should include a description of the environment, of the methods by which the site was dug, and of the artifacts found. Finally, there should be a synthesis describing the way people at the site lived. An archeologist will usually include a chapter telling how his findings relate to those from other sites and how they fit into the history of a region. All reports should begin with a clear statement of what was attempted and what was accomplished. This statement tells the reader immediately whether the report describes a test excavation, a probing of graves to get a ceramic sequence, the uncovering of a temple complex to determine its development, or the excavation of a whole site, or a portion of it, to get a representative picture of the prehistoric community.

The report should be clear and concise. It should begin with a geographical description and include maps and plans of the site and its environs. The method of excavation should be described in sufficient detail to allow the reader to judge whether, from his knowledge of similar sites, the approach was adequate. Unless this is done, the layman as well as the professional may be seriously misled. The progress of the excavation should be detailed in drawings or photographs, and the stratigraphic relations of one area to another should be clearly shown.

The artifacts and special features—walls, fireplaces, and so on—should be clearly described and illustrated. Sometimes it is possible to refer to other reports and merely say that certain of the new artifacts are similar to others that have been reported before. Usually artifacts are described in accordance with standardized principles of classification. The results should then be tabulated so that quantities can be readily determined.

One can judge a report by the kind of things reported. Certain things, like bones, which are usually present in sites, should be detailed in a report. If they were discarded or not analyzed, the reader can be sure that valuable information was lost. If an archeologist overlooks information of this kind, he may have overlooked other things as well. For example, preoccupation with burials or houses may have blinded the archeologist to the very small but significant objects that can be recovered only by special techniques. Such items as tiny flint tools are often overlooked because the dirt is not screened. Similarly, plant remains are often missed because the archeologist does not recognize the importance of saving them or does not know the techniques for recognizing and recovering them. And, let us emphasize once more, all data must be recorded stratigraphically and horizontally.

It is well to mention here that many archeologists publish "preliminary" reports summarizing the findings of one season's work, or the essentials of a dig before the fully documented final report can be published. Publication of detailed, well-illustrated reports is both time-consuming and expensive; the preliminary report serves to bridge the gap between the inevitable delay in getting a final report published and the undesirable results of not publishing anything for years after a site has been dug. Many archeologists also publish short articles dealing with a single facet of their excavations. For example, if the writer finds new types of projectile points that he believes should be brought to the attention of fellow archeologists, he may simply describe their occurrence. Good examples of the power of such suggestion are the first articles dealing with microblades and burins in America. As an immediate consequence of this work, archeologists suddenly became aware of what to look for, and there has followed a wealth of articles reporting similar finds in other sites.

Interpretation of the evidence in a site report should be presented apart from the description, so that a minimum of bias will be introduced into the basic data. Interpretations can be personal, and even wholly erroneous ones will not affect the quality of the report if they are kept separate from the basic description. There are, in fact, many archeologists who wish to prove pet theories—and do so—but their reports are written in such a way that their interpretations do not alter their data. Other archeologists are then free to interpret the factual data in their own ways.

This discussion avoids the issue of "objectivity" in reporting the results of any investigation. It is clear that no scientist begins his work with an empty head. His method of work, his choice of a subject, and his reporting of the results all depend on what he considers proper and worthwhile. Some scholars have invented elaborate procedures for recording their data "objectively," but if we examine their position we find that any such attempt represents a sophisticated theoretical bias—the very thing they are trying to avoid. Because we recognize this danger, what we are stressing here is that certain standards of reporting should be observed. These standards are based on what we believe to be the most fruitful approach to prehistory. In any event, we cannot conceive of a reasonable defense for sloppy or incomplete reporting.

Regional Histories

When enough sites in an area have been excavated and reported, archeologists can construct the framework of a regional sequence. For this, one needs only the chronological arrangement of assemblages. It is fair to say that most archeology is concerned with this essential task. The size of a "region" varies, depending on the archeologist's interests. It may be a little valley, a drainage of a major river, such as the Missouri, a major physiographic area, such as the American Southwest, or a continent. Larger regions lend themselves to subdivision, and many archeologists spend their lifetimes studying minor parts of larger areas. If there are suitable ways to date sites, it is easy to set up regional sequences. But establishing relative chronologies bears the same relation to history that the arranging of prime numbers in order of ascending size bears to mathematics.

Changes in regions are usually expressed as a series of successive **phases** or *cultures* or *stages* of development. These three terms imply chronological differences within a region, but each emphasizes a different aspect of change. A phase implies a time when artifacts in a region were similar and when people had a related way of life. Phases usually occur in a sequence that can be specified. For example, in the Deh Luran region of southwest Iran, there are ten successive phases that have been excavated at three sites. These ten phases comprise the outline of the archeological history of this region over a span of some 4000 years. Each phase can be identified by its chronological position (based on stratigraphy and radiocarbon dates), by the artifacts in use during its time, and by the specific mode of subsistence. Frequently we suspect that one phase grew out of the last and that there is no change in culture. What we have recorded is often only changes that come inevitably with time and perhaps the development of better techniques of farming, hunting, making pots, or whatever.

The implication of successive cultures is that different people appear in the same locale. In areas where there was movement of peoples, it may be preferable to look at the successive changes in this way than to think of gradually changing phases. Certainly when we look at the linguistic evidence of America and can see how speakers of different Native American language families are mixed among one another, we have evidence of the actual movement of

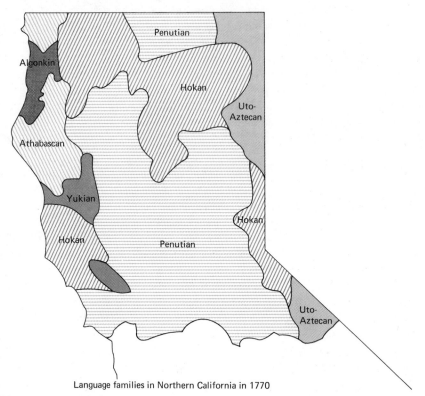

Language families in Northern California in 1770

FIG. 14.1 *The northern part of California had some of the greatest linguistic diversity in North America. Concentrated in this small area in 1770 were the speakers of five language families. The differences among these families are like that between English and Chinese. Within these families there were many dialects that were related to each other as languages of western Europe are today.*

different cultures (Fig. 14.1). Insofar as the speakers of these different languages left distinct artifacts in their sites, we ought to be able to trace the histories of cultures. When several of these peoples passed through a region, we might find not continuous and gradually changing phases, but distinct and clearly separate cultures expressed in the archeological remains.

Finally, we can consider stages of development. These imply successively more complex or sophisticated methods of coping with the local situation. For example, an early stage might be of nomadic hunters and gatherers, a later stage consist of settled horticulturalists, and a final one of full-scale farmers.

The way an archeologist arranges his data relates to the kinds of interpretations he would like to make. In any single region he might arrange his archeological evidence according to all three of these schemes for different interpretive purposes. Ultimately, however, he will probably want to find out why the remains change in the ways they do. Changes, whether in economy, pottery design, or house type, demand an explanation. In fact, were there no change for a considerable period, one would wonder why there had been none. The prehistorian's task is to answer the questions of "how" and "why" about his sequences.

Models of Prehistory

Speaking broadly, two quite different kinds of models have been used by archeologists and historians to conceptualize and synthesize their data: descriptive and causal. The former have been used much more extensively and can be subdivided into those that are essentially atemporal in their emphasis (that is, they do not consider change) and those that focus on change.

Descriptive Models

The atemporal descriptive models are exemplified by Thomsen, who arranged the museum collections of Denmark into stone, bronze, and iron, thereby unwittingly providing terms that, set in chronological sequence, could be used to describe the course of a part of culture history. Although Thomsen devised his organization before accurate dating was known, it was not long before others adopted his divisions as chronological stages, and soon such terms as "Paleolithic," "Mesolithic," and "Neolithic" were coined to describe subdivisions of the Stone Age. From that point most work in the Old World was concerned with describing temporal change.

Quite a different history of work in the Americas led to the widely used "Midwestern Taxonomic Method," first described by McKern (1939). The method resulted when archeologists recognized that they were using terms like "culture" so loosely that it was hard to communicate to one another about what they had excavated. Accordingly, there arose an interest in making more precise systems for classification of artifacts and cultures. The first formal descriptive terminology for use over a wide area reflected this concern for classification, and at the same time the lack of interest in development. The "Midwestern Taxonomic Method" was based entirely on the degree to which an assemblage from one site resembled that from another. In other words, there was no implication of time or space in the taxonomic labels. Beginning with the smallest unit, the system grouped components (assemblages of artifacts from one site or cultural level within a site) into **foci**. Foci were said to be somewhat equivalent to what ethnologists call tribes. A grouping of similar foci produced an **aspect**; groups of aspects became phases, which in turn were grouped into **patterns**, and these finally into **bases**. A base was the most general classification, and patterns were included in it largely on subsistence similarities; for example, "sedentary-fishing base" or "horticultural base."

A system could hardly be devised that was less adequately directed toward culture history than this one. Even though the sites could be described by this system, its disregard of time and space put the emphasis on classification for the sake of classification. These shortcomings caused arguments over whether something was an aspect or a phase; indeed, the designations had to be changed frequently as more was learned.

Within the Midwestern Taxonomic Method was a designation of cultures that began with "Paleo Indian," "Early Man," or "Big Game Hunter" and was followed by "Archaic," "Desert Culture," and "Woodland." Again there was no necessary implication of development, although the distinctions of time and economy were emphasized.

The lack of a sense of cultural development in much American thinking seems odd to many Old World archeologists, but there were reasons for the prevailing attitude. In the first place, in many areas there was no discernible "development" over the whole time of occupation. That is, economy, being in fine adjustment with the physical and cultural environment, remained stable. The changes that could be seen were stylistic, and their causes could hardly be directly related to the broader development of culture. Perhaps partly responsible for the lack of change in many areas is the relatively short duration of occupation in the Americas, which saw few major climatic changes and gave little time for diffusion of peoples or ideas into more remote areas.

A second factor was that most Native Americans, the descendants of the prehistoric men whose remains were being unearthed, had not advanced much beyond savagery or early barbarism on Morgan's (1875) ethnographic scale. Any developments seen archeologically would have seemed relatively minor.

Third, archeologists were greatly influenced by ethnographic descriptions. In many instances their purpose was to produce for prehistory the kind of description that an ethnologist writes of a present-day tribe. For the most part, ethnologists viewed culture without a time dimension. Many archeologists, paralleling the ethnographic use of the "ethnological present," thought of the "prehistoric present" and discounted the importance of historical factors in that momentary slice of life.

Long before the Midwestern Taxonomic Method was devised to describe Native American cultures, European archeologists had taken the initiative to work out evolutionary models. These followed logically on the discovery that Thomsen's "Three Ages" were in fact chronologically successive in much of Europe, and that biological evolution was a powerful new concept that had far-reaching ramifications.

In ethnology, models were made that described man's progession from savagery through barbarism to civilization (Morgan 1875). The archeological and enthnological models were complementary, dealing with technology and culture. All these early models, based on very scanty evidence, were "in large part the outcome of the doctrines of optimism, the inevitability of progress, and the perfectibility of man current in the eighteenth century" (Piggott 1960:20).

For some archeologists, the models were viewed as proofs of cultural laws. To G. de Mortillet (1903) the "law of similar development" was no mere model, nor would Morgan (1875, 1878:vi) have entertained much doubt that man had really advanced by his postulated stages. He contended that "the history of the human race is one in source, one in experience, and one in progress."

Theories of cultural evolution were confined for the most part to the Old World, where the cultural sequence was long enough to contain evidence of man's biological as well as his cultural evolution. In the 1930s archeologists began to see that, even though there was a general increase in technological efficiency in prehistoric times, culture did not everywhere go through precisely the same stages in the same way.

Although this statement is generally true, Soviet archeologists have continued to follow a stricter evolutionary scheme than their colleagues in other countries. Whereas most evolutionary models assume that progressive change is normal or inevitable, the Russians go a step further by declaring that social changes are caused by technological changes. Their model is based on Marx and Engels' incorporation of Morgan's ethnographic data of the late nineteenth century into a picture of the past. It purports to demonstrate the close ties between technology and society. Instead of dividing prehistory into technological stages or economic stages, the Marxist thinkers have set up a series of social stages wherein society changes from a family based on communism to a matrilineal clan, and finally, after techniques of farming are learned, into a series of degenerate class societies. The idea was that the "whole structure of society is determined in the long run by the mode (method) of production which in turn is dependent on the 'means of production'—that is, on the technical forces at the disposal of society for the satisfaction of socially recognized needs" (Childe 1951b:10). As Childe goes on to show, such a viewpoint is untenable in the face of evidence. "The Russian scheme of classification assumes in advance precisely what archaeological facts have to prove" (Childe 1951b:29) and hence is foredoomed. Some sort of causal relation between technology and society is not denied; what is denied is that a kind of technology inevitably results in a kind of society. It is nearer to the truth to say that with a given technology there are certain alternate forms that society may take.

The classic evolutionary approach is often called "unilinear," to emphasize the idea that it purports to describe an invariable chain of events. Even a brief glimpse of human history, however, confirms the fact that there are considerable differences in both the steps by which advanced societies were achieved, and in the complex societies themselves.

Julian Steward, in *Theory of Culture Change*, proposed a divergent approach to the study of evolution that he calls "multilinear evolution." His approach was "based on the assumption that significant regularities in cultural change occur, and it is concerned with the determination of cultural laws" (1955:18). The approach "simply poses the question of whether any genuine or meaningful similarities between certain cultures exist and whether these lend themselves to formulation" (1955:19).

Steward, like most of the archeologists who have followed his lead (Adams 1966; Sanders and Price 1968), emphasizes a cultural core of sociocultural integration. In other words, he emphasizes the organizational aspects of society.

In his search for regularities in the development of cultures he selects "special constellations of causally interrelated features which are found among two or more, but not necessarily among all, cultures" (1955:23). The real heart of his problem is to determine causal relations that can account for the growth of more complex levels of sociocultural integration. These then become the processes of evolution and can be expressed as laws when they are sufficiently refined.

Robert Adams' book, *The Evolution of Urban Society,* presents a carefully considered alternative to a unilinear evolutionary approach. Adams, like Steward, sees social complexity, rather than material variables such as temples, international trade, writing-craft specialization, or standing armies, as the core of the issue, because the latter are symptomatic and often unique, permitting of only limited comparison between separated cultural entities. As he puts it (1966:12),

> Social institutions lend themselves more easily to the construction of a brief paradigm than do the tool types or pottery styles with which the archeologist traditionally works. But I also believe that the available evidence supports the conclusion that the transformation at the core of the Urban Revolution lay in the realm of social organization. And, while the onset of the transformation obviously cannot be understood apart from its cultural and ecological context, it seems to have been primarily changes in social institutions that precipitated changes in technology, subsistence, and other aspects of the wider cultural realm, such as religion, rather than vice versa.

Accordingly, Adams tried to show how the processes of development of two historically separate civilizations were similar, despite their overt and impressive cultural differences. He examined major transformations in detail, reasoning that the growth of civilization was not simply incremental but rather a series of steps by which *qualitatively* different levels of sociocultural complexity were attained.. Therefore the subject of his study was what happened at each crucial step; and underlying his analysis was the theoretical position that the adaptation of society within its larger ecosystem was the controlling or guiding factor.

In contrast to those who have constructed universal or particular evolutionary models, many archeologists have been concerned with stages of development represented in certain areas. The intellectual dependence of these studies on ideas of evolution should be clear, although the authors usually disavow any overt intent at traditional evolutionary thinking. In recent years the trend has been to describe culture history in terms suitable to each geographic or cultural region. That is, archeological stages are named for the places where sites exist rather than for some pancontinental or universal stage of development. This sidesteps the issue of assigning every episode in history to one of the theoretical steps in the evolutionary ladder, but in so doing it also incurs the problem of using specific cultural, rather than presumably universal, aspects of the cultures for description. In other words, it is difficult if not impossible to make direct comparisons among areas. Attempts to avoid this difficulty are seen in Willey and Phillips (1958) and Willey (1966a, 1971) where stage *names* such as Lithic, Archaic, and Formative are applied across cultures.

At this point it is useful, as an aside, to mention that the practice of describing areas in their own terms was initiated to do away with identifying sites as "middle Paleolithic," "Mesolithic," or "Archaic" when such terms have long since, by indiscriminate use, lost their original precision. Using terms invented in France to describe sites found in the Gobi Desert is sheer nonsense. Among a small group of specialists, shortcut terms may be useful, but they only cause confusion for most of us. To take a notorious example, the word "Neolithic" in various contexts has meant: a self-sufficient food-producing economy; an assemblage in which pottery is found; an assemblage in which polished stone tools are found; and a culture in which the people are settled but have no polished stone or pottery. In short, there are several definitions of "Neolithic," yet many archeologists of sound reputation continue to use the word indiscriminately and wonder what the confusion is all about.

A reaction to evolutionary thinking began with the "direct historical approach" that involved working back through time from the known present to the less well-known prehistoric past. This technique has not yet had the attention it deserves, and consequently much valuable insight has been overlooked. However, it is also possible to begin with the earliest cultures and work toward the present by trying to connect successive archeological periods. The first attempts of this sort were made by Irving Rouse (1954, 1957), who developed the idea of a "**co-tradition**" in an effort to trace the historic development of the Peruvian civilizations. Instead of considering Peruvian history as a number of discrete episodes appearing in time, the workers emphasized the continuity of the episodes. In so doing, they discerned parallel sets of traditions. This was an important step in historical reconstruction, because it gave a framework that had meaning in culture as well as in time. But an interest in time and culture alone does not lead to historical interpretation.

The next necessary step was to view the separate traditions and try to understand them against a backdrop of environment and the other traditions with which they came in contact. It is out of this kind of study, based on solidly established regional traditions, that archeologists have been able to discern regularities in cultural development. To some persons, these regularities suggest the validity of cultural evolution. The contrast with nineteenth-century archeologists is that today the stages are discovered by examining data. They are not a priori theories to which data are fitted, although the concept that there are stages to discover harks back to earlier approaches.

The stimulus for a nontaxonomic, nonevolutionary approach came initially from the Old World but it was soon adapted to the Americas. It is worth reviewing these efforts and comparing them with a taxonomic approach (Willey and Phillips 1958) to show how they fit into the general studies of culture history.

All thinking about long-range history begins with the obvious assumption that man originally had relatively simple equipment and social organization, and eventually developed the complicated technology and society that we know today. Though some will argue with the use of the term, this change from simple to complex is "progress." It might also be called the "course of culture history," "cultural evolution," or simply "development." Because development (that is, towards more complex, more differentiated, or larger) is undeniable in the long run, any description of culture history must somehow accommodate and, if possible, help explain it.

The most elaborate systematic summaries of New World prehistory have been written by Willey and Phillips (1958), and Willey (1966a, 1971). The former describes culture history by putting all archeological remains into five "stages," which are variously defined on the basis of technology, economy, settlement, society, and esthetics. The stages are ahistorical in the sense that their relative chronological placement is not a primary factor in their definition; yet they are historical in the sense that in some areas they appeared successively. The Willey and Phillips attempt is impressive for its scope, but the fact that its main concern is with classification makes it hard to use for historical interpretation (see Caldwell 1959).

While Willey and Phillips were arranging American prehistory into stages, Robert Braidwood (1958) was considering the developments that had led to the Old World civilizations. His interest was mainly in Southwest Asia, and the models he devised reflected this interest. In essence he described a series of subsistence-settlement "eras," each of which reflected man's increasing mastery over his environment and his increasing social complexity. The eras were based as much on hindsight as on the evidence at hand. In other words, Braidwood worked from the relatively known to the relatively unknown, but at the same time, as he established each era, he thought of it as a step from the simple to the more complex. Following Braidwood, Willey (1960) described American prehistory in much the same terms. Their jointly edited volume, *Courses toward Urban Life* (1962), clearly demonstrates that although both see progress—but they do not call it that—they recognize that it took place only when the environmental, social, and historical factors were favorable. In other words, they see culture history resulting from a complex interplay of natural and cultural variables. They stress the "cultural alternates" that man could and did choose. Their conclusions clearly indicate that the authors see history as a cultural, and not as a biological or supernatural, phenomenon. They also show that there is a discernible direction in man's development that can be understood only by taking a dynamic developmental, rather than a static taxonomic, approach.

Willey's volumes of *An Introduction to American Archeology* (1966a, 1971) take a different tack. This was an attempt to "follow through the histories of the *major cultural traditions* . . . the principal native cultures or major cultural groupings as these can be discerned in geographical space and in chronological time" (Willey 1966a:4). In this book Willey treated the traditions in each area in their own terms so that, whereas in Meso-America he dealt with the Pre-Classic, Classic and Post-Classic of each civilization, in the Eastern Woodlands he found it useful to describe the Archaic, Woodland, and Mississippian traditions. This approach follows the definitions of significant periods developed by local archeologists; it does not attempt to impose on an area a set of stages that could be considered comparable from one area to another, and universal in scope.

In contrast to these works, some of the most popular and influential descriptions of prehistory ever written are *Man Makes Himself* (1951a) and *What Happened in History* (1954) by the late V. Gordon Childe. Childe's success lies as much in his masterly understanding of Old World prehistory—to a degree unparalleled—as in the sheer volume of his work. It is instructive to consider some of his viewpoints.

Childe described culture history by referring to the major technological and social advances as "revolutions" that enabled man to make better use of his environment. For Childe, man's social evolution went hand in hand with his technology. The first revolution, the "Neolithic" (that is, food-producing), allowed man to amass surpluses that allowed a dramatic increase in population and the support of craft specialists. Childe roughly equated his Neolithic stage with Morgan's (1878) "barbarism," but he subdivided it to allow for the effects of other technological advances, such as the use of copper and bronze.

Childe's *Social Evolution* (1951b) is an earlier, one-man summary of the same evidence that was compiled later by Braidwood and Willey (1962), and the conclusions are essentially that cultures have taken diverse roads but are tending in the same direction. In the sense that man has continuously improved his adaptation to his environment and thereby increased his numbers, Childe says that he "progressed," and he calls this progress social evolution. Although their conclusions were similar, Braidwood and Willey were little interested either in progress per se or in revolution.

The descriptive models used by Childe, Braidwood, and Willey attempt to tell what happened in prehistory and how it happened; they do not, except secondarily, try to tell *why* any particular event occurred.

Causal Models

Models of causation are quite different in their intent from descriptive models, although in some descriptive models there may be implied cause, as for example in cultural evolution. Concerning major changes in cultural orientation, causes like stimulus and response, environmental determinism, and racial qualities have been proposed. On a somewhat smaller scale climatic changes, invention, and diffusion have also been suggested as particular causes.

As an example of the broader approach we can cite Arnold Toynbee, who, in his *Study of History* (1934–1960), contended that cultural progress resulted from man's meeting the challenges placed before him. His point of view has strong religious overtones, and for this and other reasons has not been generally accepted. In many instances he relied on data that are now known to be incorrect, and in others he had no data and only assumed certain challenges where there may have been none. In any event, ex post facto it is difficult to know what a "challenge" would have meant to prehistoric man. In short, Toynbee's work fails to give much insight into the course of prehistory.

Ellsworth Huntington, a geographer, also made an attempt to organize culture history (1959). He tried to demonstrate the role of environment in determining civilization. In environment he saw opportunities that would be exploited by people who had the proper genetic makeup. Huntington believed vigorous civilizations could be developed only under rigorous climatic conditions. Albright (1957:121) proposes a series of six stages in the history of culture based on greater or less integration and differentiation through time. According to this approach, "the Graeco-Roman civilization of the time of Christ represented the closest approach to rational unified culture that the world has yet seen and may justly be taken as the culmination of a long period of relatively steady evolution." Culture history has also been written to demonstrate racial superiority. Hitler had his archeologists excavate extensively in Germany to trace the origins of the Aryan race, and he had his historians write histories that showed how the Nordics had led the world from the beginning of time. In expressing the view that Nordics are racially superior and thus bound to advance over their brethren, the Nazi archeologists were stating a biological theory of cultural progress.

Persons who take the view that cultures are basically conservative must often seek explanations for changes in influences from outside the culture. This is the position of many **diffusionists**, who hold that stronger or more advanced cultures exert important influences on lesser cultures. This view says nothing about the development of the strong cultures, but it may help one to understand the direction of transmission of certain ideas and techniques. Gordon Childe's book, *The Dawn of European Civilization* (1957), is a good example of diffusionist thinking. In that volume he attempted to show how Oriental civilization had influenced the course of European history. Childe's basic position went unchallenged until the recent assessments of radiocarbon dating that now show cultures in Europe to be at least as old as their supposed sources in Greece and Egypt. Childe and virtually all archeologists who followed him had managed to make rather tenuous archeological evidence fit what they considered to be a reasonable model of change: that "advanced" cultures of the Mediterranean had diffused their ideas and techniques to the less developed peoples of Europe. The influence of the diffusionist view of culture is so strong that today many people, especially laymen, can hardly understand the independent invention of such complex cultural items as metallurgy or agriculture in several parts of the world. To adopt the view that all important elements of culture were diffused, however, reduces the problem to ridiculous proportions and leaves one groping for suitable diffusionary mechanisms that could have sped the ideas round the globe.

Migration is one such possible mechanism, and it has been invoked so many times to explain the unexplained that its mere mention is enough to cause one to stop and ask, "Why would people have migrated, and by what route?" Merely finding burned levels in towns and new types of pottery is insufficient to prove a case of migration (or even of invasion). It is very much to the point to consider seriously just what kind of evidence migration would leave. An example from historically documented times is the famous Hyksos invasion of Egypt, which, so far as anyone can tell, left no tangible remains; yet historical records suggest it was of fundamental importance in the disintegration of the thirteenth dynasty. Many authors now wonder whether there ever was a real invasion. There seems no logical home for a large invasion force and no remains other than myth and story to evidence a people who struck terror into the hearts of Egyptians some 3800 years ago.

Migrations and invasions have certainly occurred in human history, but the point we wish to make is that they must be proved and based on something more substantial than a wild guess that people may have come from an unexplored part of the prehistoric world. It all too often happens that when the unexplored areas come to be known there is nothing there from which an invasion force could have been mounted. In actual practice it seems most economical to look at each development in its own terms, assuming that most change will have been engendered locally. That is to say, a very close regard to chronology must be paid, and disjunctions in sequences treated from a solid base of evidence rather than from a brave use of guesswork. As we noted before, an incorrect interpretation of dates coupled with the idea of diffusion resulted in an erroneous interpretation of the cultural development of western Europe in the third and fourth millennia B.C.

Necessity is frequently invoked as the mother of *invention*, but the nature of "necessity" is one that requires considerable thought. Obviously, if ice descended on a previously warm area, people would have to leave or invent ways to stay alive in quite a different environment, but the immanence of most necessities is less obvious. It is well known from anthropological studies that what may seem vital to us would not seem so for other persons. We are gadget-ridden and hence limited in our mobility. It is not stretching the point to say that many people in America would have a hard time adjusting if they were deprived of electricity. It is necessary for them to have power to run their toothbrushes, radios, lawnmowers, and dishwashers. But what are these to a hunter? He feels no necessity to have any of the artifacts mentioned here and would hardly be likely to invent electric generators so that he could have them. It is sufficient to say here that natural events that would impair the ability of a people to survive will usually be counteracted (see Chapter 15 for a discussion of these adaptive adjustments). People do, of course, invent things in time of crisis, but there is good evidence that more changes, or at least a greater variety of changes, will take place when people are relatively secure (Barnett 1953:81–82).

We have talked at length in previous chapters about adaptation, which is only another way of looking at invention. Inventions are often thought of as new kinds of tools, or houses, but the invention of appropriate forms of society is likewise relevant and must not be overlooked. In the course of human history social adjustments, particularly after basic technology was developed, were probably more important than innovations and style changes in tools. This follows from the concept that organization is what is important in cultural change.

Climatic changes are known to have had effects on human populations, especially during the Pleistocene; however, their effect on hunting peoples may not have been drastic. Of course, if ice covered an area, people would not have been able to live there, but advances and retreats of glaciers were relatively slow compared to the duration of a human generation. In other words, the oscillations of climate during the Pleistocene may have caused people to move without substantially disrupting their lives. When the precise climatic sequence, coupled with detailed archeological evidence, has been worked out in western Europe, it will provide a good case study of the degree to which climate affected the lives of the people. It looks at this time as though the change was not very substantial.

On the other hand, for people who were committed to agriculture, several years of drought and even very minor climatic changes in marginal areas may have had serious consequences within the lifetimes of individuals (Raikes 1967). The more specialized the economic adaptation, the more likely it is that environmental changes will affect the lives of people. This follows closely from theories of ecosystems (Harris 1969). Some of the effects may be seen in technology. For example, it has been suggested that woodworking tools spread with the advance of forests in Africa. We might also expect to find some people shifting the balance of their subsistence according to the proportion of hunting or gathering or farming.

Climatic changes are best understood in limited areas where there are good data on both climate and archeology. That is, we need to know changes in rainfall and temperature in sufficient degree so that their precise effect on the distribution of soils, plants, and animals can be specified. And we need archeological dating precise enough to permit us to relate specific horizons in sites to the corresponding environmental conditions. Probably nowhere in the world have data been refined to a sufficient degree, but the best evidence comes from the American Southwest.

Turning now from extracultural to cultural factors, we can discuss the influence of invention and diffusion. These aspects partly represent possible cultural responses to factors like climatic change, but they may, and usually do, take place quite independently. Although many anthropologists and archeologists argue that culture is basically conservative, changing only when necessary, some students of culture change (Barnett 1953, for instance) have pointed out that change is inevitable in the long run. They do not insist, however, that change necessarily takes a continuous path in any particular direction. Changes that might be called inevitable are ordinarily in the realm of unconscious stylistic or dialectic changes (to use an analogy from language). The implications are that there is imperfect transmission of information from one person to another and that it is impossible to duplicate anything precisely. That is to say, the minor changes that have accumulated may, over a period of years, seem striking.

Beginning with some rather simple statements—that is, that cultures change and that on a worldwide basis they tend to change from simple to complex both technologically and socially—we can see that in order to understand change we must first find out what happened in the past, but we cannot do so without taking into account what we want to find out.

We can begin by recognizing that most of any culture's artifacts and activities are likely to be only partly, if at all, related to the cause for the general form that culture has developed. This idea suggests that, for understanding trends and long-range changes, there may be aspects of culture that are more important than others. Given our interest in the general history of culture, our problem is twofold: to discover which changes were important in the long run and what caused them. It is here that we find System Theory relevant, because it emphasizes the organizational aspects of society. By this line of reasoning, for example, we should be more interested in the fact that large groups of laborers were brought together to build the pyramids than in the changes in the architecture of the structures themselves. On the one hand, we have a mobilization for common effort of people who might otherwise have minded their own businesses. On the other hand, we have architectural and artistic changes that although they may help us identify particular cultures, seem to tell us little about the crucial changes in society itself.

Perhaps we should here reemphasize the point that we must make our own choices about what is important. For this example we assumed that, over the long run, changes in the organization of society were more important than changes in technological efficiency or in style alone. This assumption in no way minimizes any efforts to trace the causes of the technological and artistic changes; it suggests only that for our present example these efforts seem peripheral.

A number of aspects of the development of human culture might be investigated by archeologists, although perhaps not simultaneously. Changes in technology and subsistence are obvious, and their causes may be discernible. Changes in the organization of society are not directly observable until graphic art and status symbols announce them, but they are "visible" in such structures as pyramids, which imply the mobilization, direction, and maintenance of laborers drawn from outside the range of any single community. We might consider organized warfare as also being closely related to, and an indication of, the establishment of an impersonal and complex rank- or class-oriented society.

Still another aspect of human history is the "decline and fall" of certain societies and the changing importance of others relative to neighboring societies. The apparent collapse of the Classic Maya is an example of the former; an example of the latter is the emergence of powerful and colorful societies in the southeast United States or in coastal British Columbia that outstripped their formerly equal neighbors in social organization and wealth. As archeologists, we can ask why these particular changes occurred and, if we can discover their causes, whether our reasons are applicable to general statements about human history. In essence the procedure is to eliminate as many secondary factors as possible so that we can see the more fundamental issues.

We must therefore try to understand particular situations in terms of the situations themselves rather than in terms of some arbitrary set of stages or theories of trends. In any situation there are physical conditions (geographic and demographic) that can be specified. At the same time, it is usually possible to specify many of the technical skills of prehistoric people by observing the tools they used, the things they made, the things they ate, and the things they traded. To this we can add knowledge of social organization and relations to surrounding people. When these factors have been specified, even though we are ignorant of language, customs, and beliefs, we can still, by trying to see how each of these elements relates to the others, make tentative attempts in the direction of understanding. In this way we begin to see how people in the past acted and interacted with their physical and social environments. When we have listed these factors for a number of sites, we may begin to see recurrent situations. This is the traditional approach exemplified by Steward and Adams in their works on the evolution of society, and another good example is the work of Michael Coe (1961), who compared the ancient Maya and Khmer civilizations and found similarities in the environmental situations that suggested possible causes for the form that each society took.

In Coe's view, geographic homogeneity, even distribution of resources, difficulty of travel, and an easily produced surplus of food, predisposed both civilizations to develop "unilineal" societies with a strong religious focus. He contrasts this society with that of highland Mexico and Mesopotamia, where, except for abundant food production, opposite factors prevailed and the civilizations were "organic," held together by economic needs. This analysis, incidentally, relieves one of the problem of trying to relate very similar developments to migration or other sorts of influences of one population on another.

Similar studies might be made—not of moments in time, but of sequences where changes are dramatic, and even of sequences where changes are not evident. In these instances we should focus on determining the causes for change or stability. When dependable data covering long periods of change or stability are not available, archeologists have resorted to picking examples from a variety of places, and trying to account for what they find in the various situations. This task is exceedingly difficult because of the many variables involved. It would seem more fruitful to concentrate these kinds of analyses on sequences where the basic situations remain relatively unchanging and where the influence of specific factors can be assessed. That is, within an unbroken sequence in one region, it is relatively easy to detect things like climatic change, the influx of new people, new technology, and the like, and to see reactions by the local people to them.

This review of the ways archeologists have described and interpreted culture history was intended to show how models can be used and to show how the different kinds of models relate to scientific method. The overall tenor of this book has been that there are some ways to do archeology that have more chance of success than others. The techniques described are only aids or tools that contribute to a realization of the ultimate goals. The proper methods, we reason, are those of science, and the strategies those appropriate to archeological interests. Many problems in human history are too complex to handle today, but the large problems can usually be broken into smaller, more manageable ones. When the small problems are clearly stated in relation to the overall goals, they can often be solved quickly and efficiently. The problem for archeologists is to learn to state the problems accurately, in such a way that they can be solved. Usually this procedure means framing an hypothesis and testing it. On the scaffolding of solid, tested hypotheses we can expect to erect a structure of culture history that will be not only as good as any other but perhaps better. In the end, any structure may fail, but the best structures stand firm in the light of current data and theory. Only revolutionary discoveries and great theoretical advances should call well-built structures into question. But we should remember that "ideas are to be used, not believed." Belief converts ideas to unquestioned ritual, a luxury we can ill afford. Fact is the closest approximation to the truth at any moment, but the world has seen one treasured fact after another fail the test of new ideas.

15

CONCEPTS AND METHODS
OF PROCESSUAL INTERPRETATION

Our final chapter is primarily theoretical, dealing with concepts that have become important in prehistoric studies only in recent years. At the time of this writing relatively few substantive results have come from the use of new models of thought. We are concerned here primarily with the way cultures operate as systems and the ways in which they change. Most of this book has been concerned with the acquisition and interpretation of data from sites and only the preceding chapter has dealt explicitly with the historical course or development of cultures. In that chapter the methods discussed were derived in part from history and from the historical natural sciences such as paleontology. The emphasis on developing taxonomic frameworks of culture history comes directly out of these fields. In preceding chapters we also dealt principally with particular cultures rather than with general cultural development and the principles that underlie it. Now we turn to unifying concepts based on principles of organization that attempt to place all studies of cultures in a common perspective.

We begin with a discussion of the contrasting viewpoints of science and history as they have been expressed by archeologists, and then we turn to the question of processes. Next we deal with concepts of culture and cultural processes, especially as they relate to general system theory. Finally we give some examples of processual studies in archeology today and some suggestions for further work.

Science and history are two approaches to the study of prehistory. The choice of one or the other of the approaches determines the concepts that are used and the manner in which they are employed. The two approaches are not opposed to one another, although they are sometimes so characterized. The historical approach implies a concern for arranging events in sequential order and interpreting the unique events that make each history distinct. Science starts with the premise that the past can be understood rationally, and it attempts to get at general principles of human behavior and explanations of particular events through the testing of hypotheses.

History versus Science

Archeologists have debated whether history is or can be scientific and whether historical explanations are grounded in a well-defined set of concepts and theory. Archeologists sometimes claim that history is basically a descriptive discipline whose chief activity is to set down in chronological order events that happened in the historic past. Historians usually write about things they think are interesting and so exercise their judgment about what to include or leave out, just as archeologists select certain aspects of their data to report and interpret. Thus even a descriptive account must be an interpretation. But most historians do not leave it at that; they go on to tell why they think the course of history was as it is written, and so they enter the realm of explanation. What constitutes explanation in history strikes some archeologists as inadequate, and this would seem to be a fair appraisal if we examine the writings of some authors—chiefly in the nineteenth and early twentieth century—who imposed their own moral or economic doctrines on their accounts of the course of history. Today historians employ social science theory and are much less bound by their own cultural heritage in devising explanations.

Trigger (1970:30) criticizes some archeologists' views of the nature of historical research and explains what he thinks are the principal differences between history and the social sciences.

> History differs from the social sciences in that it aims to explain individual situations in all their complexity rather than to formulate general laws for indefinitely repeatable events and processes. . . . This does not mean that historians deny the existence of general rules: rather they seek to employ them to gain an understanding of individual (i.e. unique and non-recurrent) situations. The social sciences, on the other hand, extract recurrent

variables from their socio-cultural matrix so that relationships of general validity can be established between them.

Trigger (1970:31) goes on to say that there is no basic dichotomy between science and history. "History and the social sciences are like the two sides of a coin—complementary rather than antagonistic."

In the writing of new archeology, history has been called ideographic (particularizing), and social science, nomothetic (generalizing). These terms usually have been used without explanation, but their origin is in the presumed antithesis of the two approaches, an antithesis that serves little useful purpose since many archeologists and historians use both. An article by Sabloff and Willey (1968) has provoked much of the discussion (L. Binford 1968a; Erasmus 1968; Trigger 1970; Watson, Leblanc, and Redman 1971) about the differences in approach and the resulting explanations. It is worth mentioning the arguments for purposes of illustration.

Sabloff and Willey, following the general sequence of investigation advocated by Willey and Phillips in *Method and Theory in American Archaeology* (1958), contend that one must first learn what happened, then determine why. In the case they discuss, the collapse of Lowland Maya civilization is attributed to an invasion, a particular historic event (see Fig. 15.1). They find this historic explanation more satisfying than a processual explanation which attempts to account for the reasons an invasion was successful. That is, they were not very concerned with possible problems in the economic, social, technological, or ideological sectors of Maya life that might have allowed an invasion to result in a sudden and widespread collapse. It has rightly been pointed out that total collapse is not a common consequence of invasion. Why in this instance? L. Binford (1968a) argues that Sabloff and Willey have simply offered a common-sense explanation and have not attempted to test its implications; in consequence it stands solely as an opinion, not as fact. We may see the disagreement as concerning two questions: (1) Has an invasion been adequately demonstrated? and (2) If an invasion occurred, does it explain the collapse of the Maya?

The discussion of these questions has occupied many pages of print in books and professional journals and has ranged from off-hand opinions to attempts to set a series of hypotheses that can be tested with archeological data. There is no point here is going into these debates, but it is useful to mention that additional fuel continues to be added to the fires by archeologists who have proposed new historical and social factors which might have led to a collapse (Culbert 1974), and by those who deny that there was ever a real collapse. The debate will continue simply because at the moment there is no way to answer the questions to the satisfaction of all. The data do not yet lend themselves to formal scientific testing so that most archeologists seem willing to stick with plausible "historic" explanations.

These explanations have not been well received by the followers of Binford, but as Trigger (1970:35) remarks, "The archaeologist who is primarily interested in formulating laws about sociocultural processes might better become a social

FIG. 15.1 (top) *The Temple of the Inscriptions at Palenque, a Maya site in southern Mexico.* (bottom) *The Palace group at Palenque. Sites with elaborate structures such as these were abandoned and the area allowed to revert to jungle after the Maya "collapse." Many details of Maya life and of the uses of these buildings remain to be discovered.*

anthropologist or an ethnologist and work with existing or historically well-documented peoples rather than with the more refractory material of archaeology." Trigger's opinion is shared by many who feel that if archeology has anything to offer it is the particular and the unique events of the past. Until such time as one can infer all the courses of human history from the present (an unlikely possibility) much of the appeal of archeology will lie in its ability to tell—by reference to the things that remain—what happened in the past.

Those who feel that archeology should be as much a science as a history prefer to think that explanations for events conform to general laws of human behavior and that one of the goals of archeology should be to discover these underlying laws. Once discovered, the laws should provide adequate explanation of historical events:

> If we can all agree that one important goal is explanation of particular events and processes in the past, then we must agree first on what we mean by explanation. If we agree that explanation means subsumption of the particular events and processes under appropriate general or covering laws, then we must agree on the source of these laws: Do the necessary confirmed laws already exist, or must we formulate and test them? If the former, what are they? If the latter, how do we go about it? Can we use the archeological record to help us formulate and to test hypothetical laws about particular events in human prehistory and processual aspects of human behavior, and about major aspects of culture and cultural processes? Yes, of course, to the extent that archeology is pursued as a science (Watson, LeBlanc, and Redman 1971:171–172).

To the extent that archaeology is a science, it must be able to ask the correct questions. "If we ask something without knowing what the possible answers are, then we have not really posed a question; we have instead requested help in formulating a question" (Tribus and McIrvine 1971:179). To the historian interested in explaining why Maya society collapsed, one answer is invasion. To Watson and her co-authors, the answer is that the Maya conformed to a general law. In other words, the question as stated has no meaning because it does not suggest answers that might be tested to reduce the uncertainty about which is correct. At least, as L. Binford (1968a) points out, one can test an invasion hypothesis. Similarly one could test whether disease, depletion of the environment, emigration, or internal revolt contributed to the decline. But it is not clear that one can answer the question by invoking a law whose essentials are unfathomed. One might just as well say, "it happened," and let it go at that. For some time we shall probably have to be content to recognize that there are two distinct levels of operation with which we may be concerned: description of particular events and an accurate interpretation of the factors that accompany them; and an attempt to discover underlying principles of human behavior. In the latter we should probably deal with contemporary events and processes that are readily controlled, while keeping in mind that if they have been correctly interpreted, they should also pertain to events in the past.

The Scientific Method

A scientific approach in prehistory is inextricably linked with the methods of science. For the most part science is analytic and attempts to isolate and explain the relationships between two or more variables. It does this by reducing problems to the smallest units that have the properties we wish to explain, and by controlling or holding constant any extraneous variables. The next step is to test various hypotheses concerning the causal relationships. If this is carried out successfully, one hypothesis that cannot be rejected will remain. Subsequent tests of other relationships enable a scientist to build up a set of laws that can be combined into a general law covering all the variables that have been under investigation. This procedure has worked exceptionally well in the physical sciences, and has its applications in the biological and social sciences, although it has not been so notably effective there. Buckley (1968:xvi–xvii) suggests reasons for this. Biology and social science depend on concepts outside the scope of physical concepts: "organism, life, birth, death, sex, viability, adaptation, behavior, cell, organ, evolution, . . . mutation, selection, . . . etc." Although physical sciences are making some contributions toward understanding these things, "still an irreducible residue remains. Biological processes are simply too complex to yield to the scientific method" (Buckley 1968). The problem is even more complex when we try to deal with human behavior, where motives play an important role; what we can perceive is a person or a group acting in a certain context but we find it virtually impossible to analyze the event into its constituent parts.

The crucial point is that when we are dealing with prehistoric peoples we are concerned with whole entities—tribes, societies, and cultures—or subsets such as social organization or economics. What is characteristic about these is that they imply organized relationships among people and among the activities denoted by the subsets. In other words, we are dealing with systems in which the "whole functions as a whole by virtue of the interdependence of its parts" (Buckley 1968: xvii). It follows from this definition that we cannot understand systems simply by analyzing their component parts. Together the parts do not add up to a system. We will take this up in detail in the section on system analysis.

This is not to say that the analytic methods of science have no use in the study of systems; on the contrary, they do, but primarily to test hypotheses about particular happenings. We have mentioned invasion in connection with the Maya collapse as a happening. Let us look at another problem of a type that is common in archeology, whose solution is crucial if we are to make accurate interpretations of culture processes.

Let us say that a new type of pottery appears abruptly in a sequence and we wish to explain its sudden appearance. We make the hypothesis that it was traded into the site from elsewhere. (Until we have determined whether it had an external origin, it is fruitless to consider the factors that may have allowed it to be incorporated into the local inventory.) We should also make the counter-hypothesis that the pottery was locally made. Then we can set up some test implications for which we need the following kinds of information.

1. Is the chronological sequence into which the pottery appears complete, or does it have significant gaps?
2. Is there continuity with respect to some types of pottery and perhaps other artifacts in the sequence?

3. Do the "foreign" types of pottery have designs or shapes different from the presumed locally made wares?
4. Are the clays of the "foreign" pots different from the clays used to make the local wares?
5. Are the "foreign" wares functionally similar to the local wares, or are they special types that might have been used in ceremonies?
6. Are the "foreign" wares and local wares found in the same kinds of archeological contexts?
7. If the clays, designs and/or styles of pots are different, can they be shown to be typical of pots made in other areas?
8. Can a mechanism of trade be postulated or demonstrated? That is, what was traded for the pots? For example, if site A manufactured shell beads for trade to site B in exchange for pots, are the beads found at site B?

Answers to this list of questions should show that one of the hypotheses is false and may raise other hypotheses which can be similarly tested. Once the problem of diffusion or local invention has been resolved one can turn to a consideration of the processes that may have accounted for this fact.

Processes and Systems

The term "process" or "processes" crops up frequently in the writings of scientific archeology, and it is also used in history, in manufacturing, and in analysis. As we understand the term colloquially it refers to the sequential set of operations that lead from A to B. Thus the process of manufacturing an automobile includes the mining and smelting of the raw materials, the fabrication of parts, the assembly on a moving line, the testing that accompanies the various stages, and finally the road test of the completed car. Similarly, we have referred to the sequential steps involved in an archeological project. This is the process of doing archeology. In discussing biological evolution we mentioned three processes—natural selection, drift, and mutation—that account for changes in the genetic composition of populations over time. In history certain processes are similarly mentioned: diffusion, invention, warfare, and emigration. We can readily see that process means two quite different things. First, it may refer to a *sequence of events*. Second, it may refer to the *causes* of the sequence of events. In both meanings, process is conceptually linked with the states or conditions of the things under observation at different times.

As process is used in archeology (cf. processual analysis, process archeologists), it refers to an analysis of the factors that cause changes in **state**, such as from "barbarism" to "civilization," or "**band**" to "**chiefdom**." Processual archeology is an analysis of causes by reference to stated relationships between variables and the testing of these postulated causes with archeological data.

The nature of the relationships between variables depends on one's conception of how the thing under observation—in this case prehistoric cultures—works.

This kind of analysis is sometimes considered an example of General System Theory, which has provided a formal set of concepts and models that describe systems. In principle, General System Theory has great potential in archeology, but important concepts and theories remain to be developed before it can be properly exploited. In archeology, we may abstract from these ideas some which are of particular relevance now. In its most basic terms, "a system is a set of objects together with relationships between objects and between their attributes" (Hall and Fagan 1956:18). The particular system under investigation will have its own set of objects. Thus, an archeological study of settlement pattern may ignore the color of houses, but in a study of the political organization of the community, color of houses might be important.

Before we turn to culture systems in particular, it is useful to outline some of the basic concepts of systems that are relevant to archeological problems. These concepts are most useful when we are dealing with interpretations of explanations of changes in organization.

Organizations have some or all of the following properties: wholeness, growth, differentiation, hierarchical order, dominance, control, centralization, and competition.

The wholeness of organizations suggests that they are more than the sum of their parts and therefore not amenable to analysis as *organizations* by considering the parts separately. The emphasis must be on the relations rather than on the parts. In stressing the relational links between elements in the human society (or in any organization) we are concerned with *communication,* a topic that has been intensively studied in relation to regulatory mechanisms of machines. This study, generally called **cybernetics**, uses communications and feedback to explain how systems regulate themselves to maintain a steady state, or homeostasis. Temperature-controlling mechanisms in mammals are the classic example of homeostatic systems. In these systems, deviations from the norm are counteracted: When the animal gets too hot it sweats, pants, dilates its blood vessels, or looks for a cool place. Machines also do this: we are all familiar with thermostats. When a room gets too cool, the thermostat activates the heater. A simple diagram will illustrate this feedback principle of self-regulation.

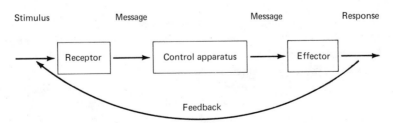

The stimulus "too cold" is received by the thermostat, which acts as a stimulus to initiate the response of turning on the heater. When the temperature has risen to the prearranged degree, the thermostat through the feedback loop initiates the response of turning the heater off. There are many analogous regulatory mechanisms in the human body and in organizations generally. Note, however, that if organizations always operated this way there would be no change without a change in the organization itself. In homeostatic systems the outcome is determined by initial conditions. Obviously, organizations change; hence the simple homeostatic model is insufficient to explain such characteristics as growth or differentiation. The mechanical model covers special conditions, but is too simple for many human situations. This model, however, puts the stress on maintenance of a predetermined condition. Feedback-induced changes are a simple form of adaptation, although they do not allow for a change in structure that is implied in our view that *human organizations are adaptive systems:* ". . . they possess the ability to react to their environment in a way that is favorable, in some sense, to the continued operation of the system" (Hall and Fagen 1956:23).

This problem is covered by the concept that *human organizations are dynamic,* containing the potential for change.

> The dynamic-system model denies that the sociocultural system can be adequately characterized as a pre-programmed machine; the notion of complex adaptive organization suggests rather the generation of alternatives which are continually being selected during the process of operation by decision-making units. In this process, sociocultural structures of all levels of complexity may be generated, maintained, elaborated, or changed (Buckley 1967:159).

Buckley's complex adaptive organizations are "goal-directed," and achieve the direction not only from preprogrammed instructions but also from on-the-spot decision making. Decisions result in behavior that can run the range from adaptive to maladaptive. When the new behavior is significantly more adaptive, a new form of organization may result. This happens in cases where we see increasing differentiation and evolution. In the contrary situation, maladaptive organisms die or, perhaps more realistically with human societies, lose their relative competitive position. Importantly, however, they may be able to regain their position by making more appropriate decisions, if the first mistake did not finish them off.

Another interesting concept is that of *equifinality,* in which "the final state may be reached from different initial conditions and in different ways" (von Bertalanffy 1956:4). This concept is opposed to the idea that the final state is unequivocally determined by the initial conditions. In human history, of course, we find numerous examples of the fact that peoples with different histories do arrive at the same end result, insofar as the organization of society is concerned. The concept of equifinality or convergent development has important implications for the archeological study of the growth of societies.

In system analysis a basic assumption is that *systems are complex* and can only be understood in their complexity. If a system is more than the sum of its parts, it follows that one cannot understand a system by reducing the analysis to the parts alone. It is the relationship among the parts—the organization of the system—that is central to system analysis. In archeology this means that we should study variation in sites and among sites and above all, the relationships among sets of data. It cannot be presumed that any one aspect of the archeological record is necessarily in itself informative about the system that produced it. Artifacts as such are of only minimal interest in system analysis; it is the information that the artifacts may give about the organized behavior that produced them that is important. A system perspective thus shifts our focus from things to relationships that are informative about organization.

Principles of Growth

In archeology we are often concerned with the development of cultures. Such an interest is expressed in many ways: cultural evolution of several types has been proposed by authors as early as Lewis H. Morgan in *Ancient Society* (1878), and more recently by Robert Adams in his book, *The Evolution of Urban Society* (1966). Another view is to treat the stages through which cultures progressed. Such a view has been treated comparatively in a symposium volume edited by R. Braidwood and Willey, *Courses toward Urban Life* (1962), and this approach is especially prevalent in American archeology. All these attempts stem ultimately from the idea that cultures have tended to become progressively more complex, and the attempt has been to chart this change. The evolutionary nature of such changes is, of course, historically related to similar concepts in biology. However, most of these attempts have been based on a typology of steps rather than on the processes by which the steps were attained, and none was explicitly developed from a general theory of organic growth.

From a study of growth processes in a variety of contexts, system theorists have abstracted some apparently universal characteristics that can serve as testable hypotheses so far as archeological or culture-historical data are concerned. Of course, it is first necessary to have a suitable body of data with which to work. At the time of this writing such data are not available to archeologists, but with the theory in mind it should be relatively easy to construct a research design to test some of the hypotheses.

Principle of Progressive Segregation

"The system changes in the direction of increasing division into subsystems and sub-subsystems or differentiation of function. This kind of segregation seems to appear in systems involving some creative processes or in evolutionary and developmental processes" (Hall and Fagen 1956:22).

Returning now to Willey and Phillips (1958), we find a Formative stage in the archeology of America. If the principle of progressive segregation is correct, we should find that archeological cultures during the Formative stage become increasingly differentiated. That this is true seems assured from results reported from Meso-America, but increasing differentiation is more difficult to prove with the existing data from other areas. In any event, a corollary to the principle might be that if progressive segregation does not appear, the society has reached a point of either equilibrium or of progressive desegregation—it is declining in complexity. Where cultures appear to "fall" (or, perhaps more correctly, to "fade away"), a clue to the onset of such a condition would be at the moment progressive segregation ceases. This aspect has not been examined archeologically thus far in any explicit fashion.

Principle of Systematization

In systematization there is a change toward wholeness, which "may consist of strengthening of preexisting relations among parts, the development of relations among parts previously unrelated, the gradual addition of parts and relations to a system, or some combination of these changes" (Hall and Fagen 1956:22). The process of systematization should be seen archeologically in the development of political orbits of larger size or in the integration of even politically simple societies through a process like the extension of **ramified lineages**. The former example is more familiar in archeology and is especially pronounced in the growth of city states and empires. On a less spectacular level, we might also expect to find it in the growth of market centers, evidence of systematic interregional trade, or in temple or political centers that drew their support from a wide region.

It is important to note that segregation and systematization can occur simultaneously, but that this need not be the situation. One suspects, for example, that the developing societies in Mesopotamia show both processes, whereas those in the Classic Maya area, because of their politico-religious nature, would show more systematization. What is more, the processes may occur in sequence. Following maximum differentiation, systematization could occur. It will be interesting in the future to see whether we can determine what the sequences of development in these terms were in various areas. In this way we may come closer to a cross-cultural appreciation of the processes that led to civilization.

Principle of Centralization

In centralization one element becomes dominant in the system to the point that a change in this part greatly affects the whole system (Hall and Fagen 1956:22). A social analogue would be the dictator in a totalitarian regime. M. Coe (1961), following Durkheim, has described a totalitarian society as a mechanical society, and he thinks it can be found in the Maya area. Certainly there is evidence that the ceremonial centers were erected in honor of important political or religious persons (Proskouriakoff 1960), and there is relatively little evidence that there was a substantial group of other persons who comprised anything like a balance of "power." In this sense the chief would be dominant. One would expect, then, that his demise would shake the structure of society, at least in the parts of society that depended on him. Again the Maya offer a possible illustration. Many authors have speculated on the possibility that the end of Classic Maya culture occurred about A.D. 1000, when the ruling class was overthrown. The rapid decline of the Maya in the Peten is suggestive that such a hypothesis (following the principle of centralization) may be correct. Archeological data to support this notion may be hard to find, but if it should be determined that the lineages of ruling families died out, and were not replaced, the hypothesis would seem bolstered, even though not proved, because a great variety of counterhypotheses could be offered (environmental change, disease, and invasion, for example).

Principle of Nonproportional Change

Many of our archeological data, especially from surface survey, are in the form of numerical expressions of size. It is worth noting that as the linear dimensions of a site double, the area enclosed is squared. In other words, a site that is twice as big in outline has four times as much space inside. If we simply divide the area by the assumed amount of space taken up by a house we can arrive at an estimate of the number of houses. However, the geometric increase in space raises certain questions about the growth of the structure whose answers are not obvious from surface alone. "As some of the essential functions and variables of structure depend on its linear dimensions, some on its areal dimensions, and some on its volumetric dimensions, it is impossible to keep the same proportions between all significant variables and functions as the structure grows" (Boulding 1956a: 71).

Especially important is the question of communication among the various parts of the structure. In a small community, face-to-face contact ensures communication. A compensatory change in a larger community, whose total population increases geometrically as a function of its linear dimensions, might be to add to the bureaucracy, whose individual members can maintain face-to-face contacts with the constituents. In any event, it is clear that as any society grows larger there must be increased communication distance between the leaders and the followers. In a tribal society, communication is effectively handled through councils, whose members represent their constituent bands or clans, and by heads of families who meet in caucus with the clan leaders. In larger societies a more formal governmental structure is required, but the principle remains: a single representative of government can meet with only so many constituents; therefore, as the population grows, so must bureaucracy. The effectiveness of the communication between government and governed determines the point at which it is no longer feasible to allow the polity to grow. In economic terms, the "law of diminishing returns" applies.

The precise form that government will take to cope with a burgeoning population may be hard to predict, but it is certain, if we follow the principle of nonproportional change, that some compensatory adjustments will need to be made. Archeologically, we should see this in signs—for example, rank becomes more widespread—and perhaps also in the greater distribution of wealth as a bureaucratic middle class emerges.

Another kind of compensatory change would be to make the parts of society functionally separate, following a previous principle of progressive segregation. In this event, needs for communication could be reduced by developing autonomy of parts or rigid and ritualistic patterns of behavior. The development of a segment (for example, castes or classes) whose position in society goes unquestioned would be a good example. Archeological evidence of such behavior would be found in clear-cut differences among segments of the society; however, if members of castes were not kept separate spatially, evidence of this kind of social structure might be hard to infer.

Principle That Growth Creates Form, but Form Limits Growth

"This mutual relation between growth and form is perhaps the most essential key to the understanding of structural growth" (Boulding 1956a:72). A structure builds from what it has. Once a structure has certain characteristics, it must take these into account in subsequent changes. Some structures are probably more limiting than others in terms of ultimate growth. In other words, diminishing returns may set in at different stages of growth, depending on the nature of the structure. The truth of this principle is suggested by the principles already discussed.

Archeologically, we might find evidence of the limits of certain forms of structure in the size typically reached. If significantly larger polities came to be incorporated, they might suggest a fundamental change in the structure.

Principle of Equal Advantage

"The advantage of a unit in any location is an inverse function of the relative quantity of units in that location" (Boulding 1956a:73). That is, it is more advantageous to have no competition. One would therefore expect to find that units of society would bud off until unused space of equal advantage had been used; then units of larger size, accompanied by progressive segregation and/or systematization, would emerge if the population continued to grow.

An archeological example is provided by the spread of prehistoric settlements of fairly uniform size in western Iran following the beginnings of agriculture. In this instance each settlement appears to be self-sufficient and retains in its immediate surroundings enough land to maintain self-sufficiency. In time there was no more land of equal advantage, and compensatory changes had to ensue if the population was to continue growing. The data suggest that nucleation occurred and, with it, progressive systematization, but these beliefs have not yet been demonstrated beyond doubt.

The principles stated above can be considered hypotheses that one can test with data from surface reconnaissance and excavation. They serve to point up the fact that the stating of hypotheses suggests things to look for archeologically.

Culture Systems

After this very general review of some of the concepts of system theory that are relevant to archeology, we may turn to the nature of culture systems and the analysis of processes that affect them.

A culture system consists of sets of behavior and the interrelations among them.

For purposes of analysis it is permissible to isolate separate sets, even though they are known to be interrelated. We can analyze several levels simultaneously, from the organization of the family to the entire society, depending on the purposes of analysis. A different archeological problem, ascertaining the behavior sets involved in the production of a single type of artifact, requires quite different theories and data, and they are directed toward quite different ultimate interpretive ends.

A culture system represents a balance between opportunities and the satisfaction of neccessities.

The precise form of a culture system depends on a multiplicity of factors, many of which have never been assessed accurately either archeologically or ethnographically. There are many factors that we may never be able to assess. Among those we might mention, for example only, are a host of perished material culture, precise climatic conditions, and psychological or social factors in the minds of the extinct peoples.

A culture system tends toward higher levels of integration.

That a culture system tends toward higher levels of integration is another way of saying that it strives for greater efficiency, particularly with respect to obtaining food or other energy, and with respect to competition with neighboring peoples. In both contingencies we might expect to see changes in technology and in social organization.

If behavior tends to be adaptive, changes in behavior should be relatable to the factors adapted to.

If behavior is nonadaptive, or any set of behavior is nonadaptive, it should be replaced ultimately by more adaptive behavior.

Cultures change and different aspects of culture (again expressed in sets of behavior) change differentially.

Changes in sets of behavior, such as styles of artifacts, types of artifacts, residence rules, and the organization of society, will require different kinds of explanations.

Cultures tend to change in the direction of least possible effort, but incremental change is pervasive because of the impossibility of exact replication.

As was stated earlier; there are different kinds of changes, and they require different kinds of explanation.

The beliefs about culture remain beliefs for the most part, because in their stated form they are hard to test. We shall see in the final parts of this chapter how these beliefs can be restated as principles of systematic organization, and in such a way that they are amenable to analysis.

Communities

Population and Community

Population and community are key concepts in ecology and are equally applicable in system analysis because the processes of adaptation, growth, diversity, and change operate on aggregates of individuals over time. They do not operate directly on single members of the species. However, as we read in ecology and anthropology, we find that the words "population" and "community" have been used in different ways. This factor may cause confusion unless we recognize that the basic differences in usage have to do with the size of the groups under consideration and the number of different species and inorganic factors that are included in the community.

Populations have the following general characteristics: a finite number of people, likeness of kind, aliveness, and limitation of universe in space and time (Allee and others 1949:265). A living biological population can be defined if we can specify how many persons it comprises, what kind of species are included, and where the members of the population are. We shall use the word "population" here to refer to what ethnologists call bands, tribes, or ethnic entities as distinct and identifiable groups of people.

The word "community" implies several things, and it may be used in different ways for different purposes. At the heart of any definition, however, is the concept that the community has functional integrity. It is composed of "ecologically compatible species populations whose collective ecological requirements of food, shelter, and reproduction are satisfied, in the last analysis, by a certain range of environments" (Allee and others 1949:437). "Community" thus introduces the notions of self-sufficiency that are not claimed for populations. Moreover, it implies that several distinct populations are in mutual interaction, and that the separate species which comprise them cannot be considered in isolation. To understand the processes of culture, then, we must consider the relation between people and the many facets of their self-sustaining world.

If a community embraces more than simply a population of one species or of one village, how big or inclusive need we make it? Here the decision belongs to the person making the analysis, because only he has the intimate knowledge of data necessary to determine the range of factors that will be required to solve his problem. If we take the broadest view of "community," it "may be defined as a natural assemblage of organisms which, together with its habitat, has reached a survival level such that it is relatively independent of adjacent assemblages of equal rank; to this extent, given radiant energy, it is self-sustaining" (Allee and others 1949:436). As stated earlier, this view varies from the usual anthropological or archeological conception of a community, which is taken to be the tribe or village under investigation. In the broadest sense, however, an ecological community (or ecosystem) consists of all the species that interact to form a self-sustaining entity. One or more of the species must be capable of utilizing an inorganic energy source because, obviously, people do not directly convert radiant energy and minerals to food; they do so through the intermediary plants and animals that they consume. Moreover, a village of people ordinarily interacts through marriage, trade, or similar social relations with other villages and groups of people. The concept of the biological community thus forces us to expand our traditional focus to regard things that are not "cultural" as integral parts of any viable cultural system.

In practice, ecologists and archeologists deal mostly with communities that are not too complex or diverse. We may consider, for example, that all the people who are related through marriage, trade, or political ties form a viable social system that we may liken to a biological community. This is a convenient frame of reference, and we often find that our problems do not require us to consider the rainfall, soil conditions, growth of grass, or insect parasites; however, this chapter should serve as fair warning that such factors are important to some aspects of the human community. In archeology we usually select to study from the total ecosystem the portions that we can readily manage and that contribute to the solution of our problems.

The Ecology of Social Differentiation

A basic premise is that a community has organizational structure. One way in which this structure is accomplished is through differentiation. Within the higher orders of organisms, members of groups are differentiated by sex, age, size, and behavior. Such differentiation is usually expressed in physical distinctiveness and by dominant and submissive behavior. In other words, some animals have greater influence over other animals and consequently gain priority of access to food, females, or other desirable things. In the differentiation of human populations, dominance is important.

Ecologists recognize two basic kinds of social communities—monospecific and polyspecific—referring, respectively, to those composed of one species and to those of more than one species. We cannot relate this directly to human groups, because all humans are of one species, but it is useful to substitute culture for species to see the implications of the distinction.

We find that most human societies are monospecific, being made of members of the same culture, but that most complex societies (especially civilizations) are polyspecific. Both the size of the group and the cultural homogeneity of the population will determine to some degree what sort of dominance hierarchy will occur. In societies where the hierarchy is linear, a single person dominates the others. Such a situation is uncommon in human societies, but examples may be found from simple bands to dictator-led civilizations. In small populations there literally may be no designated "leader," but the larger the group, the more likely it is that someone will take charge or be designated leader. His status will then be underscored by his dominant behavior and/or by symbols that express his difference. "Once a hierarchy has become established, the ability to recognize individuals greatly reduces the number of conflicts" (Klopfer 1962:133).

In human societies we find that people are usually divided by family and by occupation. Within each family and within each occupation there is a hierarchy, and each of these units may be ranked relative to all others so that some families may be dominant, and some businesses more important. The influence of the various members of the population will ordinarily be in relation to certain tangible aspects of dominance like size and wealth. In most complex societies too much power is held by several segments of the population to make a linear-dominance hierarchy enduringly feasible. Accordingly, we find many gradations along the scale of dominance.

Ecology gives us some reasons why social organization is necessary and some of the basic ways in which organization is accomplished. It also indicates some of the problems inherent in a differentiated society. A major problem in a human society is to organize the people so that they can do their jobs with a minimum of mistakes and conflicts. In a simple society, where people are jacks-of-all-trades, this is no real problem, but it can be in a society which has many specialized segments. Ecologists have found that, as societies become more complex and statuses and roles (ranked jobs, for example) are added, it becomes more difficult for one person to recognize and react properly toward the statuses of all other people. This condition is especially true in a monospecific community when dominance differences are not physically obvious and when there are more individuals than any one person can know personally. People solve this problem by creating status symbols. These artifacts are to people what size, aggression, and color are to members of other animal communities. We can thus see status as a device to facilitate the orderly operation of a social system.

How do we use these ideas archeologically? In a monospecific culture there are two ways to express status—through the use of symbols and by creating castes or feudal classes. Anthropologists have found that the most elaborate symbols are used in societies where there is the greatest relative difference between the most dominant and the most submissive member. Should the symbols be preserved archeologically, they will be obvious, because they will be restricted to a very few of the total group. In a monospecific society without castes or great relative differences between top and bottom, status symbols will be common objects but perhaps of better quality or different material for the more important people (for instance, copper tools instead of stone). Because they restrict certain kinds of activities to each caste, castes are an alternative way of differentiating people. In this way the society comes to be made up of mutually interacting and interdependent specialized parts. In the most rigid of these societies there is no movement of people between castes. Archeologically, castes would be recognized by the nonrandom distribution of artifacts related to the activities of the caste, and probably also by the relative wealth of members of different castes. Physically, however, the people might all look the same. And it might also be very hard to distinguish members of a caste from persons who belong to occupationally specialized groups.

The most complex societies are multicultural, a situation analogous to different species of animals in a symbiotic relation. An important ecological principle is that two species cannot occupy the same niche; one will drive the other out. If we were to find evidence of two cultural groups coexisting in the same system we should expect to find that they occupied different occupational niches.

Ecological System Analysis

The discussion of differentiation and dominance raises the issue of relations among members of communities or populations. As we stated earlier, human societies, and the ecosystems of which they are a part, work in their own self-interest. Behavior is directed toward survival, which is effected only through a balance among cooperation, competition, exploitation, and predation. Klopfer (1962) put this in sharp focus in his chapter, "Why Don't Predators Overeat Their Prey?" The fact is, as students of cybernetics explain it, there are mutual causative factors involved; changes in one factor always cause changes in another factor. If a predator overate his prey he would die also, unless he had an alternative food source. If the number of predators is a function of the number of prey, a decrease in the prey will result in a decrease in the predators; in this way an effective balance is maintained. This is another way of stating that, to ensure survival, mutually beneficial interactions among the total set of factors in an ecosystem must obtain. Of course, this remark does not preclude the fact that the relations between any *two* species may be detrimental to one and advantageous to another.

The interrelations described above are a statement of organization, because the pattern of relations can be abstracted and the links between the elements specified. Consequently, ecology is amenable to investigation through the concepts of system theory. Inasmuch as the emphasis is on the interrelations among elements, ecology must ignore an analysis that uses culture as its major determinant. It does so because one cannot easily count or describe cultures in ways that are commensurable for comparative or analytic purposes. As Vayda and Rappaport (1968:494) say, one must make a tangible unit, such as population, the focus of ecological studies, because "no such commensurability obtains if cultures are made the units, for cultures, unlike human populations, are not fed upon predators, limited by food supplies, or debilitated by disease."

To an anthropologist, culture is many things, whereas, to an ecologist, culture is an adaptive mechanism expressed in behavior. It is the same kind of variable as body size or speed in running, traits that are selected in the complex interplay of factors that ultimately make any kind of animal better or less suited to survival. In the same fashion, human behavior (culture) is constantly tested and modified in the course of human experience. What is more, culture seems no more important as a primary cause of human behavior than is, for example, climate. To make this statement, however, is only to deny primacy to any *one* cause, not to argue that either culture or climate is all-important or unimportant.

The preceding may sound contradictory, but it is only when you adopt a position that there are clearly specified simple relations of cause and effect. System theorists and ecologists take the view that there are no such relations, at least in such complex areas as human behavior. They would stress that biological, physical, social, and cultural factors all play parts in effecting outcomes through a process of mutual causation or circularity. There is no chicken or the egg paradox, because the issue is phrased so that both are necessary for the maintenance of the life system. It also points up the fact that one must consider processes rather than points or static terminal conditions. Process and organization, rather than causes, lend themselves most readily to archeological and anthropological analysis. We can come much closer to figuring out how an ecosystem works than why it definitely has certain characteristics and not others.

In much archeological writing, ecology is used synonymously with environment. This view was taken by Steward (1937) when he related Great Basin subsistence practices to certain environmental factors. As we have already implied, however, such a view of ecology is overly narrow and, for most purposes, insufficient. The important point is that ecology involves much more than a set of physical conditions. It is only in the broadest view, where environment is treated as the totality of animate and inanimate objects that affect human societies, that we can equate environment with ecology.

The term "ecological niche," as used by many archeologists, implies that people utilize and are adjusted to a particular well-defined environmental area or set of areas. All species are adapted to certain environments, and this is no less true for human groups. To understand effectively the workings of an archeological culture we must ascertain the particular ways in which the environment was used. No less, we must also consider the space within communities as it concerns relations among individuals, because space and the objects in it indicate modes of relations among people and the land they live on.

Population density is another concept that has implications of efficiency in exploiting an environment, of relations among people within a village, and of a settlement to those outside it; and vacant spaces or lightly exploited spaces inform on the degree of specialization (narrow-spectrum exploitation of food sources such as agricultural products as opposed to broad-spectrum exploitation exemplified by hunting and collecting), as well as relations among groups of people (buffer zones, territorial boundaries, and the like).

Differentiation of members of a single population or of people who comprise a polyspecific community is likewise an indication of higher levels of integration, where the group seeks to maximize its potential through dividing the labor among specialists, thereby gaining an advantage in converting raw materials to energy (principally through farming and manufacturing) or in opposition to outside peoples who impinge with hostile intent.

This division of labor raises the issue of dominance, which has been partly implicit in some of the foregoing remarks. Dominance is expressed when relatively few members of a community have greater access to certain resources than do others, and when one community prevails over another either by eliminating it or by placing it in a subservient position. The principle is that where there is competition for the same niche, two groups (or species) cannot coexist, and one will prevail, owing to its dominance. The less well adapted group will then have to shift its ecological niche, merge with the dominant group, or be destroyed. Numerous examples of just this situation abound both in historical and ethnographic literature.

The ecological implication in this example is that advantages gained by one group will be exploited to the disadvantage of other groups, who in turn will have to adopt countermeasures if they are to survive. Elman Service (1962) describes this process well in his discussion of the genesis of tribal societies, which he ascribes more to competition among peoples than to any qualities inherent in their physical environmental or social circumstances. Following the expansion of a dominant groups, there will be countermeasures and ultimately a return to stable conditions, with new boundaries and new relations, until the next advantage restores the process to a state of disequilibrium. Even over periods measured in the hundreds of years, equilibrium may not be achieved— this is a reason why short-term studies can be misleading, and it serves as a warning against a too rapid appraisal of any seemingly adjusted system.

Systems in Archeology

Formal system analysis introduces terms that are not familiar to most students of archeology. However, these terms precisely describe the interactions and relationships within certain systems. Of particular interest here are systems that archeologically appear to be stable over long periods, those which grow or evolve into more complex forms, and those which decline and fall. In system terms, the first are systems that tend to maintain equilibrium: they are "deviation-counteracting mutually causal relationships." The second type are "deviation-amplifying systems" in which positive feedback causes growth. The third are "negative deviation-amplifying systems" that decline, perhaps into extinction. Diagrams that illustrate each of these situations are given in Figures 15.2, 15.3, and 15.4.

We can recognize each of these situations in archeology. For long terms, many cultures remain stable and appear to be unchanging. We might say that they are in balance internally and with their physical and social environments. In the course of human history, however, there has been a trend toward growth and more complexity. In these systems that have ultimately led to our own civilization, deviations have been encouraged (amplified) rather than discouraged (counteracted). Finally there are instances when cultures have declined and disappeared, such as the Maya. In these instances the people made choices that put them at a disadvantage, or circumstances over which they had no control, such as environmental change, put them out of business. The negative or disadvantageous deviations were amplified.

Archeologists have tended to focus on situations of growth and to look for conditions that would provide an impetus for it. The development of new technology such as agriculture or of new social relations such as trade is the kind of thing that has been invoked as a "kick" to the system. The idea is that these new things provided an initial stimulus or "kick" and that other ad-

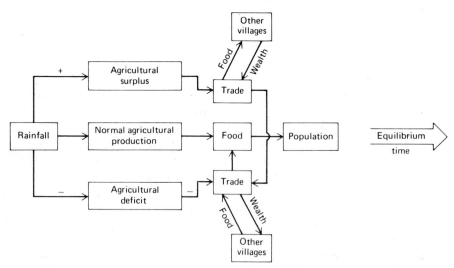

FIG. 15.2 Diagram of a deviation-counteracting system. (Based on analysis of archeological findings in Oaxaca, Mexico.)

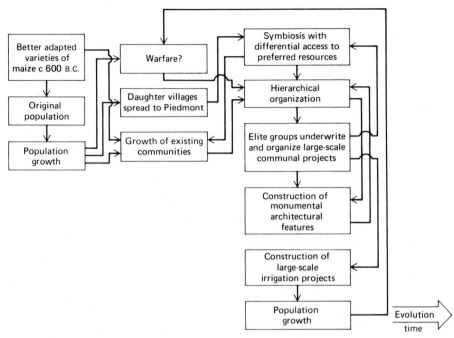

FIG. 15.3   Diagram of a deviation-amplifying system. (Based on analysis of archeological data from the Valley of Mexico.)

justments amplified these deviations and enabled the system to grow and sustain itself at new levels of size and competitive efficiency.

We can illustrate this point with a hypothetical example. Assume a population at some point in its history in which there is an invention (recall our loose equation of invention in culture with mutation in biology). In system terms the invention affords the possibility of deviation from the previous state. Should an innovation such as the invention of clothing or the use of fire prove viable, it might allow expansion into new territory that had been climatically inhospitable before. In turn this expansion could result in the growth of population, as previously untapped food resources were put to use. In this example we can see how an invention that in itself has nothing to do with the food quest may enable people to use a potential source of food that was previously denied them. The effects of such an invention will then be amplified as people take advantage of it, perhaps refine it still further, and in the process once again amplify the effect. Once started toward manufacturing forms of protection from the cold, rather than relying on body heat alone, the culture system further elaborates and develops this new adaptation. In both biological and cultural terms the people are evolving: there are more of them and they have added to their inventory of cultural things.

The concepts of drift and selection are included in the discussion above. The population that moves into a new environment with a new set of techniques

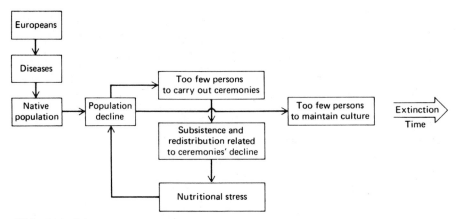

FIG. 15.4 Diagram of a negative deviation-amplifying system. (Based on an ethnographic example from central Brazil.)

develops further along lines laid out by the initial invention. The invention is the "kick" in the system, which is amplified by continued use and elaboration. Metaphorically and physically, the population drifts farther and farther away from the parent group. Selection, of course, rests in the advantage (expressed in the numbers of people who can be supported) gained by employing the invention.

Human history has seen many such changes and the deviation-amplifying processes that followed. There is more to this development, however. In human as among other species, there is competition from outside. Let us say that one group adopts firearms and uses them to take advantage of its neighbors. The group that is being preyed upon may counteract this situation by also adopting firearms, thus hoping to return to a state of equilibrium. In this case we would have a deviation-counteracting effect. However, as we know from modern history, an arms race may ensue, in which case we have a deviation-amplifying relationship.

The way human societies actually operate to control deviation is through minor adjustments that are usually not thought to have long-range implications of their own. However, as Forrester (1971:95) puts it, "There is usually a conflict between the goals of a subsystem and the welfare of the broader system." Minor tinkering with the system seems to be characteristic, but "a policy which produces improvement in the short run is usually one which degrades the system in the long run" (Forrester 1971:94). This is a dire prediction that seems not to be borne out by our knowledge of human evolution, but the apparent paradox is solved by recognizing that as long as growth is possible, short-term errors may be solved with short-term solutions. The problem facing mankind today is that continued growth no longer seems possible.

A system perspective forces us to look at the way the subsystems interact and to consider that as a whole, a culture system will attempt to counteract deviations and thereby remain stable or in equilibrium. Our knowledge of human evolution, on the other hand, requires us to take note of the fact that change is customary. It is instructive to examine situations in which change cannot be detected in the essentials of a system over a long duration. Early in human history there were few perceptible changes. Hundreds of thousands of years passed without notable changes in technology or in biology. Gradually changes that culminated in biologically modern man did occur and with his appearance so did a great acceleration in the rate of cultural change as it is expressed in archeological remains. There are circumstances, however, in which even modern peoples seem scarcely to change.

We have seen that culture is transmitted through symbolic communication which allows it to move rapidly and to be cumulative. It is transmitted within and between distinct groups. The fact that it is cumulative means that as time passes there is potentially much more information available to be used and to serve as the basis for inventions. This process of cumulation is accelerated by growth in the total population of mankind. Thus, the potential for change has developed at an ever-increasing rate, as today's "information" explosion testifies.

Were it not for the potential advantage such changes afforded, however, they would not have been retained. If we recall biological principles, which have been translated into cultural terms by Service (1968) as the "law of evolutionary potential," we see that the larger the inventory of ideas and things a people have, the more likely will they be able to respond to disequilibrating factors. This is another way of saying that diversity, rather than specialization, is adaptive.

If systems tend to counteract deviation, we should expect to find that they change relatively little (except through drift) unless they are faced with disequilibrating factors that cannot be shrugged off. Such factors may be generated internally, as with a population that expands to the limits of the system's ability to feed it, or externally, as in the case of climatic change or warfare. Archeologically we need to look for potential sources of disequilibration in systems that are known to have been undergoing change, and conversely to see what factors inhibit disequilibration in systems that are not changing.

Sanders and Price (1968), in their study of the evolution of Meso-American civilization, see three factors or, as they call them, three "basic ecological processes": population growth, competition, and cooperation.

It is easy to put these into systems terms. Population growth puts stress on resources and creates a greater density in living arrangements. Consequently there is competition for the resources that may encourage warfare and the elaboration of social stratification. In turn, these effects may lead to increased cooperation, both in the construction of facilities for irrigation, defense, and ceremony on the one hand, and in the unification under central direction of previously separate groups on the other. These actions then feed back upon the population and set up further sources of competition. Thus we find, in very simple outline, a set of factors that result in a deviation-amplifying system, which, expressed in cultural terms, is the evolution of Meso-American civilization.

In our discussion of systems we have had no need to mention ceramics, graves, houses, or bone tools, which are what we mostly deal with in archeology. Have we then effectively abandoned archeology as an empirical analytic science grounded in the observation and analysis of things, in favor of freewheeling theoretical speculation? It may seem so to many readers but this is not the case. The concepts on which system analysis stands are accepted as useful working hypotheses and serve as an embracive framework in which we can view science as a whole. The validity of this model must be tested with empirical evidence dug from the ground in such a manner that we can test specific propositions. This is a new direction of archeology, and it remains to be seen whether it will become only a short-term gain or whether this initial kick in our system of thought will be positively amplified toward the generalizing science that many expect it to become.

CONCLUDING REMARKS

We have attempted to present a basic and systematic picture of archeology: what it is, how it is done, and what its underlying rationale is. Our exposition has moved from the simple and descriptive to the interpretive and explanatory. Much of archeology is hidden from the view of the layman, who can easily understand and carry out certain aspects of fieldwork, but who seldom sees the much more complex and time-consuming process of formulating problems, selecting appropriate sites to excavate, carrying through analysis, and testing relevant hypotheses. These latter are the concern of professional archeologists, who themselves find it increasingly difficult to keep up with the latest techniques and ideas.

Many archeologists have become administrators rather than diggers, so that they can coordinate the multidisciplinary teamwork so essential today in order to extract and analyze the diverse data from a site. To the extent that this trend has taken some archeologists away from direct participation in digging, it is regrettable; however, in the sense that the work becomes more efficient and the results become more accurate, it is salutary. The responsibility for making the decisions and for finally integrating the results rests squarely on the archeologist, who must have enough command of the various facets of his operation to communicate fruitfully with his technical experts and guide their work toward a realization of the archeological goals.

In the history of the discipline, most archeologists have been concerned with their site, their region, and the changes they saw expressed in tangible artifacts such as settlement patterns, houses, skeletons, and tools. Most archeological effort has been directed toward refining classifications and toward working out the detailed chronological sequences and interrelations of cultures within areas. These data are valuable, because they are readily understood and will ultimately provide us with the kind of information we need to test our theories. However, we shall reiterate here what we have said before: that *the facts of prehistory do not speak for themselves*. There are two logical procedures open to us in interpreting prehistory. We can make inferences about the implications of the archeological data, or we can pose hypotheses based on our understanding of cultures or of systems and then test these against our data. The latter approach is directed at exposing the underlying characteristics and causes of cultural phenomena, whereas the former is largely a translation of data into familiar cultural terms. Through inference we see archeological cultures as an ethnologist sees modern peoples. Through the use of testable hypotheses we see the operation of society laid bare sometimes at the expense of stripping it of its human and particular cultural significance. In this approach, we penetrate deeper and deeper into the inner structure and processes of human organizations.

At the base of all of this inquiry is our fascination with the past, with the history of mankind. Grahame Clark said it this way in *Aspects of Prehistory* (1970:127–128):

> If one asks why he should want an explanation, one answer might be that he does so in order to meet the apprehensions that accompany self-awareness. The price of knowledge is anxiety or at least an awareness of ignorance. Is this not the nemesis of education? The more we have of it, the more keenly we are or ought to be aware of our ignorance. Yet it is precisely because of this awareness that we feel the need to know more by asking questions and by seeking to understand what we observe. The thirst for knowledge is a direct outcome of self-awareness. And of all the mysteries that confronted man as he emerged from the womb of instinctive life into the world of self-awareness and culture, none can have been more frightening or more poignant than the mystery of time.

We call this study archeology because we are concerned with the mystery of time, but in the largest sense it is history, sociology, anthropology, economics, geography, and all of the disciplines that study man and his works. Our dimension is time and our data lie buried and mostly undiscovered. The more we learn about the present, the more we can hope to learn about the past. Anthropology has revealed and taught us to appreciate the panorama of cultures around the world, and archeology has begun to reveal the stages of mankind and the achievements of cultures far removed from our own. We can marvel at the feats of people whom we can never know and we can probe their remains for clues about their origins and fates. What we learn is far from trivial. Man in his characteristically human ways has repeatedly coped with recurring problems of diminishing resources and competition between groups, and with the opportunities of geographic or technological frontiers. There are lessons in the past if we can see them. The world changes, and mankind with it. We need studies of the past to appreciate how transitory the present is and, if we will face it, how traditional our supposedly "modern" responses to crises often are. As we learn to interpret the past, perhaps we can also begin to learn from it. A world that is changing as rapidly as ours needs a global no less than a historical perspective.

GLOSSARY

Adaptation   Adjustment by a culture or organism to changing circumstances.

Aficionado   A devotee or fan, in archeology, of antiquities.

Alluvium   Sandy or silt soil that has been carried in suspension by a swiftly moving river and then deposited when the river entered a plain or open valley, where its velocity was no longer sufficient to carry the sand or silt.

Altamira   A cave with polychrome paintings, mostly **Magdalenian*** in origin, discovered in 1879 in the Cantabrian region of northeastern Spain.

Altiplano   A high mountain plain in the central Andes.

Analogy   An inference that if two or more things agree with one another in some respects they will probably agree in others. Example in archeology: determining the use of an ancient **artifact** by comparing it with a similar object in use today.

Antediluvian   Literally, "pre-flood." Once used to refer to archeological finds that dated back to before the presumed time of the biblical flood.

* Words in boldface are defined elsewhere in this glossary.

Anthropology The scientific study of man in his biological, linguistic, and social aspects, both now and in the past.

Arable Suitable for cultivation.

Archeological culture Similar **assemblages** found at several sites of the same age in the same region.

Artifacts Objects made, modified, or used by man.

Aspect In North American archeology, a grouping of similar **foci**.

Assemblage All of the different **artifacts** found together in one layer, regardless of the materials from which they are made.

Aswan Dam A dam on the Nile at the first cataract, where international cooperation has saved many valuable archeological monuments from destruction by the rising waters.

Atlatl **Aztec** word for a spear thrower, a device that gives increased leverage to the arm when hurling a spear. It is basically a short stick with a hook or spear on one end where the cupped end of the spear is socketed.

Australopithecus The oldest and most primitive grade of man, dating back five million years in East Africa.

Aztec The native civilization of central Mexico, whose capital lay at Tenochtitlan in what is now Mexico City. The Aztecs were conquered by Cortez in 1521.

Band The most basic form of group social structure. Bands are small groups of **nuclear families** that carry out all subsistence and economic activities together, without any formal system of authority or law.

Bank An embankment of earth, which results from the digging of a ditch, as in an **earthwork.**

Base In North American archeology, a group of similar **patterns;** a general classification usually defined in terms of subsistence (such as hunting or farming).

Belzoni, Giovanni Battista (1778–1823) A circus strong man and hydraulic engineer, who later turned his attention to discovering and looting sites in Egypt. He did incalculable damage in his two years of work between 1817 and 1819.

Bronze Age The period in human history when bronze became the primary metal for the manufacture of tools. This period coincides with the advent of the historical period in Southwest Asia.

Cahokia A group of **mounds** near East St. Louis in southern Illinois that were constructed during the Mississippian period (A.D. 900–1550).

Calyx krater A large bowl used for mixing wine. These two-handled vessels were made in Greece but exported into Europe as well.

Central America A geographic term referring to the lands between Guatemala and Columbia.

Chiefdom A society in which a person's rank depends on the rank of parents and order of birth (heredity). Chiefs serve as agents of coordination and redistribution of goods and services.

Childe, V. Gordon (1892–1957) A leading prehistorian in the first half of this century, whose many books emphasized the interrelations among cultures.

Circumvallation Wall around a city.

Clan A social unit of related people, defined differently for different **cultures.**

Classical archeology Study of the civilizations of ancient Greece and Rome through their archeological remains.

Codex (pl. codices) Latin for "book"; usually refers to the few surviving written documents of the **Maya** and **Aztecs.**

Connectivity A term used in locational analysis to express relationship between places.

Conquistadors Spanish soldiers who invaded Mexico and Peru in the 1520s and 1530s and conquered the **Aztec** and **Inca** civilizations.

Context The spatial, temporal, and cultural environment of an **artifact**, from which we can derive interpretations and significance.

Contract archeology Archeological investigation or interpretation done in response to legal requirements in connection with the management of cultural resources. Sometimes called "public archeology" or "conservation archeology."

Corinth A city of ancient Greece whose graves were robbed in Roman times by veterans of Caesar's army.

Co-tradition A concept that attempts to relate ethnological and archeological culture classifications in a well-defined area. As defined by Bennett (1948:1), "only the territory is considered within which the component cultures formed a culture area at every time period, and not the territory of maximum expansion during a particular time period." His example was the central Andes.

Cross dating A technique whereby the age of one **artifact** is inferred from the age of a similar one that has been dated.

Crusades Military expeditions by European Christians of the Middle Ages to recover the Holy Land from the Moslems.

Cultural association The archeological **culture** to which a collection of **artifacts** belongs.

Cultural Resource Management (CRM) A branch of archeology that is concerned with developing policies and action in regard to the preservation and use of cultural resources such as archeological sites.

Culture In anthropology, a set of customs and **artifacts** that characterizes a people.

Cultures The different manifestations of culture.

Cultural evolution A term that has been applied to the changes that have taken place in human history. In a more specific sense it has been used to imply that cultures have evolved in ways analogous to biological evolution.

Cumulative histogram A graph employed in archeology to plot the percentages of tool types. As each type is plotted, its percentage of occurrence is added to the accumulating total, so that the final entry on the graph is 100 percent.

Cuneiform Literally "wedge-shaped"; it refers to the style of early Mesopotamian writing. The wedge-shaped form resulted from the use of a triangular reed pressed into soft clay to form the words.

Cuneiform tablets Clay tablets from Mesopotamia with cuneiform ("wedge-shaped") inscriptions of various early languages, dating from approximately 3000–1000 B.C.

Cybernetics The study of systems of communication and regulation.

Deductive A course of action in which an archeologist devises hypotheses and then looks for evidence to substantiate or refute his theory: cf. **inductive.**

Degrade   To wear down, as by erosion.

Demic expansion   A geographical spread of people as a result of increasing population.

Demography   The study of population numbers through vital statistics.

Diffusion   The spread of cultural concepts, ideas, or **artifacts** from their place of origin to another area.

Diffusionists   People who believe that ideas occur rarely and spread widely: stronger, more advanced, or innovative cultures affect those around them.

Dig   Colloquial reference to an archeological excavation.

Dilettanti   Amateurs who collect **artifacts** for their artistic value alone. Especially applied to wealthy collectors during the Renaissance.

Direction   In locational analysis, orientation to a point in a settlement **system.**

Distance   In locational analysis, can be measured in a number of units, including shortest distance, easiest route, and number of hours.

Ditch   A trench dug to provide material for an **earthwork**. Ditches added to the effective height of a defensive earthwork.

Earthwork   An embankment of earth constructed by man to enclose **sites** and serve as defensive walls.

Ecological niche   The type of environment inhabited by a species.

Ecosystem   The interplay of organisms with their biological and physical environments.

Environmental impact statement (EIS)   An analysis of the impact that industrial or other development may have on the natural resources of an area.

Epigraphist   One who studies inscriptions.

Epimerization   The process of changing into an epimer—a change in chemical structure involving carbon atoms.

Ethnoarcheology   An approach by which archeologists conduct studies of contemporary peoples as an aid in interpreting the past.

Ethnographer   An anthropologist who does or writes ethnographies.

Ethnography   The description of a living **culture** in the framework of **anthropology.**

Eustacy   The alternate raising or lowering of the worldwide sea level due to changes in the size of the polar ice caps.

Exogamous   Marriage to a person from outside your own particular social group, such as a **clan** or **moiety.**

Extended family   A family in which older relatives of the adults live with the **nuclear family.**

Extracorporeal   Nonbiological, residing outside the body; such as **culture**, which is intangible.

Field   Location of study, usually a **site** or area, outside laboratories and libraries.

Fieldwork   Study done in the field.

Flotation   A method of obtaining seeds and other organic materials from the soil of a **site** by means of liquid separation.

Fluted point   A flint projectile point with a longitudinal channel on each face made by a technique called "**fluting.**"

Fluting   The technique of applying pressure to the base of a flint point so as to remove a long sliver of flint that leaves a longitudinal channel.

Focus   In North American archeology, a term used to represent the **assemblage** of a **site** or cultural level within a site; roughly equivalent to an ethnological "**tribe.**"

Folsom point   A type of chipped stone projectile point that has a concave base and a longitudinal **flute** or channel on each face. These points are found on the High Plains in North America and date to 9000–8000 B.C.

Gene flow   The transmission through hybridization of genes from one group to another.

Gene pool   The sum of all the genes contained within a biological population.

Genetic drift (= Sewall Wright effect)   In small breeding populations, changes in the genetic structure of a population's gene pool because of chance factors.

Geochronology   Dating by relations to geologic features.

Glottochronology   A linguistic technique that calculates how long ago two present-day languages split apart by measuring the number of cognates (similar words).

Grid (a verb)   To lay out a network of lines that intersect at right angles across a site (as N–S and E–W). These lines subdivide the surface of the site and serve as a guide to the location of **test pits** and excavation areas.

Hand-stone (= mano)   Stone held in the hand and used with another, and larger, nether stone (**metate**) in grinding of grain.

Herculaneum   A Roman city that, along with **Pompeii**, was buried by the ash from the eruption of Mount Vesuvius in A.D. 79.

Hieroglyphs   In a strict sense, the **pictographic** script of the Egyptians, but can be applied to other nonalphabetic writing systems.

Hominid   Any of the family Hominidae, which includes modern man and his ancestral forms.

Horizon   (a) **Stratigraphic** context of artifacts, synonymous with stratum and layer; (b) a period during which a specified set of **artifacts** was used.

Horizon markers   **Artifacts** with a short span of existence, which therefore are good indications of age.

Howard, Thomas, Earl of Arundel   Famed seventeenth-century collector of ancient Greek art.

Ideographic   Concerned with particular instances of general laws.

Inca   The final native civilization of the Central Andes. Founded around A.D. 1200, it lasted until its conquest in 1532 by Pizarro's Spanish troops.

Index fossils   In archeology, **artifacts** whose historical life span was short and whose presence in a **site** therefore indicates its age.

Inductive   A nonrigorous, intuitive method of discovery, where one constructs theories out of data already collected; cf. **deductive.**

Intaglio   Design cut into stone or metal.

Iron Age   The period when iron replaced bronze as the primary metal for the manufacture of tools. In Europe this period begins about 1100 B.C. and lasts until the industrial revolution.

Isohyet   A line on a rainfall map that connects points receiving equal amounts of rain.

Isostacy   Alternate raising and lowering of the land relative to the sea; the weight of glaciers causes the land to sink, and their melting allows it to rise again.

Isotope   One of two or more species of a chemical element that differ in atomic mass or mass number (such as C^{13} and C^{14}).

Khafajeh   An important early Sumerian site near Baghdad in Mesopotamia, which was excavated by American archeologists in the 1930s. The site is especially notable for its temples.

Kiva An underground room, used for men's clubhouses and religious ceremonies; found in **ethnographic** and **prehistoric** Pueblo villages in the Southwest.

Layard, Sir Austen H. (1817–1894) An early British archeologist who discovered Nimrud in Mesopotamia.

Lexicostatistics A linguistic technique similar to **glottochronology.**

Loessland Land formed by deposits of loess, a fine soil that was transported by the wind, usually during the Pleistocene (Glacial) period.

Logical positivist A school of philosophy; as used by archeologists it refers to the attempt to explain particular cases in terms of general laws.

Lower Paleolithic The time from the first tools made by hominids about 2.6 million years ago until about 100,000 years ago. The crude pebble tools, flake tools, and later choppers and hand axes were made by the **Australopithecus** and *Homo erectus* forms of fossil **hominids.**

Magdalenian The last culture of the **Upper Paleolithic** in western Europe, c. 15,000–10,000 B.C. The Magdalenians are famous for their beautifully carved bone **artifacts** and their cave art.

Magnetometer An instrument that measures the magnetic intensity of the earth and is used to detect objects of iron and sometimes pits or walls in **sites**, through the changes in the magnetic intensity they induce.

Mastodon An extinct elephantlike mammal of the genus *Mammut*, which differs from mammoths and elephants chiefly in the form of the molar teeth.

Matrilineage A social system in which inheritance is traced back through the females.

Maya A **pre-Columbian** civilization in what is now southern Mexico, Guatemala, and Honduras. It is notable for its temple architecture, ceramics, and advanced writing system.

Maya Classic The period during which Maya civilization reached its peak—A.D. 200–900.

Mayan Pertaining to the people and archeological cultures of the Yucatan peninsula of Southern Mexico, Guatemala, and Honduras.

Medicine men Religious specialists in some societies, who are reputed to have powers of healing the sick.

Megalithic Built of large stones. Refers especially to monuments and tombs built by prehistoric peoples in Europe and elsewhere.

Mesa Verde Located in southwestern Colorado; the site of the most impressive surviving cliff dwellings.

Meso-America A geographic area extending from central Mexico to Nicaragua. This is the area in which the Olmec, Teotihuacan, **Aztec**, and **Maya** civilizations developed. The term has cultural rather than strictly geographic connotations.

Metate A shaped slab of stone on which corn or other seed are ground, usually with the aid of a **mano**, a stone held in the hand that crushes the grain against the metate.

Micro-stratigraphy Study of layers much smaller than the grossly recognizable ones in archeological sites.

Midden   An accumulation of household refuse. Trash deposits.

Middle America   A geographic term that includes all the land between central Mexico and northwestern Columbia.

Middle Paleolithic   A time from about 100,000 to 35,000 years ago during which stone tools were made from flakes. The period is associated with **Neanderthal** forms of fossil **hominids.**

Minimal socioeconomic unit   The smallest set of people who function together socially and economically.

Minoan   The people of **Bronze Age** Crete from 2500–1400 B.C. Best known from their great palaces (such as Knossos).

Mohenjo-daro   One of the twin capitals (with Harrapa) of the Indus civilization which stretched over 400 miles along the Indus river in Pakistan. The city was occupied between 2300 and 1700 B.C.

Moiety   One of two basic tribal divisions.

Mound   (a) An accumulation of debris resulting from occupation of a **site**. The largest mounds are found in southwest Asia, where buildings were made of mud. (b) An artificial hill built of dirt to cover a burial or to serve as an elevated platform on which to site a temple.

Mousterian   A culture of the **Middle Paleolithic** of Europe and Southwest Asia. Tools of this culture are associated with **Neanderthal** forms of fossil **hominids** (100,000–35,000 years ago).

Mutation   Spontaneous change in genetic structure.

Mycenaean civilization   A late **Bronze Age** civilization of eastern and southern Greece, which flourished around 1400 B.C. Named from the **site** of Mycenae, excavated by Heinrich Schliemann.

Nabonidus   King of Babylon (555–538 B.C.), who conducted the first recorded archeological excavations.

Native American   A person whose ancestors were in America before European and other colonists arrived in the sixteenth century. In short, Indian.

Natural level   A visually recognizable stratum, usually indicating a definite period of occupation or activity in a **site.**

Natural selection   The breeding out of unsuitable genes by elimination of the individuals who have them before they are able to reproduce.

Neanderthal   An archaic form of **hominid** who lived in Europe and western Asia during the late **Pleistocene** (100,000–35,000 years ago).

Neolithic   "New **Stone Age**." Originally referred to the use of tools that were ground and polished rather than chipped. Now usually used to indicate early agricultural cultures.

Nimrud   Important ancient Babylonian city, discovered by **Layard** in 1845. From Sennacherib's palace Layard recovered a library of **cuneiform tablets.**

Nineveh   Important Mesopotamian site from which A. H. **Layard** recovered a large number of winged bull sculptures and reliefs carved in stone.

Nomothetic   Concerned with general laws.

Nuclear family   A residential, economic, reproductive, and socializing unit composed only of a father, a mother, and their children.

Nuestra Señora de Atocha   A Spanish galleon (ship) that sailed from Havana in 1622 and sank off Florida.

Numismatist   One who studies coins and medals.

Obelisk   A stone pillar of tapering square section with a pyramidal top. In Egypt they were usually erected for religious or commemorative purposes and had **hieroglyphs** carved on them. Many were taken to Rome after the conquest of Egypt.

Olduvai Gorge A canyon cut through **Pleistocene** deposits in northern Tanzania, where L. S. B. and Mary Leakey found a series of examples of early forms of fossil **hominids.**

Paleoanthropology Another name for **prehistoric** archeology; an emphasis on ancient peoples and not merely on **artifacts.**

Paleobotany The study of ancient plant remains.

Paleolithic The Old **Stone Age.** Generally used to refer to the long period of human development before the advent of agriculture and the use of metal: cf. **Lower Paleolithic, Upper Paleolithic.**

Paleontology The study of fossil remains of animals.

Palynologist One who studies pollen.

Papyrus The reed that grows along the Nile. Also, the paper made of interwoven strips of the papyrus reed.

Particularist One who is concerned with details and unique events rather than with general laws.

Pattern In North American archeology, a grouping of similar **phases.**

Peat Partially carbonized moss and vegetation, usually found in acidic bogs; occasionally an excellent preserver of archeological material.

Pedologist A soil scientist.

Petroglyph A rock painting or engraving.

Petrographer A person who describes, identifies, and classifies rocks.

Petrographic microscope Instrument used to reveal the mineralogic composition of pottery and rocks.

pH A measure (from 0 to 10) of acidity or alkalinity. pH 7.0 is neutral; values over 7.0 indicate a basic or alkaline medium; those below 7.0 are acid.

Phase In North American archeology, a grouping of similar **aspects.**

Photogrammetry Making measurements and maps with the aid of aerial photos.

Pictographic An early style of writing in which a picture was drawn of the thing mentioned.

Piedmont Foothills; lower slopes of a mountain range.

Playa A low-lying area or basin that fills with water after heavy rains and then reverts to desert when the water has evaporated.

Pleistocene A geologic period, usually thought of as the Ice Age, which began about 1.6 million years ago and ended with the advent of the Holocene about 11,500 years ago.

Pompeii A Roman city that was covered and preserved by the ash from the eruption of nearby Mt. Vesuvius in A.D. 79.

Pre-Columbian Literally, before Columbus discovered America. The term usually refers to archeological remains older than the 1520s, the time of the conquest of Mexico by Hernando Cortez.

Prehistory History before written records, as inferred from archeological remains.

Process The operation of factors that result in a change of **culture.**

Processual analysis An approach to archeology that looks for processes resulting in culture change.

Profile Usually, a drawing of a stratified deposit in section.

Protohistory   History, either of nonliterate people who were written about by their contemporaries, or of peoples, such as the **Maya**, whose writing is scarce and/or undeciphered.

Provenance (=provenience)   Place of finding.

Quaternary   A geologic era that includes the **Pleistocene** and Holocene periods.

Quipu   An Incan method for keeping records that consisted of a system of knots on colored cords.

Racemization   The action or process of changing from an optically active compound into a racemic compound or mixture (optically inactive toward polarized light).

Ramified lineages   (Also known as conical **clans** or branching clans.) All collateral lines of descent as well as individuals in the families are ranked in terms of birth order.

Rassam, Hormuzd   An archeologist whose primitive excavation techniques at sites in Mesopotamia in the mid-nineteenth century produced a wealth of objects but caused irreparable harm.

Rawlinson, Henry Creswicke (1810–1895)   The "Father of **Cuneiform**," who deciphered Darius the Great's rock inscriptions in Old Persian at Bisitun in western Iran.

Relative dating   Dating one object only in relation to another: older, the same age, or younger.

Resistivity surveying   A method of locating underground features in **sites** by measuring the electrical resistance of the earth. Walls, pits, and other features in a site may impede or enhance the electrical conductivity of the earth and hence be detectable.

Rich, Claudius (1787–1820)   Appointed as the British Resident in Baghdad in 1808, Rich visited sites, made collections, and published several books on his experiences, which served to stimulate the development of Mesopotamian archeology.

Rosetta Stone   A stone found in Egypt at Rosetta in 1779 by Napoleon's troops. The stone has a decree of Ptolemy V (196 B.C.) written in three forms: Greek, demotic, and **hieroglyphic.**

Salvage archeology   The digging of **sites** to obtain some information before they are destroyed by construction, inundation, and so forth.

Salvor   One whose business is to salvage material from shipwrecks.

Sampling   Selecting representative **sites**, portions of sites, or **artifacts** to be analyzed.

Sepulcher   A tomb.

Sequence dating   A method devised by Sir Flinders Petrie in 1901, which identified and traced minor changes in pottery found in graves in Egypt and allowed him to set up a series that had chronological significance.

Seriation   A method of placing **artifacts** in a chronological sequence.

Shaman   In some societies, a person who employs techniques of magic in the treatment of sick individuals: cf. **medicine man.**

Sherds   Pieces of pottery or glass.

Side scan sonar   An instrument that emits a high-frequency sound that bounces off objects it hits. A "picture" of the objects can be recorded on a paper chart. Side scan sonar looks sideways on each side of the instrument.

Site   Location of archeological remains.

Sondage (=sounding)   A French word often used to indicate a **test pit.**

State In archeology, the condition of a people, defined culturally, technologically; examples: **band, chiefdom**.

Stela(e) A carved or inscribed stone pillar usually erected for commemorative
purposes.

Steno's Law Nicolaus Steno (1638–1686), a Danish medical doctor who explained the principle of stratigraphic succession ("Steno's Law") in his
Prodromus, first published in 1669.

Step trench A method of excavation in which a pit is dug to one level near
the center of a **mound**; then another is dug in an adjacent section to the
next level; and so on in staircase fashion down the hill. The method is
especially suited to sample deeply stratified sites such as Mesopotamian
tells.

Stone Age Popular term for the long span of human history during which
people made tools of stone rather than of metal: cf. **Paleolithic, Neolithic**.

Stratification The flat-lying layers visible in an excavation **profile**.

Stratigraphy Interpretation of the cultural significance of strata in an archeological site.

Subdiscipline A special topic within a larger area of academic study; for example, prehistoric archeology within the discipline of **anthropology**.

Superposition The principle behind **stratigraphy**, that in a layered deposit the
oldest material is at the bottom.

Survey Reconnaissance of an area to determine its archeological potential.

System A group of objects or organisms under consideration together with
their interrelations.

Talus The weathered rock and gravel that lies at a slope against the base of
cliffs.

Taxonomic Dealing with the systematic classification of objects or organisms.

Tectonic Relating to the motion of land masses.

Tektites Small, chemically distinct drops of glass, thought to be of meteoric
origin. When found in **sites**, they may provide a relative date.

Tell Same as **mound**. Ususally applied to Near Eastern town sites.

Test pit, test trench A small exploratory pit designed to provide a quick view
of the contents of a **site**.

Thermo-remanent magnetism (TRM) A record of the magnetic declination, inclination, and magnetic intensity of the earth, which is preserved in
material such as baked clay. During the baking of the clay the TRM is
"frozen" in place and will not change unless the clay is reheated.

Three-Age System A method of classifying **artifacts** (developed in the last
century in the Danish National Museum) according to the material out of
which they were made. Led to the naming of the **Stone Age, Bronze Age**,
and **Iron Age** when it was discovered that they succeeded one another
historically.

Tipi rings Rings of stone used to hold down the bottom edges of **tipis.** When
the camp moves, the stone rings remain in place.

Tipis Structures of poles and skins that were used by many native American
tribes, especially those on the Great Plains.

Topographic map A map of the elevation relief of the land by means of contour
lines.

Trait list A compilation of items, elements, or features of a culture. **Ethnog-**

raphers and archeologists have compared such lists to help establish relationships.

Troy A site in southeastern Turkey, known today as Hissarlik, that was the location of the story of Homer's *Iliad*. Discovered by Schliemann in 1871.

Tufa (travertine) A deposit of calcium carbonate produced by a spring rich in lime; the calcium carbonate was originally disolved in the water and then deposited when the water evaporated. Calcareous tufa may be deposited by blue-green alga at their anchor-spots on rocks.

Tuff Rock consisting of volcanic ash.

King Tut (=Tutankhamen) An Egyptian pharaoh of the late 18th Dynasty, whose rich and well-preserved tomb was discovered in the Valley of the Kings at Thebes by Howard Carter in 1922.

Upper Paleolithic A span from about 35,000 to 10,000 years ago when the art of making stone tools on blades became widespread and well developed. Modern forms of man are associated with these tools. Cave art, carved bones, and human figurines show esthetic sensibilities and artistic skills.

Varves Layers of sediments, usually two annually, that are deposited in a lake and reflect the seasonal thawing and freezing of the water source.

Vesuvius A volcano in central Italy that buried **Pompeii** and **Herculaneum** in A.D. 79.

Weathering horizons In geologic or archeological deposits, layers that were once exposed to the atmosphere and were weathered by chemical action.

Woolley, Sir Leonard (1880–1960) An outstanding British archeologist, who did his major work at Ur, a site of early civilization in southern Mesopotamia.

READINGS

Chapter 1

What is archeology?

The story of large-scale archeology in the Middle East, and of the intellectual significance of prehistory, is well told by C. L. Woolley (1934, 1958, 1959). Other books dealing with the general subject of prehistory are by V. G. Childe (1956, 1962), Grahame Clark (1960, 1970), G. Clark and S. Piggott (1965), B. Fagan (1972), Willey and Sabloff (1974), and D. Wilson (1975).

What is meant by the commonly used word "culture" is amply treated in A. L. Kroeber (1952) and A. L. Kroeber and C. Kluckhohn (1963); a recent critical review is J. W. Bennett (1976).

Archeology as a career is discussed by J. Rowe (1954), though things have changed considerably since this was written. Autobiographies or biographies of archeologists are interesting to read. See Breasted (1947), Brunhouse (1971, 1973). Ceram (1966), Crawford (1955), Layard (1903), Petrie (1931), Poole and Gray (1966), J. E. S. Thompson (1963), and Wheeler (1955).

Additional works referred to in this section are G. Clark (1954—see also 1972 for a follow-up essay) on the excavation of an English Mesolithic hunters' site; J. Hodgson (1822) is an early statement on the value of systematic study of the past; W. Taylor (1948) is a methodological study of archeology; M. Wheeler (1956) provides a general survey of methods, emphasizing the need for control in excavation, keeping proper records, and publishing the results; G. Isaac (1971b) is a prize-winning essay on new directions in archeology.

Prehistory

T. Wilson (1899) is an essay of the end of the last century on the beginnings of prehistoric archeology. J. Deetz's (1967) book is a small but important treatise on what archeology can inform us about and some of the ways of interpreting archeological data.

There are a number of readily available books or articles that trace, by example, the development of our knowledge of prehistory. The following are recommended: Bibby (1956), Brevil (1941), R. Carpenter (1933), Ceram (1958), Chang (1967a), Childe (1947, 1951a, 1953a, 1962), G. Clark (1957), Clark and Piggott (1965), Cottrell (1957), G. Daniel (1962), Hawkes and Woolley (1963), Heizer (1969), Lynch and Lynch (1968), and Shorr (1935).

History and archeology

The relationship between these two subjects has led to the creation of a considerable literature. See, for example, Bagby (1963), Childe (1953b), Finley (1971), Griffiths (1956), Jones (1967), and Kroeber (1957a).

V. Gordon Childe's *Piecing Together the Past* (1956) is a methodological treatise written by a master of the subject.

Why study archeology?

G. Clark (1957, 1970) has written perceptively on the larger purpose that archeology serves, as has V. Childe (1947). The changing view of what prehistory has meant in the larger arena of intellectual knowledge is discussed by Daniel (1971).

The importance of archeology as a direct source of information about the human past can also be examined by reading one or more of the several histories of the development of the subject. See, for example, Casson (1939), Daniel (1950, 1962, 1967, 1968a, 1968b), Pallottino (1968), and Peake (1940).

Goals of archeology

Works referred to in this section deal generally with the variety of ways in which archeology is done. Aims are reached only if they are defined in advance and the methods for reaching them are applied with the particular goals in mind. See Binford (1962, 1964, 1968a, 1968b), Caldwell (1959), G. Clark (1953a), Fritz and Plog (1970), Hole (1972), Isaac (1971b), Watson, Le Blanc, and Redman (1971; see also review by Schuyler 1973), and Watson and Watson (1969).

What archeologists do

There are, of course, thousands of detailed published reports on what was recovered from particular archeological sites, and the interpretation of the data recorded. Some sites—such as Ur of the Chaldees with its royal tombs, which was excavated by L. Woolley (1934), or H. Schliemann's (1875, 1878) digging of the sites of Troy and Mycenae, or Howard Carter's (1930) discovery of the tomb of King Tutankhamen in Egypt—are well known to the general public. Less ostentatious sites are reported by archeologists and read by their collegues.

A useful organized list of the kinds of archeological sites that exist has been compiled by Nelson (1938). Major periodicals that publish results of archeological work include *American Antiquity, Archaeology, Historical Archaeology, Journal of Field Archaeology, The Plains Anthropologist, Science, Antiquity, World Archaeology,* and *Proceedings of the Prehistoric Society.* There are perhaps a hundred or more other publications that are more specialized by area or topic, which readers can consult to acquire the latest information.

Underwater archeology

This kind of archeology is developing rapidly. There are survey articles and books (Bascom 1971, Bass 1963, 1966, Borhegyi 1961, Frost 1963, Goggin 1960, Holmquist and Wheeler 1964, Marx 1975, and Silverberg 1964).

In addition to finds, a specialized set of underwater-adapted methods of photography, surveying, and recording is being developed. For some of these see Ryan and Bass (1962). A bibliography of the subject has been compiled by Kapitan (1966).

The *International Journal of Nautical Archaeology and Underwater Exploration* publishes articles dealing with the latest techniques and discoveries.

Culture history

Grahame Clark's (1975: 256–261) discussion of how archeology has become important in emerging nations is excellent. As more archeologists are trained in Latin America it is increasingly difficult for U.S. archeologists to secure excavation permits.

Key problems in human history

On the beginnings of urbanism see, for example, R. McC. Adams (1966, 1970, 1972), R. Adams and H. Nissen (1972), and Braidwood and Willey (1962).

Examples of interdisciplinary archeological research are the Tehuacan Valley project in Mexico (MacNeish 1967a) and the Deh Luran project in Iran (Hole, Flannery, and Neely 1969, Hole n.d.).

Testing hypotheses

A sample of the rich variety of publications that deal with scientific approaches to archeology is in the following books and publications: L. R. Binford (1964, 1972), D. Clarke (1972, 1973), Leone (1972), C. Morgan (1973,

1974), Mueller (1975), Reid, Schiffer, and Rathje (1975), Salmon (1975), Schiffer (1975b, 1976), Watson, LeBlanc, and Redman (1971, 1974), and Woodall (1972). R. McC. Adams (1974a), Flannery (1967a, 1972), and Hawkes (1973) review some aspects of these works.

Experiments

General papers on experiments by archeologists are by Ascher (1961a), Coles (1967), Keeley (1974), and Proudfoot (1967). A bibliography on experimental archeology has been prepared by Hester and Heizer (1973).

Making inferences on how prehistoric stone tools were used by studying edge wear is now done as a regular part of archeological analysis. Semenov (1964) was instrumental in instituting this kind of work; better methods are described by Tringham (1974).

Experimental earthwork construction in England is described by Ashbee and Cornwall (1961), Dimbleby (1965), and Jewell and Dimbleby (1966).

Ethnoarcheology

Ethnoarcheology is a rapidly developing branch of archeology. Although many projects are in progress or recently completed, there is not yet a large body of published literature. On ethnographic analogy as applied to archeological materials see Ascher (1961b), Dozier (1970), and Orme (1974). A useful collection of papers on ethnoarcheology has been assembled by Donnan and Clewlow (1974). References in these papers can be consulted for details on specific projects. Examples of one kind of such projects are the various studies of pottery and pot-making, including David (1972), DeBoer (1974), Foster (1960a,b), Longacre (1974), and Stanislawski (1973, 1975). Examples of living people whose ways of life have been studied for archeological reasons are given in Gould (1973), Hole (n.d.), and Yellen (1973).

A mission for archeology: cultural resource management

The history of the federal Antiquities Act of 1906 is amply treated by Lee (1970); state and federal statutes covering antiquities on public lands are printed in McGimsey (1972). There is already a large literature on contract archeology. See, for example, Heizer (1975), McGimsey (1972), and Schiffer (1975).

Chapter 2

Some references to histories of archeology have been suggested in the readings for Chapter 1. Chronological lists of important persons, events, and discoveries can be found in Ceram (1958:307-315), Daniel (1975), Eydoux (1968:106–110), Laming-Emperaire (1963:197–205), Michaelis (1906:293-300), and Potratz (1962:310-320).

There are several anthologies in which are reprinted experiences and exciting discoveries described by archeologists. The following are recommended: Ceram (1966), Deuel (1961, 1967), Hawkes (1963), Heizer (1959), Silverberg (1964), Wauchope (1965), M. Wheeler (1957, 1959), Willey (1974), and Woolley (1958).

Dilettantes, bargain hunters, and deep-sea divers

W. Emery's (1961) book is a lively and authoritative account of the earlier Egyptian dynasties. Egyptian tomb-robbing of the 20th Dynasty is described by Peet (1943). Greek and Roman interest, including digging to recover objects, in archeological materials is detailed in Wace (1949).

On early gentleman-students of the past and collectors see Kendrick (1950), Piggott (1950), Smith (1916), and Walters (1934). An excellent historical survey of archeological work in the Middle East is by Pallis (1956), to which the student can turn for the activities of early workers such as Rich, Rawlinson, Layard, Botta, and Loftus. Lloyd (1955) covers much the same ground, but in less detail. Layard's own writings (1849, 1853) are most interesting reading in terms of his experiences; as archeological reports they are little more than the recounting of murdered evidence.

The story of the finding and subsequent history of the Rosetta Stone and its decipherment by Champollion can be found in Cleator (1962), Friedrich (1957), and Heizer (1969).

Belzoni's escapades are described by himself (1820), and retold by Mayes (1961).

King Tutankhamen's undespoiled tomb in the Valley of the Kings is described by Carter (1930) and Carter and Mace (1923–1933). An illustrated catalogue of the tomb contents has been assembled by Desroches-Noblecourt (1963) and Edwards (1972).

Eighteenth-century Spanish archeological exploration in the New World is discussed in Bollesteros (1960). Stephens' (1842) lively account of the discovery of Maya cities should be read not only because it is a remarkable adventure story, but also for the marvellous engravings by Frederick Catherwood, the artist. On Catherwood himself see von Hagen (1947). J. E. S. Thompson, the great scholar of Maya hieroglyphs, is author of the best single book on the ancient Maya (1954).

The Lartet-Christy team activities are summarized in Daniel (1950). Nordenskiold's (1895) account of the Mesa Verde ruins is still good reading but bad archeology.

Borhegyi (1961) is a readable account of underwater archeology. Additional works on this subject are listed in the readings for Chapter 1.

Lyell (1872: Vol. II) is about geology in the broadest sense of the word. As a geology text it is outdated, but any student today can learn a lot about man and the world by reading it.

Prehistory and protohistory

Thomsen's formulation of the Three Age System is translated in Heizer (1969). Earlier efforts in this direction, going back as far as the Greeks, are summarized in Daniel (1943) and Heizer (1962a).

Steno's *Prodromus* is translated in part in Heizer (1969). On the Scythians and
their royal tombs in the Altai Mountains see Rice (1957) and Rudenko
(1970).

Renfrew (1970) proposes that the Mediterranean area may have been the
receptor, rather than the donor, of many features of early European
civilization.

Adam and beyond

The work of the several British geologists is summarized in Daniel (1975).
Sections of the writings of Boucher de Perthes, Prestwich, and Flower
can be found in Heizer (1969).

Mortillet's (1867) ideas, we now know, were too simplistic. But they were
among the first real efforts to digest and synthesize the deluge of new
facts that came in the first decade of prehistoric archeology in Europe.

The geologists, after about 1800 when this science took form, helped provide
archeologists with a time scale for cultural and biological evolution.
Their calculations were much too short, but they were a start. On this
see Bowen (1958), Haber (1959a, 1959b), and Lyell (1863).

Wauchope (1965) wrote an obituary of Alfred V. Kidder, who contributed
importantly to the development of southwestern American archeology
and for long directed the Carnegie Institution of Washington's anthropological program in Middle America.

Some of the crazy speculations on the origin of the Native Americans are
surveyed in a book by R. Wauchope (1962). It is entertaining reading,
but the theories are all wrong.

There are several good summaries of Native American prehistory. The volume
assembled by Jennings and Norbeck (1964) is still sound. Others are
by Jennings (1968) and Willey (1966a, 1971). The history of development
of American archeology is well covered in Fitting (1973) and Willey and
Sabloff (1974).

Landmarks in archeology

Among books dealing not only with archeology, but rather with science in
general, we recommend Planck (1949) and Platt (1962). Many of the
landmark finds in archeology are treated both in the original reports
and in briefer form in the anthologies or readers cited for Chapter 1.

Techniques

Thomas Jefferson's report of the excavation (using black slave labor) of a
Virginia burial mound is reprinted in Heizer (1959), as is N. C. Nelson's
systematic stratigraphic excavation at Tano, New Mexico—an excavation
which, as pointed out by Woodbury (1960), revolutionized American
archeology.

Remote sensing and satellite photos are discussed by Gumerman and Lyons
(1971). Aerial photography in the service of archeology has, of course, a
long history. Useful introductions to this subject are by Cameron (1958),
Chevallier (1957, 1964), Colwell (1956), Deuel (1969), Matheny (1962),

Miller (1957), St. Joseph (1966), and Solecki (1957). In the New World there are two outstanding applications of this technique. One is the settlement pattern survey of the Viru Valley in Peru by Willey (1953); the second is the making of the photomosaic map of the ancient Mexican city of Teotihuacan (Millon 1964, 1970, 1973).

Water flotation of site soils to recover small bones, charcoal, carbonized seeds, and other items is described by Struever (1968a).

Braidwood's pioneering multidisciplinary approach to the archeology of the Middle East is illustrated in the volume by Braidwood and Howe (1960).

Interpretation

There are numerous works on Paleolithic cave art. An available and excellent survey is by Ucko and Rosenfeld (1967)—this contains an extensive bibliography.

On ecology, anthropology, and archeology the reader can start with Bresler (1966), Butzer (1972), Helm (1962), Odum (1963), and Wagner (1960).

R. McC. Adams's (1968) article on archeological research strategies in historical perspective can be read with profit.

Chapter 3

Antiquity and change

The story of how the discovery of fossil bones and geology helped awaken men to the fact of the immense span of geological time is well told in Greene (1961) and Haber (1959).

Stratigraphy and sequence

Reference has been made in Chapter 2 to Steno, the first stratigrapher. A full treatment of archeological stratification is provided by E. Harris (1975) and Pyddoke (1961).

Culture

On what culture is, and how anthropologists use the concept, see Bennett (1976), Keesing (1974), Kluckhohn and Kelly (1945), Kroeber (1917, 1952), Kroeber and Kluckhohn (1952), and White (1949, 1959b). The several kinds of evolution are discussed by Huxley (1955), Mellor (1972), Steward (1955), and White (1947, 1959b). Culture patterns are discussed by Kroeber (1943). Invention is treated in Barnett (1953) and Boas (1938: 238–281).

The relation between biological and cultural process

On this subject see Bordes (1971), Bray (1972), Kroeber (1943), Simpson (1964), Washburn (1960), and Washburn and Lancaster (1968).

Archeological cultures

This subject is treated by Childe (1947) and Rouse (1968). Behavior as inferred from archeological evidence is one of the focal aims of the new archeology. See, for example, Binford (1962) and Longacre (1970b).

Chapter 4

Archeological sites

We cannot overemphasize the value to any archeologist of reading as widely as possible in the literature of ethnography. Archeologists will, of course, read *all* the ethnological accounts written about peoples in the area in which they are excavating. But beyond this, as wide a perspective as possible will prove to be useful so that the prehistorian is aware of some of the great variety of ways earlier people lived, with what and how they made material items, the forms of their houses, and so on. For the North American archeologist references arranged by area and tribe can be found in the Murdock and O'Leary (1975) *Ethnographic Bibliography of North America*. For Middle America and South America see the *Handbook of Middle American Indians* (Wauchope 1964–1976), and for South America Steward's (1946–1950) *Handbook of South American Indians*.

Kinds of sites

Ethnographic Maya village farmers are far better known than their prehistoric ancestors are. For efforts to understand the lifeway of these earlier people see Culbert (1973), Haviland (1968, 1972a), and Vogt (1968).

Kill sites

There are some first-rate studies of ancient kill sites. Among these are Leonhardy (1966) and Wheat (1967, 1972), which describe in detail bison mass kills in Paleoindian times; and J. D. Clark and Haynes (1970), who describe an African instance.

Butchering pattern examples are discussed by Kehoe and Kehoe (1960) and White (1952, 1953, 1954, 1955).

Trading centers

Such towns did exist in Meso-America. See Chapman (1957), Parsons and Price (1971), Polyani et al. (1957), and West et al. (1969). Casas Grandes in northern Mexico is thought to have been a trading center (Di Peso 1974). In the Near East, as judged by the ancient trade in obsidian, there were also such sites (Renfrew 1968a).

Burial sites

There are hundreds of published reports on burials. Since death is strongly affect-laden it is not surprising to find that there is evidence of this in the way people were buried and what was placed in their graves. The Pennsylvania children's cemetery is reported by Farrabee (1919); the men's graveyards in the Fayum of Egypt by Caton-Thompson and Gardner (1934); the Roman cemetery in Austria by Kloiber (1957); and the Carter Ranch site by Longacre (1964).

Petroglyphs and pictographs

A very large literature has developed on this topic. C. Grant (1965, 1967) has written on what is perhaps the most elaborate prehistoric painted cave art of the New World, and a broader-based volume on the rock art of North America. The rock art of Nevada and California is reported on by Heizer and Baumhoff (1962) and Heizer and Clewlow (1973). An excellent review of Paleolithic cave art is by Ucko and Rosenfeld (1967).

Much has been written, most of it nonsense, by such charlatans as Erich von Daniken and others of his ilk on the "Nazca lines" in Peru. A salutary assessment of reality of these linear designs is provided by G. Hawkins (1973). There is a growing fad to account for these various ground designs as evidence for a highly sophisticated astronomical knowledge of what must have been peoples with quite simple cultures—simple at least in the sense that it is inconceivable that these peoples would have spent so much time and energy in perfecting a knowledge of astronomical matters which could not have been put to any use.

How is a site made?

On Near East tells see Lloyd (1963). The Naco and Lehner kill sites in Arizona are carefully described by Haury et al. (1933, 1959).

One method for trying to find out how an occupational deposit was formed is by passing a substantial amount of earth through a fine screen and segregating the components retained in the screen. Examples can be found in Ambrose (1967), Colyer and Osborne (1965), Cook and Heizer (1951), and Cook and Treganza (1947).

What is preserved?

The "bog bodies" that are preserved in "pickled" form in the acid peat bogs of northern Europe are described by Glob (1954, 1969) and Schlabow (1958). The frozen Scythian tombs are described in great detail by Rudenko (1970). The cold environment of Norway has inhibited bacterial decay and thus helped to preserve the thousand-year-old Viking ships (Brogger et al. 1917).

What is willfully destroyed?

The work of the Coptic iconoclasts in Egypt is described by Moorehead (1961), and Duignan (1958) reviews the immense labors of Catholic priests in destroying Aztec sculptures.

What is recovered?

The recovery by water flotation of carbonized seeds that would have otherwise escaped notice in the earth is described by Hole, Flannery, and Neely (1969), Renfrew, Monk, and Murphy (1975), Struever (1968), and Williams (1974).

Chapter 5

Archeological context

For numerous examples of plundered sites and what was recovered from them and commercially sold see Coggins (1970), Ford (1971), Grant (1966), Meyers (1973), and Sheets (1973).

Stratigraphy and stratification

On stratification, its varieties, causes, and methods of recording vertical sections see Adams (1975), Harris (1975), Pyddoke (1961), and Wheeler (1956). Most archeological site reports contain drawings of stratigraphic profiles and interpret these.

Deriving stratigraphy from stratification

The reversed stratigraphy of the Chetro Ketl site is explained in detail by Ellis (1934). Pueblo Bonito was excavated over a number of years by N. M. Judd of the U.S. National Museum. For the particular instance cited here see Judd (1959: 176–177).

On the subject of slash-and-burn agriculture and its effect on human settlement see Carneiro (1956), Conklin (1961), O. F. Cook (1921), and Dumond (1961).

G. Foster's (1960b) "census" of pots in a Mexican village has important implications to archeologists who study ceramics. Along the same lines see David (1972a, 1972b).

The deliberate return to the form of older models ("archaism") is familiar to us in the fashions of the eighteenth century in Europe, when dress and furniture reverted to the style of classical models. The two archeological Egyptian examples referred to here are more fully described by Aldred (1961: 155) and W. S. Smith (1958). The Eskimo example comes from Ford (1959: 22).

Time

The site of Stonehenge is well described by R. Atkinson (1956). The later work of the astronomer G. Hawkins (1965) is interpretation based on what is known of the great concentric stone circles.

The unusual instance of dating by matching tektites that come from extra-terrestrial space with those found in association with ancient human fossils is described by Gentner and Lippolt (1969: 82).

Cultural associations and space

Moving the obelisk now in Paris from Luxor in Egypt is a most interesting
story, which can be found, in retold form, in Dibner (1970).
On the concept of culture areas see Driver (1962) and Kroeber (1936, 1963: 16).
Still very well worth reading for archeologists is the early monograph
by E. Sapir (1916) on time perspective.

Chapter 6

Finding sites

On methods for site survey see Hester, Heizer, and Graham (1975: Chap. 3).
Ruppé (1966) discusses reasons for surveys and their importance. A
good example of the need for a thorough site survey is demonstrated
by MacNeish (1967a), in the first of a series of volumes reporting results
of the Tehuacan Valley Project in Mexico. R. McC. Adams's (1965, 1972)
surveys are excellent examples from Mesopotamia.

Age and cultural association

The important matter of sampling—how much to collect in order to secure
a representative lot—is only briefly touched on here. The student should
read one or more of the following publications in order to become
familiar with the ways available to accomplish this: Alcock (1951), Cowgill (1964, 1970), Hill (1967), Jelks (1975), Mueller (1974, 1975), Ragir
(1975), Redman (1974), Redman and Watson (1970), Rootenberg (1964),
and Vescelius (1955).
A few archeologists have taken the trouble to compare the kinds of potsherds found on a site surface with those excavated from pits in order
to estimate to what extent surface materials reflect the variety of ceramics
that lie buried. L. Spier (1917) did this in the Southwest; P. Tolstoy (1958)
in the Valley of Mexico; and J. Ford and G. Willey (1949) made such tests
in the Viru Valley in Peru.

Structural features

Sampling with an auger that brings up a solid core is illustrated by the work
done at Monk's Mound, Cahokia, site in Illinois by Reed, Bennett, and
Porter (1968).
The "periscope camera" for inspecting underground Etruscan tomb chambers
is described by Lerici (1959).
Magnetometers and what they can reveal beneath the surface are treated by
Aitken (1970), Breiner (1965, 1973), Morrison (1971), and Tite (1972).
Two Olmec sites in southeastern Mexico have been surveyed with a
magnetometer with positive results. See Breiner and Coe (1972) for the
site of San Lorenzo, and Morrison, Clewlow, and Heizer (1970) for the
survey of the earth pyramid at the La Venta site.

Resistivity surveying is described by Atkinson (1963), Hesse (1966), and Tite (1972).

Excavation

W. Sears' (1954, 1961) attempts to determine the social and religious systems of the prehistoric people of the southeastern United States do not get very far because earlier archeologists failed to make the proper kinds of observations.

How to dig

There are numerous guides and handbooks on this subject, but one can learn more in a week's practice under proper guidance than one can from reading fifty books. But as an introduction on techniques of excavation see Atkinson (1953), Hester, Heizer, and Graham (1975:2–3), Kenyon (1961), and M. Wheeler (1956). There is even an instruction book on directing archeological excavations (Alexander 1970).

Kenyon (1957) provides an interesting historical account of the several attempts to unravel the story of the occupation of the biblical city of Jericho.

Keeping records

On this see, for example, Hester, Heizer, and Graham (1975) and Wheeler (1956). Reading of good excavation reports will illustrate the kinds of detail that must be recorded. Photography as part of record keeping is covered in Frantz (1950), Harp (1975), John (1965), McFadgen (1971), Matthews (1968), Schaber and Gumerman (1969), and Schwartz (1965).

Chapter 7

Description

The preparation of archeological reports is something one learns by practice, first as a student learner and later under tutorial guidance. Some suggestions on the organization and writing of reports by experienced archeologists are worth reading. See Atkinson (1953: 173–206), Grinsell, Rahtz, and Warhurst (1966), Harrison (1945), Webster (1963: 131–166), and Wheeler (1956: 182–199).

Classification

A great deal has been written on this subject, much of it over the head of the beginning student. The following, however, we think will not be unduly confusing: Epstein (1964), Ford (1954b), Krieger (1944, 1960), and Rouse (1939, 1960).

Functional types, convenient types, cultural types

On this complicated but important matter see the discussions by Chang (1967a), Deetz (1967: 43–52), Ford (1954a), Hole (1971), Rouse (1944, 1970, 1972b), Spaulding (1953, 1973), and Willey and Sabloff (1974: 142–145).

Description and illustration of artifacts

On description, using various methods, see Bohmers (1956, 1969), Irwin, Hurd, and LaJeunesse (1971), Movius et al. (1968), Sackett (1966), and Son-neville-Bordes (1960).

Nonphotographic illustration techniques are described by Brodribb (1970), Hope-Taylor (1966, 1967), Isham (1965), Kenrick (1971), Kobayashi and Bleed (1971), Platz (1971), Ridgway (1938), Rivard (1964), R. H. Smith (1970), Staniland (1953), Vinnicombe (1963), and Young (1970).

Determining the uses of artifacts

For the techniques and results of microscopic examination of stone tools to determine use wear, see the following: Frison (1968), Hester (1970), Hester and Heizer (1972), Semenov (1964), Wilmsen (1968), and Wit-thoft (1967). A bibliography of wear pattern studies can be found in Hester and Heizer (1973:23–26).

Ethnographic analogy

There are some good general discussions of the usefulness and limitations of ethnographic analogy: Anderson (1969), Ascher (1961b), Heider (1967), Holmes (1913), Orme (1974), Service (1964), M. A. Smith (1955), and R. Thompson (1956).

On the methods of the direct-historical approach see Baerreis (1971), Clauson (1973), Phillips (1974), Strong (1940), and Wedel (1938).

Replicative experiment

A great deal has been written on this subject. For an extensive bibliography of experiments see Hester and Heizer (1973), and for a general discussion see Coles (1967, 1973). The kinds of replication that can be done are almost limitless, and all that is needed is time, materials, and ingenuity.

Analysis

The *Journal of Archaeological Science* and *Archaeometry* publish articles on various kinds of analysis and should be consulted for new developments. Aitken (1974) is a good general reference.

Analysis of pottery

A standard handbook of ceramic analysis is Shepard (1956—see also Shepard 1971). Useful also are works by Courtois (1976), Dufournier (1976), Matson (1951, 1960, 1965, 1971), and Van der Leeuw (1976).

Analysis of metal and stone

Petrographic analysis of stone is well treated by Stelcl and Malina (1970). A Mesoamerican archeological application is in Williams and Heizer (1965). Precise determination of the composition of various stones or pottery clays often makes it possible to identify the geologic source of the stone or the clay (Jope 1953, Shotten 1969, and Stelcl and Malina 1970). On this kind of study of pottery see Perlman and Asaro (1970, 1971), and Winter (1971). Obsidian lends itself readily to such analysis; for examples of Mediterranean area artifacts and sources see Dixon, McCann, and Renfrew (1968) and Wright (1969). Meso-American obsidians have been studied by Hester, Heizer, and Jack (1971) and Sidrys, Andresen, and Marcucci (1976). Flint can be analyzed in this fashion (Sieveking et. al. 1972), as can quartzite (Heizer et al. 1973). Metallurgical analysis is given a general treatment by Coghlan (1960) and Pittioni (1960).

Analysis of weaving

For an introduction to the technical analysis of weaving (cloth, basketry, and so on) see Balfet (1952), Emery (1966), and Weltfish (1930, 1932). For examples of analyses of archeological textiles see Heizer and Krieger (1956), I. Johnson (1967), Mason (1904), and Morris and Burgh (1941).

Analysis of soils

Soil science in the service of archeology is treated in Arrhenius (1963), Cook (1962, 1965), Cornwall (1958, 1960, 1963), Dauncey (1952), Dietz (1957), Eddy and Dregne (1964), Heizer (1960), Lee (1969), Limbrey (1972), Lotspeich (1961), R. Parsons (1962), Saucier (1966), and Simonson (1954). An excellent example of soil analysis is in Bordes (1972).

Analysis of animal and plant remains

Inferences about earlier climate from animal bones are considered by Garrod and Bate (1937, I: 139–153), Harris (1963), Higgs (1965), Hokr (1951), and Soergel (1939). An ancient bison kill analyzed in great detail is the Olson-Chubbock site in Colorado (Wheat 1972). The methods of identifying and counting numbers of individuals from the bones recovered in an archeological site are treated in Chaplin (1971), Cornwall (1974), Flannery (1967b), Gabel (1967), Gilbert (1973), Glass (1951), Olsen (1961a, 1971), Reed (1963), and Ziegler (1973).

Palynology (pollen analysis) requires expert knowledge and special laboratory facilities. For what is involved see Anderson (1955), Bryant (1975), M. B. Davis (1963), Dimbleby (1969), Erdtman (1943), Faegri and Iverson (1964), Gray and Smith (1962), Jelinek (1966), Martin (1963), and Martin and Gray (1962).

Plant remains (seeds, leaves, and so on) perserved in carbonized form in open sites or in dry cave and shelter sites can provide important clues to cultural practices (Barghoorn 1944). For a review of such materials from archeological sites east of the Rocky Mountains see Cutler and Blake (1973). For the near East see Renfrew (1973).

Human coprolites provide a direct lead into human diet. For analyses of coprolites from the United States, Mexico, and Peru see Bryant (1974), Callen (1965, 1967, 1969), Callen and Cameron (1960), and Heizer and Napton (1970). Coprolites may contain pollen that helps indicate certain plant foods that were eaten (Bryant 1975; Martin and Sharrock 1964).

The technique of passing the soil of the site through very fine screens, often aided by water washing, extracting the material held by the screen, and analyzing it is illustrated by Cook and Heizer (1951), Coutts (1970), Shawcross (1967), and Terrell (1967).

Hoaxes and fakes

There is a lot written about fakes. The reader can start with Cooney (1963), Ekholm (1964), Plenderleitn (1952), Pradenne (1932), Reith (1970), Sachs (1973), Von Bothmer and Noble (1961), and Wakeling (1912).

Chapter 8

Radiocarbon dating

The story of the discovery and first application of measuring the age of organic materials through their radiocarbon content is told in Arnold and Libby (1949) and Kamen (1963, 1972). Analytical techniques, their applications to dating various materials (wood, bone, shell, humic acid, and so on), sources of error in radiocarbon dates, and other matters are discussed by Anderson and Levi (1952), Bender (1968), Berger, Horney, and Libby (1964), Berger, Taylor, and Libby (1966), Broecker (1964), Broecker and Kulp (1956), Broecker and Olson (1960), Burleigh (1974), Carpenter (1955), Catch (1961), Coles (1975), Craig (1954), Evans (1969), Haynes (1966), Keith and Anderson (1963, 1964), Libby (1961, 1963), Rafter (1965), Rubin, Likens, and Berry (1963), Rubin and Taylor (1963), Sellstedt, Engstrand, and Gejvall (1966, 1967), Stuckenrath (1965), Waterbolk (1971), and Weber and La Rocque (1963). Calibration curves and comments on them are in Burleigh, Switsur, and Renfrew (1973), Damon, Long, and Wallick (1972), Suess and Clark (1976), and Switsur (1973). Some of the major effects of the new calibrations are detailed in Atkinson (1975) and Renfrew (1973).

Potassium-argon dating

On the techniques, limitations, and results of K-A dating see Carr and Kulp. (1957), Curtis (1961), Curtis and Reynolds (1958), Evernden and Curtis (1965), Evernden, Savage, Curtis, and James (1964), Faul (1971), Lipson (1958), and Schaeffer and Zähringer (1966).

Thermoluminescence

More extended discussions of thermoluminescence dating of ceramic materials can be found in Aitken (1961), Aitken and Alldred (1972), Aitken and Fleming (1972), Dort et al. (1965), E. T. Hall (1969), Mazess and Zimmerman (1966), Ralph and Han (1966, 1971), Tite and Waine (1962), and Winter (1971). Current research and results achieved can be followed by reading two current journals: *MASCA Newsletter,* published by the Applied Science Center for Archaeology, University of Pennsylvania (Vol. 12, 1976) and *Archaeometry,* published by the Oxford Research Laboratory for Archaeology and the History of Art.

Natural low-level radioactivity

On the application of this method see Bowie and Davidson (1955), Jelinek and Fitting (1965), Oakley (1961, 1963a, 1963b), Oakley and Howells (1961), and Oakley and Rixon (1958).

Fission track dating

For a more detailed treatment of this technique see Faul and Wagner (1971), Fleischer, Price, and Walker (1965), Walker, Fleischer, and Price (1971), Watanabe and Suzuki (1969), and Zimmerman (1971).

Amino acid dating

For the amino acid dating method see Bada (1972) and Hare (1974). For the results of aspartic-acid racemization age determinations on human skeletal material from California and Olduvai Gorge see Bada and Protsch (1973), Bada, Schroeder, and Berger (1974), and Bada, Schroeder, and Carter (1974).

Paleomagnetic dating

Here, as in so much of archeology, there is a plethora of publication but few concrete results. This indicates merely that work is continuing at refining techniques to secure uniform and accurate results. On paleomagnetic dating see Aitken (1960, 1961), R. Cook (1969), Kopper and Creer (1976), Tite (1972), Watanabe (1959), and Weaver (1967).

Fluorine and nitrogen analyses

On the methods and results of fluorine analysis of bones see Baud (1960), Cook (1960), Cook, Brooks, and Ezra-Cohn (1961), Cook and Ezra-Cohn (1959), Cook and Heizer (1953), Groff (1971), Heizer and Cook (1952), and Oakley (1955, 1963c, 1964, 1969). Nitrogen analysis of bone and its usefulness in relative dating is treated by Cook (1952, 1960).

Patination

The best single discussion of this subject is by Goodwin (1960). The chemical nature of rock patina is treated by Engel and Sharp (1958). Hurst and Kelly (1961) present an analysis of differentially patinated Georgia flint implements; a study of English flint tools is by Schmalz (1960).

Other dating methods

On dendrochronology see Bannister (1962, 1969), Bannister and Smiley (1955), Fritts (1965), Giddings (1962), Glock (1955), McGinnies (1963), Schulman (1940, 1941), and Stokes and Smiley (1968). On obsidian hydration dating see Friedman and Long (1976), Friedman, Smith, and Clark (1969), Katsui and Kondo (1965), Michels (1967, 1973), and Michels and Bebrich (1971).

Chapter 9

For general surveys of archeological dating methods the reader may consult the following: Aitken (1960, 1961), Alibone (1970), Brothwell and Higgs (1969: 35–108), Griffin (1955), Heizer (1953), Hester, Heizer, and Graham (1975: 275–282), Michael and Ralph (1971), Michels (1973), Oakley (1953, 1964b), Pewe (1954), Smiley (1955), Tilton and Hart (1963), Tite (1972), and Zeuner (1958, 1959, 1960).

Dating by use of artifacts

For Petrie's sequence-dating method see the reprint of his demonstration in Heizer (1975: 376–383). A number of other examples of seriation are in this book. Seriation of pottery styles for chronological purposes is treated by Ford (1938, 1962), Gifford (1960), Phillips, Ford, and Griffin (1951), and Tolstoy (1958). On cross-dating see the discussion, with citations, in Hester, Heizer, and Graham (1975: 275–277).

Dating by using plants and animal remains

Pollen analysis of site soils is generally treated by R. Anderson (1955), Bryant and Holtz (1968), Butzer (1964: Chaps. 16, 17), M. Davis (1963), Dimbleby (1969), Erdtman (1943), Faegri and Iversen (1964), Gray and Smith (1962), Martin (1963), and Martin and Gray (1962).

Dating by using animal remains

On the methods of study of animal bones in archeological sites see Butzer (1964) and Ziegler (1973). Also useful is the summary in Heizer (1960).

Dendrochronology

Basic principles of tree-ring dating are explained in Bannister (1969), Fritts (1965), and McGinnies (1963). For results the reader can consult archeological reports. Climatic change, traced through pollen and tree rings, in the American Southwest is summarized by Martin (1963).

Correlation of Pleistocene features

This subject is fully discussed by Butzer (1964) and Zeuner (1958, 1959). Geologic dating is discussed by Antevs (1948), Pewe (1954), and Oakley (1964b). Analysis of soil aimed at archeological explanation is illustrated by Arrhenius (1934) and Eddy and Dregne (1964), who examined Southwestern sites; and by Cook and Heizer (1965), who examined California and west Mexican occupation site soils.

Location of sites

On this see Chang (1968) and Willey (1956).

Chapter 10

Concepts relating to reconstruction

Insight into the theoretical aspects of concepts introduced here can be gained from the following sources: Bayard (1969), Chang (1967a), D. Clarke (1968, 1972), Deetz (1967), Hole (1972), Rouse (1972a, 1972b), Trigger (1968a, 1968b, 1970, 1971), and Watson, Le Blanc, and Redman (1971). For a broad review of anthropological theory see Harris (1968).

Ethnographic analogy

Although considerable use of ethnographic analogy in archeological interpretation is implicit, it is useful to be aware of the theory underlying the concept, and cautions on its application. For general discussions see K. Anderson (1969), Ascher (1961b), L. Binford (1967b), S. Binford (1968), Chang (1967b), G. Clark (1951, 1957), J. D. Clark (1968), Dean (1970), Freeman (1968), Heider (1967), Kehoe (1958), Lee and DeVore (1968), Orme (1972), Service (1964).

Ethnohistory and ethnography in the service of archeology

The close connection between practices of extinct and living societies makes the knowledge of the latter essential to the archeologist. The following references are relevant: Ackerman and Ackerman (1973), Balfet (1965), L. Binford (1967a), Calnek (1972), Campbell (1968), Charlton (1969), Clauson (1973), Cranstone (1971), Dozier (1970), Friedrich (1970), Gould (1968, 1969, 1971), Harlan (1967), Kroeber (1957b), Lauer (1971), Mulvaney and Golson (1971), C. Nelson (1972), Parsons (1940), Phillips (1974), Rowlands (1971), Ucko (1969), Van der Merwe and Scully (1971), and C. White and Peterson (1969).

Ethnoarcheology

Archeologists who study the refuse left at occupation sites by primitive peoples are attempting to observe the kinds and distribution patterns of what will ultimately become archeological materials. Studies of the longevity of household pottery by David (1972) and Foster (1960a, 1960b) are pertinent. Ascher (1962) studied the Seri Indians of Baja California from this standpoint; Stanislawski (1969) made an ethnoarcheological study of Hopi pottery; Oswalt and Van Stone (1967) excavated an Alaskan Village using this approach. Related also are experiments in soil changes and artifacts deliberately buried in artifactual earthworks—such experiments are going on in England, and the reader is referred to Ashbee and Cornwall (1961), Bowen (1967), Dimbleby (1965), Jewell (1961), and Jewell and Dimbleby (1966). Other studies are by Isaac (1967), Longacre and Ayres (1968), Puleston (1971), and Shaw (1970).

Technology

A good grounding in technology is essential to the archeologist. There are numerous detailed studies of the material culture of individual societies. General surveys of technology are Daumas (1962), Hodges (1970), Leroi-Gourhan (1943), Oswalt (1973), Sayce (1963), and Singer, Holmyard, and Hall (1954–1958). An example of a detailed material culture study of a social group is Blackwood (1950).

Adaptation and ecology

These topics are referred to elsewhere in this volume. On the larger relation of the earth to man see Baker (1962), Bennett (1944, 1976), Bray (1972), J. D. Clark (1965), Dubos (1976), and Hardesty (1972).

Chapter 11

What is economy?

Helpful discussions on this subject can be found in G. Clark (1952, 1953b), Higgs (1972, 1975), Jarman (1971), Lee (1968), Malinowski (1932), Mauss (1954), Nash (1966), and Polanyi (1957).

Diet—its variety and archeological traces

The most direct evidence of what people ate can be recovered from feces (coprolites) preserved under favorable conditions, usually in dry sites. An excellent bibliography of analyses of ancient coprolites is by Wilke and Hall (1975). The problem of how dependent ancient man, say of the Paleolithic period, was on plant foods is discussed by Heizer (1975), Isaac (1971a), Jolly (1970), and Kliks (1975).

Recovery of dietary information

On this subject the information is so great that it is impossible to reference it. The following publications are cited as deserving careful reading: Aschmann (1959), Bird (1943), Coon (1951), Goodall (1946), Heizer (1960), Helbaek (1951, 1964, 1969), Isaac (1971a), Lartet and Gaillard (1907), MacNeish (1967b), Morin (1911), Reed (1959, 1960, 1961, 1962), Saffiro (1972), Struever (1962, 1968b), Van Buren (1939), Wedel (1961), T. E. White (1953b), Wood (1968), Wulsin (1941), and Ziegler (1973).

Ethnographic studies of the food-quest can be helpful to the archeologist. Examples are Bennett (1955), Carneiro (1961), Hawley, Pijoan, and Elkin (1943), Krogh and Krogh (1915), McCarthy and McArthur (1960), Malkin (1962), Parker (1910), Scott (1958), Scudder (1971), Simoons (1961), and Sullivan (1942).

Trade

Ethnographic trade situations can serve as models for archeological ones. See Berndt (1951), Colton (1941), Dixon, Cann and Renfrew (1968), Flannery et al. (1967), Grace (1961), Haines (1938a, 1938b), Hermann (1968), W. Hill (1948), Hole (1966), Polanyi (1957), Mallowan (1965), Navarro (1925), Piggott (1959b), Renfrew (1968a), Shepard (1948), Stone and Thomas (1956), Tower (1945), and Wright (1969).

Archeological trade is discussed by R. McC. Adams (1974), Bradley (1971), Brand (1938), de Cardos (1959), Chapman (1957, 1959), Davis (1961), Ewers (1955), Malinowski (1932), Sabloff and Lamberg-Kavlosky (1973, 1975), Sahlins (1965), D. F. Thompson (1949), and Webb (1974).

Chapter 12

Locational analysis

Further exploration of this subject can be followed in Berry (1968), Berry and Marble (1968), Chorley (1968), Chorley and Haggett (1969), Christaller (1966), Garner (1967), Harvey (1967), Lösch (1954), Nystuen (1968), Nystuen and Dacy (1968), and Zipf (1949).

Population statistics

Much has been written on this subject, perhaps because it is so important. The following will introduce the reader to problems of determining prehistoric population numbers and vital statistics: Angel (1947), Ascadi and Nemeskeri (1970), Ascher (1959), Baker and Sanders (1972), Birdsell (1957, 1968), Casselberry (1974), Cook (1947, 1972), Cook and Borah (1963, 1971), Dobyns and Thompson (1966), Genoves (1969b), Haviland (1969, 1972), Howells (1960), Kryzwicki (1934), McArthur (1970), Senyurek (1947), Swedlund (1975), Vallois (1960), and Wiessner (1974).

Factors affecting population size

Environmental factors, in the widest sense of the word, can encourage or limit numbers of people. See, for example, the discussions by Baumhoff (1963), A. Brown (1967), Casteel (1972), Carneiro (1956, 1961), Cook (1946, 1947, 1949a), Cook and Heizer (1965), G. Cowgill (1975a, 1975b), U. Cowgill (1961, 1962), Gumerman (1971), Harpending and Bertram (1975), Hassan (1973), Laslett (1965), and Swedlund (1975).

Factors affecting settlement pattern

Adams (1965, 1970b, 1972), Adams and Nissen (1972), W. Adams (1968), Burch (1971), Coe (1961), Coe and Flannery (1964), Conklin (1961), Derricourt (1972), Dumond (1961), Drucker and Contreras (1953), Fitzhugh (1972), Flannery et al. (1967), Gumerman (1971), Hack (1942), Hall (1966), Heizer (1962b), Higgs (1975), Hodder and Hassal (1971), Hole (1962b), Meggers (1954), Meggers and Evans (1957), Michels (1968), Steward (1936, 1937, 1938), and Struever (1965, 1968b).

Settlement patterns

Some general studies, useful for orientation, are by Chang (1968, 1972), Parsons (1972), Trigger (1967), Willey (1965b), and the members of SARG (1974). Examples of settlement-pattern determination can be found in Adams (1962, 1965, 1970b, 1972), Chang (1958, 1962), G. Clark (1952), Crumley (1976), Fitting (1969), Haviland (1965), G. Johnson (1973, 1975), Jones (1966), McCartney (1975), Millon (1973), Nietsch (1939), Peterson (1975), Sears (1968), Trigger (1965), Ucko, Tringham, and Dimbleby (1972), Voorhies (1972), Willey (1973), and Young (1966). Analyses of various levels of settlement, from the household and community to the region, are in Flannery (1976).

Chapter 13

Prehistoric peoples and cultures

There is some most interesting writing on this subject. See Caldwell (1964), Childe (1951b, 1956), Gladwin and Gladwin (1928a), Kroeber (1962, 1963), and Rouse (1965).

Direct historical approach

The methodological principles are presented by Steward (1942). Its application can be examined and evaluated in Caldwell (1958), G. Clark (1957: 256–

261), Eggan (1952, 1966), Heizer (1941a), Hester (1962), Hoijer (1956b), Jett (1964), Lipe (1970), Murdock (1959), Nelson (1972), Rowe (1945, 1946), Strong (1940), and Wedel (1936).

Linguistic approaches

The indirect approach to peoples' histories through language has borne some good results. A basic study is that of Sapir (1916), and more sophisticated techniques developed since that time are presented by Bergsland and Vogt (1962), Clauson (1973), Crossland (1957), Hoijer (1956a), Hymes (1960), Swadesh (1959, 1960), Traeger (1955), and Van der Merwe (1966). For applications see Baumhoff and Olmsted (1963), Finley (1970), Gimbutas (1963), Hencken (1955), Hoijer (1956b), Elsasser and Heizer (1966: 1–6), Krober (1955), Phillips (1974), Pulgram (1959), Swadesh (1953), Taylor and Rouse (1959), and Thieme (1958).

Migrations

For general discussions see Rouse (1958). For applications see Ammerman and Cavalli-Sforza (1972a), Byers (1957), Chard (1958), Giddings (1960), Gladwin (1947), Greenman (1963), Griffin (1960, 1962), Heine-Geldern (1954), Heine-Geldern and Ekholm (1951), Hester (1962), Heyerdahl (1959, 1963), Hopkins (1959), Linne (1955), McBurney (1960), MacWhite (1956), Mather (1954), Meggers (1975), Meggers, Evans, and Estrada (1965), Pearson (1968), Renfrew (1972a), Stewart (1960), Swadesh (1962), Thompson (1958b), Wendorf (1966), and Willey (1956a).

Skeletal and burial evidence

Disregarding the great royal tombs of Meso-America, Egypt, the Middle East, and China, we cite here more prosaic studies of more ordinary people. For a broad discussion of information that can be extracted from mortuary practices see Binford (1971) and Brown (1971); and for the argument that disposal of the dead can be likened to fashion see Kroeber (1927).

For examples of graves, their contents and interpretation, the reader can browse in the following: Brogger, Falk, and Schetelig (1917), Kidder (1958), Lewis and Kreberg (1946), Lothrop (1942), Ragir (1972), Reisner (1932), Rudenko (1970), and Woolley (1934). Social inferences from graves can be found in Anderson (1965), Brothwell (1965), Brothwell and Sandison (1967), Daniel (1960), Durand (1960), Farabee (1919), Hoffman and Brunker (1976), Kerley and Bass (1967), Rathje (1970), and Lane and Sublett (1972).

Archeological traces of religion and magic

A great deal of crazy writing on this subject exists. In our opinion, the following can be recommended as sound: Bergouinoux and Goetz (1958), Blanc (1961), Breuil (1951), Elsasser (1961), Engnell (1967), Heizer (1951b), Heizer and Baumhoff (1961), James (1962), Maringer (1960), Sears (1961), and Stevens (1975).

Intellectual developments and attainments

It is inconceivable that only in the third quarter of the twentieth century did man suddenly become so intelligent that he was able to send living, encapsulated, programmed men to the moon and unmanned vehicles to Mars. There was, of course, a long-range preparation, both mentalistic and technological, for these events. This preparation was the experience learned by man during the long period of prehistory. Some hints to what very simple-cultured societies, well endowed in thinkers, had managed to achieve in terms of astronomy, technology and cosmology can be seen in: Aveni (1974), Blacker and Lowe (1975), Hatch (1971), and Hoyle (1972) on astronomy; Barber (1900) and Heizer (1966) on the transport of stones weighing up to 1000 tons in ancient times; Edwards (1961) and Mencken (1963) on building the Egyptian pyramids; Thompson (1950) on Maya hieroglyphic writing; Leon-Portilla (1973) on Maya thought; Colton and Martin (1969), Hawkins (1965a, 1965b), and Hoyle (1966) on Stonehenge as an eclipse computer; Thom (1967, 1971) on megalithic sites and their uses; Dewez (1974) and Marshack (1972, 1976) on the significance of engraved notations on Paleolithic bone artifacts.

Chapter 14

Historical reconstructions in archeology

For broad presentations the reader can consult R. Adams (1966), Bagby (1953), Bernal (1969), Caldwell (1966), Chang (1967a), G. Clark (1953a), Coulborn (1959), Daniel (1968), Dray (1957), Flannery (1967a), Heizer and Graham (1971), Kroeber (1953, 1957a, 1962), MacWhite (1956), Melko (1969), Quigley (1961), Renfrew (1968b, 1972a, 1972c), Riley (1969), Rouse (1953), Service (1968), Taylor (1948), Willey (1966b), Willey and Phillips (1958), and Wolf (1967).

Site reports—their preparation and illustration

Useful guides to procedures exist, but practice with archeological data is the only way to learn how to do this. See Atkinson (1953: 173 ff.), Brodribb (1970), Bryant and Holz (1965), Grinsell, Rahtz, and Warhurst (1966), Harrison (1945), Lester (1967), Piggott and Hope-Taylor (1965), Ridgway (1938), Rivard (1964), R. Smith (1970), Staniland (1953), Webster (1963: Chap. V), and Wheeler (1956: Chap. XVI).

Regional histories

There are numbers of these, and a good place to start is in the *Ancient Peoples and Places* series published by Thames and Hudson, London, under the general editorship of Glynn Daniel of Cambridge University. For North America there is the regionally organized volume edited by Jennings and Norbeck (1964) and the two-volume work by Willey, Vol. 1 (1966a) of which concerns North America, and Vol. 2 (1971) South America. The book-review sections of *American Antiquity* and *American Anthropologist* are excellent sources of information on books that deal with particular areas or topics.

Models of prehistory

On *descriptive models* see R. Adams (1966), Binford (1966), Bordes (1971), Braidwood (1958, 1960), Braidwood and Reed (1957), Braidwood and Willey (1962), Caldwell (1958), Childe (1944a, 1944b, 1951a, 1951b, 1954), D. Clarke (1972), J. D. Clark, Cole, Isaac, and Kleindienst (1966), Collins (1970), Culbert (1974), Daniel (1943, 1971b), Flannery (1972, 1973, 1976), Gathercole (1971), Klejn (1972), Kroeber (1962), McKern (1939), Meggers (1959), Morgan (1875, 1878), Piggott (1960), Rouse (1955, 1957), Rowe (1966), Sherratt (1972), Steward (1949, 1955, 1968), Vogt (1964), Willey (1960), and Willey and Phillips (1958).

Causal models are discussed or applied in Albright (1957), Bagby (1963: Chap. 6), Barnett (1953), Binford (1968a), Childe (1957), G. Clark (1966), J. D. Clark (1960, 1964), Coe (1961), Culbert (1973), Dray (1957), Erasmus (1968), Flannery (1966, 1972b), Fleming (1972), Harner (1970), Huntington (1959), Kikuchi (1976), Kossina (1941), Kroeber (1943, 1944), Plog (1974), Raikes (1967), Renfrew (1967, 1968b, 1970a, 1973), Sabloff and Willey (1968), P. Smith (1972), Spengler (1926–1928), Tortelot and Sabloff (1972), Toynbee (1934–1960), Willey (1953), and Willey and Shimkin (1971).

Civilization—its definitions and methods of analyzing it

R. Adams (1966), Bagby (1963), Bernal (1969), Bohannan (1971), Carneiro (1974), Daniel (1968), Heizer (1960), Heizer and Graham (1971), Hole (1966), Kroeber (1953, 1962), MacNeish (1964), Melko (1969), Quigley (1961), Rathje (1971), Renfrew (1972a), Riley (1969), Sanders (1965), Sanders and Price (1968), Service (1975), Smith and Young (1972), and Wolf (1967).

Chapter 15

History and science in archeology

Both sides of the famous debate on this subject, though dealing with anthropology in general rather than archeology in particular, are worth reading. See Boas (1936) and Kroeber (1935). See also Binford (1968a), Childe (1953b), Erasmus (1968), Kroeber (1931, 1957a), Trigger (1970), and Watson, LeBlanc, and Redman (1971).

Scientific method

The student can learn much from reading the following: R. McC. Adams (1974), L. R. Binford (1964, 1972), Buckley (1968), Chamberlin (1965), D. Clarke (1972, 1973), Flannery (1967, 1972), Hawkes (1973), Hayek (1955), Hempel (1951, 1952, 1965, 1966), Hempel and Oppenheim (1948), Kluckhohn (1939); T. Kuhn (1962), Leach (1961), Leone (1972), C. Morgan (1973,

1974), Mueller (1975), Platt (1962, 1964), Reid, Schiffer, and Rathje (1975), Rudner (1966), Salmon (1975), Schiffer (1975, 1976), Tribus and McIrvine (1971), P. Watson (1972a), Watson, LeBlanc, and Redman (1971), Wilson (1952), and Woodall (1972).

General system theory

Recommended are Ackoff (1960, 1963), R. Adams (1968), von Bertalanffy (1956, 1962), Blalock (1971), Boulding (1956b), Buckley (1967, 1968), Flannery (1968), Hall and Fagen (1956), and Rashevsky (1967).

BIBLIOGRAPHY

Aberle, D. F., 1970, Comments. In *Reconstructing prehistoric pueblo societies,* W. A. Longacre, ed. Albuquerque: University of New Mexico Press, pp. 214–223.

Ackerman, R. E., and L. A. Ackerman, 1973, Ethnoarchaeological interpretations of territoriality and land use in Southwestern Alaska. *Ethnohistory* 20: 315–334.

Ackoff, R. L., 1960, Systems, organizations, and interdisciplinary research. *General Systems* 5:1–8.

Ackoff, R. L., 1963, General system theory and systems research contrasting conceptions of systems science. *General Systems* 8: 107–122.

Adams, R. E. W., 1975, Stratigraphy. In *Field methods in archaeology,* T. R. Hester, J. A. Heizer, and R. F. Graham, eds. Palo Alto, Calif.: Mayfield Press, pp. 147–162.

Adams, R. McC., 1962, Agriculture and urban life in early southwestern Iran, *Science* 136: 109–122.

Adams, R. McC., 1965, *Land behind Baghdad*. Chicago: University of Chicago Press.

Adams, R. McC., 1966, *The evolution of urban society*. Chicago: Aldine.

Adams, R. McC., 1968, Archeological research strategies: past and present. *Science* 160: 1187–1192.

Adams, R. McC., 1970, The study of ancient Mesopotamian settlement patterns and the problem of urban origins. *Sumer* 25: 111–124.

Adams, R. McC., 1972, Patterns of urbanism in early southern Mesopotamia. In *Man, settlement and urbanism*, P. J. Ucko, R. Tringham, and G. W. Dimbleby, eds. London: Duckworth, pp. 735–749.

Adams, R. McC., 1974a, Anthropological perspectives on ancient trade. *Current Anthropology* 15: 239–258.

Adams, R. McC., 1974b, Review of *An archaeological perspective* by L. R. Binford. *American Anthropologist* 76: 649–651.

Adams, R. McC., and H. J. Nissen, 1972, *The Uruk countryside*. Chicago: University of Chicago Press.

Adams, W. Y., 1968, Settlement pattern in microcosm: the changing aspect of a Nubian village during twelve centuries. In *Settlement archaeology*, K. C. Chang, ed. Palo Alto, Calif.: National Press Books, pp. 174–207.

Aitken, M. J., 1960, Magnetic dating. *Archaeometry* 3: 41–44.

Aitken, M. J., 1961, *Physics and archaeology*. New York: Interscience.

Aitken, M. J., 1970, Magnetic prospecting. In *Scientific methods in medieval archaeology*, R. Berger, ed. Berkeley: University of California Press, pp. 423–434.

Aitken, M. J., 1974, *Physics and archaeology*, 2d ed. Oxford: Clarendon Press.

Aitken, M. J., and J. C. Alldred, 1972, The assessment of error limits in thermoluminescent dating. *Archaeometry* 14: 257–267.

Aitken, M. J., and S. J. Fleming, 1972, Thermoluminescence dosimetry in archaeological dating. *Topics in radiation dosimetry* Supplement I (ed. Attix) 1–78.

Albright, W. F., 1957, *From the Stone Age to Christianity: monotheism and the historical process*, 2d ed. Baltimore: The Johns Hopkins Press.

Alcock, L., 1951, A technique for surface collecting. *Antiquity* 98: 75–76.

Aldred, C., 1961, *The Egyptians*. New York: Praeger.

Alexander, J., 1970, *The directing of archaeological excavations*. New York: Humanities Press.

Alibone, T. E., et al., 1970, *The impact of the natural sciences on archaeology*. New York: Oxford University Press.

Alland, A., 1970, *Adaptation in cultural evolution: an approach to medical anthropology*. New York: Columbia University Press.

Allee, W. C., O. Park, A. E. Emerson, T. Park, and K. P. Schmidt, 1949, *Principles of animal ecology*. Philadelphia: Saunders.

Allen, D. C., 1971, The reconstruction of kinship from archaeological data: the concepts, the methods, and the feasibility. *American Antiquity* 36: 41–53.

Ambrose, W. R., 1967, Archaeology and shell middens. *Archaeology and Physical Anthropology in Oceania* 2: 169–187.

Ammerman, A. J., and L. L. Cavalli-Sforza, 1972a, Measuring the rate of spread of early farming in Europe. *Man* 6: 674–688.

Ammerman, A. J., and L. L. Cavalli-Sforza, 1972b, A population model for the diffusion of early farming in Europe. In *The explanation of culture change,* C. Renfrew, ed. London: Duckworth.

Anderson, E. C., and H. Levi, 1952, Some problems in radiocarbon dating. *Det Kongelige Danske Videnskabernes Selskab,* Copenhagen, 27 (6).

Anderson, J. E., 1965, Human skeletons of Tehuacan. *Science* 148: 496–497.

Anderson, K. M., 1969, Ethnographic analogy and archeological interpretation. *Science* 163: 133–138.

Anderson, R. Y., 1955, Pollen analysis: a research tool for the study of cave deposits. *American Antiquity* 21: 84–85.

Angel, L., 1947, The length of life in ancient Greece. *Journal of Gerontology* 2: 18–24.

Antevs, E., 1948, Climatic changes and pre-white man. Salt Lake City: *University of Utah Bulletin* 38: 168–191.

Archaeometry. Oxford: Research Laboratory for Archaeology and the History of Art. Annual, Vol. 1, 1958.

Arnold, J. R., and W. F. Libby, 1949, Age determinations by radiocarbon content: checks with samples of known age. *Science* 110: 678–680.

Arrhenius, D., 1934, *Fosfathalten i Skånska Jordar.* Stockholm: Sveriges Geologiska Undersökning Ser. C, No. 383 (Årsbok 28, No. 3).

Arrhenius, D., 1963, Investigation of soil from old Indian sites. *Ethnos* Nos. 2–4: 122–136.

Ascàdi, G., and J. Nemeskéri, 1970, *History of human life span and mortality.* Budapest: Akadémìai Kiadó.

Ascher, R., 1959, A prehistoric population estimate using midden analysis and two population models. *Southwestern Journal of Anthropology* 15: 168–178.

Ascher, R., 1961a, Experimental archeology. *American Anthropologist* 63: 793–816.

Ascher, R., 1961b, Analogy in archaeological interpretation. *Southwestern Journal of Anthropology* 17: 317–325.

Ascher, R., 1962, Ethnography for archeology: a case from the Seri Indians. *Ethnology* 1: 360–369.

Aschmann, H., 1959, *The central desert of Baja California: demography and ecology.* Berkeley: University of California Press. Ibero-Americana, No. 42.

Ashbee, P., and I. W. Cornwall, 1961, An experiment in field archaeology. *Antiquity* 35: 129–135.

Atkinson, R. J. C., 1953, *Field archaeology,* rev. ed. London: Methuen. (1st ed., 1946.)

Atkinson, R. J. C., 1956, *Stonehenge.* London: Hamish Hamilton.

Atkinson, R. J. C., 1963, Resistivity surveying in archeology. In *The scientist and archaeology,* E. Pyddoke, ed. London: Phoenix House, pp. 1–30.

Atkinson, R. J. C., 1975, British prehistory and the radiocarbon revolution. *Antiquity* 49: 173–177.

Aveni, A. F., 1974, *Archaeoastronomy in pre-Columbian America.* Austin: University of Texas Press.

Bada, J. L., 1972, Amino acids and their use in dating fossil bones. San Diego Museum of Natural History: *Environment Southwest* No. 448, pp. 1–4.

Bada, J. L., and R. Protsch, 1973, Racemization reaction of aspartic acid and its use in dating fossil bones. *Proceedings of the National Academy of Sciences* 70: 1331–1334.

Bada, J. L., R. A. Schroeder, and G. F. Carter, 1974, New evidence for the antiquity of man in North America deduced from aspartic acid racemization. *Science* 184: 791–793.

Bada, J. L., R. Schroeder, R. Protsch, and R. Berger, 1974, Concordance of collagen-based radiocarbon and aspartic-acid racemization ages. *Proceedings of the National Academy of Sciences* 71: 914–917.

Baerreis, D. A., 1971, The ethnohistoric approach and archaeology. *Ethnohistory* 8: 49–77.

Bagby, P. H., 1953, Culture and the causes of culture. *American Anthropologist* 55: 535–554.

Bagby, P. H., 1963, *Culture and history*. Berkeley: University of California Press.

Baker, P. T., 1962, The application of ecological theory to anthropology. *American Anthropologist* 64: 15–22.

Baker, P. T., and W. T. Sanders, 1972, Demographic studies in anthropology. B. J. Siegel, ed., *Annual Review of Anthropology* 1: 151–178.

Balfet, H., 1952, La vannerie: essai de classification. *L'Anthropologie* 56: 259–280. (English translation in *Reports of the University of California Archaeological Survey* No. 37: 1–21, 1957.)

Balfet, H., 1965, Ethnographical observations [on pottery making] in north Africa and archaeological interpretation. New York: *Viking Fund Publications in Anthropology* No. 41: 161–177.

Ballesteros Gaibrois, M., 1960, Spanische Archaologische Forschungen in Amerika im 18 Jahrhundert. *Tribus* 4: 185–190.

Bannister, B., 1962, The interpretation of tree-ring dates. *American Antiquity* 27: 508–514.

Bannister, B., 1969, Dendrochronology. In *Science in archaeology*, D. Brothwell and E. Higgs, eds., rev. ed. London: Thames and Hudson, pp. 191–205.

Bannister, B., and T. L. Smiley, 1955, Dendrochronology. In *Geochronology, with special reference to the southwestern United States*, T. L. Smiley, ed. Tucson: University of Arizona Bulletin 26: 177–195.

Barber, R. M., 1900, *The mechanical triumphs of the ancient Egyptians*. London: Kegan Paul.

Barghoorn, E. S., Jr., 1944, Collecting and preserving botanical materials of archaeological interest. *American Antiquity* 9: 289–294.

Barnett, H. G., 1953, *Innovation: the basis of cultural change*. New York: McGraw-Hill.

Bascom, W., 1971, Deep-water archeology. *Science* 174: 161–169.

Bass, G. F., 1963, Underwater archeology: key to history's warehouse. *National Geographic Magazine* 124: 138–156.

Bass, G. F., 1966, *Archaeology underwater*. New York: Praeger.

Baud, C. A., 1960, Dating of prehistoric bones by radiological and optical methods. New York: *Viking Fund Publications in Anthropology* No. 28: 246–264.

Baumhoff, M. A., 1963, Ecological determinants of aboriginal California populations. Berkeley: *University of California Publications in American Archaeology and Ethnology*, 49: 155–236.

Baumhoff, M. A., and D. L. Olmsted, 1963, Palainihan: radiocarbon support for glottochronology. *American Anthropologist* 65: 278–284.

Bayard, D. T., 1969, Science, theory and reality in the "new archaeology." *American Antiquity* 34: 376–384.

Belzoni, G., 1820, *Narrative of the operations and recent discoveries within the pyramids, temples, tombs, and excavations in Egypt and Nubia*, 2 vols. London: J. Murray.

Bender, M. M., 1968, Mass spectrometric studies of carbon 13 variations in corn and other grasses. *Radiocarbon* 10(2): 468–472.

Bennett, J. W., 1944, The interaction of culture and environment in the smaller societies. *American Anthropologist* 46: 461–478.

Bennett, J. W., 1976, Anticipation, adaptation, and the concept of culture in anthropology. *Science* 192: 847–853.

Bennett, M. K., 1955, The food economy of the New England Indians, 1605–1675. *Journal of Political Economy* 63: 369–397.

Berger, R., A. B. Horney, and W. F. Libby, 1964, Radiocarbon dating of bone and shell from their organic components. *Science* 144: 999–1001.

Berger, R., R. E. Taylor, and W. Libby, 1966, Radiocarbon content of marine shells from the California and Mexican west coast. *Science* 153: 864–866.

Bergounioux, F.-M., and J. Goetz, 1958, *Les religions des préhistoriques et des primitifs*. Paris: Fayard.

Bergsland, K., and H. Vogt, 1962, On the validity of glottochronology. *Current Anthropology* 3: 115–153.

Bernal, I., 1969, *The Olmec world*. Berkeley: University of California Press.

Berndt, R. M., 1951, Ceremonial exchange in western Arnhem land. *Southwestern Journal of Anthropology* 7: 156–176.

Berry, B. J. L., 1968, Approaches to regional analysis: a synthesis. In *Spatial analysis: a reader in statistical geography*, B. J. L. Berry and D. F. Marble, eds. Englewood Cliffs, N.J.: Prentice-Hall, pp. 24–34.

Berry, B. J. L., and D. F. Marble, eds., 1968, *Spatial analysis: a reader in statistical geography*. Englewood Cliffs, N.J.: Prentice-Hall.

Bertalanffy, L. von, 1956, General system theory. *General Systems* 1:1–10.

Bertalanffy, L. von, 1962, General system theory—a critical review. *General Systems* 7: 1–20.

Bessaignet, P., 1956, An alleged case of primitive money (New Caledonian beads). *Southwestern Journal of Anthropology* 12: 333–345.

Bibby, G., 1956, *The testimony of the spade*. New York: Knopf.

Binford, L. R., 1962, Archeology as anthropology. *American Antiquity* 28: 217–225.

Binford, L. R., 1964, A consideration of archaeological research design. *American Antiquity* 29: 425–441.

Binford, L. R., 1966, The predatory revolution: a consideration of the evidence for a new subsistence level. *American Anthropologist* 68: 508–512.

Binford, L. R., 1967a, An ethnohistory of the *Nottoway, Meherrin* and *Weanock* Indians of Southeastern Virginia. *Ethnohistory* 14: 104–218.

Binford, L. R., 1967b, Smudge pits and hide smoking: the use of analogy in archaeological reasoning. *American Antiquity* 32: 1–12.

Binford, L. R., 1968a, Some comments on historical versus processual archaeology. *Southwestern Journal of Anthropology* 24: 267–275.

Binford, L. R., 1968b, *New perspectives in archaeology*. Chicago: Aldine.

Binford, L. R., 1971, Mortuary practices: their study and their potential. In *Approaches to the social dimensions of mortuary practices*, J. A. Brown, ed. Salt Lake City: University of Utah, Society for American Archaeology, Memoir No. 25: 6–29.

Binford, L. R., 1972, *An archaeological perspective*. New York: Seminar Press.

Binford, S. R., 1968, Ethnographic data and understanding the Pleistocene. In *Man the hunter*, R. B. Lee and I. DeVore, eds. Chicago: Aldine, pp. 274–275.

Bird, S. B., 1943, Excavations in northern Chile. New York: *Anthropological Papers of the American Museum of Natural History* 38: 171–318.

Birdsell, J. B., 1957, Some population problems involving Pleistocene man. *Cold Spring Harbor Symposia on Quantitative Biology* 22: 47–69.

Birdsell, J. B., 1968, Some predictions for the Pleistocene based on equilibrium systems among recent hunter-gatherers. In *Man the hunter*, R. B. Lee and I. DeVore, eds. Chicago: Aldine, pp. 229–240.

Blacker, C., and M. Lowe, eds., 1975, *Ancient cosmologies*. London: Allen and Unwin.

Blackwood, B., 1950, *The technology of a modern stone age people in New Guinea*. Oxford, England: Oxford University, Pitt-Rivers Museum, Occasional Papers on Technology, No. 3.

Blalock, H. M., ed., 1971, *Causal models in the social sciences*. Chicago: Aldine-Atherton.

Blane, A. C., 1961, Some evidence for the ideologies of early man. In *Social life of early man*, S. L. Washburn, ed. New York: Viking Fund Publications in Anthropology, 31: 119–136.

Boas, F., 1936, History and science in anthropology: a reply. *American Anthropologist* 38: 137–141.

Boas, F., 1938, *General anthropology*. New York: Heath.

Bohannan, P., 1971, Beyond civilization. *Natural History* 80: 50–67.

Bohmers, A., 1956, Statistics and graphs in the study of flint assemblages. *Palaeohistoria* 5:1–5ff.

Bohmers, A., 1969, A statistical analysis of flint artifacts. In *Science in archaeology*, D. Brothwell and E. Higgs, eds. London: Thames and Hudson, pp. 564–566.

Bonomi, J., 1853, *Nineveh and its palaces*. London: Ingram, Cooke.

Bordes, F., 1971, Physical evolution and technological evolution in man: a parallelism. *World Archaeology* 3: 1–5.

Bordes, F., 1972, *A tale of two caves*. New York: Harper & Row.

Borhegyi, S. F. de, 1961, *Ships, shoals, and amphoras: the story of underwater archaeology*. New York: Holt, Rinehart and Winston.

Boulding, K. W., 1956a, Toward a general theory of growth. *General Systems* 1: 66–75.

Boulding, K. W., 1956b, General systems theory—the skeleton of science. *General Systems* 1: 11–17.

Bradley, R., 1971, Trade competition and artifact distribution. *World Archaeology* 2: 347–355.

Bowen, H. C., 1967, Corn storage in antiquity. *Antiquity* 41: 214–215.

Bowen, R. N. C., 1958, *The exploration of time*. New York: Philosophical Library.

Bowie, S. H. U., and C. F. Davidson, 1955, The radioactivity of the Piltdown fossils. London: *Geology*, Bulletin of the British Museum of Natural History 2(6): 276–282.

Braidwood, R. S., 1958, Near Eastern prehistory. *Science* 127: 1419–1430.

Braidwood, R. S., 1960, Levels in prehistory: a model for the consideration of the evidence. In *The evolution of man: mind, culture and society*, Vol. 2, S. Tax, ed. Chicago: University of Chicago Press, pp. 143–151.

Braidwood, R. S., and B. Howe, 1960, *Prehistoric investigations in Iraqi Kurdistan.* Chicago: Oriental Institute of the University of Chicago, Studies in Ancient Oriental Civilization, No. 31.

Braidwood, R. S., and C. A. Reed, 1957, The achievement and early consequence of food-production: a consideration of the archeological and natural-historical evidence. *Cold Spring Harbor Symposia on Quantitative Biology* 22: 19–32.

Braidwood, R. S., and G. R. Willey, eds., 1962, *Courses toward urban life: archeological considerations of some cultural alternates.* Viking Fund Publications in Anthropology No. 32.

Brainerd, G. W., 1951, The place of chronological ordering in archaeological analysis. *American Antiquity* 16: 301–313.

Brand, D. D., 1938, Aboriginal trade routes for sea shells in the Southwest. *Association of Pacific Coast Geographers* 4: 3–10.

Bray, W., 1972, The biological basis of culture. In *The explanation of culture change*, C. Renfrew, ed. London: Duckworth.

Breasted, C., 1947, *Pioneer to the past; the story of James Henry Breasted, archaeologist.* London: Jenkins.

Breiner, S., 1965, The rubidium magnetometer in archeological exploration. *Science* 150: 185–193.

Breiner, S., 1973, *Applications manual for portable magnetometers.* Palo Alto: Geometrics.

Breiner, S., and M. D. Coe, 1972, Magnetic exploration of the Olmec civilization. *American Scientist* 60: 566–575.

Bresler, J. B., ed., 1966, *Human ecology: collected readings.* Reading, Mass.: Addison-Wesley.

Breuil, H., 1941, The discovery of the antiquity of man: some of the evidence. Huxley Memorial Lecture for 1941. Published separately by Royal Anthropological Institute, London. (Reprinted in the *Journal for the Royal Anthropological Institute of Great Britain and Ireland*, 1945, 75: 21–31.)

Breuil, H., 1951, Pratiques religeuses chez les humanités quaternaires. *Scienza e Civilita*, pp. 45–75.

Briggs, L. J., and K. F. Weaver, 1958, How old is it? *National Geographic Magazine* 114: 234–255.

Brodribb, C., 1970, *Drawing archaeological finds for publication.* London: John Baker.

Broecker, W. S., 1964, Radiocarbon dating: a case against the proposed link between river mollusks and soil humus. *Science* 143: 596–597.

Broecker, W. S., and J. L. Kulp, 1956, The radiocarbon method of age determination. *American Antiquity* 22: 1–11.

Broecker, W. S., and E. A. Olson, 1960, Radiocarbon from nuclear tests, II. *Science* 132: 712–721.

Brogger, A. W., H. Falk, and H. Schetelig, 1917, *Osebergfundet*, Vol. I. Kristiana, Norway. (Reprinted in part in Heizer 1959: 29–53.)

Bronson, B., 1966, Roots and subsistence of the ancient Maya. *Southwestern Journal of Anthropology* 22: 251–279.

Brothwell, D. R., 1965, *Digging up bones*. London: British Museum of Natural History.

Brothwell, D. R., and E. Higgs, eds., 1969, *Science in archaeology*, rev. ed. London: Thames and Hudson.

Brothwell, D. R., and A. T. Sandison, eds., 1967, *Diseases in antiquity: a survey of the diseases, injuries and surgery of early populations*. London: Thomas (Thorson's).

Brown, A. K., 1967, *The aboriginal population of the Santa Barbara channel*. Berkeley: Reports of the University of California Archaeological Survey, No. 69.

Brown, J. A., ed., 1971, *Approaches to the social dimensions of mortuary practices*. Washington, D.C.: Society for American Archaeology, Memoir No. 25: 1–5.

Brunhouse, R. L., 1971, *Sylvanus G. Morley and the world of the ancient Mayas*. Norman: University of Oklahoma Press.

Brunhouse, R. L., 1973, *In search of the Maya: the first archaeologists*. Albuquerque: University of New Mexico Press.

Bruning, H. H., 1898, Moderne Topferei der Indianer Perus. *Globus* 74: 254–260.

Bryant, V. M., 1968, The role of pollen in the reconstruction of past environments. *Pennsylvania Geographer*, Vol. 6 (reprint, 8 pp., n.p.).

Bryant, V. M., 1974, The role of coprolite analysis in archeology. *Bulletin of the Texas Archaeological Society* 45.

Bryant, V. M., 1975, Pollen as an indicator of prehistoric diets in Coahuila, Mexico. *Bulletin of the Texas Archaeological Society* 46: 107–126.

Bryant, V. M., and R. K. Holtz, 1965, A guide to the drafting of archaeological maps. *Bulletin of the Texas Archaeological Society* 36: 269–285.

Bucha, V., 1971, Archaeomagnetic dating. In *Dating techniques for the archaeologist*, H. N. Michael and E. K. Ralph, eds. Cambridge, Mass.: MIT Press, pp. 57–117.

Buckley, W., 1967, *Sociology and modern systems theory*. Englewood Cliffs, N.J.: Prentice-Hall.

Buckley, W., ed., 1968, *Modern systems research for the behavioral scientist*. Chicago: Aldine.

Builday, J., and P. Parmalee, 1962, Aboriginal butchering techniques at the Eschelman site, Lancaster Co., Pa. *Pennsylvania Archaeological Bulletin of the Society for Pennsylvania Archaeology* 22: 59–83.

Bullard, W. R., Jr., 1960, Maya settlement pattern in northeastern Petén, Guatemala, *American Antiquity* 25: 355–372.

Burch, E. S., Jr., 1971, The nonempirical environment of the Arctic Alaskan Eskimos. *Southwestern Journal of Anthropology* 27: 148–165.

Burleigh, R., 1974, Radiocarbon dating; some practical considerations for the archaeologist. *Journal of Archaeological Science* 1: 69–88.

Burleigh, R., V. R. Switsur, and C. R. Renfrew, 1973, The radiocarbon calendar recalibrated too soon? *Antiquity* 47: 309–316.

Burnham, P., 1972, The explanatory value of the concept of adaptation in studies of culture change. In *The explanation of culture change*, C. Renfrew, ed. London: Duckworth.

Butzer, K. W., 1964, *Environment and archaeology: an introduction to the Pleistocene*. Chicago: Aldine.

Butzer, K. W., 1972, *Environment and archaeology.* London: Methuen.

Byers, D. S., 1957, The Bering-bridge—some speculations. *Ethnos* 22: 20–28.

Caldwell, J. R., 1958, *Trend and tradition in the prehistory of the eastern United States.* Washington, D.C.: American Anthropological Association, Memoir No. 88.

Caldwell, J. R., 1959, The new American archeology. *Science* 129: 303–307.

Caldwell, J. R., 1964, Interaction spheres in prehistory. In *Hopewellian Studies*, J. R. Caldwell and R. L. Hall, eds. Illinois State Museum Scientific Papers 12: 135–143.

Caldwell, J. R., ed., 1966, *New roads to yesterday: essays in archaeology.* New York: Basic Books.

Callen, E. O., 1965, Food habits of some Pre-Columbian Mexican Indians. *Economic Botany* 19: 335–343.

Callen, E. O., 1967, Analysis of Tehuacan coprolites. In *The prehistory of the Tehuacan Valley*, Vol. 1, D. S. Byers, ed. Austin: University of Texas Press, pp. 261–289.

Callen, E. O., 1969, Diet as revealed by coprolites. In *Science in archaeology*, D. Brothwell and E. Higgs, eds., rev. ed. London: Thames and Hudson, pp. 235–243.

Callen, E. O., and T. W. M. Cameron, 1960, A prehistoric diet revealed by coprolites. *New Scientist*, July 7, pp. 229–234.

Calnek, E. E., 1972, Settlement pattern and chinampa agriculture at *Tenochtitlan. American Antiquity* 37: 104–115.

Cameron, H. L., 1958, History from the air. *Photogrammetric Engineering* 24: 366–375.

Campbell, J. M., 1968, Territoriality among ancient hunters: interpretations from ethnography and nature. In *Anthropological Archaeology in the Americas.* Washington, D.C.: Anthropological Society of Washington, pp. 1–21.

Cardos, de M. A., 1959, El commercio de los Mayas antiguos. *Acta Anthropologica*, Epoca 2, Mexico City, 2(1).

Carneiro, R. L., 1956, Slash-and-burn agriculture: a closer look at its implications for settlement patterns. *Selected Papers of the Fifth International Congress of Anthropological and Ethnological Sciences.* Philadelphia: University of Pennsylvania Press, pp. 229–234.

Carneiro, R. L., 1961. Slash-and-burn cultivation among the Kuikuru and its implications for cultural developments in the Amazon Basin. *Antropologica* (Supplement No. 2), pp. 47–67.

Carneiro, R. L., 1974, A reappraisal of the roles of technology and organization in the origin of civilization. *American Antiquity* 39: 179–186.

Carneiro, R. L., and D. F. Hilse, 1966, On determining the probable rate of population growth during the Neolithic. *American Anthropologist* 68: 177–181.

Carpenter, E. F., 1955, Astronomical aspects of geochronology. In *Geochronology*, T. L. Smiley, ed. University of Arizona Physical Sciences Bulletin 2:29–74.

Carpenter, R., 1933, *The humanistic value of archaeology*, Martin Classical Lectures IV. Cambridge, Mass.: Harvard University Press.

Carr, D. R., and J. L. Kulp, 1957, Potassium-argon method of geochronometry. *Bulletin of the Geological Society of America* 68: 763–784.

Carter, H., 1930, *The tomb of Tutankhamun*. London: Cassell.

Carter, H., and A. C. Mace, 1923–1933. *The tomb of Tut-ank-Amen, discovered by the late Earl of Carnavon and Howard Carter*; 3 vols. London: Cassell.

Casson, S., 1939, *The discovery of man: the story of the inquiry into human origins*. London: Hamish Hamilton.

Casteel, R. W., 1972a, Some biases in the recovery of archaeological faunal remains. *Proceedings of the Prehistoric Society* 38: 382–388.

Casteel, R. W., 1972b, Two static maximum population-density models for hunter-gatherers: a first approximation. *World Archaeology* 4: 19–40.

Catch, J. R., 1961, *Carbon-14 compounds*. London: Butterworth.

Caton-Thompson, G., and E. W. Gardner, 1934, *The desert Fayum*. London: Royal Anthropological Institute of Great Britain and Ireland.

Ceram, C. W., 1958, *The march of archaeology*, Richard and Clare Winston, trans. New York: Knopf.

Ceram, C. W., 1966, *Hands on the past: pioneer archaeologists tell their own story*. New York: Knopf.

Chamberlin, T. C., 1965, The method of multiple working hypotheses. *Science* 148: 754–759. (Originally printed in *Science* [Old Series] 15: 92 [1890].)

Chang, K.-C., 1958, Study of the Neolithic social grouping: examples from the New World. *American Anthropologist* 60: 298–334.

Chang, K.-C., 1962, A typology of settlement and community patterns in some circumpolar societies. *Arctic Anthropology* 1:28–41.

Chang, K.-C., 1967a, *Rethinking archaeology*. New York: Random House.

Chang, K.-C., 1967b, Major aspects of the interrelationship of archaeology and ethnology. *Current Anthropology* 8: 227–243.

Chang, K.-C., ed., 1968, *Settlement archaeology*. Palo Alto, Calif.: National Press.

Chang, K.-C., 1972, Settlement patterns in archaeology. *Addison-Wesley Module in Anthropology*, no. 24. Reading, Mass.: Addison-Wesley.

Chaplin, R. E., 1971, *The study of animal bones from archaeological sites*. New York: Seminar Press.

Chapman, A. M., 1957, Trade enclaves in Aztec and Maya civilizations. In *Trade and market in the early empires*, K. Polanyi, C. M. Arensberg, and H. W. Pearson, eds. New York: Free Press, pp. 114–153.

Chapman, A. M., 1959, *Puertos de intercambio en Mesoamerica prehispanica*. Instituto Nacional de Antropologia e Historia, Serie Historia No. 3, Mexico.

Chard, C. S., 1958, *New World migration routes*. Fairbanks, Alaska: Anthropological Papers of the University of Alaska 7: 23–26.

Charlton, T. H., 1969, Ethnohistory and archaeology: Post-Conquest Aztec sites. *American Antiquity* 34: 286–294.

Chevallier, R., 1957, Bibliographie des applications archéologiques de la photographie aérienne. *Bulletin d'Archéologie Marocaine*. Tome II (Supplement), Edita-Casablanca.

Chevallier, R., 1964, *L'avion et la découverte du passe*. Paris: Fayard.

Childe, V. G., 1944a, Historical analysis of archaeological method (a review of G. Daniel, "The three ages"). *Nature* 153: 206–207.

Childe, V. G., 1944b, *Archaeological ages as technological stages*. London: Royal Anthropological Institute of Great Britain and Ireland, Huxley Lecture. (*Man* 65: 19–20.)

Childe, V. G., 1947, Archaeology as a social science: an inaugural lecture. London: University of London, Institute of Archaeology, Third Annual Report, pp. 49–60.

Childe, V. G., 1951a, *Man makes himself*. New York: New American Library.

Childe, V. G., 1951b, *Social evolution*. New York: Henry Schuman.

Childe, V. G., 1953a, The constitution of archaeology as a science. In *Science, medicine and history*, Vol. 1, E. A. Underwood, ed. London: Oxford, pp. 2–15.

Childe, V. G., 1953b, *What is history?* New York: Abelard-Schuman.

Childe, V. G., 1954, *What happened in history*. Baltimore: Penguin.

Childe, V. G., 1956, *Piecing together the past; the interpretation of archaeological data*. New York: Praeger.

Childe, V. G., 1957, *The dawn of European civilization*. New York: Knopf.

Childe, V. G., 1962, *A short introduction to archaeology*. New York: Collier.

Chorley, R. J., 1968, Geography and analog theory. In *Spatial analysis: a reader in statistical geography*, B. J. L. Berry and D. F. Marble, eds. Englewood Cliffs, N.J.: Prentice-Hall, pp. 42–52.

Chorley, R. J., and P. Hagget, eds., 1969, *Models in geography*. London: Methuen.

Christaller, W., 1966, *Central places in Germany*. C. W. Baskin, trans. Englewood Cliffs: Prentice-Hall.

Clark, G., 1951, Folk-culture and European prehistory. In *Aspects of archaeology in Britain and beyond*, W. Grimes, ed. London: Edwards, pp. 49–65.

Clark, G., 1952, *Prehistoric Europe; the economic basis*. London: Methuen.

Clark, G., 1953a, Archaeological theories and interpretations. In *Anthropology today*, A. L. Kroeber, chairman. Chicago: University of Chicago Press, pp. 343–360.

Clark, G., 1953b, The economic approach to prehistory. *Proceedings of the British Academy* 39: 215–238.

Clark, G., 1954, *Excavations at Star Carr*. London: Cambridge.

Clark, G., 1957, *Archaeology and society; reconstructing the prehistoric past*. London: Methuen.

Clark, G., 1961, *World prehistory: an outline*. London: Cambridge.

Clark, G., 1966, The invasion hypothesis in British archaeology. *Antiquity* 40: 172–189.

Clark, G., 1970, *Aspects of prehistory*. Berkeley: University of California Press.

Clark, G., 1972, *Star Carr: a case study in bioarchaeology*. Addison-Wesley Modular Publications, Module 10. Reading, Mass.: Addison-Wesley.

Clark, G., 1975, *The earlier Stone Age settlement of Scandinavia*. New York: Cambridge University Press.

Clark, G., and S. Piggott, 1965, *Prehistoric societies*. New York: Knopf.

Clark, J. D., 1960, Human ecology during Pleistocene and later times in Africa south of the Sahara. *Current Anthropology* 1: 307–324.

Clark, J. D., 1964, The influence of environment in inducing culture change at the Kalambo Falls prehistoric site. *South African Archaeological Bulletin* 19: 93–101.

Clark, J. D., 1965, Culture and ecology in prehistoric Africa. In *Ecology and economic development in tropical Africa*, D. Brokensha, ed. Berkeley: University of California Press, pp. 13–28.

Clark, J. D., 1968, Studies of hunter-gatherers as an aid to the interpretation of prehistoric societies. In *Man the hunter*, R. B. Lee and I. DeVore, eds. Chicago: Aldine, pp. 276–280.

Clark, J. D., G. H. Cole, G. L. Isaac, and M. R. Kleindienst, 1966, Precision and definition in African archaeology. *South African Archaeological Bulletin* 21: 114–121.

Clark, J. D., and C. V. Haynes, 1970, An elephant butchery site at Mwanganda's Village, Karonga, Malawi, and its relevance for Paleolithic archaeology. *World Archaeology* 1: 390–411.

Clark, W., 1946, *Photography by infrared: its principle and application.* New York: Wiley.

Clarke, D. L., 1968, *Analytical archaeology.* London: Methuen.

Clarke, D. L., 1972, *Models in archaeology.* London: Methuen.

Clarke, D. L., 1973, Archaeology: the loss of innocence. *Antiquity* 47: 6–18.

Clauson, G., 1973, Philology and archaeology. *Antiquity* 47: 37–42.

Cleator, P. E., 1962, *Lost languages.* New York: New American Library.

Coe, M. D., 1961, Social typology and the tropical forest civilizations. *Comparative Studies in Society and History* 4: 65–85.

Coe, M. D., and K. V. Flannery, 1964, Microenvironments and Mesoamerican prehistory. *Science* 143: 650–654.

Coggins, C., 1970, The Maya scandal: how thieves strip sites of past cultures. *Smithsonian*, October, 2: 8–17.

Coghlan, H. H., 1960, Metallurgical analysis of archaeological materials: I. New York: Viking Fund Publications in Anthropology No. 28: 1–20.

Coles, J., 1967, Experimental archaeology. *Proceedings of the Society of Antiquaries of Scotland* 99: 1–20.

Coles, J., 1973, *Archaeology by experiment.* London: Hutchinson.

Coles, J., 1975, Timber and radiocarbon dates. *Antiquity* 49: 123–125.

Collins, D., 1970, Stone artefact analysis and the recognition of culture traditions. *World Archaeology* 2: 17–27.

Colton, H. S., 1941, Prehistoric trade in the Southwest. *Scientific Monthly* 52: 308–319.

Colton, R., and R. L. Martin, 1969, Eclipse prediction at Stonehenge. *Nature* 221: 1011–1012.

Colwell, R. N., 1956, The taking of helicopter photographs for use in photogrammetric research and training. *Photogrammetric Engineering* 22: 613–621.

Colyer, M., and D. Osborne, 1965, Screening soil and fecal samples for recovery of small specimens. *American Antiquity* 31(2:2): 186–192.

Conklin, H. C., 1961, The study of shifting cultivation. *Current Anthropology* 2: 27–61.

Cook, O. F., 1921, Milpa agriculture: a primitive tropical system. *Smithsonian Report for 1919*: 307–326.

Cook, R. M., 1969. Archaeomagnetism. In *Science in archaeology*, D. Brothwell and E. Higgs, eds., rev. ed. London: Thames and Hudson, pp. 76–87.

Cook, S. F., 1946, A reconsideration of shellmounds with respect to population and nutrition. *American Antiquity* 12: 50–53.

Cook, S. F., 1947, The interrelation of population, food supply, and building in preconquest central Mexico. *American Antiquity* 13: 45–52.

Cook, S. F., 1949, *The historical demography and ecology of the Teotlalpan.* Berkeley: University of California Press, *Ibero-Americana* No. 33.

Cook, S. F., 1950, The quantitative investigation of Indian mounds. Berkeley: *University of California Publications in American Archaeology and Ethnology* 40: 223–261.

Cook, S. F. 1952, The fossilization of bone: organic components and water. Berkeley: Reports of the University of California Archaeological Survey No. 17.

Cook, S. F., 1959, The chemical analysis of fossil bone: individual variation. *American Journal of Physical Anthropology* 17: 109–115.

Cook, S. F., 1960, Dating prehistoric bone by chemical analysis. New York: Viking Fund Publications in Anthropology No. 28: 223–245.

Cook, S. F., 1962, Chemical analysis of the Hotchkiss site. Berkeley: Reports of the University of California Archaeological Survey No. 57, Part 1: 1–24.

Cook, S. F., 1965, The quantitative approach to the relation between population and settlement size. Berkeley: Reports of the University of California Archaeological Survey No. 64: 1–97.

Cook, S. F., 1966, Human sacrifice and warfare as factors in the demography of precolonial Mexico. In *Ancient Mesoamerica*, J. A. Graham, ed. Palo Alto, Calif.: Peek Publications, pp. 279–298. (Reprinted from *Human Biology* 18: 81–102 [1946].)

Cook, S. F., 1968, Relationships among houses, settlement areas, and population in aboriginal California. In *Settlement archaeology*, K.-C. Chang, ed. Palo Alto, Calif.: National Press, pp. 79–116.

Cook, S. F., 1971, *Essays in population history: Mexico and the Caribbean*, Vol. 1. Berkeley: University of California Press.

Cook, S. F., 1972, Prehistoric demography. *McCaleb Module in Anthropology.* Reading, Mass.: Addison-Wesley.

Cook, S. F., and W. Borah, 1963, *The population of central Mexico on the eve of the Spanish Conquest.* Berkeley: University of California Press, *Ibero-Americana* No. 45.

Cook, S. F., S. T. Brooks, and H. Ezra-Cohn, 1961, The process of fossilization. *Southwestern Journal of Anthropology* 17: 355–364.

Cook, S. F., and H. C. Ezra-Cohn, 1959, An evaluation of the fluorine dating method. *Southwestern Journal of Anthropology* 15: 276–290.

Cook, S. F., and R. F. Heizer, 1951, The physical analysis of nine Indian mounds of the Lower Sacramento Valley. Berkeley: *University of California Publications in American Archaeology and Ethnology*, 40: 281–312.

Cook, S. F., and R. F. Heizer, 1965, Studies on the chemical analysis of archaeological sites. *University of California Publications in Anthropology 2.* Berkeley.

Cook, S. F., and A. E. Treganza, 1947, The quantitative investigation of aboriginal sites: comparative physical and chemical analysis of two California Indian mounds. *American Antiquity* 13: 135–141.

Coon, C. S., 1951, *Cave explorations in Iran, 1949.* Philadelphia: University of Pennsylvania Museum, Museum Monographs.

Cooney, J. F., 1963, Assorted errors in art collecting. *Expedition* 6: 20–27.

Cornwall, I. W., 1958, *Soils for the archaeologist.* London: Phoenix House.

Cornwall, I. W., 1960, Soil investigations in the service of archaeology. New York: *Viking Fund Publications in Anthropology* No. 28: 265–299.

Cornwall, I. W., 1963, Soil-science helps the archaeologist. In *The scientist and archaeology*, E. Pyddoke, ed. London: Phoenix House, pp. 31–55.

Cornwall, I. W., 1974, *Bones for the archaeologist*, rev. ed. London: Dent.

Cottrell, L., 1957, *Lost cities*. London: R. Hale.

Coulborn, R., 1959, *The origin of civilized societies*. Princeton, N.J.: Princeton University Press.

Courtois, L., 1976, Examen au microscope petrographique des ceramiques archéologiques. *Notes et Monographies Archéologiques* No. 8. Paris: Centre de Recherches Archéologiques.

Coutts, J. F., 1970, The archaeology of Wilson's Promontory. *Australian Aboriginal Studies* No. 28. Canberra.

Cowan, R. A., 1967, Lake-margin ecologic exploitation in the Great Basin as demonstrated by an analysis of coprolites from Lovelock Cave, Nevada. Berkeley: *Reports of the University of California Archaeological Survey* No. 70: 21–35.

Cowan, T. M., 1970, Megalithic rings: their design construction. *Science* 168: 321–325.

Cowgill, G. L., 1964, The selection of samples from large sherd collections. *American Antiquity* 29: 467–473.

Cowgill, G. L., 1970, Sampling and reliability problems in archaeology. In *Archeologie et Calculateurs*, Paris: Editions du Centre National de la Recherche Scientifique, pp. 161–175.

Cowgills, G. L., 1972, Models, methods and techniques for seriation. In *Models in archaeology*, D. Clarke, ed. London: Methuen.

Cowgill, G. L., 1975a, On causes and consequences of ancient and modern population change. *American Anthropologist* 77: 505–526.

Cowgill, G. L., 1975b, Population pressure as a non-explanation. In *Population studies in archaeology and biological anthropology: a symposium*, A. C. Swedlund, ed. Memoir 30, Society for American Archaeology, pp. 127–131.

Cowgill, U. M., 1961, Soil fertility and the ancient Maya. *Transactions of the Connecticut Academy of Arts and Sciences* 42: 1–56.

Cowgill, U. M., 1962, An agricultural study of the southern Maya lowlands. *American Anthropologist* 64: 273–286.

Cowgill, U. M., 1971, Some comments on *Manihot* subsistence and the ancient Maya. *Southwestern Journal of Anthropology* 27: 51–63.

Craig, H., 1954, Carbon-14 in plants and relationships between carbon-13 and carbon-14 variations in nature. *Journal of Geology* 62: 115–149.

Cranstone, B. A. L., 1971, The Tifalmin: a 'Neolithic' people in New Guinea. *World Archaeology* 3: 132–142.

Crawford, O. G. S., 1955, *Said and done: the autobiography of an archaeologist*. London: Weidenfeld and Nicolson.

Crone, D. R., 1963, *Elementary photogrammetry*. London: Edward Arnold.

Crossland, R. A., 1957, Indo-European origins: the linguistic evidence. *Past and Present* 12: 16–46.

Crumley, C. L., 1976, Toward a locational definition of state systems of settlement. *American Anthropologist* 78: 59–73.

Culbert, T. P., ed., 1973, *The Classic Maya collapse*. Albuquerque: University of New Mexico Press.

Culbert, T. P., 1974, *The lost civilization: the story of the Classic Maya*. New York: Harper & Row.

Curtis, G. H., 1961, A clock for the ages: potassium-argon. *National Geographic Magazine* 120: 590–592.

Curtis, G. H., and J. H. Reynolds, 1958, Notes on the potassium-argon dating of sedimentary rocks. *Bulletin of the Geological Society of America* 69: 151–160.

Cutler, H. C., and L. W. Blake, 1973, *Plants from archaeological sites east of the Rockies*. St. Louis: Missouri Botanical Garden.

Damon, P. E., A. Long, and E. I. Wallick, 1972, Dendrochronological calibration of the carbon-14 time scale. *Proceedings of the Eighth International Conference on Radiocarbon Dating, Lower Hutt City*, 1: 45–59.

Daniel, G. E., 1943, *The three ages; an essay on archaeological method*. London: Cambridge.

Daniel, G. E., 1950, *A hundred years of archaeology*. London: Duckworth.

Daniel, G. E., 1960, *The prehistoric chambered tombs of France*. New York: McKay.

Daniel, G. E., 1962, *The idea of prehistory*. London: Watts.

Daniel, G. E., 1967, *The origins and growth of archaeology*. Baltimore: Penguin.

Daniel, G. E., 1968a, *The first civilizations: the archaeology of their origins*. London: Thames and Hudson.

Daniel, G. E., 1968b, *Man discovers his past*. New York: Crowell.

Daniel, G. E., 1971, From Worsaae to Childe: the models of prehistory. *Proceedings of the Prehistoric Society* 27: 140–153.

Daniel, G. E., 1975, *A hundred and fifty years of archaeology*, 2nd ed. London: Duckworth.

Dannenfeldt, K., 1959, Egypt and Egyptian antiquities in the Renaissance. *Studies in the Renaissance* 6: 7–27.

D'Aquili, E. G., 1972, *The biopsychological determinants of culture*. McCaleb Module in Anthropology. Reading, Mass.: Addison-Wesley.

Daumas, M., 1962, *Historie générale des techniques:* Vol. 1. *Les origines de la civilization technique*. Paris: Presses Universitaires.

Dauncey, K. D. M., 1952, Phosphate content of soils on archaeological sites. *Advancement of Science* 9: 33–36.

David, N., 1971, The Fulani compound and the archaeologist. *World Archaeology* 3: 111–131.

David, N., 1972, On the life span of pottery, type frequencies, and archaeological inference. *American Antiquity* 37: 141–142.

David, N., and H. Hennig, 1972, *The ethnography of pottery: a Fulani case seen in archaeological perspective*. Addison-Wesley Module in Anthropology No. 21. Reading, Mass.: Addison-Wesley.

Davis, J. T., 1960, An appraisal of certain speculations on prehistoric Pueblo subsistence. *Southwestern Journal of Anthropology* 16: 15–21.

Davis, J. T., 1961, Trade routes and economic exchange among the Indians of California. Berkeley: *Reports of the University of California Archaeological Survey No. 54.*

Davis, M. B., 1963, On the theory of pollen analysis. *American Journal of Science* 261: 897–912.

Dawkins, W. B., 1880, *Early man in Britain and his place in the Tertiary period.* London: Macmillan.

Dean, J. S., 1970, Aspects of Tsegi Phase social organization: a trial reconstruction. In *Reconstructing prehistoric pueblo societies*, W. A. Longacre, ed. Albuquerque: University of New Mexico Press, pp. 140–174.

DeBoer, W. R., 1974, Ceramic longevity and archaeological interpretation: an example from the Upper Ucayali, Peru. *American Antiquity* 39: 335–342.

Deetz, J., 1967, *Invitation to archaeology.* New York: Doubleday.

Deevy, E. S., Jr., R. F. Flint, and I. Rouse, 1967, *Radiocarbon measurements: comprehensive index, 1950–1965.* New Haven, Conn.: Yale University Press.

Derricourt, R. M., 1972, Human ecology and site resource analysis. Capetown, S.A.: South African Archaeological Society Goodwin Series No. 1: 21–25.

Desroches-Noblecourt, C., 1963, *Tutankhamen: life and death of a pharaoh.* London.

Deuel, L., 1961, *The treasures of time.* New York: Avon.

Deuel, L., 1967, *Conquistadors without swords.* New York: St. Martin's Press.

Deuel, L., 1969, *Flights into yesterday: the story of aerial archaeology.* New York: St. Martin's Press.

Dewez, M. C., 1974, New hypotheses concerning two engraved bones from LaGrotte de Remouchamps, Belgium. *World Archaeology* 5: 337–345.

Dibner, B., 1970, *Moving the obelisks.* Cambridge: MIT Press.

Dietz, E. F., 1955, Natural burial of artifacts. *American Antiquity* 20: 273–274.

Dietz, E. F., 1957, Phosphorus accumulation in soil of an Indian habitation site. *American Antiquity* 22: 405–409.

Dimbelby, G. W., 1965, Overton Down experimental earthwork. *Antiquity* 39: 134–136.

Dimbelby, G. W., 1967, *Plants and archaeology.* London: John Baker.

Dimbelby, G. W., 1969, Pollen analysis. In *Science in archaeology*, D. Brothwell and E. Higgs, eds., rev. ed. London: Thames and Hudson, pp. 167–177.

Di Peso, C., 1974, *Casas Grandes: a fallen trading center of the Gran Chichimeca*, 3 vols. Flagstaff: Northland Press.

Dittert, A. E., Jr., and F. Wendorf, 1963, *Procedural manual for archeological field research projects of the Museum of New Mexico.* Santa Fe: Museum of New Mexico, Papers in Anthropology, No. 12.

Dixon, J. E., J. R. Cann, and C. Renfrew, 1968, Obsidian and the origins of trade. *Scientific American* 218: 38–46.

Doberenz, A. R., and P. Matter, 1965, Nitrogen analyses of fossil bones. *Comparative Biochemistry and Physiology* 16: 253–258.

Dobyns, H. F., and H. Paul Thompson, 1966, Estimating aboriginal American population: an appraisal of techniques with a new hemispheric estimate (pp. 395–416); a technique using anthropological and biological data (pp. 417–449). *Current Anthropology* 7: 395–449.

Donnan, C., 1971, Ancient Peruvian potters' marks and their interpretation through ethnographic analogy. *American Antiquity* 36: 460–466.

Donnan, C. B., and C. W. Clewlow, 1974, *Ethnoarchaeology.* Institute of Archaeology Monograph No. IV. University of California at Los Angeles.

Dort, W., et al. 1965, Paleotemperatures and chronology at archaeological cave sites revealed by thermoluminescence. *Science* 150: 480–482.

Dozier, E. P., 1970, Making inferences from the present to the past. In *Reconstructing prehistoric pueblo societies*, W. A. Longacre, ed. Albuquerque: University of New Mexico Press, pp. 202–213.

Dray, W. H., 1957, *Laws and explanations in history*. London: Oxford.

Drier, R. W., 1961, Archaeology and some metallurgical investigative techniques. Ann Arbor: University of Michigan, *Anthropological Papers of the Museum of Anthropology*, No. 17: 134–147.

Driver, H. E., 1962. The contribution of A. L. Kroeber to culture area theory and practice. Bloomington: *Indiana University Publications in Anthropology and Linguistics*, Memoir No. 18.

Drucker, P., and E. Contreras, 1953, Site patterns in the eastern part of Olmec territory. *Journal of the Washington Academy of Science* 43: 389–396.

Dubos, R., 1976, Symbiosis between the earth and humankind. *Science* 193: 459–462.

Dufournier, D., 1976, Recherches sur la signification et l'interpretation des resultats des analyses chimiques des poteries anciennes (elements majeurs et mineurs). *Notes et Monographies Techniques No. 6*. Paris: Centre des Recherches Archéologiques.

Duignan, P., 1958, Early Jesuit Missionaries: a suggestion for further study. *American Anthropologist* 60: 725–732.

Dumas, F., 1962, *Deep water archaeology*. London: Routledge.

Dumond, D. E., 1961, Swidden agriculture and the rise of Maya civilization. *Southwestern Journal of Anthropology* 17: 301–316.

Durand, J. D., 1960, Mortality estimates from Roman tombstone inscriptions. *American Journal of Sociology* 65: 365–373.

Durkheim, É., 1949, *The division of labor in society*. New York: Free Press.

Eardley, A. J., 1942, *Aerial photographs: their use and interpretation*. New York: Harper & Row.

Eddy, F. W., and H. W. Dregne, 1964, Soil tests on alluvial and archaeological deposits, Navajo reservoir district. *El Palacio* 71: 5–21.

Edeine, B., 1956, Une methode pratique pour la détection aérienne des sites archéologiques, en particulier par la photographie sur films en couleurs et sur films infrarouges. *Bulletin de la Société Prehistorique Française* 53: 540–546.

Edwards, I. E. S., 1961, *The pyramids of Egypt*. Baltimore: Penguin.

Edwards, I. E. S., 1972, *The treasures of Tutankhamun*. New York: Viking.

Efimenko, P. P., 1958, *Kostienki I*. Leningrad: Akademia Nauk SSSR, Institut istorii materialnoi kulturj.

Eggan, F., 1952, The ethnological cultures of eastern United States and their archaeological backgrounds. In *Archeology of eastern United States*, J. B. Griffin, ed. Chicago: University of Chicago Press, pp. 35–45.

Eggan, F., 1966, *The American Indian*. Chicago: University of Chicago Press.

Ekholm, G. F., 1964, The problem of fakes in Pre-Columbian art. *Curator* 7: 19–32.

Ellefson, J. O., 1968, Personality and the biological nature of man. In *The study of personality*, E. Norbeck, D. Price-Williams, and W. M. McCord, eds. New York: Holt, Rinehart and Winston, pp. 137–149.

Ellis, Florence M., 1934, *The significance of the dated prehistory of Chetro Ketl.* Albuquerque: University of New Mexico Bulletin, Monograph Series, 1(1).

Elsasser, A. B., 1961, Archaeological evidence of shamanism in California and Nevada. Berkeley, Calif.: *Kroeber Anthropological Society Papers,* 24: 38–48.

Elsasser, A. B., and R. F. Heizer, 1966, Excavation of two northwestern California Coastal Sites. *University of California Archaeological Research Reports,* 67, pp. 1–149.

Emery, I., 1966, *The primary structure of fabrics: an illustrated classification.* Washington, D.C.: The Textile Museum.

Emery, W. B., 1961, *Archaic Egypt.* Baltimore: Penguin.

Emlen, J. M., 1966, Natural selection and human behavior. *Journal of Theoretical Biology* 12:410.

Emlen, J. M., 1967, On the importance of cultural and biological determinants in human behavior. *American Anthropologist* 67: 513–514.

Engel, C. G., and R. P. Sharp, 1958, Chemical data on desert varnish. *Bulletin of the Geological Society of America* 69: 487–518.

Engnell, I., 1967, *Studies in divine kingship in the ancient Near East.* Oxford: Blackwell.

Epstein, J. F., 1964, Towards the systematic description of chipped stone. Mexico City: *Actas y Memorias,* XXXV Congreso Internacional de Americanistes 1: 155–169.

Erasmus, C. J., 1968, Thoughts on upward collapse: an essay on explanation in anthropology. *Southwestern Journal of Anthropology* 24: 170–194.

Erdtman, G., 1943, *An introduction to pollen analysis.* New York: Ronald.

Evans, E. E., 1956, The ecology of peasant life in western Europe. In *Man's role in changing the face of the earth,* W. L. Thomas, ed. Chicago: University of Chicago Press, pp. 217–239.

Evans, J. G., 1969, Land and freshwater molluscs in archaeology: chronological aspects. *World Archaeology* 1: 170–183.

Evans, Joan, 1943, *Time and chance; the story of Arthur Evans and his forebears.* New York: McKay.

Evernden, J. F., and G. H. Curtis, 1965. The potassium-argon dating of late Cenozoic rocks in east Africa and Italy. *Current Anthropology* 6: 343–385.

Evernden, J. F., D. E. Savage, G. H. Curtis, and G. T. James, 1964, Potassium-argon dates and Cenozoic mammalian chronology of North America. *American Journal of Science* 262: 145–198.

Ewers, J. C., 1955, *The horse in Blackfoot Indian culture.* Washington, D.C.: Bulletin of the Bureau of American Ethnology, No. 159.

Eydoux, H. P., 1968, *History of archaeological discoveries,* London: Leisure Arts.

Eyre, S. R., and G. R. J. Jones, eds., 1966, *Geography as human ecology: methodology by example.* London: E. Arnold.

Faegri, K., and J. Iversen, 1964, *Textbook of modern pollen analysis.* Copenhagen: E. Munksgaard.

Fairman, H. W., 1972, Tutankhamun and the end of the 18th Dynasty. *Antiquity* 44: 15–18.

Farabee, W. C., 1919, Indian children's burial place in western Pennsylvania. *Museum Journal,* University of Pennsylvania, 10: 166–167.

Faul, H., 1971, Potassium-argon dating. In *Dating techniques for the archaeologist*, H. N. Michael and E. K. Ralph, eds. Cambridge, Mass.: MIT Press, pp. 157–163.

Faul, H., and G. A. Wagner, 1971, Fission track dating. In *Dating techniques for the archaeologist*, H. N. Michael and E. K. Ralph, eds. Cambridge, Mass.: MIT Press, pp. 152–156.

Finley, M. I., 1970, *Early Greece: The Bronze and Archaic Ages*. London: Chattos & Windus.

Finley, M. I., 1971, Archaeology and history. *Proceedings of the American Academy of Arts and Sciences* 100: 168–186.

Fitting, J. E., 1969, Settlement analysis in the Great Lakes region. *Southwestern Journal of Anthropology* 25: 360–377.

Fitting, J. E., 1973, *The development of North American archeology*. New York: Anchor Press/Doubleday.

Fitzhugh, W. W., 1972, Environmental archaeology and cultural systems in Hamilton Inlet, Labrador: a survey of the Central Labrador Coast from 3000 B.C. to the present. *Smithsonian Contributions to Anthropology* 16.

Flannery, K. V., 1966, The Postglacial "readaptation" as viewed from Mesoamerica. *American Antiquity* 31: 800–805.

Flannery, K. V., 1967a, Culture history v. cultural process: a debate in American archaeology. *Scientific American* 217: 119–122.

Flannery, K. V., 1967b, The vertebrate fauna and hunting patterns [in Tehuacan Valley]. In *The prehistory of the Tehuacan Valley*. Vol. 1, D. S. Byers, ed. Austin: University of Texas Press, pp. 132–177.

Flannery, K. V., 1968, Archeological systems theory and early Mesoamerica. In *Anthropological archeology in the Americas*, B. J. Meggers, ed. Washington, D.C.: The Anthropological Society of Washington, pp. 67–87.

Flannery, K. V., 1969, Origins and ecological effects of early domestication in Iran and the Near East. In *The domestication and exploitation of plants and animals*, P. J. Ucko and G. W. Dimbleby, eds. Chicago: Aldine, pp. 73–100.

Flannery, K. V., 1972a, Archeology with a capital S. In *Archeology today*, C. L. Redman, ed. New York: Wiley.

Flannery, K. V., 1972b, The cultural evolution of civilizations. *Annual Review of Ecology and Systematics*, F. Johnston and Michener, eds., pp. 399–426. Palo Alto: Annual Reviews, Inc.

Flannery, K. V., 1973, The origins of agriculture. *Annual Review of Anthropology* 2: 271–310. (B. J. Siegel, ed.)

Flannery, K. V., ed., 1976, *The Mesoamerican village*. New York: Seminar Press.

Flannery, K. V., A. V. T. Kirkby, M. J. Kirkby, and A. W. Williams, Jr., 1967, Farming systems and political growth in ancient Oaxaca. *Science* 158: 445–454.

Fleischer, R. L., P. B. Price, and R. M. Walker, 1965, Tracks of charged particles in solids. *Science* 149: 383–393.

Fleming, A., 1972, Models for the development of aristocratic society in the Early Bronze Age. In *The explanation of culture change*, C. Renfrew, ed. London: Duckworth.

Ford, J. A., 1938, A chronological method applicable to the Southeast. *American Antiquity* 3: 260–264.

Ford, J. A., 1954a, Comment on A. C. Spaulding, "Statistical techniques for the discovery of artifact types." *American Antiquity* 19: 390–391.

Ford, J. A., 1954b, On the concept of types. *American Anthropologist* 56: 42–54.

Ford, J. A., 1959, Eskimo prehistory in the vicinity of Point Barrow, Alaska. New York: *Anthropological Papers of the American Museum of Natural History* 47(Part 1).

Ford, J. A., 1962, *A quantitative method for deriving cultural chronology.* Pan American Union, Technical Manual, No. 1.

Ford, J. A., and G. R. Willey, 1949, Surface survey of the Viru Valley, Peru. New York: *Anthropological Papers of the American Museum of Natural History* 43(Part 1).

Ford, R. I., 1971a, Looting the past: an international scandal. *Science* 174: 727.

Ford, R. I., 1971b, *World dynamics.* Cambridge, Mass.: Wright-Allen Press.

Foster, G. M., 1960a, Archaeological implications of the modern pottery of Acatlan Pueblo, Mexico. *American Antiquity* 26: 205–214.

Foster, G. M., 1960b, Life-expectancy of utilitarian pottery in Tzintzuntzan, Michoácan, Mexico. *American Antiquity* 25: 606–609.

Frantz, A., 1950, Truth before beauty: or the incompleat photographer. *Archaeology* 3: 202–215.

Freeman, L. G., 1968. A theoretical framework for interpreting archeological materials. In *Man the hunter*, R. B. Lee and I. DeVore, eds. Chicago: Aldine, pp. 262–267.

Freeman, L. G., ed., 1971, New research in paleoanthropology: introduction. *American Anthropologist* 73: 1195–1197.

Fried, M. H., 1967, *The evolution of political society.* New York: Random House.

Friedman, I., and W. Long, 1976, Hydration rate of obsidian. *Science* 191: 347–352.

Friedman, I., R. L. Smith, and D. L. Clark, 1969, Obsidian dating. In *Science in archaeology*, D. Brothwell and E. Higgs, eds., rev. ed. London: Thames and Hudson, pp. 62–75.

Friedrich, J., 1957, *Extinct languages.* New York: Philosophical Library.

Friedrich, M. H., 1970, Design structure and social interaction: archaeological implications of an ethnographic analysis. *American Antiquity* 35: 332–343.

Frison, G. C., 1968, A functional analysis of certain chipped stone tools. *American Antiquity* 33: 149–155.

Fritts, H. C., 1965, Dendrochronology. In *The Quaternary of the United States*, H. E. Wright and D. G. Frey, eds. Princeton, N.J.: Princeton University Press, pp. 871–879.

Fritz, J. M., and F. Plog, 1970, The nature of archaeological explanation. *American Antiquity* 35: 405–412.

Frost, H., 1963, *Under the Mediterranean.* Englewood Cliffs, N.J.: Prentice-Hall.

Gasel, C., 1967, *Analysis of prehistoric economic patterns.* New York: Holt, Rinehart and Winston.

Garner, B., 1967, Models of urban geography and settlement location. In *Models in geography*, R. J. Chorley and P. Haggett, eds. London: Methuen, pp. 303–361.

Garrod, D. A. E., 1946. *Environment, tools, and man.* London: Cambridge.

Garrod, D., and D. M. A. Bate, 1937, *The Stone Age of Mount Carmel*, 2 vols. London: Oxford.

Gathercole, P., 1971, "Patterns in prehistory": an examination of the later thinking of V. Gordon Childe. *World Archaeology* 3: 225–232.

Gelfand, A. E., 1971, Seriation methods for archeological materials. *American Antiquity* 36: 263–274.

Genovés, S. T., 1969, Estimation of age and mortality. In *Science in archaeology*, D. Brothwell and E. Higgs, eds., rev. ed. London: Thames and Hudson, pp. 440–452.

Gentner, W., and H. J. Lippolt, 1969, The potassium-argon dating of Upper Tertiary and Pleistocene deposits. In *Science in archaeology*, D. Brothwell and E. Higgs, eds., rev. ed. London: Thames and Hudson, pp. 88–100.

Giddings, J. L., 1960, The archeology of Bering Strait. *Current Anthropology* 1: 121–138.

Giddings, J. L., 1962, Development of tree-ring dating as an archeological aid. In *Tree growth*, T. T. Koslowski, ed. New York: Ronald, pp. 119–132.

Gifford, J. C., 1960, The type-variety method of ceramic classification as an indicator of cultural phenomena. *American Antiquity* 25: 341–347.

Gilbert, B. M., 1973, *Mammalian osteo-archaeology: North America*. Missouri Archaeological Society, Spec. Publications. Columbia, Missouri.

Gimbutas, M., 1963, The Indo-Europeans: archeological problems. *American Anthropologist* 65: 815–836.

Gladwin, H. S., 1947, *Men out of Asia*. New York: McGraw-Hill.

Gladwin, W., and H. S. Gladwin, 1928, *A method for the designation of cultures and their variations*. Globe, Ariz.: Gila Pueblo Medallion Papers, No. 15.

Glass, B. P., 1951, *A key to the skulls of North American mammals*. Minneapolis: Burgess.

Glob, P., 1954, Lifelike man preserved 2,000 years in peat. *National Geographic Magazine* 105: 419–430.

Glob, P., 1969, *The bog people*. London: Faber and Faber.

Glock, W. S., 1937, *Principles and methods of tree-ring analysis*. Washington, D.C.: Carnegie Institution of Washington, Publication No. 486.

Glock, W. S., 1955, Tree growth: growth rings and climate. *The Botanical Review* 21: 73–188.

Goggin, J. M., 1960, Underwater archaeology: its nature and limitations. *American Antiquity* 25: 348–354.

Goodall, E., 1946, Domestic animals in rock art. *Transactions of the Rhodesia Science Association*, Salisbury 41: 57–62.

Goodwin, A. J. H., 1960, Chemical alteration (patination) of stone. *Viking Fund Publications in Anthropology* No. 28: 300–312.

Gould, R. A., 1968, Chipping stones in the outback. *Natural History* 77: 42–49.

Gould, R. A., 1969, Subsistence behavior among the Western Desert aborigines of Australia. *Oceania* 39: 253–274.

Gould, R. A., 1971, The archaeologist as ethnographer: a case from the Western Desert of Australia. *World Archaeology* (2): 143–177.

Gould, R. A., 1973, Australian archaeology in ecological and ethnographic perspective. *Warner Modular Publications* 7, pp. 1–33.

Grace, V. R., 1961, *Amphoras and the ancient wine trade*. Princeton, N.J.: American School of Classical Studies at Athens.

Grant, C., 1965, *The rock paintings of the Chumash*. Berkeley: University of California Press.

Grant, C., 1967, *Rock art of the American Indian*. New York: Crowell.

Grant, J., 1966, *A pillage of art*. New York: Roy.

Gray, J., and W. Smith, 1962, Fossil pollen and archaeology. *Archaeology* 15: 16–26.

Greene, J. C., 1961, *The death of Adam*. New York: Mentor.

Greenman, E. F., 1963, The Upper Paleolithic in the New World. *Current Anthropology* 4: 41–91.

Griffin, J. B., 1955, Chronology and dating processes. In *Yearbook of Anthropology*. New York: Wenner-Gren, pp. 133–148.

Griffin, J. B., 1960, Some prehistoric connections between Siberia and America. *Science* 131: 801–812.

Griffin, J. B., 1962, A discussion of prehistoric similarities and connections between the Arctic and the temperate zones of North America. In *Prehistoric cultural relations between the Arctic and temperate zones of North America,* J. M. Campbell, ed. Montreal: Arctic Institute of North America, Technical Paper No. 11, pp. 154–163.

Griffiths, J. G., 1956, Archaeology and Hesiod's five ages. *Journal of the History of Ideas* 17: 109–119.

Grigor'ev, G. P., 1967, A new reconstruction of above-ground dwelling of Kostenki I. *Current Anthropology* 8: 344–349.

Grimes, W. F., 1954, The scientific bias of archaeology. *The Advancement of Science*, London 10: 343–346.

Grinsell, L., P. Rahtz, and A. Warhurst, 1966, *The preparation of archaeological reports*. London: J. Baker.

Groff, D. W., 1971, Gas chromatography methods for bone fluorine and nitrogen composition. In *Science and archaeology*, R. H. Brill, ed. Cambridge, Mass.: MIT Press, pp. 272–278.

Gumerman, G. J., ed., 1971, The distribution of prehistoric population aggregates. *Prescott College Anthropological Reports* No. 1.

Gumerman, G. L. and T. R. Lyons, 1971, Archaeological methodology and remote sensing. *Science* 172: 126–132.

Gunda, B., 1949, Plant gathering in the economic life of Eurasia. *Southwestern Journal of Anthropology* 5: 369–378.

Haber, F. C., 1959, *The age of the world: Moses to Darwin*. Baltimore: Johns Hopkins Press.

Hack, J. T., 1942, *The changing physical environment of the Hopi Indians of Arizona*. Cambridge, Mass.: Harvard University, Papers of the Peabody Museum, 35(1).

Haggett, P., 1965, *Locational analysis in human geography*. London: E. Arnold.

Haines, F., 1938a, Where did the Plains Indians get their horses? *American Anthropologist* 40: 112–117.

Haines, F., 1938b, The northward spread of horses among the Plains Indians. *American Anthropologist* 40: 429–437.

Hall, A. D., and R. E. Fagen, 1956, Definition of system. *General Systems* 1: 18–28.

Hall, E. T., 1969, Dating pottery by thermoluminescence. In *Science in archaeology*, D. Brothwell and E. Higgs, eds., rev. ed. London: Thames and Hudson, pp. 106–108.

Hall, Edward T., 1966, *The hidden dimension*. New York: Doubleday.

Harber, F. C., 1959a, Fossils and the idea of a process of time in natural history. In *Forerunners of Darwin, 1745–1859*. B. Glass et al., eds. Baltimore: Johns Hopkins Press, pp. 222–261.

Harber, F. C., 1959b, Fossils and early cosmology. In *Forerunners of Darwin, 1745–1849*. B. Glass et al., eds. Baltimore: Johns Hopkins Press, pp. 222–261.

Hardesty, D. L., 1972, The human ecological niche. *American Anthropologist* 74: 458–466.

Hardin, G., 1968, The cybernetics of competition: a biologist's view of society. In *Modern systems research for the behavioral scientist*, W. Buckley, ed. Chicago: Aldine, pp. 449–459.

Hare, P. E., 1974, Amino acid dating—a history and an evaluation. *MASCA Newsletter* 10(1): 4–7. University Museum, University of Pennsylvania.

Harlan, J. R., 1967, A wild wheat harvest in Turkey. *Antiquity* 20: 197–201.

Harner, M. J., 1970, Population pressure and the social evolution of agriculturalists. *Southwestern Journal of Anthropology* 26: 67–86.

Harp, E., ed., 1975. *Photography in archaeological research*. Albuquerque: University of New Mexico Press.

Harpending, H., and J. Bertram, 1975, Human population dynamics in archaeological time: some simple models. *Society for American Antiquity, Memoir* 30: 82–91.

Harris, A. H., 1963, *Vertebrate remains and past environmental reconstruction in the Navajo reservoir district*. Santa Fe: Museum of New Mexico, Papers in Anthropology, No. 11.

Harris, D. R., 1969, Agricultural systems, ecosystems and the origins of agriculture. In *The domestication and exploitation of plants and animals*, P. J. Ucko and G. W. Dimbleby, eds. Chicago: Aldine, pp. 3–16.

Harris, E. C., 1975, The stratigraphic sequence: a question of time. *World Archaeology* 7: 109–121.

Harris, M., 1968, *The rise of anthropological theory*. New York: Crowell.

Harrison, M. W., 1945, The writing of American archaeology. *American Antiquity* 10: 331–339.

Harrison, R. G., and A. B. Abdalla, 1972, The remains of Tutankhamun. *Antiquity* 44: 8–14.

Harriss, J. C., 1971, Explanations in prehistory. *Proceedings of the Prehistoric Society* 37: 38–55.

Harvey, D., 1967, Models of the evolution of spatial patterns in human geography. In *Models in geography*, R. J. Chorley and P. Haggett, eds. London: Methuen, pp. 549–609.

Hassan, F. A., 1973, On mechanisms of population growth during the Neolithic. *Current Anthropology* 14: 535–542.

Hatch, M. P., 1971, An hypothesis on Olmec astronomy with special reference to the La Venta site. Berkeley: University of California, *Archaeological Research Facility, Contribution* 13: 1–64.

Haury, E. W., E. Antevs, and J. F. Lance, 1953, Artifacts with mammoth remains, Naco, Arizona. *American Antiquity* 19: 1–24.

Haury, E. W., E. B. Sayles, and W. W. Wasley, 1959, The Lehner mammoth site, southeastern Arizona. *American Antiquity* 25: 2–30.

Haviland, W. A., 1965, Prehistoric settlement at Tikal, Guatemala. *Expedition* 7: 14–23.

Haviland, W. A., 1967, Stature at Tikal, Guatemala: implications for ancient Maya demography and social organization. *American Antiquity* 32: 316–325.

Haviland, W. A., 1968, Ancient lowland Maya social organization. *Middle Ameri-*

can Research Institute Publ. No. 26. New Orleans: Tulane University.

Haviland, W. A., 1969, A new population estimate for Tikal, Guatemala. *American Antiquity* 34: 429–433.

Haviland, W. A., 1970, Tikal, Guatemala and Mesoamerican urbanism. *World Archaeology* 2: 186–198.

Haviland, W. A., 1972, Family size, prehistoric population estimates, and the ancient Maya. *American Antiquity* 37: 135–139.

Hawkes, C., 1973, Innocence retrieval in archaeology. *Antiquity* 47: 176–178.

Hawkes, J., 1963, *The world of the past.* 2 vols. New York: Knopf.

Hawkes, J., and L. Woolley, 1963, *History of mankind:* Vol. 1. *Prehistory and the beginnings of civilization.* New York: Harper & Row.

Hawkins, G. S., 1964, Stonehenge, a Neolithic computer. *Nature,* 202, 1258–1261.

Hawkins, G. S., 1965, *Stonehenge decoded.* New York: Doubleday.

Hawkins, G. S., 1973, *Beyond Stonehenge.* New York: Harper & Row.

Hawley, F. M., M. Pijoan, and C. A. Elkin, 1943, An inquiry into the food economy of Zia Pueblo. *American Anthropologist* 45: 547–556.

Hayek, F. A., 1955, Degrees of explanation. *British Journal of Philosophical Science* 6: 209–225.

Hayes, A. C., 1964, *The archaeological survey of Wetherill Mesa.* Washington, D.C.: National Park Service, Archeological Research Series, No. 7-A.

Haynes, C. V., 1966, Radiocarbon samples: chemical removal of plant contaminants. *Science* 151: 1391–1392.

Heider, K. G., 1967, Archaeological assumptions and ethnographical facts; a cautionary tale from New Guinea. *Southwestern Journal of Anthropology* 23: 52–64.

Heine-Geldern, R., 1954, Die Asiatische Herkunft der Südamerikanischen Metalltechnik. *Paideuma* 5: 347–423.

Heine-Geldern, R., and G. Ekholm, 1951, Significant parallels in the symbolic arts of southern Asia and Middle America. In *The civilizations of ancient America,* Sol Tax, ed. Selected Papers of the 29th International Congress of Americanists, pp. 299–309.

Heizer, R. F., 1941a, The direct-historical approach in California archaeology. *American Antiquity* 7: 98–122, 141–146.

Heizer, R. F., 1941b, Aboriginal trade between the Southwest and California. *Southwest Museum Masterkey* 15: 185–188.

Heizer, R. F., 1951, A prehistoric Yurok ceremonial site (Hum-174). Berkeley: *Reports of the University of California Archaeological Survey* 11: 1–4.

Heizer, R. F., 1953, Long-range dating in archaeology. In *Anthropology today,* A. L. Kroeber, chairman. Chicago: University of Chicago Press, pp. 3–42.

Heizer, R. F., ed., 1959, *The archaeologist at work.* New York: Harper & Row.

Heizer, R. F., 1960a, Agriculture and the theocratic state in lowland southeastern Mexico. *American Antiquity* 25: 215–222.

Heizer, R. F., ed., 1960b, Physical analysis of habitation residues. In *The application of quantitative methods in archaeology.* Viking Fund Publications in Anthropology, No. 28: 93–157.

Heizer, R. F., 1962a, The background of Thomsen's three age system. *Technology and Culture* 3: 259–266.

Heizer, R. F., 1962b, Village shifts and tribal spreads in California prehistory. *Southwest Museum Masterkey* 36: 60–67.

Heizer, R. F., 1963, Domestic fuel in primitive society. *Journal of the Royal Anthropological Institute* 93: 186–193.

Heizer, R. F., 1966a, Ancient heavy transport, methods and achievements. *Science* 153: 821–830.

Heizer, R. F., 1966b, Salvage and other archaeology. *Southwest Museum Masterkey* 40: 54–60.

Heizer, R. F., 1969, *Man's discovery of his past.* Palo Alto, Calif.: Peek Publications.

Heizer, R. F., 1975a, Some thoughts on California archaeology at the moment. *Journal of New World Archaeology* 1(1).

Heizer, R. F., 1975b, *The archaeologist at work.* Westport: Greenwood Press.

Heizer, R. F., In press, Man, the hunter-gatherer: food availability vs. biological factors. In *Progress in human nutrition,* Vol. 2, S. Margen, ed. Westport, Conn.: Avi Publishers.

Heizer, R. F., and M. A. Baumhoff, 1959, Great Basin petroglyphs and prehistoric game trails. *Science* 129: 904–905.

Heizer, R. F., and M. A. Baumhoff, 1962, *Prehistoric rock art of Nevada and eastern California.* Berkeley: University of California Press.

Heizer, R. F., and C. W. Clewlow, 1973, *Prehistoric rock art of California.* 2 vols. Ramona: Ballena Press.

Heizer, R. F., and S. F. Cook, 1952. Fluorine and other chemical tests of some North American human and fossil bones. *American Journal of Physical Anthropology* 10: 289–304.

Heizer, R. F., and A. B. Elasser, 1956, Excavation of two northwestern California coastal sites. *Reports of the University of California Archaeological Survey* No. 67: 1–150. Berkeley.

Heizer, R. F., and J. Graham, eds., 1971, *Observations on the emergence of civilization in Mesoamerica.* Berkeley: University of California, Archaeological Research Facility, Contribution No. 11.

Heizer, R. F., et al., 1973, The colossi of Memnon revisited. *Science* 182: 1219–1225.

Heizer, R. F., and A. D. Krieger, 1956, The archaeology of Humboldt Cave, Churchill County, Nevada. Berkeley: *University of California Publications in American Archaeology and Ethnology,* 47: 1–190.

Heizer, R. F., and L. K. Napton, 1970, *Archaeology and the prehistoric Great Basin subsistence regime as seen from Lovelock Cave, Nevada.* Berkeley: University of California, Archaeological Research Facility, Contribution No. 10.

Helbaek, H., 1951, Seeds of weeds as food in the pre-Roman Iron Age. *Kuml,* 1951: 65–74. Aarhus.

Helbaek, H., 1964, Early Hassunan vegetable food at Tell es Sawwan near Samarra. *Sumer* 20: 45–48.

Helbaek, H., 1969, Paleo-ethnobotany. In *Science in archaeology,* D. Brothwell and E. Higgs, eds., rev. ed. London: Thames and Hudson, pp. 206–214.

Helm, J., 1962, The ecological approach in anthropology. *American Journal of Sociology* 47: 630–639.

Hempel, C. G., 1951, General system theory and the unity of science. *Human Biology* 23: 313–322.

Hempel, C. G., 1952, Fundamentals of concept formation in empirical science. Chicago: University of Chicago Press, *International Encyclopedia of Unified Science, Foundations of the Unity of Science,* 2(7).

Hempel, C. G., 1965, *Aspects of scientific explanation, and other essays in the philosophy of science.* New York: Free Press.

Hempel, C. G., 1966, *Philosophy of natural science.* Englewood Cliffs, N.J.: Prentice-Hall.

Hempel, C. G., and P. Oppenheim, 1948, Studies in the logic of explanation. *Philosophy of Science* 15: 135–175.

Hencken, H. O., 1955, Indo-European languages and archeology. Washington, D.C.: *American Anthropological Association, Memoir* No. 84.

Herrmann, Georgina, 1968, Lapis lazuli: the early phases of its trade. *Iraq* 30: 21–57.

Hesse, A., 1966, *Prospections géophysiques à faible profondeur: applications à l'archéologie.* Paris: Dunod.

Hester, J. J., 1962, *Early Navajo migrations and acculturation in the Southwest.* Santa Fe, N.M.: Museum of New Mexico, Papers in Anthropology, No. 6.

Hester, T. R., 1970, A study of wear patterns on hafted and unhafted bifaces from two Nevada caves. Berkeley: University of California, *Archaeological Research Facility, Contribution* No. 7, pp. 44–54.

Hester, T. R., and R. F. Heizer, 1972, Problems in the functional interpretation of artifacts: scraper planes from Mitla and Yagul, Oaxaca. Berkeley: University of California, *Archaeological Research Facility, Contribution* No. 14: 107–123.

Hester, T. R., and R. F. Heizer, 1973, *Bibliography of archaeology I: experiments, lithic technology and petrography.* Addison-Wesley Module in Anthropology No. 29. Reading, Mass.: Addison-Wesley.

Hester, T. R., R. F. Heizer, and J. A. Graham, 1975, *Field methods in archaeology.* Palo Alto: Mayfield Press.

Hester, T. R., R. F. Heizer, and R. N. Jack, 1971, Technology and geologic sources of obsidian from Cerro de las Mesas, Veracruz, Mexico, with observations on Olmec trade. Berkeley: University of California, *Archaeological Research Facility, Contribution* No. 13, pp. 133–142.

Heyerdahl, T., 1959, *Aku-Aku: the secret of Easter Island.* New York: Rand McNally.

Heyerdahl, T., 1963, Feasible ocean routes to and from the Americas in pre-Columbian times. *American Antiquity* 28: 482–488.

Higgs, E. S., 1965, Faunal fluctuations and climate in Libya. In *Background to evolution in Africa,* W. J. Bishop and J. D. Clark, eds. Chicago: University of Chicago Press, pp. 149–157.

Higgs, E. S., 1970, The paleolithic culture sequence in western Iran. *Proceedings, VII International Congress of Prehistoric and Protohistoric Sciences, Prague, 1966,* pp. 286–292.

Higgs, E. S., ed., 1972, *Papers in economic prehistory.* Cambridge University Press.

Higgs, E. S., ed., 1975, *Paleoeconomy.* Cambridge University Press.

Hill, J. N., 1966, A prehistoric community in eastern Arizona. *Southwestern Journal of Anthropology* 22: 9–30.

Hill, J. N., 1967, The problem of sampling. *Fieldiana, Anthropology,* Chicago: Field Museum of Natural History 57: 145–157.

Hill, J. N., 1970, Prehistoric social organization in the American Southwest: theory and method. In *Reconstructing prehistoric Pueblo societies,* W. A. Longacre, ed. Albuquerque: University of New Mexico Press, pp. 11–58.

Hill, W. W., 1948, Navajo trading and trading ritual: a study of cultural dynamics. *Southwestern Journal of Anthropology* 4: 371–396.

Hodder, I., and M. Hassal, 1971, The non-random spacing of Romano-British walled towns. *Man* 6: 391–407.

Hodges, H., 1970, *Technology in the ancient world.* New York: Knopf.

Hodges, H. W., 1964, *Artifacts: an introduction to early materials and technology.* London: J. Baker.

Hodgson, J., 1822, On the study of antiquities. *Archaeologia Aeliana* 1: 9–19.

Hoebel, E. A., 1972, *Anthropology: the study of man,* 4th ed. New York: McGraw-Hill.

Hoffman, J. M., and L. Brunker, 1976, Studies in California paleopathology. Berkeley: University of California, *Archaeological Research Facility, Contribution* No. 30.

Hoijer, H., 1956a, Lexicostatistics: a critique. *Language* 32: 49–60.

Hoijer, H., 1956b, The chronology of the Athapaskan languages. *International Journal of American Linguistics* 22: 219–232.

Hokr, Z., 1951, A method of quantitative determination of the climate in the Quaternary Period by means of mammal association. *Paleontology, Sbornik Geological Survey, Czechoslovakia* 18: 209–218.

Hole, F., 1962, Archeological survey and excavation in Iran in 1961. *Science* 137: 524–526.

Hole, F., 1966, Investigating the origins of Mesopotamian civilization. *Science* 153: 605–611.

Hole, F., 1968, Prehistory of southwestern Iran: a preliminary report. *Proceedings of the Prehistoric Society* 33: 147–206.

Hole, F., 1970, The paleolithic culture sequence in western Iran. *Proceedings, VII International Congress of Prehistoric and Protohistoric Sciences,* Prague, 1966, pp. 286–292.

Hole, F., 1971, Approaching typology rationally. *The Record* 27:3.

Hole, F., 1972, Questions of theory in the explanation of culture change in prehistory. In *The explanation of culture change,* C. Renfrew. ed. London: Duckworth.

Hole, F., n.d., Pastoral nomadism in western Iran. In, *The vestigial image: explorations in ethnoarchaeology,* R. A. Gould, ed. Santa Fe: School of American Research.

Hole, F., K. V. Flannery, and J. A. Neely, 1969, *Prehistory and human ecology of the Deh Luran Plain.* Ann Arbor: University of Michigan, Museum of Anthropology, Memoirs No. 1.

Hole, F., and M. Shaw, 1967. *Computer analysis of chronological seriation.* Houston: Rice University Studies, 53(3).

Holmes, W. H., 1913, The relation of archeology to ethnology. *American Anthropologist* 15: 566–567.

Holmes, W. H., 1919, *Handbook of aboriginal American antiquities.* Washington, D.C.: Bulletin of the Bureau of American Ethnology, No. 60.

Holmquist, J. D., and A. H. Wheeler, 1964, *Diving into the past.* St. Paul: The Minnesota Historical Society and the Council of Underwater Archaeology.

Hope-Taylor, B., 1966, Archaeological draughtmanship: Part II. *Antiquity* 40: 107–113.

Hope-Taylor, B., 1967, Archaeological draughtmanship: Part III. *Antiquity* 41: 181–189.

Hopkins, D. M., 1959, Cenozoic history of the Bering Land Bridge. *Science* 129: 1519–1528.

Houghton, W., 1877, On the mammalia of the Assyrian sculptures. London: *Society of Biblical Archaeology Transactions* 5: 229–383.

Howells, W. W., 1960, Estimating population numbers through archaeological and skeletal remains. New York: *Viking Fund Publications in Anthropology* No. 28: 158–180.

Howells, W. W., 1966, Population distances: biological, linguistic, geographical, and environmental. *Current Anthropology* 7: 531–540.

Hoyle, F., 1966, Speculation on Stonehenge. *Antiquity* 40: 262–276.

Hoyle, F., 1972, *From Stonehenge to modern cosmology.* San Francisco: Freeman.

Huntington. E., 1959, *Mainsprings of civilization.* New York: Mentor.

Hurst, V. J., and A. R. Kelly, 1961, Patination of cultural flints. *Science* 134: 251–256.

Hutchinson, G. E., 1972, Long Meg reconsidered. *American Scientist* 60: 24–31, 210–219.

Huxley, J. S., 1955, Evolution, cultural and biological. In *Yearbook of anthropology, 1955.* New York: Wenner-Gren Foundation for Anthropological Research, pp. 3–25.

Hymes, D. H., 1960, Lexicostatistics so far. *Current Anthropology* 1: 3–44.

Irwin, H. T., D. J. Hurd, and R. M. LaJeunesse, 1971, *Description and measurement in anthropology.* Pullman: Washington State University, Laboratory of Anthropology Report of Investigations, No. 48.

Isaac, G., 1967, Towards the interpretation of occupation debris: some experiments and observations. Berkeley: *Kroeber Anthropological Society Papers,* No. 37: 31–57.

Isaac, G., 1971a, The diet of early man: aspects of archaeological evidence from Lower and Middle Pleistocene sites in Africa. *World Archaeology* 2: 278–279.

Isaac, G., 1971b, Whither archaeology? *Antiquity* 45: 123–129.

Isham, L. B., 1965, Preparation of drawings for paleontologic publication. In *Handbook of paleontological techniques.* San Francisco: Freeman, pp. 459–468.

James, E. O., 1962, *Prehistoric religion: a study in prehistoric archaeology.* New York: Barnes & Noble.

Jarman, M., 1971, Culture and economy in the North Italian Neolithic. *World Archaeology* 2: 255–265.

Jelinek, A. J., 1966, Correlation of archaeological and palynological data. *Science* 152: 1507–1509.

Jelinek, A. J., and J. E. Fittings, 1965, eds., *Studies in the natural radioactivity of prehistoric materials.* Ann Arbor, Mich.: University of Michigan, Anthropological Papers of the Museum of Anthropology, No. 25.

Jennings, J. D., 1957, *Danger Cave.* Salt Lake City: University of Utah, Society for American Archaeology, Memoir No. 14.

Jennings, J. D., 1964, The desert west. In *Prehistoric man in the New World,* J. D. Jennings and E. Norbeck, eds. Chicago: University of Chicago Press (for William Marsh Rice University), pp. 149–174.

Jelks, E. B., 1975, *The use and misuse of random sampling in archeology.* Normal, Illinois: Jet Publishing Co.

Jett, S. C., 1964, Pueblo Indian migrations: an evaluation of the possible physical and cultural determinants. *American Antiquity* 29: 281–299.

Jewell, P. A., and G. W. Dimbleby, 1966. The experimental earthwork on Overton Down, Wiltshire, England. *Proceedings of the Prehistoric Society* 32: 313–342.

John, D. H. O., 1965, *Photography on expeditions*. London: Focal Press.

Johnson, G. A., 1973, *Local exchange and early state development in Southwestern Iran*. University of Michigan Museum of Anthropology, Anthropological Papers No. 51. Ann Arbor: University Press.

Johnson, G. A., 1975, Locational analysis and the investigation of Uruk local exchange systems. In *Ancient civilizations and trade*, Lamberg-Karlovsky and J. Sabloff, eds. Albuquerque: University of New Mexico Press.

Johnson, I. W., 1967, Textiles. In *The prehistory of the Tehuacan Valley: Vol. 2. Nonceramic artifacts*, R. S. MacNeish, A. Nelken-Terner, and I. W. Johnson, eds. Austin: University of Texas Press, pp. 189–226.

Jolly, C. J., 1970, The seed-eaters: a new model of hominid differentiation based on a baboon analogy. *Man* 5: 5–26.

Jones, E., 1966, *Human geography: an introduction to man and his world*. New York: Praeger.

Jones, T. B., 1967, *Paths into the ancient past*. New York: Free Press.

Jope, E. M., 1953, History, archaeology and petrology. *Advancement of Science* 9: 432–435.

Judd, N. M., 1959, The braced-up cliff at Pueblo Bonito. Washington, D.C.: *Smithsonian Institution Annual Report for 1958*, pp. 501–511.

Kamen, M. D., 1963, Early history of carbon-14. *Science* 140: 584–590.

Kamen, M. D., 1972, The night carbon-14 was discovered. *Environment Southwest*, No. 448, pp. 11–112. San Diego Museum of Natural History.

Kapitan, G., 1966, *A bibliography of underwater archaeology*. Chicago: Argonaut.

Katsui, Y., and Y. Kondo, 1965, Dating of stone implements by using hydration layers of obsidian. *Japanese Journal of Geology and Geography* 36: 45–60.

Keely, L. H., 1974, Technique and methodology in microwear studies: a critical review. *World Archaeology* 5: 323–336.

Kelly, T. C., and T. R. Hester, 1976, Archaeological investigations at sites in the upper Cibolo Creek Watershed, central Texas. Center for Archaeological Research, University of Texas at San Antonio, *Archaeological Survey Report* No. 17.

Keesing, R. M., 1974, Theories of culture. *Annual Review of Anthropology* 3: 73–97. (Siegel, B. J., ed.)

Kehoe, T. F., 1958, Tipi rings: the "direct ethnological" approach applied to an archaeological problem. *American Anthropologist* 60: 861–873.

Kehoe, T. F., and A. B. Kehoe, 1960, Observations in the butchering technique at a prehistoric bison kill in Montana. *American Antiquity* 25: 420–423.

Keith, M. L., 1964, Radiocarbon dating of mollusk shells: a reply. *Science* 144: 890.

Keith, M. L., and G. M. Anderson, 1963, Radiocarbon dating: fictitious results with mollusk shells. *Science* 141: 637–638.

Kelley, D. H., 1962, A history of the decipherment of Maya script. *Anthropological Linguistics* 4(8): 1–48.

Kemp, W. B., 1971, The flow of energy in a hunting society. *Scientific American* 224: 105–115.

Kendrick, T. D., 1950, *British antiquity*. London: Methuen.

Kenrick, P., 1971, Aids to the drawing of finds. *Antiquity* 45: 205–209.

Kenyon, A. S., 1927, Stone implements on aboriginal camping grounds. *Victorian Naturalist* 43: 280–285.

Kenyon, K., 1957, *Digging up Jericho*. London: Ben.

Kenyon, K., 1961, *Beginning in archaeology*, rev. ed. New York: Praeger.

Kerley, E. R., and W. M. Bass, 1967, Paleopathology: meeting ground for many disciplines. *Science* 157: 638–643.

Kidder, A. V., 1958, Pecos, New Mexico: archaeological notes. Andover, Mass.: *Papers of the R. S. Peabody Foundation for Archaeology*, Vol. 5.

Kikuchi, W. K., 1976, Prehistoric Hawaiian fishponds. *Science* 193: 295–299.

Klejn, L., 1972, Marxism, systemic approach and archaeology. In *The explanation of culture change*, C. Renfrew, ed. London: Duckworth.

Kliks, M., 1975, Paleoepidemiological studies in Great Basin coprolites: estimation of dietary fiber intake and evaluation of the ingestion of anthelmintic plant substances. Berkeley: University of California, *Archaeological Research Facility, Contribution*.

Kloiber, A., 1957, *Die Gräberfelder von Lauriacum; das Ziegelfeld*. Linz und Donau, Austria: Oberösterreichischer Landesverlag.

Klopfer, P. H., 1962, *Behavioral aspects of ecology*. Englewood, N.J.: Prentice-Hall.

Kluckhohn, C., 1939, The place of theory in anthropological studies. *Philosophy of Science* 6: 328–344.

Kluckhohn, C., and W. Kelly, 1945, The concept of culture. In *The science of man in the world crisis*, Ralph Linton, ed. New York: Columbia University Press, pp. 78–106.

Kobayashi, T., and P. Bleed, 1971, Recording and illustrating ceramic surfaces with Tahukon rubbings. *Plains Anthropologist* 16: 219–221.

Kopper, J., 1976, Paleomagnetic dating and statigraphic interpretation in archeology. *MASCA Newsletter* 12(1). University Museum, University of Pennsylvania.

Kopper, J., and K. Creer, 1973, Cova dets Alexandres: paleomagnetic dating and archeological interpretation of its sediments. *Caves and Karsts* 15: 13–20.

Kosambi, D. D., 1967, Living prehistory in India. *Scientific American* 216: 104ff.

Kossinna, G., 1941, *Die Deutsche Vorgeschichte*. Leipzig: Barth (Mannus Bücherei). No. 9. Printed 1912, 1914, 1921, 1925, 1933, 1934, 1936.

Krieger, A. D., 1944, The typological concept. *American Antiquity* 9: 271–288.

Krieger, A. D., 1960, Archaeological typology in theory and practice. In *Selected Papers of the Fifth International Congress of Anthropology and Ethnological Sciences*, Philadelphia, pp. 141–151.

Kroeber, A. L., 1917, The superorganic. *American Anthropologist* 19: 163–213 (reprinted in Kroeber 1952).

Kroeber, A. L., 1927, Disposal of the dead. *American Anthropologist* 29: 308–315.

Kroeber, A. L., 1931, Historical reconstruction of culture growths and organic evolution. *American Anthropologist* 33: 149–156.

Kroeber, A. L., 1935, History and science in anthropology. *American Anthropologist* 37: 539–569.

Kroeber, A. L., 1936, Culture element distributions: III. area and climax. Berkeley: *University of California Publications in American Archaeology and Ethnology*, 37(3).

Kroeber, A. L., 1943, Structure, function and pattern in biology and anthropology. *Scientific Monthly* 56: 105–113.

Kroeber, A. L., 1944, *Configurations of culture growth*. Berkeley: University of California Press.

Kroeber, A.L., 1952, *The nature of culture*. Chicago: University of Chicago Press.

Kroeber, A. L., 1953, The delimitation of civilizations. *Journal of the History of Ideas* 14: 264–275.

Kroeber, A. L., 1955, Linguistic time depth results so far and their meaning. *International Journal of American Linguistics* 21: 91–104.

Kroeber, A. L., 1957a, An anthropologist looks at history. *Pacific Historical Review* 26: 281–287.

Kroeber, A. L., 1957b, What ethnography is. Berkeley: *University of California Publications in American Archaeology and Ethnology* 47: 191–204.

Kroeber, A. L., 1962, *A roster of civilizations and culture*. New York: Viking Fund Publications in Anthropology, No. 33.

Kroeber, A. L., 1963, *Cultural and natural areas of native North America*. Berkeley: University of California Press. (Originally published in *University of California Publications in American Archaeology and Ethnology* 38: 1–242.)

Kroeber, A. L., 1963, *Culture: a critical review of concepts and definitions*. New York: Random House.

Kroeber, A. L., and C. Kluckhohn, 1952, Culture: a critical review of concepts and definitions. Cambridge, Mass.: Harvard University, *Papers of the Peabody Museum*, 47(1).

Krogh, A., and M. Krogh, 1915, A study of the diet and metabolism of Eskimos undertaken in 1908 on an expedition to Greenland. *Meddelelser om Grönland* 2: 1–52.

Kryzwicki, L., 1934, *Primitive society and its vital statistics*, H. E. Kennedy and A. Truszkowski, trans. London: Macmillan.

Kuhn, E., 1938, Zur quantitativen Analyse der Haustierwelt der Pfahlbauten der Schweiz. *Vierteljahresschrift der Naturforschenden Gesellschaft Zürich* 83: 253–263.

Kuhn, T. S., 1962, *The structure of scientific revolutions*. Chicago: University of Chicago Press.

Laming-Emperaire, A., 1963, *L'Archéologie préhistorique*. Paris: Editions du Seuil.

Lane, R. A., and A. J. Sublett, 1972, Osteology of social organization: residence pattern. *American Antiquity* 37: 186–201.

Lange, F. W., 1971, Marine resources: a viable subsistence alternative for the prehistoric lowland Maya. *American Anthropologist* 73: 619–639.

Lartet, E., and C. Gaillard, 1907, La faune momifée de l'ancienne Egypte. *Archives du Musée Historie Naturelle de Lyon* 9: 1–130.

Laslett, P., 1965, The history of population and social structure. *International Social Science Journal* 17: 582–593.

Lasselberry, S. E., 1974, Further refinement of formulae for determining population from floor area. *World Archaeology* 6: 117–122.

Lauer, P. K., 1971, Changing patterns of pottery trade to the Trobriand Islands. *World Archaeology* 3: 197–209.

Lawson, C. A., 1961, Language, communication, and biological organization. *General Systems* 8: 107–116.

Layard, A. H., 1849, *Nineveh and its remains*. New York: Putnam.

Layard, A. H., 1853, *Discoveries in the ruins of Nineveh and Babylon*, New York: Putnam.

Layard, A. H., 1903, *Sir A. Henry Layard, G. C. B.; D. C. L.; Autobiography and letters*. London: J. Murray.

Leach, E., 1961, *Rethinking anthropology*. London University School of Economics and Political Science. Monographs of Social Anthropology, No. 22. (London: Athlone Press.)

Lee, G. B., 1969, Pedological investigations at Mill Creek, Iowa, archaeological sites. *Journal of the Iowa Archaeological Society* 15:318–332.

Lee, R. B., 1968, What hunters do for a living, or, How to make out on scarce resources. In *Man the hunter*, R. B. Lee and I. DeVore, eds. Chicago: Aldine, pp. 30–48.

Lee, R. B., and I. DeVore, eds., 1968, *Man the hunter*. Chicago: Aldine.

Lee, R. F., 1970, *The Antiquities Act of 1906*. Washington, D.C.: National Park Service, Office of History and Historic Architecture, Eastern Service Center.

Leone, M. P., ed., 1972, *Contemporary archaeology: a guide to theory and contributions*. Carbondale: Southern Illinois University Press.

Leonhardy, F., 1966, *Domebo: a paleo-Indian kill in the prairie-plains*. Lawton, Oklahoma: Museum of the Great Plains, Contribution No. 1.

Leon-Portilla, M., 1973, *Time and reality in the thought of the Maya*. Boston: Beacon Press.

Lerici, C. M., 1959, Periscope camera pierces ancient tombs to reveal 2,500 year old frescoes. *National Geographic Magazine* 116: 336–351.

Leroi-Gourhan, A., 1943, *L'Homme et la matière*. Paris: Albin Michel.

Leroi-Gourhan, A., 1967, *Treasures of prehistoric art*. New York: Abrams.

Leroi-Gourhan, A., 1968, The evolution of Paleolithic art. *Scientific American* 218: 58ff.

Lester, J. D., 1967, *Writing research reports: a complete guide*. Glenview, Ill.: Scott, Foresman and Clark.

Lévi-Strauss, C., 1963, *Structural anthropology*. New York: Basic Books.

Lewis, T. M. N., and M. Kneberg, 1946, *Hiwassee island*. Knoxville: University of Tennessee Press.

Libby, W. F., 1955, *Radiocarbon dating*, 2d ed. Chicago: University of Chicago Press.

Libby, W. F., 1961, Radiocarbon dating. *Science* 133: 621–629.

Libby, W. F., 1963, Accuracy of radiocarbon dates. *Science* 140: 278–280.

Limbrey, S., 1972, *Soil science in archaeology*. New York: Seminar Press.

Linné, S., 1955, The Bering Isthmus—bridge between Asia and America. *Ethnos* 20: 210–215.

Lipe, W. D., 1970, Anasazi communities in the Red Rock Plateau, Southeastern Utah. In *Reconstructing prehistoric pueblo societies*, W. A. Longacre, ed. Albuquerque: University of New Mexico Press, pp. 84–139.

Lipson, J., 1958, Potassium-argon dating of sedimentary rocks. *Bulletin of the Geological Society of America* 69: 137–150.

Lloyd, S., 1955, *Foundations in the dust: a story of Mesopotamian exploration*. Baltimore: Penguin.

Lloyd, S., 1963, *Mounds of the Near East*. Edinburgh: Edinburgh University Press.

Loftus, W. K., 1858, Warkah: its ruins and remains. *Transactions of the Royal Society of Literature* (Series No. 2) 6: 1–64.

Longacre, W. A., 1964, Archeology as anthropology: a case study. *Science* 144: 1454–1455.

Longacre, W. A., 1970, A historical review. In *Reconstructing prehistoric pueblo societies,* W. A. Longacre, ed. Albuquerque: University of New Mexico Press, pp. 1–10.

Longacre, W. A., 1974, Kalinga pottery-making: the evolution of a research design. In *Frontiers of anthropology,* M. Leaf, ed. New York: Van Nostrand, pp. 51–67.

Longacre, W. A., and J. E. Ayres, 1968, Archeological lessons from an Apache wickiup. In *New perspectives in archeology,* S. R. Binford and L. R. Binford, eds. Chicago: Aldine, pp. 151–159.

Lösch, A., 1954, *The economics of location.* New Haven, Conn.: Yale University Press.

Lothrop, S. K., 1942, *Pottery of the Sitio Conte and other archaeological sites.* Cambridge, Mass.: Harvard University, Memoirs of the Peabody Museum, Vol. 8.

Lotspeich, F. B., 1961, *Soil science in the service of archaeology.* Santa Fe, N.M.: Fort Burgwin Research Center, Publication No. 1: 137–144.

Lumley, H. de, 1966, Les fouilles de Terra Amata à Nice (A.-M.). *Bulletin du Musée d'Anthropologie Préhistorique de Monaco* 13: 29–52.

Lyell, C., 1863, *The geological evidences of the antiquity of man,* 2nd. American ed. Philadelphia: Lippincott.

Lyell, C., 1872, *Principles of geology,* 11th ed., 2 vols. New York: Appleton.

Lynch, B. D., and T. F. Lynch, 1968, The beginnings of a scientific approach to prehistoric archaeology in seventeenth and eighteenth century Britain. *Southwestern Journal of Anthropology* 24: 33–65.

MacAlister, R. A. S., 1949, *The archaeology of Ireland.* London: Methuen.

McArthur, N., 1970, The demography of primitive populations. *Science* 167: 1097–1101.

McBurney, C. B. M., 1960, *The Stone Age of northern Africa.* Baltimore: Penguin.

McBurney, C. B. M., 1961, Aspects of Palaeolithic art. *Antiquity* 35: 107–114.

McCarthy, F. D., and M. McArthur, 1960, The food quest and the time factor in aboriginal economic life. Melbourne: University of Melbourne Press *Records of the American-Australian Scientific Expedition,* 2: 145–194.

McCartney, A. P., 1975, Maritime adaptations in cold archipelagoes: an analysis of environment and culture in the Aleutian and other island chains. In *Prehistoric maritime adaptations of the circumpolar zone,* W. Fitzhugh, ed. Paris: Mouton, pp. 281–338.

McCown, T. D., and A. Keith, 1939, *The Stone Age of Mt. Carmel,* Vol. 2. London: Clarendon.

McFadgen, B. G., 1971, An application of stereophotogrammetry to archaeological recording. *Archaeometry* 13: 71–81.

McGimsey, C. R., 1972, *Public archeology.* New York: Seminar Press.

McGinnies, W. G., 1963, Dendrochronology. *Journal of Forestry* 61: 5–11.

McKern, W. C., 1939, The midwestern taxonomic method as an aid to archaeological culture study. *American Antiquity* 4: 301–313.

MacNeish, R. S., 1964, Ancient Mesoamerican civilization. *Science* 143: 531–537.

MacNeish, R. S., 1967a, An interdisciplinary approach to an archaeological problem. In *The prehistory of the Tehuacan Valley:* Vol. 1. *Environment and subsistence*, D. S. Byers, ed. Austin: University of Texas Press, pp. 14–24.

MacNeish, R. S., 1967b, A summary of the subsistence. In *The prehistory of the Tehuacan Valley*, Vol. 1. *Environment and subsistence*, D. S. Byers, ed. Austin: University of Texas Press, pp. 290–310.

MacWhite, E., 1956, On the interpretation of archaeological evidence in historical and sociological terms. *American Anthropologist* 58: 3–25.

Malinowski, B., 1932, *Argonauts of the western Pacific.* New York: Dutton.

Malkin, B., 1962, *Seri ethnozoology.* Pocatello: Occasional Papers of the Idaho State College Museum, No. 7.

Mallowan, M. E. L., 1965, The mechanics of ancient trade in western Asia. *Iran* 3: 1–7.

March, B., 1934, *Standards of pottery description.* Ann Arbor: University of Michigan, Occasional Contributions from the Museum of Anthropology, No. 3.

Maringer, J., 1960, *The gods of prehistoric man.* New York: Knopf.

Marks, A. E., 1971, Settlement pattern and intrasite variability in the Central Negev. *American Anthropologist* 73: 1237–1244.

Marshack, A., 1964, Lunar notation on Upper Paleolithic remains. *Science* 146: 743–745.

Marshack, A., 1969, New techniques in the analysis and interpretation of Mesolithic notation and symbolic art. Capo di Ponte: Centro Camuno de Studi Preistorici, Valcamonica Symposium, *Actes de Symposium International d'Art Préhistorique.*

Marshack, A., 1970a, The baton of Montgaudier. *Natural History* 79: 56–63.

Marshack, A., 1970b, Polesini: a reexamination of the ingraved mobilary materials by a new methodology. *Rivista di Scienze Preistoriche* 24: 219–281.

Marshack, A., 1970c, Le bâton de commandement de Montgaudier (Charente). Réexamen au microscope et interprétation nouvelle. *L'Anthropologie* 74: 321–352.

Marshack, A., 1970d, Notation dan les gravures du paléolithique supérieur. Bordeaux: *Publications de l'Institut de Préhistoire de l'Université de Bordeaux,* Mémoire No. 8.

Marshack, A., 1972, *The roots of civilization: a study in prehistoric cognition; The origins of art, symbol and notation.* New York: McGraw-Hill.

Marshack, A., 1976, Some implications of the Paleolithic symbolic evidence for the origin of language. *Current Anthropology* 17: 274–282.

Marshack, A., and A. Rosenfeld, 1972, Paleolithic notation. *Antiquity* 46: 63–65.

Martin, P., 1963, *The last 10,000 years: a fossil pollen record of the American Southwest.* Tucson: University of Arizona Press.

Martin, P., and J. Gray, 1962, Pollen analysis and the Cenozoic. *Science* 137: 103–111.

Martin, P., and F. W. Sharrock, 1964, Pollen analysis of prehistoric human feces: a new approach to ethnobotany. *American Antiquity* 30: 168–180.

Marx, R. F., 1975, *The underwater dig: an introduction to marine archaeology.* New York: David McKay.

Mason, O. T., 1904, Aboriginal American basketry: studies in a textile art without machinery. Washington, D.C.: *U.S. National Museum Report for 1902,* pp. 171–548.

Matheny, R. T., 1962, Value of aerial photography in surveying archeological sites in coastal jungle regions. *American Antiquity* 28: 226–230.

Mather, J. R., 1954, The effect of climate on the New World migration of primitive man. *Southwestern Journal of Anthropology* 10: 304–321.

Matson, F. R., 1951, Ceramic technology as an aid to cultural interpretation: techniques and problems. Ann Arbor: *Anthropological Papers of the University of Michigan*, No. 8: 102–116.

Matson, F. R., 1960, The quantitative study of ceramic materials. New York: *Viking Fund Publications in Anthropology* No. 28: 34–51.

Matson, F. R., ed., 1965, *Ceramics and man.* New York: *Viking Fund Publications in Anthropology* No. 41.

Matson, F. R., 1971, A study of temperatures used in firing ancient Mesopotamian pottery. In *Science and archaeology,* R. H. Brill, ed. Cambridge, Mass.: MIT Press, pp. 65–79.

Matthews, S. K., 1968, *Photography in archaeology and art.* London: J. Baker.

Mauss, M., 1954, *The gift.* New York: Free Press.

Mayer-Oakes, W. J., 1963, Complex society archaeology. *American Antiquity* 29: 57–60.

Mayes, S., 1961, *The great Belzoni (archeologist extraordinary).* New York: Walker & Co.

Mazess, R. B., and D. W. Zimmerman, 1966, Pottery dating by thermoluminescence. *Science* 152: 347–348.

Meggers, B. J., 1954, Environmental limitation on the development of culture. *American Anthropologist* 56: 801–824.

Meggers, B. J., ed., 1959, *Evolution and anthropology: a centennial appraisal.* Washington, D.C.: Anthropological Society of Washington.

Meggers, B. J., 1975, The Transpacific origin of Mesoamerican civilization: a preliminary review of the evidence and its theoretical implications. *American Anthropologist* 77: 1–27.

Meggers, B. J., and C. Evans, 1957, *Archaeological investigations at the mouth of the Amazon.* Washington, D.C.: Bulletin of the Bureau of American Ethnology, No. 167.

Meggers, B. J., C. Evans, and E. Estrada, 1965, *Early formative period of coastal Ecuador.* Washington, D.C.: Smithsonian Institution, Contributions to Anthropology, Vol. 1.

Melko, M., 1969, *The nature of civilizations.* Boston: Porter Sargent.

Melaart, J., 1967, *Çatal Hüyük: a Neolithic town in Anatolia.* London: Thames and Hudson.

Mencken, A., 1963, *Designing and building the great pyramid.* Baltimore: privately printed.

Meyers, K., 1973, *The plundered past.* New York: Atheneum.

Michael, H. N., and E. K. Ralph, 1971, *Dating techniques for the archaeologist.* Cambridge, Mass.: MIT Press.

Michaelis, A., 1906, *Die archaeologischer Entdeckungen des neunzehnten Jahrhundert.* Leipzig: E. A. Seeman.

Michels, J. W., 1967, Archaeology and dating by hydration of obsidian. *Science* 158: 211–214.

Michels, J. W., 1968, Settlement pattern and demography at Sheep Rock Shelter: their role in culture contact *Southwestern Journal of Anthropology* 24: 66–82.

Michels, J. W., 1973, *Dating methods in archaeology.* New York: Seminar Press.

Michels, J. W., and C. A. Bebrich, 1971, Obsidian hydration dating. In *Dating techniques for the archaeologist,* H. N. Michael and E. K. Ralph, eds. Cambridge, Mass.: MIT Press, pp. 164–221.

Miller, W. C., 1957, Uses of aerial photographs in archaeological field work. *American Antiquity* 23: 46–62.

Millon, R., 1964, The Teotihuacan mapping project. *American Antiquity* 29: 345–352.

Millon, R., 1970, Teotihuacan: completion of map of giant ancient city in the Valley of Mexico. *Science* 170: 1077–1082.

Millon, R., 1973, The Teotihuacan map text. In *Urbanization at Teotihuacan, Mexico,* vol. 1, part 1. Austin: University of Texas Press.

Moorehead, A., 1961, A reporter at large: the temples of the Nile. *New Yorker,* September 23, pp. 106–137.

Morgan, C. G., 1973, Archaeology and explanation. *World Archaeology* 4: 259–276.

Morgan, C. G., 1974, Explanation and scientific archaeology. *World Archaeology* 6: 133–137.

Morgan, L. H., 1875, Ethnical periods. *Proceedings of the American Association for the Advancement of Science* 24: 266–274.

Morgan, L. H., 1878, *Ancient society.* New York: Holt, Rinehart and Winston.

Morin, J., 1911, *Les dessins des animaux en Grèce d'après les vases peints.* Paris.

Morris, E. H., and R. F. Burgh, 1941, *Anasazi basketry: Basket Maker II through Pueblo III.* Washington, D.C.: Carnegie Institution, Publication No. 533.

Morrison, H. F., 1971, High-sensitivity magnetometers in archaeological exploration. Berkeley: University of California, *Archaeological Research Facility, Contribution* No. 12: 6–20.

Morrison, H. F., C. W. Clewlow, and R. F. Heizer, 1970, Magnetometer survey of the La Venta pyramid. Berkeley: University of California, *Archaeological Research Facility, Contribution* No. 8: 1–20.

Mortillet, A. de, 1903, *La classification paléthnologique.* Paris: Schleicher Frères.

Mortillet, G. de, 1867, *Promenades préhistoriques à l'Exposition Universelle: a guide to the prehistoric collections at the Paris exposition of 1867.* Paris.

Movius, H. L., Jr., and S. Judson, 1956, *The rock-shelter of La Colombiere.* Cambridge, Mass.: Harvard University, Peabody Museum, American School of Prehistoric Research, Bulletin No. 19.

Movius, H. L., Jr., et al., 1968, *The analysis of certain major classes of Upper Paleolithic tools.* Cambridge, Mass.: Harvard University, Peabody Museum, American School of Prehistoric Research, Bulletin No. 26.

Mueller, J. W., 1974, The use of sampling in archaeological survey. *Society for American Archaeology, Memoir* 28.

Mueller, J. W., 1975, ed., 1975, *Sampling in archaeology.* Tucson: University of Arizona Press.

Mulvaney, D. J., 1971, Prehistory from Antipodean perspectives. *Proceedings of the Prehistoric Society* 37: 228– 252.

Mulvaney, D. J., and J. Golson, 1971, *Aboriginal man and environment in Australia.* Canberra.

Murdock, G. P., 1959, *Africa*. New York: McGraw-Hill.

Murdock, G. P., and T. O'Leary, 1975, *Ethnographic bibliography of North America*. New Haven: Human Relations Area Files Press. 5 vols.

Naroll, 1962, Floor area and settlement population. *American Antiquity* 27: 587–589.

Nash, M., 1966, *Primitive and peasant economic systems*. San Francisco: Chandler Publishing.

Navarro, J. M. D., 1925, Prehistoric routes between northern Europe and Italy defined by the amber trade. *Geographical Journal* 66: 481–504.

Nelson, C. M., 1972, Prehistoric culture change in the intermontane plateau of Western North America. In *The explanation of culture change*, C. Renfrew, ed. London: Duckworth.

Nelson, N. C., 1938, Prehistoric archaeology. In *General anthropology*, F. Boas, ed. New York: Heath, pp. 146–237.

Neumann, G. K., 1952, Archeology and race in the American Indian. In *Archeology of eastern United States*, James B. Griffin, ed. Chicago: University of Chicago Press, pp. 13–34.

Nietsch, H., 1939, *Wald und Siedlung im vorgeschichtlichen Mitteleuropa*. Leipzig: Mannus-Bücherei.

Nordenskiöld, G. E. A., 1895, *The cliff dwellers of the Mesa Verde, Southwestern Colorado: their pottery and implements,* trans. by D. L. Morgan. Stockholm: P. A. Norstedt and Söner.

Nystuen, J. D., 1968, Identification of some fundamental spatial concepts. In *Spatial analysis: a reader in statistical geography*, B. J. L. Berry and D. F. Marble, eds. Englewood Cliffs, N.J.: Prentice-Hall, pp. 35–41.

Nystuen, J. D., and M. F. Dacey, 1968, A graph theory interpretation of nodal regions. In *Spatial analysis: a reader in statistical geography*, B. J. L. Berry and D. F. Marble, eds. Englewood Cliffs, N.J.: Prentice-Hall, pp. 407–418.

Oakley, K. P., 1953, Dating fossil human remains. In *Anthropology today*, A. L. Kroeber, chairman, Chicago: University of Chicago Press, pp. 43–57.

Oakley, K. P., 1955, *Further contributions to the solution of the Piltdown problem*. London: British Museum of Natural History, Vol. 2, Bulletin 6.

Oakley, K. P., 1961, Radiometric assays [of uranium content of bones from the Llano Estacado region]. In *Paleoecology of the Llano Estacado*, F. Wendorf, ed. Santa Fe, N.M.: Fort Burgwin Research Center, Publication No. 1: 136.

Oakley, K. P., 1963a, Relative dating of Arlington Springs man. *Science* 141: 1172.

Oakley, K. P., 1963b, Dating skeletal material. *Science* 140: 488.

Oakley, K. P., 1963c, Fluorine, uranium and nitrogen dating of bone. In *The scientist and archaeology*, E. Pyddoke, ed. London: Phoenix House, pp. 111–119.

Oakley, K. P., 1964, *Frameworks for dating fossil man*. Chicago: Aldine.

Oakley, K. P., 1969, Analytical methods of dating bones. In *Science in archaeology*, D. Brothwell and E. Higgs. eds., rev. ed. London: Thames and Hudson, pp. 35–45.

Oakley, K. P., and W. W. Howells, 1961, Age of the skeleton from the Lagow sand pit, Texas. *American Antiquity* 26: 543–545.

Oakley, K. P., and A. E. Rixon, 1958, The radioactivity of materials from the Scharbauer site near Midland, Texas. *American Antiquity* 24: 185–187.

Odum, E. P., 1963, *Ecology*. New York: Holt, Rinehart and Winston.

Olsen, S. J., 1961, A basic annotated bibliography to facilitate the identification of vertebrate remains from archeological sites. *Bulletin of the Texas Archeological Society* 30: 219–222.

Olsen, S. J., 1971, *Zooarchaeology: animal bones in archaeology and their interpretation.* Addison-Wesley Module in Anthropology. Reading, Mass.: Addison-Wesley.

Orme, B., 1972, Archaeology and ethnography. In *The explanation of culture change,* C. Renfrew, ed. London: Duckworth.

Orme, B., 1974, Twentieth-century prehistorians and the idea of ethnographic parallels. *Man* 9: 199–212.

Oswalt, W. H., 1973, *Habitat and technology.* New York: Holt, Rinehart and Winston.

Oswalt, W. H., and J. W. Van Stone, 1967, *The ethnoarcheology of Crow Village, Alaska.* Washington, D.C.: Bulletin of the Bureau of American Ethnology, No. 199.

Pallis, S. F.,1956, *The antiquities of Iraq.* Copenhagen: E. Munksgaard.

Pallottino, M., 1968, *The meaning of archaeology.* London: Thames and Hudson.

Parker, A .C., 1910, *Iroquois uses of maize and other food plants.* Albany: New York State Museum, Bulletin No. 144.

Parsons, E. C., 1940, Relations between ethnology and archaeology in the Southwest. *American Antiquity* 5: 214–220.

Parsons, J. B., 1972, Archaeological settlement patterns. *Annual Review of Anthropology* 1: 127–150. (B. J. Siegal, ed.)

Parsons, J. R., 1971, Prehistoric settlement patterns in the Texcoco region, Mexico. *University Museum Memoir* 3, Museum of Anthropology, University of Michigan.

Parsons, L. A., and B. J. Price, 1971, Mesoamerican trade and its role in the emergence of civilization. Berkeley: University of California, *Archaeological Research Facility, Contribution* No. 11, pp. 169–195.

Parsons, R. B., 1962, Indian mounds of northeast Iowa as soil genesis benchmarks. *Journal of the Iowa Archeological Society,* 12(2).

Peake, H. J. E., 1940, The study of prehistoric times. *Journal of the Royal Anthropological Institute* 70: 103–146.

Pearson, R., 1968, Migration from Japan to Ecuador: the Japanese evidence. *American Anthropologist* 70: 85–86.

Peet, T. E., 1943, *The great tomb-robberies of the twentieth Egyptian dynasty.* Oxford: Clarendon Press.

Perlman, I., and F. Asaro, 1970, Pottery analysis by neutron activation analysis. *Archaeometry* 11: 21–52.

Perlman, I., and F. Asaro, 1971, Pottery analysis by neutron activation. In *Science and archaeology,* R. H. Brill, ed. Cambridge, Mass.: MIT Press, pp. 182–195.

Perrot, J., 1955a, The excavations at Tell Abu Matar, near Beersheba. *Israel Exploration Journal* 5: 17–40ff.

Perrot, J., 1955b, Les fouilles d'Abu Matar. *Syria* 34: 1–38.

Peterson, W., 1975, A demographer's view of prehistoric demography. *Current Anthropology* 16: 227–246.

Petrie, W. M. F., 1899, Sequences in prehistoric remains. *Journal of the Royal Anthropological Institute* 29: 295–301.

Petrie, W. M. F., 1931, *Seventy years in archaeology.* London: Low, Marston.

Pewe, T. L., 1954, The geological approach to dating archaeological sites. *American Antiquity* 20: 51–61.

Phillips, C. W., 1974, The English Place-name Society. *Antiquity* 48: 7–15.

Phillips, P., J. A. Ford, and J. B. Griffin, 1951, *Archaeological survey in the lower Mississippi alluvial valley, 1940–1947.* Cambridge, Mass.: Harvard University, Papers of the Peabody Museum, Vol. 25.

Piggott, S., 1950, *William Stukely, an eighteenth-century antiquary.* Oxford: Clarendon Press.

Piggott, S., 1959a, *Approach to archaeology.* Cambridge, Mass.: Harvard University Press.

Piggott, S., 1959b, A Late Bronze Age wine trade? *Antiquity* 33: 122–123.

Piggott, S., 1960, Prehistory and evolutionary theory. In *Evolution after Darwin,* S. Tax, ed. Chicago: University of Chicago Press, pp. 85–98.

Piggott, S., 1965, *Ancient Europe.* Chicago: Aldine.

Piggott, S., and B. Hope-Taylor, 1965, Archaeological draughtsmanship: I, principles and practice. *Antiquity* 39: 165–176.

Pittioni, R., 1960, Metallurgical analysis of archaeological materials. II. New York: *Viking Fund Publications in Anthropology* No. 28: 21–33.

Planck, M., 1949, *Scientific autobiography and other papers.* New York: Philosophical Library.

Platt, J. R., 1962, *The excitement of science.* Boston: Houghton, Mifflin.

Platt, J. R., 1964, Strong inference. *Science* 146: 347–353.

Platz, K. A., 1971, Drawing artifacts for identification purposes. *Missouri Archeological Society Newsletter* 250: 5–8.

Plenderleith, H. J., 1952, Fakes and forgeries in museums. *Museum Journal* 52: 143–148.

Plog, F. T., 1974, *The study of prehistoric change.* New York: Academic Press.

Polach, H. A., and J. Golson, 1966, *Collection of specimens for radiocarbon dating and interpretation of results.* Canberra: Australian Institute of Aboriginal Studies, Manual No. 2.

Polanyi, K., 1957, The economy as instituted process. In *Trade and market in the early empires,* K. Polanyi, C. M. Arensberg, and H. W. Pearson, eds. New York: Free Press, pp. 243–262.

Poole, L. D., and G. T. Poole, 1966, *One passion, two loves: the story of Heinrich and Sophia Schliemann, discoverers of Troy.* New York: Crowell.

Potratz, J. A. H., 1962, *Einführung in die Archäologie.* Stuttgart: A. Kröner.

Pradenne, A. V. de, 1932, *Les fraudes en archéologie préhistorique.* Paris: Émile Nourry.

Proskouriakoff, T., 1960, Historical implications of a pattern of dates at Piedras Negras, Guatemala. *American Antiquity* 25: 454–475.

Proudfoot, V. B., 1967, Experiments in archaeology. *Science Journal* 3: 59–65.

Puleston, D. E., 1971, An experimental approach to the function of Classic Maya Chultuns. *American Antiquity* 36: 322–335.

Pulgram, E., 1959, Proto-Indo-European; reality and reconstruction. *Language* 35: 421–426.

Pyddoke, E., 1961, *Stratification for the archaeologist.* London: Phoenix House.

Quigley, C., 1961, *The evolution of civilizations.* New York: Macmillan.

Radcliffe-Brown, A. R., 1952, *Structure and function in primitive society.* Glencoe, Ill.: Free Press.

Radiocarbon. New Haven, Conn.: American Journal of Science. Annual; Vol. 1, 1959.

Rafter, T. A., 1965, C14 variations in nature and the effect on radiocarbon dating. *New Zealand Journal of Science and Technology*, Section B 37: 20–38.

Ragir, S., 1972, The early horizon in central California prehistory. Berkeley: University of California, *Archaeological Research Facility, Contribution* No. 15.

Ragir, S., 1975, A review of techniques for archaeological sampling. In *Field methods in archaeology*, T. R. Hester, R. F. Heizer, and J. A. Graham, eds. Palo Alto, Calif.: National Press, pp. 283–302.

Raikes, R., 1967, *Water, weather and prehistory*. London: J. Baker.

Ralph, E., 1971a, Carbon-14 dating. In *Dating techniques for the archeologist*, H. N. Michael and E. K. Ralph, eds. Cambridge, Mass.: MIT Press, pp. 1–48.

Ralph, E., 1971b, Potential of thermoluminescence dating. In *Science and archaeology*, R. H. Brill, ed. Cambridge, Mass.: MIT Press, pp. 244–250.

Ralph, E., and M. C. Han, 1966, Dating of pottery by thermoluminescence. *Nature* 210: 245–247.

Rashevsky, N., 1967, Organismic sets: outline of a general theory of biological and social organisms. *General Systems* 12: 21–28.

Rassam, H., 1897, *Asshur and the Land of Nimrod*. Cincinnati: Curtis and Jennings.

Rathje, W. L., 1970, Socio-political implications of lowland Maya burials: methodology and tentative hypotheses. *World Archaeology* 1: 359–374.

Rathje, W. L., 1971, The origin and development of lowland Classic Maya civilization. *American Antiquity* 36: 275–285.

Redman, C. L., 1974, *Archeological sampling strategies*. Addison-Wesley Module in Anthropology No. 55. Reading, Mass.: Addison-Wesley.

Redman, C. L., and P. J. Watson, 1970, Systematic, intensive surface collection. *American Antiquity* 35: 279–291.

Reed, C. A., 1959, Animal domestication in the prehistoric Near East. *Science* 130: 1629–1639.

Reed, C. A., 1960, A review of the archaeological evidence on animal domestication in the prehistoric Near East. Chicago: Oriental Institute of the University of Chicago, *Studies in Ancient Oriental Civilization*, No. 31: 119–145.

Reed, C. A., 1961, Osteological evidences for prehistoric domestication in southwestern Asia. *Zeitschrift für Tierzüchtung und Züchtungsbiologie* 76: 31–38.

Reed, C. A., 1962, Snails on a Persian hillside: ecology, prehistory, gastronomy. New Haven, Conn.: Yale University, Peabody Museum of Natural History, *Postilla* 66.

Reed, C. A., 1963, Osteo-archaeology. In *Science in archaeology*, D. Brothwell and E. Higgs, eds. London: Thames and Hudson, pp. 204–216.

Reed, E., 1956, Types of village-plan lay-outs in the Southwest. In *Prehistoric settlement patterns in the New World*, G. R. Willey, ed. New York: Viking Fund Publications in Anthropology, No. 23: 18–25.

Reed, N. A., J. W. Bennett, and J. W. Porter, 1968, Solid core drilling of Monks Mound: technique and findings. *American Antiquity* 33: 137–148.

Reid, J. J., M. B. Schiffer, and W. L. Rathje, 1975, Behavioral archaeology: four strategies. *American Anthropologist* 77: 864–869.

Reisner, G. A., 1932, A provincial cemetery of the Pyramid Age, Naga-ed-Der. *University of California Publications in Egyptian Archaeology*, Vol. 3. University of California Press.

Renfrew, C., 1967, Colonialism and *Megalithismus. Antiquity* 41: 276–288.

Renfrew, C., 1968a, Obsidian and the origins of trade. *Scientific American* 218: 38ff.

Renfrew, C., 1968b, Models in prehistory. *Antiquity* 42: 132–134.

Renfrew, C., 1969, Trade and culture process in European prehistory. *Current Anthropology* 10: 151–169.

Renfrew, C., 1970a, New configurations in Old World archaeology. *World Archaeology* 2: 199–211.

Renfrew, C., 1970b, The tree ring calibration of radio-carbon: an archaeological evaluation. *Proceedings of the Prehistoric Society* 36: 280–311.

Renfrew, C., 1972, *The emergence of civilization*. London: Methuen.

Renfrew, C., 1973a, *Before civilization: the radiocarbon revolution and prehistoric Europe*. London: J. Cape.

Renfrew, C., ed., 1973b, *The explanation of culture change: models in prehistory*. Pittsburgh: University of Pittsburgh Press.

Renfrew, C., J. E. Dixon, and J. R. Cann, 1966, Obsidian and early cultural contact in the Near East. *Proceedings of the Prehistoric Society for 1966* 32: 30–72.

Renfrew, J. M., 1973, *Paleoethnobotany: the prehistoric food plants of the Near East and Europe*. London.

Renfrew, J. M., M. Monk, and P. Murphy, 1975, *First aid for seeds*. RESCUE Publication No. 6. Dept. Anthropology, Univ. of Southampton.

Rice, T. T., 1957, *The Scythians*. New York: Praeger.

Ricketson, O. G., 1937, *Uaxactun, Guatemala Group E—1926–1931. Part I: The excavations*. Washington, D.C.: Carnegie Institution, Publication No. 477: 1–180.

Ridgway, J. C., 1938, *Scientific illustration*. Palo Alto, Calif.: Stanford University Press.

Rieth, A., 1970, *Archaeological fakes*. New York: Praeger.

Riley, C. L., 1969, *The origins of civilization*. Carbondale: Southern Illinois University Press.

Rivard, S. J., 1964, Technical illustrations applied to archaeology. *Massachusetts Archaeological Society Bulletin* 25: 44–45.

Rootenberg, S., 1964, Archaeological field sampling. *American Antiquity* 30: 181–188.

Rouse, I., 1939, Prehistory in Haiti: a study in method. *Yale University Publications in Anthropology* No. 21.

Rouse, I., 1944, On the typological method. *American Antiquity* 10: 202–204.

Rouse, L., 1953, The strategy of culture history. In *Anthropology today*, A. L. Kroeber, chairman. Chicago: University of Chicago Press, pp. 57–76.

Rouse, I., 1954, On the use of the concept of area co-tradition. *American Antiquity* 19: 221–225.

Rouse, I., 1955, On the correlation of phases of culture. *American Anthropologist* 57: 713–722.

Rouse, I., 1957, Culture area and co-tradition. *Southwestern Journal of Anthropology* 13: 123–133.

Rouse, I., 1958, The inference of migrations from anthropological evidence. Tucson: University of Arizona, *Social Science Bulletin*, No. 27: 63–68.

Rouse, I., 1960, The classification of artifacts in archaeology. *American Antiquity* 25: 313–323.

Rouse, I., 1965, The place of "peoples" in prehistoric research. *Journal of the Royal Anthropological Institute* 95: 1–15.

Rouse, I., 1968, Prehistory, typology, and the study of society. In *Settlement archaeology*, K. C. Chang, ed. Palo Alto: National Press Books, pp. 10–30.

Rouse, I., 1970. Classification for what? *Norwegian Archaeological Review* 3: 4–34.

Rouse, I., 1972a, Analytic, synthetic, and experimental archeology. In *Archeology today*, C. L. Redman, ed. New York: Wiley.

Rouse, I., 1972b, *Introduction to prehistory*. New York: McGraw-Hill.

Rowe, J. H., 1945, Absolute chronology in the Andean area. *American Antiquity* 10: 265–284.

Rowe, J. H., 1946, Inca culture at the time of the Spanish conquest. Washington, D.C.: *Bulletin of the Bureau of American Ethnology,* 2(143): 183–330.

Rowe, J .H., 1954, Archaeology as a career. *Archaeology* 7: 229–236.

Rowe, J. H., 1966, Diffusionism and archaeology. *American Antiquity* 31: 334–337.

Rowlands, M. J., 1971, The archaeological interpretation of prehistoric metalworking. *World Archaeology* 3: 210–224.

Rubin, M., R. C. Likens, and E. G. Berry, 1963, On the validity of radiocarbon dates from snail shells. *Journal of Geology* 71: 84–89.

Rubin, M., and D. W. Taylor, 1963, Radiocarbon activity of shells from living clams and snails. *Science* 141: 637.

Rudenko, S. I., 1970, *Frozen tombs of Siberia: the Pazyryk burials of Iron Age horsemen*. Berkeley: University of California Press.

Rudner, R. S., 1966, *Philosophy of social science*. Englewood Cliffs, N.J.: Prentice-Hall.

Ruppé, R. J., 1966, The archaeological survey: a defense. *American Antiquity* 31: 313–333.

Ryan, E. J., and G. F. Bass, 1962, Underwater surveying and draughting—a technique. *Antiquity* 36: 252–261.

Sabloff, J., and G. R. Willey, 1968, The collapse of Maya civilization in the Southern Lowlands: a consideration of history and process. *Southwestern Journal of Anthropology* 23: 311–336.

Sabloff, J., and C. C. Lamberg-Karlovsky, eds., 1973, *Ancient civilization and trade*. Albuquerque: University of New Mexico Press.

Sachs, S., 1973, *Fakes and forgeries*. Minneapolis Institute of Arts.

Sackett, J. R., 1966, Quantitative analysis of Upper Paleolithic stone tools. *American Anthropologist* 68 (2:2): 356–394.

Saffirio, L., 1972, *Food and food problems in prehistory*. New York: Seminar Press.

Sahlins, M. D., 1958, *Social stratification in Polynesia*. Seattle: University of Washington Press.

Sahlins, M. D., 1965, On the sociology of primitive exchange. *American Sociological Association, Monograph* No. 1: 139–236.

St. Joseph, J. K. S., 1966, *The uses of air photography*. London: J. Baker.

Saint-Perier, R. de, 1913, Gravure à contours decoupés en os et coquilles perforées de l'époque Magdalénienne. Paris: *Société d'Anthropologie de Paris Bulletin et Mémoires* (Series 6) 4: 47–52.

Salmon, M. H., 1975, Confirmation and explanation in archaeology. *American Antiquity* 40: 459–464.

Sanders, W. T., 1965, *The cultural ecology of the Teotihuacan Valley*. University Park: Pennsylvania State University, Department of Anthropology.

Sanders, W. T., and B. J. Price, 1968, *Mesoamerica: the evolution of a civilization*. New York: Random House.

Sandin, B., 1962, Gawai Batu: the Iban whetstone feast. *Sarawak Museum Journal* 10: 392–408.

Sapir, E., 1916, *Time perspective in aboriginal American culture: a study in method*. Ottawa: Canada Department of Mines, Geological Survey, Memoir 90. (Reprinted in *Selected writings of Edward Sapir*, D. G. Mandelbaum, ed. Berkeley: University of California Press, 1949.)

SARG, 1974, SARG: a co-operative approach towards understanding the locations of human settlement. *World Archaeology* 6: 107–116.

Saucier, R. T., 1966, Soil-survey reports and archaeological investigations. *American Antiquity* 31: 419–422.

Sayce, R. U., 1963, *Primitive arts and crafts: an introduction to the study of material culture*. New York: Biblo and Tannen.

Schaber, G. G., and G. J. Gumerman, 1969, Infrared scanning images: an archeological application. *Science* 164: 712–714.

Schaeffer, O. A., and J. H. Zahringer, 1966, *Age determination by potassium-argon method*. New York: Springer.

Schiffer, M. B., 1972, Archaeological context and systemic context. *American Antiquity* 37: 156–165.

Schiffer, M. B., 1975, Archeological research and contract archeology. In: *The Cache River archeological project: an experiment in contract archeology*. Arkansas Archeological Survey, Research Series No. 8, pp. 1–7.

Schiffer, M. B., 1976a, Archaeology as behavioral science. *American Anthropologist* 77: 836–848.

Schiffer, M. B., 1976b, *Behavior archaeology*. New York: Academic Press.

Schlabow, K., et al., 1958, Zwei Moorleichen Funde aus dem Domlandsmoor. *Praehistorische Zeitschrift*, Berlin, 26: 44–49.

Schliemann, H., 1875, *Troy and its remains*. London: John Murray.

Schliemann, H., 1878, *Mycenae*. London: John Murray.

Schmalz, R. F., 1960, Flint and the patination of flint artifacts. *Proceedings of the Prehistoric Society* 26: 44–49.

Schulman, E. A., 1940, A bibliography of tree-ring analysis. *Tree Ring Bulletin*, Tucson: University of Arizona, 6: 1–12.

Schulman, E. A., 1941, Some propositions in tree-ring analysis. *Ecology* 22: 193–195.

Schuyler, R., 1973, Review of Watson, LeBlanc, and Redman, *Explanation in archaeology* (1971). *American Antiquity* 38: 372–374.

Schwarz, G. T., 1965, Stereoscopic views taken with an ordinary single camera —a new technique for archaeologists. *Archaeometry* 7: 36–42.

Scudder, T., 1971, *Gathering among African woodland savannah cultivators*. University of Zambia, Institute for African Studies, Zambia Papers, No. 5.

Sears, W. H., 1954, The sociopolitical organization of pre-Columbian cultures on the Gulf coastal plain. *American Anthropologist* 56: 339–364.

Sears, W. H., 1961, The study of social and religious systems in North American archaeology. *Current Anthropology* 2: 223–246.

Sears, W. H., 1968, The state and settlement patterns in the New World. In *Settlement archaeology*, K. C. Chang, ed. Palo Alto, Calif.: National Press Books, pp. 134–153.

Sellstedt, H. L., 1967, Radiocarbon dating of bone. *Nature* 213: 415.

Sellstedt, H., L. Engstrand, and N. G. Gejvall, 1966, New application of radiocarbon dating to collagen residue in bones. *Nature* 212: 572–574.

Semenov, S. A., 1964, *Prehistoric technology*, M. W. Thompson, trans. London: Cory, Adams & Mackay.

Senyurek, M. S.. 1947, Duration of life of the ancient inhabitants of Anatolia. *American Journal of Physical Anthropology* 5: 55–66.

Service, E. R., 1962, *Primitive social organization*. New York: Random House.

Service, E. R., 1964, Archeological theory and ethnographic fact. In *Process and pattern in culture*, R. Manners, ed. Chicago: Aldine, pp. 364–375.

Service, E. R., 1968, The prime-mover of cultural evolution. *Southwestern Journal of Anthropology* 24: 396–409.

Service, E. R., 1975, *The origins of civilization and the state*. New York: Norton.

Shaw, T., 1970, Methods of earthwork building. *Proceedings of the Prehistoric Society* 36: 380–381.

Shawcross, W., 1967, An investigation of prehistoric diet and economy on a coastal site at Galatea Bay, New Zealand. *Proceedings of the Prehistoric Society* 33: 107–131.

Sheets, P., 1973, The pillage of prehistory. *American Antiquity* 38: 317–320.

Shepard, A. O., 1948, *Plumbate: a Mesoamerican trade ware*. Washington, D.C.: Carnegie Institution, Publication No. 573.

Shepard, A. O., 1956, *Ceramics for the archaeologist*. Washington, D.C.: Carnegie Institution, Publication No. 609.

Shepard, A. O., 1971, Ceramic analysis: the interrelations of methods: the relations of analysts and archaeologists. In *Science and archaeology*, R. H. Brill, ed. Cambridge, Mass.: MIT Press, pp. 55–64.

Sherratt, A., 1972, Models, theories and hypotheses. In *The explanation of culture change*, C. Renfrew, ed. London: Duckworth.

Shorr, P., 1935, The genesis of prehistorical research. *Isis* 23: 425–443.

Shotten, F. W., 1969, Petrological examination. In *Science in archaeology*, D. Brothwell and E. Higgs, eds., rev. ed. London: Thames and Hudson, pp. 571–577.

Sidrys, R., J. Andresen, and D. Marcucci, 1976, Obsidian sources in the Maya area. *Journal of New World Archaeology* 1(5): 1–14.

Sieveking, G., 1972, Prehistoric flint mines and their identification as sources of raw materials. *Archaeometry* 14: 151–176.

Silverberg, R., 1963, *Sunken history: the story of underwater archeology*. Philadelphia: Chilton.

Silverberg, R., 1964, *Great adventures in archaeology*. New York: Dial.

Simonsen, R. W., 1954, Identification and interpretation of buried soils. *American Journal of Science* 252: 705–722.

Simoons, F. J., 1961, *Eat not this flesh: food avoidances in the Old World*. Madison: University of Wisconsin Press.

Simpson, G. C., 1964, Comment on Ascher and Hockett: *The human revolution*. *Current Anthropology* 5: 151.

Singer, C., E. J. Holmyard, and A. R. Hall, 1954–1958, *A history of technology*, Vols. 1–4. London: Oxford.

Smiley, T. L., ed., 1955b, *Geochronology*. Tucson: University of Arizona Press.

Smith, A. H., 1916, Lord Elgin and his collection. *Journal of Hellenic Studies* 36: 163–372.

Smith, M. A., 1955, The limitations of inference in archaeology. *Archaeological Newsletter* 6: 1–7.

Smith, P. E. L., 1972, Changes in population pressure in archaeological explanation. *World Archaeology* 4: 5–18.

Smith, P. E. L., and T. C. Young, 1972, The evolution of early agriculture and culture in Greater Mesopotamia: a trial model. In: *Population growth: anthropological implications*, B. Spooner, ed. Cambridge, Mass.: MIT Press, pp. 101–154.

Smith, R. H., 1970, An approach to the drawing of pottery and small finds for excavation reports. *World Archaeology* 2: 212–228.

Smith, W. S., 1958, *The art and architecture of ancient Egypt*. Pelican History of Art Series. Baltimore, Penguin.

Soergel, W., 1939, Unter welchen klimatischen Verhältnissen lebten zur Bildungzeit der alt-diluvialen Kiese von Süssenborn, Rangifer. Ovibus, und Elephas trongontherii in Mittel- und Norddeutschland. *Zeitschrift Deutsches Geologisches Gesellschaft* 91: 829–835.

Solecki, R. S., 1957, Practical aerial photography for archaeologists. *American Antiquity* 22: 337–351.

Sonnenfeld, J., 1962, Interpreting the function of primitive implements. *American Antiquity* 28: 56–65.

Sonneville-Bordes, D. de, 1953, Statistical techniques for the discovery of artifact types. *American Antiquity* 18: 305–313, 391–393.

Sonneville-Bordes, D. de, 1960, *Le Paléolithique supérieur en Périgord*, 2 vols. Paris: Delmas.

Spaulding, A. C., 1973, The concept of artifact type in archaeology. *Plateau* 45: 149–163.

Spencer, R. F., 1959, *The North Alaskan Eskimo: a study in ecology and society.* Washington, D.C.: Bulletin of the Bureau of American Ethnology, No. 171.

Spengler, O., 1926–1928, *The decline of the West.* New York: Knopf.

Spier, L., 1917, New data on the Trenton argillite culture. *American Anthropologist* 18: 181–189.

Staniland, L. N., 1953, *The principles of line illustration with emphasis on the requirements of biological and other scientific workers.* Cambridge, Mass.: Harvard University Press.

Stanislawski, M. B., 1969, The ethno-archaeology of Hopi pottery making. *Plateau* 42: 27–33.

Stanislawski, M. B., 1973, Ethnoarchaeology and settlement archaeology. *Ethnohistory* 20: 375–392.

Stanislawski, M. B., 1975, Hopi and Hopi-Tewa pottery making: styles of learning. In *Experimental archaeology*, Y. Yellen, ed. New York: Columbia University Press.

Stelcl, J., and J. Malina, 1970, *Anwendung der petrographie in der archäologie.* Folia Facultatis.

Stephens, J. L., 1842, *Incidents of travel in Central America, Chiapas and Yucatan,* 2 vols. New York: Harper & Row. (Reprint of one volume: *Incidents of travel in Yucatan,* with intro. by V. von Hagen, ed., new ed. Norman: University of Oklahoma Press, 1962.)

Sterud, G., 1972, A paradigmatic view of prehistory. In *The explanation of culture change*, C. Renfrew, ed. London: Duckworth.

Stevens, A., 1975, Animals in Paleolithic cave art: Leroi-Gourhan's hypothesis. *Antiquity* 59: 54–57.

Steward, J. H., 1936, The economic and social basis of primitive bands. In *Essays in anthropology presented to A. L. Kroeber*. Berkeley: University of California Press, pp. 331–350.

Steward, J. H., 1937, Ecological aspects of Southwestern society. *Anthropos* 32: 87–104.

Steward, J. H., 1938, *Basin-Plateau aboriginal sociopolitical groups*. Washington, D.C.: Bulletin of the Bureau of American Ethnology, No. 120.

Steward, J. H., 1942, The direct historical approach to archaeology. *American Antiquity* 7: 337–343.

Steward, J. H., 1946–1950, *The Handbook of South American Indians*. Bureau of American Ethnology, Bulletin 143, 6 vols.

Steward, J. H., 1949, Cultural causality and law: a trial formulation of the development of early civilizations. *American Anthropologist* 51: 1–27.

Steward, J. H., 1955, *Theory of culture change: the methodology of multilinear evolution. Urbana:* University of Illinois Press.

Steward, J. H., 1968, Causal factors and processes in the evolution of pre-farming societies. In *Man the hunter*, R. B. Lee and I. DeVore, eds. Chicago: Aldine, pp. 321–334.

Stewart, T. D., 1960, A physical anthropologist's view of the peopling of the New World. *Southwestern Journal of Anthropology* 16: 259–273.

Stewart, T. D., and M. T. Newman, 1967, Physical types of American Indians. In *The North American Indians, a sourcebook*, R. C. Owen, J. F. Deetz, and A. D. Fisher, eds. New York: Macmillan, pp. 53–67.

Stokes, M. A., and T. L. Smiley, 1968, *An introduction to tree-ring dating*. University of Chicago Press.

Stone, J. F. S., and L. C. Thomas, 1956, The use and distribution of faience in the ancient East and prehistoric Europe. *Proceedings of the Prehistoric Society* 22: 37–84.

Strong, W. D., 1940, From history to prehistory in the northern Great Plains. Washington, D.C.: *Smithsonian Institution Miscellaneous Collections*, 100: 353–394.

Struever, S., 1962, Implications of vegetal remains from an Illinois Hopewell site. *American Antiquity* 27: 584–587.

Struever, S., 1964, The Hopewell interaction sphere in riverine-western Great Lakes culture history. Springfield, Ill.: *Illinois State Museum Scientific Papers* 12: 85–106.

Struever, S., 1965, Middle woodland culture history in the Great Lakes riverine area. *American Antiquity* 31: 211–223.

Struever, S., 1968a, Flotation techniques for the recovery of small-scale archaeological remains. *American Antiquity* 33: 353–362.

Struever, S., 1968b, Woodland subsistence-settlement systems in the lower Illinois valley. In *New perspectives in archeology*. S. Binford and L. Binford, eds. Chicago: Aldine, pp. 285–312.

Struever, S., 1968c, Problems, methods and organization: a disparity in the growth of archeology. In *Anthropological archeology in the Americas*. Washington, D.C.: Anthropological Society.

Stuckenrath, R., 1965, On the care and feeding of radiocarbon dates. *Archaeology* 18: 277–281.

Stuive, M., and H. Suess, 1966, On the relationship between radiocarbon dates and true sample ages. *Radiocarbon* 8: 534–540.

Sturtevant, W. C., 1958, *Anthropology as a career*. Washington, D.C.: Smithsonian Institution.

Suess, H., 1965, Secular variations of the cosmic ray produced carbon-14 in the atmosphere and their interpretations. *Journal of Geophysical Research* 70: 5937–5992.

Suess, H., and R. M. Clark, 1976, A calibration curve for radiocarbon dates. Antiquity 50: 61–63.

Suhm, D. A., and A. D. Krieger, 1954, *An introductory handbook of Texas archaeology*. Abilene: Texas Archaeological Society.

Sullivan, R. J., 1942, *The Ten'a food quest*. Washington, D.C.: Catholic University of America Press, Anthropological Series, No. 11.

Swadesh, M., 1953, Archaeological and linguistic chronology of Indo-European groups. *American Anthropologist* 55: 349–352.

Swadesh, M., 1959, Linguistics as an instrument of prehistory. *Southwestern Journal of Anthropology* 15: 20–35.

Swadesh, M., 1960, *Estudios sobre lengua y cultura*. Mexico City: Acta Antropologica, Epoca 2, Vol. 2, No. 2.

Swadesh, M., 1962, Linguistic relations across Bering Strait. *American Anthropologist* 64: 1262–1291.

Swedlund, A. C., ed., 1975, Population studies in archaeology and biological anthropology: a symposium. *Society for American Archaeology, Memoir* 30.

Switsur, V. R., 1973, The radiocarbon calendar recalibrated. *Antiquity* 47: 131–137.

Taylor, D., and I. Rouse, 1955, Linguistic and archaeological time depth in the West Indies. *International Journal of American Linguistics* 21: 105–115.

Taylor, W. W., 1948, *A study of archeology*. Washington, D.C.: American Anthropological Association Memoir No. 69, 50(312).

Terrell, J., 1967, Galatea Bay—the excavation of a beach-stream midden site on Ponui Island in the Hauraki Gulf, New Zealand. Wellington, New Zealand: *General Transactions of the Royal Society of New Zealand*, 2: 31–70.

Thieme, F. P., 1958, The Indo-European language. *Scientific American* 199 (October): 63–74.

Thom, A., 1964, Megalithic geometry in standing stones. *New Scientist* 21: 690–691.

Thom, A., 1966, Megaliths and mathematics. *Antiquity* 40: 121–128.

Thom, A., 1967, *Megalithic sites in Britain*. Oxford: Clarendon Press.

Thom, A., 1971, *Megalithic lunar observatories*. Oxford: Clarendon Press.

Thomas, W. L., ed., 1956, *Man's role in changing the face of the earth*. Chicago: University of Chicago Press.

Thompson, D. F., 1949, *Economic structure and the ceremonial exchange cycle in Arnhem Land*. Melbourne: Macmillan.

Thompson, J. E. S., 1950, *Maya hieroglyphic writing: introduction*. Washington, D.C.: Carnegie Institution, Publication No. 589.

Thompson, J. E. S., 1954, *The rise and fall of Maya civilization*. Norman: University of Oklahoma Press.

Thompson, J. E. S., 1963, *Maya archaeologist*. Norman: University of Oklahoma Press.

Thompson, R. H., 1956, The subjective element in archaeological inference. *Southwestern Journal of Anthropology* 12: 327–332.

Thompson, R. H., 1958b, *Migrations in New World culture history*. Tucson: University of Arizona, Social Science Bulletin No. 27.

Thompson, R. H., and W. A. Longacre, 1966, The University of Arizona Archaeological Field School at Grasshopper, East Central Arizona. *Kiva* 31: 255–275.

Tilton, G. R., and S. R. Hart, 1963, Geochronology. *Science* 140: 357–366.

Tite, M. S., 1972, *Methods of physical examination in archaeology*. New York: Seminar Press.

Tite, M. S., and J. Waine, 1962, Thermoluminscent dating: a reappraisal. *Archaeometry* 5: 53–79.

Tolstoy, P., 1958, *Surface survey of the northern valley of Mexico: the classic and post-classic periods*. Philadelphia: Transactions of the American Philosophical Society 48(Part 5).

Tortellot, G., and J. A. Sabloff, 1972, Exchange systems among the ancient Maya. *American Antiquity* 37: 126–134.

Tower, D. B., 1945, *The use of marine mollusca and their value in reconstructing prehistoric trade routes in the American Southwest*. Cambridge, Mass.: Papers of the Excavators' Club, 2(3).

Toynbee, A. J., 1934–1960, *A study of history*, 12 vols. London: Oxford University Press.

Traeger, G. L., 1955, Linguistics and the reconstruction of culture history. In *New interpretations of aboriginal American culture history*. Washington, D.C.: Anthropological Society of Washington, pp. 110–115.

Tribus, M., and E. C. McIrvine, 1971, Energy and information. *Scientific American* 244: 179–190.

Trigger, B. G., 1965, *History and settlement in Lower Nubia*. New Haven, Conn.: Yale University Publications in Anthropology, No. 69.

Trigger, B. G., 1967, Settlement archaeology—its goals and promise. *American Antiquity* 32: 149–160.

Trigger, B. G., 1968a, *Beyond history: the methods of prehistory*. New York: Holt, Rinehart and Winston.

Trigger, B. G., 1968b, Major concepts of archaeology in historical perspective. *Man* 3: 527–541.

Trigger, B. G., 1968c, The determinants of settlement patterns. In *Settlement archaeology*, K. C. Chang, ed. Palo Alto, Calif.: National Press Books, pp. 53–78.

Trigger, B. G., 1970, Aims in prehistoric archaeology. *Antiquity* 44: 26–37.

Trigger, B. G., 1971, Archaeology and ecology. *World Archaeology* 2: 321–336.

Tringham, R., et al., 1974, Experimentation in the formation of edge damage: a new approach to lithic analysis. *Journal of Field Archaeology* 1: 186–196.

Tuggle, H. D., A. H. Townsend, and R. J. Riley, 1972, Laws, systems, and research design: a discussion of explanation in archaeology. *American Antiquity* 37: 3–12.

Ucko, P. J., 1962, The interpretation of prehistoric anthropomorphic figurines. *Journal of the Royal Anthropological Institute* 92: 38–54.

Ucko, P. J., 1969, Ethnography and archaeological interpretation of funerary remains. *World Archaeology* 1: 262–280.

Ucko, P. J., and A. Rosenfeld, 1967, *Palaeolithic cave art.* London: World University Press. (Weidenfeld & Nicholson.)

Ucko, P. J., R. Tringham, and G. W. Dimbleby, eds., 1972, *Man, settlement, and urbanism.* London: Duckworth.

Vallois, H. V., 1960, Vital statistics in prehistoric populations as determined from archaeological data. *Viking Fund Publications in Anthropology* No. 28: 186–222.

Van Buren, E. D., 1939, The fauna of ancient Mesopotamia as represented in art. *Analecta Orientalia* 18: 1–113.

Van der Leeuw, S. E., 1976, *Studies in the technology of ancient pottery.* Amsterdam: University of Amsterdam Press.

Van der Merwe, N. J., 1966, New mathematics for glottochronology. *Current Anthropology* 7: 485–500.

Van der Merwe, N. J., and R. T. K. Scully, 1971, The Phalaborwa story: archaeological and ethnographic investigation of a South African Iron Age group. *World Archaeology* 3: 178–196.

Vayda, A., and R. A. Rappaport, 1968, Ecology, cultural and noncultural. In *Introduction to cultural anthropology.* J. A. Clifton, ed. Boston: Houghton Mifflin, Chap. 18, pp. 477–497.

Verpmann, H.-P., 1973, Animal bone finds and economic archaeology: a critical study of "osteo-archaeological" method. *World Archaeology* 4: 307–322.

Vescelius, G., 1955, Archaeological sampling: a problem in statistical inference. In *Essays in the science of culture,* G. E. Dole and R. L. Carneiro, eds. New York: Crowell, pp. 457–470.

Vinnicombe, P., 1963, Proposed scheme for standard representation of color in black-and-white illustrations for publication. *South African Archaeological Society Bulletin* 18: 49–50.

Vogt, E. Z., 1956, An appraisal of "Prehistoric settlement patterns in the New World." In *Prehistoric settlement patterns in the New World,* G. R. Willey, ed. New York: Viking Fund Publications in Anthropology, No. 23: 173–182.

Vogt, E. Z., 1964, The genetic model and Maya cultural development. *Desarrollo cultural de los Mayas,* E. Z. Vogt and R. L. Alberto, eds. Mexico City: Universidad Nacional Autónoma de Mexico, pp. 9–48.

Vogt, E. Z., 1968, Some aspects of Zinacantan settlement patterns and ceremonial organization. In *Settlement archaeology,* K. C. Chang, ed. Palo Alto, Calif.: National Press Books, pp. 154–173.

Von Bothmer, D., and J. V. Noble, 1961, *An inquiry into the forgery of the Etruscan terracotta warriors in the Metropolitan Museum of Art.* New York: Metropolitan Museum of Art, Occasional Papers, No. 11.

Von Hagen, V. W., 1947, *Maya explorer.* Norman: University of Oklahoma Press.

Voorhies, B., 1972, Settlement patterns in two regions of the southern Maya lowlands. *American Antiquity* 37: 115–125.

Wace, A. J. B., 1949, The Greeks and Romans as archaeologists. *Societé Royale d'Archéologie d'Alexandrie, Bulletin* No. 38: 21–35 (Reprinted in Heizer 1969: 203–216).

Wagner, P. L., 1960, *The human use of the earth.* New York: Free Press.

Wakeling, T. G., 1912, *Forged Egyptian antiquities.* London: A. and C. Black.

Walker, R., M. Maurette, R. Fleischer, and P. Price, 1971, Applications of solid-state nuclear track detectors to archaeology. In *Science and archaeology*, R. H. Brill, ed. Cambridge, Mass.: MIT Press, pp. 279–283.

Wallis, F. S., 1955, Petrology as an aid to prehistoric and medieval archaeology. *Endeavour* 14: 146–151.

Walters, H. B., 1934, *The English antiquaries of the sixteenth, seventeenth and eighteenth centuries*. London: E. Walters.

Washburn, S. L., 1960, Tools and human evolution. *Scientific American* 203: 62–75.

Watanabe, H., 1959, The direction of remanent magnetism of baked earth and its application to chronology for anthropology and archaeology in Japan. *Journal of the Faculty of Science, University of Tokyo* (Section 2) 2: 1–188.

Watanabe, N., and M. Suzuki, 1969, Fission track dating of archaeological glass materials from Japan. *Nature* 222(5198): 1057–1058.

Waterbolk, H. T., 1971, Working with radiocarbon dates. *Proceedings of the Prehistoric Society* 37: 15–33.

Watson, P. J., 1972, Explanations and models: the prehistorian as philosopher of science and the prehistorian as excavator of the past. In *The explanation of culture change*, C. Renfrew, ed. London: Duckworth.

Watson, P. J., S. A. LeBlanc, and C. L. Redman, 1971, *Explanation in archeology: an explicitly scientific approach*. New York: Columbia University Press.

Watson, P. J., S. A. LeBlanc, and C. L. Redman, 1974, The covering law model in archaeology: practical uses and formal interpretations. *World Archaeology* 6: 125–132.

Watson, R. A., and P. J. Watson, 1969, *Man and nature: an anthropological essay in human ecology*. New York: Harcourt.

Wauchope, R., 1962, *Lost tribes and sunken continents*. Chicago: University of Chicago Press.

Wauchope, R., 1964–1976, *Handbook of Middle American Indians*, 9 vols. Austin: University of Texas Press.

Wauchope, R., 1965a, Alfred Vincent Kidder, 1885–1963. *American Antiquity* 31: 149–171.

Wauchope, R., 1965b, *They found buried cities*. Chicago: University of Chicago Press.

Weaver, K. F., 1967, Magnetic clues help date the past. *National Geographic Magazine* 131: 696–701.

Webb, M. C., 1974, Exchange networks: prehistory. *Annual Review of Anthropology* 3: 357–383. (Siegel, B. J., ed.)

Weber, J. N., and A. La Rocque, 1963, Isotope ratios in marine mollusk shells after prolonged contact with flowing fresh water. *Science* 142: 1666.

Webster, G., 1963, *Practical archaeology*. London: A. & C. Black.

Wedel, W. R., 1936, *An introduction to Pawnee archeology*. Washington, D.C.: Bulletin of the Bureau of American Ethnology, No. 112.

Wedel, W. R., 1938, *The direct-historical approach in Pawnee archeology*. Washington, D.C.: Smithsonian Institution, Miscellaneous Collections, 97(7).

Wedel, W. R., 1961, *Prehistoric man on the Great Plains*. Norman: University of Oklahoma Press.

Wells, C., 1964, *Bones, bodies, and disease*. London: Thames and Hudson.

Weltfish, G., 1930, Prehistoric North American basketry and modern distributions. *American Anthropologist* 32: 454–495.

Weltfish, G., 1932, *Preliminary classification of southwestern basketry.* Washington, D.C.: Smithsonian Institution, Miscellaneous Collections, 87(7).

Wendorf, F., 1966, Early man in the New World: problems of migration. *American Naturalist* 100: 253–270.

Wertime, T. A., 1964, Man's first encounters with metallurgy. *Science* 146: 1257–1267.

West, R. C., N. P. Psuty, and B. G. Thom, 1969, *The Tabasco lowlands of southeastern Mexico.* Baton Rouge: Louisiana State University Coastal Studies Series No. 27.

Wheat, J. B., 1967, A Paleo-Indian bison kill. *Scientific American* 216(1): 44–52.

Wheat, J. B., 1972, *The Olsen-Chubbuck site: a Paleo-Indian bison kill.* Society for American Archaeology, Memoir No. 26.

Wheeler, M., 1955, *Still digging.* London: M. Joseph.

Wheeler, M., 1956, *Archaeology from the earth.* Baltimore: Pelican.

Wheeler, M., 1957, *A book of archaeology: seventeen stories of discovery.* London: Cassell.

Wheeler, M., 1959, *A second book of archaeology.* London: Cassell.

White, C., and N. Peterson, 1969, Ethnographic interpretations of the prehistory of Western Arnhem Land. *Southwestern Journal of Anthropology* 25: 45–67.

White, L. A., 1947, Evolutionary stages, progress, and the evaluation of cultures. *Southwestern Journal of Anthropology* 3: 165–192.

White, L. A., 1949, *The science of culture, a study of man and civilization.* New York: Farrar, Straus.

White, L. A., 1959a, *The evolution of culture: the development of civilization to the fall of Rome.* New York: McGraw-Hill.

White, L. A., 1959b, The concept of culture. *American Anthropologist* 61: 227–251.

White, R. C., 1963, *Luiseño social organization.* Berkeley: University of California Publications in American Archaeology and Ethnology, 48(2).

White, T. E., 1952, Observations on the butchering techniques of some aboriginal peoples, No. 1. *American Antiquity* 17: 337–338.

White, T. E., 1953a, Observations on the butchering techniques of some aboriginal peoples, No. 2. *American Antiquity* 19: 160–164.

White, T. E., 1953b, A method for calculating the dietary percentage of various food animals utilized by aboriginal peoples. *American Antiquity* 18: 396–398.

White, T. E., 1954, Observations on the butchering techniques of some aboriginal peoples, Nos. 3, 4, 5, 6. *American Antiquity* 19: 254–264.

White, T. E., 1955, Observations on the butchering techniques of some aboriginal peoples, Nos. 7, 8, 9. *American Antiquity* 21: 170–178.

Wiessner, P., 1974, A functional estimator of population from floor area. *American Antiquity* 39: 343–349.

Wilke, P. J., and H. J. Hall, 1975, *Analysis of ancient feces: a discussion and annotated bibliography.* Archaeological Research Facility, University of California, Berkeley.

Willey, G. R., 1953a, A pattern of diffusion-acculturation. *Southwestern Journal of Anthropology* 9: 369–384.

Willey, G. R., 1953b, *Prehistoric settlement patterns in the Viru Valley, Peru.* Washington, D.C.: Bulletin of the Bureau of American Ethnology, No. 155.

Willey, G. R., 1956a, An archaeological classification of culture contact situations. Beloit, Wis.: Society for American Archaeology, Memoir No. 11: 1–30.

Willey, G. R., 1956b, *Prehistoric settlement patterns in the New World*. New York: Viking Fund Publications in Anthropology, No. 23.

Willey, G. R., 1960, New World prehistory. *Science* 131: 73–86.

Willey, G. R., 1966a, *An introduction to American archaeology*, Vol. 1. Englewood Cliffs, N.J.: Prentice-Hall.

Willey, G. R., 1966b, Postlude to village agriculture: the rise of towns and temples and the beginnings of the great traditions. Spain: XXXVI International Congress of Americanists 1964, pp. 267–277.

Willey, G. R., 1968a, One hundred years of American archaeology. In *One hundred years of anthropology*, J. O. Brew, ed. Cambridge, Mass.: Harvard University Press, pp. 29–56.

Willey, G. R., 1968b, Settlement archaeology: an appraisal. In *Settlement archaeology*, K. C. Chang, ed. Palto Alto, Calif.: National Press Books, pp. 208–226.

Willey, G. R., 1971, *An introduction to American archaeology*, Vol. 2. Englewood Cliffs, N.J.: Prentice-Hall.

Willey, G. R., 1973, Man, settlement, and urbanism. *Antiquity* 47: 269–279.

Willey, G. R., ed., 1974, *Archaeological researches in retrospect*. Cambridge: Winthrop.

Willey, G. R., and P. Phillips, 1958, *Method and theory in American archaeology*. Chicago: University of Chicago Press.

Willey, G. R., and J. A. Sabloff, 1974, *A history of American archaeology*. San Francisco: Freeman.

Willey, G. R., and D. B. Shimkin, 1971, The collapse of classic Maya civilization in the southern lowlands: a symposium summary statement. *Southwestern Journal of Anthropology* 27: 1–18.

Williams, D., 1974, Flotation at Siraf. *Antiquity* 47: 288–292.

Williams, H., and R. F. Heizer, 1965, Sources of rocks used in Olmec monuments. Berkeley: University of California, *Archaeological Research Facility, Contribution* No. 1: 1–40.

Wilmsen, E. N., 1968, Functional analysis of flaked stone artifacts. *American Antiquity* 33: 156–161.

Wilson, E. B., 1952, *An introduction to scientific research*. New York: McGraw-Hill.

Wilson, D., 1975, *The new archaeology*. New York: Alfred A. Knopf.

Wilson, T., 1899, The beginnings of the science of prehistoric anthropology. *Proceedings of the American Association for the Advancement of Science* 48: 309–353.

Winlock, H. E., 1942, *Excavations at Deir el Bahri, 1911–1931*. New York: Macmillan.

Winlock, H. E., 1955, *Models of daily life in ancient Egypt from the tomb of Meket-Re at Thebes*. Cambridge, Mass : Harvard University Press for the Metropolitan Museum of Art.

Winter, J., 1971, Thermoluminescent dating of pottery. In *Dating techniques for the archaeologist*, H. N. Michael and E. K. Ralph, eds. Cambridge, Mass.: MIT Press, pp. 118–151.

Witthoft, J., 1967, Glazed polish on flint tools. *American Antiquity* 32: 383–388.

Wissler, C., 1917, The new archaeology. *American Museum Journal* 17: 100–101.

Wolf, E. R., 1967, Understanding civilizations: a review article. *Comparative Studies in Society and History* 9: 446–465.

Wood, J. J., and R. G. Matson, 1972, Two models of socio-cultural systems and their implications for the archaeological study of change. In *The explanation of culture change*, C. Renfrew, ed. London: Duckworth.

Wood, W. R., 1968, Mississippian hunting and butchering patterns: bone from the Vista shelter, 23R-20, Missouri. *American Antiquity* 33: 170–179.

Woodall, J. N., 1972, *An introduction to modern archaeology*. Cambridge, Massachusetts: Schenkman.

Woodbury, R. B., 1960, Nels C. Nelson and chronological archaeology. *American Antiquity* 25: 400–401.

Woolley, C. L., 1934, Ur excavations. *Publications of the Joint Expedition of the British Museum and the Museum of the University of Pennsylvania to Mesopotamia*, Vol. II.

Woolley, C. L., 1958, *History unearthed*. London: Benn.

Wright, G. A., 1969, *Obsidian analyses and prehistoric Near Eastern trade: 7500 to 3500 B.C.* Ann Arbor: University of Michigan, Anthropological Papers of the Museum of Anthropology, No. 37.

Wright, T., 1844, On antiquarian excavations and researchers in the Middle Ages. *Archaeologica* 30: 438–457.

Wulsin, F., 1941, *The prehistoric archaeology of northwest Africa*. Cambridge, Mass.: Harvard University, Papers of the Peabody Museum, 19(1).

Yarnell, R. A., 1969, Contents of human paleofeces. In P. J. Watson, *The prehistory of Salts Cave, Kentucky*. Springfield, Ill.: Illinois State Museum, Report of Investigations No. 16: 41–55.

Yellen, J., 1973, *The Kung settlement pattern: an archaeological perspective*. Ph.D. thesis, Harvard University.

Young, K. S., 1970, A technique for illustrating pottery designs. *American Antiquity* 35: 488–491.

Young, T. C., Jr., 1966, Survey in Western Iran, 1961. *Journal of Near Eastern Studies* 25: 228–239.

Zeuner, F. E., 1958, *Dating the past; an introduction to geochronology*, 4th ed. London: Methuen.

Zeuner, F. E., 1959, *The Pleistocene period*. London: Hutchinson.

Zeuner, F. E., 1960, Advances in chronological research. New York: *Viking Fund Publications in Anthropology* No. 28: 325–350.

Ziegler, A., 1965, *The role of faunal remains in archaeological investigations*. Sacramento, Calif.: Sacramento State College, Sacramento Anthropology Society, Paper 2, pp. 47–75.

Ziegler, A. C., 1973, *Inference from prehistoric faunal remains*. Addison Wesley Module in Anthropology No. 43. Reading, Mass.: Addison-Wesley.

Zimmerman, D. W., 1971, Uranium distributions in archeologic ceramics: dating of radioactive inclusions. *Science* 174: 818–819.

Zipf, G. K., 1949, *Human behavior and the principle of least effort*. Reading, Mass.: Addison-Wesley.

INDEX OF NAMES

INDEX OF SUBJECTS